BRITISH PISTON AERO-ENGINES
AND
THEIR AIRCRAFT

BRITISH PISTON AERO-ENGINES
AND
THEIR AIRCRAFT

Alec S. C. Lumsden M.R.Ae.S.

Airlife

England

'Merely corroborative detail, intended to give artistic verisimilitude to an otherwise bald and unconvincing narrative'.
Pooh-Bah — *The Mikado*, W.S. Gilbert.

Copyright © 1994 Alec S. C. Lumsden

First published in the UK in 1994
by Airlife Publishing Ltd

British Library Cataloguing in Publication Data
A catalogue record for this book is available from the British Library

ISBN 1 85310 294 6

Printed by Livesey Ltd., Shrewsbury.

Airlife Publishing Ltd.

101 Longden Road, Shrewsbury SY3 9EB

Dedication

This book is dedicated to Dr Nicholas F. Lawton MD, FRCP, Consultant Neurologist who diagnosed Myasthenia Gravis, at the Wessex Neurological Centre, Southampton General Hospital. Without his skill, kindness and wit and, perhaps most of all his tolerance for more than four years of an unruly patient, this book could not have been attempted. I am enormously and gratefully in his debt and also in that of his specialist team of Registrars, House Officers, Sisters and Nurses at that great teaching Hospital.

CONTENTS

Foreword

Sir Peter G. Masefield, M.A., C.Eng., Hon D.Sc., Hon D.Tech, Hon. F.R.Ae.S., F.C.I.T.,
Hon F.A.I.A.A., Hon F.C.A.S.I., Hon F.R.I.T.E., F.R.S.A.

The heart of an aeroplane is its engine, of every sort, size and configuration. Throughout the first half-century of powered flight, the internal combustion piston-engine not only made flight possible but also — in steadily increasing power, reliability and economy — brought aviation from hesitant beginnings to become a major force in World affairs.

Now, in this studiously-researched and absorbing book, Alec Lumsden has performed a service to aviation history by bringing together — and for the first time — a comprehensive record of the more than 250 basic types of British aero-engines built between 1909 and 1949. In some 900 different variants, they powered in excess of 3,000 different types of aircraft; civil and military, landplanes and seaplanes, fixed-wing and rotary-wing, both heavier and lighter-than-air. Moreover, they took into the air — and still do in a very large number of foreign aircraft as well as British.

British Piston Aero-Engines and Their Aircraft will, thus, be seen as the definitive work on this vital element of aviation history; indeed, the story of one of the wonders of the age. After centuries of human aspirations to 'fly like the birds', powered flight had to await the invention and development of the internal combustion engine and its alliance with early fixed-wing aerodynamics. The Wright Brothers brought these two elements together in 1903, with their Wright Flyer biplane and their home-built 21 hp, four-cylinder water-cooled piston-engine.

Half a century later, the piston-engine era in aviation came to a peak at 180 times the output of the first Wright engine (for only 22 times the weight), the ultimate power plant being the 3,800 hp, twenty-eight cylinder, four-row air-cooled Pratt & Whitney Wasp Major radial. Contemporary with it was the more widely used, though somewhat smaller descendant of the original Wrights' power plant, the 3,700 hp eighteen-cylinder, two-row Wright Turbo-Compound engine. This was built by the Curtiss-Wright Corporation, and linked historically with both the Wright Brothers and Glenn Curtiss.

Thus, on the way forward through the years, successive aero-engines have ranged in output from the earliest, 6 hp per litre and 8 lb dry weight per hp, of the Wright Brothers original 1903 engine, to the ultimate of around 80 hp per litre of the Rolls-Royce Eagle and of the Napier Sabre. Similar achievements were made in reaching 0.83 and 0.93 lb dry weight per hp of the Sabre and Rolls-Royce Griffon respectively. And so, after fifty-two years of development and many years of faithful service, dominating civil and military aircraft — the piston-engine was eclipsed (and gradually made obsolete for all but the smaller powers and aircraft), by the technical revolution of the gas turbine.

The inspiration and determination of Frank Whittle in England, and of Hans von Ohain in Germany brought about, from 1940 onwards, the gradual replacement of piston-engines for aircraft by jet propulsion. Further development of the piston-engine, however, continued in the quite different arena of the racing motor car business in which a new generation of high-revving, turbo-blown engines now produce more than 200 hp per litre, while derated variants of such engines are taking to the air in a new era of light aeroplanes.

Such is the broad picture. In Britain, the story — so well assembled and chronicled by Alec Lumsden — goes back to the classic four-cylinder 35 hp, 4.16 litre Green engine of 1909. Designed by Gustavus Green (1865-1964) and built by the Aster Engineering Co Ltd, it earned the distinction of a first flight in J.T.C. Moore-Brabazon's (later Lord Brabazon of Tara's) Short-Wright biplane on 30 October, 1909. On that day he won the *Daily Mail's* £1,000 prize for the first circular mile with an all British aeroplane, at the Aero Club's 'flying ground' at Leysdown on the Isle of Sheppey.

This British aero-engine was a step forward from the Wright's engine of six years before. The Green's power/weight ratio was, however, well eclipsed by the contemporary, French 50 hp Gnome, 7-cylinder air-cooled, rotary-engine designed by the brilliant French engineers, Laurent and Louis Seguin. Installed initially, in the Anglo-French Farman biplanes, it led on to a long line of rotary-engines, reduced in their effectiveness only by the fact that they burned almost as much castor oil lubricant as they consumed petrol, to provide power.

Looked at in the perspective of time, the story of British aero-engines told in this book can be seen to have evolved in six phases throughout the 40 years from 1909. The first began with the robust little Green engine, at the time of the first great Aviation Meeting at Rheims, in France, 22-29 August 1909. The existing state of the art was well shown by the 38 engines at Rheims, ranging from the, alleged, 60 hp of the eight-cylinder Franco-British E.N.V. ('En Vee'), down to the 24 hp, eight-cylinder Antoinette — likewise a water-cooled Vee.

A second phase of aero-engine development came during the five 'Golden Years' of early aviation; years which led up to the start of the First World War in August 1914. Thirty-two representative engines of that period embraced a range of powers from the 240 hp, nine cylinder water-cooled Salmson radial down to the 34 hp five cylinder air-cooled Gnome rotary — and from the 6.4 lb weight per hp of the 100 hp Vee-12 air-cooled Renault to the 2.6 lb per hp of the 80 hp, 9 cylinder air-cooled rotary Le Rhône. In this phase, 21 of the engines were water-cooled and eleven air-cooled. Although originating in France, all of these engines very soon came to be built in Britain.

Then came the leap forward in both powers and production numbers of British-built engines in 'phase three', during the four years of the First World War. Wartime demands brought Beardmore, Bentley, Siddeley, the Royal Aircraft Factory, Sunbeam and Wolseley into the large-scale design and production of piston engines for aircraft in Britain, together with a large number of sub-contractors. In France, Anzani, Hispano, Lorraine-Dietrich, Renault and Salmson, alongside Clerget, Gnome and Le Rhône built a wide range of aero-engines, while, in the United States, Curtiss and the Hall-Scott Motor Car Co built aero-engines in some numbers. At the same time, as related in the text, Mr J.G. Vincent of the Packard Co and Mr G.E.J. Hall, the Chief Engineer of Hall-Scott, came out with the outline design which eventually became the 400 hp, 12-cylinder water-cooled Liberty, built in very large numbers and supplied after the war not only to the Royal Air Force, but also to a number other European air forces.

There followed the 20 years of between-the-wars activity — from 1919 to 1939. In this 'phase four', five major British aero-engine companies — all supported by the Air Ministry to a greater or lesser degree — came to dominate much of the European scene. Those companies — Armstrong-Siddeley, Bristol, de Havilland, Napier and Rolls-Royce — produced a steady flow of both air-cooled and water-cooled engines. During this time of relative peace, aero-engine development on both sides of the Atlantic was powerfully advanced by six successive, international Schneider Trophy Contests. Between 1923 and 1931 the power and the speed of the winning seaplanes went up, from the 465 hp of the Curtiss D-12a engine and the 177 mph of the Curtiss CR-3 biplane, to the 2,350 hp of the Rolls-Royce 'R' engine and the 340 mph of the Supermarine S.6B monoplane.

Spurred on by these Schneider Contests, the Rolls-Royce 'R' 12-cylinder Vee, 36.54 litre liquid-cooled engine — developed from the 825 hp Buzzard engine of 1929 — was an outstanding example of intensive development over a short period. As a result of some detailed re-design, the permissible engine speed was increased to 3,300 rpm. Use for the first time of sodium-filled exhaust valves, a large oil capacity for pure castor oil, and a special fuel composed of methanol, acetone, benzol and TEL fuel, enabled the available engine power to be increased from the Buzzard's 825 hp to the 2,580 hp of the 'R' at +18lb boost. Installed in the Supermarine S.6B racing seaplane, on 29 September 1933 the 'R' engine set up a World's Speed Record of 407.5 mph. The 'R' engine produced 70.6 hp per litre at only 0.63 lb/hp though the life at full power was very limited.

Altogether, in the 20 years of 'phase four' of aero-engine development between 1919 and 1939, some 25 representative British engines — large and small — averaged a little more than 600 hp each (although the largest of all, the Napier Cub achieved 1,075 hp, in 1922). That average was rather more than three times the average output of the range of engines built during the First World War. The most widely-used British engines in both civil and military aircraft, during this 20-year period were Roy Fedden's series of nine-cylinder air-cooled radials, the Jupiter and Pegasus of 28.7 litres, and the Mercury and Perseus of 24.9 litres and, latterly, about 1.3 lb/hp.

For high performance aircraft at the end of the biplane era, the Rolls-Royce Kestrel V-12 liquid-cooled engine of 21.25 litres and 30.6 hp per litre, set new standards and brought single-seat fighter speeds to rather more than 200 mph. Those were the days, also, of the relatively widespread, and carefree, light aeroplane Clubs — and of much enthusiastic flying by a small band of private owners whose 'air-faring outlook' was well served by a series of reliable and fairly inexpensive in-line engines, Cirrus and Gipsy in the lead, offering between 100 and 200 hp at a modest 2.3 lb/hp.

Then, from September 1939 and the start of Second World War, a further intensive period of piston-engine development — 'phase five' brought about another trebling of average engine powers as had happened during the First World War. Cylinder capacities were increased and, with them, more horse-power per litre, and lighter specific weights. But this great upsurge in power and production of piston-engine was, however, its swan song because, on the evening of 15 May 1941, a new sound and sight was heard in British skies with the first flight of the experimental Gloster E.28/39 prototype, powered by the Whittle W.1 jet engine.

During the five-and-a-half years of the Second World War, 26 typical piston-engines of 12 different types, (at a combined total of 38,000 hp), averaged almost 1,500 hp each. By contrast, the most powerful German engine, the 2,870 hp DB 610 (two DB 601 engines coupled together) had a relatively modest specific output of 32 hp per litre for 1.2 lb/hp. In Britain, foremost among the high-power piston-engines which bore much of the wartime 'heat and burden of the day' were the 2,250 hp, 38.7 litre Bristol Hercules 14-cylinder radial, and the Rolls-Royce 1,760 hp Merlin of 27 litres. In its final form, the Hercules achieved some 58 hp/litre at 0.99 lb/hp; the Merlin registered 65 hp/litre for a specific dry weight of 0.93 lb/hp.

In the final generation of large British piston aero-engines, there were three, quite different, leaders in the state of the art. They were the Bristol Centaurus, the Napier Sabre and Rolls-Royce's Griffon and Eagle. Details of their performance are related in the text. Thus, even in its final epoch, the versatility of the piston-engine shone through in widely different variants. In the military field there was the Sabre, Griffon and Eagle, while the Bristol Centaurus went on to prove itself in civil air transport — notably in the elegant and quiet Airspeed Ambassador of British European Airways — as well as achieving 442 mph at 15,000 feet in the Hawker Sea Fury, only slightly more than its predecessor, the Tempest II single-seat fighter. Indeed, with those high powers fighter speeds went in excess of 450 mph. The Sabre attained 466 mph at 24,000 feet in the Hawker Tempest I, and the Griffon 483 mph at 21,000 feet in the Supermarine Spiteful 14, single-seat fighter. The second generation Rolls-Royce Eagle exceeded 455 mph at 23,000 feet in the massive Westland Wyvern I shipborne, single-seat fighter. All of them were nudging the edges of compressibility and its attendant control problems.

So, the piston-engine went out on a high note.

In 1944, towards the end of the piston aero-engine era, one of its greatest practitioners — Sir Roy Fedden of Bristol — suggested that the largest practicable piston-engine might be a six-row, liquid-cooled, radial of 42 cylinders of about 100 litres capacity (at 2.3 litres per cylinder). Such an engine might be expected to develop about 8,000 hp — its output limited by the ability of airscrews, of tolerable size and number of blades, to convert the power into thrust — possibly best with a contra-rotating propeller of some 15 feet diameter, with two banks of six blades each. Such a development was still-born because of the advent of jet propulsion — including turbo-prop engines.

On the way forward, among the many engines of promise which fell by the wayside, one stands out during the Second World War as a specially regrettable, missed opportunity, described in the main text, the Fairey Prince, 24-cylinder 'double' liquid-cooled engine. Either half of the engine could be run separately with its propeller capable of being feathered. Unfortunately, reluctance by the Air Ministry to commit funds to a sixth major British aero-engine company, and wartime limitations on development resources, prevented the Fairey Prince from being put into production.

Before the large piston-engine disappeared from the military scene, it had one remarkable link with the new era of turbine-power plants. That was in the form of a hybrid 'piston-cum turbo-prop' engine of high power and low specific consumption — the Napier Nomad compound engine, built in 1951 and flown briefly in the nose of an Avro Lincoln. The Nomad combined a 3,467 shp, 12-cylinder, two-cycle compression-ignition piston-engine of 41.1 litres swept-volume with a 230 lb. static thrust gas-turbine — both engines driving a single airscrew shaft. At a dry weight of 3,580 lb., the Nomad N.Nm.7 had a specific weight of 0.833 lb. per equivalent shaft horse-power at a fuel consumption of only 0.33 lb. per eshp/hour. It was, thus, a complex but highly innovative, solution to a requirement for high power and long-range.

So, over its half-century span of operation, through two World Wars, and the bridging of all the major oceans, the piston-engine made an unrivalled contribution to World affairs in both peace and War. It attained powers, economy and reliability undreamed of in its earlier days, thanks to continuous, and intensive, innovation and development on the part of skilled and dedicated teams of aeronautical engineers.

The success of the piston-engine was, indeed, made possible thanks to a wide range of innovations — all the way from substantially reduced cooling drag, brought about by aerodynamic cowlings and radiator systems, the use of vastly improved materials and fuels, the bringing into service of two-speed and two-stage gear-driven and exhaust-driven superchargers, the development of controllable pitch, constant speed airscrews driven through reduction gearing and the design of sophisticated carburettor and direct-fuel injection systems.

But, even after 50 years, problems still remained. There were weaknesses in the vital electric ignition systems and electric ignition harness. Spark plugs — though vastly improved in performance and life — were still a problem area, right to the final days of the large piston-engine. In the end, the contest between the use of engines with sodium-cooled exhaust poppet valves and those with sleeve valves remained unresolved, although the verdict seemed to be moving in the direction of the sleeves. In all of this, those concerned with British industry, British technology and British engineering expertise and ingenuity, were entitled to feel a measure of pride and satisfaction from the way in which British aero-engines of all types and sizes had been kept in the forefront of design, development, production and operation throughout the years. Moreover, they had led the way into the wholly new jet era which made obsolescent so much of the results of the immense toil and dedication which had been devoted to the piston-engine.

Against that background, Alec Lumsden's book on British aero-engines takes its place as a most valuable and comprehensive record of a long and inspired combination of people, companies, toil, tribulation and achievement, along the upwards path to the skies.

Acknowledgements

It was in a hospital intensive care unit, with nothing better to do, that the thought occurred to me that composing a book on this pet subject might be a distraction from the immediate horrors. The first words of it were composed there, on an early lap-top computer. It is due to the encouragement of Dr Lawton and his specialist staff (to whom both dedication and thanks are essential) as well as that of my long-suffering wife and innumerable stalwart friends, that this effort has come to fruition.

I have had the good fortune to operate two computers with very large memories. Using both at once, with two out of the four available kinds of software with data storage, spreadsheets and word-processing, it has been crucial to be able to compare the data in one machine with the text in the other in order to ensure, as far as possible, that there is no contradiction between them. In this connection, in addition to the help of doctors, without that of F.H. Lavender FBCO, ACT(BIRM) a former Royal Air Force pilot and now a tolerant and patient optician, the whole project might well have gone into the fire. Without the wise guidance of Mrs Isabelle Kingston, the author would probably have ended up in the same place.

After collecting data for some thirty years, the result appears to cover an enormous area when printed out. The recurring terrible decision was — what to leave out, so as to avoid making a nonsense of the whole thing and a complete waste of time. It has been possible, thanks to the help of many knowledgeable friends, to strike a reasonable balance between 'Nice to know' and 'Need to know'.

An aviation library can be a most frustrating thing. In a fairly modest one comprising about six hundred and fifty books, including a sub-library with some forty titles which include the word 'Spitfire', every book contains references to aeroplanes and, almost incidentally, to their engines. To make a cross-reference so as to list the types of aeroplane in which a particular engine was installed is a hazardous business and is also very time-consuming. The chances are that the very thing one is searching for has become lost (even if something else quite irrelevant and unexpected turns up in the process and distracts one's train of thought). How to find anything that you want requires the goodwill of friends and either a phenomenal memory, a good index, or a good computer (better still, in this instance, two of them).

The book could not have been achieved without the help of experts. These fall into two groups, who cannot possibly be called anything but friends, considering the efforts which they have made to help in this project. There is no way of listing them adequately but, broadly, there are the collectors, donors and checkers of facts and those who have made the technical side, the computers, work satisfactorily. Without either, the whole thing would have collapsed. It is quite impossible adequately to thank all the many people and organizations who have helped with contributions and permission to reproduce photographs, nor indeed to do so in order of priorities. They are all indispensable and most gratefully acknowledged. In particular, mention must be made of the enormous contributions from J.M. Bruce, Alec Harvey-Bailey, John Heaven, from the Rolls-Royce Heritage Trust at Derby, Bristol, Leavesden and Coventry, from Alvis Ltd and British Aerospace, particularly at Woodford.

The Foreword, written with characteristic kindness and generosity by Sir Peter Masefield, is much appreciated and gratefully acknowledged. The Rolls-Royce Heritage Trust has been a major contributor of information, through its various branches. In the years since the end of the Second World War, Rolls-Royce has absorbed all but one of the surviving major companies and the archivists of all of them have been wonderfully supportive in providing and checking data and several must be particularly acknowledged. In addition to Rolls-Royce, they have covered the products of Bristol, Armstrong Siddeley, de Havilland and Napier. Furthermore George T. S. Clarke, formerly Chief Engineer of Alvis Ltd and Roy Probert, Chief Inspector, have most generously sorted out the endless variations on the Leonides theme, as well as providing important facts and photographs.

Special thanks are due to Alec Harvey-Bailey who followed in his distinguished father's footsteps with equal distinction in Rolls-Royce's technical hierarchy (they gave the company a total of seventy-eight years' service between them). Nobody knows more about Merlins than Alec, who was the head of the Merlin Defect Investigation department during the war and subsequently held other senior appointments and directorships within the company, retiring in 1981. The book simply would not have been possible without the major contribution he has made to getting the engineering and historical facts and figures in this book right, particularly in the liquid-cooled engine area. Also, thanks are due to Michael H. Evans, Chairman of the Rolls-Royce Heritage Trust, for the facilities and information which he has made available.

When it comes to the field of air-cooled radial engines, John Heaven, who has held senior positions in the Engine Department of the Bristol Aeroplane Company and is the archivist and custodian of the records of the company, has made an enormous effort in checking a considerable acreage of paper, covered with facts and figures from the Bristol Branch of the Heritage Trust's records and archives, to say nothing of correcting the many early mistakes in this text. In addition, thanks are due to Filton-based Ernest Brook, Editor of the *Rolls-Royce Magazine*. The old-established Coventry company, Armstrong Siddeley lost most of its historical records in the great Blitz fire which devastated that city in the Second World War but, thanks to the work of the Committee of the Coventry Branch of the Heritage Trust and the Secretary, Walter Westacott, much information has been re-assembled to record the work of that famous company. It was with great sadness that the author learnt that Ray Cook, the branch's archivist who contributed most of the Armstrong Siddeley information collected for this book, collapsed and died while doing a good deed for a neighbour.

No account of the British aero-engine industry can exclude the great names of de Havilland and Napier, with the linking name of Halford. The records of the de Havilland company have not been easy to obtain but, fortunately, a formidable quantity of details of the complex Gipsy story has been made available, thanks to Douglas Valentine, Chairman of the Leavesden Branch of the Heritage Trust (the old de Havilland Engine Company now, sadly, closed down). The records of the old-established company of D. Napier & Son Ltd have also been hard to trace. Once again, help was at hand when an old friend kindly gave his extensive collection of data for inclusion, as also did Douglas Valentine.

The help and encouragement of several distinguished test pilots, who have always been at the forefront of engine and airframe development, is gratefully acknowledged, in particular that of Jeffrey Quill OBE, AFC, a friend whose name will for ever be associated with the Spitfire as Chief Test Pilot for Supermarine, throughout its long career. He persuaded the Spitfire to double almost everything in performance which its beautiful prototype achieved and his demonstrations of the Spitfire were poetry in motion.

Another old friend, Neville Duke OBE, DSO, DFC**, AFC, a famous wartime fighter pilot, became Hawker's Chief Test Pilot of great distinction. Principally associated in the public mind with his superb flying displays in the Hawker Hunter jet fighter, in which he also gained the World's Speed Record, he was also one of the original inspirers of this project.

Roland Beamont CBE, DSO, DFC* led, with great distinction, a formidable bunch of Hawker Typhoon and Tempest pilots, storming across northern Europe towards the end of the Second World War. As they swept away all obstacles in their path, from numerous and elusive flying bombs to tanks and locomotives, in the process they helped to overcome the technical problems of the troublesome Sabre engine, noted for its banshee howl. The only man to fly the great and lamented TSR.2, he has been of great assistance and encouragement.

The original instigator of the book was Norman Macmillan, a well-known test pilot of the 1920s. The early help of Harald Penrose, for many years the Chief Test Pilot of Westland Aircraft and a most entertaining writer and the composer of that most informative of series of books on the history of British Aviation, listed in the Bibliography is especially acknowledged.

The author is very grateful for the help of these men who have worked at the dangerously sharp end of aviation progress and who have done so much to make Britain's aircraft industry great. The experimental test pilot, whose job it is to test a new type of aeroplane or engine, is a person whose judgement and opinion in such matters is to be reckoned with and respected.

A great many official Government records are of course available from the Public Record Office at Kew and thanks are due to the helpful staff there, despite their formidable problems with the indexing system. No praise is too high for the Aeroplane and Armament Experimental Establishment at Boscombe Down, who have so willingly entered into the spirit of the research into the piston-engine era of that splendid Establishment's history and thanks are due to the present Commandant, Air Commodore John E. Houghton AFC and to his predecessors, (particularly from the time of Air Commodore R.J. 'Reggie' Spiers OBE 1979-1983). Much gratitude is also due to the Library staff, in sequence from 1973 particularly to Mrs Joan Woods, Miss Alison Whatley, Richard Lovekin, Mrs Julia Smith and Miss Sherri Carnson. From the Royal Aircraft Establishment at Farnborough has come much help, in particular from Brian Kervell.

To this acknowledgement must be added the help given by the staff of the Shuttleworth Trust, particularly by Roy Gambier. At the Royal Air Force Museum at Hendon, help given by Peter Elliott, the Librarian is particularly acknowledged, as is that given by The Curator of the Museum of Army Flying at Middle Wallop and the most helpful Archivist and Librarian, Harry Foot.

A great deal of editorial help, work and advice has been given by Michael Burns. Richard Riding and Michael Oakey, Editor and Assistant Editor of *Aeroplane Monthly* magazine have been of invaluable assistance with the provision of numerous records and photographs, as also has Alex Wright ABIPP, ARPS in his superb work, in processing of many of them from difficult and ancient originals.

Former colleagues in industry who have been an inspiration through difficult times are, particularly, Dr Norman Barfield, Peter Brooks and John Motum, all of whom may fairly be called the 'godfathers' of the book (in the old-fashioned sense). The mists of time have been cleared to a great extent by the unstinting help of Jack Bruce, the doyen of the history of aeroplanes of the Royal Flying Corps and former Deputy Director of the Royal Air Force

Museum. The author is extremely fortunate to have had his unfailing help in the ferreting-out of facts, figures and photographs from his enormous fund of expertise of the largely and sadly forgotten 'Great War' of 1914–1918. Of the same period, Harry Woodman's remarkable research into Sunbeam engines and Bill Morse's into the mysteries of rotaries are also gladly acknowledged, as also is the help of Rowland J. Christopher, Librarian of Ricardo Consulting Engineers Ltd, who kindly provided documentation, of great interest, on the remarkable work of Sir Harry Ricardo.

In addition, the number of other friends and former colleagues in the business of aeronautics, who have given so much enthusiastic help and encouragement, lent books, allowed access to private archives without demands for payment (and provided meals in the process of research and all sorts of other aid) seems to be endless. The only way to thank them, if inadequately, seems to list as many as possible of them, in alphabetical order. They include (several, sadly, having died in the many years since the project began): Monique Agazarian, Ric N. Andrews, E. Ken Barnes, John H. Blake, Brian Cocks, Dr John Collings-Wells, Alan Coster, Michael Goodall, Dr Eric Goodger, James Goulding (in particular for his artwork on performance curves), Bill Green, Mike Hooks, Joan Hughes, Derek James, Philip Jarrett, Bob Kidman, Frank Mason, Tim Mason, Eric B. Morgan, Kenneth Munson, Air Commodore G.J. (Taffy) Powell CBE, Mike Reid LRAM (for his helpful Petro-Chemical guidance, more even than his musical wizardry), Hugh Scanlan, John Stroud, Michael Stroud, Ray Sturtivant, Gordon Swanborough, Michael J. Taylor, Owen G. Thetford, Ray Williams and Derek Wood. The distinguished Naval Architect, Colin Mudie, made a notable contribution concerning the Napier Lion.

Teaching new computer techniques and keeping complicated computer equipment going and in good order has been entirely due to the combined skills, goodwill and untiring patience of Linda and Graham Harding, also Anne Juby and Charles Matthews of Beaver Business Systems Ltd, as well as George Stephenson and Alan Hankey of Dacoll Ltd. Between them, they have succeeded in defeating Murphy's Law that claims that if a thing can go wrong when trying to meet a deadline, it will (usually on a Friday afternoon or late at night and at the weekend).

That so many of these people, in their own time and at no mean effort, have taken the trouble to search and check through their old company records to ensure accuracy and completeness as far as can be ascertained is a tremendous achievement on their part. With such a backup team, any author is indeed fortunate. To the Publisher Airlife and, in particular, to Alastair Simpson and his colleagues, John Beaton and Anne Cooper, I offer my appreciation of their patience and understanding.

Although words seem inadequate to express thanks for all this sort of help, I can only echo the admirable advice of Dr Percy A. Scholes, given in his *Dictionary of Music* (Oxford, 1960). In his Introduction, he admits to having taken up six rooms in his house with manuscripts etc. Further expansion was therefore threatening to drive him and his family 'to residence, in some near future, in a tent on the lawn' and he invited readers having special knowledge or unusually keen powers of observation to let him know of any defect in either accuracy or comprehensiveness, on a post card via the publisher. Such consideration will, with the publisher's permission, be gratefully acknowledged by this author.

Author's Notes

It may be relevant to include a personal note to illustrate my interest in the inadequately-covered subject of the connection between aero-engines and their aircraft. As related elsewhere, this book originally stemmed from a chance conversation with a well-known test pilot at the Farnborough Air Show in the early 1960s, some twenty years after my first close encounter with a high-powered aero-engine. That encounter had been quite an alarming experience.

Having enlisted in the Royal Air Force at the outbreak of war early in September 1939 as an A/C Plonk, with the intention (if possible) of becoming a pilot, I was soon posted to Royal Air Force Station Kinloss, by the Moray Firth in North Eastern Scotland, where I was told there was a Flying Training School and where I should be taught to fly. I had much to learn, of the uncertainties and vagaries of Service postings, if nothing else.

Kinloss in 1940 turned out to be the home of No 19 Operational Training Unit whose function it was to train crews on large and sombre Whitley bombers. Needless to say, the posting had been a mistake but I (and several other unfortunates) had to be given useful work to do to keep us out of mischief (and out of the Station Warrant Officer's sight) while the mistake was put right. Manning a gun site and moving bombs (Norway, across the North Sea was just being invaded), sweeping hangars and cleaning latrines were the usual chores, enlivened by such orders as to locate the largest lumps of hard anthracite in the coal compound, cart them round to Station Headquarters and place them in an orderly curved line (properly dressed) to decorate the entrance approach. They were then painted white in a manner intended to impress a visiting senior Staff Officer. We later wondered if our efforts might have inspired the Drem approach lighting system which we were later to use at night, flying Spitfires. No doubt it was not so, but this story happens to be true.

Inevitably, the tedium of such fortunately temporary employment brought me to the hangars at off-duty moments, just to look at longed-for aeroplanes. On one such occasion, a Miles Master was standing on the apron and, while I was admiring this beautiful bird, a Flight Lieutenant arrived and clambered aboard. The Master did not have a self-starter, it appeared. 'Come here, airman and give me a start', a voice like that of God bellowed from the cockpit. I looked about me for support but found none. I had not the foggiest idea of what to do and had to admit it. The pilot directed me to a winding handle clipped in the rear cockpit and told me where to insert it in a small hole in the side of the engine cowling. "When I say contact, wind like hell until she starts", he commanded. "Then remove the handle and quickly pass it up to me".

The Miles Master was a big, two-seat advanced training monoplane, with a supercharged Rolls-Royce Kestrel XXX, a Vee-

After the gentle Tiger Moth, the Miles Master I was an awesome beast. An encounter such as this made the author try to understand how it worked. In fact, it was exciting to fly and very like a Hurricane. Its colour was yellow, not black, as suggested by the Ortho film used for this picture.

12 engine of nearly seven hundred horse-power — and I was expected to wind up that thing — alone? Being nineteen years of age and then of a nervous disposition, I could not help noticing, as I inserted the handle into its little hole, that the open exhaust pipes at the side of the engine were little more than a foot from my face and presumably nearly three hundred and fifty of those horses would bellow out of them in the unlikely event of my being able to start the beastly thing.

The pilot had closed his Perspex hood and I heard him yell "Contact — go on, wind like hell". I did and, much to my surprise, it was very low-geared and the propeller turned over very slowly and quite easily. After a rotation or two, with a puff of smoke, greatly to my relief, the mighty Kestrel almost purred into life. I removed the handle and gave it to the pilot who had slightly lifted his canopy. I then fled, thankfully, lest worse befell me.

I mention this trifling but, to me, alarming experience because it was exciting for a young novice and stimulated me to strive for greater things, while instilling a great respect and liking for big, powerful aero-engines. Despite their size, noise and complication, they are wonderfully delicate and expensive machines and will give of their best and get you home from a tight corner, if treated with due respect. In due course, several did.

It is perhaps appropriate that this book should be completed in the year which the Royal Air Force celebrates the seventy-fifth Anniversary of its foundation. The Service and its crews owe a great deal to their engines, designers and technicians.

Introduction
Matchmaking for Engines

The piston-engine may fairly be called a smelly, noisy, dirty but necessary evil — but the smell itself can be emotive, even exciting, as with a sports car running on Castrol 'R' oil. There is something to be said for the engine, quite apart from its sheer necessity in terms of tractive effort. It is, however, when the noise ceases (perhaps abruptly, unexpectedly and at a most inconvenient moment) that life can suddenly become more interesting, even quite exciting. As pointed out by the distinguished aviation commentator, artist and historian John Blake, the only noises remaining (of the wind in the wires and a pounding heart) can induce a fervent 'I wish I'd paid for my last coffee'.

In the early 1960s, the author had a memorable discussion on the subject of the need for a book on piston-engines with the test pilot, the late Captain Norman Macmillan. He had experienced his fair share of engine failures while testing and encouraged the author to embark on a series of articles on the subject, or a book with particular emphasis on the aeroplanes with which each engine was associated. A man of great experience and understanding of test-flying (and of engine handling and performance in particular after the First World War), he stressed the importance of matching engine performance with the requirements of the aeroplane's crew. In the 1920s, this was a field in which the practical experience of the engine industry, though limited, was growing fast.

Norman Macmillan was also a writer and historian. His series of articles on the history and testing of aero-engines and the aeroplanes they powered, particularly the series published in *Shell Aviation News*, were of considerable interest although, as he himself pointed out, a book on the subject was needed. Although several useful and detailed volumes on engines have been published in recent years, the essential object remained unfulfilled — why was such and such an engine (or version of it) put into this or that aeroplane? The term British is surrounded by 'grey areas', the original countries of origin of most early engines being anything but British. One or two which were built in Britain at that time of war with Germany even emanated originally (and not long before) from Austria or Germany itself. The grey areas grew ominously dark as research progressed and no clear, unarguable demarcation line could be laid down, except that those included should have been built in Britain, installed in an aircraft and flown.

These questions added confusion to puzzlement when trying to decide upon the sensible scope for the book. Clerget, Gnome, Hispano-Suiza, Le Rhône, Renault and several other marques of French origin but built under licence in Britain, certainly have major claims for inclusion. A large number of engines of British origin but built abroad, have been installed in foreign aircraft over the years. Not all by any means have been adequately documented anywhere but it is hoped that an adequate selection has been included, where definite information is available.

This book therefore covers, essentially, British-built piston engines, fitted to and, most importantly, flown in aircraft and range from the Green engines of around 1910 up to the Napier Nomad of the early 1950s, but the term 'British' remains a little arbitrary.

It may be a surprise that there are about nine hundred clearly definable variations of the British-built piston-engine and some three thousand one hundred installations in aircraft since 1910. There is, however, one substantial caveat on the subject. Making a readable book on the development and uses of the piston aero-engine can be a little like trying to make a light and interesting novel out of the contents of a telephone directory. It is hoped that an acceptable balance may have been achieved.

The engines are mapped out, where appropriate, in the form of families, giving basic details of each type and indicating why it was chosen to be fitted, in addition to the dry engineering details. Such important things as these need to be mentioned in suitable places of course but are not intended to be the principal purpose of the book. Although the basic types are listed, according to present-day practice, in alpha-numeric sequence, it has sometimes been necessary for the sake of clarity to list engines and aircraft in order of appearance.

Among the hundreds of books on aviation subjects, very few have dealt specifically with aircraft and their associated engines. None, so far, have dealt specifically with the combination of British engines and the airframes which they brought to life, hardly any books making more than a passing reference to the particular types of aeroplane powered by any one kind of engine. People interested in the aeroplane and its history tend to take its engine for granted, even though it is this which makes it tick and which gives the pilot a hefty push when the throttle is opened. The great days of the big piston-engine may now be over but the occasional sound of it still brings people to doors and windows, to see what is passing overhead. Shakespeare expressed a similar reaction, when 'great Pompey passed the streets of Rome' (*Julius Caesar*, Act I, Sc I).

Aeroplanes, like cars, have a magic all of their own and each individual type has its own personality. All too little has been written about the aircraft piston-engine and the combination of aeroplane and engine is indeed unique when it establishes the aeroplane's personality. Change the type of engine (a commonplace occurrence before the jet age), and a more or less marked change occurs in the visual and aural personality, quite apart from changes in the essential handling in flight and on the ground. It is the aeroplane which one notices visually, although it is the engine which draws the attention to it. Unfortunately, over the years, far too few books and magazine articles have been devoted solely to the piston aero-engine.

What has added to the incentive to write this book has been the endless examples of references, in text and in picture captions, to aircraft described as being powered by 'a Pegasus engine', or unspecified members of such large tribes as the Rolls-Royce Merlin or de Havilland Gipsy. Which one? (and why?) are the inevitable consequent questions. To redress this situation is the principal purpose of this book. Existing books have, nevertheless, been invaluable works of reference and the writer has had the great privilege of counting the authors of many of them among his friends. This volume, therefore, is not in any way intended to replace them, still less to offer criticism but rather to fill in what is seen as a wide gap in the readily available literature.

An important decision which had to be made was the period covered: the initial conclusion was to keep it to the period following the First World War. That did not last long because a substantial amount of wartime engineering (and indeed engines themselves) continued throughout the 1920s and a few of them well into the 1930s. Another decision was that the coverage should be initially of purely British engines, with perhaps another volume to cover European types and yet another American units. It did not take long to realize that this would not work either, because of the large number of French-designed engines which powered British aircraft during the 1914-1918 war, in fact almost all of the important ones being of foreign origin in one way or another. A purely British engine was something of a rarity.

The purpose of this book is to review essentially British piston-engines, beginning at the time of the early Green engines of around

1910 up to the big, complicated Napier Nomad of 1951 and, above all, to record the particular types of engine fitted to and flown in specific kinds of aircraft. Why have changes in engine installations been made in established types of aeroplane? Generally, the answer is obvious: to improve its performance, in one way or another. This applies particularly at the range of heights it was intended for, made available by an alteration or an increase in power, especially in terms of speed and climb, as well as ceiling. To assist engineers to this end, some aeroplanes have been used as specialist test-beds for new engines in order to establish their suitability for introduction into service use. It was therefore important in compiling this book to concentrate on the characteristics of the engines which contribute to making the airframe/engine combination different.

The review of engines is not, of course, confined to those for the armed Services and power plants for civilian purposes are of course included, whether for airline or private use, or simple 'pop bottle' engines for the ultra-light aircraft. Those engines in aircraft used by the Fleet Air Arm of the Royal Navy were often specially adapted for it and, in this connection, it is perhaps worth recording the rugged Senior Service independence of the naval aviator. This seems to be summed-up in the comment of a very senior engineer from industry — 'The Navy are funny people to deal with. They seem to go on the principle that, because Nelson didn't need Service Engineers, so why should they?'

There have been occasions when the reason for the very existence of an engine is not at all clear. The reason was, perhaps, because it seemed to be a good idea at the time and the maker hoped to find a market for it — not always successfully. The engines referred to are therefore those which have been built, installed in an airframe and run and, as far as can be established, at least tested in flight. The installation is quoted for each type flown. Here, it must be added, there are a few engines (particularly some very early ones), which are known to have flown but, because of the vagueness of reporting, some eighty years ago, in exactly which aircraft cannot now be positively identified. In the interests of accuracy, therefore, it has been decided to omit a very few engines where it has not been possible to unearth conclusive evidence that they have actually been flown or at least ground run in aircraft. By contrast, very successful engines, such as the de Havilland Gipsy Major, were fitted in dozens of different types of aircraft at one time or another and it cannot be claimed with certainty that even those in Britain have all been listed. Indeed, it would be tempting providence and highly inaccurate to claim that the list of engines built in Britain is totally complete. In some cases engines are known to have been built and run but, despite careful searches, it has not been possible to establish for certain in which types of aircraft they have been flown.

The conclusions drawn in every case are based on the most reliable contemporary and published information of the manufacturers (however optimistic it may now seem to have been) and on other surviving records. The author has had the good fortune to have the unstinting support of numerous friends and colleagues, experts in their own fields and branches of the aviation industry, some with an astonishing specialist knowledge. Without this help, the effort involved in compiling this work would not have been justified, nor the results of much value.

As this book is neither intended to be an engineering manual, nor a technical history of any one company, only a selection of the innumerable (and interesting) facets of engines and their handling — and thereby their performance — can be discussed. The selections may therefore appear to be subjective, but in the circumstances this is inevitable. It is extremely important to bear in mind that most, if not all, engines of a particular type or layout had a great deal in common. Therefore, to avoid needless and tedious repetition of common features of groups and types of engine, the salient points are covered in the appropriate introductory paragraphs.

Needless to say, experts in specialist fields will happily find faults and there are bound to be some who will claim that there are engines which did not fly and that there are also aircraft which have engines which are wrongly attributed to them. No doubt the author will, in due course, be provided with welcome advice, corrections or additions by reviewers, enthusiasts and other expert readers. It is to be hoped that such errors will be brought to light and so may be corrected. The sources for the information contained are both contemporary and as the result of much more recent hard labour. Published contemporary records, some of them now eighty years old, were frequently erroneous and sometimes performance figures were plainly optimistic or just advertising jargon. In many instances, there has been little hard information to go on or, worse, such historical facts as are available may seem to be tainted by the personal and more recent opinions of writers whose judgements on engine performance, satisfactory or otherwise appear to be biased or subjective. This is perhaps due to hasty misinterpretation of inaccurately published documents and sorting fact from opinion has therefore been far from easy. For this reason, if for no other, this book is an attempt to establish facts and does not set out to pass judgements, which can be a counter-productive exercise.

Engines of a particular type have always tended to run in families, with branches or major variants stemming from a basic or standard engine. Where this is so, significant variations from standard needed to be mentioned. Where the variations were minor, even apparently cosmetic, this is stated even though a variation seems to be so trivial as hardly to justify a change of type. Matchmaking between aeroplane and engine has not always been a successful operation. It is all too apparent that a few variations of type are so minor and inscrutable as to represent little more than a sales pitch on paper, hoping to tip the balance and convince a specially sought-after customer that there lay the answer to his prayer. Many such situations as this, as well as the more straightforward progression of development, need to be dealt with as briefly and concisely as possible, in the belief that such a record will fill a long-established gap on library shelves.

This leads to a major problem and it is hoped that, as time goes on, history as a subject will no longer be pushed into the background as it appears to be today. Captain J. Laurence Pritchard, the famous Secretary of the Royal Aeronautical Society wisely reminded the author, 'History begins now'. Each generation therefore has to accept the responsibility of being the custodian of the history of its own time as well as times before, in trust for generations to come.

War, sadly, is liable to hinder all that. This is no place for platitudes about the morality and tragedy of war, however worthy or just. It must be said that what tends to be overlooked in Britain is the great destruction of historical records which occurred as a result of German bombing raids, from 1940 to 1944, on major centres of British industry, such as Coventry and Liverpool, Bristol and Derby, as well as London, where bombing and fire destroyed large quantities of archive records in public libraries as well as in drawing offices. Needless to say, Britain was far from being the only sufferer. Indeed, the terrible destruction by German forces of great areas of European cities such as Warsaw which, in turn, led to wholesale conflict and the consequent destruction in Germany itself and its partners by Allied bombing, resulted in equally grievous historical losses on the losing side. Unfortunately, there can be no civilians in wartime on either side, all being caught up in the catastrophe, all suffering accordingly and their treasures, relics and culture disappearing with them.

Accidental fires are tragedies, as well as those brought about by war. Equally tragic is the regrettable, deliberate and vandalistic destruction of valuable historical records as irrelevant, ostensibly in the name of profitability, by some who are relatively new to the aircraft industry and who care little for the hard-won background of their own source of employment. This has caused a further almost irretrievable loss of essential information. (While this book was being written, the author learnt of a small building filled with undocumented glass plate aircraft negatives being destroyed as it stood, with neither fair warning nor consideration of the contents, as was the earlier use of a similar large amount of archive plates as hard-core for a car park). Without determined rescue attempts, such mindless destruction of history has therefore made the compiling of an accurate and complete record much more difficult to achieve and succeeding generations are bound to be the losers.

As an example, it was while the author was stationed at Kinloss in May 1940 and walking down a long and weary road to the nearest pub that a mechanic friend mentioned mysterious engine projects, called the Armstrong Siddeley Deerhound and Boarhound. He had, presumably, worked for the company before joining up. It was many years after the war had ended that a little more detail (frustratingly little) emerged about these intriguing and then highly secret engines. As it turned out, the only two Deerhounds to fly had been driving a Whitley up to the moment when it was destroyed in a crash, a bare six weeks before the conversation and obviously unknown to us. Such unfortunate accidents were of course all too common in Britain during the war and who was to recognize those curious and secret engines in the wreckage? When this book began, that conversation came to mind. What became of the Deerhound? The basic facts of its existence and design have been related elsewhere but no detailed drawings of the engine appear to have survived at all, as confirmed by Ray Cook, the industrious archivist of Armstrong Siddeley.

Happily, as well as private students of the subject, major institutions like the Public Record Office at Kew, the Royal Air Force Museum at Hendon, the Rolls-Royce Heritage Trust, Shuttleworth Collection and numerous other museums, collections and libraries, large and small, are doing much to preserve what is left and to fill in the gaps. It is horribly true that those who refuse to learn the lessons of history are compelled to repeat them. This book is therefore a review of the widespread uses of British aero-engines over a period of some forty-five years, within the scope available in a volume of this size, recording as much previously lost and undocumented engine history as can be found.

To review the development and the associated politics of the British aero-engine industry, though an intriguing subject in itself, is not the purpose of this book which is specifically associated with their application to aeroplanes. It does, however, provide essential background material in a survey of some of the trends of development of British engines from the years immediately preceding the outbreak of the First World War.

What data and detail had to be included and what could possibly and safely be left out was a decision not to be taken lightly. To include everything of interest would cover a football pitch and, in any case, the majority of readers will be well acquainted with much of the historical background. Few will welcome being reminded how an internal combustion engine works. Nevertheless, there are fringe areas which are worth covering, if briefly.

The great names in British aero-engine design and production were essential, both as regards designers and team leaders as well as the companies themselves. There appears to be no clear-cut line about British origins, the blurred grey area becoming very black indeed. An engine designer, knowing his own industry, was naturally well aware of the needs of the complementary airframe industry he wished to supply. He also knew just how to produce engines with the characteristics required at the time, to suit particular kinds of operation and the problems to be solved in order to do so. If he had a new power unit which he was convinced would do just what was wanted, he would try to sell the idea to a potential customer, perhaps the Air Ministry, which might be looking for just such a power unit to do a particular job. The aircraft designer would, no doubt, already be aware of this. Alternatively, the initial approach might come directly from the Air Ministry. A more likely scenario concerns both airframe and engine designers who might already have been in close touch about a projected combination of their products which could jointly be offered to Air Ministry.

Yet another situation concerns airframe and engine companies which lived virtually under a single roof, in which circumstances the alliance between the two was more or less inextricable. Bristol is the scene for one, with the Bristol Aeroplane Company and its Aero Engine Department practically under the same roof. Coventry, with Armstrong Siddeley and Armstrong Whitworth close together, is another. De Havilland at Stag Lane and Hatfield (and latterly Leavesden) is a further example, although the last example was the least rigid of these three alliances and is now, sadly, departed. Apart from such natural alliances, there was intense rivalry between engine manufacturers, competing to obtain whatever orders were available. Perhaps the most striking was that between A.H.R. Fedden (later, Sir Roy) at Bristol and John Siddeley at Coventry, each of whose companies, for nearly twenty years after the First World War, produced broadly competitive engines, although of greatly differing design.

In the piston-engine era, the aircraft industry was not organized like the motor car business — nor is it today — when the engine, chassis and bodywork are all produced by the same company, even if in different factories or different countries. Such was the way of

The inspiration for this book, Captain (as he then was) Norman Macmillan, (left), with the owner Major Wilfred Blake (centre) and navigator G.K. Malins, of a Puma-engined Airco D.H.9, at Shaibah, July, 1922, on delivery to India.

A study of engineers in conference. Royce ('R'), Hives('Hs') and Jenner ('Jn') in the garden at Royce's home at West Wittering, near Chichester, Sussex.

E.W. Hives, ('Hs') who became Lord Hives CH, MBE. He was appointed Chairman of Rolls-Royce Ltd after the death of Sir Henry Royce.

R.W. Harvey-Bailey ('By'), Alec's father. 'By' was an early associate of 'R' (Royce) and also the designer of the Rolls-Royce Falcon engine, made famous in the Bristol F.2B Fighter.

Cyril Lovesey ('Lov'), Chief Development Engineer of the Merlin during the second World War.

The winning Schneider Trophy team in 1929. L-R, Fg Off R.L.R. Atcherley, Fg Off H.R. Waghorn, Sqdn Ldr A.H. Orlebar, Henry Royce, Flt Lt D. D'Arcy Greig, Fg Off T.H. Moon, Flt Lt G.H. Stainforth.

A.A. Rubbra ('Rbr'), Rolls-Royce Technical Director and Main Board Director. He was in charge of Merlin design in the great development period during the second World War.

things in the depressed industrial period before the Second World War that there was something of a scramble to obtain orders, resulting in a flood of broadly similar products attempting to attract whatever business was available.

Which side is the more important of the two, the airframe or the engine? Were they as well matched as they might have been? It is the eternal chicken and egg situation and there appear to be no absolutes. There always have been arguments by powerful mandarins on both sides as to the merits of one combination or the other and these will no doubt continue. The demands, claims and counter claims of the aviation industry, as in any other market place, make for furious argument and implacable enmity. This book, even with the dubious benefit of hindsight, cannot set out to attempt a judgement that might have daunted Solomon. It tries to set out accurately the known facts, for the reader and historian to attempt the seemingly impossible task more easily.

There were many great and justly famous names in British aero engineering, including such as Royce, Fedden, Harvey-Bailey, Hives, Owner, Rubbra, Lovesey, Russell, Hooker, Rowledge, Siddeley, Heron, de Havilland, Halford (not necessarily in that order) and many others, far too many to record here adequately. The families of engines with which they were associated include the great names of Rolls-Royce, Bristol, Napier, de Havilland and Armstrong Siddeley, together with the numerous engines designed at the Royal Aircraft Factory (some owing much of their design to Renault).

The British aircraft industry has always gone in for emotive, sometimes almost lurid, names rather than the somewhat bleak and impersonal numerals adopted in America. The engine families are no exception. Famous names include Jupiter, Pegasus and Mercury, Perseus and Hercules, Lion and Sabre, Kestrel and Merlin, Condor and Buzzard, Hawk and Vulture, Gipsy and Ghost and a host of others. Their origins and history are recorded here as never before, together with their aircraft.

The scope is almost endless and it has been necessary to be a little selective in the examples quoted of the aircraft so powered. In the case of certain engines, a change of type of split-pin was almost enough to create a different mark of engine and, as far as possible

Major Frank Halford showing Sir Kingsley Wood, Air Minister, his Dagger VIII engine in 1939.

this is avoided. Concerning the development and use of piston aero-engines in Britain and, in particular, those engines which have been installed in aircraft and flown, there will no doubt be purists who will argue this way or that on the subject, but that is the basis on which the book has been compiled. The risk is threefold — of appearing to tell the obvious to the expert engineer, with years of experience under his belt; appearing to talk over the head of the straightforward historian who is not necessarily interested in engines, *per se*, but merely wants to find the essential bare facts; and worst of all is the risk of seeming to talk up to or down to anybody and it is hoped that something like a fair balance has been achieved. There has been a need for something such as this for a very long time and it should go some way to fill the gap, for historians, librarians and engineers, enthusiasts and modellers alike, thanks to the generous backup of highly experienced (and critical) aero engineers.

Captain Geoffrey (later Sir Geoffrey) de Havilland in his masterpiece, the Moth.

A.H.R. (later Sir Roy) Fedden.

PART 1
BRITISH PISTON AERO-ENGINE DEVELOPMENT

Chapter 1
The Power to Fly

All flight demands energy of one sort or another and all creatures that fly require power to make use of the lifting and sustaining gifts available through the most prolific elements above the Earth's surface, that mixture of gases which we call 'air'. It has been said that, if the Good Lord had intended man to fly, He would have provided wings for the purpose but, after centuries of trying, man has found ways round the problem. In man's centuries-old ambition to fly, gravity has been the only readily available motor, or source of energy, despite the discoveries of Sir Isaac Newton, gravity cannot fairly be claimed to be a British engine.

The use of gravity as a source of energy is as old as the hills themselves and so is man's struggle against it. Before the invention of a practical engine for carrying man aloft in defiance of gravity, strange ideas were devised for supporting his weight in the air, always a tremendous obstacle. His natural desire to fly, enshrined in legend (not least that of the unfortunate Icarus), is of course inspired by birds, the most intriguing and beautiful creatures whose passage through the air can appear quite effortless. The secret of this ability is the very high power that they develop for their generally light weight and their ability to use efficiently in flight the energy they store up.

The main reason for the performance of birds is the remarkable output of energy which their motor muscles can develop in relation to their weight. The rate and efficiency at which this energy is used, varies enormously from species to species. For example, the slow, lazy flap followed by a long soaring glide of the eagle and vulture can be compared with the short sharp bursts of power of the small garden birds or the very rapid wing beats of the hovering humming-bird. The energy for the muscular effort is of course provided by food. The time for which the normal movement of the particular species can be sustained depends on the rate at which the energy provided by the food can be fed to the wing muscles and then renewed following more or less brief rest periods. Birds differ greatly in the reserves of power they need. For example, a house-martin weighing a few grams will fly from an English garden, over the Alps to North Africa for the Winter and return for nesting the following Spring. Fuel of the necessary kind and in adequate quantities, is the basic requirement for providing energy for such a prodigious feat.

Man's dream of joining the birds in company with a ship far from land or wheeling round a hill-top, has been thwarted by lacking the efficient design of a bird's wing to lift him above the earth. He has thus concentrated on devising simple wings, so as to use the energy provided by gravity after first climbing to the top of a hill or tower and then gliding down the slope. The potential energy gained in climbing the hill is converted into kinetic energy, the energy of movement, in the descent. The end of the matter arrived at the bottom of the hill, entailing the laborious ascent again. The results have not always been happy. (The sad tale of Jack and Jill exemplifies the problem, even though the probability of finding water at the top of the hill seems remote).

Flight achieved through this sort of energy is one thing, whereas sustained flight without losing height in the process is quite another matter. Man's body is very feeble for its weight. Until recently, he has been incapable of the sustained power output to support and propel himself on the fragile wings at first constructed, or even to maintain gliding flight. Materials which were light and strong enough for making wings were in short supply. Using feathers, or cloth on bamboo on a simple framework to support him,

attachments were required. This is where the unfortunate Icarus, son of Daedalus came unstuck. These figures of Cretan legend from around 2,000 BC were said to have fled from the captivity of Minos, King of Crete; Icarus by means of wings attached to his body with wax. Sadly for Icarus, he flew too near to the Sun, with unfortunate if predictable results.

Many well-documented attempts to fly exist, from the eleventh century AD, when the 'Saracen of Constantinople' leapt to an equally woeful fate from a tower, supported only by a stiffened cloak. Tower-jumping persisted as a theory, but unprofitably in practice with the aid of rudimentary wings after clambering up to whatever pinnacle was handy. Several European monks, of unsurpassed faith, between the thirteenth and sixteenth centuries tried to devise satisfactory wings and one or two survived to try again. One such was the Abbot of Tongland, whose Abbey overlooked the River Dee, not far from Dumfries in South Western Scotland. This devout man took wing in 1507 from the walls of Stirling Castle. Anybody who may remember films and television series (such as *Colditz*) of which this forbidding Castle was the location of some of the scenes, will appreciate the precipitate height of those walls. That the Abbott was a survivor is itself nothing short of a miracle, for he employed goose feathers to augment his undoubted faith and blamed himself for his lack of success because he had failed to use eagles' feathers.

The urge to discover something better for the purpose than simply employing gravity persisted, with research separating into gliding and powered flight, a division which persists to this day. Enter Leonardo da Vinci, 1452-1519, probably the greatest all-round genius of history and a man with astonishing vision for his day. Born forty years before Christopher Columbus 'discovered' the West Indies, the ideas which he proposed, by any standards, were remarkable. With ambitions, an obsession and a conviction that man could sustain himself in flight by means of flapping wings, he was determined to achieve bird-like flight and devised very ingenious man-powered ornithopters which he believed could be made to flap their wings. His inventiveness led him also to propose an Archimedean-type, spring-operated, helical-screw model helicopter which could possibly have flown. As with many designs of flying machine, Leonardo's began as models, to see whether they would work.

From his surviving sketch books, it is known that, at the turn of the sixteenth century, Leonardo proposed a variety of ornithopters to be flown standing or prone and operated by a combination of arm and leg movements. One such would have had wings flapped by means of a bow-string motor which the driver would have re-wound when in flight. We now know that Leonardo's devices, had he actually built them, would not have flown, despite their mechanical ingenuity, which was remarkable. In any case, the power to make them work was not available. The weight of the incredibly ingenious contraptions which he devised was of the order of 650 lb and to this had to be added his own weight, bringing the total to something approaching 800 lb. Man's puny sustainable energy was not up to propelling such a combination, even given a start from a hill. When a man-powered machine eventually flew successfully, well over five hundred years later, scientific knowledge had enabled a machine to be built which weighed one third of this amount.

Although others, over the years, pursued the idea of powered flight by one means or another, some time passed before the first established powered flight took place, a simple model helicopter, comprising two twin rotors made of feathers, powered by a bow-string and devised in 1784 by two Frenchmen, Launoy as naturalist and Bienvenu, a mechanic. By curious coincidence, the first public demonstration of a manned hot-air balloon, made by the Montgolfier brothers, had occurred at Annonay hardly a year earlier, indicating the intensity of interest at that time in France in the possibilities of flight by one means or another.

In England, there was also keen, and more practical interest in aeronautics and the Father of Aerial Navigation may justly be given to Sir George Cayley, 1774-1857. Sir George, a most remarkable if somewhat eccentric Yorkshire baronet, had a wonderfully scientific mind which was almost as advanced for his day as Leonardo da Vinci. In 1804, he built a model glider which, with its cambered wing, first resembled what we recognize today as the shape of the aeroplane. In 1853, he built a full-size glider in which his terrified coachman was persuaded to make a short glide across a valley, an event followed almost immediately by the unfortunate man's resignation from Sir George's employment in that capacity. Cayley, like others, considered experimenting with a miniature steam engine for turning propellers, in order to power his gliders. A man with remarkable vision, he also devised perhaps the most spectacular means of providing power for flight, a motor driven by gunpowder. Happily for all concerned, he did not pursue this entertaining idea as far as installing it in a model aircraft. It fell to W.S. Henson with John Stringfellow to design an Aerial Steam Carriage and a 10-foot span model had very nearly flown under its own power in 1847 at Chard in Somerset, steam being provided by a 10-inch boiler.

In the United States, Professor Samuel Pierpont Langley, with his engineer Charles M. Manley, built and flew the first petrol-powered model 'Aerodrome' in 1901, using a small 3-cylinder rotary engine designed by a Hungarian American, Stephen Balzer. Two years later, Langley built a full-scale version which was powered by a 5-cylinder water-cooled radial engine developed by Manley and Balzer, making a brave attempt to fly across the Potomac River but it was underpowered. The Frenchman, Clément Ader and Sir Hiram Maxim both managed to clear the ground by means of steam power but sustained and controlled powered flight still eluded all of these men who shared a common purpose which can only be described as imaginative, determined and, above all courageous.

It was not until 17 December 1903 that the first practical aeroplane, powered by a simple and fairly light internal-combustion engine, was achieved by the American brothers, Wilbur and Orville Wright. They were the first men to achieve powered, sustained and controlled flights, landing on ground at the same level as the take-off point. It is from this point that the emergence and development of European and British internal-combustion engines can be traced.

At the end of the Twentieth Century, when an aircraft turbofan engine capable of producing over fifty tons of thrust is seen repeatedly and prominently in pictures by everyone, it becomes increasingly difficult to appreciate how tiny was the output of the engines with which it all began, less than a century before. With the passage of time, as its origins become more remote and blurred, the difficulty can only increase. Although this book scans the field principally of British stationary piston-engines, in the process it places in context the origins of these great modern power plants.

In the early stages of their development, gas turbines had either axial or centrifugal compressors (and one or two used a combination of both types). The essential connection between the two is that the design of the early centrifugal compressor was a direct continuation of the technology of the piston-engine's highly efficient supercharger. It led directly, as an extrapolation of the technique, to the compressor of the early gas-turbine engines. For example, the relationship between the superchargers in the Rolls-Royce Kestrel/Merlin/Griffon series and their immediate successor, the centrifugal compressor of the Dart turbo-prop, is very close. Today, when all large aircraft are powered by gas-turbines, the origins of these engines may be forgotten. The big, old piston engine supercharger is the most obvious link. In its most advanced development stages, since the end of the 1920s, the piston-engine has almost always been supercharged. Why supercharging is necessary is explained at a later stage in this narrative.

The big fan engine is but the latest in the long line of development. Any internal combustion process relies on the same principle — the ignition of a compressed mixture of air and a suitable fuel, expanded through a mechanical means of converting the resulting energy into useful work. This power can be employed mechanically by causing pistons to move in cylinders, thereby turning a crankshaft connected to a propeller, as a means of harnessing the resulting torque. Nowadays, the same principle applies when the energy of the hot gases is expanded through turbine blades so as to convert the energy partly into torque, to be applied to the common turbine-compressor shaft. The remaining energy from very hot exhaust gas is either mixed with the cool fan efflux to give the resulting thrust, or passed through a second turbine driving a co-axial shaft connected via a gearbox to a propeller or helicopter rotor shafts. The principle of converting heat into energy, whether by displacing a piston or expanding hot gas through a turbine is the same, only the application varying. Endeavouring to get the solutions to problems to come right at the right time has to be a compromise between design and behaviour.

Chapter 2

Development of a British Aero-Engine Industry

Aeronautics in Britain, as in France, started with ballooning and indeed the French Army is on record for its use of balloons for military observation as long ago as 1794. It was over eighty years before the British Army officially carried out experiments in flight with balloons, at Woolwich Arsenal, under Captain J.L.B. Templer, R.E., in 1878. The Balloon Equipment Store was moved to the School of Military Engineering at Chatham in 1882 where the Balloon Establishment was set up the following year and when the first Army balloon was made by Captain Templer. Ballooning and airship experiments continued, including the sending of balloon detachments to the Boer War. The Balloon Factory and Balloon Section, R.E. was moved to Aldershot from 1890-1892 and, in 1905, H.M. Balloon Factory was established at South Farnborough and it also accommodated the Balloon Section, Royal Engineers, which moved there the same year. Ballooning and airship design and construction were all undertaken, again principally with the idea of the enhancement of aerial observation for the Army.

Amid the many activities of the Factory involving the design, manufacture and use of dirigible airships and man-lifting kites. The name of the remarkably inventive showman, S.F. Cody, came into prominence and will always be associated with Farnborough. Following his experiments with big man-lifting kites, he interested the War Office in the idea in 1904 and was appointed Chief Instructor of Kiting at the Balloon School at Farnborough, two years later. It was only a matter of time before this imaginative man put his mind to a man-carrying powered aircraft and he devoted much energy to trying to win an order for aeroplanes of his own design for the Army.

How a British Aero-Engine Industry came into being is probably best described as: hesitantly. A group of enthusiastic and generally talented amateurs, building at several centres around Britain, experimented with some very odd-looking flying machines, from the very early years of the twentieth century. Two major events spurred them on, inevitably. On 17 December 1903, the American Wright Brothers, Wilbur and Orville, made the first acknowledged controlled powered flight at Kittyhawk, North Carolina in what a British newspaper the following day described as a 'Balloonless Airship'. The other fact that threw Britain into a state of considerable excitement was the sudden and slightly undignified arrival in a meadow below Dover Castle on 25 July 1909 of a brave Frenchman, Louis Blériot. Having persuaded his little 3-cylinder Anzani engine to keep running across the perilous Manche, or English Channel, he established beyond doubt that England was no longer an island. That raised a lot of questions, which the Tunnel does little to answer.

The success of Blériot threw open the floodgates of experiment and competition in Britain as well as in France and elsewhere on the Continent, where aviation and the inevitable flying meetings were in full spate. One of the great places where it all happened in England was the space enclosed by the new Brooklands motor racing track. Thanks to the initiative in 1909 of George Holt Thomas, a rich newspaper owner, the Locke-King family who had built the track in 1907 agreed to turn the enclosed area into a permanent aerodrome, equipped with hangars to let. Numerous pioneers of flying, such as A.V. Roe, began to make their mark there and the Aero Club Aviator's Certificate became a prize to be sought and won at Brooklands and elsewhere in Britain. The competitive world of the new and still hazardous occupation of flying brought forth not only aeroplanes but new engines. Some of the earliest of

these were of minimal power, just adaptations of motorcycle engines, driving primitive propellers via chains.

From the arrival of Blériot in 1909, among the very first British aviators was a high proportion of military and naval officers, who learnt to fly at their own expense. Several officers of the Royal Field Artillery were quick to see the possibilities of using the new aeroplanes for observation and artillery spotting. To quote a splendid phrase of J.M. Bruce in his book *The Aeroplanes of the Royal Flying Corps (Military Wing)*, 'the cavalry were not amused'. Several Gunner officers began to practice flying at Larkhill on Salisbury Plain in 1910, using their own primitive aeroplanes but with no support from the Government which, at first, accepted the advice of the Committee of Imperial Defence 'that the experiments with aeroplanes should be discontinued...'. Despite this, an Army Order authorising an Air Battalion of the Royal Engineers was issued in February 1911, creating a modest unit of two Companies.

In March 1912 a Royal Engineer officer, flown by Geoffrey de Havilland in a B.E.2, successfully spotted for artillery by wireless from the air for the first time in history, on Salisbury Plain. The following month, the standing sub-committee recommended the formation of an aerial Service designated the Flying Corps, with a Military Wing, a Naval Wing and a Central Flying School to train pilots for both. The Royal Flying Corps was created almost at once and the Air Battalion, R.E., was absorbed into the Military Wing the following month.

In August 1912, a Military Aeroplane Competition for a prize of £5,000 was held at Larkhill, to decide on an aeroplane to be built in quantity for the Army. The actual winner, on points, was S.F. Cody flying his ungainly Type V biplane. He had quickly rebuilt it from the remains of the Types III and IV, both of which had crashed the previous month, the latter in collision with a cow. The Type V was powered by the same very durable 120 hp Austro-Daimler engine, which had survived another crash the previous year in the Circuit of Britain. Despite Cody's valiant and successful efforts, the War Office decided to accept the rather more elegant and practical B.E.2, designed by Geoffrey de Havilland (not even a formal entrant in the trials) as the preferred type. This aeroplane, which had a 70 hp Renault engine, had been built at the Royal Aircraft Factory at Farnborough. The engine, however, was French and a suitable source of aero-engines in Britain was clearly needed with some urgency.

A White Paper dated 11 April, 1912 changed the name of the Army Aircraft Factory to the Royal Aircraft Factory, following which a very large number of aircraft and aero engines bearing the general 'R.A.F.' title were designed at Farnborough in the ensuing five years, through much of the Great War. Most, however, were sub-contracted to the growing aircraft industry and, according to some official records, only a total of 533 aircraft were actually built at Farnborough up to 1918. (In June 1918 the Factory, having already become a major centre for aeronautical research, was renamed the Royal Aircraft Establishment, thus preventing confusion with the Royal Air Force which had been formed two months previously).

The creative work at Farnborough of some extremely important pioneers of British aeronautics is seldom given proper acknowledgement. These include such names as Colonel J.E. Capper R.E. (the first Superintendent of the Balloon Factory) and Colonel Mervyn O'Gorman, who succeeded him when the Factory became the Army Aircraft Factory in 1911. Under O'Gorman's direction, the whole basis of a scientific method for the development of aeronautics in Britain was created and remains the foundation of methods employed to this day.

O'Gorman is also credited with employing the talented young designer and pilot, Geoffrey de Havilland in 1910 at the suggestion of F. M. Green, then Engineer in charge of design. The Factory became notable for the employment of numerous other designers, researchers and scientist test pilots, many being mentioned in the main text. The rather flamboyant style of S.F. Cody tends to overshadow other very talented men and women who were employed at Farnborough on engine and airframe development. Many were killed or injured over the years in the course of the dangerous nature of their work. Cody himself was killed in a crash but others, perhaps less well-known, should not be forgotten. They include E.T. Busk who went from Cambridge to begin valuable aerodynamics research work in 1912, only to killed in a B.E.2c two years later when the aircraft caught fire in the air. (Twelve dreadful years were to pass before the wearing of parachutes became compulsory). Others included F.W. Goodden (killed testing the prototype S.E.5 fighter). More fortunate were R.H. Mayo (remembered for his 'Composite' aircraft), J.Keith Lucas and W.S. (later Sir William) Farren and many others more or less famous for their inventive genius.

During its relatively brief existence, the Factory produced designs for a large number of aero-engines as well as aircraft, the Military Aeroplane Competition having emphasized the immediate need for an adequate supply of engines. Examples of suitable British engines were considered, many in the range of 35-80 hp, 4 and 6-cylinder upright in-line or Vee-8 cylinder units. These included Green and E.N.V. (the British-designed but initially French-built 'en V'), A.B.C. and J.A.P. units. Licence-built foreign engines, particularly the 80 hp air-cooled, Vee-8 Renault had considerable influence on design ideas at Farnborough. Most of the engines which ultimately were designed at Farnborough were, like the R.A.F. aeroplanes, farmed out to the rapidly-growing aircraft industry.

In addition, many early British aeroplanes were powered by 50, 70 and 80 hp air-cooled rotary Gnome, Le Rhône and Clerget engines. Though designed in France and imported, it was not long before these engines also were being built under licence in Britain, soon to be followed by the rotary engines designed by W.O.Bentley. In the Great War, air-cooled rotaries were used very extensively. They were light but thirsty for fuel, extravagant in the pure castor oil they used and somewhat unreliable, but the plodding reconnaissance and bombing aircraft tended to use the more reliable, though heavy 6-cylinder in line, Vee-8 or Vee-12 engines, either water or air-cooled. These engines, some designed at the Royal Aircraft Factory, were extensively used, as were the Austro-Daimler, Renault, Sunbeam and Beardmore. The adoption by Beardmore of Austro-Daimler design ideas and the subsequent production of 120 and 160 hp Beardmore engines led directly to the 260 hp B.H.P., a 6-cylinder water-cooled engine designed by Frank Halford, of whom much more anon. This, in turn, led to the complicated Galloway/Siddeley Puma story, also dealt with at greater length later.

Much use was made in fighters of the neat little water-cooled 150 hp Hispano-Suiza Vee-8 engine, designed in France by Marc Birkigt. This was built in Britain by Wolseley in several versions, the best known being the Viper. Another builder of large water-cooled Vee-shaped engines, later perhaps better associated with motor car engines was Sunbeam, whose Chief Designer was Frenchman Louis Coatalen.

Upon the outbreak of war in 1914, Henry Royce wanted to create an aero-engine, designed (as were his motor cars) as nearly as possible to perfection. His 40/50 Silver Ghost car in 1907 had aluminium castings (apart from cylinders) and alloy steels in all important ferrous components and he very much understood the use of light alloy castings and alloy steels.

Despite persuasion from the Royal Aircraft Factory that he should consider air cooling, Royce decided on a water-cooled Vee-12 engine, the Eagle, which initially delivered 275 hp and was Rolls-Royce's first and highly successful aero-engine. It was followed by the 75/95 hp 6-cylinder Hawk for coastal airships, a very rare example of the production of Rolls-Royce engines being 'farmed out' to a sub-contractor, Brazil Straker of Bristol, which gave that company's young Chief Engineer, A.H.Roy (later, Sir Roy) Fedden his chance to make a name for himself. Next appeared the remarkable and successful 260 hp Falcon, a scaled-down and lighter Eagle designed by R.W.Harvey-Bailey, used as a fighter engine and also built in considerable numbers by Brazil Straker.

There were many difficulties in producing satisfactory engines during the First World War, which is not surprising considering their relative novelty in terms of precision engineering. As examples, the quality control and performance of the American Curtiss OX-5 engine were so unsatisfactory that Brazil Straker in Bristol had virtually to redesign the engine, to make it safely usable. As well as this, no account of the less successful engines can omit the A.B.C. Dragonfly which was, at the end of the war, the subject of much critical, if unkind comment — such as a disaster waiting to happen. This is probably true in many respects, because it had been due to power a large proportion of the newly-formed Royal Air Force from April 1918 and turned out, mechanically, to be a failure of dramatic proportions.

Towards the climax of the war, the demand for ever more powerful engines increased with the emphasis beginning to grow not just on power but on economy as well, which meant a heavier emphasis on greater power per pound of installed weight. The success of the three Rolls-Royce engines, Eagle, Hawk and Falcon, led to a really powerful development, the big 650 hp Condor which was begun in 1917. The Condor was not without its troubles and, at first, was also rather too heavy. D.Napier & Son undertook sub-contract work on the R.A.F.3a for the Government. This was rather unsatisfactory work for Napier, as a result of which A.J.Rowledge, the company's Chief Designer, assumed responsibility for the design of the twelve-cylinder Napier Lion of 1918, a 450 hp 'broad-arrow' (W-shape) power unit which was extensively used in bombers and long-range flying-boats. He subsequently joined Rolls-Royce, initially to work on improvements to the Condor.

The end of the war in 1918 found the aircraft and aero-engine industry confused and there could hardly have been a more difficult situation. With the Armistice of 11 November 1918, almost every warlike contract was terminated very abruptly, leaving the industry gasping. It was bloated with production, much of it in store and industry was desperate for new orders. Official records show that fifty-eight thousand engines had been made in Britain or purchased abroad. Engine production from August 1914 to December 1918, ordered, delivered and cancelled or suspended as officially recorded by the Ministry of Munitions at the end of the war, were meticulously researched by Jack Bruce and Mike Goodall for *Cross and Cockade* and are here reproduced with the Society's permission. It has to be noted, however, that, in the course of later research among original documents, it became apparent that the exactness of some of the figures should be treated with caution.

The Dragonfly débâcle had done little to help and a real disaster was avoided — just. All was not lost, however, for the R.A.F.8, 14-cylinder air-cooled radial, designed to take a supercharger and which had been started at Farnborough in 1916, was waiting to appear as the Siddeley-Deasy Jaguar, after the company sorted out the problems which had occurred in making the water-cooled 230 hp B.H.P./Galloway Adriatic engine into a workable engine, as the Siddeley-Deasy Puma.

The end of the First World War was also the beginning of long-running battles between the designers and manufacturers of rival air-cooled engines in the 400-450 hp class and the protagonists of similarly powered water-cooled engines. Coolant leaks, rigidity and stiffness, as well as the relative installed weights were among disputed points. Siddeley-Deasy at Coventry (soon to become Armstrong Siddeley) had a powerful rival at Bristol, initially in the Cosmos Engineering Company whose Jupiter engine had been designed by Roy Fedden and, shortly after, by the Engine Department of the Bristol Aeroplane Company, which took the whole concern over.

During the First World War, the relatively heavy though powerful German water-cooled engines of around 200 hp had a low fuel consumption and, at first until the arrival of Rolls-Royce's Eagle, were rather more efficient than the Allied equivalents.

Gradually, developments by British manufacturers and the Royal Aircraft Factory overtook the German advantage and the need for supercharging became ever more obvious. In France, Professeur Rateau worked on exhaust-driven centrifugal blowers and had made a start on the problem. With low compression ratios, the exhaust was too hot for the materials then available for turbines, which tended to disintegrate under heat and stress with alarming and potentially disastrous consequences.

The supercharging of engines to compensate for the drop in atmospheric pressure with the gain of height was the subject of much work at Farnborough, particularly by J.E. Ellor from 1915 onwards. He began with an engine-driven impeller, installed at the rear of an R.A.F.1a in a B.E.2c in December of that year. The R.A.F.8 14-cylinder radial had, from the outset, been intended to incorporate a gear-driven blower and its successor, the Armstrong Siddeley Jaguar, was the first production-type engine to have one. In addition, Farnborough also did much experimental work on exhaust-driven turbo-compressors after the French Professeur Rateau had sent over an experimental set, following promising bench tests in 1917. This was mounted on an R.A.F.4d engine in an R.E.8 and, for work in conjunction with this equipment, a remarkable variable-pitch propeller, weighing 100 lb, was designed and made at the Royal Aircraft Factory, in order that the power might be absorbed at a constant speed of rotation. Fortunately, a photograph of this unique installation has survived.

The story of supercharging is a complex and interesting subject but this is not the place to go into its history in depth. A detailed account of these early experiments is recorded in the Internal Combustion Engine Sub-Committee Report on the Rateau turbo-compressor, No 36, dated June 1918. A number of test flights were made with and without this variable-pitch propeller and, on the last flight, the turbine rotor failed at 26,500 rpm. Ground air pressure could be maintained up to 13,500 feet, at which height a release valve was operating, to maintain the proper mixture. It was estimated that the rated altitude would have been 17,000 feet. The Report may look like dry reading but, in the days before parachutes were in regular use, some of the flight tests must have been alarming and are proof that explosive turbine failure is not a new phenomenon. In the end, Farnborough left most of the development work to industry, Ellor eventually joining Rolls-Royce in 1928, being referred to as 'Lr' in that company's terminology.

Frank Bernard Halford is a name which has appeared and reappeared throughout the history of the British aero-engine industry, well into the gas turbine era. Halford was the 'H' in the B.H.P. saga of the First World War, which is related at greater length elsewhere. Following the war, Halford and Geoffrey de Havilland collaborated in engine and airframe design and integration to a remarkable degree for a very long time. At the end of the war, Halford worked as an associate with Ricardo & Co., engine consultants. This firm, which undertook research into fuel, combustion, supercharging and the uses of the Burt-McCollum sleeve-valve system, was founded and run by Harry R.(later, Sir Harry) Ricardo, an extremely inventive engineer.

In 1923, Halford left Ricardo and, shortly after, became a consultant to A.D.C. (the Aircraft Disposal Company) to make whatever use could be made of the very large number of engines left over after the war. This work led Halford, initially, to adapt the 80 hp Renault, modified with aluminium cylinder heads, to become the 120 hp Airdisco. The A.D.C. Nimbus and Airsix project both owed much of their origin to the Siddeley Puma. Subsequently, by using half the Airdisco and a new crankshaft and crankcase, Halford created the little A.D.C. Cirrus, which was first used to power de Havilland's new Moth light aeroplane. The Airdisco company soon ceased trading and Cirrus engines continued to be made by the Hermes Engineering Company until 1934, when Blackburn Aircraft took the concern over and a new series of Blackburn Cirrus engines emerged.

It was not long after the end of the war that the large numbers of demobilized former R.F.C. pilots and others, like-minded, turned their attention to the possibilities of getting back into the air. Gliding was the obvious first step and meetings became popular occasions, especially on hill tops. Most of the pre-war engines, based on motorcycle power units, were heavy and out-dated and there was much interest in providing new power for some of the gliders.

Competitions, with fairly substantial prizes were arranged and several little engines derived from motor cycle units were produced by A.B.C., Blackburne and Douglas, their capacities ranging from 350 to 750 cc. The Motor Glider competition, using engines not exceeding 750 cc, took place at Lympne in Kent in October 1923, the ANEC I aircraft achieving 87.5 miles on a single gallon of petrol and subsequently reaching a height of 14,400 feet. The Air Ministry, partly with an eye to an ultra-light two-seater trainer, encouraged the development of light aeroplanes and engines more suited to running at high power than previously and sponsored a second competition a year later, for engines of 1,100 cc. This was again held at Lympne and some two-seat entrants were rather underpowered, important exceptions being those powered by Roy Fedden's little Bristol Cherub flat-twin.

The Air Ministry recommended a minimum of 34 hp, and, for training purposes, around 45 hp, the fitting of dual ignition and type-testing, to improve reliability. Another competition, the second organized by the Air Ministry, was for engines weighing up to 170 lb (which at around 3 lb/hp would provide almost 60 hp) was organized in 1925 for two-seaters, but was postponed until 1926. De Havilland formed his own company in 1920 and, with the encouragement of the Air Ministry, began work on several light aircraft designs. Two of the competitors were de Havilland Moths but, because their 65 hp A.D.C. Cirrus engines were well over the limiting weight, they were excluded from performance trials. However, Armstrong Siddeley had by then produced the 75 hp Genet, which was light enough to allow the Genet Moth to be entered. This series of competitions was the beginning of the British light engine industry for light and ultra-light aeroplanes. Examples which extended up to the late 1930s are the A.B.C. Scorpion and Hornet, the Scott Flying Squirrel, the Carden Ford adaptation of a motor-car engine, Aero Engines Sprite and Pixie, Blackburne Thrush and Tomtit, the Bristol Cherub I and III. Also, there were the little radials, the compact and smooth-running geared Pobjoy 'R', Niagara and Cataract, and British versions of the French Salmson series.

Following the initial success of the Genet and Cirrus Moths, Halford, as a consultant, collaborated with de Havilland in the design of a more powerful yet similar engine but using new and lighter parts, resulting in the Gipsy I. It was an immediate success in the celebrated Gipsy Moth and was the beginning of a long line of Gipsy engines, including the Major which powered almost innumerable but at least eighty different types of aircraft.

In the early 1920s, Armstrong Siddeley joined battle with Bristol for orders for aircraft of all kinds and they remained arch-rivals for nearly twenty years. The company's numerous air-cooled radial engines ranged from the little Genet, through the workhorse Jaguar, Lynx and Panther and the big Leopard of the 1930s. The end of the Armstrong Siddeley line came with the Tiger, another big radial which never quite made the top grade but pioneered two-speed supercharging. A modestly powered but very successful engine was

The Armstrong Siddeley Tiger cylinder and its two-valve head.

the Cheetah (developed from the Lynx), and the 5-cylinder Mongoose led to its double-row derivative the Serval. Armstrong Siddeley retained two-valve cylinder heads, whereas Bristol, Rolls-Royce and Napier had opted for the more complex four-valve layout.

The two-valve cylinder head of an Armstrong Siddeley Jaguar.

Henry Royce, assisted by A. J. Rowledge who had left Napier, worked on getting the Condor to turn into a reliable if still rather heavy engine. In addition, experiments that were conducted in 1924 on a very advanced engine pointed to what was to come a decade later on, particularly as regards supercharging. Although still called an Eagle, this complex X-shaped, supercharged 16-cylinder engine, was no longer a true Eagle.

Meanwhile, Fedden at Bristol continued the successful Jupiter line, as well as the Lucifer and two or three other less successful engines. He was gathering round him a small but enthusiastic team, headed by L.F.G. 'Bunny' Butler, who was his very meticulous designer. There is no doubt that, though Fedden was a man of ideas and a brilliant entrepreneur, it was Butler who put the integrity and skill into the design of Bristol engines and a man whose work was also very much respected by Rolls-Royce.

The development of the 9-cylinder radial, air-cooled series continued the success of Bristol, with the emergence of the Mercury and Pegasus. The latter was a long-stroke version of the Mercury, which was a fighter engine while the Pegasus distinguished itself in the hard-working bomber-type field, as a kind of grown-up Jupiter for powering the long-range bomber and transport. The Phoenix was a diesel experiment, from the Pegasus design, while the Draco was an experimental petrol injection version of the same basic engine.

Fedden, determined as ever, saw a future in the Burt-McCollum sleeve-valve for air-cooled engines. Despite formidable production problems, particularly with the emergence of 'shadow factories' run

by the motor-car industry before and, during the Second World War, he managed to create a successful series of light, powerful 9, 14 and 18-cylinder engines, the Perseus, Hercules and Centaurus respectively. The civil Hercules and Centaurus, big engines running at modest power, set remarkable records for economy of operation, reaching three thousand hours between overhauls. In all, one and a half million Bristol sleeve-valve engines were turned out.

Halford's inventiveness put Napier back on the aero-engine map in a modest way, after the Lion had been outclassed by Rolls-Royce's 'F' engine. In 1929 he devised an upright 16-cylinder H-shaped engine of 350 hp, named Rapier, effectively gearing together four scaled-down Gipsy engines. It was successful but only saw very limited use. A larger 24-cylinder version, the Dagger, initially of 675 hp, also saw limited service in the Royal Air Force. Halford also tried out the Napier Javelin, an inverted 6-cylinder engine to compete with the Gipsy Six but without great success.

C.R. (later Sir Richard) Fairey imported fifty of the compact and lightweight Curtiss D-12 engines from the United States and, for British use, re-named the engine the Fairey Felix. The D-12 was developed from the power unit which had enabled the United States to win the Schneider Trophy twice. When fitted to a squadron of Fairey Foxes, these day bombers proved to be faster than the fighters intended to intercept them and gave rise to some thought at Derby. Henry Royce did a careful analysis of the D-12 and felt that he could substantially improve on certain aspects of the design of the American engine.

The ideas which rapidly emerged as a result of Royce's study resulted in the 'F' series engine, later to become the illustrious Kestrel and which quickly became available in normally-aspirated and supercharged versions, for medium and high-altitudes. This splendid 550 hp engine appeared in the Hawker Hart in its innumerable versions, as well as the Fury and many other types of aircraft in the 1930s. The Kestrel, which outshone all others of its kind before the war, also appeared in an experimental evaporatively-cooled version named Goshawk and was ultimately developed into the Peregrine.

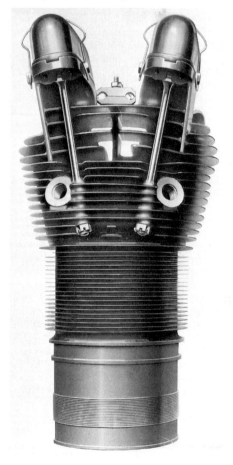

A modernized version of the Armstrong Siddeley Jaguar cylinder and two-valve head which was adapted for the Tiger.

With the Kestrel, Rolls-Royce really put the 60 degree Vee-12 liquid-cooled engine once more on centre stage. The Buzzard, a bigger engine of similar design and produced in small numbers, also had great potential. The 'H' engine, or Rolls-Royce Buzzard, was the basis for the spectacular 'R' model, of which Rowledge was the chief designer and which enabled R.J.Mitchell's Supermarine S.6B seaplane finally to win outright the Schneider Trophy and, albeit temporarily, gain the World's Speed Record in 1931. The 'R' engine had an important influence on the development of the Merlin, with the idea of getting military-type lives with Schneider Trophy-type powers, an achievement which in fact occurred during the Second World War.

Royce (by then, Sir Henry) died in the spring of 1933 after much ill-health and was in due course succeeded by Ernest Hives (later, Lord Hives). As head of that great company, E.W.Hives ('Hs', in the curious terminology adopted by Royce for his senior executives) was supported by a team of engineers who gained fame in their own right. The Rolls-Royce Merlin has a place in history and its story is too well-known to need a detailed repetition here. In its many versions, it powered fighters and bombers in vast numbers throughout the Second World War, performing great feats of endurance and power, which doubled in the course of its development and gave remarkably little trouble throughout its life, which ended honourably ploughing across the Atlantic with passengers.

The Griffon was another development of the Buzzard and the racing 'R' engine and was similar in design to a Merlin but 10 litres bigger and turned the other way. It successfully powered the later Spitfires, succeeding in catching the elusive and fast-flying German V-1 flying bomb. In its contra-prop version, it has also ground its reliable but noisy way into Royal Air Force history, powering the 'ten thousand rivets flying in close formation' called the Avro Shackleton. The X-shaped 24-cylinder Vulture was reminiscent in some respects to the Kestrel and Peregrine series but was not so successful. The second Eagle, a very high powered horizontal H-shaped 24-cylinder sleeve-valve engine, ended the production line, although there were other Rolls-Royce engines of great interest coming along, when the gas turbine overtook everything and swept all else aside.

Halford developed a really powerful engine in the Napier-Halford, H-shaped Sabre. This was a horizontal H-shaped, liquid-cooled 24-cylinder sleeve-valve engine, which began life in the Royal Air Force in 1940 in the Hawker Typhoon at just over 2,000 hp. Manufacturing problems with the sleeves and subsequent lubrication troubles and seizures inhibited the initial success of the Typhoon and resulted in several serious accidents but, after sleeve redesign and other modifications, the Typhoon and Tempest were formidable fighters in the last two years of the war.

The names of Alvis and Wolseley cannot be omitted from this review. Makers of sports and high class touring cars, both turned their attention to the medium-powered air-cooled radial engine in the years immediately preceding the Second World War. Wolseley produced three types of engine, notably the sweetly-running Aries. Alvis, despite rather elaborate plans to rival neighbouring Armstrong Siddeley in Coventry, only produced one flyable engine before war overtook the industry in September 1939. By a strange fate, Wolseley withdrew leaving Alvis to challenge Armstrong Siddeley for the medium power market and scooped up what business was to be had after the war, in light transports and helicopters.

THE AMERICAN CONTRIBUTION

This account cannot omit the massive American contribution to the production of engines for wartime use in Britain. The big 12-cylinder Liberty was neither designed nor built in Britain in 1917 but it was used so extensively by the Royal Air Force and overhauled in what became known as Maintenance Units in such large numbers that it cannot fairly be ruled out. For years, Royal Air Force D.H.9As powered by these remarkably reliable engines and, bristling with extra radiators, spare wheels and much besides, ploughed their reliable, monotonous and unspectacular way through some of the most spectacular and inhospitable terrain in the World, the North-West Frontier Province of India (now Pakistan).

Unlike the justly famous Liberty, the not so celebrated American Curtiss OX series was extensively modified (amounting to a redesign) and rebuilt in Bristol by Brazil Straker, subsequently becoming adequately reliable. The Curtiss D-12, some of which as previously mentioned were imported into Britain by Richard Fairey and installed in Fairey Fox I light bombers, was a successful engine when used by the Royal Air Force and was renamed the Fairey Felix.

In the Second World War, the enormous engine-building programmes by Ford in Britain and Packard in the States, famous names more clearly associated with motor cars, must be acknowledged. Vast numbers of Rolls-Royce Merlins and their American equivalents, Packard V-1650 engines, were progressively developed and modified in closely monitored parallel engine programmes as the war progressed. Even if previous relations with American engine manufacturers had at times lacked the intimate understanding which war can induce, the collaboration by Ford and Packard with Rolls-Royce in building the Merlin during the Second World War was magnificent. This, however, does not apply to Ford in the U.S.A., because Henry Ford in fact turned down the idea of making Merlins. The Merlin engine variants and American equivalents in the V-1650 series were produced in larger numbers than any other piston engine the World has ever seen, including all the big American radials, this huge production effort justifying a book on its own.

Chapter 3
The Design of Engines

This book is not intended to be a detailed study of the workings of the internal combustion engine but the subject must be touched on, however briefly. The following notes on the design and operating characteristics may serve as an *aide memoire* to help to clear the air for readers whose interest is historical rather than technical, or for those who have neither the time nor need to study the subject but just require a quick reference book. To answer some of the commonest questions which have cropped up in the course of research, it seemed therefore worthwhile to note down the two most important types of engine and a series of functions of the engine, from the moment the air enters the intake to the exit, via the exhaust.

To begin at the beginning may be a cliche, but it helps. In addition to the almost universally adopted four-stroke engine, it is necessary also to refer to the two-stroke engine, uncommon as it has been as an aircraft propulsion unit. The basic operation of the four-stroke (or four-cycle) engine, first devised by the German engineer Nikolaus Otto in 1876 and used in most motor vehicles is too well-known to require more than a brief mention here. The basic 'suck, squeeze, bang, blow' process is more correctly and more elegantly known as the Otto cycle and the four piston strokes are referred to as the induction, compression, power and exhaust strokes; they operate in the course of two crankshaft revolutions. Almost all piston aero-engines recorded in this book are therefore in the four-stroke category. The lighter, simpler and ingenious two-stroke engine has never, so far, found much favour as an aircraft power unit although some have flown and the type may yet reappear in quantity production with improved design. So a brief description of the basic valveless two-stroke cycle cannot here be omitted.

It is worth recording that for some years from about 1960, the Japanese firm of Honda won international motor-cycle races with monotonous regularity. By chance in 1967, the author met one of Honda's senior engineers who was visiting Europe for a conference. In the course of discussing the two-stroke engine, the engineer remarked inscrutably (and perhaps not too seriously) 'Of course nobody really understands quite how a two-stroke engine works'. Despite such proclaimed ignorance, the Japanese were effectively sweeping the low-power board at the time and developed valved two-stroke racing engines. However true that claim of ignorance may have been, Britain also had considerable success over the years in the design and production of small two-stroke engines and, clearly high performance two-stroke engines are viable.

When describing any continuous cycle, or rotation, the best starting point is as debatable as the cycle itself. In either the two- or the four-stroke cycle, if the cylinder is filled with a compressed mixture of fuel and air and this is ignited (by either of the two usual methods), the resulting burning and released energy forces the piston downwards, best described as the power stroke. At this point, the two-stroke and four-stroke engine cycles part company.

The simple two-stroke cylinder has upper and lower ports, the lower one being for inlet and the upper one for exhaust. There is no mechanical valve gear in the basic type of two-stroke because the piston itself, moving past the ports, takes the place of this by exposing and closing each in turn. The fuel and air is mixed in the crankcase, in a manner reminiscent of some of the rotary engines. Below the piston, after its upward compression stroke and ignition mentioned above, a fuel and air mixture has been sucked in through the inlet port when the piston passed it on the upward compression stroke. Following ignition, therefore, beneath the piston on the power stroke, the fuel and air mixture now present is forced downwards into the crankcase. This compresses it because the inlet port is then covered by the piston on its down-going stroke. At the same time, the top of the piston is uncovering the exhaust port which is starting to evacuate the burnt gases. Simultaneously, the piston uncovers an internal passage which connects the crankcase (with its compressed mixture) to the cylinder. The mixture rushes into the cylinder and this not only helps in the evacuation or scavenging of the previous burning but fills the cylinder in preparation for the upward compression stroke. As the piston rises, it covers both the exhaust port and the inlet passage from the crankcase, thus sealing the cylinder for compression. As the piston rises, it creates a depression in the crankcase and as its base passes the fuel and air inlet, it sucks in the next charge to be compressed into the crankcase and so, at the top of the stroke, ignition starts the process again.

The valveless two-stroke is therefore a very simple engine, cleverly designed with few moving parts. It is a lot smaller and lighter for its power. Given the advanced technology now available, the two-stroke, in valved form, may yet make a come-back in the aero-engine field. For whatever reason, the two-stroke is at present notable for its almost total absence from the aviation scene. Despite several imaginative and brave projects, it has so far failed to achieve its predicted place in the engine market. The rampant development of the four-stroke piston engine during the Second World War led directly to the gas turbine and absorbed enormous expenditure of Government and private money, leaving little scope, incentive or finances for pursuance of an engine with such an uncertain future. (See Footnote). Nevertheless, it is worth recording the dry comment by the then Dr (later Sir Stanley) Hooker that the four-stroke produced one stroke to produce power — and three strokes to wear it out! The Rolls-Royce Crecy, a sleeve-valve, direct-injection two-stroke engine, which could have been a superb power plant, was a distant dream sadly overtaken by the cold light of the dawn of the gas turbine.

NOTE: (The particular reasons why such a situation should have come about are discussed in greater detail in other books listed in the Bibliography).

If it had been intended from the outset that man should fly, he would not only have developed wings for the purpose but the provision of a constant atmospheric pressure would also have helped. As it is, the laws of physics unfortunately preclude such a convenient solution to the problem and the engines which man has developed to give him the energy to rise from the surface do not work equally well at height as on the ground. Robert Boyle concluded, some thirty years before his death in 1691, that the volume of a gas is inversely proportional to the pressure, if the temperature remains constant. This may be a simple definition to the engineer or physicist but may be confusing to the lay reader, and it is perhaps worth a thought as to what it actually involves.

Boyle's Law, as it has become known, came from his realization that, as height is gained, the temperature and pressure fall and the volume increases. If the volume increases, the density of the gas must at the same time decrease. When air is passed through a tube at sea level and is kept flowing at a steady rate, the pressure and temperature of the gas also remain constant. When the tube begins to rise above the earth's surface, the air passing through it, at the same steady rate, will register a drop in pressure and temperature in step with the increase in height. Therefore, when this flow remains at the same steady rate and the pressure and temperature drop with the increase of height, the density of the air must also drop. In other words, the number of molecules of oxygen gas passing at the steady rate through the tube also drops (oxygen being only a part of the mixture of gas which we call 'air'). An engine's air intake is just such a tube and, through it, the oxygen in the air flows, after which the fuel in the form of petroleum gas is mixed by suction in a carburettor or injection by means of a pump. Keeping the fuel/air mixture 'correctly proportioned' as air density decreases with height becomes critically important. In other words, the higher the aircraft flies, the thinner the air.

By comparison with the engine of a motor vehicle the aeroplane's engine, though similar in operation, is far more complex. This is because of the third dimension, height and the consequent loss of atmospheric pressure and density as height is gained.

If the simplest kind of aero-engine is considered, driving a fixed-pitch propeller, the carburettor is set for the correct fuel and air mixture so as to give the required rpm at full-throttle and therefore the engine will be delivering its maximum horse-power, at ground level (or sea level). The engine is therefore developing this maximum power and developing the maximum thrust of which the propeller is capable while stationary on the ground. The drag of the blades, stirring up stationary air is considerable. Once the chocks or brakes are released and the aeroplane accelerates through the surrounding air, the drag on the propeller decreases, the engine's rpm increases and as the rpm is a measure of the engine's rate of doing work, so the horse-power increases slightly up to the maximum rpm for which it is designed. Another small benefit is a reduction of the back-pressure on the exhaust as the aircraft accelerates. While it is stationary, there is an inertia in the exhaust as well as the air surrounding the pipes. Once the machine gets going, this is reduced to a small but significant degree, adding further to the rpm and therefore the developed horse-power.

After take-off, the temperature begins to fall as the aircraft climbs but the fall in atmospheric pressure does not immediately have much effect, or adversely affect the engine's power. Instead, for about the first 2,000 feet of climb, the decrease in temperature slightly increases the air density, more or less balancing the effect of the reduction in atmospheric pressure, thereby maintaining the take-off horse-power up to this height. From this height upwards, the reduction of pressure and temperature begin to take effect. For this reason the A. & A.E.E. at Martlesham, in many of its Performance Test Reports, adopted 2,000 feet as the Rated Altitude of the normally aspirated or unsupercharged engine.

The supercharged aero-engine was initially invented to overcome the problems associated with the reduction of air pressure with increase of height, so as to maintain the maximum sea-level power permissible for the engine up to the maximum height to which the supercharger was capable of maintaining it, while keeping the fuel-air mixture in the correct proportions. The height so achieved is the Rated Altitude.

The simple in-line engine is usually a four or six-cylinder machine, whereas all but a few early radials were air-cooled. There have always been strong protagonists for both air-cooling and liquid-cooling and the arguments one way or another chiefly concern installed weight and cooling drag. Liquid-cooled engines are normally upright, whereas the air-cooled type (typified by the Gipsy and Cirrus range) is much more frequently in the inverted position because this can give the pilot a somewhat better view ahead. In-line engines come in various other shapes, ranging from the familiar Vee-8s of the Royal Aircraft Factory and Renault or Vee-12s of Rolls-Royce (even a few little Vee-twins for the ultra-lights) to the upright H-shaped type adopted by Halford with his Napier engines. These latter were air-cooled and were followed by the massive horizontally mounted H-shaped Sabre, while their predecessor off the Napier line was the famous Lion, an engine in a 'broad arrow' or W formation.

Although the majority of the radials and rotaries were air-cooled, a notable exception was the French engineered Salmson range, developed by Canton-Unné. In the First World War, these were water-cooled radials, some of them having vertical crankshafts driving their propellers through right-angle gearing. This type of engine appeared in most cases with cylinders in odd numbers, from three upwards, except for some of the early Anzanis, which had six in a single row. Nearly all the rest of British radials had single rows of up to 9 cylinders and then went into multiple rows of odd numbers. Thus, there were 3, 5, 7 and 9-cylinder single-row engines and 10, 14 and 18-cylinder staggered double-row units. (In the U.S.A. Pratt & Whitney achieved adequate cooling with the 28-cylinder, four-row Wasp Major). There were exceptions, of course and these were mostly experimental and not very successful. These included the 15 and 21-cylinder, three-row Armstrong Siddeley Hyena and Deerhound engines and an odd 'Double Octagon' from Bristol, called Hydra. The rotaries followed the same general trend as the more conventional radials, although Clerget managed to squeeze eleven cylinders more or less successfully into a single row.

SOME OF THE ODD ONES

Axial or barrel-type engines, often called wobble-plate or swash-plate engines may be unfamiliar to some but they cannot be omitted altogether. Several companies looked at them and most looked away again, hastily. These engines work on the principle of mounting the cylinders axially, that is, parallel to the crankshaft, exerting their turning moment via ball-ended piston rods operating in sockets in an inclined disc connected to the propeller shaft.

Two axial types are here recorded as having been built and flown in Britain and there are no doubt others. One type was similar to a radial engine, although with axial cylinders. Called the Redrup Fury and designed by C.B. Redrup, it was flown in a Simmonds Spartan in 1929. Redrup also designed an air-cooled, rotary axial engine, although there is yet to appear proof that it was flown. Another rotary axial engine which did fly was the 40 hp Statax, mounted in a Caudron G.III biplane. A possible connection between Statax and Redrup has not been established — yet. Two-stroke and four-stroke variants are possible. The essential advantage of this type of layout is its light weight, small diameter and 'head resistance' or drag for its potential power which theoretically can be considerable, a figure of 5,000 hp at 3,000 rpm for a weight of 3,000 lb having been mentioned.

Mention should also be made of some of the stalwart aeroplanes which were used as test-beds for new engines. The Hawker Hart probably takes the prize for having, in one form or another, been used as a test-bed for practically every kind of British engine (and quite a few foreigners) from 450 hp, up to the 1,030 hp Merlin prototypes, sharing the latter work with the big Hawker Horsley torpedo bomber. There were others, including the big, clumsy-looking Folland Fo.108 43/37, several of which were built purposely for testing the biggest engines during the Second World War. Others included the Armstrong Siddeley Deerhound Whitley, the Hyena-engined A.W.XVI. In the Bristol camp, there were the Westland Wapiti with the Draco and the Phoenix diesel engine, while the Hawker Harrier flew with the Bristol Hydra (Double Octagon) engine.

In the early 1930s, a period of imminent end radical changes in the thinking of engine/airframe designers. The cantilever monoplane, with all its great possibilities for clean design and speed was typified and led by Lockheed's single-engined Orion. This was introduced on European routes by Swissair and led Heinkel in Germany to plan the handsome He 70. Its B.M.W. VI engine, though reliable and powerful, was heavy and old-fashioned, its combination with the He 70 seeming to lead nowhere, despite German Air Ministry hope for export orders for it. Rolls-Royce supplied a Kestrel V to an order from Germany and this was fitted to He 70G D-UBOF. The result was the export of the aircraft to Rolls-Royce at Hucknall early in 1936, its registration as G-ADZF and subsequent use as a test-bed for several Kestrel engines and the Peregrine. The other, rather more significant, result was Germany's very watchful eye on developments at Derby and Hucknall.

The ultimate in complication, though not entirely a piston engine, was the Napier Nomad. This immensely complex, compound engine, combined a very advanced sleeve-valve diesel engine, connected with a gas turbine, as a turbo-prop power plant which flew in the nose of an Avro Lincoln.

Initially, engines were very simple affairs, use being made of well-known and easily-worked materials. Forged or stamped steel and cast-iron were commonly used, although the obvious weight problem had to be tackled as soon as it was realized how great were the penalties involved. Aluminium was in its infancy as an engineering material when aero-engines were first introduced but castings in this material were bedeviled by porosity until casting techniques improved generally. The loads imposed on steel components, which were highly stressed or subject to continual vibration, made research into stronger alloy steels a matter of great urgency. So the period of development of the aero-engine at the time of the Great War was also the time of great strides in the development of new, stronger and lighter materials. The old, time-honoured substances used up to the beginning of the twentieth century had to be replaced by materials with properties far better suited to the demanding environment of the inner workings of a powerful engine. The methods of producing new materials had to be improved in step with the possibilities they offered.

There are far too many to describe here but one or two examples may illustrate the situation. Early pistons were usually made of cast-iron. Since it is a heavy material, the inertia resulting from its use in pistons contributed much to the low rpm and accordingly low horse-power of early engines. This was a particularly significant factor in the running of rotary engines. During the 1914-1918 war, the National Physical Laboratory developed a high-strength aluminium-based alloy, containing 4 per cent copper, 2 per cent nickel, 1.5 per cent magnesium, the remainder being aluminium. This was to become well-known as Y-alloy, and was subsequently used extensively in highly stressed parts of aero-engines. It was far lighter than cast-iron and the firm of Peter Hooker Ltd, who built Gnome rotary engines in Britain under licence, made forged pistons for these engines in Y-alloy. Their running became smoother and at the same time more reliable.

Henry Royce had used aluminium alloys, as well as alloy steels extensively in his 40/50 Silver Ghost car engines and was therefore no stranger to the materials when he started work on aero-engines. All production Rolls-Royce aero-engines had aluminium pistons and it was W.O.Bentley who had suggested the aluminium piston, from his racing experience with the D.F.P. car. It has been said that it took 10 per cent inspiration and 90 per cent perspiration on the part of Royce, in order to make the alloy piston work and it was very successful indeed.

This useful material was also used for forged cylinder heads and other components (not always so successfully). Together with great improvements in the qualities of steel forgings in general, it greatly contributed to increased reliability and reduced weight. Such improvements did not happen overnight and some components took many years to perfect. Both aircraft and motor racing engineers have persevered over the years towards achieving the power output and reliability expected today.

Porosity was a severe problem in casting early aluminium cylinder heads. It occurred when gas bubbles formed in the molten metal during the casting process, fatally weakening the finished component. Until the difficulty was overcome, cast aluminium heads were subject to a very high rejection rate (at one time up to 90 per cent). The pressures within a cylinder are extremely high and it must be strong enough to withstand quite a hammering. Where weight is not a problem, fairly crude and substantial components are acceptable but, in an aircraft, weight-saving is naturally of great importance. Therefore cylinder wall thickness has to be reduced to an absolute minimum to save weight and, with early materials, the compromise between weight and strength presented difficulties. Improvements in materials were therefore important.

Great stress concentrations occur in the cylinder head because of the intensity of heat, as it contains both the exhaust and the inlet ports as well as the sparking plugs. The heat of the exhaust has to be evacuated through the exhaust port very smartly indeed, both the heat and the expansion which goes with it being besetting problems. The exhaust valve is, literally, in the thick of it and burnt-out valves have always been a source of trouble. Corrosion caused by the chemistry of combustion, coupled with the physical laws which govern motion and heat, are a formidable combination as well. The cylinder head is therefore a component of the greatest importance and much attention has had to be given to keeping it as cool as possible, hence the elaborate finning of the air-cooled cylinder and the complex internal coolant passages of a liquid-cooled engine.

At the beginnings of the internal combustion engines, the cylinder heads were castings, usually of iron or steel. These were subsequently replaced towards the end of the First World War by aluminium castings and, latterly, forgings. It would be impossible, here, adequately to deal with the problems of cylinders and heads except to draw attention to some of the difficulties of getting the hot exhaust away in adequate time for the next charge to enter the cylinder — at, say, 3,000 rpm which is 750 exhaust strokes a minute, or 12.5 per second. (In these terms, a racing car engine peaking at perhaps 14,000 rpm hardly bears thinking about and the Appendix on valve overlap is indeed thought-provoking).

The burnt gases on the exhaust stroke having to emerge through the port, past the valve in the cylinder head, have been the object of much study. S.D. Heron, a senior engineer at the Royal Aircraft Factory, worked from 1915 to 1916 with Professor A.H. Gibson on carrying out the first systematic research into the design of air-cooled cylinders. Three principles emerged from this research: that the head should be of aluminium for the rapid conducting away of heat; that the head should be of one piece, since metal to metal contacts ensuring good thermal conductivity were difficult to maintain; and that the design of the head should provide the shortest possible escape path for heat at the hottest points, across the greatest possible cross-section.

Until he joined Siddeley-Deasy in 1917, Heron had worked at Farnborough on devising ways of cooling exhaust valves, particularly those in air-cooled cylinders, by filling the stems partially with the soft and inflammable metal sodium, or a compound of it. This element has the ability to transfer heat very rapidly, assisting in keeping the temperature within limits. Heron did further work on valve cooling after he went to the United States and there is much to be learned about this from the book which he wrote with Robert Schlaifer (see Bibliography).

The cylinder is a hollow forging, machined inside to the exact dimensions required for the bore and stroke. At one end, there is naturally the opening for the piston, with its sealing and scraper rings to be inserted and for the movement of the connecting rod; at the other end, there is the cylinder head. As the action which takes place within the cylinder is very hot, very rapid and under very great pressure, there is a major problem of attaching the cylinder to its head while ensuring a gas-tight joint. There are two basic types of cylinder. One is like an opened tin can which has been inverted, the base thus becoming the top, while the other type is open at both ends. In the former case, apertures are machined in the top for inlet and exhaust ports (one of each in some engines, two or more in others) and for sparking plugs (normally two of them). This top is machined smooth externally and the cylinder head, equally smooth, is bolted tightly to it, with its valve gear. This type is called a 'poultice' head (a borrowed medical term indicating a tightly attached hot bandage).

It is difficult to get a quick and efficient transfer of heat between the components, the big problem being adequate cooling, whether by air or liquid. Even when surfaces are in the tightest possible contact with each other, heat transfer is inefficient. The effectiveness of the contact between the two surfaces determines the success of the heat transfer and this success is even harder to achieve when there are different metals involved, with differing co-efficients of expansion. It is thus doubly difficult to achieve a good transfer of heat from the cylinder to the head.

As shown above, it was normal for cast heads to be bolted to the top of a poultice-type air-cooled cylinder whereas, in the case of the open-ended cylinder, a forged head is screwed, shrunk and locked onto the top of the cylinder. The valve gear is fitted afterwards. With the head sitting on the top of an open-ended tube, the outward heat transfer achieved is therefore direct and quicker, keeping the head cooler and so allowing the engine to run continuously at a higher rpm. As a result, the engine with a forged head can develop a greater horse power than a similar engine with a cast (poultice) head. It might be thought that the forged head, being stronger, would allow a higher compression ratio. Although this might be so, the Bristol Jupiter for example, which was produced initially with cast heads, when fitted with forged heads could, in many cases, be run at a slightly lower compression ratio, for a similar output because of the higher rpm.

As already indicated, the transfer and dissipation of combustion heat is of crucial importance if the cylinder is to operate continuously and reliably. The air-cooled cylinder itself is usually a forging in poppet-valve and sleeve-valve engines. It is machined to the exact dimensions required and is also machined outside so as to provide cooling fins of adequate area and spacing for the necessary dissipation of heat. In some early cases, the steel exterior was copper-plated in an attempt to speed the heat transfer to the cooling air, not always successfully. Most were turned circular but there was an exception in the case of the Bristol Jupiter, which was turned eccentrically so as to provide greater fin area at the rear of the cylinder and therefore better balanced cooling. It could not therefore be used as a pusher, at least partly accounting for the use of the Siemens-geared Jupiters on the huge 12-engined Dornier Do X. Siemens turned their cylinders circular.

The cylinder and cooling system of a liquid-cooled engine has, over the years, taken several very different forms, according to the ideas and preferences of the designers. The cylinder, which is also a steel forging, must be machined inside and out to a minimum acceptable wall thickness. It must be able to transfer the heat outwards to its cooling liquid at an adequate rate from the combustion chamber above the piston at its lowest point, while being strong enough to resist distortion by pressure, heat and other stress. It has to be surrounded as much as possible with the cooling liquid, so that a pump may carry it away to a radiator.

From the end of the First World War, the two major British exponents of liquid-cooling were Rolls-Royce and Napier. Once the early problems of casting in aluminium and porosity had been overcome, Henry Royce designed the engines in aluminium, apart from the individual cylinders of forged steel, with sheet steel water jackets. With individual cylinders and water jackets, six in a row, the engine tended to be long and heavy. At Hispano-Suiza (whose Vee-8 engines were built under licence by Wolseley) Marc Birkigt used an aluminium block employing dry steel liners and, to get round some of the acknowledged porosity problems, all blocks were enamelled inside and out. The resulting short, compact and somewhat lighter engine, when compared with the Rolls-Royce Eagle, had the better power/weight ratio although the more robust Rolls engine had the edge in terms of power per litre.

Early liquid-cooled engines had separate, forged poultice-head cylinders, with water jackets usually of welded steel, the cooling system with its numerous joints connecting the cooling circuit being both heavy and a constant source of trouble such as leaks. The dry-lined monobloc-type of water-cooled engine retained the closed-top type of cylinder liner, which was screwed upwards into the head, via the base of the cast aluminium skirt, with water-ways so as to give as much cooling as possible. Heat transfer problems still kept occurring between the metal surfaces with uneven heat distribution, before the coolant could be reached. This resulted in distortion and numerous other troubles, including internal and external coolant leaks.

The Napier Lion, a 'broad-arrow' type engine, designed by A.J. Rowledge, had three rows of four cylinders and was short and compact for a 12-cylinder engine. It also benefited from an equally short and stiff crankshaft. Unlike Royce's approach using individual cylinders and heads, the Lion had each row of individual cylinders screwed into a single cast aluminium head. Cooling such a layout was complicated because each head and cooling jacket had to be fed individually from the radiator, resulting in a rather heavy installed weight.

A 'wet' liner is the most efficient, with the coolant in direct contact with the greater part of the outside of the liner. An open-ended cylinder liner, threaded and screwed directly into the head but lacking a flat base (or top), demands careful machining and assembly because distortion would be disastrous. The type of wet-liner design devised by Royce and used from the Kestrel onwards, set and remained a standard for subsequent engines of this type. The really major development in cylinder design on Rolls-Royce engines was the introduction of the two-piece block on the Merlin.

ROTARY ENGINES

The satisfactory operation of a rotary has been described as something of a black art. In this engine, the crankshaft remains stationary while the cylinder assembly (with the propeller) rotates round it. The movements of the pistons inside the cylinders take place in exactly the same manner as in a stationary engine, the valves being operated by cams. The odd number of cylinders, five, seven, nine or even eleven (occasionally in double rows) were fired alternately and the complete cycle was made in two revolutions.

Although a substantial mainstay of the air forces on both sides during the First World War, the rotary engine almost completely disappeared from the scene fairly soon afterwards. Over twenty different types of rotary were at one time used in Britain and, when first introduced, were far lighter for their power (about 3:1 lb/bhp) than the stationary type and therefore at first had considerable appeal. However, their fuel consumption was high, oil consumption very high indeed and their running time between overhauls, which should have been about twenty-five to forty hours, could be as low as six hours. In spite of this, although unreliable, they were simple to maintain although an overhaul meant effectively a complete rebuild. The very high stresses caused by their rotating mass restricted their rpm and prevented rotary engines greatly exceeding about 230 hp. An examination of the two types of operating systems used in rotary engines cannot be omitted from a survey such as this, forming as they did a substantial part of early aero-engine history. There are few still operating, in antique aircraft or replicas of them.

At first sight and before the rotary engine is started, its appearance is similar to that of an air-cooled radial but when it is running, the comparison naturally ceases. It runs as a four-stroke engine and works in more or less the same way as any other but with such important differences as to justify explanation. The first production type rotary engine to appear was the two-valve 50 hp Gnome, designed in France by Laurent Seguin and his brother, in 1908 and featured an inlet valve in the piston head and a push-rod operated exhaust valve. It was followed by the 'Monosoupape' type engine, some five years later. In 1912, the Le Rhône engine appeared, a two-valve engine of basically similar design but differing in mechanical detail and incorporating a single push-pull valve rod and rocker.

The following year, there appeared the 80-150 hp series of Clerget engines, designed near Paris by Clerget, Blin et Cie. This introduced for the first time two independently operated inlet and exhaust valves. The Clerget, as well as Gnome and Le Rhône engines were subsequently built in large numbers in Britain during the First World War. Like all rotaries, the Clerget tended to overheat and it fell to W.O. Bentley, on behalf of the Admiralty, to introduce major modifications to the Clerget engine design and these were reflected in his own, subsequent engine, at first known in 1916 as the Admiralty Rotary A.R.1. and, in due course the Bentley B.R.1. This was followed in 1917 by the ultimate British rotary, the 230 hp Bentley B.R.2.

The other major difference between the stationary and the rotary type engines was the method of getting the fuel and air mixture into the cylinders. In a stationary engine this is straightforward, via induction pipes from the intake and carburettor to the inlet ports. In the design of a rotary engine, it presented a problem. In the Gnome, as in other rotaries, the solution lay in a carburettor of the 'Bloctube' type, mounted on the hollow rear end of the stationary crankshaft, thus sealing it but admitting air as required. The throttle lever adjusted the fuel flow and a 'fine adjustment' enabled the pilot to keep the fuel/air mixture correct for the engine speed, height and air temperature. It could be tricky to operate because, without careful adjustment, even after a climb of a few hundred feet, the engine could fail with little or no warning. When cruising, fuel consumption could vary by as much as fifty per cent, with consequent effects on range if the mixture were not adjusted properly.

The explosive fuel and air mixture from the carburettor passed straight into the crankcase, where it was well mixed ready for admission to each cylinder. In the two-valve Gnome, the inlet valve from the crankcase into the cylinder was via a spring-loaded and weighted valve in the cast-iron piston itself, simply operated by differential pressure. Thus, the explosive mixture of gas and air passed through the piston as the inlet valve in its crown opened, entered the cylinder where it was fired by a single sparking plug and exhausted. Ignition was by a single magneto. This system gave a lot of trouble, particularly when inlet valves did not work properly, and it could cause dangerous back-fires into the cockpit.

A continuous film of oil was provided for the works by a gear-driven pulsating pump, some of it going to the main and thrust ball-races and the rest entering the crankcase, mixed with the fuel and so entering the cylinders. It was essential that the lubricating oil could withstand both the heat and the centrifugal force and would not dissolve in the petrol and so become diluted. For these reasons, only pure pharmaceutical castor oil was suitable to be used. The rotary engine was enormously wasteful with oil, throwing it out through the exhaust ports and over everything down wind of it. Oil consumption could reach up to two gallons per hour, causing oiled-up plugs and much else besides.

The exhaust ports of all rotaries were open, without stubs, the valves in the cylinder heads being mechanically operated via cams and pushrods. The exhaust valve mechanisms, being unprotected from the heat, were therefore very susceptible to failure. Some rotaries had inlet pipes carrying the explosive mixture outward from the crankcase mixing chamber to the cylinder head and the inlet valve, the curved copper pipes to each cylinder of the 110 hp Le Rhône engine being a notable example.

The B.R.1 and B.R.2 rotary engines designed by W.O.Bentley (later to design well-known touring and sports cars — 'the fastest lorries in the world', according to Ettore Bugatti) were two-valve machines and featured forged aluminium alloy pistons rather than the usual cast-iron, thus saving considerable weight and permitting slightly higher rpm and greater power. The 230-240 hp achieved by the B.R.2 was about the peak power for a British rotary.

From this point, the two very different systems of rotary engine operation diverged and the 'Monosoupape', which worked in a rather different way from the others, has to be considered. The 'Mono' engine, to give it its more usual name, was a term particularly applying to some of the other Gnome engines designed in 1913 by the Seguin brothers, notably Laurent. This French term, meaning a single valve, referred to the simple and clever alternative to the more usual two-valve cylinder head. The 'Mono' engine had only an exhaust valve in each cylinder head and this was unusual in performing dual functions. When it acted as an exhaust valve, its temperature was naturally raised. It then admitted enough air into the cylinder by suction, for combustion of the next charge while, at the same time slightly cooling the valve. It appeared to work somewhat in the manner of a two-stroke but, in fact, it was a four stroke engine.

'Mono' engines had no mechanically operated inlet valves, the fuel charge entering the cylinders in a different manner. The fuel entered the crankcase, like the oil, via the hollow shaft but, in the 'Mono' engine, the crankcase was only filled with fuel gas, no air being admitted at this point and it was therefore not explosive (and considerably safer). The cylinders were set rather more deeply into the crankcase than the ordinary Gnome and each had a ring of holes in the wall which were uncovered and so opened by the crown of the piston in its downward path, passing at about 20 degrees before bottom dead centre. This sucked the fuel vapour from the crankcase straight into the cylinder via the holes in the cylinder walls, where it met and mixed with the air already admitted via the exhaust port. It was then fired and exhausted.

Throttle control, as such, was almost non-existent in the 'Mono' engine, power being controlled by a fine-adjustment of the fuel flow and was anything but fine in its effect on the speed of the engine. Therefore it had a 'blip' switch, in the form of a button on the control column which cut out the main ignition switch, the inertia of the engine and propeller carrying it along for a second or two before the button was released for another burst of power. A 'Mono' engined aircraft could thus be recognized by these alternating brief bursts of power on the ground or approach, as the blip switch was operated.

In a rotary engine, the open exhaust port rotated through the hot gases trapped (if briefly) within the cowling and any cooling factor at the cylinder head was nominal, minimal and contributed to the general unreliability of the type. The whole assembly was inadequately and unevenly cooled because each cylinder followed so closely behind the one ahead of it, causing cylinder distortions and all sorts of trouble. In any case, in nautical terms, the 'windage' of the rotating mass of cylinders absorbed some twenty-five per cent of the gross power available. Its development and its life were inevitably strictly limited. The static radial was obviously a more efficient way of developing air-cooled power, with far greater potential than the whirling mass of the rotary engine.

Chapter 4
Valves, Ignition and Exhaust

As has already been discussed briefly, the problems of cylinder head design combined with efficient exhaust valve cooling were not easy to solve and S.D.Heron's work on sodium-cooling for valve stems and seats went a long way to help. So did the development of the very hard 'Stellite' facings for valve inserts and, for the head and seat, the less-hard 'Brightray' which was more resistant to heat corrosion. When it came to cooling a four-valve head on a two-row engine, the difficulties were considerable.

The vigorous argument for and against the very widely-used sleeve-valve engines, perfected by Roy Fedden at Bristol and typified by the Hercules and Centaurus, will no doubt continue as long as there are engineers with great experience in the design and operation of either system, poppet or sleeve. There were two types of sleeve valve, the Knight type having double concentric sleeves, each with a purely oscillating action and the Burt-McCollum type single sleeve, combining semi-rotary and reciprocating actions, as exemplified by the Argyll engine. The double sleeve presented difficulties in lubrication and manufacture and, because of their nature, both seemed more suited to liquid cooling.

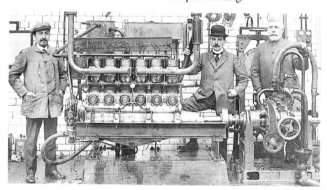

The 120-130 hp Argyll sleeve valve engine of 1914, which inspired Roy Fedden to examine the possibilities of a similar system in an air-cooled engine.

Fedden was, above all, an acknowledged master of the air-cooled engine. Although he had first been interested in an Argyll water-cooled engine in 1914, he was satisfied that an air-cooled sleeve valve engine would work. Bristol therefore took the British rights for and concentrated on the development of the Burt-McCollum type of single sleeve-valve. Although the Bristol Aeroplane Company's Aero-Engine Department and some of its shadow factories produced the poppet-valve Mercury and Pegasus in considerable numbers during the Second World War, they moved to the sleeve valve Hercules as the war progressed. Right at the end of the war, eighteen-cylinder sleeve-valve Centaurus engines were introduced.

The wartime production of Bristol radial engines, poppet and sleeve-valve, together rivalled but did not equal that of the Rolls-Royce Merlin. In round figures, they were: Mercury, 32,000; Pegasus, 32,000; Hercules 65,000; Taurus, 3,400; Perseus, 8,000; and Centaurus, 2,800; a total in excess of 143,000 engines.

Napier had the Sabre with sleeve-valves, not without many early difficulties. Rolls-Royce also explored the possibilities of sleeves with the big 46-litre Eagle. The Rolls-Royce Exe engine, designed by A.J.Rowledge, was a small sleeve-valved and pressure air-cooled engine for Fleet Air Arm operation which was intended for

the Fairey Barracuda. It was dropped by Hives when the war started, because he saw it was too big a diversion and effort. This engine did a lot of flying in a 'hack' Fairey Battle of Rolls-Royce at Hucknall and was quite reliable, though thirsty for oil.

Other sleeve-valve engines were run (but did not fly). These included the Rolls-Royce Pennine, which was intended for civil operation but was dropped after being run on the bed, as was the Crecy, a direct-injection supercharged two-stroke engine. It gave a lot of trouble and Hives asked Hooker and Lovesey to examine the engine and see whether it had a future, because there was clearly an enthusiastic following for this kind of engine. They spent three months on it and one of the things that Hooker did was to ask for an examination of sleeve-valves versus poppet-valves. An analysis of all the results that could be obtained from single-cylinder operation suggested that there was no real advantage in the sleeve-valve and that, in certain conditions, it was less effective than the poppet-valve.

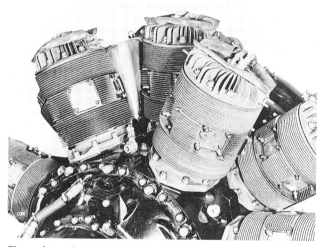

The uncluttered sleeve valve look. A Bristol Taurus II, here seen with its ports blanked off.

The junkhead and piston from the original Perseus rig.

A show-piece sectioned Bristol Hercules, revealing the works, closely-spaced cooling fins, piston, sleeve and sparking plug. The gears in the centre operate the sleeve drives.

A typical Bristol sleeve, showing the shape of the ports and cylinder details. This example was used in the original Perseus 6-cylinder rig for a proposed Vee-12 engine.

The link which operated the Bristol variable-timing gear used on the Jupiter IV and early VI, is located on the front of the crankcase.

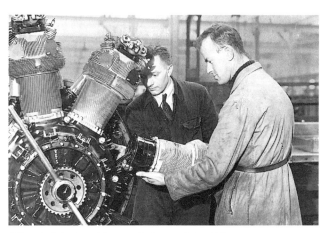

'I hope it fits'. Assembling a cylinder in a Bristol Mercury.

A superbly sectioned Bristol Pegasus, showing the epicyclic reduction gear and poppet valves.

The fact remains that, efficient or otherwise, Bristol and its shadow factories produced a very large number of satisfactory sleeve-valve air-cooled engines, largely for use in wartime bombers, although they were really the only company to do so. Napier produced the fast-running and high-powered liquid-cooled Sabre, after a great deal of early trouble which was much reduced by Bristol expertise in making sleeves. The Germans and Americans used poppet-valves and the Americans stayed with two-valve heads. The sleeve-valve engine really owed its success entirely to Fedden's great determination to press on with it.

Fedden, who had always used four-valve heads, saw the difficulty of making such a head with a two-row radial engine, particularly the practical problems of the valve gear. He experimented, briefly, with variable valve-timing in high-compression versions of the Bristol Jupiter (the IV and early VIs). By means of an adjustable, crank-operated cam drive which

Bristol Jupiter IV with a cast four-valve poultice head. Between the push-rods is the Bristol expansion compensating link, preventing differential expansion of head and cylinder affecting the valve settings and timing.

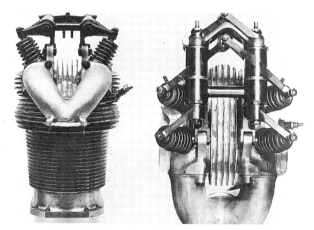

An example of a cast Bristol penthouse cylinder head. It is from the Orion engine.

retarded the inlet valve timing, the pilot could use full throttle for take-off without the risk of detonation when using the fuel then available. This successful but rather complex system was abandoned on high-compression engines, in favour of a simple gated throttle, which prevented the pilot from blowing off his cylinders, limiting the power of the engine below 5,000 feet. The supercharger, with automatic boost control, was clearly needed.

The sleeve-valve was made to work well but this had entailed a great deal of research work and it has been suggested that the additional manufacturing effort seemed hardly worthwhile. One of the other assets of the sleeve-valve engine which had been mentioned was the fact that a smaller diameter engine could be made for the same capacity, without valve gear. This theory has been countered by the claim that the junkhead, that part of the cylinder head which sealed the top of the sleeve, took up all the space required by the usual valve mechanism, the conclusion being that there was really nothing in it. The suggestion has also been made that the sleeve-valve engine required more man-hours to manufacture than the equivalent poppet-valve engine, giving no advantage. What has not been made clear in this comparison is whether this comparison was between the big two-valve American

engines, made by Wright and Pratt & Whitney and the four-valve engines of comparable power favoured on this side of the Atlantic. Bearing in mind Fedden's attempt to resolve the problem presented in designing a two-row, four-valve radial, it is essential that like be compared with like and this is not the place to adjudicate. The fact remains that far fewer parts were required to assemble a sleeve-valve engine than a poppet-valve of equivalent horse-power.

If it had not been for Fedden's single-mindedness, the sleeve-valve air-cooled engine would not have happened. Napier, with its Sabre, had severe sleeve trouble, giving rise to piston failures in its early days in 1940 and Rolls-Royce also had problems several years later with the Eagle 22, the engine intended to replace the Sabre. In order to get 3,500 hp, the Eagle ran at +28 lb boost, giving about the same specific power as a Merlin on 150 grade fuel at +25 lb, showing that comments about the sleeve-valve not being as effective as claimed had some substance. Where the sleeve-valve scored, particularly in civil operation with the Centaurus engine running at very modest cruise powers, was the life that was obtained from the valve gear.

Leaving out the RM17.SM, the Merlin effectively doubled its power over the war years, without altering valve-timing and with a small change in ignition timing, to make the engine less prone to back-fires. Rolls-Royce went from the inlet magneto firing 45 degrees before top dead centre (T.D.C.) and the exhaust magneto firing 50 degrees before T.D.C. to 38-45 ignition timing. The compression ratio remained at 6:1, which is obvious with using a lot of supercharge. Rolls-Royce did introduce a parabolic acceleration cam but, in fact the true valve openings were not very different. Packard thought that Rolls closed the inlet valve too late and just clocked the cam round five degrees so that the inlet valve opened a little earlier but it made no difference to the power of the engine. It was just the way they saw it. Because of the fierce accelerations on the valve, it is desirable to bring the cam ramps, either by bucket tappet or rocker, into contact with the valve relatively gently and then bang the valve open. So there is quite a period when the valve opening is quite small.

NOTE: For a note on Valve Overlap, see Appendix 2.

The Merlin was always limited on exhaust valves. Cruising at 800 hp, a single-stage Merlin 500 could run for a thousand hours but the two-stage engines, running at higher cruising powers, required a block-change in their life, although this was slowly increased. Later, six hundred and fifty to seven hundred hours were achieved between block changes but the problem with the Merlin was that, with its very compact four-valve head, there was not much room to develop revised exhaust valves. Valves with cooled stems were of course standard from the beginning and cooling in the valve head was also tried. The Merlin was developed specifically as a combat engine and it met all the requirements of life and reliability at very high powers. The fact that it was successfully used as a commercial engine after the war was due to the fact that it existed in large quantities, was relatively inexpensive, well-known and easy to maintain. Rolls-Royce, having such an enormous amount of Merlin experience, learnt a lot of useful lessons from the civil operation of the Merlin.

Whichever way the argument goes, in civil operations the sleeve-valve Centaurus, running at very conservative cruise ratings, well under 50 per cent, had a much longer valve life than did the Merlin. The time between overhauls on the sleeve-valved civil Hercules and Centaurus was finally three thousand hours.

Ignition of the fuel-air mixture in the cylinder releases the energy so contained but only the briefest reference to ignition is appropriate in the present work. Dual ignition, through two sparking plugs has been mandatory since the end of the First World War, ignition usually being by means of dual magnetos, rather than the coil normally used in motor vehicles. Plug insulators, having to resist very high voltages, were originally made of mica, a well-known British type of plug bearing the initials of racing driver Kenelm Lee Guinness. Years later, thanks to the alertness of Rod Banks on a pre-war visit to Germany, he realized the value of the aluminium oxide plug insulators made by Siemens for high-powered engines and brought some home in his baggage. The sintered-bodied plugs were then made in Britain and in the United States during the war.

In the case of the Rolls-Royce Griffon, the same reliability of ignition provided by twin magnetos was achieved with a single unit with two independent magnetic circuits giving similar electrical reliability. The single magneto casing saved space within the cowling and variable spark timing was achieved by means of a fixed contact breaker and an oil-operated servo-piston moving a sliding sleeve in the magneto drive with helical splines responding to throttle control. Coil ignition has been used infrequently, a notable exception being the Rolls-Royce Exe (the experimental engine previously mentioned, which did not achieve production status but was full of innovative ideas) but it has not found wide acceptance in the aero-engine industry. Variable ignition timing became progressively more necessary early in the development of the aero engine, particularly as rpm increased. It was at first adjusted to determine the best setting for each engine, for example the 1,250 rpm of a wartime Bentley rotary, to about 1,800 of a Jupiter VI of 1927. From the Jupiter VIII, two years later, there was initially a separate advance/retard ignition control and then a direct link into the throttle control, the latter becoming standard until the present, as in motor vehicles.

Compression ignition engines, diesel in other words, have been rare but Rolls-Royce flew a compression-ignition variant of the Vee-12 Condor in a Hawker Horsley. The Bristol Phoenix, a variant of the early Pegasus was another exception, gaining the World's altitude record for diesel engines at 27,430 feet in a Westland Wapiti. Napier imported a few Junkers Jumo six-cylinder opposed-piston diesels in the late 1920s for trial purposes. Mention must also be made here of the other Napier diesel engine, that most complicated of all piston engines, the Nomad compound which was flown in an Avro Lincoln.

The long exhaust tail pipes of the Cirrus-engined Moth gave a gentle purr.

Exhaust collector-boxes on a Merlin I installed in a Fairey Battle in 1938. The fitters here had the unenviable task of working under a simulated gas attack.

The stoutly braced 'chimney' of the Sunbeam Maori II exhaust, serving the inside exhausts of both cylinder banks. In this picture, the engine was the central pusher of the three-engined Grahame-White Ganymede.

The 24-cylinder Napier Dagger III installed in the Hawker Hector Army Co-operation aircraft was fitted with exhaust collector boxes. Each row of six cylinders discharged through four ports.

Exhaust system power losses, caused by silencers in motor cars, can be quite significant unless the silencers are properly designed for the job which they have to do. However desirable they may be environmentally, in aero-engines they are a considerable hindrance to good performance. For this reason, combined with the brief period during which an aero-engine is generally a nuisance, they are almost unknown. That is not to say that exhaust pipes do not have a silencing effect. Many early engines had vertical stove-pipe exhausts, often in pairs and reminiscent of the funnels of ocean liners. Long tail-pipes were introduced towards the end of the First World War and later became fashionable in light aircraft, notably

those in the various types in the de Havilland family of Moths, masking the already gentle purr of their Cirrus and Gipsy engines. Those in the Hawker Audax and Demon cut down the usual crackle from the open stubs of the Rolls-Royce Kestrel engine to some extent but none of these installations very significantly increased the exhaust back-pressure or reduced the engine's power output. An odd anomaly was the so-called 'rams-horn' type of exhaust stubs, installed on certain Kestrels notably in the Hawker Hind. These were

Open stub exhausts of the Armstrong Siddeley Jaguar were exceedingly noisy.

Ejector exhausts, familiar on Merlins, were introduced on the Kestrel XXX used on the Miles Master I advanced trainer. Seen here with a Rotol propeller on a test rig, these exhausts gave a small but useful additional thrust.

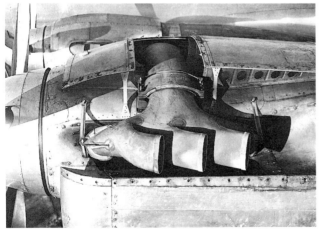

Merlin exhausts were noisy and cabin sound-proofing for passenger aircraft was heavy and expensive. Rolls-Royce's ingenious 'cross-over' exhaust system carried much of the noise away to the outside of the engine, while keeping cowling temperatures within acceptable limits.

large and rather ugly collector boxes, three mounted on each side of the engine. They smoothed out the noise a little but did nothing for the appearance of the aeroplane nor the pilot's view ahead.

When the Merlin first appeared in service, the exhaust emerged through slits in three streamlined collector boxes, connecting pairs of exhaust outlets on either side of the cowling. Soon, the ejector type of exhaust was adopted on the engine, again entailing coupling the six exhaust ports on either side in pairs, but turning the hot gases rearwards, so giving a significant extra amount of thrust and consequently some useful additional speed at the top end. Ultimately, individual exhaust stubs became standard fittings.

There were two important considerations during wartime operations governing exhaust, the first being the reduction of the visible blue flame and bright red glow at night and, most important of all, the elimination of exhaust gases from the cockpit and fuselage. Exhaust contains a high proportion of carbon monoxide, a highly toxic gas which cannot be smelled and, if inhaled, rapidly congeals the blood, inhibiting its flow. Air in the cockpit, which was so contaminated has certainly resulted in many deaths over the years and, in some circumstances pilots have been warned to breathe oxygen from start-up to switch-off.

Flame-damping exhaust trials, two different types installed on a Centaurus VII in a Bristol Buckingham.

The air-cooled engine was at first a very noisy machine, the early Armstrong Siddeley Jaguar being particularly noticeable with its open exhaust stubs. It became a little quieter with long tail pipes but it was not until exhaust collector rings round the front of radial engines became commonplace that things became a little quieter. There was, as always, a price to pay not only in weight. Being very hot and exposed to the effects of rapid and localized temperature changes, there was always the problem of corrosion and of welds giving way and allowing a jet of flame to play on something vulnerable or inflammable on the airframe.

An ingenious solution was devised at Bristol, installing an exhaust collector ring in the front of the engine leading smoothly into a cowling ring in turn making the most efficient use of the cooling air. This resulted to a large extent in the characteristically musical Bristol hum, or howl, according to the musical ear. Eventually the Bristol system was improved still further. By keeping the exhaust pipes from individual cylinders separate but in groups and arranging their discharge so as to add to the venturi effect of the cowling on the cooling air past the cylinders, the combination added a significant amount of extra thrust, as well as better cooling. This shows that individual items of an engine's installation cannot be taken in isolation and, in a well-planned installation, they should all contribute to the success of the whole.

Chapter 5
Lubrication and Cooling System

Aero-engines, like other machines, need lubricating oil. The oil pressure gauge is always the first thing to watch when starting an engine, in order to ensure that pressure begins to build up immediately the engine starts. Otherwise, if the pressure does not reach a set minimum within a given time, there is something seriously wrong and the engine has to be stopped down at once. The oil temperature and pressure gauges in flight are 'required reading' for any pilot or flight engineer who wishes to return home as safely as possible. (Even some very advanced engines have suffered lubrication problems, particularly those with early sleeve-valves, notably the Bristol Perseus and Napier Sabre, and the Rolls-Royce Exe gained a rather unkind reputation for tending to run out of oil before it ran out of petrol).

Early engines were lubricated with pure pharmaceutical castor oil. This congealed like treacle when cold, was expensive and some engines used a lot of it, most of all the rotaries. Oil was even known to burst a full tank when cold and under pressure. If dirt and grit were allowed to accumulate in oilways in the crankcase and elsewhere, it endangered the engine which usually wrecked itself, to say nothing of the aircraft and its crew. The uniform distribution of lubricant within the engine with suitable air and oil filters were of the greatest importance, to keep engines running reliably in hostile environments.

As a very early and rather extreme example, apart from the normal and universal need for workshop cleanliness, the problems of servicing in the field in the appalling conditions experienced by the British Expeditionary Force in parts of the Western Front in 1917-1918 are hard to imagine. Even at some flying grounds, not far behind the front line where men, horses and guns could disappear without trace in a shell-blasted sea of deep mud, absolute cleanliness still had to be demanded in the workshops. More often than not, these were merely large unprotected canvas tents, euphemistically referred to as Bessonneau hangars. Cleanliness in such terrible circumstances was naturally an engine fitter's nightmare. That such a high standard of serviceability was achieved at all is remarkable testimony to the skill, dedication and, above all the stamina of the engineering personnel, particularly of squadrons in the field. Their endurance deserves to be remembered.

Maximum running times between complete overhauls of comparatively simple rotary engines was sometimes only about five hours. For the more complicated water-cooled Hispano-Suiza engines, whose complete dismantling for cleaning was recommended at sixty hours, this was a very optimistic figure indeed and to achieve one tenth of that figure was quite good going at the time. (Ricardo has credited Rolls-Royce engines as averaging a remarkable one hundred hours between removals on the Western Front).

A very large proportion of Hispano engines became unserviceable owing to damage to crankshaft journals caused by lubrication failure, the engines being wrecked beyond repair. Every effort had to be made by all concerned to prevent the entry into oil systems, from all sources, of particles of dirt and grit and to ensure the cleanliness of engine interiors. Once inside, grit could not be extracted before reaching a filter — meanwhile it could do irreparable damage to bearings. Standing Orders included such minutiae as keeping oil funnels separate from anything else, not allowing them to touch anything else, including the bench and especially the floor. In frosty weather, the oil from each machine was to be emptied after flight into petrol tins, kept for each, the

balance to be made up and heated before transfer back to the tanks. 'As cleanliness is so essential, it is recommended that each oil funnel should be kept in a tin box when not actually used for filling the tank. It should never be laid on the ground or bench. If the tin is formed with an internal ledge, the funnel is supported vertically and the oil upon it can drain to the bottom of the tin'. Further, 'Rigorous disciplinary measures will be taken to enforce this'. The cleaning daily of all oil containers under such conditions was no soft life nor was the above to be taken other than seriously — in other words a court martial could well follow any lapse.

Such was the eventual demand for lubricating oil that an easier-made and cheaper substitute had to be found, resulting in the mineral-based oil whose specification became universally known as DTD 109, in place of pure castor oil. Engine oil, by the very nature of the job it has to do, becomes very hot indeed, requiring a radiator or cooler of its own. The Vickers-Potts type oil cooler was a familiar sight under the noses of Bristol, Rolls-Royce and Armstrong

5028

Westland Wapiti J8495 with a standard Bristol exhaust ring, as used on the Jupiter. Prominent beneath it is a 9-element Vickers-Potts oil cooler, as also are the Hucks starter claw and Hele-Shaw adjustable-pitch propeller.

Siddeley engines, taking the form of a stack of five to ten flat plates, edge-on to the slipstream, through which the oil was circulated. Although not so liable to resemble treacle when cold, as was castor oil, DTD 109 still suffered from stickiness when very cold, needing to be thinned with petrol before engine starting and an oil dilution system was used in high-powered engines. Filters to protect oil systems as well, in dusty environments, were a vital necessity. The wear on expensive engines and the resulting decrease of time between overhauls, caused by sand getting into everything capable of movement, was of great and continuous concern to the engineering and overhaul workshop people. This says nothing of the concern felt by pilots and crews flying over featureless and seemingly endless desert, forest, jungle or sea, or the jaggedly mountainous Hindu Kush or Nepal and the inevitable and hideous consequences of engine failure in the latter circumstances, despite the best endeavours of the maintenance engineers. The Merlin never had effective oil filters and depended on air filters stopping most of the sand getting into the engine.

COOLING

Engine cooling, by means of liquid circulated through the cylinder block and head, results in a compact engine profile and, when carefully designed, perhaps resulted in the best of them all with the beautifully-sculpted, low-drag installation of the Rolls-Royce Merlins in the de Havilland Hornet of 1945. Liquid-cooling by water coped adequately until the advent of the Rolls-Royce Merlin. Experiments were made in the alternative use of pressure cooling, evaporative cooling and glycol cooling and, when A.C.Lovesey (who became Deputy Director of Engineering at Rolls-Royce, Derby) visited the United States in 1933, he was impressed by the use of glycol cooling in the Curtiss D-12 engine. This permitted the use of temperatures up to 150 degrees Centigrade and reduced the size of radiator needed and thus cooling drag.

Much research work had gone on before in the improvement of radiator design, particularly at Farnborough. The aircraft radiator, like that of the motor vehicle, is a fairly primitive heat-exchanger. Adjustable, venetian-blind type shutters helped to control extremes of temperature change, especially at high altitudes. Experience in the Middle East in the 1920s resulted in D.H.9As and Bristol Fighters sporting two radiators to dispose of the extra heat. Obviously, such extras carried a penalty in terms of added drag and installed weight and this, combined with a reduction of power brought about by the hot atmosphere, imposed severe handicaps on efficient aircraft performance in a hot climate. With the increase of power in the 1930s, adjustable and retractable radiators were introduced and, later still, ducted low-drag radiators with controllable outlets were devised so that their expanded cooling air, so far from adding drag to the airframe, actually added a small amount of thrust upon ejection after cooling. At the same time, the search for more efficient cooling led to a better form of cylinder head design.

Rolls-Royce, in an effort to reduce still further the already low drag of their engine installations, made a study of the possibilities of evaporative cooling, using several early Kestrel installations and the Goshawk, a derivative of the Kestrel IV. This was basically a system from which it was hoped to eliminate the radiator altogether. It worked by making the cooling water absorb a great deal of heat and then boil, making steam which would be passed through a large condenser and so return to the engine. The system was expected to be more efficient than a more normal one. The condenser was tried out and the system proved, notably on the Hawker High-Speed Fury fighter, on which the condenser was mounted in the upper wing leading edges. There were however problems with steam separation causing vapour locking, quite apart from leaks in the plumbing system.

When the Rolls-Royce Merlin first went into service, it used 100 per cent ethylene-glycol as the coolant. This allowed the engine to be run with the coolant at 135 degrees Centigrade without boiling and, therefore, a smaller radiator could be fitted. Unfortunately, it also resulted in inconveniently high cylinder-head metal temperatures. It was also prone to leakages and was very inflammable, a highly inconvenient snag in a tightly enclosed cowling. The ultimate solution and a great advantage, lay in the use of a non-inflammable 70/30 per cent water/glycol mixture, under pressure. If such a mixture is raised to 15 lb/sq in, a temperature of 135 degrees Centigrade can be reached without boiling, thereby reducing the cylinder-head temperature by 30 degrees. This was first used in the Merlin IV and was a significant factor later when greatly improved fuel permitted really high boost pressures. This coolant subsequently became standard in all pressure liquid-cooled engines. Incidentally, the glycol was doubly useful as an anti-freeze but, to prevent corrosion and hot spots in the cooling system, the water had to be kept clear of impurities and inhibited ethylene-glycol (DTD 344A) was used.

As has been discussed previously, an air-cooled engine relies on a sufficient rate of air flow round its cylinders, particularly round the heads to disperse the heat of combustion. There is a large amount of metal in the piston head where the heat is most concentrated and, at sustained high power and a relatively slow forward speed in a climb, cylinder head temperatures need to be watched. The cowling ring produced by Dr H.C.H. Townend in 1928, in conjunction with the National Physical Laboratory, not

A Vickers Vespa VII, which broke the altitude record with a Pegasus IS.3

A Townend ring on an Armstrong Siddeley Panther VII in the Armstrong Whitworth XVI, an inner guide ring directing the air flow. Before cylinder baffles were perfected, the rear row of cylinders and exhaust ring needed careful cooling.

The Douglas DC-2 was usually powered by rear-exhausted Wright Cyclones. Those ordered by the Polish Airlines LOT had Pegasus IVs with long-chord cowlings. The Hawker Hart K3020 was used as a test-bed.

only helped to increase the cooling effect of the airflow but also reduced the drag of the air-cooled radial engine. This development was broadly in line with the similar cowl produced by the National Advisory Committee on Aeronautics (N.A.C.A.) in the United States at about the same time.

Shaped baffles led the air through the cooling fins, the design of whose area, shape and location had to be controlled so as to ensure adequate cooling where needed, in all likely circumstances. To aid this, the rear of the cowling ring had a circular row of small flaps, gills as they were called, which could be opened or closed manually by the pilot turning a handle or by an electric motor. This allowed the cooling air to escape from the rear of the cowling at a higher or lower rate, as required, thus keeping the cylinder head temperature within limits. The venturi effect of the air being accelerated through the cowling and so adding to the cooling had to be weighed against the added drag of the opened gills on an engine running at high power on take-off and initial climb. An unusual and clever installation, flown in 1938 was, once more, that of the Rolls-Royce Exe, whose ram-air cooling intake was efficient and had a very low drag penalty.

It should not be assumed that all air-cooling was from the front. In the case of the de Havilland Gipsy Twelve (and its Service equivalent, the Gipsy King), the cooling air was collected from ducts in the wing leading edges and led forward through carefully-shaped cooling ducts and discharged below the engine. The de Havilland Albatross airliner and D.H. Don trainer were examples of this. It is widely supposed that the capture of a German B.M.W. 801 radial engine in the Focke-Wulf Fw 190, with its fan-assisted cooling, was something of a shock in Britain. In fact Bristol had similar, closely-cowled engines well advanced at the time and, so far from the theory that the rear row of tightly-packed cylinders of the Centaurus must have been hard to cool, its cowling, baffles and exhaust pipes were so cunningly shaped that the rear cylinders actually ran cooler than those in the front row.

The works. The DC-2 Pegasus IV installation, with cowling removed.

The DC-2's Pegasus IV installed in the ultimate long-chord cowling developed by Bristol, incorporating a leading-edge exhaust ring, with a semi-enclosed tail pipe. This is the DC-2 installation.

The reverse-flow cooling rig for a Bristol Centaurus. The rear row of cylinders of this 18-cylinder engined actually ran cooler than the front row, thanks to the cunningly devised wing-mounted air intakes.

Chapter 6
Air Intake and Carburation

The induction system may be normally or naturally aspirated, (unsupercharged) or blown (supercharged) to varying degrees. Early unsupercharged engines did not always have forward-facing carburettor air intakes, their air intakes being merely conveniently-placed tubes or holes in the sides of the cowlings, cut to accommodate the carburettor inlet. The fuel/air mixture may be carried into the induction system via the induction pipes, breathing through the induction (suction) stroke, either by natural aspiration or, aided when the aircraft was moving, by any available ram air into the carburettor intake or by supercharging. As power increased and drag was reduced with the progressive refinement of airframe design, so a more direct form of entry into the carburettor became necessary.

Two problems manifested themselves in the design of air intakes, one from a very early stage. These were sand and ice. The Royal Air Force and the emerging airliners were based in or regularly passed through the Middle and Far East where sand and dust are a perpetual problem. Air filters were gradually improved so that they did not significantly restrict the flow of air into carburettors, so causing an unwelcome enrichment of the mixture coming from the carburettor. They tended to be bulky and heavy, as for example the tropical filters mounted under the noses of the early Spitfires, Seafires and Hurricanes. With experience, the design of air filters improved and became less obtrusive. Debris guards were also provided, in the form of a wire mesh mounted in a small frame a few inches ahead of the intake, so that they caused no obstruction if icing occurred, that was the important thing, rather than to stop ice getting into the engine.

It can be quite a problem getting large volumes of air and fuel mixture (though not very great compared with the great gulps of air consumed by today's jet engines) into and through multi-choke carburettors and into long induction pipes, evenly distributed among twenty-four, or even more, cylinders. Several ingenious means were devised for ensuring even distribution in 'Normally Aspirated' or unsupercharged engines. (The latter, simpler term is adopted throughout this book, as it means the same thing). The early Bristol radials, for example the unsupercharged Jupiter, had an unique type of spiral induction distributor. This took the form of a three-start spiral, dependent on three carburettors, each in turn feeding three induction pipes. This resulted in a reasonably even mixture distribution. When the supercharged Jupiter VII was introduced, with a single carburettor and the fan effect of the blower, the spiral was redundant and discontinued.

Armstrong Siddeley entered the high-powered engine market with the two-row, fourteen-cylinder Jaguar. It was designed from the outset to have a supercharger but, until the blower's development reached production status, efficient mixture distribution was an immediate problem. The solution adopted by Armstrong Siddeley in its unsupercharged radials was to mount a plain fan driven off the tail of the crankshaft, at the same speed and contained within a fan casing at the rear of the crankcase. The mixture streaming from the carburettor passed through this casing, was thoroughly churned up and passed out through the induction pipes to the inlet valves.

Most, if not all, of the higher-powered multi-cylinder engines were supercharged. In the case of Armstrong Siddeley engines, there were two types of fan, the 'geared-fan' and the supercharger. The geared-fan gave a slight pressure in the induction pipes and thereby maintained the power at sea-level up to about three thousand feet rated altitude. After the introduction of the Jupiter VII, Bristol also adopted the engine-speed plain fan for its

unsupercharged engines, the fan-effect of the rotor ensuring that the fuel/air was mixed evenly. The geared-fan may be compared with the moderate supercharge adopted by Rolls-Royce, although in that case, the rated altitude of a moderately supercharged Kestrel engine was a little higher. In all cases, fully-supercharged engines had rated altitudes well in excess of 10,000 feet. There is however a caveat even on this, because it was still not easy to ensure that the mixture was always evenly distributed, particularly at the far end of a long induction pipe like that of the Merlin. So difficult was the problem that fuel injection was eventually the solution.

CARBURETTORS
Carburettor design is very complex: maintaining a correct and steady supply of mixture in all circumstances is crucial to obtaining the best performance from an engine. It presents major difficulties. Not only variations in height and temperature have to be considered but humidity is also a major problem, even today. Carburettor icing can build up very quickly indeed, with little warning for the unwary pilot and a build-up of ice in the throat, restricting the flow of air, can cause a rich cut unless the carburettor is fed with warm air. This is done either by passing hot engine oil round the carburettor inlet or by taking the air from behind the oil-cooler or behind an air-cooled cylinder. In any event, an engine delivers its best power when fed with cold (and therefore dense) air and warming it so as to prevent icing can also result in a loss of power, perhaps when it is most needed. Icing is potentially very dangerous and therefore a matter to be taken seriously, some types of engine suffering from the problem worse than others.

The throttle control is normally simply a 'butterfly', or plate which is mounted in the throat of the carburettor and is rotated as the throttle is opened, so as to open the throat permitting a greater or lesser stream of air to pass through, the fuel flow being adjusted accordingly so as to permit a rich or weak mixture, according to circumstances as demanded and selected by the pilot. In later carburettors, mixture strength was automatically adjusted. When, at the very end of the war, the Merlin 134 and 135 were introduced into service, they were fitted with Corliss throttles. These engines were similar to the earlier Merlin 130-series. The Corliss throttle is a steam-engine-type control, having the effect of providing an unrestricted air-intake when the throttle is fully open. It has cylindrical ends with a middle sector blanked in. It rotates in the throttle body and gives the effect of an unrestricted intake with a very low opening torque on the throttle levers. The other advantageous factor about it, when flying the aircraft, was that the reduction of torque on the throttle levers also reduced the tendency of a plate throttle to snap open when the control was advanced.

Carburettors can be fed from gravity tanks or by engine-driven fuel pumps. A major problem, in the past, has been the reaction of a carburettor-fed engine to negative-g forces acting on the fuel float in its chamber, a matter which used to be particularly prevalent in fighters until the early 1940s. In this connection, it is worth outlining what happened during the Battle of Britain. The Royal Air force fighters, mostly powered by Rolls-Royce Merlin II and III engines, had the problem with the so-called 'negative-g cut'. This occurred when a sudden dive was made, causing the carburettor float in the opening phase, abruptly to reduce the fuel flow, thus delivering a weak mixture. An equally inconvenient rich-cut immediately followed it when order was restored. This was caused partially by the fact that the Merlin gear-type fuel pump originally fitted had twice the capacity needed by the engine, plus 20 per cent on each separate pump unit. There was therefore a tendency for the rich-cut when the carburettor float was not controlling because of the great amount of over-fuelling provided. The total duration of the cut was of the order of 1.5 seconds only.

At Farnborough a Scientific Officer, Miss Beatrice Shilling, known privately to some as 'Tilly', introduced a clever gadget which simply limited the amount of over-fuelling caused by surges in the flow, through a carefully-calibrated orifice in a metal disc placed downstream of the fuel pump. (See the entry under Rolls-Royce Merlin 50). This simple and cheap solution to the problem, officially called the 'R.A.E. restrictor', was promptly and ribaldly named after Miss Shilling to whom the credit was due. It was followed by the anti-g carburettor, also developed at the R.A.E., which was fitted retrospectively in a modification conversion programme on the early AVT.40, S.U. carburettors and worked very well. At about the same time, Rolls-Royce had also developed a diaphragm type of negative-g carburettor, which was flown on trial in two squadrons of Spitfire VIs at North Weald, powered by Merlin 50s. This carburettor was found to be unsatisfactory because it could not sense zero-g and was therefore rejected. As a result, the carburettors which were subsequently used as the war progressed, (generally S.U.-types), were built either to the R.A.E. anti-g standard or were retrospectively modified up to that standard, as also were other makes. The S.U.-type carburettor was later cleared potentially for +21 lb boost on 150 grade fuel.

The general difficulties involved during wartime, concerning the availability of materials, planning and production resulted in very tight restrictions on everything. Bureaucracy tended to reign supreme, with the usual possibilities of confusion between industry and Government departments. An example of one of the difficulties and controls incurred by the formidable demands of production, is related by the famed Air Commodore F.R.(Rod) Banks in his autobiography *I Kept No Diary*. There was some confusion about the production of a new type of S.U. carburettor early in 1941. It was at first believed by Rolls-Royce that the S.U. carburettor was an Embodiment Loan item, that is to say any item so described was Government-owned or furnished equipment, issued strictly on loan to a manufacturer for a set purpose. Somewhere along the line, confusion as to whose was the actual responsibility for producing the required type of carburettor in the required quantities at the right time had resulted in crossed wires and the items most urgently required were not in fact on Embodiment Loan but the responsibility of industry. Accordingly, a production programme for S.U. carburettors was set up very rapidly, under the impetus of the boot of the Minister of Aircraft Production, Lord Beaverbrook. This programme was therefore run jointly by the S.U. Company and Rolls-Royce, with the collaboration of the Nuffield organization, thereby resolving the problem.

INJECTORS

Supercharged radial engines, thanks to their star-shaped layout, did not greatly suffer from uneven fuel/air distribution, thanks to the fan-effect of the rotor. However, the more powerful in-line engines were not so easy to ensure even distribution of mixture, particularly at the far end of a long induction pipe like that of the Merlin. In order to eliminate the g-effects, a Rolls-Royce development of the Bendix injection carburettor, as used in the later Packard-built Merlins, was introduced at Derby. This sprayed fuel into the eye of the supercharger at about 5 lb/sq in. It did have problems at first, however, if pilots allowed drop tanks to run dry before jettisoning them, the resulting airlock making the engine cut and difficult to restart. This was cured by fitting an improved fuel pump and a metering chamber (D-chamber) bleed. The R.A.E. also introduced a fuel injection system, as did Hobson using an injector, designed at the R.A.E. as well, the latter being adopted by Bristol for the Hercules and Centaurus.

FUEL — WHY TEL?

Oil is found in many parts of the world, from the Far and Middle East to the American continents, to say nothing of huge deposits in the former Soviet Union and elsewhere and the quality, and constituents of oil samples found in different areas vary considerably. Aviation-grade petrol, refined to the standard degree required from crude oil, wherever found, is expensive to produce. The variation and therefore the constituents of motor fuel (particularly of aviation grade) and its characteristics, have been the source of much confusion and misunderstanding about the subject outside the world of chemistry. The standards required for fuel suitable for high-powered engines have, in the past, varied between Britain and the United States with regard to such matters as the nature and proportion of additives to reduce or prevent detonation. It does not help, when researching to establish the very small quantity of TEL (tetra-ethyl-lead) which is added to a gallon of fuel to make it comply with a standard specification, when the type of gallon is not quoted. It may be forgotten that a U.S. gallon is smaller than an Imperial gallon. (i.e. there are 1.2 U.S. gallons to an Imperial gallon).

Much has been written, loosely, about TEL and 100 or 87-Octane fuels, some accounts referring simply to 'DTD 230' fuel, not always with total clarity (DTD was the Directorate of Technical Development of the Air Ministry). There is much of interest on the subject in three of the books listed in the Bibliography. One is, as mentioned previously, *I Kept No Diary*, by F.R. Banks, whose exotic fuel cocktails enabled the Rolls-Royce 'R' engines, driving R.J. Mitchell's Supermarine S.6B seaplanes, to win the Schneider Trophy outright for Britain in 1931 and, subsequently, to gain the World's Speed Record. The second book, a monumental work by Schlaifer and Heron called *The Development of Aircraft Engines and Fuels*, is required (and very interesting) reading for anyone intent on learning more of this very complicated subject.

The third book, *Memories and Machines, The Pattern of My Life* is the autobiography of that most distinguished research engineer, Sir Harry Ricardo (republished to mark the 75th anniversary of the founding of the company, Ricardo Consulting Engineers Ltd). Reading this is particularly rewarding. All three books are devoted to the development of aero-engines and, in particular, the fuels that enable them to tick.

High-powered aero-engines are inevitably associated with high-Octane fuels, complicated products of organic chemistry and are a subject calculated to glaze the eyes of all but a dedicated few. Others are excused reading the Appendix on the subject, which is actually necessary to explain, as briefly as possible, what this involved and important subject is all about.

Chapter 7
Compression Ratio and Supercharging

There are various degrees of supercharge. In most cases, the fuel/air mixture is carried from the carburettor via the induction pipes, and rammed into the cylinders at a pressure provided by an engine-driven fan (compressor or blower). The supercharger is driven by a gear train from the crankshaft, with a spring system or clutch to protect it in the event of sudden accelerations of one sort or another. The V-1650 Merlin built by Packard incorporated an epicyclic supercharger drive. Both types step up the crankshaft rpm, driving one or more centrifugal compressors whose speed and diameter produce the required boost in the induction pipe. An alternative is to use an exhaust-driven turbine connected to a compressor, the earliest experiments of which produced results which were both dramatic and explosive because of the inability of contemporary metals to stand up to the heat and stresses. Mention must also be made of the ingenious supercharging method which was devised by Ricardo even before the First World War.

In the Performance tables, there are many possible variations in the induction system. These include unsupercharged engines, with or without a fan (for mixture distribution). Supercharged engines are here categorized as; LS = Low Supercharged; MS = Medium or Moderate Supercharged; FS = Fully Supercharged; 2S = Two-Speed Supercharged; 3S = Three-Speed Supercharged engines and 2ST = Two-Stage supercharged with inter-cooling (sometimes called after-cooling). In most unsupercharged engines, F/T = Full-Throttle was allowed when required for take-off and continuously thereafter. High-compression engines, which were capable of delivering more power than the engine could safely withstand without risking detonation, required the protection of a gated throttle = GT.

ENGINE HANDLING, COMPRESSION RATIO AND DETONATION
Basically, the compression ratio is increased so as to improve the efficiency of the engine. The higher the cylinder pressure that can be obtained, the more efficient will be the burning, provided that it does not result in pre-ignition or detonation. Such factors as hot spots in the combustion chamber or at a sparking plug or excessive cylinder pressures, are influences which can give rise to detonation, an extremely damaging situation. Early engines were unsupercharged and were run at as high a compression as was practical. Certain engines which could be run at higher compression ratios than were usable on the ground were therefore throttled, so that the breathing was restricted, discussed below under 'Gated Throttle'. Cylinder pressures were then not so great, so it was possible from about three thousand feet to open the throttle fully and gain more power from fully using the effects of the high-compression engine.

With unsupercharged engines therefore, the most effective way of getting more power is to raise the compression ratio, particularly so when uprating older engines. With the use of modern fuel, the compression ratio can be raised considerably, giving a lot more power. Increases in compression ratio have always been limited by the availability of suitable fuel, just as to some extent it limited the power available from supercharged engines.

GATED THROTTLE
In a gated throttle, the throttle lever moved in a slot which, in many engine installations, had a stop which prevented the lever travelling beyond it without the pilot first consciously pushing it slightly sideways. This was referred to as the gate and prevented the pilot inadvertently opening the throttle too far or at least warning him not to do so. It then could enter another slot which allowed it to attain its full travel.

The following note is attached to many A. & A.E.E., Martlesham Reports — 'In normally aspirated engines . . ., in an ungated engine the rated altitude will be taken as 2,000 ft. In a gated engine the rated altitude will be the lowest height at which the throttle is fully opened'. The point of having a gated throttle in an unsupercharged engine was that, if allowed to do so, some engines could develop more power than was good for them. For example, Air Publication AP.832 dated May 1921, stated that Napier Lion engines must have a gate, to prevent the throttle being opened beyond it, below 5,000ft. The actual critical height varied to some extent between 3,000 and 5,000 feet, according to the type of engine. At that time, fuel quality could be a doubtful factor and the rigorous quality control applied today would have been of equally doubtful value with the consequent risk of detonation which could have resulted from the use of full throttle. The technique therefore was to open the throttle on take-off, as far as the gate would allow (ensuring that the proper engine rpm was not exceeded), up to the 'gated' height. Above this, the rpm would start to drop and the throttle lever could then progressively be advanced past the gate, while still keeping the rpm within the limits stated for the climb, or whatever circumstances were appropriate.

Still using the Lion as an example, its fixed-pitch propeller was supposed to have a pitch, profile and efficiency which would give a maximum thrust at the maximum crankshaft rpm allowed for take-off, climb (normal) and full-throttle level — inevitably a compromise. Quoting the A.P., 'Propellers should in all cases be designed to give a crankshaft speed of 1900-1950 rpm at full throttle, stationary on the ground'. This was all fairly approximate and so it was up to the pilot to watch his revs as well as his airspeed.

ENGINE HANDLING, SUPERCHARGED ENGINES
The use of gated throttles was not confined to high-compression naturally-aspirated engines. On supercharged engines, particularly in fighter installations, there was often far more power available for take-off than was actually needed on a normal airfield. The throttle lever was gated, usually marked 'RATED' and 'TAKE-OFF', the actual take-off normally being made at rated power, except when only a very short run was available. This was simply to prevent more power than necessary being used, to save wear and tear as well as fuel. With the big Rolls-Royce Griffon engine and a five-bladed propeller, a Spitfire on take-off showed a distinct inclination to rotate round the propeller if the throttle was not operated with due caution. Not only that, the aeroplane tried to slide sideways, with consequent scuffing damage to the tyres and it could be quite a handful. Of course, when full power was really needed, the gate could be passed.

Engines were supercharged in various ways. The superchargers were, initially, single-speed types mechanically driven by gearing from the crankshaft with step-up ratios arranged according to the boost pressure required. Moderately supercharged engines drove their blowers at about six times crankshaft speed, whereas in fully supercharged engines, this figure was nearer ten. Driving the mechanical supercharger at the high speeds required, could itself absorb quite a large amount of the extra power which the engine could provide. The additional energy also required safeguards within the supercharger mechanism, such as a spring drive or a clutch, set to slip when a pre-determined torque was exceeded. This enabled the clutch to slip so as to protect the drive mechanism and so reduce the risk of shock loading the engine in the event of a back-fire or minor accident. It also dampened any twisting or torsional vibration in the driving shafts. Designing a suitable supercharger was a very specialized art.

In the engine industry, between the wars, the generally accepted rated altitude for medium supercharged engines was 3,000-5,000 feet and, for full supercharge, 10,000 feet or slightly above. As superchargers became more efficient, MS could be quoted as high as 10,000 feet and FS appropriately higher.

SUPERCHARGER BOOST PRESSURE

When supercharging was first brought in, it was intended to give sea-level powers at altitude and nothing more. The engine with a normal compression ratio could therefore run with a supercharger to offset the effects of the reduction in atmospheric density as the aircraft rose. It was towards the end of the Schneider Trophy contests that a rather different emphasis was placed on supercharging. For the first time, supercharging was used to increase the power at sea-level. The Schneider engines were therefore an example of virtually a full-throttle engine at sea-level, with a high degree of supercharge. Under such conditions, there are limitations on the compression ratio that can be used. Technically, the effect of a high-compression engine is to produce very high peak pressures in the indicator diagram which can be destructive to the engine. In a supercharged engine, the indicator diagram does not have the same peaks but is, in fact, fatter. It gives more effective operation by pressure on the piston further down the stroke.

Following the Schneider Trophy, supercharging was used both to increase the power at ground level and also to increase the power at altitude. This meant that, if the engine was run at full-throttle at ground level, it would be over-boosted and would fail. It was necessary to introduce some form of boost regulation so that the throttle was not fully open until an altitude had been reached where the required power was given and was given at a safe level. This resulted in the introduction of an automatic boost control system, controlled by an aneroid capsule, in British engines. A pilot-controlled cut-out was available in an emergency. (In American engines without such a system, it was necessary to keep a fairly hawk-like eye on the boost indicator to avoid over-boosting).

One of the advantages of the liquid-cooled engine is its ability to run for short periods at what would otherwise be regarded as excessive boost pressures, thanks to the reserve of heat capacity in its cooling system. This was put to good use through a variable-datum and over-riding cut-out unit in the automatic boost control, for pilot's use in an emergency. He could thus obtain the full operation of the throttle, the cut-out valve being located alongside the throttle lever. When operated, a lead sealed wire was broken. This indicated to the aircraft's fitter that the cut-out had been operated, certain engine components needing to be inspected before further flight.

TWO-SPEED, THREE-SPEED OR TWO-STAGE?

There has long been confusion between the expressions 'two-speed' and 'two-stage' superchargers, due in part to many-times repeated misleading or entirely incorrect statements which have appeared in print. 'Two-speed' or 'three-speed' means just that and refers to a gear-driven supercharger which is engaged, by means of a clutch, at one gear ratio or another, the gear being selected according to the height of the aircraft either automatically or by the pilot. A few engines, including the 100 series of Rolls-Royce Griffons, had three-speed blowers, for low, medium or high-altitude operation.

Entirely different are the gear-driven 'two-stage' superchargers, irrespective of whether they may be driven at two or three speeds. These have blowers with two rotors of different compressing capacities, mounted in series and driven together on a single shaft. The output of the first stage of compression is fed to the eye of the second blower, to be compressed still further. This is quite irrespective of the speed at which they are driven. This degree of compression naturally leads to considerable heating of the charge and requires an intercooler (or aftercooler, as it is sometimes called) and the cooling of inter-stage passages, as described below.

TWO-SPEED SUPERCHARGERS

The two-speed supercharger, taking advantage of both medium and full supercharge possibilities and controlled (which may be by means of a hydraulic clutch, manually or automatically) at the height at which a change-over was required, was patented in 1932. It must be emphasized that any clutch-slip can only be momentary. Continued slip will cause the clutch to burn out. An engine so powered first appeared in production form in the Armstrong Siddeley Tiger VIII in 1936. The Rolls-Royce Kestrel had been the subject of preliminary work by A.A.Rubbra from 1931, but had not been without troubles. After a subsequent visit to Paris, a licence agreement was made with the Farman Company to incorporate their two-speed drive in Rolls-Royce engines. Although slightly longer than the original design by Rolls, this was regarded as a worthwhile penalty.

Two-speed superchargers were subsequently widely used in certain types of engine, starting with, for example the Bristol Pegasus XVIII in the Wellington and a two-speed supercharger was also introduced by Rolls-Royce in the Merlin X for the Whitley, both aircraft being bombers. Two-speed Merlins, starting with the Mark XX (a modified Mark X) were used in both bombers and fighters. The Merlin did not use a hydraulic clutch. The clutch load came from centrifugal load on the bob-weights. The hydraulic mechanism was purely an act of withdrawal or engagement. (Later, as mentioned previously, Griffon and Napier-Halford Sabre engines with three-speed superchargers were flown experimentally).

It is worth quoting here the Air Ministry's advice contained in AP 1729A and referring to the Bristol Hercules 100. Resulting from the increase in engine power due to a decrease in the inlet air temperature and exhaust back-pressure which occur during a climb, at a given altitude the throttles in the injector are fully open and above this height there is a drop in boost and therefore the power falls. The altitude at which more power can be obtained by changing to high gear varies according to the rpm, boost, airspeed, installation and the prevailing atmospheric conditions. Take-off is therefore normally made in low gear (or MS) since high gear (S) can consume considerably more power without giving any advantages. If, when climbing, the boost given in the operational limitations for this condition has fallen by about 2½ lb/square inch, an increase in power can be obtained by changing to high gear.

In almost every case, MS gear was used for take-off and climb but there was a notable exception. The Avro Shackleton, the famous maritime patrol aircraft was capable of a twenty-four hour endurance and took-off at a very high gross weight. It was powered by two-speed, single-stage Rolls-Royce Griffon 57/58s and needed all of the 2,455 hp available, requiring +25 lb boost and 100/130 grade fuel plus water/methanol injection for charge-cooling. It took-off in S gear but cruised in M gear on long patrols and was the only Rolls-Royce piston-engine to use water/methanol injection.

It will be noted that, in a few Bristol engines, the supercharger is recorded as 'locked in M gear'. This occurs in the case of standard two-speed supercharged engines, which were operated at medium and low levels. The full supercharge facility was not needed, hence the modification. An example is the Pegasus 38 which was intended for low-level maritime reconnaissance or on civil routes for flying-boat operations in areas where only modest altitudes were required. The Pegasus 48, an otherwise similar engine, which powered flying-boats on routes down the length of Africa, had to cross much high ground and also cope with high ambient temperatures. It therefore needed its two-speed blower and all the power it could deliver at high altitude.

Several low-level versions of the Hercules were used to power torpedo-dropping Beaufighters (the 'C', or Coastal Command versions). At the other end of the scale, an unusual engine, the Hercules VIII, a very high-altitude unit with a single-speed medium supercharger, remained basically medium-supercharged but had an auxiliary high-altitude single-speed 'S' supercharger, giving its maximum 1,100 hp at 32,000 feet. It was designated HE-8MAS (Medium supercharged, auxiliary 'S' blower) and, modified, its maximum power level was subsequently raised to 40,000 feet. This is not to be confused with the Hercules XVMT, with a turbo-blower, referred to below.

TWO-STAGE SUPERCHARGERS, INTERCOOLING AND CHARGE-HEATING

The compression given by a supercharger to the fuel/air mixture raised its temperature before its admission to the cylinders. In engines with two-stage superchargers, the charge could be raised to such a degree that it needed to be cooled, a common method being passing it through an intercooler, or aftercooler as it is sometimes called. This was installed in the form of a heat-exchanger with its own radiator, so as to reduce the charge temperature before its admission from the second stage of the induction system into the cylinders, so reducing the risk of detonation. The inter-stage passages also required cooling. A very early example was the Bristol Pegasus PE.6S special high-altitude, fully-supercharged engine mounted in a Bristol 138A, which had an extra second-stage supercharger driven by a flexible shaft and clutch, with an intercooler (mounted externally, below and behind the cowling). The auxiliary blower was engaged at about 35,000 feet and the aircraft attained the World's Altitude Record, at 53,937 feet, in 1937. The Bristol Hercules XVMT, like the Hercules VIII, was another very high-altitude development of the Hercules II but had a single auxiliary, high-altitude, turbo-supercharger. Basically, it remained a moderately supercharged engine (MT = Medium/Turbine) but, when so equipped, became a hybrid two-speed, two-stage fully/medium supercharged unit, producing 1,230 hp at 38,000 feet.

Increases in compression ratio have always been limited by the availability of suitable fuel, which also to some extent limited the power available from supercharged engines. Rolls-Royce found that they could use +18 lb boost on 100 Octane fuel on two-stage engines with intercooling or on single-stage engines without intercooling but, for +20 to +25 lb boost, which was used during the war (and +30 lb, for which the Merlin was eventually cleared), 150 grade fuel was needed, all of which had to be taken into account.

There was also a risk, with high Octane rating fuel in fighter installations, of lead-fouling of the sparking plugs if power was not substantially increased immediately after a take-off at reduced boost. This technique did not apply so much on heavily-laden bomber aircraft which needed all the power they could get on take-off and climb, differential throttle control taking care of the directional problems. This factor was, however, encountered on long-range bombing and fighter-escort sorties during the war, as well as in the later civil Merlins when there was also a continuing risk of plug-leading at cruising power. This could later be reduced by charge-heating, a technique which, in turn, could also be achieved by halving the depth of the intercooler. In addition, if the unit could provide both full-depth intercooling for take-off and climb, as well as charge-heating at cruise, an increase in maximum power could be achieved, while retaining freedom from plug-leading at cruise. Rolls-Royce designed such a mixing scheme, used together with a modest extra ½ lb boost. Measuring boost pressure downstream of the intercooler allowed the Merlin 626 series engines to develop 1,765 hp at take-off, while providing a useful extra ton of disposable weight on Canadair DC-4M aircraft.

Chapter 8
Starting and Propeller (Airscrew) Drive

An R.E.8 at Farnborough in 1918, powered by a R.A.F.4d, with a Rateau turbo-supercharger. To use the remarkable potential of this power unit, Farnborough designed a variable-pitch propeller. The enormous scoop for cooling air can be seen.

The Townend cooling ring was easily combined with an exhaust collector ring, in most Bristol engines at the leading edge. This unusual rear-mounted installation was on a Pegasus II in the Gloster Goring J8674 in 1933.

The long-chord NACA cowling here encases a Pegasus IM.2 with a rear-mounted exhaust in a trial for a Swedish Hawker Hart. Also notable is the big, beautifully sculpted Watts wooden propeller.

The Rotol controllable-pitch propeller, with an internal piston, as fitted to Pegasus XXII engines of the Long-Range Development Unit Wellesleys.

The most familiar Bristol long-chord cowling, seen here on a Hercules II with the cooling gills open. The upper intake is to the down-draught carburettor, the lower to the oil cooler.

An early Hercules VI power plant, with a Rotol electrically-operated propeller.

de Havilland Hydromatic propeller, fitted to Bristol Perseus engines of the D.H. Flamingo.

The High-Speed Spitfire, serialled N-17, with a Merlin II special, intended for an attempt on the World's Speed Record.

The big five-blade propeller on a Spitfire PR.XIX, with a Rolls-Royce Griffon 66. The enormous power available on take-off could result in a tendency for the aeroplane to rotate round the propeller. A 170 gallon extra fuel tank is fitted.

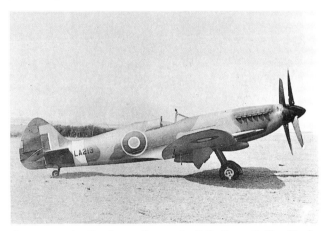

Counter-rotating Rotol propellers on the Rolls-Royce Griffon 85 of a Spitfire 21 used for engine/propeller trials.

As rebuilt in recent years, the D.H. Comet has been fitted with the more modern de Havilland constant-speed propellers and appropriate spinners.

The Hercules of this late type typically incorporated fan-cooling. Here, it is installed in a Bristol 170 Freighter Mk 31 for the R.C.A.F.

The de Havilland Comet, winner of the MacRobertson Mildenhall-Melbourne Air Race in October, 1934. The flat operating discs on the propeller spinners are just visible.

The Series II version of the Gipsy Major I, with increased power and a bracket-type de Havilland variable-pitch propeller.

Armstrong Siddeley Cheetah XV, with a Rotol constant-speed propeller, in an Anson XII

When considering the performance of the propeller at various altitudes, if the engine is not supercharged, as previously mentioned, its power falls off as height increases. Also, the lower density of the air at high altitudes reduces the drag on the propeller blades, consequently lessening the propeller torque. If the propeller torque remained constant at all altitudes, the reduction in engine power would cause a drop in rpm. The combined effect of reductions in both engine power and propeller torque is therefore small, the loss of rpm due to the former being counter-balanced by the gain of rpm due to the latter.

If the engine is supercharged, it can be assumed that the power at the rated height is the same as at sea level. Thus, if an aircraft is flying at the engine's rated height, there is a decrease in propeller torque but not of engine power. The resistance to turning the propeller is therefore reduced and it rotates faster than at sea level, thereby allowing the engine to run faster, even to 'race'. To prevent this, the pilot is compelled to throttle back and the benefit of supercharging is, to a great extent, lost.

It follows that, if the full benefit of supercharging is to be obtained, some method of maintaining the propeller torque constant at high altitudes is required. The variable-pitch propeller, in which the blade angles can be increased, or coarsened — thus increasing thrust and drag on the blades — fulfils these conditions. Initially, a two-position (bracket-type) propeller was made in Britain by de Havilland, under licence from Hamilton Standard in the United States. Another type of propeller was made by Rotol, a company formed jointly by Rolls-Royce Ltd and Bristol Aeroplane Company. Rotol produced a type of variable-pitch propeller based on Hele-Shaw Beacham patents. Just in time for the Battle of Britain in 1940, both these types of propeller had been converted to control by constant-speed units and, thanks to remarkable work by Rolls-Royce and the propeller manufacturers, as well as by engineers in Royal Air Force units, constant-speed propellers were fitted to the Merlin engines in Hurricanes and Spitfires.

A propeller's principal characteristics, apart from the number of blades, are the diameter, chord, camber, blade angle and pitch. The diameter chosen is, inevitably, a compromise resulting from considering a number of conflicting factors. A large diameter produces a high efficiency but only if the tip speed is not excessive. The tips of a propeller's blades of course have the greatest velocity, this velocity being in most cases well below the speed of sound. In certain cases, however, tip speed can reach the speed of sound, resulting in an ear-piercing, high-pitched howling noise. This din is unpleasant, due to compression waves set up at the tips, which greatly increase the propeller's torque, without a large alteration of thrust, efficiency thus being reduced.

In order to keep tip speeds low, the diameter and rpm of the propeller must be carefully restricted. A reduction gear between the crankshaft and the propeller will of course decrease the propeller rpm, thus permitting the use of a larger diameter propeller. There is a limit to the reduction practicable, however, as the diameter is still limited by the ground, fuselage or water clearance available.

The chord and camber are usually determined by considerations of strength required to resist the bending moments and the tension due to centrifugal forces. From the point of view of efficiency, the aspect ratio (i.e. the ratio of propeller radius to mean chord) should be about six. Blade angle and pitch are determined by the intended maximum and cruising speeds of the aircraft, as already indicated.

The propeller torque must also be taken into consideration in its design. It is quite possible that a two-bladed propeller, designed in accordance with these conditions, may give insufficient torque, if it is to be fitted to a high-powered engine. For this reason, most of the powerful engines were fitted with three-bladed propellers, as by this means sufficient torque is obtained without much reduction in efficiency. The use of four and five-bladed propellers may be explained in the same manner. Where very high powers have to be absorbed and propeller diameter needs to be restricted, the solution can be a pair of counter-rotating propellers, or 'contra-props'. These have the added advantage of eliminating torque and were therefore used to good effect on aircraft carriers.

The main disadvantages of the fixed-pitch propeller are that a large portion of the blade is stalled during take-off, resulting in low efficiency and it cannot satisfactorily be used with supercharged engines if the full benefit of supercharging is to be obtained, except at the expense of take-off. The variable pitch propeller overcomes both of these difficulties and the constant-speed variety which holds the engine speed where the pilot sets it (within limits) was the next stage in its development. Propellers became more and more sophisticated, at first feathering so as to stop a damaged engine turning in the slipstream and degenerating further or catching fire in flight and then ultimately the reversing and braking action. With extra sophistication came greater risks of failure, such as run-away propellers, stuck in fine pitch and leading to catastrophic engine failure.

Root failure, mostly from fatigue, was not unknown and accounted for a number of accidents resulting from the loss of a blade. A particular example concerns a twin-engined bomber, several of which crashed unaccountably just after the Second World War. On landing approach, at least one was found to have shed one of its four propeller blades on one side, at high power with wheels and flaps down. The resulting vibration caused the engine to tear itself out before it could be stopped and the working engine's throttle 'chopped'. The instant asymmetric power and drag resulted in the aircraft's becoming rapidly uncontrollable. Fortunately, some of the pieces were found and root fatigue diagnosed, corrective action being taken.

Suitable materials, both heat-treated and compressed wood, as well as metal (duralumin and steel) have evolved over the years, both being widely used. Wooden blades are made up of laminated and glued sheet, covered with fabric and varnished, often with metal-reinforced leading edges. Recent research of old records, particularly invoices, has revealed that during the First World War, the Bristol Company made over nineteen thousand propellers, mostly in laminated mahogany or walnut and a few in teak. They were machine profiled and roughly milled, the finishing being done mostly by women using planes and sand-paper, completing the job with varnish. Balance was of course crucial. The big, elegantly sculpted blades of the Watts propeller in the Hawker Hind and Gloster Gladiator are fine examples of later models. Later still, in the Second World War, blades had a protective plastic outer sheath, which could however mask internal cracks resulting in vibration with serious results. Fixed-pitch metal propellers were made in Britain, chiefly by Fairey under licence from Dr S.A.Reed in the U.S.A., being machined to suitable profiles from forged duralumin slabs. Perhaps the most notable examples were those for the Supermarine S.6 series of Schneider Trophy racing seaplanes.

Before the Second World War, most propellers were of fixed pitch and so the reduction gear ratio had to be a compromise, carefully chosen to suit in the best manner possible the overall range of work for which each type of engine was designed. (By comparison, the satisfactory selection of suitably-spaced gear ratios in a motor vehicle's gearbox is rather more a matter for the designer's inspiration and perhaps more straightforward). Naturally, the reduction gear ratio option related directly to the optimum crankshaft speed (and therefore the propeller rpm)

required for normal regimes of flight — take-off, climb, cruising and maximum available ('Combat', in contemporary parlance). This of course had a major influence on the operator's choice when selecting an appropriate engine for an aircraft for a particular task.

PROPELLER DRIVE — SPUR GEARED
There were several methods of matching crankshaft speeds to acceptable propeller rpm. The simplest method was the spur type, whereby a small gear turned a larger one, the ratio between them being chosen to match the engine rpm to the particular type of propeller. A variation of this was the co-axial drive, as used on the racing Napier Lions. In this, the crankshaft drove a geared layshaft, which in turn drove the propeller shaft, again via gearing making it co-axial with the crankshaft. Counter-rotating propellers had co-axial shafts which were driven through two spur trains, one of which had an idler that reversed the rotation. In a few aircraft, such as the de Havilland Hornet, left and right-hand propellers were used so as to counteract the effect of torque. This was done in one engine by inserting an idler pinion in the reduction gear.

PROPELLER DRIVE — EPICYCLIC GEARED
The 'epicyclic reduction gear' is a mechanical device which is spoken of far more easily than accurately described. Quite strenuous debates have arisen as to the best wording to describe its functions and the following seems the simplest way in which it may be visualized. An epicyclic-type propeller reduction gear transmits the crankshaft torque to the propeller, co-axially with the crankshaft, a speed-reduction being made in the process.

Epicyclic propeller reduction gears, as used in the Rolls-Royce Eagle, Falcon and Condor I.

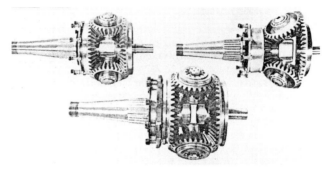

Epicyclic gears for Bristol Jupiter, Pegasus and Mercury engines.

It consists of an annulus gear driven by the crankshaft, with three or more double spur gears, on bearings located in arms fixed to the propeller shaft and a fixed gear attached to the front of the reduction gear casing. The spur gears are driven in one set of spurs by the annulus gear but are made to rotate the propeller shaft at a speed differential by means of the second set of spurs which mesh with the front fixed gear.

It is a neat, compact unit, needing little or no more diameter than the crankcase itself. Two versions of epicyclic reduction gear have been used, with a straight or a bevelled spur, the latter type having been patented by the Farman company in France. Whether a straight spur or a bevelled spur, the result is similar, although the choice between the two is a matter of the designer's preference for the particular engine. The degree of reduction (or even increase) in the resulting rpm depends on the angles set and the relative diameters (and, naturally, the numbers of teeth) of the meshing gears.

In the geared Cosmos Jupiter II of 1919, Fedden used the straight spur type. The big French aero-engine concern, Gnome-Rhône, acquired a licence in 1921 to make Bristol Jupiters and subsequently incorporated the Farman reduction gear. Fedden also considered the design of the French gear and, when he introduced the Bristol Jupiter VIII in 1927, he too adopted the bevelled type. As a result, Bristol paid royalties until the company bought the manufacturing entitlement outright in 1931, staying with this type of gearing thereafter.

Rolls-Royce used a straight spur-type epicyclic reduction gear on the Eagle and Falcon engines. (Incidentally, an Eagle IX was tested with a two-speed reduction gear, this being controlled by the pilot, through a clutch which diverted scavenge oil through an operating cylinder, a similar arrangement being used to operate the two-speed supercharger drive on the Merlin). Alvis Ltd, which had close pre-war links with Gnome-Rhône, used both types of gear in versions of the Leonides.

ENGINE STARTING

Before the days of electric self-starters, it was usual to swing a propeller by hand, a big engine requiring the combined strength of up to three men to turn it over. An aid to this method of propeller-swinging was the R.A.E. 'Bag Starter', an ingenious if rather 'low-tech' device, comprising a canvas bag attached to a rope and placed over the upper propeller tip. There were other ingenious mechanical devices, such as the Noakes starter. Of course, propeller-swinging continues still, with small engines of up to about 150 hp. Most big engines were provided with winding handles for starting, often requiring two men to wind the engine over compression. They were very low-geared and sometimes connected via a clutch to an inertia fly-wheel. A starting system was needed for engine installations which were too high above the ground, too dangerous or otherwise impracticable and too slow and cumbersome to operate satisfactorily. There was one ingenious idea which was used in the Handley Page Heyford biplane bomber of 1933. In this, the engines were mounted on the upper wing, making starting a problem. It was neatly solved by means of portable shafts which could be mounted on each undercarriage wheel casing in turn, connecting it to the engine some eight feet above and safely winding it by hand until the engine started.

A gas starter was devised at Farnborough, comprising what appeared to be a small vee-twin motor cycle engine. In fact it used a single cylinder for power and the other was a pump, which passed a rich fuel/air mixture round the cylinders in turn and the ignition was switched on when the engine turned. This R.A.E. device was not altogether satisfactory but Fedden went one better and produced the Bristol gas starter which worked on similar principles and became widely used.

Mention must of course be made of the famous Hucks starter, one of which is still in use today at the Shuttleworth Collection. This strange-looking device, invented by B.C.Hucks, was strictly practical and the last working model has been in use since the 1920s and is based on the chassis of a Model 'T' Ford car. The starter is driven up to the propeller of an engine fitted with a special 'claw' on its hub and its driving shaft is engaged in the propeller's claw. By the engagement of a special clutch, the car engine drives the shaft, thus turning the propeller so that the aircraft's engine starts. The claw automatically throws out the shaft and the car's own clutch is then engaged so that it can be driven away.

The electrical starter has been a standard fitment in the majority of engines for decades but there was an exception in the case of the cordite cartridge-operated Coffman starter which was used in several types of engine during the Second World War and subsequently, chiefly in military aircraft.

It was ever thus. Starting by hand-swinging a 150 hp Gnome Monosoupape in a Sopwith F.1 Camel.

Starting from the cockpit. A novel idea for winding up a Gnome 100 hp 14-cylinder Omega-Omega. It did not catch on, for engine starting at least.

Propeller swinging, even with a relatively light rotary engine was not always easy, worst of all in the confined space of a pusher, as here in Airco D.H.2 with a Gnome Monosoupape 100 hp.

Cold-weather starting, aided by a blow-lamp — an unusual aspect but all too common in the unprotected conditions experienced in the first World War. This was a R.A.F.1a engine in an Airco D.H.6.

Strictly low-tech, the R.A.E. Bag-starter on the Hispano-Suiza 8B series engine in an S.E.5a fighter. (Above and below.)

R.A.E. Bag-starter on a Lion-engined Airco D.H.9a.

B.C. Hucks, the genius who invented the engine starter bearing his name, with his Blériot XI, Gnome 70 hp.

The simple hand-operated Noakes starter, attached to a Liberty-engined Airco D.H.9a. The inventor Jack Noakes joined the Royal Flying Corps on its formation, retired as a Group Captain and was 99 years old on the R.A.F's 75th Anniversary.

A Hucks engine starter at Abingdon, at the 50th Anniversary of the Royal Air Force, April, 1958. This survivor, belonging to the Shuttleworth Collection, like most, is mounted on a Ford Model T chassis. Others used the Crossley chassis.

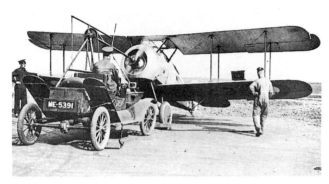

Starting a Sopwith Snipe with a Hucks starter (Ford chassis).

The Pegasus engine of the Bristol 138A, started with the Hucks starter on a Crossley chassis.

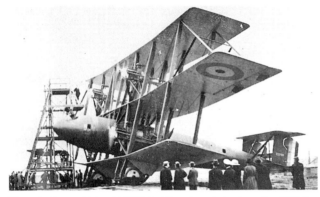

The only Tarrant Tabor, F.1765, had been intended to have four Siddeley-Deasy Tigers. These were not ready and, instead, it was fitted with six Napier Lions, the lower four being paired, tractor/pusher. It crashed on its first attempted take-off on 26.5.19 killing the two pilots.

Starting the engines of the Tarrant Tabor almost defies description. The elaborate scaffolding held a Ford Hucks starter, which was moved from one engine to another. The Ford chassis is here seen hoisted to about first-floor level and the tractor engines are running. The whole edifice then had to be moved to start the rear pusher engines.

The ingenious starting arrangement on a Handley Page Heyford, a vertical drive shaft connecting the starting handles to the Kestrel engines above.

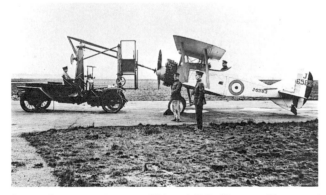

Starting the prototype Armstrong Whitworth Siskin III, powered by a geared Jaguar III, J6583. This Hucks starter was mounted on a Crossley chassis.

A Spitfire II. The Coffman cartridge engine starter can be seen here as the drum-shaped attachment to the crankcase of the Merlin XII, with the drive to the reduction gear casing.

The two-handed starting handles of a Merlin II in a Hawker Hurricane I.

Chapter 9
Engine Designations and Ratings

Engines are usually designated in such a way as to indicate in some way their power output. When reviewing the progress of engines, perhaps the most difficult aspect of the subject to approach and, quite the most important of all, is the horse-power developed in various conditions. Half a dozen figures may have been given for the power of a type of engine (particularly the supercharged variants) and exactly what was meant by variations of power is not always explained. It is not so much that there were errors of fact but, rather, that at the time records were published the people concerned knew exactly what was meant, though the facts published seemed to be imprecise and could even appear contradictory. There are now all too few people left who are able to explain from personal experience but, of course, the inconsistencies persist in published papers. There is therefore a need for the facts to be restated before it is too late and circumstances change. This thorny problem, together with the other, equally prickly, as to why the type of engine was selected for a particular use, needs explanation and is not an easy matter to portray simply and accurately.

Much confusion and argument has been caused by the inaccessibility or lack of available official definitions, as far as they concern engines. Widely and commonly-used terms all too often mean different things to different people, leading to confusion and argument. Furthermore, there is nothing new in the tendency of salesmen to place emphasis on the positive aspect of a product, be it soap or a sophisticated engine. Correct definitions do exist but, all too often, are to be found only deep within official publications, too deep perhaps even for the interested layman to have time to reach. In addition to the desire to prevent needless uncertainty and because of the complexity of the whole subject of power output in relation to induction, whether naturally aspirated or supercharged, fuel and other factors, much condensation and cross-referencing has been necessary in an attempt to make it as manageable as possible. Basically, therefore, the information in the Tables of Performance Figures relates to engine type, take-off power, climb or normal power and maximum power at maximum rpm, compression ratio, dimensions and dry weight (the latter as an aid to judging power/weight ratios). Notes are added where appropriate concerning propeller reduction gear ratios.

Differences between engines of the same basic type can be very numerous for a variety of reasons. Some versions of a type were supercharged (to different degrees, for different Rated Altitudes) and some were not. Propeller reduction gears, where fitted, varied quite widely, each acquiring a different, identifiable engine sub-type. Some had auxiliary drives, such as hydraulic pumps for undercarriage retraction, flaps, gun-turret operation etc. and some did not. An engine of a particular type number or mark, might differ from the next in its series principally or solely by virtue of having a hydraulic pump for undercarriage and flap operation. The Armstrong Siddeley Cheetah IX/X series was a typical example, in that the Mark X had a hydraulic pump, whereas the Mk IX did not.

The majority of wartime aircraft used by the Royal Air Force had differentially-operated compressed-air brakes, which became ever more necessary with the constant increase in aircraft weights and the widespread introduction of hard-surfaced runways. The Spitfire had flaps and retractable landing lamps which were pneumatically-operated as well. Engine-driven air-compressors thus became necessary and the fitting of such equipment frequently resulted in a different engine designation of one kind or another from the previous model. (Earlier, simpler aircraft had relied largely on the drag of a steerable tail-skid which also acted as a brake on a grass surface, perhaps with a panting airman trotting at the wing-tip, attempting to provide steerage in a cross-wind).

Certain aircraft had a radiator layout which necessitated a reversed-flow coolant system; this is mentioned in the Rolls-Royce Merlin section for de Havilland Mosquito, Hornet and Westland Welkin installations. Improvements and variations in supercharger and carburettor design, to meet the continual improvements in fuel quality on which the engine would give its best performance, resulted in alterations in engine design and had a great influence on whether or not a new type-number should be issued. This is referred to under Engine Ratings. It was a matter for consideration of the possible issue of a new number, or mark, when an existing engine was modified and possibly upgraded. Similarly, when an engine was derated so as to deliver less than its designed power (for training purposes, so as to prolong its useful life, or in places in the world where a suitably high grade of fuel was not available), a revised designation would be applied.

The installation of a particular version of an engine in an aeroplane, whether it be for reasons of confined space within a tight cowling or for the need of a special type of starting system (such as the Coffman cartridge-starter and the attendant need for quick access to it for replacement of used cartridges on the draughty decks of aircraft carriers) could also give rise to a different type and the same applied to changes in the appropriate electrical system or plumbing, whether for liquid cooling, pneumatics or hydraulics. For obvious reasons also, a clearly identifiable type-name facilitated Stores requisitioning and the quick issue, in times of urgency, of the appropriate mark of engine to the unit making provision for the aeroplane requiring it. When major overseas stores units had literally stacks of engines in packing cases, it was also vital that the correct types were available (and properly labelled). Otherwise they simply would not fit the job and an engine supplied as a replacement without appropriate modifications was worse than useless.

To mount a particular mechanical component, appropriate for the engine, usually required a modification to the front or rear cover, crankcase or auxiliary-drive gearbox of the engine itself and this was one of the principal causes of alterations in mark numbers. The adoption of a more or less self-contained 'power-egg', such as the Rolls-Royce Merlin XX or the Bristol Hercules XVI and their successors, naturally gave rise to particular problems and demanded precise attention to installations.

How an engine acquired its correct designation requires some explanation but, because of local variations in procedure, is not claimed to be comprehensive. When an engine was first introduced into the works, it was accompanied by a 'Drawing Introductory Sheet' (DIS), or a comparably-named list. This was a list of parts, whose drawings were then frozen and could not be altered without going through strict formalities. These, called Mods (Modifications), ensured that no unauthorized alterations were made which might be dangerous or interfere with the flow of production. The engine would be issued with a log book containing its DIS and serial identification numbers and a list of the Mods already incorporated. This told the user of the up-to-date standard of the particular engine. All subsequent Mods were given priorities, according to their urgency and were noted in the log book when incorporated.

The engine mark number indicated to the user the engine rating, as it was known and also told what particular features, accessories etc were particularly applicable to the mark. Ratings were established and laid down by the Ministry of Aircraft Production, generally known as M.A.P. These would include, where relevant, fundamental characteristics, such as the method of starting (electric or Coffman cartridge), cabin supercharger, propeller hand rotation etc. In addition, the incorporation of a number of special Mods might justify the issue of a separate mark number, i.e. the Merlin Mark 24, when modified so as to improve its service life, was re-designated the Mark T.24. This partly explains why several Marks of engine could have the same rating. A change in the propeller reduction gear ratio or the coolant flow would alter the mark number but not the rating. Another example is the Bristol engine built to Rating PE-9M50. The PE stood for Pegasus, this particular engine being a revised Pegasus Mark X, with a 0.5:1 propeller reduction gear and a 100 mm propeller shaft, thus becoming a Pegasus Mark XXII. As in other cases, the degree of supercharging is also indicated in the rating, the letter 'S' (sometimes FS) meaning fully supercharged, medium or moderately supercharged ratings bearing the letter 'M'. Two-speed supercharged engines were therefore designated 'SM'.

When major changes were made internally to a supercharged engine which affected its operation, a new Rating Number was given, an example being the change from single-stage to two-stage supercharging. Another example, changing the supercharger gear ratios of the Rolls-Royce Merlin Mark 61 (Rated RM8.SM, the 'RM' indicating Rolls Merlin), so as to give more power at lower altitudes, created a new series of engines which began with the Merlin Mark 65. This bore the new Rating RM10.SM, which was developed specifically for the Mustang project (the 'SM' designation indicating that it still retained a two-speed supercharger). A different kind of change (similar to that in the Pegasus referred to above), which simply altered the propeller reduction gear particularly to suit Spitfire operations, resulted in the Merlin Mark 66. As there were no other significant differences between the engines, they both therefore remained at Rating RM10.SM. Experimental engines which did not enter production were still given ratings, such as the RM17.SM. Clearly an advanced Merlin (in fact, it was capable of operating at +30 lb boost), it was type-tested but, because the war ended it was not needed and therefore dropped before baptism, not having been given a mark number.

ENGINE POWER — BRAKE HORSE-POWER

The proper definitions of various aspects of engine power can be both bewildering and exasperating to those unfamiliar with them. Indeed, this is one of the principal causes of the writing of this book. The term horse-power (referred to in this book as 'hp')simply relates to the engine's rate of doing work. In fact there is nothing simple about it, as there are many variable factors which affect the engine's performance.

The precision of specifications and mechanical tolerances, which are taken for granted today, was comparatively rare in the general run of engineering prior to the Second World War. This apparent lack of precision, left unexplained, leaves us today with a legacy of doubt which has repeatedly been encountered in the course of preparing this book. Tables of published engine performance figures are all too often mutually contradictory or, at best, so imprecise as to be unsatisfactory for inclusion in the history of the engine concerned. The question so raised is, which source is to be relied upon for accuracy and for completeness?

Examples of imprecision are so many that suitable ones are difficult to select for quotation. Probably the worst and most frequently discovered are figures quoted for horse-power. All too often an engine is quoted, for example, as a '350 hp Cheetah' or a '450 hp Jupiter', leaving the reader with a very vague notion of the power of the engine. Other examples quote variously from figures under the headings of Take-off, Climb and Maximum, sometimes with Economical, Continuous and Rated added for good measure. All should be (but seldom are) related to the appropriate rpm, if they are to make any sense and yet seldom are the figures published in context.

Differences between published comparable performance figures of particular engines are, on the whole, minor if it is assumed that the basis for all figures is the same. Air Ministry approval for the issue of a Type Certificate for an engine (via whatever agency was appropriate at the time) was based on a tolerance of +/-2.5 per cent in the Declared Power of each batch of engines. The Declared (or usable) Power for a given batch of engines could vary between engine batches and was not itself governed by the +/-4 per cent tolerance which was acceptable to the Air Ministry.

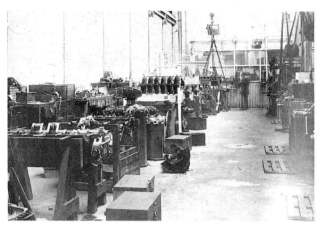

The Test-Shop, fairly primitive conditions at the Royal Aircraft Factory at Farnborough.

Bench-testing a Napier Lion on a Heenan and Froude dynamometer.

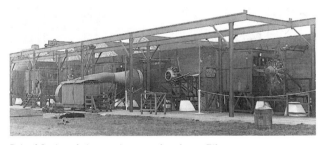

Bristol Jupiters being run-in on test-benches at Filton.

A Rolls-Royce Buzzard being tested on a Heenan and Froude dynamometer.

Provided that the actual performance of all engines in a batch delivered to Air Ministry orders was within 5 per cent of the declared figures, it was within acceptance limits. Understandably, the upper figure achieved was usually quoted. This was assumed until about the beginning of the Second World War and, broadly, the manufacturers' figures and those determined by the Aeroplane and Armament Experimental Establishment agreed to this extent. So, if the figure of 695 brake horse-power is quoted and, the other figure of 665 is about 4.3 per cent down and this was within the tolerance allowed.

The A. & A.E.E. at Martlesham used a form of dynamometer devised at Farnborough, by the Royal Aircraft Establishment (re-named from the Royal Aircraft Factory in June, 1918). This simple but ingenious instrument was mounted on the propeller-shaft, for direct measurements of power output and the figures so realized were reasonably accurate. They certainly accounted for the small discrepancies between individual engines of the same type or batch and the figures published by the makers. The results were also a basis for the Air Ministry to judge whether or not the performance of the engines under flight test were within contractual limits

The manufacturers' brochures, issued to the technical Press are (or should be) the ultimate guide and, yet, salesmanship seems to have changed little over the years. Editorial acceptance of the figures issued with advertising material has been known to be coloured by the need for continued advertising support and the consequently confusing performance figures for a new engine can take some time to clear up after half a century. The figures published are frequently open to interpretation, according to what you want to read or what you want your potential customer to read. You can either swamp him with figures about your new engine, so that he has to be very perceptive in finding out what he needs to know, or send him a carefully prepared set of figures which tell him what you want him to know, leaving him to find out, if he can, what you possibly hope he won't discover until you have put it all right in the Mark III version. This sounds all very cynical but it has happened and amounts to a battle of wits between the two sides, between whom there is an understanding of mutual skulduggery.

In the 1930s, perhaps the most interesting development period of all (with war looming ever nearer), engine powers were frequently quoted in two figures for a given rpm, i.e. 575/600 hp at 2,500 rpm, or 665/695 hp at 2,500 rpm. An understandable reaction to such figures, when quoted from official Air Ministry documents, for example, is 'which'? So, why were there so many examples of engine powers quoted in such a manner? The answer was no doubt obvious to the experts for whom such things were a daily occurrence but, these days, to others who have neither the time nor the inclination to go into the matter, it may be helpful to explain briefly why this should come about. Even today, it is hard enough to find the answers.

Quite apart from minor and purely mechanical differences between one engine and the next off the production line (tolerances being not quite as tight as they are today), the revolutions at which an engine will run at full-throttle, while the aeroplane is on the chocks, is limited by various factors. These include such things as exhaust back-pressure and the drag of a big (perhaps fixed-pitch) propeller turning in air which may well be static or even blowing in the reverse direction in which the slipstream must go.

Once the thing gets going, the rpm can go up because of reducing propeller drag. As the horse-power developed (or the work done) depends on the rpm, so the reducing drag allows the revolutions to increase and the power to increase proportionately, up to the point when the resistance of the propeller is equal to the energy applied to it at the throttle setting and fuel supplied. This partly explains why the power output of an unsupercharged engine actually increases, with the initial climb, as discussed in an earlier chapter.

Power Rating — Declared (or usable) Power, from the manufacturer.

1. The Rated Power of the engine is the corrected hp developed at the Rated Altitude (see 4) at the International rpm (see 2).
2. International rpm has been quoted variously over the years, all amounting to the same figure, i.e. Continuous, Maximum Continuous Climb, 'Normal', or Rated rpm.
3. In a supercharged engine, International Boost is the Maximum Continuous Climbing or Rated Boost at International rpm. (see 2) and is often 'gated', the gate position on the throttle usually marked 'RATED'.
4. The Rated Altitude is the lowest height at which full-throttle at International rpm (see 2) is permissible, or may be obtained through automatic boost control. It is also the highest altitude at which International or Rated Boost (see 3) at International rpm can be maintained by the supercharger.

Power Rating — Civil

The boost pressure and rpm of a 'C' rated (Civil) engine — i.e. the Perseus XIIc, were set at reduced figures for international and cruising power, principally for fuel economy reasons. In consequence, engine wear and resulting maintenance costs were also reduced slightly at lower continuous power.

Power Rating — Economical Cruise

The maximum permissible boost pressure for economical cruising without a constant-speed propeller, is that which gives a 2.5 per cent drop in rpm from Maximum Continuous power. Another criterion in the Air Ministry's advice for judging maximum economical cruising power, with a two-speed supercharger, is to change from low to high gear, when the boost given in the operational limitations has fallen by 2 lb/square inch.

Chapter 10
Standards

This account has been put together using, as far as possible, manufacturers' designations for their engines. Regrettably, there was little or no co-ordination between them. Some are known to be reliable, but there are notable exceptions, Armstrong Siddeley being one of them. Following the damage done during the air raids on Coventry, the remaining records of the Company are woefully incomplete. Contradictions have been checked so as to eradicate them as far as possible. A somewhat idealistic approach, with no guesswork as to the most reliable source of information, has been the aim. Where information was uncertain or unproven, it has been left out — sometimes accounting for unwelcome gaps. Where, for example, there is no reliable record of an engine being run, tested and fitted to an airframe, the engine is listed as 'Not recorded'. This should not be interpreted as a definite claim one way or the other. In any case, engines were often interchangeable, for example within the Rolls-Royce Kestrel and Bristol Jupiter families. Many engines were built and test-bed run, never to have been mounted in airframes, if contemporary records are to be believed — which is a doubtful premise in any case. Basic criteria has therefore to be based on the best possible accuracy, after many years' neglect or loss.

Each engine recorded has details in accordance with the following sequence, as far as possible.

1. Name, type and horse-power (i.e. a convenient approximate figure, usually maximum continuous or 'International' power but, in some cases where this is not known, take-off power) and year of introduction. General similarities to other engines of the same type or 'family', with modifications to suit particular installations.
2. Number of cylinders and layout of the engine.
3. The method of cooling — liquid (including type) or air.
4. Type of valve-gear — poppet or sleeve.
5. Bore and stroke, Swept Volume (Vol).
6. Compression ratio.
7. Induction — Normally Aspirated (Unsupercharged), Supercharging, Full or Medium in one, two or three-speeds and in one or two stages.
8. Propeller drive, direct or geared. In the latter case, epicyclic, spur, co-axial, double-reduction, torquemeter-type with the reduction ratio :1, relative to crankshaft speed. Direction of rotation, as viewed from behind, left-hand (L.H.) — anti-clockwise; right-hand (R.H.) — clockwise), tractor or pusher drive; propellers may be of variable or controllable-pitch, of the constant-speed type, or counter-rotating, some with reversible pitch or braking capability.
9. Fuel, Octane rating or grade. DTD Specification.
10. Production, where known. Ordered, Delivered, Cancelled or suspended,
11. Aircraft known to have been powered by the engine, either experimentally or in service.

Dry weights frequently need to be considered in relation to power output — the important power/weight ratio. Where available, weights are to be found in the performance tables. The figures quoted are those published by manufacturers, Government sources or, in their absence, in the most reliable technical press. Dry weights and dimensions may vary considerably between models of a basic engine, according to accessories fitted and many engines in series production appear in a bewildering number of variants. Some involve major differences, such as superchargers and propeller reduction gears and others relate to major accessories. The differences may be relatively small, internal and therefore invisible, though important and this inevitably results in a considerable degree of repetition, particularly in certain dimensions. Relevant figures, where known, are listed in the text and tables. Radial and rotary engines are marked according to diameter and length. In-line engines are marked in length, width and height.

Some idea of the importance of knowing the dimensions and weights of engines and power-packs may be judged by the necessity of being able to transport them by air, as replacements for failed units, as illustrated.

A Spare Napier Lion II engine under the port wing of a Vickers Victoria bomber-Transport, showing the mounting cradle attached to bomb-rack points.

A Supermarine Scapa flying boat, carrying a spare Kestrel engine on its back.

Another example of a Lion II engine under the starboard wing of a Vickers Victoria. The opening cabin windows were a blessing to the embarked troops in Middle-Eastern hot and bumpy weather.

A spare Bristol Hercules engine, being carried on bomb crutches in the bomb-bay of a Handley Page Halifax. The flame-damping exhausts of the Hercules are noteworthy.

Although the figures for dimensions, as well as for dry weights, are based on the figures and units published by the manufacturers, it should also be noted that wartime security restrictions prevented the publication of some details until the end of hostilities. By then, as mentioned previously, some (and occasionally all) details had become lost, destroyed by enemy action or otherwise obscured, or even the makers themselves had lost interest in publishing details, thus making a complete and accurate compilation impossible, despite the best endeavours of many helpers. Fortunately, towards the end of the 1914-18 war, the Aeronautical Inspection Department of the Ministry of Munitions issued brief contemporary engine Specifications and rare copies of these survive and are included in this text.

It is believed that every significant engine type and sub-type which was built in Britain and which actually flew, is included. Inevitably, by the nature of things, there will also be omissions. Very many experimental engine installations were tried out which resulted in some strange anomalies. Certainly, there were 'grey areas' in this respect. The criterion, 'Did it fly?' is flexible, to the extent that an engine which was mounted in an airframe and ground-run on test, may have failed to come up to expectations and

then have been modified, consequently being given a different name or mark number. Many such engines were built and test-bed run, but never mounted in airframes and flown, if contemporary records are to be believed — which is a doubtful premise in any case. In cases where engines which were used as development steps towards subsequent types which were flown and eventually went into production, both may be included. In such circumstances, the relevance of both can justify their inclusion but a hard and fast rule is unreasonable. Where there is reasonable doubt about this however, an engine may be included in the 'Not Recorded' list.

The engines are listed as logically as possible, alpha-numerically where possible, under type names and not necessarily chronologically. This is most important. Engines of a particular type, with numerous sub-variants, tended to be produced for several years, in the course of which other variations and indeed other engines appeared and a strict chronological record can become extremely confusing. For this reason, it is not always desirable to retain the alpha-numerical order, although where possible, with the year of first appearance being recorded (where the information is available). The full and correct published designations of engines and airframes are given. In cases where there are families of engines, sections of which have much in common with each other (i.e the Rolls-Royce Merlin), a table of the family groups also precedes the relevant text, so that the researcher may more easily find the group and individual type under review.

The original source of information was normally the manufacturer, who ought to know. Despite this, careful researches have revealed published performance figures which appear to be rather over-optimistic. They are, perhaps, slanted towards sales but seem not to tally with other figures of uncertain origin but published in reputable books and magazines. The situation has proved to be a very difficult one to resolve in many cases. Which was correct? It was important that this difficulty be resolved, if possible. One solution of course lay in the study of the numerous Reports prepared in the 1920s and 1930s, for the Air Ministry by the Aeroplane and Armament Experimental Establishment at Martlesham Heath, as well as those emanating from the nearby Marine Aircraft Experimental Establishment at Felixstowe. Extracts, such as figures from power curves, from selected Reports of the A. & A.E.E. will be found under their appropriate engine headings in the text, using slightly adjusted terminology simply to clarify the contents.

Similar records, just as valuable, have been kept at Farnborough and the Air Ministry's official Air Publications handbooks. Many of these Reports may be seen at the Public Record Office at Kew. The meticulous testing in the air, using dynamometers developed both at the R.A.E. and in the United States, enabled power outputs in flight to be recorded with a high degree of accuracy, even highlighting minor differences between nominally identical engines, particularly before the widespread use of constant-speed propellers.

It should be remembered that, in the 1920s and 1930s, aircraft intended for Service as well as civil use were subjected to rigorous flight testing of their strength and performance, just as it is today. The major difference was that training in the art and skill of judging an aeroplane's performance and suitability for the job for which it was designed was, until the Second World War, to a considerable degree a matter of the pilot's opinion and judgement based on his experience rather than, as now, a rather more exact science arising out of the vast accumulation of experience. In this connection, the skill expected of and displayed by test pilots today is of course no less than it was. Further, the demands on their courage and dedication are certainly no less and it is also worth remembering that the compulsory wearing of parachutes in Service aeroplanes was not required until as late as 1925.

The most obvious difficulty, therefore, has simply been the lack of really reliable published information on performance figures, even on design and methods of construction and variations between otherwise similar engines. Where information is still lacking after long searches, an educated guess has occasionally had to be adopted but, in the interests of historical accuracy has, as far as possible, been avoided. The endless inconsistencies in published work concerning engine power cannot all be attributed to the writers or publishers because the manufacturers themselves have in the past tended to confuse the issue with repeated examples of terminological inexactitude and inconsistencies. It has therefore been necessary to sort out these inconsistencies and, where possible, to explain them.

At the very beginning of this book, some twenty years before its publication, it was obvious that some sort of order was going to be needed in the presentation of the mass of facts and figures which would accumulate. The biggest question of all was whether to put figures in Imperial or metric measurements. The book was largely intended to cover the period up to the 1950s, when big piston engines were becoming ever rarer, the turbine sweeping all before it. With the likelihood of a broadly European (and therefore metric) standard being adopted increasingly widely, it was evident that future readers would probably become more and more oriented towards metric measurements.

A fact that is not always appreciated is that the earliest aero-engines, most of which had their origins in France or Germany were, naturally, made to metric measurements. Examples are the 80 hp Renault and the 120 hp Austro-Daimler, both subsequently built in Britain, well into the First World War. The Renault cylinders were measured in metric units which subsequently found their way into the post-war Cirrus and the similar de Havilland Gipsy, both of which of course owed their origin to Renault. The Austro-Daimler engine gave birth to the succession of Beardmore, B.H.P. and Siddeley-Deasy engines and metric measurements again were used. Firms which built engines which were developments, more or less, of power units of European origin tended therefore to retain their metric measurements. The dimensions of engines designed in Britain were usually quoted in Imperial measures, sometimes involving sixteenths or thirty-seconds of an inch, to say nothing of the omni-present 'thou'. There is a notable example of an engine of French (and therefore metric) origin which had measurements heavily Anglicised into thousandths of an inch. For a close approach to a state of lunacy is a British manufacturer's brochure measurement of an engine's height is quoted as '(overall approximate) 52 29/32 in'!

As ever, there was resistance in Britain to anything which was suspected of being foreign, even the humble decimal being rejected, as were 'those damn dots' so despised by Randolph Churchill, the father of the great wartime leader, Winston Churchill. Even in the 1990s, there are some who find decimals uncomfortable and disagreeable to live with, even converting them back to fractions and thus easier to visualize. To others, clearly decimals rather than sixteenths of an inch are preferable. In converting fractions to decimals in this book, a maximum of three decimal places has been used. Although it has to be reasonably accurate, it is not intended to be an engineer's reference book.

Taking into account the probability that future generations will use mathematical units which, even at the end of the twentieth century, still seem strange, some increasingly common units have been avoided. Horse-powers are quoted in the usually accepted unit of Brake Horse-Power, abbreviated to 'hp'. One unit which is avoided is the kilowatt, when applied to engine power. Although its use may be academically correct, it might also be regarded as showing-off. It is not given to everybody to be convinced that 'There is only Physics. The rest is Stamp-Collecting', this being attributed to the great nuclear physicist, Lord Rutherford. It is believed that the majority of readers would be put to needless mental agility to assess the horse-power value of a kilowatt, in the same way that few people now would recognize an old-fashioned Cheval Vapeur (even if seen grazing in a field). More readily understandable is the difference between a 120-130 hp de Havilland Gipsy Major and a Rolls-Royce Merlin of rather more than 1,200 hp. Similarly, readers are likely to appreciate the difference between a 1.3 litre motor-car engine and, say, a Merlin of 27 litres, or a hefty 37-litre Griffon. American engines have, in the past, tended to be given cubic capacities in cubic inches but the metric system is now accepted in the United States, largely thanks to that great country's membership of NATO and litres are now quoted for modern American engines.

Thereby hung a dilemma, an anomaly which had to result in a compromise and the decision was made to use whichever system, Imperial or metric, was published by the manufacturers themselves. There were several reasons for this decision. It avoids the risk of needless errors occurring in the very many hundreds of conversions required in the figures for some nine hundred types of engine. It also saves a great deal of time, space and expense in the course of printing and publication. In any case, few will require such exactitude and, for those hardy souls who wish to do so, a straightforward conversion table is provided, a pocket calculator with a constant facility doing the rest. It is hoped that this decision will emerge as correct in the circumstances.

Historical Notes

HISTORICAL NOTE ON ENGINE NAMES

One of the possible disadvantages of a semi-classical upbringing is an insatiable curiosity about the origins of names. The frustrations are about equalled by the discoveries. The allocation of names deemed to be suitable for military engines was the prerogative of the Air Ministry, its heirs and successors, who must have burned much oil digging up several of them. For example —

Alvis Leonides. Leonidas was the King of Sparta who defended the Pass of Thermopylae against the Persians in 480 BC. The connection with the Alvis Leonides, an engine of modest output is obscure.

Alvis Maeonides Major. Lydian Maeonian. The poet Homer was Maeonian, born in Maeonia — Asia Minor. There is no obvious connection.

Alvis Pelides. No bets offered on the origin of the name, except the possibility of a corruption of Pleiades, the seven daughters of Atlas and Pleione who were all transformed into stars, one of them being invisible, out of shame for various inscrutable reasons.

Yet, these curiosities are as nothing compared with the obscure origins of the name given to the German Mercedes engine. Mercedes, is anything but a German name. It has been suggested elsewhere that it is French, owing to the addition of accents. One of the stories about Daimler-Benz is that they adopted the name because it was the name of the daughter of a very good French customer of theirs. The word is in fact Spanish, of ancient origin. A German engineer from Daimler-Benz at Stuttgart, when questioned about why the name was adopted for cars built by his company, was uncertain but said it was his understanding that the three-pointed star within a ring meant 'The Three Graces, Land, Sea and Air' (all of which are appropriate to their engines).

A further explanation is connected with three goddesses of Greek legend, Aglaia, Euphrosyne and Thalia, who personified light, joy and fertility, as exemplified in the group sculpture by Antonio Canova (1757-1822). The Spanish connection therefore, allowing for possible errors of syntax, comes from the polite form of address 'usted', expressed in full 'vuestra merced' (written, Vd). It means 'your grace', or 'your honour', plural 'vuestras'. ('Las Mercedes', or 'The Graces', no accents being required in the original language). However, there are other possible explanations, less agreeable and more Wagnerian. This deduction is naturally open to correction but seems reasonable.

If this explanation may appear not to be strictly applicable to a book on British aero-engines, the Mercedes connection did (at least initially) give Mr Henry Royce food for thought, even though he preferred to pursue his own ideas.

It is hoped that these accounts, will not result in what has been described as the `Three stages of a Naval Argument; direct assertion, followed by flat contradiction, resulting in gross personal abuse'.

HISTORICAL NOTE ON ENGINES AND THEIR AIRCRAFT

The engine and airframe combinations listed are, as far as possible, those recorded as having flown. There were very many trial installations and inclusion in the list does not imply that a particular engine was standard in its airframe, although the great majority were. As engine improvements were made, resulting from experience in service, they were frequently modified, the alteration usually resulting in a change in the designation not only of the engine but also of the aeroplane itself. (A policy decision was made,

early in the Second World War that, in view of the ever-increasing complication of Roman numerals as Mark numbers progressed, after the figure for Twenty (XX) the more easily understood and tidier figures in the Arabic numeral system were to be adopted. There were a few exceptions, viz. Pegasus XXII, Kestrel XXX).

For more explicit information, reference should be made to the records of the engine and aircraft manufacturers listed in the Bibliography. Regrettably, with over 3,100 installations, in some cases space does not permit more than the briefest description of each type, nor the inclusion of more than a token of the very large number of foreign aircraft powered by British engines. In a number of cases, there are no available records to complete even the briefest questionnaire, so gaps are bound to occur, rather than resorting to guesswork. Set against this, as stated previously, an engine that is known to have run, probably flown but there is 'No Record' of positive proof that it was actually flown, cannot with certainty be excluded, resulting in an uncomfortable fence-sitting exercise. The Appendix therefore ensures that the published details are not discarded or lost should further information come to light following the publication of this book.

Before the outbreak of the Second World War, almost all new land and seaplanes were sent for testing at one or other of the two Government testing stations, the Aeroplane and Armament Experimental Establishment and the Marine Aircraft Experimental Establishment (M.A.E.E.). The A. & A.E.E. at Martlesham Heath, near Ipswich, Suffolk and the M.A.E.E. at nearby Felixstowe were, for the sake of security, moved respectively to Boscombe Down on the edge of Salisbury Plain and to Helensburgh, on the North side of the Firth of Clyde. A number of performance figures which are included in the text have been taken from official test Reports of both Establishments and it will be seen that some of the figures are at variance with the published manufacturers' figures quoted in the text and tables. This is at least partly because Martlesham used standard calibrated dynamometers for measuring power output, instruments which were not always available to the manufacturers. These instruments were developed at the Royal Aircraft Establishment and reflected consistently (and remarkably accurately in the inter-war period) the permitted variations in power between otherwise identical engines. Prior to this, in the early 1920s, the quoted brake horse-power (hp) was a very nominal figure, frequently optimistic and not to be taken too literally. The '80 hp Gnome' rotary, on a good day, would usually produce about 70 hp. The great majority of published engine performance figures and even their terminology varied alarmingly for anyone trying to make sense of them. Criticism is therefore inevitable.

Unfortunately, the moves away from Martlesham Heath and Felixstowe upon the outbreak of war in 1939, happened to coincide with the beginning of the era of variable-pitch and constant-speed propellers and a totally different form of presentation by both Establishments of their engine power Reports. This is the reason for the absence of the old-established Reports from about the end of that year.

Engines which were supercharged to varying degrees are referred to as such. It follows, therefore, that all others were unsupercharged or, to use the old term, 'normally aspirated'.

Engine production figures, 8/1914-12/1918 by a variety of manufacturers and sub-contractors, ordered, delivered, cancelled or suspended, are quoted as officially recorded in 1918 but the exactness of some of the figures needs to be treated with some caution.

PART 2
BRITISH PISTON AERO-ENGINES AND THEIR AIRCRAFT

(The companies are listed in the Index on page 318)

A.B.C. MOTORS LTD, LONDON

The engine company of this name originated under the name of W.L.Adams, in a small workshop at Redbridge, Southampton, about 1900. The name was changed to The Aeroplane Engine Company Ltd in 1909. In 1910, the Government was inclined to give cash rewards for aircraft and engines of British construction and 21-year-old Granville Eastwood Bradshaw, recently appointed Chief Designer, suggested changing the name to the All British Engine Co. A.B.C. Motors Ltd was formally founded in 1912, by which time it had entered the motor-cycle and aero-engine business and moved from Southampton to Hersham, near Walton-on-Thames, Surrey, so as to be near the new centre of aviation and motor racing at Brooklands. Selsdon Engineering Ltd of Croydon, took over the sole manufacturing rights of A.B.C. aero-engines from 1918, on behalf of Walton Motors Ltd, which was by then the design authority.

Between 1919 and 1923, A.B.C. Motors Ltd produced little in the way of aero-engines but then the company began to develop engines for use in light aircraft, beginning with converted air-cooled motor-cycle engines.

A.B.C., 30 hp, (1912), an upright 4-cylinder water-cooled in-line engine with copper water-jackets. One push-rod operated inlet and exhaust valve per cylinder, camshaft-operated. Bore/stroke 3.74 x 3.15 in, vol 138.4 cu in. (95 x 80 mm, vol 2.2 litre).
Aircraft:
    Burgess-Wright (Winner, British Empire Michelin Cup 1912, pilot Harry Hawker).

A.B.C., 60 hp, (1912), an upright 90-degree Vee-8 water-cooled engine, with a direct tractor-drive. Bore/stroke 3.75 x 3.125 in. Vol. 276 cu in. The cylinder body was of forged steel with a jacket of steel, plated on the inside with copper welded to it by oxy-acetylene. Overhead valves, via push-rods. Cast-iron pistons. Nickel chrome crankshaft, steel connecting rods and cast steel crankcase.
Aircraft:
    Avro Type E

A.B.C., 100 hp, (1912), an upright 90-degree Vee-8 engine water-cooled poppet-valve engine with a direct tractor-drive. Bore/stroke 5.0 x 4.25 in. Vol. 706.88 cu in.
Aircraft:
    Avro 504, 504A
    Flanders Biplane

GNAT I, 30/35 hp, (1916), a 2-cylinder horizontally-opposed air-cooled poppet-valve, it had a direct R.H. tractor-drive. Bore/stroke 4.33 x 4.72 in. Vol. 139.06 cu in. (110 x 120 mm. Vol. 2.28 litre). Compression ratio 3.8:1. One A.B.C. carburettor, one magneto. Production, 8/1914-12/1918, from:-
A.B.C. Motors Ltd, Walton-on-Thames,
Ordered, 18; Delivered, 17; Cancelled/suspended, 1
Aircraft:
    B.A.T. F.K.28 Crow
    Blackburn Sidecar
    Grain (P.V.7) Kitten
    Sopwith Bee/Tadpole/Sparrow

MOSQUITO, (1916), this was a 6-cylinder air-cooled single-row radial, poppet-valve engine. Direct R.H. tractor-drive. It is said to have originated from a bet by Harry Hawker that Bradshaw could not design a six-cylinder radial engine. It used Gnat cylinders but was not a success. Its steel cylinders were copper-plated to assist cooling and it had one inlet and two exhaust valves per cylinder. Bore/stroke 4.33 x 5.51 in. Vol. 487 cu in.
Production, 8/1914-12/1918, Ordered/delivered, 1.
Aircraft:
    B.A.T. F.K.22

The seven-cylinder A.B.C. Wasp in the prototype Sopwith Snail.

The A.B.C. Gnat flat-twin in a Sopwith Tadpole.

An A.B.C. Wasp in an Avro 504K in May, 1920.

WASP I, 160 hp, (1918). A 7-cylinder single-row radial, air-cooled poppet-valve engine, it had a direct R.H. tractor-drive. Bore/stroke 4.53 x 5.9 in. Vol. 667.1 cu in. (115 x 150 mm. Vol. 10.78 litre). Compression ratio 4.05:1. Two Claudel-Hobson carburettors, two magnetos. Diameter 42.0 in.
Production, 8/1914-12/1918, from:-
Crossley Motors Ltd, Ordered, 12; Cancelled/suspended, 4
Galloway Engineering Co Ltd, Dumfries,
Ordered, 12; Delivered, 12; Cancelled/suspended, 0
Delivered, 8, by 18 March, 1918;
Guy Motors Ltd, Wolverhampton, Ordered, 12; Delivered, 1; Cancelled/suspended, 11
Gwynnes Ltd, Hammersmith, Ordered, 12; Delivered, 11; Cancelled/suspended, 1
Sheffield Simplex Motor Co Ltd, Sheffield,
Ordered, 20; Delivered, 12; Cancelled/suspended, 8
Vickers Ltd, London SW3,
Ordered, 212; Delivered, 4; Cancelled/suspended, 208
Aircraft:

      Avro 504K
      B.A.T. F.K.23 Bantam
      B.A.T. F.K.24 Baboon
      Sopwith 8F.1 Snail
      Westland Wagtail

WASP II, 200 hp, (1919), this was similar to the Wasp Mk I but with increased bore/stroke and swept volume (4.75 x 6.25 in. Vol. 775.59 cu in. 120.65 x 158.75 mm. Vol. 12.71 litre). Direct R.H. tractor-drive. Compression ratio .457:1. Diameter 42.7 in, length 45 in.
Aircraft:

      Avro 504K
      B.A.T. F.K.23 Bantam
      B.A.T. F.K.27
      Saunders Kittiwake
      Sopwith 8F.1 Snail
      Westland Wagtail

DRAGONFLY I, 320 hp, (1918) 9-cylinder single-row radial, air-cooled poppet-valve engine, it had a direct R.H. tractor-drive.

Bore/stroke 5.5 x 6.5 in. (139.7 x 165.1 mm)
Swept Volume 1,390.4 cu in. (22.80 litres).
Compression Ratio 4.42:1.
Diameter 48.8 in. Length 47.80 in.
Weight — *see* Performance tables.

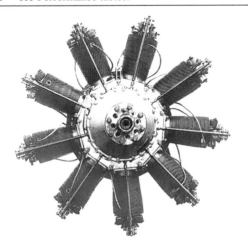

The A.B.C. Dragonfly I which was an unsatisfactory engine and nearly turned out to be a disaster owing to massive over-ordering by the Government.

The Dragonfly has for many years been the subject of much critical comment, such as a disaster waiting to happen. This is probably true in many respects because, had all gone according to the Government's original plans, a large proportion of the newly-formed Royal Air Force from April 1918 would have been powered (at least, nominally) by Dragonfly engines. As it turned out, the highly unsatisfactory engine was over-sold to a credulous Government, on the basis of initial (quite successful) test runs. The lesson, which the Government should have learnt on the basis of the lack of proper and adequate testing of the Sunbeam Arab I and which itself had brought about an engine crisis a year earlier, had not been absorbed. In effect the manufacture of all engines, other than Roll-Royce's Eagle and Falcon and Siddeley's Puma was to be terminated immediately after the 1918 Armistice, in favour of the Dragonfly.

The first Dragonfly is believed to have been made by Guy Motors at Wolverhampton, in just under a month in February 1918. In all, an incredible total of well over 11,930 were ordered, although only 1,147 were delivered and nine or ten were actually flown, before the programme was cancelled altogether. The engine turned out to be low on power, high on fuel consumption and overweight. It also overheated and vibrated so badly as to verge on disintegration after a few hours' running. The vibration was subsequently attributed to the provision of static balance only. Synchronous torsional vibration was not at all properly understood at the time but this happened, by ill-luck, to be an extreme case. Bradshaw had inadvertently designed the engine to run just at its major critical vibration frequency which, perhaps more by luck than judgement, other designers had escaped. Although rated at 320 hp at 1,750 rpm, with a potential of 340 hp, it seldom achieved 295 hp at a maximum of 1,650 rpm. The steel forged cylinders had integral heads, the cooling fins being coated with copper to aid cooling, in which it was ineffective. The pistons were of aluminium alloy and each cylinder had one large inlet and two smaller exhaust valves, the ports being bolted to the head. Two Claudel-Hobson H.C.8 carburettors, two magnetos.

It would have taken such a long time to correct the Dragonfly's many design faults that the remaining orders were cancelled. As designed, it has been said to have been as much use as a stick with two wrong ends and that the First World War ended only just in time to save the fledgling Royal Air Force from, potentially, a mechanical catastrophe.
Production, 8/1914-12/1918, from:-
Beardmore Aero Engine Ltd, Glasgow,
Ordered, 1,500; Delivered, 0; Cancelled/suspended, 1,500
Belsize Motors Ltd, Manchester
Ordered, 1,000; Delivered, 0; Cancelled/suspended, 1,000
F.W. Berwick & Co Ltd, Park Royal, London.
Ordered, 1,000; Delivered, 0; Cancelled/suspended, 1,000
Clyno Engineering Co, Wolverhampton,
Ordered, 500; Delivered, 4; Cancelled/suspended, 496
Crossley Motors Ltd,
Ordered, 1,000; Delivered, 0; Cancelled/suspended, 1,000
J.B. Ferguson, Belfast,
Ordered, 12; Delivered, 1; Cancelled/suspended, 11
Guy Motors Ltd, Wolverhampton,
Ordered, 600; Delivered, 14; Cancelled/suspended, 586
Humber Ltd, Stoke, Coventry,
Ordered, 850; Delivered, 0; Cancelled/suspended, 850
Mather & Platt Ltd, Manchester,
Ordered, 750; Delivered, 0; Cancelled/suspended, 750
Maudslay Motors Co Ltd, Coventry,
Ordered, 512; Delivered, 5; Cancelled/suspended, 507
North British Locomotive Co Ltd, Glasgow,
Ordered, 12; Delivered, 4; Cancelled/suspended, 8
Ransomes, Sims & Jeffries, Ipswich,
Ordered, 500; Delivered, 0; Cancelled/suspended, 500
Ruston Proctor & Co Ltd, Lincoln,
Ordered, 1,500; Delivered, 0; Cancelled/suspended, 1,500
Sheffield Simplex Motor Co Ltd, Sheffield,
Ordered, 500; Delivered, 7; Cancelled/suspended, 493
Vickers Ltd, London SW3
Ordered, 1,000; Delivered, 1; Cancelled/suspended, 999
Vulcan Motor & Engineering Co,
Ordered, 600; Delivered, 0; Cancelled/suspended, 600
Wolseley Motors Ltd, Birmingham,
Ordered, 12; Delivered, 1; Cancelled/suspended, 11
Aircraft:

      Armstrong Whitworth Ara
      Austin Greyhound
      Avro 533 Manchester I

Boulton & Paul P.7 Bourges IA
de Havilland D.H.11 Oxford I
Sopwith Rainbow
Sopwith 2FR.2 Bulldog

DRAGONFLY IA, 330/360 hp, (1920). This was similar to the Mk I but had revised pistons and cylinder heads, designed at Farnborough, as the R.A.F.22W, by S.D.Heron and had a revised oil system. Attempts to improve cooling and to reduce vibration and weight were largely unsuccessful, the engine persisting in suffering from imbalance and torsional vibration. Diameter 50.6 in, length 47.8 in.

The Sopwith Dragon with an A.B.C. Dragonfly IA

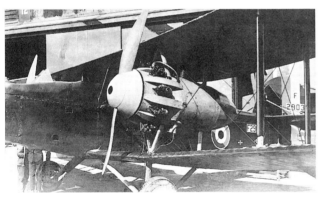

The Boulton & Paul P.7 Bourges IA, powered by an A.B.C. Dragonfly IA.

The A.B.C. Dragonfly IA, following modifications at Farnborough. These did little to make it a satisfactory engine.

Aircraft:

Austin Greyhound
B.A.T. F.K.25 Basilisk
Boulton & Paul P.7 Bourges IA
Bristol 23 Badger I
Nieuport Goshawk
Nieuport Nieuhawk
Nieuport Nighthawk
Siddeley S.R.2 Siskin
Sopwith Dragon
Sopwith Snark
Sopwith R.M.1 Snapper
Sopwith Cobham I
Westland Weasel

A.B.C. Dragonfly IA.

The tiny A.B.C. engine of a nominal 8 h.p., with considerable commotion, just manages to get the English Electric Wren off the ground.

GADFLY, 60 hp, (1920) 5-cylinder single-row radial, air-cooled poppet-valve. Very little information published.
Aircraft:

Bristol Babe, possibly flew with a Gadfly (contemporary records suggest this, although it is still uncertain).

A.B.C., 8 hp, (1923), a specially-tuned, converted 2-cylinder motor-cycle design, horizontally-opposed air-cooled poppet-valve. Direct R.H. tractor-drive. Bore/stroke 2.72 x 2.13 in. Vol. 24.76 cu in. (69 x 54 mm. Vol. 404 cc).
Aircraft:

English Electric S.1 Wren
Handley Page H.P.22

SCORPION I, 30 hp, (1923), 2-cylinder horizontally-opposed, air-cooled poppet-valve engine. Direct R.H. tractor-drive. Bore/stroke 3.6 x 3.7 in. Vol. 73.32 cu in. (87.5 x 91.5 mm. Vol. 1.1 litre). Compression ratio 4:1.
Aircraft:

Boulton & Paul P.41 Phoenix I
de Havilland D.H.53 Humming Bird
Hawker Cygnet
Kay 32/1 Gyroplane
Parmentier Wee Mite
Westland Woodpigeon

Heath Parasol
Henderson-Glenny HSF II Gadfly I & II
Hendy 281 Hobo
Mignet HM 14N Pou du Ciel
Parmentier Wee Mite
Short S.4 Satellite
Wheeler Slymph

HORNET, 75 hp, (1929), effectively a double Scorpion 4-cylinder, horizontally-opposed air-cooled poppet-valve. Direct R.H. tractor-drive. Bore/stroke 4.02 x 4.8 in. Vol. 243.18 cu in (102 x 124.5 mm. Vol. 4.0 litre). Compression ratio 5.6:1. Length 25.5 in; width 39.0 in; height 28.0 in.
Aircraft:

Civilian Coupe I
Robinson Redwing I
Southern (Miles) Martlet
Westland Widgeon III

The A.B.C. Hornet, really a 75 hp double Scorpion was used in light aircraft from 1929.

The flat-twin A.B.C. Scorpion I, of 30 hp.

The A.B.C. Hornet.

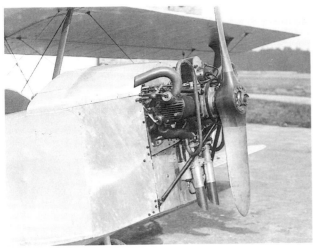

The A.B.C. Scorpion I in a Hawker Cygnet.

SCORPION II, 34 hp, (1924), as Mk I with slightly increased bore. Direct R.H. tractor-drive. Bore/stroke 4.02 x 3.6 in. Vol. 91.42 cu in. (102 x 91.4 mm. Vol. 1.49 litre). Compression ratio 6:1. Length 26.0 in; width 32.0 in; height 15.5 in.
Aircraft:

A.B.C.Robin
Comper C.L.A.7 Swift

AIRCRAFT DISPOSAL COMPANY LTD (A.D.C.).

F.B. Halford was the 'H' in the B.H.P. saga of the First World War, at the end of which in 1918 (by now promoted Major), he joined forces as an associate with Engine Patents Ltd, consultants, the name which H.R. Ricardo first adopted for his firm in July 1917, later to become Ricardo & Co. They undertook research into combustion problems, supercharging and the possible uses of the Burt-McCollum sleeve-valve system. In order to continue his work on combustion research, in 1923 Halford formed an independent design Company, becoming well-known again as a consultant for his design work, from 1924, with the Aircraft Disposal Company, or A.D.C. The object of A.D.C. was to make whatever use possible of the large number of engines left over after the war. This work led Halford, initially, to adapt the 80 hp Renault, modified with aluminium cylinder heads, so as to become the 120 hp Airdisco. The modestly-successful A.D.C. Nimbus and the proposed air-cooled Airsix both owed much of their origin to the Siddeley Puma. Subsequently, by using half the Airdisco with a new crankshaft and crankcase, Halford created the little A.D.C. Cirrus which was first used to power de Havilland's new Moth light aeroplane. The Cirrus series is described under CIRRUS. The Airdisco company soon ceased trading but Cirrus engines continued to be made by the Hermes Engineering Co until 1934. Blackburn Aircraft then took the concern over and Blackburn Cirrus engines appeared.

A.D.C. AIRDISCO, 120 hp, (1925), 8-cylinder, upright 90-degree Vee, air-cooled poppet-valve, geared spur .5:1 R.H. tractor-drive. Bore/stroke 4.13 x 5.12 in. Vol. 548.94 cu in. (104.90 x 130.05 mm. Vol. 9.00 litre). The Airdisco was derived from the 80 hp Renault with aluminium cylinder heads. Compression ratio 4.6:1. Length 46.0 in; width 21.3 in; height 31.1 in.
Aircraft:

    Avro 548A
    Cierva C.11 Parnall Gyroplane
    de Havilland D.H.51
    Royal Aircraft Factory S.E.5a

A.D.C. Airdisco, a re-designed 80 hp Renault which produced 50% more power.

An Airdisco-powered Avro 548, a 504K in disguise.

A.D.C. CIRRUS. *see* **CIRRUS AERO ENGINES** (CIRRUS-HERMES) and **BLACKBURN CIRRUS.**
Because of confusion caused by the changes in the ownership of the name 'Cirrus', A.D.C. Cirrus, Cirrus and Cirrus-Hermes engines are listed together under 'Cirrus'. Blackburn Cirrus engines are listed separately.

A.D.C. NIMBUS, 300 hp, (1926). The Nimbus was a 6-cylinder upright in-line water-cooled poppet-valve engine. It had one large inlet and two smaller exhaust valves per cylinder with a direct R.H. tractor-drive. Bore/stroke 152 x 190 mm. 18.85 litre. Compression ratio 5.4:1. It was a redesign by F.B. Halford of the 230 hp Siddeley-Deasy Puma (q.v.) which, after much time, effort and modification eventually achieved its designed power output. Length 70.0 in; width 17.5 in; height 44.0 in.
Aircraft:

    Airco D.H.9 srs
    de Havilland D.H.37A
    de Havilland D.H.50
    Martinsyde (Nimbus)
    Vickers 133 Vendace II
    Vickers 157 Vendace II

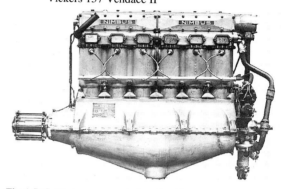

The A.D.C. Nimbus was a redesigned and improved Siddeley-Deasy Puma.

A.D.C. AIRSIX, a 6-cylinder, upright in-line air-cooled poppet-valve engine generally similar to the Airdisco. Direct R.H. tractor-drive.

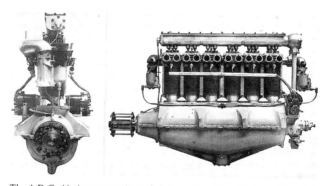

The A.D.C. Airsix was an air-cooled derivative of the Nimbus, although it did not achieve production.

ADMIRALTY ROTARY

A.R.1. (150 h p), *see* Bentley B.R.1.

AERO ENGINES LTD, KINGSWOOD, BRISTOL.
Formed in 1935, incorporating and taking over the Bristol works of DOUGLAS (William Douglas (Bristol) Ltd). They were, initially, manufacturers of motor-cycle engines and whose aero-engine interests taken over by Aero Engines Ltd in 1935. Subsequently, WEIR (G. & J. WEIR Ltd, of Glasgow) were incorporated. Douglas also produced a two-cylinder opposed air-cooled engine of 45 cu in, which developed 22 hp at 3,500 rpm and a maximum of 30 hp at 5,500 rpm. It was chain-geared and had an outside fly-wheel weighing 72 lb. Few details are available but the engine enabled a Parnall Pixie to attain 90 mph at the 1923 Lympne meeting and an Avro Avis to reach 13,859 feet.

DRYAD, 40 hp, (1932), similar to Sprite below. Bore/stroke 92 x 92 mm. Vol. 1.2 litre. Geared, spur via camshaft, .55:1.
Aircraft:

    Weir C.28 W.1, W.2 Autogiro

The Aero Engines (Douglas) Dryad, 40 hp was a geared engine, similar to the Sprite.

PIXIE (built formerly by J & G WEIR of Cathcart, Glasgow, taken over in 1938), 50 hp, 4-cylinder inverted in-line air-cooled poppet-valve. The valves are operated by an underhead-type camshaft. Y-Alloy pistons. Direct L.H. tractor-drive. Bore/stroke 3.15 x 3.94 in. Vol. 122.87 cu in. (80.77 x 100 mm. Vol. 2.048 litre). Compression ratio 5.58. Length 32.3 in; width 10.5 in; height 26.5 in.
Aircraft:

    Weir W.3 Autogiro
    Weir W.4 Autogiro
    Weir W.5 Helicopter

The Aero Engines (formerly Weir) Pixie.

SPRITE I (formerly DOUGLAS), 23 hp, (1936), 2-cylinder horizontally-opposed air-cooled poppet-valve. Direct R.H. tractor-drive. Bore/stroke 3.11 x 3.23 in. Vol. 49 cu in. (79 x 82 mm. Vol. 804 cc). Compression ratio 6:1. Length 19.7 in; width 25.7 in; height 11.7 in.
Aircraft:

    B.A.C. Super Drone
    Gordon Dove
    Helmy Aerogypt I, II, III

    Luton Buzzard II
    Luton Minor
    Mignet HM 14N Pou du Ciel
    Tipsy S.2
    Vickers 89 Viget

The Aero Engines (Douglas) Sprite, fitted to a B.A.C. Super Drone.

ALVIS LTD, COVENTRY.

In 1919, following the First World War, T.G.John Limited, later to be known as Alvis Limited, was formed to design and manufacture specialist sports and racing motor cars. The Company specialized in manufacturing engine parts in the relatively new industrial metal, aluminium. Mr John, from a well-known southern Welsh family, had set up a factory in Coventry and, seeking financial backing from Welsh businessmen in the high unemployment situation after the war, undertook to give work to his countrymen who were skilled in aluminium smelting. As a result, for a time the Welsh language was far more familiar in the Coventry foundry than English. The name Alvis is derived from the aluminium which the Company used in its manufacture and the Latin word indicating power. Alvis soon became well-known for its sports cars, particularly those featuring the front-wheel drive type of transmission which has become so familiar today, as well as for producing high-quality saloon and touring cars, featuring the inverted red triangle motif which still distinguishes the Company's name.

Alvis entered the aero-engine business in order to extend the power output range of British engines, then around 1,000 hp, up to 1,500 hp and possibly to 2,000 hp. By the end of 1935, new aero-engine shops had been completed next to the Alvis motor car factory at Coventry, the Company having also taken out a licence for the production, in England, initially, of two powerful air-cooled radial engines originally designed and built by the French firm of Gnome et Le Rhône, better known as Gnome-Rhône, in their 'K' series. All of the resulting engines were, in accordance with Air Ministry instructions, given rather unlikely star-constellation names, associated with Greek mythology. Two two-row engines were intended to be produced. These were the 14-cylinder, 1,100 hp Pelides, built in 1937 and the 18-cylinder Alcides, proposed but not built in 1938, each design being moderately supercharged and each having a fully-supercharged 'Major' version. Further, each was proposed either in a direct-drive version, or in two different degrees of propeller reduction, .5:1 or 13:19 (epicyclic).

Every component in the original French design had been carefully examined, numerous modifications embodied to conform with British requirements and the latest techniques and metallurgical practises were brought together to ensure satisfactory performance, especially regarding all moving parts.

Initially, the French-designed one-piece, Maneton-type bolt crankpin was retained but, in 1944, Alvis introduced a redesigned two-piece crankpin, the bearing being a part of the crank assembly. Other differences between French and British threads (nut, bolt and stud sizes) had to be resolved, the main engine dimensions in the Pelides being kept metric. Threads for small bolts and studs were converted to B.S.F., except for studs in the softer alloys, which required Whitworth threads.

Ring-nuts inside the engines were kept metric, however. Farman-type bevelled epicyclic reduction gears, of a type preferred and extensively used in Britain from 1927 onwards, notably by Bristol, were used but the accessory drive units were Anglicized. The somewhat confused picture thus conjured up does not suggest an easy or economical design. The Pelides was a two-valve engine with a supercharger drive protected from acceleration stresses by three centrifugal clutches. A compressor, hydraulic pump, electric starter and generator, Constantinesco gun gear and a v.p. propeller unit together with a heated Zenith carburettor and automatic boost control unit combined to make the Pelides a credible power unit. The Alvis Pelides passed a 50-hour Air Ministry civil type-test, producing 1,065 hp, in 1937 but, sadly, only fifteen of these engines were built.

Although so few Pelides were built and ground-run, together with parts for a prototype of the Maeonides Major fourteen-cylinder two-row engine, as well as components for other types, none of them found favour with the hoped-for market in Air Ministry or airline circles and further development was dropped. Competition with the formidably well-established Armstrong Siddeley firm, virtually next door, was a brave if forlorn effort. Nevertheless, despite this disappointing start, these engine projects paved the way for an entirely new nine-cylinder engine, the Alvis 9ARS which, eventually, was to enjoy some success after the Second World War, in several versions as the Leonides. This first ran early in 1938 and was flown in a two-seat Bristol Bulldog in January 1939 but, with the onset of war, all further development was temporarily dropped, in favour of other more pressing work.

The war with Germany, beginning in September 1939, brought Alvis a great deal of aero-engine overhaul work, particularly of the Merlin for Rolls-Royce and for propeller hub assembly for de Havilland, as well as development testing and servicing of American engines in service with the Royal Air Force. As was the case of so many parts of the British defence industry during the war, this work involved no fewer than twenty-one dispersed factory sites, employing 3,160 people.

In 1944, Alvis was awarded a development contract for the Leonides which, by then had acquired a Hobson fuel-injection system in place of its original Zenith carburettor. The Leonides began to show promise as a substitute for the Armstrong Siddeley Cheetah and, in November 1945, the re-emergence of the Alvis engine coincided with its passing a 112-hour type acceptance test at 500 hp. Ultimately, both engines began to fade away together in the 1960s, with the advent of a new generation of moderately-powered, economical gas turbine engines. Finally, there appeared the Leonides Major, a two-row, 14-cylinder development of the original 9-cylinder engine, seeing service in Westland S.55 Whirlwind helicopters and in the prototype Handley Page (Reading) Herald.

ALVIS — THE FIRST GENERATION.
Although none of the following Alvis engines ever flew, they were at an advanced stage of development when, with the onset of the Second World War, all further progress had to be abandoned. Nevertheless, they need to be mentioned because their existence at the time was widely known and advertised and their development led, via the 9ARS engine, directly to the successful post-war Leonides.

The **ALVIS ALCIDES, of 1,300 hp**, (1937) was a projected 18-cylinder two-row air-cooled radial. It was a poppet-valve medium supercharged engine, bevel-geared epicyclic .5:1 with L.H. tractor-drive. Fuel 87 Octane. (Many of its components were interchangeable with the Alvis Pelides). The ALCIDES MAJOR was similar to the Alcides except that the Major would have been fully-supercharged, bevel-geared epicyclic .5:1 L.H. tractor-drive. Fuel 87 Octane. Bore/stroke 5.75 x 7.087 in. Vol. 3,314 cu in. (146 x 180 mm. Vol. 54.24 litre). Compression ratio 5.5:1.

The **MAEONIDES MAJOR, 650 hp**, (1937), was a proposed 14-cylinder two-row radial air-cooled, poppet-valve engine. It would have been single-speed fully supercharged and geared, epicyclic .656:1. Fuel 87 Octane. Bore/stroke 4.8 x 4.567 in. Vol. 1,158.4 cu in. (122 x 116 mm. Vol. 19 litre). Compression ratio 6:1.

The **PELIDES, of 1,000 hp**, (1936) was the first aero-engine to be built by Alvis. A 14-cylinder air-cooled two-row radial air-cooled poppet-valve. It was single-speed medium supercharged, geared epicyclic 21:32 with L.H. tractor-drive. Fuel 87 Octane. Fifteen were built and the engine was type-tested in 1937. Bore/stroke 5.75 x 6.5 in. Vol. 2,359.8 cu in. (146 x 165mm. Vol. 38.7 litre). Compression ratio 5.5:1.

The **PELIDES MAJOR, of 1,000 hp**, (1936), was a proposed 14-cylinder air-cooled two-row radial, poppet-valve. It was a fully supercharged engine, bevel-geared epicyclic .5:1 L.H. tractor-drive. Fuel 87 Octane. Identical to Pelides except for supercharger ratio. Bore/stroke 5.75 x 6.5 in. Vol. 2,359.8 cu in. (146 x 165mm. Vol. 38.7 litre). Compression ratio 5.5:1.

ALVIS 9ARS, 430/450 hp, (1937), 9-cylinder single-row radial, air-cooled poppet-valve. It was a single-speed medium supercharged engine, bevel-geared epicyclic .5:1, L.H. tractor-drive. Fuel 87 Octane. Zenith carburettor. The engine was named 'Leonides' in 1938. Bore/stroke 4.8 x 4.41 in. Vol. 719 cu in. (122 x 112 mm. Vol. 11.78 litre). Compression ratio 6.3:1. Diameter 41.5 in; length 52.0 in.
Aircraft:
    Bristol 124 Bulldog TM

The first Alvis engine to fly was this 9ARS, fitted to a two-seat Bristol Bulldog.

POST-WAR ALVIS ENGINES.
LEONIDES, the post-war derivative of the Alvis 9ARS appeared in numerous sub-variants, each associated principally with one installation.

The **LEONIDES** was a 9-cylinder, air-cooled single-row radial poppet-valve engine. It was available for fixed-wing installations and some variants had oblique drives for helicopter use.

Alvis standard Leonides engines had the following in common:-
Bore/stroke 4.80 x 4.41 in. (122.0 x 112.0 mm)
Swept Volume 718.6 cu in (11.80 litres)
Compression Ratio 6.8 :1
Dimensions vary according to accessories.
Diameter 41.5 in.   Length 54.4 in   Weights 790-810 lb.

The Leonides engine was medium-supercharged, geared epicyclic .5:1 or .625:1. L.H. tractor-drive. The suffixes 'A' and 'B' indicate increased fuel flow rates.

Alvis long-stroke Leonides, 530 Series.
Bore/stroke 4.80 x 4.80 in. (122.0 x 122.0 mm).
Swept Volume 782 cu in. (12.80 litres).
Compression Ratio 6.5 :1
Dimensions vary according to accessories.
Diameter 43.0 in.   Length 54.4 in.
Weights, where published — *see* Performance tables.

The suffix 'B' in the 530 Series indicates a supplementary fuel injection system.

Leonides helicopter engines had either vertical or oblique, direct or reversing drive with a .8:1 reduction. Fuel 100 Octane 100/130 grade.

All standard Leonides ran at 3,000 rpm on take-off with the exception of the 524/1 (Mk 173) which ran at 3,200 rpm and +7 lb boost. There was a normal 20-second peak emergency limit of 3,150 rpm.

The precise identification of the numerous variants of the Leonides engine has for many years been much of a mystery. For reasons best known to the Air Ministry, no fewer than three types of designation were current at various times, frequently overlapping and seldom being cross-referred leading to much confusion. It is hoped that the listing below will go some way towards resolving it. Leonides engines are therefore listed, first under Alvis Type Numbers followed by the equivalent Military Mk. Nos. and, finally Engine Specifications, (the LE-numbers) where available.

In the 1960s Alvis aero-engine production gradually faded out and the Company concentrated its work on the production of armoured military vehicles.

LEONIDES 501/1, 520 hp, bevel-geared epicyclic, reduction .5:1. LE-1M.

LEONIDES 501/2, 520 hp, as 501/1 but geared, epicyclic, reduction .625:1. Accessories mounted on remote-drive gearbox. LE-2M.

LEONIDES 501/3, 520 hp, as 501/2 but bevel-geared, epicyclic reduction .5:1.
Aircraft:
  Percival Prince 1, 2
  Percival P.54 (As designed. Percival was changed to
   Hunting Percival in April 1954)
  Scottish Aviation Pioneer 1

LEONIDES 501/4, 500/520 hp, as 501/1 but geared, epicyclic reduction .625:1. Non-essential accessories mounted on the engine. LE-4M.
Aircraft:
  Airspeed A.S.41 Oxford
  Cunliffe-Owen Concordia
  Handley Page (Reading) H.P.R.2
  Percival Prince 1, 2
  Percival P.54
  Scottish Aviation Pioneer 1

The Alvis Leonides 501/4 displaying its easy accessibility for servicing.

The Leonides 501/4 installed in a Percival Prince.

LEONIDES 502/1, 520/540 hp, bevel-geared, epicyclic reduction .5:1.

LEONIDES 502/2, 520/540 hp, as 502/1 but geared, epicyclic reduction .625:1. Accessories mounted on remote drive gearbox.

LEONIDES 502/3, 520/540 hp, as 502/2 but bevel-geared, epicyclic reduction .5:1.

LEONIDES 502/4, 520/540 hp, as 502/2 but geared, epicyclic reduction .625:1. Non-essential accessories mounted on the engine.
Aircraft:
  Airspeed A.S.65 Consul
  de Havilland (Canada) D.H.C.2 Beaver 2
  Percival Prince 3, 3A, 3E
  Scottish Aviation Pioneer C.C.1

LEONIDES 502/5, 520/540 hp, geared, epicyclic, reduction .625:1. Non-essential accessories mounted on the engine. Altered generator drive on rear cover.
Aircraft:
  Percival Prince 3B, 3D

LEONIDES 502/7, 560 hp, geared, epicyclic reduction .625:1. Non-essential accessories mounted on the engine. Altered generator drive on rear cover and a high-pressure priming system embodied.
Aircraft:
  Scottish Aviation Pioneer C.C.1

LEONIDES 503/2, Mk 22, 520/540 hp, geared, epicyclic reduction .625:1.

LEONIDES 503/4, Mk 24, 520/540 hp, geared, epicyclic reduction .625:1. Non-essential accessories mounted on the engine.
Aircraft:
  Percival Prince 4, 4E.

LEONIDES 503/5, Mk 125 01/2, 520/540 hp, (1950), geared epicyclic reduction .625:1. Non-essential accessories mounted on the engine, altered generator drive on rear cover.
Aircraft:
  Percival President 1
  Percival Prince 4, 4D
  Percival P.66 Sea Prince T.1.

An Alvis Leonides 503/4 in a Percival Prince 4 having an engine test-run in darkness.

LEONIDES 503/6A, Mk 126, 520/540 hp, (1950), geared, epicyclic reduction .625:1. Non-essential accessories mounted on the engine and an altered generator drive on rear cover. High-pressure priming system and this engine provided continuous power during inverted flight in the basic trainer for the Royal Air Force.
Aircraft:
   Percival P.56 Provost T.1, T.51.

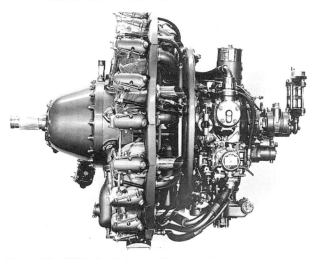

The Leonides 503/6A for the Percival Provost trainer.

LEONIDES 503/7, Mk 130, 500/520 hp, (**1950**), geared, epicyclic reduction .625:1. Non-essential accessories mounted on the engine. Altered generator drive on rear cover and a high-pressure priming system embodied.
Aircraft:
   Percival P.66 Pembroke C.C.1.

LEONIDES 503/7A, Mk 127 01/2, 540/560 hp, (1950), geared, epicyclic reduction .625:1. Non-essential accessories mounted on the engine. Altered generator drive on rear cover and a high-pressure priming system embodied.
Aircraft:
   Percival President 1
   Percival P.66 Pembroke C.1., C(PR) Mk.I
   Scottish Aviation Pioneer C.C.1.

LEONIDES 503/8, 540 hp, (1950), bevel-geared, epicyclic reduction .5:1. Non-essential accessories mounted on the engine. Altered generator drive on rear cover and a high-pressure priming system embodied.

Aircraft:
   Scottish Aviation Twin Pioneer prototype

LEONIDES 504/5, Mk 125, 540 hp, (1950), geared, epicyclic reduction .625:1. Non-essential accessories mounted on the engine, altered generator drive on rear cover.
Aircraft:
   Percival President 1
   Percival Prince 6B

LEONIDES 504/8B, Mk 128, 520/540 hp, bevel-geared, epicyclic reduction .5:1. Non-essential accessories mounted on the engine. Altered generator drive on rear cover and a high-pressure priming system embodied. 'B' refers to increased fuel flow rate.
Aircraft:
   Scottish Aviation Twin Pioneer C.C.1., 2

LEONIDES 514, 550 hp, geared, epicyclic reduction .625:1. Engines bearing 510 series numbers signified the inclusion of extensive design changes and refinements. In particular, these related to much of the lubrication system, the cylinders and heads, crankcase and supercharger drive.
Aircraft:
   Scottish Aviation Pioneer C.C.1.

LEONIDES 514/2A, 560 hp, as 514/8A, non-essential accessories mounted on the engine. Altered generator drive on rear cover and a high-pressure priming system embodied. Drive for remote accessories gearbox. Geared, epicyclic reduction .625:1. 'A' refers to increased fuel flow rate.

LEONIDES 514/4A, 560 hp, as 514/8A, with low-pressure priming. Non-essential accessories mounted on the engine.

LEONIDES 514/5A, 560 hp, as 514/4A with altered generator drive. Geared, epicyclic reduction .625:1. Non-essential accessories mounted on the engine, altered generator drive on rear cover.
Aircraft:
   Percival President 2

LEONIDES 514/6A, 560 hp, geared, epicyclic reduction .625:1. Non-essential accessories mounted on the engine and an altered generator drive on rear cover. Provision for inverted flight lubrication.

LEONIDES 514/7A, 560 hp, as 514/8A but geared, epicyclic reduction .625:1. Non-essential accessories mounted on the engine. Altered generator drive on rear cover and a high-pressure priming system embodied.

LEONIDES 514/8, 560 hp, bevel-geared, epicyclic reduction .5:1. Non-essential accessories mounted on the engine. Altered generator drive on rear cover and a high-pressure priming system embodied.
Aircraft:
   Scottish Aviation Pioneer C.C.1

LEONIDES 514/8A, 560 hp, bevel-geared, epicyclic reduction .5:1. Non-essential accessories mounted on the engine. Altered generator drive on rear cover and a high-pressure priming system embodied. 'A' refers to increased fuel flow rate.
Aircraft:
   Scottish Aviation Pioneer C.C.1

LEONIDES 521/1, Mk 50, 480/500 hp, helicopter vertical drive. Reversing reduction gear .8:1. Oil pump driven at .5:1 crankshaft speed. LE-24HMV.
Aircraft:
   Westland WS-51 Mk I & IA Dragonfly H.R.1, 3, H.C.4

LEONIDES 521/2, 520/540 hp, as 521/1, helicopter direct vertical drive. Reversing reduction gear .8:1. Modified oil pump driven at .75 times crankshaft speed. Oil jets in crankpin bosses.
Aircraft:
   Westland S-51 Srs 2 Widgeon

LEONIDES 522/1, 550/570 hp, helicopter direct vertical drive. LE-21HMV

LEONIDES 522/2, 520/540 hp, similar to helicopter direct horizontal drive, LE-12 HMH. Also similar to LE-21 & LE-23HMV.

Aircraft:

Fairey Gyrodyne

LEONIDES 523/1, Mk 70, 520/540 hp, as 521/2, helicopter vertical drive. Reversing reduction gear .8:1. Oil system as in 521/2.
Aircraft:

Westland WS-51 Dragonfly H.R.5

LEONIDES 524/1, Mk 173, 500/520 hp, (1955), helicopter direct vertical drive. Centrifugal clutch, 16 inch. Oil pumps integral with rear cover. LE-23HM.
Aircraft:

Bristol 171 Sycamore 3, 4, H.C.14.

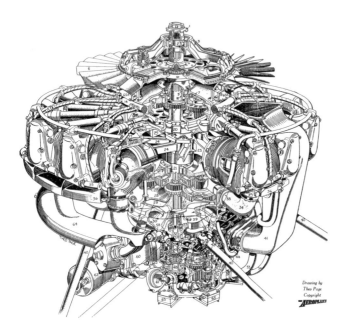

Alvis Leonides 524/1, Bristol Sycamore installation, drawing by Theo Page.

Alvis Leonides 524/1, Bristol Sycamore installation.

LEONIDES 525/1, Mk 173, 500/520 hp, as 524/1, helicopter direct vertical drive. Centrifugal clutch, 16 inch. Oil system as in 524/1.
Aircraft:

Bristol 173 prototype

LEONIDES 531/8, 640 hp.

LEONIDES 531/8B, Mk 138, 640/650 hp, (1957), long-stroke version, as 531/8. Bevel-geared, epicyclic, reduction .5:1. Supercharger ratio 6.5:1. Non-essential accessories mounted on the engine. Altered generator drive on rear cover and a high-pressure priming system embodied. 'B' refers to increased a supplementary fuel injection system and increased flow rate. The more powerful Leonides 530 series was developed from the 510 series, the additional power being derived from the 10 mm increase in stroke and by the improved fuel injection system. Some of the improvements made in the 510 series were retained, with the exception of the supercharger drive, so that the engines were generally interchangeable with earlier types.
Aircraft:

Scottish Aviation Twin Pioneer C.C.2, 3

LEONIDES 532, 620 hp, as 531 but with supercharger ratio 7.92:1.

LEONIDES MAJOR, 14-cylinder, two-row radial, air-cooled, poppet-valve.

Alvis Leonides Major engines had the following in common:-
Bore/stroke 4.80 x 4.41 in. (122.0 x 112.0 mm).
Swept Volume 1,118.0 cu in. (18.30 litres).
Compression Ratio 6.80:1.
Dimensions vary according to accessories.
Diameter 38.9 in   Length 62 in.
Weights, where published — *see* Performance tables.

LEONIDES MAJOR 702/1, 850 hp, (1950), medium-supercharged single-speed, geared planetary bevel reduction .533:1. L.H. tractor-drive. Fuel 100/130 grade. A.LE.M.1–1.
Aircraft:

Handley Page (Reading) H.P.R.5 Herald.

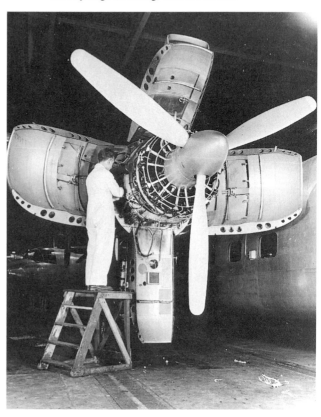

Alvis Leonides Major 702/1; note the easy accessibility in the prototype Handley Page H.P.R.5 Herald.

Alvis Leonides Major 700 series (fixed wing), the two-row version.

Alvis Leonides Major 702/1, fitted to the prototype Handley Page H.P.R.5 Herald.

LEONIDES MAJOR 755/1, Mk 155, 780 hp, (1951), 14-cylinder, two-row radial air-cooled poppet-valve medium supercharged, derated. Helicopter, oblique (approx 35 degrees to horizontal), direct-drive. Fuel 100/130 grade. A.LE.M.1–6.
Aircraft:
    Bristol 173 Mk III
    Westland S-55 srs 2 Whirlwind H.A.S.7, 8

All Alvis engines were designed for easy access. This Leonides Major 755/1 is fitted to a Westland Whirlwind H.A.S.7.

The oblique drive of the Alvis Leonides Major 755/1 for a Westland Whirlwind H.A.S.7.

LEONIDES MAJOR 755/2, Mk 160, 780 hp, (1951), 14-cylinder, two-row radial air-cooled poppet-valve, medium supercharged. Helicopter vertical direct-drive. Fuel 100/130 grade. A.LE.M.1–6.
Aircraft:
    Bristol 173 Mk III
    Bristol 191 Belvedere
    Westland S-55 Srs 2 Whirlwind H.A.S.5, 6, 7, H.C.C.8

ANZANI (BRITISH) — *see also* Anzani (British/Luton).
Vee-shaped Anzani motor-cycle engines were well-known in France before the dramatic arrival of M. Louis Blériot in a field below Dover Castle in 1909. In his case, the engine was a three-cylinder fan-shaped engine. The upright fan shape came about largely because of troubles associated with oiled-up sparking plugs, a problem not unknown ninety years later but largely overcome, thanks to pressure lubrication and the radial that took its place. Anzani in France and Italy continued to make air-cooled and water-cooled Vee and W-shaped engines, with 2, 3, 4 and 6 cylinders, rated up to 60 hp until the outbreak of the First World War. There was an unusual design feature in the induction system. The carburettor fed a mixing chamber in the crankcase, from which extended a tangential induction pipe to the inlet valve in each cylinder. The idea was to impart a swirl and outward force which would improve even mixing to each cylinder.

Anzani radial six and ten-cylinder radial engines have often been regarded as unusual because odd-numbered cylinders are usual. In fact, these were double threes and fives, with cast-iron cylinders, with automatic inlet and push-rod and rocker arm-operated exhaust valves. The two-throw crankshafts had two bearings and the connecting rods ended in portions of a hollow shoe, which where clamped together from the outside by a bronze collar, thus making up the bearing.

BRITISH ANZANI ENGINEERING CO LTD, was based, initially, at Willesden, London and subsequently at Kingston-on-Thames, Surrey.

ANZANI (BRITISH), 45 hp, (1916), 6-cylinder two-row radial air-cooled poppet-valve. Direct R.H. tractor-drive. Bore/stroke 3.54 x 4.72 in. Vol. 278.85 cu in. (90 x 120 mm. Vol. 4.58 litre).

Aircraft:
>   Austin Whippet
>   Blackburn Mercury III
>   Caudron Biplane, 45 hp
>   Leopoldoff L.7 Colibri

ANZANI (BRITISH), 60 hp, (1916), 6-cylinder two-row radial air-cooled poppet-valve. Direct R.H. tractor-drive. Bore/stroke 4.1 x 4.7 in. Vol. 372.5 cu. in (105 x 120mm. Vol. 6.2 litre).
Aircraft:
>   Austin Whippet
>   Grahame-White VIII
>   Westland Woodpigeon II

ANZANI (BRITISH), 100 hp, (1917), 10-cylinder two-row radial. air-cooled, two poppet-valves, initially with cast-iron and, later, steel cylinders with integral cooling fins. Direct L.H. or R.H. tractor/pusher-drive (either rotation). Bore/stroke 4.13 x 5.71 in. Vol. 765.14 cu in. (105 x 145 mm. Vol. 12.1 litre). One Zenith 42 D.E.F. carburettor, two magnetos. Compression ratio 4.48:1.
Production, 8/1914-12/1918, from:-
British Anzani Engine Co Ltd, Willesden,
Ordered, 125; Delivered, 125; Cancelled/suspended, 0
Aircraft:
>   Blackburn Land/Sea
>   Blackburn White Falcon
>   Caudron G.III, G.IV
>   Central Centaur IVA, IVB
>   Curtiss H.4 Small America
>   Handley Page Type G
>   L & P 4
>   Mann & Grimmer M.1
>   Pemberton Billing P.B.31E Nighthawk
>   Sopwith Anzani Tractor Seaplane
>   Sopwith Grasshopper
>   Vickers F.B.12C

The Mann & Grimmer M.1 powered by a 100 hp Anzani.

ANZANI (BRITISH), 35 hp, (1924, 1938) 2-cylinder, inverted 60-degree Vee air-cooled, poppet-valve. Direct R.H. tractor-drive. Bore/stroke 3.23 x 3.95 in. Vol. 64.76 cu in. (83.0 x 101.5 mm. Vol. 1,100 cc). Compression ratio 5.5:1. As French-built engine of 1923 but with roller-bearing valve rockers. Length 16.0 in; width 19.0 in; height 22.0 in.
Aircraft:
>   ANEC I, IA, II
>   Bristol Prier-Dickson
>   Hawker Cygnet

ANZANI (BRITISH/LUTON), Gerrards Cross, Buckinghamshire. Luton Aircraft Ltd was formed in November 1935 by C.H. Latimer-Needham to build ultra-light aircraft. In 1938, the company acquired the manufacturing rights for the former Anzani inverted Vee-twin (above), which subsequently had modified valves and ignition.

ANZANI (BRITISH/LUTON), 35 hp, (1924, 1938) 2-cylinder inverted 57-degree Vee, air-cooled, poppet-valve. Direct R.H. tractor-drive. Bore/stroke 3.27 x 3.95 in. Vol. 67.6 cu in. (83.0 x 101.5 mm. Vol. 1.1 litre). Compression ratio 5.25:1. Length 16.0 in; width 19.0 in; height 22.0 in.

Aircraft:
>   Luton Buzzard I, II
>   Luton L.A.4A Minor
>   Mignet HM 14 Pou du Ciel

A very early British ultra-light aeroplane, the A.N.E.C. II, of 1924.

The reliable little 35 hp Anzani two-cylinder engine.

The Luton Minor of 1938, powered by a later version of the 35 hp Anzani.

ARMSTRONG SIDDELEY MOTORS LTD, COVENTRY.

See also Royal Aircraft Factory and Beardmore.

During 1917, following the Report of the Burbidge Committee of Inquiry into alleged shortcomings on the part of the Royal Aircraft Factory at Farnborough, its substantial design and construction capabilities were dismantled and its functions redirected in 1918, principally to research as the Royal Aircraft Establishment. This change led to some very experienced, senior designers leaving Farnborough and joining other aircraft and engine constructors. Among these were Major F.M.Green, who had been in charge of design, John Lloyd, head of the Stress Department and S.D.Heron, the engine designer. At Farnborough, Green and Heron had been responsible for what would otherwise have emerged as the 300 hp, R.A.F.8, a fourteen-cylinder, two-row air-cooled radial engine, which had first run in September 1916.

Thus, in 1917 this team joined what was, initially, the Siddeley-Deasy Motor Car Co. at Coventry, taking the designs for the new engine with them. The Company was headed by John D. Siddeley, a man accustomed to having his own way and noted for being both energetic and somewhat autocratic. So came the opportunity for the former Farnborough team to continue their development work, particularly on the promising new radial engine. There was however a condition. First of all, the Siddeley-Deasy Puma, a development of the 230 B.H.P., had to be made into a more satisfactory engine. Siddeley, a man of inventiveness, as an engineering employer required his senior staff to do as they were told, even when this was against their own judgement and experience. One of the things which he demanded was a change in the design of the cylinder head of the new radial engine from two valves to three, two exhausts and one inlet. This principle would have followed the line of the 230 B.H.P./Puma saga, which Siddeley was then building in an attempt to rescue an important but ailing engine.

Sam Heron would not agree with this and other matters of design policy. Subsequently, following a major dispute on matters of principle with Siddeley, Heron left for the U.S.A., where he was employed at first as a civilian research engineer by the Engineering Division of the U.S. Army Air Corps. With the Wright Aeronautical Corporation, he designed the cylinder of the J-5 engine. He concentrated on the 'hot' end of engine design and developed the salt-cooled and sodium-cooled valve. He was a great loss to Britain and was replaced at Siddeley-Deasy by F.R. Smith. There was, accordingly, some delay to the development of the new radial engine which was eventually to become the Armstrong Siddeley Jaguar, the Company's first really successful engine, to power the Siddeley Siskin.

S.M. Viale joined Major F.M. Green at Siddeley-Deasy (and its successor Armstrong Siddeley) in mid-1919 and, following Sam Heron's successful invention of the sodium-cooled valve stem, Viale worked on a satisfactory method of operating it. He was subsequently involved in the design of the Armstrong Siddeley Lynx and Cheetah engines. After designs left the drawing board, Viale's Latin temperament seemed to predominate and he tended to lose interest and, in 1932, he returned to Italy for several years.

Peter Hooker Ltd, a company in Walthamstow, London, had built Gnome engines during the 1914-1918 war and had subsequently developed a method of forging Y-alloy pistons. This kind of piston, with conventional rings, replaced the cast-iron type and obturator ring. When Armstrong Siddeley Motors received a large order for Jaguar engines after the war, Peter Hooker supplied the pistons. Unfortunately the company was in receivership and there was no suitable alternative piston. Hooker's Works Manager, W.C. Devereux proposed to Siddeley the setting up of a forge and machine shop to make the thousands of Y-alloy pistons required. Siddeley lent him the money to buy back the hammers, stamps and other tools which Alfred Herbert Ltd, the machine tool company had purchased from the receiver. Devereux and former colleagues set up a factory at Slough, so starting High Duty Alloys Ltd. This company was licensed by Rolls-Royce Ltd to produce a series of light, high-strength forging alloys which it had developed under the general heading of 'RR', with the name of Hiduminium.

In October 1919, John D. Siddeley, was determined to remain in the aircraft and engine industry, despite the drastic post-war curtailment of orders and re-organization in design work. The Sir

W.G. Armstrong Whitworth Development Company formed a subsidiary, Armstrong Siddeley Motors Ltd, to take over the car and aircraft businesses of Armstrong Whitworth and the Siddeley-Deasy Motor Car Co and to concentrate the business at the Parkside Works, Coventry. The Chairman was J.D. Siddeley (later to become Sir John Siddeley and, eventually, Lord Kenilworth).

NOTE: Because of the large number of different types of Armstrong Siddeley engine produced in under twenty years, many of them overlapping each other, chronological order has been quite difficult to achieve and, in an attempt to prevent needless confusion the types are here listed in approximate order of appearance.

In general, Mark numbers of Armstrong Siddeley engines were ill-defined and could be highly confusing. Letters which were often added after the type names, gave an indication of the specific type of engine. Some explanation is needed. Changes in the designations of several engines, as they developed, did little to clarify the position, which the following attempts to do.

Armstrong Siddeley engines compared. The 10-cylinder Serval; 7-cylinder Lynx and Cheetah.

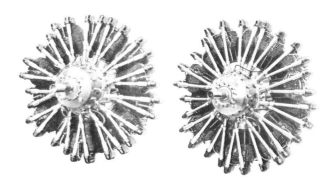

Armstrong Siddeley engines compared. The 14-cylinder Panther VI and Tiger IV.

Engines, such as the Jaguar and Panther (q.v.) could be supplied geared (G) or ungeared, direct drive; geared and supercharged (GS); ungeared and supercharged (S). In unsupercharged engines, a plain fan (PF) driven off the tail of the crankshaft at engine-speed, churned up and distributed the mixture delivered by the carburettor; a geared fan (GF), gave slight supercharge to about 3,000 ft; a supercharged (S) engine, gave a full supercharge to about 11,500 ft. Confusion reigned supreme when the exact type letters were omitted from the basic text of information released to the technical Press or in advertising, making accurate historical research a difficult problem.

JAGUAR originated as the 300 hp R.A.F.8, originally designed at the Royal Aircraft Factory at Farnborough in 1917. (*see* Royal Aircraft Factory and also Siddeley-Deasy). It was a two-row, fourteen-cylinder engine, intended from the outset to be provided with the type of gear-driven supercharger on which Farnborough put much faith. A Government development contract was granted in June 1919 and the engine's type-test run was started on 21 June 1922. It did not initially develop the power expected and, after the stroke was increased in the second version, this became possible.

Throughout its long and useful military and commercial service, the Jaguar suffered from the lack of a centre bearing and from torsional vibration.

JAGUAR I, 300 hp, (1923), 14-cylinder, two-row radial air-cooled engine with two poppet valves. Two-piece master rod. Coil and accumulator ignition. Direct L.H. tractor-drive. Bore/stroke 5.0 x 5.0 in. Vol. 1,375 cu in. (127.0 x 127.0 mm. Vol. 22.5 litre). Compression ratio 5:1. Diameter 43.0 in; length 41.0 in.
Aircraft:

    Airco D.H.4
    Armstrong Whitworth/Siddeley S.R.1 Siskin I
    Nieuport Nighthawk
    Parnall Plover

The first Armstrong Siddeley Jaguar, a direct-drive engine evolved from the R.A.F.8. It was intended from the beginning to have a gear-driven supercharger.

Armstrong Siddeley Jaguars, after the Mk I, had the following in common:-
Bore/stroke 5.0 x 5.5 in. (127.0 x 139.7 mm)
Swept Volume 1,512.5 cu in. (24.8 litres).
Compression Ratio varied 5.0:1 — 5.1:1 — see text.
Dimensions, approximate, vary according to accessories.
Diameter 45.6 in,
Length (direct-drive) 48.25 in.   (Geared) 58.83 in.
Weights, where published — *see* Performance tables.

JAGUAR II, 385 hp, (1923), as Mk I, but with the stroke increased from 5.0 in to 5.5 inches, plain fan. Direct L.H. tractor-drive. Lubrication, as was usual for engines of the period 'for summer use, is by means of pure pharmaceutical castor oil'. Compression Ratio 5.0:1.
Aircraft:

    Airco D.H.4
    Armstrong Whitworth Siskin II
    Fairey Flycatcher prototype
    Gloucestershire Mars VI Nighthawk
    Hawker Woodcock I
    Nieuport Nighthawk
    Westland Weasel

A Jaguar II powered the Armstrong Whitworth Siskin III, making the fastest time in the 1924 King's Cup Air Race.

JAGUAR III & IV

The Jaguar III and IV have been bones of contention for many years, as regards performance and aircraft installations. A lack of precision, even in contemporary publications, has made positive identification very difficult and caused confusion even among the most idealistic writers. Much research has revealed the following, which may go some way towards satisfying the need to straighten out the record.

It has been recorded that Armstrong Whitworth aircraft, notably the Siskin, could be fitted with either version of the engine and each of them in several of its variants. The choice of variant depended on the requirements and duties of the particular operator or Squadron equipped with the Jaguar engine. An examination of the engine specification throws a little light on the problem of identification. All of these engines were interchangeable in respect of their mountings. The mounting ring was 25 inches in diameter and the number of mounting bolts was sixteen, each being 3/8 inch diameter, in all cases. Their power-range was between 380 and 410 hp on take-off, with a maximum varying between 445 and 510 hp. The Jaguar IIIA, with a compression ratio of 5.1:1 (marginally higher than the 5.0:1 of the Mk III series) but with a lower rpm, was slightly lower powered than the Mk IV. Their weights varied between 798lb for the plain Mk III and 1,048 lb for the geared and supercharged Mk IV. Their interchangeability was obvious, the only restriction being the installation of the heaviest engine.

It follows therefore that despite arguments to the contrary, apart from the obvious reduction gear casing, there can be no absolute certainty about which aircraft had which version of the engine, whether new, repaired or rebuilt engines and the modification note about the Jaguar IV* highlights this. (The author had the good fortune to accompany the late A.J. Jackson and E.J. Riding, on visits in 1948-50 to the old Air Registration Board, to examine the massive card index of civil aircraft registrations, on which were not only details of the aircraft but also a photograph of each. The details recorded are therefore as stated by the owner, which is by no means an absolute guarantee of accuracy and, in any case, engines were often changed in the course of time).

JAGUAR III, 385 hp, (1923), engine-speed fan. Direct or geared /L.H. tractor-drive. Compression ratio 5.0:1.
Aircraft:

    Airco D.H.9J
    Armstrong Whitworth Ajax
    Armstrong Whitworth Argosy I
    Armstrong Whitworth Atlas I, DC
    Armstrong Whitworth Siskin II, III, IIIA, IIIDC, IV, V
    Armstrong Whitworth Wolf
    Blackburn R.2 Airedale
    de Havilland D.H.50J
    de Havilland D.H.56 Hyena
    Gloucestershire Grebe I
    Martinsyde A.D.C.1

A supercharged Armstrong Siddeley Jaguar III in an Armstrong Whitworth Siskin IIIA, of the Royal Air Force Meteorological Flight, Duxford. The pilot was Dick Reynell and, with him the Orderly Officer, Flying Officer Jeffrey Quill.

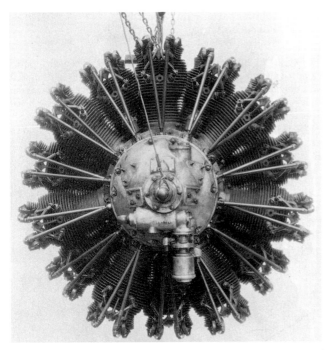

A direct-drive Armstrong Siddeley Jaguar III, as used in the de Havilland D.H.50J.

A Jaguar III fitted to the Martinsyde A.D.C.1

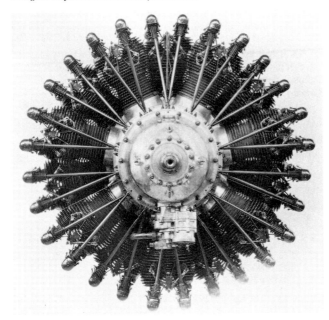

A geared Armstrong Siddeley Jaguar III.

A geared Jaguar III in the prototype two-seat Armstrong Whitworth Siskin IIIDC trainer, J7000.

JAGUAR IIIA, 380 hp, (1923), precursor of the Mk IV series. Cylinders identical with Mk IV engine. Engine-speed fan. Zenith carburettor. Direct L.H. tractor-drive. Increased compression ratio 5.1:1.
Aircraft:

    Armstrong Whitworth Argosy I
    Gloucestershire Grebe I

JAGUAR IV, 385 hp, (1925), engine-speed fan. Armstrong Siddeley dual carburettor. Compression ratio 5.0:1. Direct, L.H. tractor-drive.
Aircraft:

    Armstrong Whitworth A.W.XIV Starling II
    Armstrong Whitworth Atlas I, DC
    Armstrong Whitworth Siskin III, IIIA
    Armstrong Whitworth Wolf
    Avro 636
    de Havilland D.H.42 Dormouse
    de Havilland D.H.56 Hyena
    Fairey Ferret I
    Fairey Flycatcher I, III
    Gloucestershire Grebe II
    Handley Page H.P.27 W.9a Hampstead
    Hawker Danecock (Dankok)
    Larkin (Lasco) Lascowl (ANEC III)
    Supermarine Nanok
    Supermarine Solent
    Vickers 134 Vellore I
    Vickers 156 Vimy Trainer

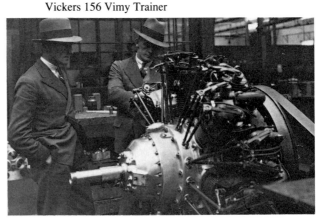

A geared Jaguar IV ready to be fitted to the Vickers 134 Vellore I G-EBYX to be flown by Flt Lt S.J. Moir and P/O H.C. Owen on a flight to Australia in March 1929.

JAGUAR IVA, 420 hp. Geared, epicyclic .657:1, L.H. tractor-drive.
Aircraft:

    Armstrong Whitworth Argosy II
    Armstrong Whitworth Atlas DC
    Armstrong Whitworth A.W.XVII Aries

JAGUAR IV*, 400/410 hp, engine-speed fan. Direct L.H. tractor-drive. The Jaguar Mk IV* engine was a Mk IV, reconditioned to a standard a little below that of the Jaguar IVC and fitted to any aircraft normally powered by a Jaguar IV. Fuel 73 Octane (DTD 134).
Aircraft:
> Any, powered by unsupercharged Jaguars

JAGUAR IVC, 400 hp, (1928), engine-speed fan. Direct L.H. tractor-drive. New one-piece master rod and enclosed valve gear. R.A.E. Mk II starter. Claudel Hobson A.V.T.70G carburettor. Compression ratio 5:1. Power Curve at rated altitude 2,000 ft from A.I.D. Test Record, dated 23.6.31.

RPM	1,870	1,800	1,700	1,600	1,500
BHP	443	432	410	387	360

Fuel 73 Octane (DTD 134).
Aircraft:
> Airco D.H.9J
> Armstrong Whitworth Atlas I, DC
> Blackburn C.6/29 Biplane and C.6/29 Monoplane
> Fairey Flycatcher
> Westland Wapiti IV

JAGUAR IV(S), 365 hp, (1925), fully supercharged. This was the world's first production engine to have a supercharger, which was geared at 12.9 times crankshaft speed. Compression ratio 5.0:1. Claudel Hobson AVT.70E carburettor. Direct L.H. tractor-drive.
Aircraft:
> Armstrong Whitworth Siskin IIIA, IIIB, V

JAGUAR V, (1928), Compression ratio 5:1. Engine-speed fan. L.H. tractor-drive.
Aircraft:
> Hawker Hawfinch
> Hawker Hoopoe (N.21/26)

JAGUAR VI, (1927). Compression ratio 5.0:1. Direct L.H. tractor-drive.
Aircraft:
> Armstrong Whitworth Atlas I
> Blackburn F.1 Turcock
> Boulton & Paul P.71A Mailplane
> Boulton & Paul P.71A-1 Mailplane
> Supermarine Air Yacht
> Vickers 166 Vellore I
> Westland Wapiti III

JAGUAR VI(S), (1928), supercharged version of Jaguar VI. No details.
Aircraft:
> Fairey IIIF

JAGUAR VIC, 470 hp, (1927), geared .657:1 epicyclic version of Jaguar VI. Compression ratio 5.0:1
Aircraft:
> Armstrong Whitworth Atlas I
> Avro 667
> de Havilland D.H.61 Giant Moth
> Supermarine Southampton X
> Vickers 193 Vespa IV
> Vickers 199 Viastra III
> Vickers 208 Vespa V

JAGUAR VID, (1928).
Aircraft:
> Avro 642/2

JAGUAR VIIA, 400 hp, (1929). Fully supercharged. Direct L.H. tractor-drive.
Aircraft:
> Armstrong Whitworth A.W.XIV Starling I N.21/26

JAGUAR VIII, 405 hp, (1928). Compression ratio 5:1. Fully supercharged. Geared, epicyclic .657:1, L.H. tractor-drive.
Aircraft:

> Armstrong Whitworth Siskin IIIB
> Gloster Gnatsnapper II
> Westland Wapiti

OUNCE, 45 hp, 2-cylinder, horizontally-opposed air-cooled poppet-valve engine, its valve rockers being unusual in design. It was intended for what is now called 'ultra-light' aircraft but was not much used. It had two cylinders as used in the original R.A.F.8 and Jaguar I engines. It had direct L.H. tractor-drive. Bore/stroke 5.0 x 5.0 in. Vol. 196 cu in, 3.2 litre. Compression ratio 5:1. Length 20.5 in; width 39.5 in; height 24.5 in.
Aircraft:
> Bristol 46 Babe II
> R.A.E. Aerial Target

The Little 45 hp, flat-twin, Siddeley Ounce, as installed in the radio-controlled R.A.E. Aerial Target.

LYNX.

This was in effect half a Jaguar and the first engine, like the Mk I version of the Jaguar, had a shorter stroke than the Lynx I and subsequent marks. It was a two-valve 180-215 hp, 7-cylinder, air-cooled single-row radial poppet-valve engine, with a plain fan. Its propeller drive was direct L.H. tractor-drive.

> Armstrong Siddeley Lynx engines had the following in common (prototype engine first):-
> Bore/stroke 5.0 x 5.0 in.   Mk I & others 5.0 x 5.5 in.
> Swept Volume 11 litre. Mk I & others 756 cu in. 12.4 litre.
> Compression Ratio 5.0:1 — 5.1:1.
> Dimensions vary according to accessories.
> Diameter 42.0 in.   (Mk I) 43.0 in.   Others 45.6 in.
> Length 43.3 in. (Mk I)   Others 45.6-48.25 in (supercharged)
> Weights, where published — *see* Performance tables.

LYNX I, 150 hp, (1920). Direct L.H. tractor-drive. Early engines had cast pistons, later replaced by forged pistons. Plain fan. Fuel 74 Octane. Diameter 43.0 in.
Aircraft:
> Avro 504K
> Westland Wagtail

LYNX II, 184 hp, (1920). Plain-fan, direct L.H. tractor-drive.
Aircraft:
> Avro 504N, 504Q
> Cierva C.8L Mk I Autogiro (Avro 611)
> Gloucestershire Grouse II
> Vickers (Canada) Vedette (pusher Lynx)
> Westland Wagtail

LYNX III, 200 hp, (1924). Plain fan, direct L.H. tractor-drive.
Aircraft:
> Armstrong Whitworth Ape
> Avro 504N

LYNX IV, 180 hp, (1929), the Mk IV Lynx introduced into the series, Y-alloy forged pistons, in place of castings. Direct L.H. tractor-drive. Fuel 77 Octane (DTD 224).

The Lynx Engine

Armstrong Siddeley Lynx II.

The Armstrong Siddeley Lynx II in an Avro 504N trainer, in a crazy flying display.

Avro 504O seaplane with an Armstrong Siddeley Lynx II.

Canadian Vickers Vedette reconnaissance flying-boat, powered by a pusher Lynx II.

Aircraft:
    Avro 504N, R Gosport
    Avro 621 Tutor
    Blackburn F.2 Lincock I
    Boulton & Paul P.31 Bittern
    Cierva C.8L Mk II, III (Avro 617)
    Supermarine Seamew

LYNX IV(G), geared, epicyclic .657:1, plain fan engine.
Aircraft:
    Blackburn F.2 Lincock II

LYNX IV (MOD), 190 hp, (1929), plain fan. Direct L.H. tractor-drive. This is a reconditioned Lynx IV to a standard between that of the Mk IV and the IV*, in particular the piston crown being flat, as opposed to the concave crown of the IV*.
Aircraft:
    Avro 504N
    Avro 621 Tutor

LYNX IV(S), (1928), similar to Mk IVC, compression ratio 5:1. Fully supercharged. Direct L.H. tractor-drive.
Aircraft:
    Avro 584 Avocet (17/25)
    Parnall Parasol
    Vickers 125 Vireo

LYNX IV*, 210 hp, (1930). Direct L.H. tractor-drive. In effect, half a Jaguar IV*. Air Publication 1287, regarding the seven-cylinder Lynx engine states 'It will be realised by those conversant with the Jaguar IVC engine, that the Lynx IV* is in effect a Jaguar IVC engine employing but a single row of cylinders...'. The Air Publication goes on to list the more important components in which the two engines differed, these essentially being the crankshaft, connecting-rod assembly, and other things like the engine body, carburettor and ignition, appropriate to halving a two-row engine. Power Curve at rated altitude sea level from A.& A.E.E., Martlesham, Report M.624, dated 21.6.33.

R.P.M.	2,090	2,000	1,900	1,800	1,700	1,600
B.H.P.	227	221	213	203	192	181

Fuel 73 Octane (DTD 134).
Aircraft:
    Airspeed A.S.5 Courier
    Avro 504N
    Avro 621 Tutor

LYNX IVA, 188 hp, (1930). Direct L.H. tractor-drive.
Aircraft:
    de Havilland D.H.75 Hawk Moth.

LYNX IVC, 208/225 hp, (1929), fuel 77 Octane.
Aircraft:
    Airspeed A.S.5, 5A Courier
    Airspeed A.S.6A Envoy II
    Avro 504N, 504O
    Avro 618 Ten
    Avro 621 Tutor
    Avro 626 Prefect

Avro 641 Commodore
Avro 642/4m
Avro 646 Sea Tutor
Blackburn F.2 Lincock I
Fokker F.VIIA/3m
Handley Page H.P.32 Hamlet (Type D)
Saro A.17 Cutty Sark
Saro A.19 Cloud

GENET, a 5-cylinder single-row radial, air-cooled poppet-valve engine. This was one of the earliest practical radial engines for the rapidly developing light aeroplane industry in the mid-1920s.

Armstrong Siddeley Genet I, II & IIA. Early engines had the following in common:-
Bore/stroke 4.0 x 4.0 in. (101.6 x 101.6 mm)
Swept Volume 251.43 cu in. (4.1 litre)
Compression Ratio (Mk I) 5.2:1;   (Mk II) 5.25:1
Dimensions vary according to accessories.
Diameter 34 in Length 28.5 in.
Weights, where published — *see* Performance tables.

GENET I, 65 hp, (1926). Direct L.H. tractor-drive.
Aircraft:

Avro 581 Avian prototype
Blackburn L.1 Bluebird I
Cierva C.9 Autogiro (Avro 576)
Cierva C.10 Autogiro
de Havilland D.H.60 Moth
Junkers A.50 Junior
Westland Widgeon II
Westland-Hill Pterodactyl IB, IC

The little Armstrong Siddeley Genet I.

The Westland-Hill Pterodactyl IB, J9251, powered by an Armstrong Siddeley Genet I pusher engine.

Avro 594B Avian II, powered by an Armstrong Siddeley Genet I on display at a German show.

Flying inverted, a D.H.60 Genet Moth of the Royal Air Force Central Flying School.

Armstrong Siddeley Genet I powered a German Klemm L.25.

GENET II, 80 hp, (1930), — as Genet I but more powerful, with compression ratio slightly increased to 5.25:1.
Aircraft:
> ANEC IV Missel Thrush
> Avro 594B Avian II
> Blackburn L.1A Bluebird II
> Cierva C.19 Mk I Autogiro
> de Havilland D.H.60 Moth
> Junkers A.50 Junior
> Klemm L.25
> Parnall Imp
> Robinson Redwing I
> Southern (Miles) Martlet
> Westland Widgeon III

GENET IIA, 80 hp, (1930), as Genet I, with minor differences.
Aircraft:
> Robinson Redwing II, III.

The **ARMSTRONG SIDDELEY MONGOOSE** of 1926 was unusual in appearance for a small radial engine, seeming to be upside-down, with the 'odd' cylinder at the bottom of the circle, risking oiling-up of the lower plugs.

MONGOOSE I, 135 hp, (1926), 5-cylinder, single-row radial air-cooled poppet-valve plain fan. Direct L.H. tractor-drive. Front-mounted magnetos. Bore/stroke 5 x 5.5 in. Vol. 540 cu in. (Vol. 8.9 litre). Compression ratio 5:1. Diameter 45.6 in; length 36.6 in.
Aircraft:
> Avro 504R Gosport
> Parnall Peto

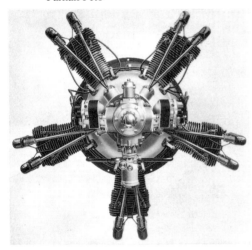

The five-cylinder Armstrong Siddeley Mongoose.

The remarkable performance of the slotted-wing Handley Page Gugnunc, low-speed research aircraft, under the modest power of a Mongoose engine It was flown by Major J.L.B.H. Cordes, Chief Test Pilot of Handley Page.

MONGOOSE II, 155 hp, (1930) increased power, similar to Mk I.
Aircraft:
> Handley Page H.P.32 Hamlet (Type D)
> Handley Page H.P.39 Gugnunc
> Hawker Tomtit
> Parnall Peto

An Avro 504R Gosport, with an Armstrong Siddeley Mongoose engine. Note the exposed and unprotected magneto behind the propeller.

MONGOOSE III, (1929). Plain fan. Service engine.
Aircraft:
> Handley Page H.P.39 Gugnunc

MONGOOSE IIIA, (1929). Civil engine. Diameter 45.6 in; length 35.65 in.
Aircraft:
> Avro 504N, R
> Avro 621 Tutor
> Hawker Tomtit

MONGOOSE IIIC, (1929). Military engine, similar to Mk IIIA.
Aircraft:
> Avro 504N
> Avro 621 Trainer
> Hawker Tomtit
> Parnall Peto

The **LEOPARD** was a big, powerful 14-cylinder, air-cooled single-row radial, poppet-valve engine. The only Armstrong Siddeley engine to have a four-valve head, except the Leopard III. It was either unsupercharged or had a geared fan and its propeller drive could be direct or geared with epicyclic-type reduction, L.H. tractor.

Armstrong Siddeley Leopards had the following in common:-
Bore/stroke 6.0 x 7.5 in. (152.4 x 190.5 mm)
Swept Volume 2,970.0 cu in. (48.6 litre).
Compression Ratio 5.0:1.
Dimensions vary according to accessories.
Diameter Mks I-III 58.0 in.   Length 60.75 — 60.85 in
Weights, where published — *see* Performance tables.

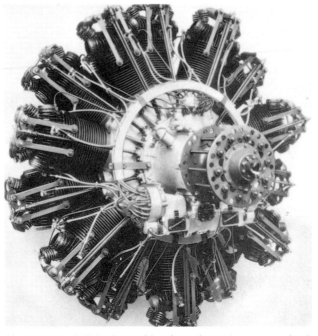

The Armstrong Siddeley Leopard I, a four-valve engine, an exception in engine design from this company and in this case a direct-drive type.

The Armstrong Siddeley Leopard I mounted in a Hawker Horsley test-bed.

Junkers Ju 52 seaplane, with an ungeared Leopard I engine.

LEOPARD I, 700 hp, (1927). Geared fan medium supercharged. Direct L.H. tractor-drive. Compression ratio 5:1. Diameter 58.0 in; length 60.85 in.
Aircraft:

> Hawker Horsley (test-bed)
> Junkers Ju 52

LEOPARD II, 700 hp, (1927), 14-cylinder two-row radial air-cooled engine. Geared, epicyclic, .633:1. L.H. tractor-drive. Compression ratio 5:1. Diameter 58.0 in; length 66.75 in.
Aircraft:

> Hawker Horsley (test-bed)
> Hawker Dantorp

The Armstrong Siddeley Leopard II, a geared four-valve engine.

LEOPARD III, 800 hp. Compression ratio 5:1. Cylinder head changed to incorporate two poppet valves. Geared fan medium supercharged. Direct L.H. tractor-drive.
Aircraft:

> Blackburn R.B.1 Iris IV
> Hawker Horsley

LEOPARD IIIA, 800 hp. Compression ratio 5:1. Medium supercharged geared fan. Geared, epicyclic .633:1, L.H. tractor-drive. Diameter 59.5 in; length 66.75 in.
Aircraft:

> Hawker Dantorp
> Hawker Horsley

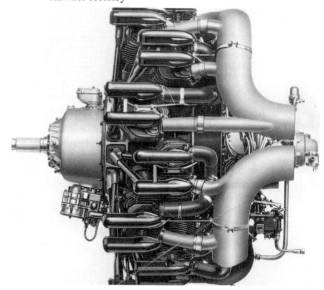

The Armstrong Siddeley Leopard IIIA, geared, two-valve.

A Danish variant of the Hawker Horsley torpedo-bomber, the Dantorp, powered by a geared two-valve Armstrong Siddeley Leopard IIIA.

GENET MAJOR series. This name has given rise to much confusion, because it was available in both five and seven-cylinder versions.

GENET MAJOR I, 105 hp, (1929). This was a 5-cylinder engine similar to the Genet I but was higher-powered by virtue of having larger cylinders and therefore a greater capacity than the Genet I. Direct L.H. tractor-drive, Fairey-Reed propeller. Bore/stroke 4.25 x 4.5 in. Vol. 319.32 cu in. (107.95 x 114 mm. Vol. 5.2 litre). Compression ratio 5.35:1. Power Curve at rated altitude sea level, from Armstrong Siddeley Inspection Certificate dated 17.11.30.

RPM	2,420	2,200	2,100	1,800
BHP	113	106.3	102.5	89.9

All-out level flight (5 min) 110 hp, 2,420 rpm. Fuel 73 Octane (DTD 134) or 80/20 Service fuel/benzol. Diameter 38 in; length 36.2 in.

Aircraft:

Avro 616 Avian IVM
Avro 619 Five
Avro 624 Six
Avro 625 Sports Avian (monoplane)
Avro 638 Club Cadet
Blackburn L.1C Bluebird IV
Cierva C.19 Mk II, IIA, III, IV, IVP Autogiros
Cierva C.30 prototype
Civilian Coupe II
Saro A.17 Cutty Sark
Southern (Miles) Martlet
Westland Wessex

GENET MAJOR IA, 145 hp, (1936), a seven-cylinder Genet Major originally to be called the Genet Super Major. It was a considerably more powerful version of the Genet Major I. It had enclosed push-rods and had an engine-speed fan. Direct L.H. tractor-drive. The Royal Air Force adopted it as the 'CIVET I'. Bore/stroke 4.25 x 4.50 in. Vol. 452.01 cu in. (107.95 x 114.3 mm. Vol. 7.3 litre). Compression ratio 5:1. Fuel 77 Octane. Diameter 38.15 in; length 38.8 in.

Aircraft:

Avro 616 Avian IVM
Avro 631 Cadet
Avro 639 Cabin Cadet
Avro 640 Cadet Three-Seater
Avro 643 Cadet Mk II
Cierva C.30A (Avro 671) Autogiro (Rota I)
Cierva C.30P Autogiro
Fleet F.7D-2
Saro A.17 Cutty Sark
Westland Wessex

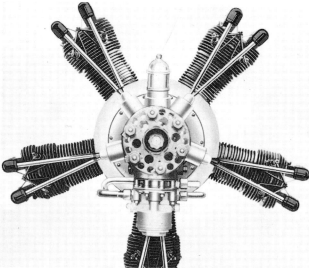

The five-cylinder Armstrong Siddeley Genet Major I, fitted to many light aircraft in the 1930s.

Armstrong Siddeley Genet Major 01A

The Genet Major I, fitted to a Westland Wessex.

Cierva C.19 Autogiro G-AAHM.

The seven-cylinder version of the Armstrong Siddeley Genet Major was the Mk IA, here installed in an Avro 640 Cadet Three-Seater.

Saro A.17 Cutty Sark light flying-boat G-ACDP, powered by Genet Major IA engines, was used by Air Service Training at Hamble and here seen on Southampton Water.

CIVET I was the Royal Air Force name for the Genet Major IA. (1931), a 7-cylinder single-row radial, air-cooled poppet-valve engine. Direct L.H. tractor-drive. Bore/stroke 4.25 x 4.5 in. Vol. 447.05 cu in. (107.95 x 114.3mm. Vol. 7.3 litre). Compression ratio 5.25:1.
Aircraft:

   Cierva C.30A (Avro 671) Rota I Autogiro

Avro 671 (Cierva C.30A) Rota I Army Co-operation autogiro, with flotation bags inflated.

GENET MAJOR III, as Mk IA, except that the cylinders were of the Mk IV type with integral cast rocker boxes. Compression ratio 5.25:1.
Aircraft:

   Avro 631 Cadet

GENET MAJOR IV, 160 hp, a geared version of the Genet Major IA. A 7-cylinder single-row radial. Geared epicyclic .663:1, L.H.tractor-drive, basically as Mk IA. Bore/stroke 4.25 x 4.5 in. Vol. 447.05 cu in. (107.95 x 114.3mm. Vol. 7.3 litre). Compression ratio 5.25:1.

The **ARMSTRONG SIDDELEY PANTHER**, of 1929 was originally called the JAGUAR MAJOR, having an increased power output of some 25 per cent. It was a fourteen-cylinder air-cooled two-row radial poppet-valve engine. Generally similar to the Jaguar, it had cylinders of slightly increased bore (5.25 inches), similar to those of the Cheetah and retaining the same 5.5-inch stroke.

JAGUAR MAJOR I, a geared engine, prototype of the Panther, compression ratio 5:1.

Armstrong Siddeley Genet Major IV was a geared version of the Mk IA engine.

Armstrong Siddeley Panthers had the following in common:-
Bore/stroke 5.25 x 5.5 in
Swept Volume 27.3 litre
Compression Ratio varied, 5.0:1, 5.2:1, 6.35:1.
Dimensions vary according to accessories.
Diameter 46.45 in, Mks I-III;   47.7 in, Mks VI-XI.
Length varied 62.86 in, to 64 in.
Weights, where published — *see* Performance tables.

PANTHER II (PF), (1929), similar to the Panther IIA but with a plain fan. Geared, epicyclic .657:1, L.H. tractor-drive.
Aircraft:

   Handley Page H.P.34 Hare (Type H)
   Westland Wapiti V

PANTHER IIA (GF), 605 hp, (1930), medium supercharged (Geared Fan, GF). Compression ratio 5:1. Geared, spur epicyclic .657:1, L.H. tractor-drive. Gated throttle. Claudel Hobson A.V.70.H. carburettor. Power Curve at rated altitude 3,000 ft from A.& A.E.E., Martlesham, Report M.617, dated 24.1.33. Boost, rated -.625 lb/sq in.

RPM	2,300	2,200	2,100	2,000	1,900	1,800
BHP	605	579	554	529	501	469
BOOST	zero		-.625lb			

Max boost, zero lb/sq in. Fuel 73 Octane (DTD 134). Diameter 46.45 in; length 63.25 in.
Aircraft:

   Armstrong Whitworth Atlas II
   Armstrong Whitworth Starling
   Avro 627 Mailplane
   Blackburn T.5 Ripon IIF
   Fairey IIIF
   Fairey Gordon I, II
   Fairey Seal
   Handley Page H.P.34 Hare (Type H)
   Hawker Hart
   Hawker Hoopoe
   Heinkel He 46
   Supermarine Air Yacht
   Supermarine Southampton X

Vickers 204 Vildebeest IV
Vickers 206 Vildebeest VI
Vickers 216 Vildebeest VII
Westland Wapiti III, V, VIII

The geared, moderately-supercharged Armstrong Siddeley Panther IIA.

Fairey Seal with a Panther IIA.

W.R.N.S. trainee mechanics, working on the Panther IIA of a Fairey Seal, during the second World War.

PANTHER III, 560 hp, (1931), Fully supercharged version of the Mk IIA. Geared, epicyclic .657:1 L.H. tractor-drive.
Aircraft:
    Armstrong Whitworth Atlas II
    Hawker Hoopoe

PANTHER IIIA, 502 h.p, (1931), generally similar to the Mk III. It was fully supercharged and had a geared, epicyclic, L.H. tractor propeller drive. (A piston was burnt, causing engine failure — see Panther VII). Power at rated altitude 12,000 ft from A.& A.E.E., Martlesham, Report M.598, dated September, 1932. Boost, rated -0.5 lb/sq in.

RPM	2,000
BHP	501.8
BOOST	-0.5lb

Fuel 73-77 Octane (DTD 134).
Aircraft:
    Armstrong Whitworth Atlas II
    Armstrong Whitworth A.W.XVI (F.9/26, N.21/26)
    Gloster S.S.18B, 19
    Hawker Fury (Norway)

The Norwegian Hawker Fury, powered by a Panther IIIA.

PANTHER VI, 560 hp, (1930). Medium supercharged, geared fan 5.88:1. Compression ratio 5.2:1. Geared, epicyclic .594:1 L.H. tractor-drive. Fuel 77 Octane (DTD 224).
Aircraft:
    Fairey IIIF Mk IIIM
    Fairey Seal
    Fairey TSR I

PANTHER VIA, 560 hp (1932), medium supercharged, geared fan, 5.88:1. Compression ratio 5.2:1. Geared, epicyclic .594:1 L.H. tractor-drive. Fuel 77 Octane (DTD 224). Diameter 47.7 in; length 64.03 in.
Aircraft:
    Hawker Audax/Nisr (Avro 674) for Egypt

PANTHER VII, 565 hp, (1934), Compression ratio 5.1:1. Fully supercharged, gear ratio 12.4:1. Geared, epicyclic .657:1 L.H. tractor-drive. Power Curve at rated altitude 12,000 ft, from A.& A.E.E., Martlesham, Report M.598, dated August 1933 and A.I.D. Inspection Certificate dated 1.5.33. Fully supercharged, 12.4:1. Boost, rated zero lb/sq in., 2,100 rpm

RPM	2,400	2,300	2,100	1,900	1,800
BHP	638	615	588	490	453
BOOST	+0.5lb		zero		

Max boost +0.5 lb/sq in. 2,400 rpm Fuel 73-77 Octane (DTD 134). (Note — after a burnt piston caused the failure in June 1933, of a Panther VII engine, written instructions were issued by Air Ministry stated '. . . the maximum boost allowable for this engine on take-off and climb until rated altitude was reached, provided that fuel having an Octane value of 77 was used. The A.& A.E.E. suggested to the Air Ministry that, in view of the fact that standard fuel had an

Octane value between 73 and 76, the engine was operating dangerously close to critical conditions if a decrease in Octane value of at most 4 causes failure').
Aircraft:

    Armstrong Whitworth A.W.XVI F.9/26
    Armstrong Whitworth A.W.35 Scimitar
    Westland Wapiti

PANTHER IXA, 580/605 hp, compression ratio 6.35:1. Medium supercharged, 5.88:1. Geared, epicyclic .594:1 L.H. tractor-drive. Power Curve at rated altitude 5,000 ft from A.& A.E.E., Martlesham Report M.681, dated 22.6.35. Medium supercharged. Boost, rated -.125 lb/sq in.

RPM	2,450	2,350	2,250	2,100	1,850
BHP	696.3	668.4	644.6	597.7	522.6
BOOST	+1.25lb		-.125lb		

Max boost +1.5 lb/sq in., (subsequently raised to +.25 lb, normal at 2,250 and +2.5 lb at 2,600 rpm, 29.7.35). Fuel 87 Octane (DTD 230).
Aircraft:

    Armstrong Whitworth A.W.35 Scimitar.

PANTHER X, 700 h.p, (1934). Compression ratio 6.35:1. Medium supercharged 5.88:1. Geared, epicyclic 5.94:1 L.H. tractor-drive. Fuel 87 Octane (DTD 230). Diameter 47.7 in; length 59.03 in.
Aircraft:

    Hawker Audax (Osprey tail)

PANTHER XI, 600 hp, (1936). Modified Mk X, for Norway. Compression ratio 6.35:1. Medium supercharged. Geared, epicyclic .594:1 L.H. tractor-drive. Fuel 87 Octane.
Aircraft:

    Armstrong Whitworth A.W.35 Scimitar
    Avro 636A
    Hawker Fury (Norway)

LYNX V, (1930), This engine is a typical example of the confusion surrounding Armstrong Siddeley engine names. First, its name was changed to 'LYNX MAJOR' and then to 'CHEETAH'. This engine used the same 5.25 x 5.5 inch cylinders as the Jaguar Major, which was renamed 'Panther'. It follows therefore that the Lynx V/Lynx Major/Cheetah was, effectively, half a Panther.
Aircraft:

    Blackburn Lincock III
    Vickers 160 Viastra I

CHEETAH.
The seven-cylinder Cheetah was a very widely used, reliable and well-trusted power unit, particularly during World War II and evolved into a big family of engines. A modestly powered engine, the Cheetah was developed from the Lynx, an earlier seven-cylinder engine with five-inch cylinders (virtually half a 14-cylinder Jaguar). The variants of the Lynx itself also comprised quite a large family and, in the natural course of events, it might be assumed that the Lynx IV would be followed by the Lynx V. However, it was followed by the 'Lynx Major' which had cylinders with a slightly greater bore (5.25 inches), as used in the Panther VI (or, to tease the reader, the 'Jaguar Major'), but still retaining the Lynx's stroke of 5.5 inches. Two versions of the Lynx Major became available with either direct or epicyclic reduction drive to the propeller and weighed 535 and 605 lb respectively. They were both engines with geared fans, delivering 260 hp at sea-level, with a compression ratio of 5:1. In a confusing situation, the Lynx Major became known as the Cheetah, the geared version being the Mk IIA.

From this point on, the Cheetah range evolved from the Mk V and, at first, only direct-drive models were produced. They were available, in the usual manner adopted by Armstrong Siddeley, either as unsupercharged engines with the mixture distributed by a plain (engine-speed) fan driven directly from the rear end of the crankshaft or moderately supercharged, using a geared fan. It was not until the Mk XI Cheetah that the geared propeller drive reappeared. Over 40,000 Cheetahs were built.

Armstrong Siddeley Cheetah V, onwards, 7-cylinder, air-cooled 1-row radial, poppet-valve engines had the following in common:-
Apart from the Mk V which had a plain fan, the Cheetah was medium supercharged (Geared Fan).
Bore/stroke 5.25 x 5.5 in. (133.35 x 139.7 mm).
(The Cheetah XI had a 5.0 inch stroke).
Swept Volume 833.77 cu in. (13.66 litres)
Compression Ratio varied, 5.2 or 6.35:1
Dimensions varied, according to accessories.
Diameter 47.6 Length varied, 48.75 — 49.6 in.
Weights, where published — *see* Performance tables.

CHEETAH V, 270 hp, (1935), (PF). Compression Ratio 5.2:1. The cylinders were as those for the Panther VI. Direct L.H. tractor-drive. The fuel specified was 77 Octane and the carburettor a Claudel-Hobson A.V.70A.
Aircraft:

    Airspeed A.S.5B Courier
    Airspeed A.S.6 Envoy I
    Avro 626 Prefect
    Avro 637 Trainer
    Avro 652

An Armstrong Siddeley Cheetah V installed in an Avro 637 trainer fuselage.

CHEETAH VA, 285 hp, (1935), similar to the Mk V, with minor differences.

CHEETAH VI, 307 hp, (1935), similar to the Mk V but medium supercharged (GF), Compression Ratio 5.2:1. Direct L.H. tractor-drive. Power Curve at rated altitude 6,000 ft from A.& A.E.E., Martlesham, Report M.663, dated 16.2.35. Boost, rated +0.5 lb/sq in.

RPM	2,300	2,200	2,100	2,000	1,980	1,800
BHP	313	298	282	265	248	228
BOOST	+1.5lb		+0.5lb			

Max boost +1.5 lb/sq in., 2,300 rpm take off to 1,000 ft or 1 min. Fuel 77 Octane (DTD 224).
Aircraft:

    Airspeed A.S.6 Envoy
    Avro 652, 652A

CHEETAH VIA, (1936), as the Mk VI, fitted with Mk IX cylinders, using 77 Octane fuel (DTD 224). Six accessories provided for.
Aircraft:

    Airspeed A.S.8 Viceroy
    Avro 652A Anson I

CHEETAH IX, 310 hp, (1937), a more powerful version of the Mk VI. Compression ratio 6.35:1, medium-supercharged geared 6.52:1. Fuel 87 Octane. Direct L.H. tractor-drive. Power Curve at rated altitude 6,000 ft from A.& A.E.E., Martlesham, Report M.658, dated 3.4.36. Boost, rated +0.5 lb/sq in, 2,100 rpm.

RPM	2,425	2,300	2,200	2,100	2,000	1,900
BHP	353	341.8	322.9	305.8	288.7	269.2
BOOST	+0.5lb		+0.5lb			

Max boost +2.5 lb/sq in., 2,425 rpm take off to 1,000 ft or 1 min. Fuel 87 Octane (DTD 230).

Aircraft:

> Airspeed A.S.5J Courier
> Airspeed A.S.6JM/C Envoy III
> Avro 652 Mk II
> Avro 652A Anson I, X
> Bristol 124 Bulldog TM
> de Havilland D.H.75 Hawk Moth

A Cheetah IX fitted to an early Avro 652A Anson.

CHEETAH X, 360 hp, (1938), medium supercharged, similar to the Mk IX, the main difference being provision for an electric or hand starter, hydraulically-operated accessories, including a V.P. propeller, the first medium-powered engine to have this feature. Power Curve at rated altitude 6,750 ft from A.& A.E.E., Martlesham, Report M.718, dated 1.6.37. Boost, rated +.5 lb/sq in at 2,300 rpm.

RPM	2,425	2,300	2,100	2,000	1,900
BHP	367	345	304	281	253
BOOST	+0.84lb	+0.62lb	+0.23lb	zero lb	-0.2lb

Max boost 2.5 lb/sq in., 2,425 rpm take off to 1,000 ft or 1 min. All-out level flight (5 min) +.5 lb, 2,425 rpm. Fuel 87 Octane (DTD 230).

Aircraft:

> Airspeed A.S.10 Oxford I, II
> Airspeed A.S.30 (30/35)Queen Wasp
> Airspeed A.S.65 Consul
> Edgar Percival Prospector

A Cheetah VI, fitted to the early Avro Anson.

The distinctive engine cowlings of the original Avro Anson, powered by Armstrong Siddeley Cheetah VI engines.

The Armstrong Siddeley Cheetah X, renowned for its training role in the Airspeed Oxford.

CHEETAH XI, 415 hp, a geared version of the Mk X, with a short stroke (5.0 inches, instead of the standard 5.5 inches, Vol. 12.42 l) and provision for a V.P./constant-speed propeller. Compression ratio 6.35:1. Medium-supercharged geared 6.52:1. Geared, epicyclic .597:1 L.H. tractor-drive. Diameter 43.38 in; length 52.73 in.

A Cheetah XI, a short-stroke, geared version of the Mk X.

CHEETAH XII, similar to the Cheetah X, adapted for the radio-controlled target aircraft, with screened ignition.
Aircraft:
>   Airspeed A.S.30 Queen Wasp

CHEETAH XV, 420 hp, reverted to the data of the Mk X, with compression ratio 6.35:1, medium-supercharged geared 6.35:1. Geared, epicyclic .732:1, driving fixed-pitch or Rotol 2-blade constant-speed feathering propellers, L.H. tractor-drive. The crankshaft had Saloman dampers. Boost, rated +2.75 lb/sq in., 6,000 ft. Max boost 4.0 lb/sq in. 2,550 rpm take off to 1,000 ft or 1 min. All-out level flight (5 min) +2.75 lb, 2,425 rpm Fuel 87 Octane (DTD 230).
Aircraft:
>   Airspeed A.S.10 Oxford III
>   Avro 652A Anson XII, XVIIIC, XIX ('Nineteen')
>   Avro 652A Anson XX, T.21, T.22

CHEETAH XVII, 385 hp, (1948), compression ratio 6.35:1. As the Mk XV but with single-lever A.V.70MH carburettor, medium-supercharged geared 6.52:1. Geared, epicyclic .732:1 L.H. tractor-drive, Rotol 2-blade VP/CS feathering propeller.
Aircraft:
>   Avro 652A Anson XII, XVIII
>   Handley Page (Reading) H.P.R.2
>   Percival Provost prototype

CHEETAH XVIII, 385 hp, as Mk XVII, the main difference being the carburettor modified for aerobatics.
Aircraft:
>   Handley Page (Reading) H.P.R.2

CHEETAH XIX, direct-drive propeller as Mk IX, with a Mk X rear cover and an auxiliary-drive gearbox. Max 2,300 rpm take off at full-throttle to 1,000 ft or 1 min. Continuous climb +2.25 lb at 2,300 rpm. All-out level flight (5 min) 2,425 rpm, +2.25 lb/sq in. Maximum emergency, 1 minute 2,900 rpm, +2.25lb boost.
Aircraft:
>   Avro 652A Anson I, X, XI.

CHEETAH 25, 385 hp, similar to the Mk XV, with a modified constant-speed unit. The other main differences were a higher take-off rating, compression ratio 6.35:1, geared, epicyclic .732:1 L.H. tractor-drive. Fuel (DTD 230), 87 Octane.
Aircraft:
>   I Ae D1 22C (Argentine)

CHEETAH 26, 385 hp, as the Mk 25, the main difference being geared, epicyclic .60:1 L.H. tractor-drive and automatic boost and mixture controls.

CHEETAH 27, 385 hp, (1948), as the Mk 25, the main difference being an automatic single-lever carburettor.

HYENA, 618 hp, (1933), 15-cylinder, 3-row radial air-cooled poppet-valve. Bore/stroke 5.3 x 4.88 in. Vol. 1,615.58 cu in (137 x 125 mm. Vol. 26.6 litre). Medium supercharged. Geared, epicyclic L.H. tractor-drive. Cylinders 3 rows, in-line. It has been suggested that each row had one overhead camshaft but this is doubtful. Surviving records indicate short push-rods with five camshafts between cylinder banks. However, neither push-rod nor camshaft drawings appear to have survived to prove the matter either way, nor G.A. drawings.
Aircraft:
>   Armstrong Whitworth A.W.XVI.

The Armstrong Siddeley Hyena, 15-cylinder, three-row air-cooled radial in the Armstrong Whitworth A.W.XVI G-ABKF. There were cooling problems with the rear-row of cylinders.

The Armstrong Siddeley Hyena air-cooled radial in the Armstrong Whitworth A.W.XVI G-ABKF, following modifications to improve cooling air-flow over the rear row of cylinders.

DEERHOUND I, 1,115 hp, (developed 1,500 hp on test). (1935-38), 21-cylinder, 3-row radial, air-cooled poppet-valve. Fully supercharged. Geared, epicyclic .432:1, L.H. tractor-drive. Cylinder rows in-line, each row having one overhead camshaft. Bore/stroke 5.26 x 4.95 in. Vol. 2,259.75 cu in. (135 x 127 mm. Vol. 38.19 litre). Fuel DTD 230 87 Octane.

Armstrong Siddeley Deerhound I, three-row, 21-cylinder air-cooled engines Nos 1-5 in assembly at Coventry. The cowling intake on No 2 shows the original design, resembling that of the Hyena. The design was unsatisfactory on both, for cooling the rear row of cylinders.

First installation of the Armstrong Siddeley Deerhound I, in its original form, in the Whitley II. The original overhead camshaft covers are notable.

Armstrong Siddeley Deerhound I, 21-cylinder engine.
Note the revised camshaft covers and reduction gear cover. Reverse-flow cooling required extensive redesign.

Armstrong Whitworth Whitley II, with Armstrong Siddeley Deerhound I engines, fitted with a reverse-flow cowling and large intake scoop, to improve the cooling of the rear row of cylinders, instead of the original conventional type of cowling.

The unfortunate end of the Deerhound Is, in the crashed Whitley II, K7243. An inexperienced crew is believed to have taken-off with the tail-trim fully back and sadly did not survive.

DEERHOUND III, (1940), a slightly larger version of the Mk I, 21-cylinder, 3-row radial, air-cooled poppet-valve. (Bore/stroke 140 x 127 mm. vol. 41.07 litre). It would have been two-speed supercharged, ratios 5.19:1 and 7.54:1, with a rated altitude in S gear of 15,000 ft, at which it would have delivered 1,440 hp at 2,825 rpm. It was not completed because the factory was bombed in April 1941.
Aircraft:

    Armstrong Whitworth A.W.38 Whitley II (K7243, crashed 3/40)

SERVAL I, 326/340 hp, 1931 (Formerly DOUBLE MONGOOSE), 10-cylinder, 2-row radial, air-cooled, poppet-valve. Serval radial engines had the following in common:-

Bore/stroke 5.0 x 5.5 in.
Swept Volume 1,080. cu in. (17.7 litres).
Compression Ratio was 5.0:1, except in the Serval III for Imperial Airways which was 5.24:1 and the Serval IIIB and V which had a 5.15:1 ratio.
Dimensions vary according to accessories.
Diameter 45.6 in. Length (geared) 58.4 in, (direct) 54.25in
Weights, where published — *see* Performance tables.

Geared, spur epicyclic .657:1 L.H. tractor-drive. Engine speed plain fan. Power Curve at rated altitude sea level to 2,000 ft, from M.A.E.E. Felixstowe, Report F.88, dated 18.6.32.

RPM	2,200	2,100	2,000	1,900	1,800	1,700
BHP	369	363	353	338	324	307

Max 342/356 hp, 2,200 rpm, all-out level flight (5 min). Fuel 80/20, or 74 Octane (DTD 134).
Aircraft:
  Saro A.19 Cloud

The geared, ten-cylinder Serval I, or Double Mongoose.

SERVAL III, (1932), Compression ratio 5.24:1. Geared fan, medium supercharged (GF) 4.97:1. Direct L.H. tractor-drive.
Aircraft:
  Armstrong Whitworth A.W.XV Atalanta
  Saro A.19 Cloud

SERVAL IIIB, 310 hp, (1932), Compression ratio 5.15:1. Medium supercharged (GF) 4.97:1. Direct L.H. tractor-drive.
Aircraft:
  Armstrong Whitworth A.W.XV Atalanta

SERVAL IV, 310 hp. Compression ratio 5.0:1. Direct L.H. tractor-drive.
Aircraft:
  Airco D.H.9J

SERVAL V, 340 hp, (1933). Compression ratio 5.15:1. Medium supercharged (GF), ratio 6.52:1. Direct L.H. tractor-drive.
Aircraft:
  Fairey Fox II

The **ARMSTRONG SIDDELEY TIGER** originating in 1932, though not the largest, was the most powerful of the Company's air-cooled radial engines. Although it was the final type to emerge in production form, it was outlived by several years by the smaller Cheetah. It was intended for bomber use and, as such, the Mk VIII version was the first production-type engine to employ a two-speed supercharger, for the design of which Armstrong Siddeley held a patent.

Armstrong Siddeley Tigers had the following in common:-
Bore/stroke 5.5 x 6.0 in.
Swept Volume 32.7 litres
Compression Ratio 5.2 — 6.2:1.
Dimensions vary according to accessories.
Diameter 50.8 in; length varies 61.42—68.3 in.
Weights, where published — *see* Performance tables.

TIGER I, 570 hp, (1932), 14-cylinder, air-cooled, 2-row radial poppet-valve. Bore/stroke 5.5 x 6.0 in. (Vol. 32.7 litre). Compression ratio 5.2:1. Medium supercharged. Geared, epicyclic .657:1 L.H. tractor-drive.
Aircraft:
  Blackburn T.5 Ripon IIF
  Blackburn B.5 Ripon V

TIGER III, 610 hp, Compression ratio 5.35:1. Medium supercharged. Geared, epicyclic .594:1 L.H. tractor-drive.

TIGER IV, 720 hp, (1934). Compression ratio 5.35:1. Medium supercharged. Geared, epicyclic .657:1 L.H. tractor-drive.
Aircraft:
  Armstrong Whitworth G.4/31
  Avro 654
  Blackburn B.6
  Blackburn T.9 Shark I S.15/33
  Blackburn B-7, G.4/31
  Fairey G.4/31 Mk II
  Handley Page H.P.51

Avro 654, powered by an Armstrong Siddeley Tiger IV.

TIGER VI, 760 hp, (1936). Compression ratio 6.25:1. Geared fan, medium supercharged, ratio 5.4:1. Geared, epicyclic .594:1. L.H. tractor-drive. Power Curve at rated altitude 6,250 ft from A.& A.E.E., Martlesham, Report M.710, dated April 1937. Figures are for engines experimentally fitted with 2-pitch propellers. Medium supercharged M Gear. Boost, rated +0.25 lb/sq in.

Armstrong Siddeley Tiger VI.

RPM	2,450	2,150
BHP	760	744
BOOST	+2.5lb	+0.25lb

Max boost 2.5 lb/sq in., 2,450 rpm Fuel 87 Octane (DTD 230).
Aircraft:

Armstrong Whitworth A.W.19
Armstrong Whitworth A.W.23 C.26/31
Armstrong Whitworth G.4/31
Blackburn T.9A Shark II, IIA
Blackburn T.9B Shark III
Fairey G.4/31
Short S.8 Calcutta

TIGER VIC,
Aircraft:

Blackburn T.9A Shark IIA

TIGER VIII, 860 hp, (1936), was the first engine of any description, in full production, to be fitted with a two-speed supercharger, an Armstrong Siddeley patented device. Otherwise, similar to Mk IX. Compression ratio 6.2:1, two-speed M/S F/S supercharged. Geared, epicyclic .594:1 L.H. tractor-drive. Power Curve at rated altitude 6,250 ft from A.& A.E.E., Martlesham Report M.699, dated 18.8.38. Medium supercharged. Boost, rated +.5 lb/sq in.

RPM	2,450	2,375	2,100	2,000	1,870
BHP	838	815	711	665	602
BOOST	+0.5lb	+0.20lb	-0.5	-0.66lb	-0.87lb

The Armstrong Siddeley Tiger VIII, the first production- type engine to be fitted with a two-speed supercharger.

Max boost, take-off, +2.5 lb, 2,450 rpm, 860 hp, take off to 1,000 ft or 1 min. All-out level flight (5 min), +0.5lb, 2,450 rpm. Power Curve at rated altitude 12,750 ft. Fully supercharged. Boost, rated +.5 lb/sq in. Max +.5 lb/sq in.

RPM	2,450	2,200	2,100	2,000	1,870
BHP	814	742	685	622	542
BOOST	+0.5lb	+0.5lb			

All-out level flight (5 min), +0.5 lb, 2,450 rpm, 780 hp. Fuel 87 Octane (DTD 230).

Aircraft:

Armstrong Whitworth A.W.23 C.26/31
Armstrong Whitworth A.W.29
Armstrong Whitworth A.W.38 Whitley II, III

Armstrong Siddeley A.W.38 Whitley III, being fitted with its Tiger VIII engines while under final assembly at Coventry.

The first production Armstrong Whitworth A.W.38 Whitley III, K8936, about to be delivered to Royal Air Force Bomber Command, powered by Tiger VIII engines.

TIGER IX, 810 hp, (1936). Compression ratio 6.2:1. Medium supercharged. Geared, epicyclic .594:1, L.H. tractor-drive, fitted with variable-pitch propeller. Power Curve at rated altitude 6,250 ft from A.& A.E.E., Martlesham, Report M.699, dated 17.7.36. Medium supercharged. Boost, rated +.25 lb/sq in.

RPM	2,450	2,375	2,150	1,925	1,715
BHP	832.2	808.3	732.8	630.5	527.6
BOOST	+0.59lb	+0.4lb	+.08lb	-0.6lb	-1.1lb

Max boost +2.5lb/sq in., 785/815 hp, 2,375 rpm, take off to 1,000 ft or 1 min. All-out level flight (5 min), +0.25lb, 815 hp, 2,450 rpm. Fuel 87 Octane (DTD 230). Diameter 50.8 in; length 68.33 in.
Aircraft:

Armstrong Whitworth A.W.27 Ensign I
Armstrong Whitworth A.W.38 Whitley I, III B.3/34

TIGER IXC, 805 hp, (1938), civil-rated, similar to Mk IX, compression ratio 6.2:1. Medium supercharged. Geared, epicyclic .594:1, L.H. tractor-drive. Power Curve at rated altitude 6,250 ft from A.& A.E.E. Report M.726, dated 26.3.38. Medium supercharged. Boost, rated +.25 lb/sq in.

RPM	2,450	2,375	2,150	1,925	1,715
BHP	807.6	789.6	716.1	629.5	529.0
BOOST		+0.25lb	-0.75lb		

Max boost +2.5lb/sq in, 805 hp, 2,375 rpm, take off to 1,000 ft or 1 min. All-out level flight (5 min), +0.25lb, 785/810 hp, 2,450 rpm. Fuel 87 Octane (DTD 230).
Aircraft:
    Armstrong Whitworth A.W.27 Ensign I.

The Armstrong Siddeley Tiger IX, a medium-supercharged version of the Mk VIII.

The Armstrong Whitworth A.W.27 Ensign I with Armstrong Siddeley Tiger IXCs, a civil version of the Mk IX.

TIGER X. Fully/medium supercharged. Geared, epicyclic L.H. tractor-drive. At Tiger VIII rating.
Aircraft:
    Armstrong Whitworth A.W.38 Whitley I, III B.21/35,

ASPIN, F.M. & CO LTD. The Company was formed in 1937, to build a new type of engine. Each cylinder had a rotating conical head, containing a valve port which opened the inlet and exhaust alternately. The valve system was gear-driven from the crankshaft. The engine ran at very high speed and had a compression ratio of 10:1. The Aspin was a 4-cylinder, horizontally-opposed, air-cooled rotary-valve engine. Unsupercharged, its propeller drive was geared, spur reduction .4:1. L.H. tractor-drive. Bore/stroke 83 x 80 mm. Vol 1.71 l. Length 26.38 in; width 36.87 in; height 17.25 in. There is uncertainty as to whether this engine actually flew.

AUSTRO-DAIMLER, also called '**AUSTRIAN DAIMLER**' (*See also* BEARDMORE).
The early 6-cylinder, water-cooled Austro-Daimler aero-engines were designed in Austria by Ferdinand Porsche. Fitted to an Etrich monoplane, one 120 hp engine (q.v.) was brought to England by Leutnant H. Bier for the 1911 Circuit of Britain.

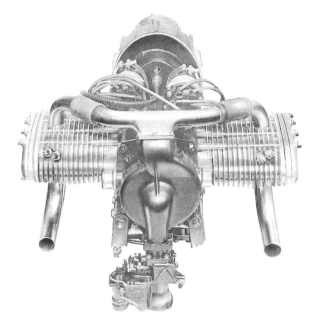

The Aspin engine was very unusual in the design of its valves and had an exceptionally high compression ratio.

AUSTRO-DAIMLER 90 hp, a 6-cylinder, upright in-line water-cooled poppet-valve engine, unsupercharged and its propeller drive was direct R.H. tractor/L.H. pusher drive. Bore/stroke 120 x 140 mm, Vol 578.46 cu in.a 6-cylinder, upright in-line water-cooled poppet-valve engine, unsupercharged and its propeller drive was direct R.H. tractor/L.H. pusher drive. Single magneto. Length 48.6 in; width 18.1 in; height 27.2 in.
Aircraft:
    Pemberton Billing P.B.29E Nighthawk
    Sopwith Bat Boat I

AUSTRO-DAIMLER 120 hp. The reliable 6-cylinder, water-cooled 120 hp Austro-Daimler aero-engine, fitted to an Etrich monoplane, was brought to England by Leutnant H.Bier for the 1911 Circuit of Britain but crashed. The engine was however salvaged, bought and subsequently used by S.F. Cody in his Type IV monoplane (in which it survived another crash) and Type V biplane, in the 1912 Military Aeroplane Competition, for £5,000, which Cody nominally was to win. The engine was also to power the D.F.W. biplane which gained the world's altitude record in 1914, by climbing to 24,800 ft near Leipzig. A licence to build a modified version was taken out by Wm Beardmore & Son, (q.v.) in Glasgow. Bore/stroke 130 x 175 mm. Vol. 850.5 cu in.

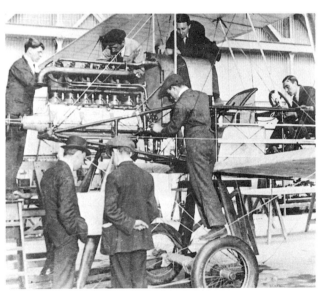

A 120 hp Austro-Daimler installed in a Royal Aircraft Factory R.E.5.

AUSTRO-DAIMLER 160 hp, a 6-cylinder, upright in-line water-cooled, poppet-valve engine. It was generally similar to the 120 hp engine. It was unsupercharged, and its propeller drive was direct R.H. tractor/L.H. pusher drive. Adopted as a model by Beardmore, q.v.
Aircraft:
    Royal Aircraft Factory R.E.5
    Royal Aircraft Factory R.E.7

AVRO. The pioneer aviator A.V. Roe, having used a J.A.P. engine, delivering a doubtful 10 hp, for his first experiments, in 1910 designed a small 20 hp air-cooled flat-twin two-stroke. The mixture was drawn into the crankcase by both pistons and both were fired together.

AVRO ALPHA, 90 hp, (1927), 5-cylinder radial, air-cooled engine.
Aircraft:
    Avro 504R Gosport
    Avro 594A Avian II (Alpha)
    Cierva C.12 Autogiro
    Cierva C.17 Mk II Autogiro

Avro 504R Gosport G-EBPH, powered by an Avro Alpha.

BEARDMORE, B.H.P. (BEARDMORE-HALFORD-PULLINGER), GALLOWAY, SIDDELEY-DEASY.

The B.H.P. and Puma story is extremely complicated and, to understand how it evolved, entails grouping together these Companies out of alphabetical order.

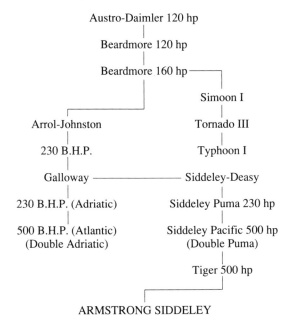

ARMSTRONG SIDDELEY

Avro 504R Gosport G-EBPH, Avro Alpha. The same aircraft/engine combination, only seven years later. The engine was first produced in 1927 and the last was installed in the last Avian in 1935.

Following the invention of the practical internal combustion engine for road vehicles, it follows that the earliest applications of the power unit to a flying machine was a direct development of the motor-car engine. The first such practical engine was developed by the brothers Wilbur and Orville Wright who achieved the first controlled, powered, man-carrying flight in the United States in 1903. The inventors of engines to power aeroplanes subsequently came thick and fast, just as had such inventors of motor-cars, not many years before. It follows that the earliest aeroplane engines were the direct descendants of automotive power units. The greatest problem was that of weight for, obviously, the lightest, most reliable and suitably robust engine for the power output required would win and then, as today, sales were important.

An early 6-cylinder, water-cooled 120 hp Austro-Daimler aero-engine, designed in Austria by Ferdinand Porsche and fitted to an Etrich monoplane, was brought to England by Leutnant H. Bier for the 1911 Circuit of Britain. Following a crash, the engine was salvaged, bought and subsequently used by S.F.Cody in his Type IV monoplane and Type V biplane, in the 1912 Military Aeroplane Competition, which Cody won.

Arrol-Johnston Ltd, of Dumfries, an associated Company with the Scottish engineering firm of William Beardmore & Son, undertook to build under licence a version of the sturdy and reliable 120 hp Austro-Daimler. However, the outbreak of war in 1914 intervened, as a result of which deliveries of the improved engine were still well below expectations, even early in 1916. The arrival at Beardmore's works of Frank Bernard Halford, seconded as a Captain in the Royal Flying Corps from the A.I.D. in France, quickly resulted in improvements. Under Halford's guidance, Arrol-Johnston produced a more powerful development of this engine, delivering 160 hp. Production problems continued at Dumfries and the War Office placed further orders for the 160 hp engine with Crossley Motors Ltd. Because of wartime delays, this Company too was beset with hold-ups and could not meet its full target delivery rate until October 1917, four months late.

Halford had been born in Nottingham on 7 March 1894. He was a remarkable aeronautical engineer and engine designer who, over some four decades, left an indelible mark on the British aircraft industry. After leaving Felstead School, he studied for an Engineering Degree at Nottingham University, learnt to fly at Brooklands and briefly acted there as a flying instructor, then aged 19. He was employed as an examiner in the War Office Inspection Department and, upon the outbreak of war with Germany in August 1914, enlisted in the Royal Flying Corps. He went to France as a Sergeant and was soon commissioned. After joining the new Aeronautical Inspection Department (A.I.D.), headed by General Bagnall-Wilde, he was soon posted home, in uniform and nominally attached to Wm Beardmore & Co Ltd, of Parkhead Steelworks, Glasgow.

Halford's first work was with Arrol-Johnston Ltd (an associated Company of Beardmore, and motor-car makers of Dumfries) and was to improve the poor rate of production of the 120 hp Beardmore. He also began to devise ways of increasing its power to at least 160 hp. As well as building a developed version of the 120 hp Austro-Daimler, Arrol-Johnston was also involved in the production of a smaller 90 hp engine. Beardmore acquired appropriate licences from Austro-Daimler before the war, following Cody's success in 1912.

With the example of the obviously reliable German and Austrian 6-cylinder water-cooled engines, a still more powerful engine was urgently needed for the Royal Flying Corps. Halford was asked urgently to design, as a private venture, a suitable British power unit of at least 200 hp, the project being financed by Sir William Beardmore (later to become Lord Invernairn). Beardmore instituted a development programme, to be undertaken by Arrol-Johnston under the guidance of Halford, using the 160 hp Beardmore, the upright, six-cylinder engine which he had been involved with previously, as a basis for the design (though much modified and not an exact copy). Early in 1916, Arrol-Johnston undertook the building, initially, of the 200 hp engine. This culminated in the 200/230 hp B.H.P. The B.H.P. story itself is extremely complicated and involves several Companies, the best-known name linking them all together is that of Halford himself, the 'H' in B.H.P. It is a name which, necessarily, appears time and time again in the history of British aeronautics.

With the support of T.C.Pullinger, Beardmore's Chief Engineer and the Managing Director of Arrol-Johnston, the design was completed in June 1916, when the new engine underwent bench testing, developing a little over 200 hp. This was at the Heathall Works, on the edge of what was to become Dumfries aerodrome. The engine was given the name 'B.H.P.', the initials of Sir William Beardmore Bt, Frank Halford and T.C.Pullinger — hence the B.H.P. name (the 'Brake Horse Power' allusion was, co-incidentally, both convenient and confusing).

Instead of individual cylinder heads, the 230 B.H.P. (as it was known) had cylinders grouped in threes, each cylinder comprising a forged steel liner, like an inverted tin with a closed end but with apertures for the inlet and exhaust ways. It was threaded over its full length and screwed into the cast aluminium cylinder-head. Difficulties with the production of these units caused a temporary reversion to cast-iron. This type of head, which suffered from poor heat transfer between the cylinder and the head itself, tended to suffer also from burnt-out exhaust valves. The water jacket surrounding the block was of sheet steel. This arrangement was a different solution of the problems of assembly and cooling from the manner used by Hispano-Suiza, but it employed some of the simple principles devised and patented by Marc Birkigt, much favoured by Halford following his experience with the R.F.C. in France but, as suggested above, turned out to be unsatisfactory.

The well-known problems, then associated with porosity in aluminium casting, had yet to be overcome satisfactorily for mass-production in England and the 'monobloc' cylinder design adopted by Hispano was yet to be perfected. Beardmore, as well, had trouble with twisting of crankshaft forgings. Instead of the more usual single inlet and exhaust valves, the 230 B.H.P. engine had a large single inlet valve, operated by a rocker arm and two smaller cam-operated exhaust valves per cylinder. The single overhead camshaft was mounted in an aluminium casing extending the whole length of the cylinders.

The prototype B.H.P. engine first flew in August 1916, in the prototype Airco D.H.4. The aircraft was intended originally intended to be powered by a 160 hp Beardmore, with which it would have been very under-powered. However, the prototype B.H.P. was delivered just in time for fitting, instead, to the first D.H.4, hence the temporary 'step' in the top line of the forward fuselage of this unique aircraft. Arrol-Johnston's Heathall production capacity was limited by space, much of which was already taken up with war contracts. Partly because of this and also because of confidence in the Government's continuing interest in the new engine, the Galloway Engineering Co Ltd was set up in 1916 by Beardmore to build it at Tongland, just to the north of Kirkudbright and some twenty miles from Dumfries.

As recalled in the Introduction, the Abbott of Tongland had made a brave attempt to fly from the ramparts of Stirling Castle in 1507. Four hundred and ten years later, in January 1917, in a hope of sustaining flight (which now seems almost as forlorn) the War Department chose the production-type 230 B.H.P. engine, now called the Galloway Adriatic (one of four engines of similar power for major production) and agreed the Tongland factory in which to

build it. The Works was opened in February 1917. Despite the expectation of very large orders, production was disappointingly slow and, in the event, of the 560 ordered from the Company, only 94 of these engines were built. Nor was the potential and intended output of at least 300 hp reached at this stage.

Beardmore and the Galloway Engineering Co were nevertheless still unable to meet the output of 230 B.H.P./Galloway Adriatic engines which the war effort demanded in 1916-1917. There were also management problems, and Pullinger decided to leave the firm. At the end of 1916, J.D.Siddeley had visited Dumfries to see the new engine running and had been assured by Pullinger (in the presence of Sir William Beardmore) that the initial troubles, particularly regarding the aluminium castings, had been overcome. Siddeley, when offered a production contract to build the engines, agreed that Siddeley-Deasy Motor Car Co at Coventry, where there was greater capacity available, would build fifty per week, subject to further satisfactory tests and a total of 3,000 engines by 31 January 1918.

Four engines were delivered by Siddeley-Deasy to the Air Department at the end of July 1917. Further tests were not at all satisfactory, despite Pullinger's earlier assurances about overcoming the imperfections in the aluminium castings and Siddeley-Deasy continued to have difficulty in obtaining acceptable units. Siddeley therefore asked to be relieved of the contract but agreed to carry on provided that he could introduce major modifications to the engine. The opportunity to do so occurred following the Report, published during 1917, of the Burbidge Committee of Inquiry into the Royal Aircraft Factory at Farnborough, its functions being redirected principally towards research, as the Royal Aircraft Establishment, (or, later, the Royal Aerospace Establishment). This change led to senior designers leaving Farnborough and joining other aircraft and engine constructors, among them being Major F.M.Green, who had been in charge of design; John Lloyd, head of the Stress Department and S.D.Heron, the engine designer.

Thus, in 1917 this team joined, initially, the Siddeley-Deasy Motor Car Co. at Coventry, taking the designs for a proposed R.A.F.8 radial engine with them. However, before the former Farnborough team could continue this development work, there was a condition. First of all, the engine which Siddeley had taken on from Galloway, originally to be called the Siddeley 1S, later the Puma, had to be developed into a satisfactory engine. After trials and tribulations, which led to substantial modification, the much-revised engine became known as the Siddeley-Deasy Puma, as related below. The Air Board Technical Department, reluctantly, accepted Siddeley's insistence on these innovations, provided that he accepted personal responsibility for the outcome. This was all greatly to the annoyance of Halford.

A great deal of hasty redesign work had first to be undertaken by the former Farnborough team, at Siddeley's insistence. This resulted in the cast-iron cylinder heads being replaced by completely new aluminium heads and the sheet steel water jackets replaced by detachable cast aluminium units, supplied by Weir & Co. The big problem was the very high proportion of the aluminium castings received which had to be rejected because of porosity, the rejection rate at one time being over 90 per cent. This was still a relatively new technique and, despite Halford's favouring of the Hispano-Suiza 'monobloc' design technique, the practice of stove-enamelling the castings inside and out, which might have helped in reducing, if not eliminating the problem altogether, was not adopted. This material was, rather belatedly, beginning to be understood and the problems of casting overcome.

Instead of inserting fully-threaded, closed cylinder liners the new design had open-ended, short-threaded sleeve-type liners which were screwed and shrunk into the head. The separate aluminium water jacket surrounding the 'hot', upper half of the cylinder liner barrels was bolted to the head and was tightened at the lower end against rubber sealing glands.

These substantial modifications resulted in the Siddeley-Deasy Puma, the first aero-engine to bear the Siddeley name, becoming virtually a different engine. The design of the Puma was started in January 1917 and the engine was complete in March. There were delays in delivery, many resulting from production problems and the burning-out of exhaust valves. It is frequently assumed that the 230 hp, B.H.P./Galloway Adriatic and the Siddeley Puma were interchangeable but this is far from the case, for indeed they were not interchangeable in any way. The Airco D.H.9, like the D.H.4 had been designed to take either the Adriatic or the Puma, on the false assumption that this and the Puma were alternative power units. However, the Technical Department General Notes on the two engines published at the beginning of 1918 made it clear that, though both followed the same principle of design and had the same bore and stroke, they were quite dissimilar and very few parts were interchangeable, the engines also being different dimensionally. It was not expected that any more Galloway engines would be sent to the Expeditionary Force, although contemporary official records seldom distinguished one engine from another.

In a Report of a meeting of the Progress and Allocation Committee held on 20 September 1917, Col Fletcher stated that the 'E.F.' had asked which parts were interchangeable between Siddeley and Galloway engines, to which the reply had to be that the two should be considered as separate engines. At a meeting held on 6 November in answer to the question whether the B.H.P. engine, to be produced by Beardmore and Crossley, would be of the Galloway or Siddeley type, the answer was that Beardmore (as sub-contractors to the Galloway Engineering Co) would produce cylinder blocks for the Galloway B.H.P. engine only and that the contract with Crossley for Siddeley-type B.H.P. engines had been cancelled.

The 230 B.H.P./Galloway engine had originally been intended for the Airco D.H.4 and indeed the prototype engine had first flown in the prototype airframe. Following the redesign of the engine by Siddeley-Deasy, as the Puma, it was found that the process had so altered the Puma that the engines would not fit the airframes for which they had been intended. The Airco D.H.9 was ordered in large numbers as an improvement on the D.H.4 from which it was evolved. The Internal-Combustion Sub-Committee of the Advisory Committee for Aeronautics considered a suitable choice of engine of about 200 hp. The engines considered comprised an Hispano-Suiza, the Sunbeam Arab and Saracen and the B.H.P., the last of these being selected, theoretically including either the B.H.P. or the Puma. The many shortcomings of the Puma had yet to become apparent. Clearly as it turned out, this was not a practical option because the D.H.9 was actually inferior in performance to its predecessor. Nevertheless, its front fuselage had been modified so as to accept the changed mounting requirements of the Puma and, thus powered it did achieve extensive if rather undistinguished service with the fledgling Royal Air Force (formed on 1 April 1918) as indeed did the D.H.4 (duly modified).

The chapter on the B.H.P./Puma story cannot be concluded without reference to the 12-cylinder, 'double' versions of each. In 1918, there was a great demand for a 'bomb-Berlin bus'. The only way in which the Great War could be won was perceived as by means of destroying the heart of the German attacker. Handley Page and Vickers had the big aircraft to do the job, with the necessary range and needed great power to lift a worthwhile load for the great distance involved. Engines of rather greater horse-power than the existing Rolls-Royce Eagle were needed and it was known that the big Condor was coming along at Derby. After Siddeley had taken over the 230 B.H.P./Galloway Adriatic, the Galloway Company turned its attention to a V-12 engine, the 500 hp Galloway Atlantic which was virtually a double Adriatic, with two banks of cylinders working on a single crankshaft. Similarly inspired, Siddeley made the Pacific engine, also of 500 hp. from a pair of Pumas. In the event, neither achieved much success, owing to the ending of the war and the wholesale cancellation of Government contracts.

There was a third V-12 engine which has lurked practically in hiding and about which little is known, tending to trip the unwary. This was the Siddeley Tiger, a slightly more powerful engine, of a nominal 600 hp. It was a major clean-up in design, using some Puma components. It had a larger bore and a shorter stroke and therefore could achieve higher rpm and power, partly because it was a geared engine. Atlantic and Pacific engines, due to their ancestry were direct-drive engines. The quoted power figures for the Tiger are those published by the manufacturer in 1921 and should be regarded as optimistic. This engine bore little more than a

superficial relationship, either to the 500 hp, B.H.P./Galloway Atlantic or to the 500 hp Siddeley Pacific. In the event, none of them was to achieve success.

BEARDMORE AERO ENGINE LTD, PARKHEAD STEEL WORKS, GLASGOW.

BEARDMORE 90 hp, (Built to Austro-Daimler design), a 6-cylinder, upright in-line water-cooled poppet-valve engine, unsupercharged and its propeller drive was direct R.H. tractor/L.H. pusher drive. Bore/stroke 120 x 140 mm, Vol 578.46 cu in.

BEARDMORE 120 hp, (1915), (Built to Austro-Daimler design), 6-cylinder, upright in-line water-cooled, poppet-valve. Bore/stroke 5.12 x 6.89 in. Vol. 851 cu in. (130 x 175mm. Vol. 13.145 litre). Compression ratio 4.85:1. Direct R.H. tractor/L.H.pusher-drive. The design differed from other stationary engines in particular because the cast-iron cylinders were slightly offset from the line of the crankshaft, allowing a spur-wheel within the deep crankcase to drive the camshaft via an idler wheel at half engine speed, in turn operating one long tappet-rod per cylinder. This operated single inlet and exhaust valves via an overhead rocking bell-crank. Pistons were of mild steel, slightly concave. Two Beardmore carburettors, two magnetos. Length 57.0 in; width 19.9 in; height 31.9 in.

A Royal Aircraft Factory F.E.2b of No 25 sqn, R.F.C. captured by Germans.

A Royal Aircraft Factory R.E.7, with a large bomb.

Production, (unit cost £825), 8/1914–12/1918, from:-
Arrol-Johnston & Co Ltd, for Beardmore Aero Engine Ltd,
Glasgow, Ordered, 188; Delivered, 188.
Daimler Co Ltd, Coventry, Ordered, 212; Delivered, 212;
Aircraft:

>   Airco D.H.1A
>   Airco D.H.3
>   Armstrong Whitworth F.K.3
>   Armstrong Whitworth F.K.8
>   Bristol 6 T.T.A
>   Cody V
>   Martinsyde G.100 Elephant
>   Royal Aircraft Factory F.E.2a, b, c
>   Royal Aircraft Factory R.E.5
>   Royal Aircraft Factory R.E.7
>   Vickers F.B.14
>   White & Thompson No 3

A 120 hp Beardmore fitted to a R.E.7 at Filton.

120 hp Beardmore engine.

Airco D.H.3 with 120 hp Beardmore pusher engines and folded wings.

BEARDMORE 160 hp, (1917), developed by Arrol-Johnston Ltd
of Heathall, Dumfries, Scotland, an associated Company, from the
licence-built 120 hp Austro-Daimler. 6-cylinder, upright in-line,
water-cooled, poppet valve. Bore/stroke 5.59 x 6.93 in. Vol. 1,020
cu in. (142 x 176 mm. Vol. 16.635 litre). Compression ratio 4.56:1.
Direct R.H. tractor/L.H pusher-drive. Two Zenith 48R.A.
carburettors, two magnetos. Length 57.0 in; width 19.9 in; height
31.9 in.

Production, (unit cost £1,045), 8/1914–12/1918, from:-
Arrol-Johnston & Co Ltd, for Beardmore Aero Engine Ltd,
Glasgow,
Ordered, 2,037;   Delivered, 1,656; Cancelled, 381
Crossley Motors Ltd,
Ordered, 900;   Delivered, 900.
Aircraft:

>   Airco D.H.3A
>   Armstrong Whitworth F.K.7, 8
>   Austin Kestrel
>   Avro 547
>   Beardmore W.B.IIB
>   Beardmore W.B.X
>   Central Centaur IIA
>   Martinsyde G.102
>   Norman Thompson N.T.2B
>   Royal Aircraft Factory F.E.2b, c
>   Royal Aircraft Factory R.E.7
>   Short 'Shrimp' Sporting Seaplane
>   Supermarine Channel I
>   Supermarine Sea King I
>   Vickers F.B.14

SIMOON I, 1,100 hp, (1922), an 8-cylinder, inverted in-line water-
cooled poppet-valve engine. It was generally similar to the 6-
cylinder Typhoon, water-cooled poppet-valve, unsupercharged,
with direct R.H. tractor-drive. Bore/stroke 8.56 x 12.0 in. Vol 5,528
cu in. Compression ratio 5.25:1. Length 98.0 in; width 37.6 in;
height 72.6 in.
Aircraft:

>   Blackburn T.4 Cubaroo

TORNADO III, 585 hp (1929), a very heavy 8-cylinder, upright in-
line. Cooling was by means of water evaporation, in conjunction with
a condenser. An airship engine, originally intended to develop 720 hp
but achieved little better than 585 hp at 900 rpm. Bore/stroke 8.25 x
12.0 in. Vol. 5,132 cu in. Compression ratio 12.25:1. Fuel: Diesel.
Aircraft:

>   R101 (Royal Airship Works) H.M. dirigible airship

TYPHOON I, (1923), a 6-cylinder, inverted in-line water-cooled
poppet-valve engine. It was generally similar to the upright
Beardmore Cyclone. It was unsupercharged and its propeller was
direct R.H. tractor-drive. Bore/stroke 8.63 x 12.0 in. Vol 4,207 cu
in. Compression ratio 5.25:1. Length 80.3 in; width 38.5 in; height
59.2 in.
Aircraft:

>   Avro 549 Aldershot IV

200 B.H.P. (1916), prototype of the 230 hp series. 6-cylinder,
upright, in-line water-cooled, poppet-valve. Bore/stroke 5.71 x 7.48
in. Vol. 1,149 cu in. (145 x 190 mm. Vol 18.832 litre). Compression
ratio 4.96:1. Direct R.H. tractor-drive,
Aircraft:

>   Airco D.H.4

230 B.H.P. The production version was built as the GALLOWAY
ADRIATIC, (1917), a modified B.H.P. 230 hp, 6-cylinder, upright
in-line water-cooled poppet-valve. Bore/stroke 5.71 x 7.48 in. Vol.
1,149 cu in. (145 x 190 mm. Vol 18.832 litre). Compression ratio
4.96:1. Two Zenith carburettors, two magnetos. Unsupercharged,
although an experimental version incorporating a Ricardo
supercharger was built and flown at Farnborough. Direct R.H.
tractor-drive. Length 67.2 in; width 18.7 in; height 43.7 in.
Production, 8/1914–12/1918, from:-
Crossley Motors Ltd, Ordered, 500; Delivered, 0; Cancelled 500
Galloway Engineering Co, Dumfries, Ordered, 560;
Delivered, 94; Cancelled/suspended, 466
Aircraft:

>   Airco D.H.4,
>   Airco D.H.9
>   Avro 529A
>   Bristol 14 F.2B Fighter
>   de Havilland D.H.10 Amiens I
>   Sopwith 2B.2 Rhino.

The 'straight-eight' Beardmore Tornado III, which propelled the airship R101 on its attempt to reach India in 1931, ending in disaster at Beauvais, near Paris.

The Avro 594, powered by a Beardmore Typhoon engine.

The airship R101 was powered by five somewhat heavy Beardmore Tornado III engines. Experiments were made to provide it with a reversing gear.

The prototype B.H.P. engine was of 200 h.p and flew in the prototype Airco D.H.4. It can be recognized by the 'step' line on the top cowling.

The inverted, six-cylinder Beardmore Typhoon.

The second prototype Sopwith Rhino, powered by a 230 hp B.H.P.

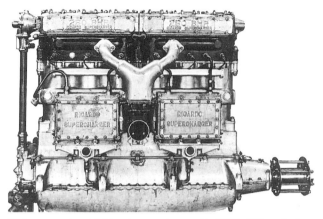

With an experimental Ricardo supercharger, the B.H.P. 230's output was increased to 260 hp.

GALLOWAY ATLANTIC 500 hp, (1918). A double Adriatic, two B.H.P. 230 hp blocks, mounted as a 12-cylinder, upright 60-degree Vee water-cooled poppet-valve. 230 B.H.P. cylinder assemblies. Bore/stroke 5.71 x 7.48 (main rod) 7.95 (articulated rod) in. Vol. 2,370 cu. in (145 x 190/202 mm). Vol. 37.7 l. Compression ratio 4.9:1. Direct R.H. tractor/L.H. pusher-drive. Effectively, a double Adriatic in Vee-form. Length 74.1 in; width 34.1 in; height 43.5 in. Production, 8/1914–12/1918, from:-
Arrol-Johnston Ltd, Dumfries, Ordered, 600; Delivered, 0; Cancelled/suspended, 600
Galloway Engineering Co Ltd, Dumfries,
Ordered, 200; Delivered, 72; Cancelled/suspended, 128
Aircraft:
    de Havilland D.H.15 Gazelle
    Handley Page H.P.15 V/1500

Paired Galloway (B.H.P.) Atlantics in a Handley Page V/1500.

The de Havilland D.H.15 Gazelle with a B.H.P. Atlantic engine.

SIDDELEY-DEASY PUMA, 236 hp, (1918), a much-modified 230 B.H.P./Galloway Adriatic 6-cylinder, upright in-line water-cooled, poppet-valve. Bore/stroke 5.71 x 7.48 in. Vol. 11.49 cu in. (145 x 190 mm. Vol. 18.832 l.). Compression ratio 4.95:1. Direct R.H. tractor-drive. Length 69.9 in; width 24 in; height 43.6 in. Fuel 80/20.

Production, 8/1914–12/1918, from:-
Siddeley-Deasy Co Ltd, Coventry,
Ordered, 11,500; Delivered, 4,288; Cancelled/suspended, 7,212
Aircraft:
    Airco D.H.4
    Airco D.H.9 srs
    Avro 539, 539A
    Avro 547A
    Bristol 23X Badger
    Bristol 28
    Bristol 29
    Bristol 34 Seaplane
    Bristol 36 Seely
    Bristol 40 F.2B Fighter
    Bristol 47
    Bristol 81 Puma Trainer
    Bristol 86 Greek Tourer
    de Havilland D.H.10 Amiens
    de Havilland D.H.50
    Fokker F.III
    Handley Page H.P.17
    Handley Page H.P.26 W.8e/f Hamilton
    Henderson H.S.F.1
    Larkin (L.A.S.Co) Lascoter
    Royal Aircraft Factory F.E.2h
    Short 'Shrimp' Sporting Seaplane
    Short Silver Streak
    Supermarine Channel II
    Supermarine Sea King I

The 230 hp Siddeley-Deasy Puma.

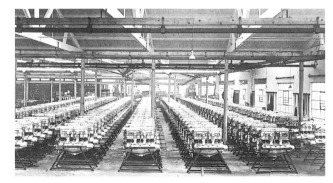

Siddeley-Deasy Pumas awaiting delivery at Coventry in 1918. There are at least 250 visible in the shop.

PUMA, 240/249 hp (H.C.), (1918), a derated production version of the proposed 300 hp, Puma, 6-cylinder, upright in-line water-cooled, poppet-valve. Bore/stroke 5.7 x 7.41 in. Vol. 11.49 cu in. (145 x 190 mm. Vol. 18.82 l.). Compression ratio originally 5.4:1, reduced to 4.95:1. High-speed camshaft, strengthened con-rods and modified exhaust valves. Direct R.H. tractor-drive. Dimensions as standard Puma.
Aircraft:

    Airco D.H.9 srs
    Avro 533 Manchester II
    Avro 539A
    Avro 547A
    Bristol 40 F.2B Fighter
    Bristol 24 Braemar I (double Pumas)
    Sopwith Cobham II

The double mounting for Siddeley-Deasy Pumas, for the Bristol Braemar I

Double mounting for Siddeley-Deasy Pumas, for the Bristol Braemar I

PACIFIC, 500 h.p. (1919), a Vee-12, (double Puma), upright Vee-12 water-cooled, poppet-valve engine. Bore/stroke 5.71 x 7.48 in. Vol. 2,298 cu in. (145 x 190 mm. Vol. 37.65 litre). Compression ratio 5.4:1. Direct R.H. tractor-drive. Length 69.9 in; width 32 in approx; height 43.6 in. Fuel 80/20.

TIGER, 600 hp, (1918). The first Tiger to bear the name of Siddeley was a big Vee-twelve water-cooled engine of a nominal 600 hp which, effectively, comprised a couple of bored-out, short-stroke Puma blocks and heads on a common crankcase and running at a slightly higher rpm. Equipped with an electric starter and an automatic friction clutch, it was spur-geared .559:1. It was a 12-cylinder, upright 60-degree Vee shaped, water-cooled, poppet-valve. Bore/stroke 6.3 x 7.1 in. Vol. 2,657.0 cu in. (160 x 180 mm. Vol 43.5 litre). Compression ratio 5.2:1. Direct L.H. tractor-drive. Length 81.34 in; width 33.46 in; height 39.57 in. The quoted power figures are those published by the manufacturer in 1921 and should be regarded as optimistic. The Tiger bore little more than a superficial relationship, either to the 500 hp, B.H.P./Galloway Atlantic or to the 500 hp Siddeley Pacific. In the event, none were to achieve success.

The only two Tigers to fly were installed in the prototype Siddeley Sinaia, a large bomber, of which three were planned in 1918.

As an example of how failure of Government interest and funding can result in near disaster at the conclusion of hitherto hectic hostilities, the unfortunate Sinaia and its equally luckless Tiger engines seem to be worthy of a special mention. The well-known (and extremely courageous) R.A.E. test pilot Frank T.

Courtney, in his book *Flight Path* (William Kimber, 1973) made some memorable remarks about this aircraft, which came near to ending his life. The engines, he said, had only undergone 'sketchy' bench tests and no air tests at all. Both they and the Sinaia were experimental and could be counted on for delays and troubles. '. . . nobody was any longer interested in planes or engines; the whole project had been started during the war and had never been cancelled and there was now no prospect for a further contract. All anybody cared about was to complete this contract — which included test flights — with the least possible effort and expense. Under these conditions, nobody consciously neglected anything but, on the other hand, nobody could work up much enthusiasm for making the changes or corrections that the pilot thought necessary for the completion of the flight tests'. Courtney flew the big bomber on several flights at Farnborough, which were short because, as he commented, 'the engines could never be persuaded to run simultaneously for any length of time'.

The sad and ill-fated Siddeley Sinaia I.

At the conclusion of a test flight, during which he noticed an increasing slackness in the elevator control, he suggested an inspection of the control cables. As he says in his book, 'We never arrived at that inspection — for, while the plane was being wheeled into the hangar, the main fuselage buckled wearily in the middle'. This would have happened in the air, had the flight lasted a few minutes longer and the results would have been catastrophic. Dryly, Courtney comments 'Nobody was interested in making repairs and the Sinaia and its Tiger engines vanished into almost-forgotten history'. Not quite forgotten, however, for the Siddeley Tiger represents the end of the difficult line which was started when Beardmore undertook the licence-building of Austro-Daimler engines, pursued through the B.H.P., Arrol-Johnston, Galloway, Siddeley Puma saga. This was not a happy episode but much good was eventually to come from it when the inevitable lessons came to be learnt.
Aircraft:
    Siddeley Sinaia Mk I

BEATTY.
George W. Beatty was an American who arrived at Hendon with a two-seat version of the Wright biplane in the summer of 1913. He is believed to have built the aircraft himself and fitted it with a 50 hp American Gyro rotary pusher engine, which he proceeded to demonstrate and use as an instructional machine. He built several aircraft based on the Wright pattern, for several years after it had been proved to be unsatisfactory both as regards stability and control. Most were powered by the 50 hp Gnome but one at least was powered by an engine designed and built by Beatty himself.

BEATTY 50 hp, a 4-cylinder, upright in-line, water-cooled poppet-valve engine, unsupercharged, the propeller drive was direct. R.H. tractor/L.H pusher drive. Bore/stroke 4.375 x 4.5 in. Vol 270.6 cu in.
Aircraft:
    Beatty-Wright

BENTLEY.
The B.R.1 and B.R.2 rotary engines designed by W.O.Bentley were intended to be lighter and more efficient than the existing Clerget

rotaries in wide scale use. Bloctube carburettor and plunger oil pump. Two A.D.S. magnetos. They were both two-valve machines and the B.R.2 featured forged aluminium alloy pistons rather than the usual cast-iron and no obturator ring was necessary. This saved considerable weight and permitted slightly higher rpm and greater power. The 230-240 hp thus achieved by the B.R.2 was about the peak power for a British rotary.

The 50 hp Beatty engine tested by George Beatty at Hendon.

B.R.1 150 hp, (1917), formerly ADMIRALTY ROTARY A.R.1., 9-cylinder, 1-row rotary, air-cooled poppet-valve. Bore/stroke 4.72 x 6.69 in. Vol. 1,053 cu in. (120 x 170 mm. Vol. 17.3 l.). Compression ratio 5.8:1. Direct R.H. tractor/L.H. pusher drive. Bloctube carburettor, two magnetos. Diameter 42.0 in; Length 43.5 in.

A 150 hp Bentley B.R.1 rotary fitted to a Sopwith F.1 Camel.

Production, 8/1914–12/1918, from:-
Peter Brotherhood Ltd, Peterborough,
Ordered, 180;   Delivered, 0;   Cancelled/suspended, 180
Humber Ltd, Stoke, Coventry,
Ordered, 1,000;   Delivered, 600;   Cancelled/suspended, 400
Vickers Ltd, London SW3,
Ordered, 550;   Delivered, 523;   Cancelled/suspended, 27
Aircraft:
  A.D.1 Navyplane (Pemberton Billing)
  Avro 504K, 504L
  Avro 536
  Avro 538
  Avro 546
  Boulton & Paul P.7 Bourges I
  Bristol 10 M.1A

Sopwith F.1 Camel
Sopwith 2F.1 (Ship) Camel
Sopwith 7F.1 Snipe (prototype)
Westland 1N.1B

BENTLEY B.R.2, 200 hp, (1918), 9-cylinder, 1-row rotary, air-cooled poppet-valve. Bore/stroke 5.51 x 7.09 in. Vol. 1,521 cu in. (140 x 180 mm. Vol. 24.9 litre). Compression ratio 5.26:1. Direct R.H tractor/L.H. pusher drive. Bloctube carburettor. Diameter 42.6 in; length 44.5 in.
Production, 8/1914-12/1918, from:-
Crossley Motors Ltd,
Ordered, 600;   Delivered, 83;   Cancelled/suspended, 517
Daimler Co Ltd, Coventry,
Ordered, 4,000;   Delivered, 1,415; Cancelled/suspended, 2,585
Gwynnes Ltd, Hammersmith,
Ordered, 1,000;   Delivered, 82;   Cancelled/suspended, 918
Humber Ltd, Stoke, Coventry,
Ordered, 700;   Delivered, 391;   Cancelled/suspended, 309
Ruston Proctor & Co Ltd, Lincoln,
Ordered, 1,000;   Delivered, 596;   Cancelled/suspended, 404
Aircraft:
  Airco D.H.6 (Alula)
  Armstrong Whitworth F.M.4 Armadillo
  Austin Triplane
  Boulton & Paul Bobolink
  Gloucestershire Mars III Sparrowhawk I, II, III
  Gloucestershire Mars X Nightjar
  Gloucestershire Grouse I
  Grain (Port Victoria) Griffin
  Handley Page H.P.21 (Type S)
  Nieuport B.N.1.
  Nieuport Nightjar
  Parnall N.2A Panther
  Sopwith F.1 Camel
  Sopwith 7F.1 Snipe
  Sopwith T.F.2 Salamander
  Sopwith Buffalo
  Sopwith Gnu
  Vickers F.B.26A Vampire II

A 200 hp Bentley B.R.2 in a Sopwith 7F.1 Snipe.

BENTLEY B.R.2, 245 hp, (1918), similar to B.R.2 200 hp. Compression, ratio 5.3:1. Direct R.H. tractor-drive. Diameter 42.6 in; length 44.5 in.
Aircraft:
  Sopwith 7F.1 Snipe
  Sopwith 7F.1a Snipe Ia (LR)

BLACKBURN CIRRUS. (BLACKBURN AIRCRAFT LTD, CIRRUS ENGINE DEPT, BROUGH, YORKSHIRE).

In 1931, the Cirrus-Hermes Engineering Co took over trading in Cirrus engines. In February 1934, Phillips & Powis Aircraft (Reading) Ltd acquired the existing stocks of the Cirrus Mks I, II and III engines, together with their spare parts and rights to build.

Two years later, Blackburn Aircraft took the Cirrus-Hermes concern over and a new range of Blackburn Cirrus inverted four-cylinder engines began to appear, beginning with the Cirrus Minor.

BLACKBURN CIRRUS MAJOR I, 150 hp, (1936), a 4-cylinder, inverted in-line engine. Air-cooled, it was generally similar to the Cirrus-Hermes IVA poppet-valve, unsupercharged, its propeller drive direct R.H. tractor. Steel forged cylinders. Forged Hiduminium heads and connecting rods, forged Y-alloy full-skirted pistons. Bore/stroke 4.72 x 5.51 in. Vol 385.64 cu in (120 x 140 mm). Compression ratio 5.1:1. Length 50.0 in; width 17.5 in; height 30.0 in.
Aircraft:

   Blackburn B-2

BLACKBURN CIRRUS MAJOR II, 145 hp, (1939), similar to Cirrus Major III, 4-cylinder, inverted in-line air-cooled poppet-valve. Bore/stroke 4.72 x 5.5 in. Vol. 386 cu in. (120 x 140 mm. Vol. 6.3 litre). Compression ratio 5.8:1. Direct R.H. tractor-drive. Length 42.2 in; width 18.3 in; height 30.6 in.
Aircraft:

   Auster J/5H Autocar
   General Aircraft G.A.L.42 Cygnet II
   General Aircraft G.A.L.45 Owlet

Hendy 302A
Miles M.2S Hawk Major
Miles M.14A, B Hawk Trainer
Miles M.28 Mercury II

Blackburn Cirrus Major II in the General Aircraft G.A.L.45 Owlet.

THE BLACKBURN CIRRUS MAJOR SERIES III ENGINE
(155 b.h.p. for take-off)

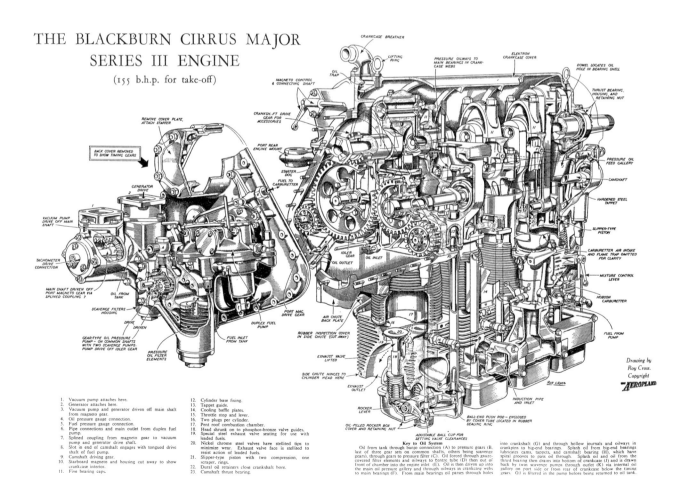

1. Vacuum pump attaches here.
2. Generator attaches here.
3. Vacuum pump and generator driven off main shaft from magneto gear.
4. Oil pressure gauge connection.
5. Fuel pressure gauge connection.
6. Pipe connections and main outlet from duplex fuel pump.
7. Splined coupling from magneto gear to vacuum pump and generator drive shaft.
8. Slot in end of camshaft engages with tongued drive shaft of fuel pump.
9. Camshaft driving gear.
10. Starboard magneto and housing cut away to show crankcase interior.
11. Five bearing caps.
12. Cylinder base fixing.
13. Tappet guide.
14. Cooling baffle plates.
15. Throttle stop and lever.
16. Two plugs per cylinder.
17. Pent roof combustion chamber.
18. Head shrunk on to phosphor-bronze valve guides.
19. Special steel exhaust valve seating for use with leaded fuels.
20. Nickel chrome steel valves have stellited tips to minimize wear. Exhaust valve face is stellited to resist action of leaded fuels.
21. Slipper-type piston with two compression, one scraper, rings.
22. Dural oil retainers close crankshaft bore.
23. Camshaft thrust bearing.

Key to Oil System

Oil from tank through banjo connection (A) to pressure gears (B, last of three gear sets on common shafts, others being scavenge gears), through gears to pressure filter (C). Oil forced through gauze-covered filter elements and oilways to centre tube (D) then out of front of chamber into the engine inlet (E). Oil is then driven up into the main oil pressure gallery and through oilways in crankcase webs to main bearings (F). From main bearings oil passes through holes into crankshaft (G) and through hollow journals and oilways in crankpins to big-end bearings. Splash oil from big-end bearings lubricates cams, tappets, and camshaft bearing (H), which have spiral grooves to pass oil through. Splash oil and oil from the thrust bearing then drains into bottom of crankcase (J) and is drawn back by twin scavenge pumps through outlet (K) via internal oil gallery on port side or from rear of crankcase below the timing gears. Oil is filtered in the pump before being returned to oil tank.

The Blackburn Cirrus Major III. A sectioned drawing by Roy Cross.

BLACKBURN CIRRUS MAJOR III, 135 hp, (1945), 4-cylinder, inverted in-line air-cooled poppet-valve. Bore/stroke 4.72 x 5.5 in. Vol. 386 cu in. (120 x 140 mm. Vol. 6.3 litre). Compression ratio 6.5:1. Direct L.H. tractor-drive. Power Curve at rated altitude S/L from A.& A.E.E., Martlesham, Report M.714, dated 11.8.37.

RPM	2,450	2,400	2,300	2,200	2,100	2,000
BHP	148.3	146.2	143.8	137.5	132.2	126.6

Length 42.5 in; width 16.9 in; height 29.7 in.
Aircraft:

    Auster J/5G Cirrus Autocar
    Auster J/5K Aiglet
    Blackburn B-2
    Chrislea CH.3 srs 4 Skyjeep
    Fairey Primer
    Foster Wickner F.W.3 Wicko
    Miles M.2S Hawk Major
    Miles M.14A Hawk Trainer
    Miles M.18 Mk II, III
    Miles M.28 Mercury II, III, V, VI
    Miles M.38 Messenger I, IIA, IIB, III
    Miles M.48 Messenger
    Miles M.57 Aerovan 1, 2, 3, 4
    Miles M.65 Gemini 8
    Miles M.75 Aries
    Miles (Hurel Dubois) H.D.M.105
    Portsmouth Aerocar Major

The Blackburn Cirrus Major III.

BLACKBURN CIRRUS MIDGET, 55 hp, (1937), 4-cylinder, inverted in-line, air-cooled, poppet-valve. Bore/stroke 85 x 100 mm. Vol. 6.33 litre). Compression ratio 6:1. Direct L.H. tractor-drive. Length 33.6 in; width 14.18 in; height 21.65 in.
Aircraft:

    Chilton Monoplane

The 55 hp Blackburn Cirrus Midget.

BLACKBURN CIRRUS MINOR I, 82 hp, (1937). After taking over the Cirrus-Hermes Engineering Co Ltd in 1937, the first engine to be designed and built at the Blackburn works at Brough, Yorkshire, the Cirrus Minor was a 4-cylinder, inverted, in-line air-

cooled poppet-valve. Bore/stroke 3.94 x 5.0 in. Vol. 243 cu in. (100 x 127 mm. Vol 4.0 litre). Compression ratio 5.8:1. Direct L.H. tractor-drive. Length 39.9 in; width 17.9 in; height 25.6 in.
Aircraft:

    Arpin A-1 Mk 2
    Auster J/3A Adventurer
    Auster J/4
    B.A.Swallow II
    C.W. Cygnet
    Deekay Knight
    Foster Wickner F.W.2 Wicko
    General Aircraft G.A.L.26
    General Aircraft G.A.L.42 Cygnet Minor
    General Aircraft G.A.L.47
    Hillson Helvellyn
    Marendaz Trainer
    Moss M.A.2
    Taylor Experimental
    Taylorcraft D Auster I
    Taylorcraft Plus C.2
    Taylorcraft Plus D

The 90 hp Blackburn Cirrus Minor.

BLACKBURN CIRRUS MINOR II, 100 hp, (1945), similar to Mk I but higher compression ratio, 6.25:1. Can use leaded fuel 4 cc/imp gall.
Aircraft:

    Auster J/1 Autocrat
    Miles M.65 Gemini 1, 1A, 1B, 4
    Miles M.68 'Boxcar'
    Newbury A.P.4 Eon

The Blackburn Cirrus Minor II in the prototype Miles Gemini.

BLACKBURN CIRRUS BOMBARDIER 203, (1960), 4-cylinder, inverted in-line air-cooled poppet-valve, fuel-injection engine. Bore/stroke 4.8 x 5.5 in. Vol. 398 cu in. (122 x 140 mm. Vol. 6.5 litre). Compression ratio 7:1. Direct L.H. tractor-drive. Unsupercharged. Provision for VP/CS propeller. Military engine. Length 45.3 in; width 19.0 in; height 30.95 in.
Aircraft:
    Auster A.O.P.9
    Auster B.5

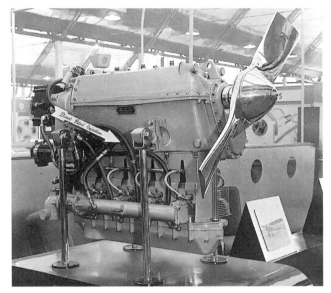

The fuel-injected Blackburn Cirrus Bombardier 203, as fitted to an Army Auster A.O.P.9.

BLACKBURN CIRRUS BOMBARDIER 702. Minor differences in design from Mk 203, fuel-injection engine. Bore/stroke 4.8 x 5.5 in. Vol. 398 cu in. (122 x 140 mm. Vol. 6.5 litre). Compression ratio 7:1. Unsupercharged. Direct R.H. tractor/L.H pusher-drive. Provision for VP/CS propeller. Civil version of 200 series. Length 45.3 in; width 19.0 in; height 30.95 in.
Aircraft:
    Auster B.4
    Cierva W.14 Skeeter IIIB (prototype), V
    Miles M.38 Messenger 5

BLACKBURNE (Burney and Blackburne) were makers of motor-cycle engines, at Bookham, Surrey.

THRUSH, 38 hp, (1924), 3-cylinder, 1-row radial air-cooled poppet-valve. Bore/stroke 3.16 x 3.78 in. Vol. 88.97 cu in. (91.5 x 97 mm. Vol. 1,500 cc). Direct R.H. tractor-drive.

The three-cylinder 1,500 cc Blackburne Thrush.

Aircraft:
    ANEC IV Missel Thrush
    Avro 562 Avis
    Blackburn L.1 Bluebird I
    Clarke Cheetah (Monoplane & Biplane)
    Parnall Pixie III

    Supermarine Sparrow I
    Vickers 89 Viget
    Vickers 98 Vagabond
    Westland Widgeon I

TOMTIT, 26 hp, (1923), 2-cylinder, initially upright converted motor-cycle engine, later inverted and named Tomtit. 60-degree Vee-twin, air-cooled poppet-valve. Bore/stroke 2.77 x 3.43 Vol. 41.36 cu in. (71 x 88 mm. Vol. 697 cc). Compression ratio 6.2:1. Direct R.H. tractor-drive.
Aircraft:
    ANEC I (inverted)
    Avro 558 (inverted)
    Avro 560 (upright & inverted)
    de Havilland D.H.53 Humming Bird (inverted)
    Gloucestershire Gannet (inverted)
    Gnosspelius Gull (upright)
    Handley Page H.P.23 (inverted)
    Heath Parasol (inverted)
    Parnall Pixie II (inverted)
    Short S.1 Cockle (Satellite) (upright)
    Wheeler Slymph (inverted)

Powering an Avro 560, the tiny 26 hp two-cylinder Blackburne motor-cycle engine, in its initial upright form, later to be inverted and named the Tomtit.

BRISTOL AEROPLANE COMPANY LTD, AERO-ENGINE DEPARTMENT AND ITS FOREBEARS, BRAZIL STRAKER LTD AND COSMOS ENGINEERING LTD.
In military terms, 'for the sake of good order and discipline' and at the undoubted risk of incurring the terminal wrath of purists, to say nothing of that of helpful historians, it has been decided to combine the very complicated and involved story of these three companies. If a reason has to be given for this impossibly difficult decision, it must be the continuity provided by that most remarkable and formidable character, Roy Fedden the genius who linked and ruled them all.

COSMOS ENGINEERING COMPANY, FISHPONDS, BRISTOL.
Brazil Straker Ltd, motor-car makers of Fishponds, Bristol was formed by an Irish engineer, J.P.Brazil and Sydney Straker, a London motor agent who specialized in steam-powered and motor vehicles, in partnership with L.R.L.Squire. A.H.Roy Fedden, while still a student, had designed a two-seat light car. He joined Brazil in 1906, after an apprenticeship with Bristol Motor Co. Ltd. and night school at Merchant Venturers Technical College. He completed the design for his little 'Shamrock' car the following year. In 1906, Straker Squire in Bristol entered a programme for building German buses for London, making 1,000 in three years, in addition to 150 Straker Squire cars in the latter year. Fedden was appointed chief of the design staff and, in 1914 aged 29, he was appointed Chief Engineer and Technical Director of Straker Squire. That year he saw and was impressed by the 120 hp Argyll 6-cylinder water-cooled aero-engine, which used an ingenious single sleeve-valve system, which had been patented in 1909, jointly by Scotsman Peter

Burt and Canadian James McCollum. The Argyll Motor Co went into liquidation, so nothing much eventually came of this engine but the germ of an idea remained in Fedden's mind.

Fedden had an enthusiastic team to support him, headed by L.F.G. 'Bunny' Butler. Then, immediately following outbreak of the First World War resulted in the new Royal Naval Air Service training pilots on American Curtiss JN-4s, powered by the 90 hp Curtiss OX-5, a most unsatisfactory engine. Fedden and his team were given a free hand in rectifying its numerous shortcomings and, by the end of 1914, he and Butler had virtually redesigned the engine to the Admiralty's satisfaction. The Admiralty took over the Fishponds works the following month and the Director of Aeronautical Supplies at the Ministry of Munitions proposed that Brazil Straker should build a small new engine designed by Rolls-Royce for coastal airships. Thanks to Royce's faith in the integrity of Fedden and his close associates, this was the only British company to be entrusted with the job of manufacturing Rolls-Royce aero-engines and, indeed, they also built numerous Falcons and supplied parts for Eagles.

The problems of water-cooling and leakage concerned Fedden and he turned more and more towards air-cooling, on the grounds that it was lighter for its power, simpler and need not necessarily incur greater drag. In 1916, the Director of the Admiralty Air Department issued a draft specification for a radial air-cooled engine of at least 300 hp. Fedden and Butler entered the competition for this job with enthusiasm, designing an engine initially called the Brazil Straker Mercury. In addition, they designed the air-cooled Jupiter and Lucifer radials. These engines were notably light in their installed weight.

In the course of 1918 and 1919, Brazil Straker's business was bought by Cosmos, an Anglo-American group (its origins being in coal and shipping in South Wales). Fedden was informed (by letter) that Cosmos had taken over Brazil Straker's aero-engine business, that the company would henceforth be known as the Cosmos Engineering Co and its products as Cosmos engines. Fedden was understandably annoyed at the way events had turned out and, with Butler, seriously contemplated even returning to the motor car business. He also learned that he was expected to continue in his post, although no Cosmos director appeared on the scene. However, in the event, Cosmos Engineering Company itself went into liquidation in February 1920.

The liquidation in quick succession, within some 18 months, of Brazil Straker and Cosmos Engineering was a shattering blow to Fedden and Butler. After an initial unsuccessful approach to John Siddeley whose Jaguar engine was to be the Jupiter's principal rival, Fedden was also at first faced with a rebuff from the neighbouring Bristol Aeroplane Company at Filton. He managed to keep his design team intact and the work quietly under way, during which time he sought a buyer for the Company. He was not a man easily put off and, as a result of encouraging suggestions from the Air Ministry and after playing 'hard to get', the board of the Bristol Aeroplane Company eventually agreed to take over the remaining Brazil Straker engine project, the Jupiter (later referred to as Cosmos) and the Cosmos Lucifer, as the nucleus of an Aero Engine Department. This took place just in time for showing the Jupiter and Lucifer on the Bristol stand at the Olympia Aero Show in August 1920.

With Air Ministry approval, A.H.R.Fedden continued Jupiter development and production at Bristol, now as Chief Engineer of the Engine Department of the Bristol Aeroplane Company. He thus retained the post he had previously held at Cosmos, ensuring continuity of design. He was a man of imagination and a formidable determination and had now gained much valuable experience while working for Brazil Straker. He already had the small Lucifer ready for production, a three-cylinder engine similar to the Jupiter. However, peacetime orders were hard to come by, the industry was reduced and there was a struggle everywhere for survival, not least at Bristol. The success of the Jupiter, in civil and military roles saved the situation and, in addition, licence manufacturing agreements for the Bristol engine were made with foreign companies, notably the French firm Société des Moteurs Gnome et le Rhône and, in Belgium, S.A.B.C.A.

It was from this point that Fedden's design team began to build up, perhaps most notable of all being F.M.Owner, who joined him

as the stressman in 1922 and went on to become Chief Engineer twenty-five years later, after Fedden's enforced retirement at the end of 1942.

FEDDEN'S EARLIEST ENGINES,
from STRAKER SQUIRE, via COSMOS to
BRISTOL AEROPLANE COMPANY
Details taken from the Company's own Records, are as follows.

COSMOS MERCURY, 345 hp, (1918). The original Mercury was built at Bristol by Brazil Straker, under Roy Fedden's direction. It was a 14-cylinder, 2-row radial air-cooled poppet-valve engine and of unusual design. Instead of having a master rod and six articulated rods on each of the two crankpins, it had seven narrow connecting-rods on each, resulting in a double helical formation of each row of cylinders. Bore/stroke 4.375 x 5.8 in. Vol. 1,223 cu in. (111 x 147.6 mm. Vol. 20.0 litre). Compression ratio 5.3:1. Direct L.H. tractor/R.H pusher-drive. It ran well and smoothly, setting an unofficial record by climbing to 10,000 feet in 5.4 minutes, going on to reach 20,000 feet in 16.25 minutes. Originally, 200 production Mercuries were ordered but were cancelled after the armistice.
Aircraft:
    Bristol 21A Scout F.1

COSMOS JUPITER I & II, 400 hp, (1918). Three were completed, the first two being called Brazil Straker Jupiter I, until renamed after the company was sold to Cosmos Engineering. The third built was called the Cosmos Jupiter II, until taken over by the Bristol Aeroplane Co's Engine Department as the Bristol Jupiter. (*See below*).

The Jupiter was a 9-cylinder, 1-row radial air-cooled poppet-valve engine and Jupiter engines had the following in common:-

---

Bore/stroke 5.75 x 7.5 in. (146.0 x 190.0 mm)
Swept Volume 1,753.0 cu in. (28.7 litres).
Compression Ratio varied according to type.
Dimensions varied according to accessories.
Diameter 54.5 in; length varies according to equipment.
Weights, where published — *see* Performance tables.

Direct L.H. tractor-drive (engine Nos.1 & 2). Geared, epicyclic spur geared 0.666:1, L.H. tractor-drive (engine No.3). Fitted with three separate Claudel Hobson HC.8 carburettors, each feeding three equally-spaced cylinders, by means of a three-start spiral in the induction chamber. This ensured even running in the event of a failure of a carburettor.
Aircraft:
    Bristol 23A Badger II
    Bristol 32 Bullet
    Sopwith Schneider
    Westland Limousine II (geared engine)

The first of the three Cosmos Jupiters built, the direct-drive Jupiter I (engine No 1), fitted to the Bristol 23 Badger.

Cosmos direct-drive Jupiter I (engine no 2).

Sopwith Schneider seaplane with Cosmos direct-drive Jupiter I (engine no 2).

The epicyclic, spur-geared Cosmos Jupiter II (engine no 3).

The Avro 504K, G-EAJB with the Cosmos Lucifer engine.

COSMOS LUCIFER I, 80/100 hp, (1919). As the Jupiter, taken over by Bristol, see below. It was a 3-cylinder, 1-row radial air-cooled poppet-valve engine, using Jupiter-type cylinders but with a shorter stroke. Bore/stroke 5.75 x 6.25 in. Vol 487 cu in. (146 x 159 mm. Vol. 8.0 litre). Compression ratio 4.8:1. Direct L.H. tractor-drive. Diameter 48.0 in.
Aircraft:

        Avro 504K Lucifer
        Boulton & Paul P.10

Bristol air-cooled radial engines, whether in poppet or in sleeve valve form, appeared in many variants but all engines of each type had a great deal in common. They are shown in approximate order of appearance, because there were numerous overlaps:-

1. **Bristol Poppet-Valve Family Group.**
   JUPITER, ORION, LUCIFER, CHERUB, TITAN, NEPTUNE, MERCURY, PEGASUS, DRACO, PHOENIX, HYDRA (DOUBLE OCTAGON).

2. **Sleeve-Valve Family Group**.
   PERSEUS, AQUILA, TAURUS, HERCULES, CENTAURUS.

NOTE: Engine Specifications can be complex but, where identifiable, the Specification is quoted i.e. PE-9M50 = a revised Pegasus X, with 0.5:1 propeller reduction gear and 100 mm propeller shaft = Pegasus XXII.

NOTE: Reduction gears and torquemeters. Reference is made to these instruments under Centaurus and Hercules entries. All these engines had epicyclic bevel propeller drives, the reduction ratio being specified where one engine differed from a previous one specified. Later engines, of both types, having odd type numbers also had a torquemeter built into the reduction gear. In this assembly the front bevel gear was held in position by two pistons in the Hercules and by three in the Centaurus. These pistons worked in cylinders cast in the casing. High-pressure oil was supplied to the cylinders and a bleed hole which was uncovered by movement of the pistons caused the pressure in the cylinders to be proportional to engine torque; thus, knowing rpm, engine power could always be measured. The torquemeter casings may be just seen on the reduction gear of both Hercules and Centaurus.

POPPET-VALVE FAMILY GROUP.

BRISTOL JUPITER — continuation of Cosmos Jupiter (q.v.).

UNSUPERCHARGED JUPITER. JUPITER II, III, IV, V, VI, VIII, IX, XI

1-SPEED, 1-STAGE SUPERCHARGED JUPITER. JUPITER VII, X variants

Bristol Jupiter, air-cooled 1-row 9-cylinder, 1-row poppet-valve radial engines had the following in common:- Bore/stroke 5.75 x 7.5 in. (146.0 x 190.0 mm) Swept Volume 1,753 cu in. (28.7 litres) Compression Ratio varies — *see* text L.H. tractor-drive. Diameter 53.6 in; length varied according to equipment Weights, where published — *see* Performance tables.

The very successful Bristol Jupiter series was designed by Fedden as the Brazil Straker Jupiter and, following the sale of the aero-engine business, built as the Cosmos Jupiter, three being built in total. The Cosmos Jupiter I, two of which were built, was first run at the end of October 1918. The second engine had been intended to have a propeller reduction gear but this was not fitted. In 1921, an ungeared Jupiter II built by Bristol gained the first Air Ministry Type Test Certificate to be issued. The Jupiter subsequently underwent progressive development for over a decade, also being built under licence abroad in over a dozen countries, notably in France, Germany and Japan.

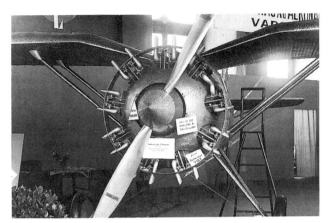

A licence-built Bristol/P.Z.L. Jupiter VIFH in a Polish P.Z.L. VI fighter.

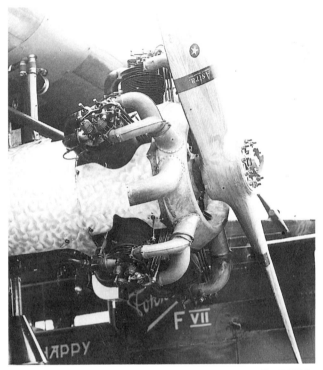

A licence-built Bristol/Gnome-Rhône Titan I, installed in a Fokker F.VII/3m of K.L.M. Royal Dutch Airlines.

In France, the licensee was Gnome-Rhône and, in Germany, Siemens. A notable difference between engines built by Bristol and Siemens was that the British engines had cylinders with cooling fins which were deeper at the rear than in the front, to even-out the cooling. (The heat distortion experienced in rotary engines, on the 'down-wind' side of the cylinders, was still a fresh memory). The Bristol-built Jupiter was therefore intended only be used in tractor installations. This was in the 1920s, before the advent of closely-cowled engines with ingenious cooling baffles. By contrast, the German-built engines were redesigned, so as to be able to run either as pushers or tractors, their cylinders being truly circular. A notable example was the huge Dornier Do X twelve-engined flying-boat, which had six pairs of geared Jupiters, mounted in tandem above the wing. A trade-off in the other direction was the adoption by Gnome-Rhône of the Farman-type epicyclic propeller reduction gear which was adopted for production engines at Bristol when the Jupiter VIII was designed.

Gear-driven supercharging was introduced in production Jupiter VIIs but interesting experiments in collaboration with R.A.E. were made in exhaust-driven turbo-superchargers fitted to jupiter III, IV and a derivative, the Orion, between 1922 and 1928.

BRISTOL (COSMOS) JUPITER I, II — *see* Cosmos, above. Early Bristol records refer to all Bristol-built Jupiters as Mk I series II, III, IV . . . etc.

BRISTOL JUPITER II, 400 hp, (1923). A 9-cylinder, 1-row radial air-cooled poppet-valve. Bore/stroke 5.75 x 7.5 in. Vol. 1,753 cu in. (146 x 190 mm. Vol. 28.7 litre). Compression ratio 5:1. Direct L.H. tractor-drive.
Aircraft:

      Boulton & Paul P.25 Bugle I 30/22
      Bristol 32A Bullet
      Westland Weasel

JUPITER III, 400 hp, (1923); Compression ratio 5:1, unsupercharged except for provision of a special turbo-supercharger in the Bristol 36 Seely (S). Direct L.H. tractor-drive.
Aircraft:

      Boulton & Paul P.25 Bugle I
      Bristol 36 Seely (S)
      Bristol 52 MFA Bullfinch I
      Bristol 53 MFB Bullfinch II
      Bristol 89
      de Havilland D.H.42A Dingo I
      Gloucestershire Mars VI Nighthawk
      Handley Page H.P.12 O/400 Type O
      Hawker Woodcock II

A licence-built Bristol/Siemens Jupiter VI, as used in the Dornier Do X twelve-engined flying-boat.

Jupiter III, exhibition cut-away, Wembley Exhibition, 1925. It was outwardly similar to the Mk II, the first to have compensated valve gear.

Production line of Bristol Jupiter IIIs and IVs and a couple of Lucifers, 1924.

JUPITER IV, 430 hp, (1926). Compression ratio 5:1. Direct L.H. tractor-drive. Some had a variable valve timing gear (see also early Jupiter VIs) and all, unlike previous Jupiters, had a Bristol Triplex carburettor, which consisted of three Claudel-Hobson HC 8 carburettors fitted in a common casing, with a single control operating all three. As a civil engine and principally for insurance purposes, the Jupiter IV could be derated to 320 hp.

The Bristol Jupiter III, of 1922, with an experimental exhaust-driven turbo supercharger for the Bristol 36(S) Seely.

Aircraft:

        Boulton & Paul P.25 Bugle II
        Bristol 52 MFA Bullfinch I
        Bristol 53 MFA Bullfinch II
        Bristol 72 Racer
        Bristol 72 Racer (special Jupiter IV racing engine)
        Bristol 75 Ten-seater
        Bristol 75A Express Freighter
        Bristol 76 Jupiter Fighter
        Bristol 79 Brandon
        Bristol 84 Bloodhound
        Bristol 84A Bloodhound (Variable-Timing Engine)
        Bristol 84B Bloodhound (Turbo-supercharged Engine)
        Bristol 89, 89A (Derated Engine), advanced trainer
        Bristol 93 Boarhound I
        Bristol 93A Beaver
        Bristol 93B Boarhound II
        de Havilland D.H.42 Dormouse
        de Havilland D.H.42B Dingo II
        de Havilland D.H.50

        Fairey Flycatcher I
        Gloucestershire Mars VI Nighthawk
        Gloucestershire Grebe I
        Gloucestershire Gamecock I
        Handley Page H.P.12 O/400
        Hawker Duiker 7/22
        Hawker Hedgehog 37/22
        Hawker Woodcock II 25/22
        Parnall Plover
        Short S.3 Springbok I, II
        Short S.3b Chamois
        Vickers F.B.27 Vimy
        Vickers 113 Vespa I
        Vickers 144 Vimy Trainer

The turbo-supercharged version of the Jupiter IV of 1928, for the Bristol 84B Bloodhound.

The Bristol Orion of 1926, with a cast penthouse head, was another experimental development of the Jupiter with an exhaust-driven turbo-supercharger.

An early example of a removable power plant, a Bristol 75 Ten-seater G-EBEV with a Jupiter IV on a swinging mount, 1922.

JUPITER V, 480 hp, (1925), Compression ratio raised to 5.3:1. Direct L.H. tractor-drive.
Aircraft:
        Bristol 84 Bloodhound
        Gloster Goring 23/25

JUPITER VI, 480/520 hp, (1927, also built in France as the Gnome-Rhône 9A). This was a very important and widely-used engine, visually similar to the Mk IV with which it had much in common. It was produced in three versions, low compression (5.3:1), high compression (6.3:1) and a small number of early, high compression engines with variable valve-timing. The first two were identical apart from their compression ratios. The variable valve-timing gear, fitted to the early Jupiter VIs (and to some IVs), was operated by a cam ring which could be controlled by the pilot, enabling him to run the engine at full throttle at ground level. This would have resulted in detonation, when using standard service fuel in the high compression engine, if the variable timing were not fitted.

On later high compression engines, this gear was deleted and the engines were modified to fixed timing, early engines so equipped being similarly modified. In place of this gear, a gated throttle was substituted, restricting the power of the engine to a safe figure up to 4,000 initially and, later 5,000 feet. The operating instructions were that, with the high compression engine, full-throttle power at sea-level could only safely be obtained when using a fuel mixture of 60 per cent benzol and 40 per cent petrol, to avoid the risk of detonation. When using standard service fuel at sea-level with the fixed timing engine, the gate setting should not be exceeded below 5,000 feet. With the early, variable timing, the timing had to be retarded appropriately up to 5,000 feet.

Bristol Bloodhound on an endurance trial, powered by a Jupiter VI, flown by Bristol's Chief Test Pilot, C.F. Uwins.

The steel cylinder barrels had aluminium 'poultice'-type heads, as in earlier Jupiters. (NOTE — There has been much confusion over the designations of Bristol cylinders. As a guide, the following may clarify matters and be an aid to their recognition. There were two kinds of cylinder heads produced at Bristol, 'Poultice' and 'Penthouse'. Poultice heads were always cast and their valve stems were parallel, standing vertically out of the heads. Penthouse heads had their valves clearly set at an angle of 45 degrees to the centre-line of the cylinder and could be cast or, usually, forged having the 'F' designation. Cast penthouse heads were hard to recognize without close inspection, the give-away being a rougher finish of the fins. Forged heads had a much finer finish). The overall diameter of the Jupiter VI was slightly smaller than before, connecting rods and cylinders being shortened (the latter by means of raising the spigot heads), the crankshaft throw remaining unaltered. Other differences included a two-piece crankshaft, enabling a one-piece master rod bi-end and one-piece floating bush to be incorporated, in place of the earlier split big-end bearing. The Jupiter VI which, like the Mk IV, incorporated a Bristol three-start spiral mixture distributor from the single triplex carburettor, unsupercharged with a direct L.H. tractor-drive. As a civil engine and principally for insurance purposes, the Jupiter VI could be derated to 320 hp.

Bristol 93 Beaver, powered by a Jupiter VI

Aircraft:
        Airco D.H.9 (M'pala I)
        Airco D.H.9AJ Stag
        Boulton & Paul P.29 Sidestrand I
        Bristol 84 Bloodhound (normal and derated engine)
        Bristol 89, 89A (normal and derated engine)
        Bristol 92 'Laboratory'
        Bristol 93A Beaver
        Bristol 93B Boarhound II
        Bristol 95 Bagshot
        Bristol 99, 99A Badminton
        Bristol 99A Badminton (short-stroke 525 hp racing
           engine)
        Bristol 101
        Bristol 107 Bullpup
        Bristol 124 Bulldog TM
        de Havilland D.H.50
        de Havilland D.H.61 Giant Moth

de Havilland D.H.66 Hercules
de Havilland D.H.67 Survey (see Jupiter VIII, IXF and
    Gloster A.S.31)
Fairey Ferret II, III
Gloster Gamecock II
Gloster Goring
Gloster Gambet
Handley Page H.P.27 W9a Hampstead
Hawker Hawfinch
Hawker Heron
Junkers F.13
Saunders A.4 Medina
Short S.6 Sturgeon I
Vickers 113 Vespa I
Vickers 119 Vespa II
Vickers 121 Wibault Scout
Vickers 131 Valiant
Vickers 149 Vespa III
Vickers 159 Vimy Trainer
Westland Wapiti prototype
Westland Wapiti I
Westland Westbury
Westland Witch I

JUPITER VIA, 415/440 hp (1927). The Mk VIA was similar to the Mk VI but was not a Service engine. Compression ratio 6.3:1. Direct L.H. tractor-drive. It was however used as the basis for the supercharged Mk VII.
Aircraft:
Bristol 101
Bristol 105A Bulldog II
Gloster Goral
Vickers 143 Bolivian Scout

Bristol Jupiter VIA, showing the valve rocker covers over the poultice heads.

JUPITER VIFH, 415/440 hp, (1932), Compression ratio 5.8:1. Direct L.H. tractor-drive. Danish Bulldog IIs had Viet gas-starters. Fitted with forged 'penthouse'-type cylinder heads, screwed and shrunk on to the barrels.
Aircraft:
Bristol 105A Bulldog IIA
Bristol 124 Bulldog TM

JUPITER VIFL, 415/440 hp, (1932), Compression ratio 5.15:1. Direct L.H. tractor-drive.

JUPITER VIFM, 415/440 hp, (1932), Compression ratio 5.3:1. Direct L.H. tractor-drive.
Aircraft:
Vickers 220 Viastra VIII

JUPITER VIFS, 415/440 hp, (1932), Compression ratio 6.3:1. Direct L.H. tractor-drive.

JUPITER VII, 375 hp, (1928), compression ratio 5.3:1, fully-supercharged. Direct L.H. tractor-drive. Also built by Gnome-Rhône as the 9ASB.
Aircraft:
Boulton & Paul P.33 Partridge
Bristol 99 Badminton
Bristol 105 Bulldog I
Bristol 105A Bulldog II, IIA
Gloster Gamecock (Special)
Gloster Gnatsnapper I
Junkers W.34
Vickers 143 Bolivian Scout
Westland Interceptor F.20/27

The supercharged Bristol Jupiter VII, with (cast) poultice heads, shown by their vertical valves.

JUPITER VIIF (forged head), 480 hp/1,775 rpm,(1929), similar to Mk VII but with Y-alloy screwed-on cylinder heads. Compression ratio 5.3:1, fully-supercharged. Direct L.H. tractor-drive. Power Curve at rated altitude 9,000 ft from A.& A.E.E., Martlesham, Report M.588, and A.I.D. Inspection and Acceptance Test Report, dated 20.2.30. Fully supercharged. Boost, rated -0.5lb/sq in. Max zero lb/sq in., 1,950 rpm.

The supercharged Jupiter VIIF. The picture shows the angled valves, indicating the penthouse heads and the unshrouded rockers.

The aggressive nose of the well-named Bristol Bulldog IIA, with a supercharged, direct-drive Jupiter VIIF.

RPM	1,950	1,850	1,775	1,675	1,575
BHP	549	505	481	438	405
BOOST	+.15lb	-.25lb	-.53lb	-.85lb	-1.2lb

Max boost + lb/sq in. hp, rpm take off to 1,000 ft or 1 min. All-out level flight (5 min), + lb, hp, rpm. Fuel 77 Octane (DTD 224).
Aircraft:

> Bristol 105A Bulldog IIA
> Bristol 107 Bullpup
> Gloster Goldfinch
> Gloster S.S.18A, S.S.19
> Handley Page H.P.33 Hinaidi I
> Hawker Hawfinch
> Vickers 161 C.O.W. Gun Fighter F.29/27
> Vickers 171, 196 Jockey
> Vickers 210 Vespa VI

JUPITER VIIF.P., 480 hp/1,775 rpm, (1930), similar to Mk VIIF. (P. indicates pressure-feed lubrication to the wrist-pins).
> *Aircraft:*
> Bristol 105A Bulldog IIA.
> Gloster Gamecock (Special)

JUPITER VIII, 440 hp, (1929), similar to Mk VI but compression ratio 6.3:1. Bevel-geared drive, epicyclic .5:1, L.H. tractor-drive. Power Curve at rated altitude 4,000 ft from A.& A.E.E., Martlesham, Report M.490, dated 1930.

RPM	2,200	2,000
BHP	563	440

Max 563 bhp, 2,200 rpm, all-out level flight (5 min), S/L. Fuel 73–77 Octane (DTD 134).

Prototype Handley Page Hinaidi J7745, powered by geared Jupiter VIIIs.

Aircraft:
> Airco D.H.9 ('M'pala II')
> Blackburn T.5 Ripon IIF
> Boulton & Paul P.29 Sidestrand
> Bristol 84 Bloodhound
> Bristol 109
> de Havilland D.H.67B Survey (*see* also Gloster A.S.31)
> Fairey IIIF
> Handley Page H.P.33 Hinaidi prototype I, II (Type M)
> Handley Page H.P.34 Hare (Type H)
> Hawker Harrier
> Hawker Hart
> Vickers 132 Vildebeest I
> Vickers 150 B.19/27
> Westland Wapiti I, IA, II, IIA
> Westland Westbury
> Westland Witch

A Jupiter VIII with cast poultice heads, the first geared Jupiter.

The Bristol 84 Bloodhound with a Jupiter VIII with shrouded valve gear.

JUPITER VIIIF, 460 hp, (1929), similar to Mk VIII with forged heads. Compression ratio 5.8:1. Bevel-geared drive, epicyclic .5:1, L.H. tractor-drive. Jupiter VIII.FA was geared .656:1.
Aircraft:

    Blackburn B.T.1 Beagle
    Boulton & Paul P.29 Sidestrand III
    Handley Page H.P.33 Clive I
    Vickers 192 Vildebeest
    Westland Wapiti I, IA, II, IIA

The Jupiter VIIIF, with forged heads and unshrouded valve gear.

The Jupiter VIIIF with semi-shrouded valve gear, giving limited anti-ice protection.

JUPITER VIIIF.P., 460 hp, (1929), similar to Mk VIIIF. (P. indicates pressure-feed lubrication to the wrist-pins of the articulated connecting-rods)). Following repeated failures of Jupiter VIIIs in Wapitis of No. 55 Squadron Iraq, time between overhauls was reduced to 150 hrs. Such failures, which in almost every case resulted in a complete engine write-off, continued after this and re-equipping Jupiter VIIIF-powered Wapitis with the Jupiter VIIIF.P. was recommended.
Aircraft:

    de Havilland D.H.65J Hound
    Gloster Goring

    Handley Page H.P.33 Clive I
    Westland Wapiti I, IA, II, IIA
    Westland Witch II

The Boulton & Paul P.29 Sidestrand III powered by the Jupiter VIIIF.

JUPITER IX, 525 hp, compression ratio 5.3:1.
Aircraft:

    Handley Page H.P.35 Clive II, III
    Supermarine Seagull II
    Vickers 134, 166 Vellore I
    Vickers 145 Victoria
    Vickers 173 Vellore IV

A sectioned Jupiter IX, showing the cast poultice head and exposed valve gear.

JUPITER IXF, 550 hp, forged heads, compression ratio 5.3:1, bevel-geared, epicyclic .5:1. Jupiter IX.FA geared .656:1.
Aircraft:

    Blackburn C.B.2. Nile
    Handley Page H.P.36 Hinaidi II (Type M)
    Short S.8 Calcutta
    Short S.8/8 Rangoon
    Supermarine Solent
    Vickers 167 Virginia X
    Vickers 203 Viastra VI
    Vickers 242 Viastra IX
    Westland Wapiti VI

JUPITER X, 470 hp, compression ratio 5.3:1. Bevel-geared, epicyclic .5:1.
Aircraft:

    Short S.10 Gurnard I
    Vickers 192 Vildebeest

JUPITER XF, 540 hp, compression ratio 5.3:1. Bevel-geared, epicyclic .5:1. Forged cylinder heads.
Aircraft:
> Blackburn B.T.1 Beagle
> Boulton & Paul P.32 (B.22/27)
> Bristol 118
> Fairey Hendon prototype
> Gloster Goring
> Handley Page H.P.34 Hare (Type H)
> Hawker Hart
> Vickers 192 Vildebeest

JUPITER XFA, 483 hp. It was fully supercharged single-speed, single-stage. Its propeller drive was geared, epicyclic-type reduction .656:1. L.H. tractor-drive. Compression ratio 5.3:1. Power Curve at rated altitude 11,000 ft from A.& A.E.E., Martlesham, Report dated 3.3.31. Boost, rated zero lb/sq inch.

R.P.M.	2,200	2,000	1,600
B.H.P.	506	476	410
BOOST	zero	zero	zero

Fuel 73 Octane (DTD 134).
Aircraft:
> Bristol 118
> Westland Wapiti IIA, III, V
> Westland-Houston P.V.3

JUPITER XFAM, 580 hp, geared, epicyclic .656:1, L.H. tractor-drive. As XFA, medium supercharged.
Aircraft:
> Hawker Hart

JUPITER XFBM, 580 hp, as Mk XFAM, bevel-geared, epicyclic .5:1. Medium supercharged.

A Jupiter XFBM, with valve gear fully protected, shrouded anti-ice and anti-oil.

Servicing the Jupiter XFBMs of a Handley Page 42W, Heracles type

Aircraft:
> Boulton & Paul P.32 (B.22/27)
> Handley Page 42W Heracles
> Short S.8 Calcutta
> Short S.17 Kent
> Short L.17 Scylla
> Supermarine Southampton X
> Vickers 214 Vildebeest IV
> Vickers 241 Victoria V

JUPITER XFS, fully supercharged.
Aircraft:
> de Havilland D.H.72
> Vickers 177 Fighter (F.21/26)

JUPITER XI, compression ratio 5.15:1, bevel-geared, epicyclic .5:1.
Aircraft:
> de Havilland D.H.50
> Fokker F.VIIA
> Vickers 147 Valiant

A Fokker F.VIIA powered by a Bristol Jupiter XI, at Croydon Airport in 1929. The Jupiter XI was the low-compression version of the Jupiter X engine, which was also adopted for the Handley Page H.P.42E (Eastern version, Hannibal-type).

JUPITER XIF, 500 hp, compression ratio 5.15:1, bevel-geared, epicyclic .5:1. Jupiter XI.FA geared .656:1.

Hannibal, the first Handley Page H.P.45, G-AAGX, usually known as the H.P.42E (Eastern version). The engines were low-compression Jupiter XIFs.

Aircraft:
> Bristol 109
> de Havilland D.H.61 Giant Moth

Gloster A.S.31 Survey
Handley Page H.P.42E (H.P.45) Hannibal class
Short S.8 Calcutta
Short S.8/8 Rangoon
Short S.11 Valetta
Vickers 172 Vellore III
Vickers 198 Viastra II
Vickers 209 Vildebeest III

JUPITER XIF.P., 525 hp, similar to Mk XIF, compression ratio 5.15:1. (P. indicates pressure-feed lubrication to the wrist-pins). Power Curve at rated altitude 2,000 ft from A.& A.E.E., Martlesham, Report M.612, dated 31.10.32. Power Curve at rated altitude sea level to 2,000 ft.

RPM	2,200	2,100	2,000	1,900	1,800	1,600
BHP	549	532	512	494	473	429

Max 549 bhp, 2,200 rpm, all-out level flight (5 min). Fuel 73 Octane (DTD 134).
Aircraft:
Saro A.7 Severn
Short S.11 Valetta

ORION I, (1926), based on Jupiter III, 9-cylinder, single-row radial, air-cooled, poppet-valve. Bore/stroke 5.75 x 7.5 in. Vol. 1,753 cu in. (146 x 190 mm. Vol. 28.7 litre). Compression ratio 5.3 :1, exhaust-driven turbo-supercharger. L.H. tractor-drive. Diameter 51.0 in. 9 engines built, 5 delivered. Ceiling at first only 6,000 ft on Goring but, after modification, design performance was obtained, maintaining constant power up to 24,000ft. Metallurgy problems caused programme to be abandoned.
Aircraft:
Gloster Gamecock I
Gloster Goring

LUCIFER I — *see* Cosmos, above.

LUCIFER II, 122 hp, similar to Mk I, 3-cylinder, single-row radial air-cooled, poppet-valve. Bore/stroke 5.75 x 6.25 in. Vol. 487 cu in. (146 x 159 mm. Vol. 8.0 litre). Compression ratio 4.8:1. Direct L.H. tractor-drive. Diameter 48.0 in.

Aircraft:
Avro 504N
Bristol 73 Taxiplane
Bristol 83 School Machine

LUCIFER III, 118 hp, (1923), as Mk II. Compression ratio 5.0:1.
Aircraft:
Bristol 73 Taxiplane
Bristol 83 School Machine
Parnall Peto

LUCIFER IV, 140 hp, (1925). Higher compression ratio, 5.3:1. Special racing version in Bristol 77 M.1D
Aircraft:
Avro 504N
Bristol 77 M.1D (Special Engine)
Bristol 83 School Machine
Handley Page H.P.32 Hamlet (Type D)
Parnall Peto

The high-compression racing Bristol Lucifer IV.

CHERUB I, 32 hp, (1923), 2-cylinder, horizontally-opposed, air-cooled, poppet-valve. Bore/stroke 3.35 x 3.8 in. Vol. 67 cu in. (85 x 96.5 mm. Vol. 1,095 cc), compression ratio 6:1. Direct L.H. tractor-drive. Width 25.6 in.

Bristol direct-drive Cherub I.

The three-cylinder Bristol Lucifer II.

Aircraft:
> Avro 562 Avis
> Beardmore W.B.XXIV Wee Bee
> Bristol 91 Brownie I
> Cranwell C.L.A.2, C.L.A.3
> Granger Archaeopteryx
> Messerschmitt M.17
> Short S.4 Satellite
> Supermarine Sparrow I
> Westland-Hill Pterodactyl I

CHERUB II, 34 hp, (1924), 0.5:1 spur-geared drive, R.H. tractor.
Aircraft:
> Avro 562 Avis
> Short S.1 Cockle
> Short S.4 Satellite

CHERUB III, 36 hp, (1924), similar to Mk I, Bore/stroke 3.54 x 3.8 in. Vol. 75 cu in. (90 x 96.5 mm. Vol. 1,228 litre), compression ratio 5.75:1. One with chain-driven reduction gear supplied to R.A.E. in 1925.

The unique chain-geared Bristol Cherub III, supplied to R.A.E. Farnborough.

The spur-geared Bristol Cherub II.

Aircraft:
> ANEC II
> B.A.C.Drone
> Beardmore W.B.XXIV Wee Bee
> Bristol 91A Brownie I
> Bristol 91B Brownie II
> Bristol 98 Brownie III
> Cranwell C.L.A.4, 4A
> De Bruyne-Maas Ladybird
> de Havilland D.H.53 Humming Bird

> Halton H.A.C.1 Mayfly
> Hawker Cygnet
> Heath Parasol
> Martin Monoplane
> Mignet HM 14 Pou du Ciel
> Parnall Pixie III, IIIA
> R.A.E. Hurricane
> R.A.E. (P.B.) Scarab
> Supermarine Sparrow II
> Vickers 98 Vagabond
> Westland Woodpigeon I
> Westland-Hill Pterodactyl IA

TITAN I, 205 hp, (1928), 5-cylinder, single-row radial air-cooled poppet-valve. It was made as the Titan I with cast poultice heads and Titan IF, with forged penthouse heads. Bore/stroke 5.75 x 6.5 in. Vol. 844 cu. in (146 x 165 mm. Vol. 13.8 litre). Compression ratio 5.0:1. Direct L.H. tractor-drive. Diameter 48.4 in.
Aircraft:
> Avro 504N
> Bristol 83 Trainer
> Bristol 110A

Bristol Titan I, with cast poultice heads.

The Halton H.S.C.1 Mayfly, with a Cherub III.

Avro 504N G-EBKQ with A Bristol Titan I.

TITAN IIF, similar to IF but with altered valve operating gear.

TITAN IV, 205 hp, (1928), 5-cylinder, single-row radial air-cooled poppet-valve. Bore/stroke 5.75 x 6.5 in. Vol. 844 cu. in (146 x 165 mm. Vol. 13.8 litre). Compression ratio 5.0:1. Geared (standard Jupiter reduction gear .5:1), L.H. tractor-drive. Was originally known as Titan II (Special)
Aircraft:
    Bristol 83E Trainer

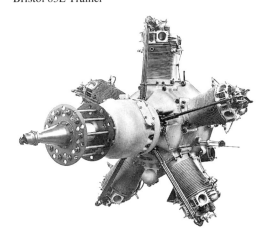

Geared Titan IV with cast poultice heads.

Titan IF, forged penthouse heads.

NEPTUNE I, 290 hp, (1930) 7-cylinder, single-row radial air-cooled poppet-valve. Bore/stroke 5.75 x 6.5 in. Vol. 1,182 cu. in (146 x 165 mm. Vol. 19.3 litre). Compression ratio 5:1. Instead of the spiral induction system previously used by Bristol, a fan was used to ensure even distribution. Cast penthouse heads. Direct drive, L.H. tractor-drive. Diameter 48.4 in.
Aircraft:
    Bristol 110A

Bristol Neptune I, with cast penthouse heads.

BRISTOL MERCURY. The first Mercury to be designed under Roy Fedden's direction, was a Brazil Straker engine but, for a complexity of reasons, appears under the Bristol Aeroplane Co., (Cosmos) title (q.v.) and was a two-row, 14-cylinder radial engine, totally different from the Bristol engine of that name.

Titan IIF, with forged heads but altered valve operating gear.

More familiar is the Bristol engine of that name, a nine-cylinder, single-row radial. It will be seen that there is some apparent confusion between the designations of some of the early Mercury and Pegasus (q.v.) engines. Both were evolved from the nine-cylinder, air-cooled Jupiter which, as Roy Fedden's masterpiece, had been developed at the end of the First World War. Continuing the same 5.75-inch bore, the 9-cylinder Mercury had a 6.5 inch stroke, one inch shorter than that of the Jupiter. The rpm was raised and so was the power output and this engine was intended for the then new concept of the fast-climbing interceptor fighter. A Mercury was also modified to have a very short (5 inch) stroke, this being tried out on the Bristol Bullpup but the experiment was not pursued further. New developments in materials and cooling techniques helped to make a success of the Mercury and the A and B versions of the Mercury V, VI, VII and VIII reverted to the 7.5 inch stroke of the faithful old Jupiter.

The longer stroke, combined with a similar piston speed combined to keep crankshaft rotation speed at a level suitable for gearing to the plodding requirements of the long-range bomber and reconnaissance flying-boat. These variants therefore formed the basis for the lengthy and successful series of Bristol engines named Pegasus. It is worth recording that the total number of Mercury engines produced by Bristol and its shadow factories between 1939 and 1945 was about 32,000. A similar number of Pegasus was also built.

The combinations of numbers and letters which follow the names of Mercury (and Pegasus) engines have a definite meaning, indicating the principal characteristics of the respective engines. The first Roman numeral indicates the Series, or Mark of the engine. Difference of a major character result in a different Series, or Mark. This is followed by a letter showing whether the engine is naturally aspirated (unsupercharged) or supercharged and to what degree. Following this, the numeral 2, or 3 indicates the propeller reduction gear ratio.

Thus, I, II, III etc, is the Series.

F.   Engine-speed Induction Fan.
U.   Induction fan, geared 4.5:1, better mix, to about 500ft.
L.   Low Duty fan, geared 5.7:1, supercharged to 1,500 ft.
M.   Fan geared 7:1, Moderately Supercharged to 5-7,000 ft.
P.   Persia. Ran on locally available DTD 134 fuel.
S.   Fan geared 10:1, Fully Supercharged to 10-15,000 ft.

2.   Airscrew Reduction Gear ratio .655:1.
2A. Airscrew Reduction Gear ratio .666:1.
3.   Airscrew Reduction Gear ratio .5:1.
4.   Airscrew Reduction Gear ratio .572:1.

UNSUPERCHARGED MERCURY
MERCURY VIA, VIB, VIIIA, VIIIB

SINGLE-SPEED, SINGLE-STAGE SUPERCHARGED
MERCURY
MERCURY I, II , III , IV , IVS.2, V , V, VIS, VISP, VIS.2,
VIIA, VIIB, VIII, IX, XI, XII, XV, XVI, XX, 25, 30, 31

Bristol Mercury 9-cylinder, single-row, air-cooled, poppet-valve radial engines had the following in common:-
Bore/stroke (standard engine) 5.75 x 6.5 in. (146.0 x 165.0 mm)
Swept Volume 1,520 cu in (24.9 litre).
Compression Ratio — see text.
Dimensions vary according to accessories.
Diameter 51.5 in; length 47.0 in.
Short stroke engine, diameter 47.0 in.
Weights, where published — see Performance tables.

Compression ratio, supercharge and boost (see text). Epicyclic-geared — reduction ratio as in text, all having L.H. drive. Those from the Mk VIII onwards had controllable-pitch propellers, the later Mercuries being equipped with constant-speed units or converted to them. Long-stroke versions of the engine were later renamed Pegasus, q.v. The experimental short-stroke engine had a 5 inch stroke and a correspondingly smaller diameter, q.v.

Fuel. Initially DTD 224, 77 Octane and the first Mercury to be able to use DTD 230, (87 Octane) fuel was the Mk VI.S of 1933. A

strengthened engine was required for using this fuel but a 'lightened' series was introduced two years later. The first of these were the Mks VII, VIII and IX. After 100 Octane fuel became available, from early 1940, it was used in the Mercuries 30 and 31.

Dry weight and dimensions, which varied from one Mark to another, depended on the type of engine and the accessories fitted, whether geared or not, all being supercharged (single-speed, single-stage). Examples, as above, basically, were:-

UNGEARED MERCURIES, Mks I, II & IIA. Dry Wt. 680 lb.
GEARED MERCURIES, Mks III to 31. Dry Wt. 940 — Dry Wt. 1,065 lb.

After the Mk VII, standard Mercuries in service ran at a maximum 2,650 rpm on take-off and, when diving, had a 20-second peak limit, diving, of 3,120 rpm.

MERCURY I, 808 hp, (1926), 9-cylinder, single-row radial air-cooled poppet-valve engine, resembling the Jupiter VI but having a reduced diameter, due to a reduced stroke and redesigned cylinder head. At the same time, the rpm was increased. Bore/stroke 5.75 x 6.5 in. Compression ratio 6.25:1, ground boosted. Direct L.H. tractor-drive. This was a supercharged racing engine, designed for the 1926 Schneider Trophy Contest and developed 960 hp for a short period on the test-bench.
Aircraft:
Short-Bristow Crusader (7/26)

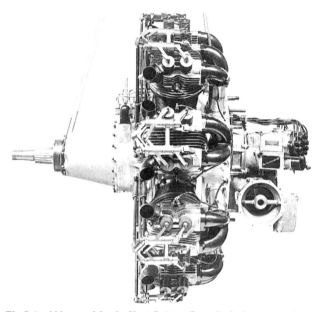

The Bristol Mercury I for the Short-Bristow Crusader had a cast penthouse head, a single compensating gear and direct drive. The extended drive shaft reduced torsional vibration and gave a smooth entry for the big radial engine.

The Mercury engine of the Short-Bristow Crusader with cylinder 'helmets' lifted.

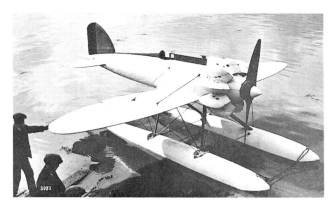

The Short-Bristow Crusader, a 1927 Schneider Trophy entry powered by the supercharged Bristol Mercury I. It crashed at Venice before the race, due to crossed aileron controls.

MERCURY II, 420 hp, (1928), Compression ratio 5.3:1, fully supercharged. Direct L.H. tractor.
Aircraft:
    Bristol 101

MERCURY IIA, 440 hp, (1928), Compression ratio 5.3:1, fully supercharged. Direct L.H. tractor-drive.
Aircraft:
    Bristol 107 Bullpup
    Fairey Flycatcher II
    Gloster Gamecock I
    Gloster Gnatsnapper I
    Gloster S.S.18 (F.10/27)
    Hawker Hoopoe
    Vickers 151 Jockey F.20/27
    Westland Interceptor F.20/27

MERCURY III, 485 hp, (1929), compression ratio 4.8:1, bevel-geared, epicyclic reduction .5:1. Fully supercharged. L.H. tractor-drive.
Aircraft:
    Bristol 105A Bulldog III
    Westland Interceptor F.20/27

MERCURY IIIA, generally similar to Mk III, with modifications to suit particular installations. Compression ratio .5:1, fully supercharged. Geared, epicyclic reduction .5:1. L.H. tractor-drive.
Aircraft:
    Westland C.O.W. Gun F.29/27

MERCURY IV, 485 hp, (1929), compression ratio 4.8:1, fully supercharged. Geared, epicyclic reduction .656:1. L.H. tractor-drive.
Aircraft:
    Bristol 105A Bulldog IIIA
    Gloster S.S.37 Gladiator prototype
    Hawker Audax

MERCURY IVA, 510 hp, (1931), compression ratio 5.3:1. Fully supercharged. Geared, epicyclic reduction .656:1. L.H. tractor-drive.
Aircraft:
    Bristol 105A Bulldog IIIA

MERCURY IVS.2, 510 hp, (1932), compression ratio 5.3:1. Fully supercharged. Geared, .655:1, epicyclic reduction L.H. tractor-drive. Power Curve at rated altitude 13,000 ft from A.& A.E.E., Martlesham, Report M.606, dated 9/32. Fully supercharged. Boost, rated zero lb/sq inch. Max 1.5 lb/sq inch., 2,600 rpm.

RPM	2,600	2,450	2,350	2,250	2,150	2,050
BHP	635	585	551	515	468	435
BOOST	+1.5lb			zero		

Max boost +1.5lb/sq inch. 635 bhp, 2,600 rpm take off to 1,000 ft or one minute. Fuel 73 Octane (DTD 134).
Aircraft:
    Bristol 105A Bulldog IV

The Bristol 105A Bulldog IV with a Mercury IVS.2, an early long-chord cowling with cooling-gills open.

MERCURY (Short stroke), 390 hp, similar to other engines in the series, apart from the reduced stroke. This was a 'one-off' experiment, flown in a Bristol 107 Bullpup and was not successful enough to pursue further. 9-cylinder, single-row radial, air-cooled, poppet-valve. Bore/stroke 5.75 x 5.0 in. Vol. 1,169 cu in. (146 x 127 mm. Vol. 19.1 litre). Compression ratio 5.3:1. Fully supercharged. Geared, epicyclic reduction .656:1. L.H. tractor-drive. Initial power rating, before blower drive gear ratio was modified — Take-off 400 hp/2,500 rpm, +1.5 lb.; Normal 390 hp/2,500 rpm, +.25 lb., 12,000 ft; Max 480 hp, 2,750 rpm, 12,000 ft. Diameter 47.0 in.
Aircraft:
    Bristol 107 Bullpup.

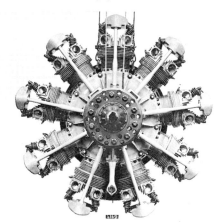

The geared, blown short-stroke Bristol Mercury.

MERCURY V, 546 hp, compression ratio 5.3:1, geared, epicyclic reduction .656:1. This engine became the Pegasus IS.2.
Aircraft:
    Bristol 118A

MERCURY VIS, 605 hp, (1933), compression ratio 6:1. Fully supercharged. Bevel-geared, epicyclic reduction .5:1. L.H. tractor-drive. Power Curve at rated altitude 12,500 ft from A.& A.E.E., Martlesham, Report M.654, dated 26.3.36.

RPM	2,750	2,600	2,500	2,400	2,300	2,200
BHP	752	694	663	604	568	532
BOOST	+2.5lb			+1lb		

Max boost +2.5 lb/sq inch. 750 bhp, 2,750 rpm take off to 1,000 ft or one minute. All-out level flight (five minutes), +1 lb, 2,750 rpm. Fuel 87 Octane (DTD 230).
Aircraft: Gloster S.S.19B
        Gloster Gauntlet I (F.24/33), II

A Bristol Mercury VIS, as fitted to the Gloster Gauntlet. This engine was developed into the widely-used MKVIII

Bristol Mercury VIS in a Gloster Gauntlet I.

MERCURY VISP, 605 hp, (1931), compression ratio. Fully supercharged. Geared, epicyclic reduction .5:1. L.H. tractor-drive. Designation 'P' is 'Persia'. Engine de-rated for fuel, locally available, equivalent to DTD 134, 73 Octane.
Aircraft:
        Hawker Fury (Persia) F.13/30.

MERCURY VIS.2, 605 hp, (1933), compression ratio 6:1. Fully supercharged. Geared, epicyclic reduction .655:1. L.H. tractor-drive. Power Curve at rated altitude 12,500 ft from A.& A.E.E., Martlesham, Report M.677, dated 28.8.36. Boost, rated +1 lb/sq inch. (Note, by its reduction gear, this was strictly a Mercury VIS.2A but the gear was easily changed).

RPM	2,750	2,600	2,500	2,400	2,300	2,200
BHP	738	688	646	610	570	538
BOOST	+2.5lb			+1lb		

Max boost +2.5 lb/sq inch. 738 bhp, 2,750 rpm take off to 1,000 ft or one minute. Fuel 87 Octane (DTD 230).
Aircraft:
        Bristol 105A Bulldog IVA
        Bristol 133
        Bristol 142 'Britain First'
        Gloster S.S.37 Gladiator prototype F.7/30

Bristol 133 fighter, with a Mercury VIS.2 engine.

MERCURY VIA, 575 hp, (1928), Compression ratio 5.3:1, Geared, epicyclic reduction .656:1. This engine was renamed the Pegasus IU.2.
Aircraft:
        Hawker F.20/27
        Hawker Hoopoe
        Hawker Hart

MERCURY VIIA, 560 hp, Compression ratio 5.3:1, Geared, epicyclic .656:1. Was renamed Pegasus IM.2.
Aircraft:
        Fokker G.1 ('Le Faucheur')
        Gloster Goring

MERCURY VIII, 825 hp, (1935), compression ratio 6.25:1. Fully supercharged. Geared, epicyclic reduction .572:1. L.H. tractor-drive. Lightened engine, ME-3S(a)57. Power Curve at rated altitude 13,000 ft from A.& A.E.E., Martlesham, Report M.668, dated 8.3.38. Boost, rated +5 lb/sq inch.

RPM	2,750	2,650	2,400
BHP	837	802	694
BOOST	+5lb	+5lb	+3.5lb

Max boost +5 lb/sq inch. 840 bhp, 2,750 rpm take off to 1,000 ft or one minute. All-out level flight (five minutes), +5 lb, 840 bhp, 2,750 rpm. Fuel 87 Octane (DTD 230).
Aircraft:
        Airspeed A.S.45 Cambridge (T.4/39)
        Bristol 142M Blenheim I
        Bristol 149 Blenheim IV, Bolingbroke I, III
        Gloster F.5/34,
        Hawker Hart
        Hawker Hind (Persia)

MERCURY VIIIA. This engine was the Mercury VIII when fitted with the Constantinesco gun-gear for the Gloster Gladiator and was renamed MERCURY VIIIA (not to be confused with the second MERCURY VIIIA, below.
Aircraft:
        Gloster Gladiator I (F.7/30)
        Gloster Sea Gladiator I

The starboard Mercury VIII of a Bristol 142M Blenheim I.

The uncowled Mercury VIII of a Bristol 142M Blenheim I, showing cooling gills which were hand-operated by the pilot. Though effective, they could cause considerable drag.

The Gloster Gladiator I with a Mercury VIIIA. This is the same engine as the Mk VIII except for the C.C. interrupter gear for the twin synchronized fuselage guns.

The ingenious way Mercury VIIIs were transported in pairs to be mounted in a Blenheim I.

MERCURY VIIIA, 535 hp, Compression ratio 5.3:1, unsupercharged. Geared, epicyclic .656:1. Was renamed Pegasus IU.2P.

MERCURY IX, 825 hp, (1935), compression ratio 6.25:1. Fully supercharged. Geared, epicyclic reduction .5:1. (experimentally .572:1), L.H. tractor-drive. Lightened engine, ME-3S(a)50. Power Curve at rated altitude 13,000 ft from A.& A.E.E., Martlesham, Report M.666, dated 10.9.37. Boost, rated +5 lb/sq inch. Max +5 lb/sq inch., 2,650 rpm.

RPM	2,750	2,650	2,500	2,400	2,200
BHP	852	820	730	685	589
BOOST	+5.66lb	+5.08lb	+3.73lb	+3.17lb	+1.73lb

Max boost +5 lb/sq inch. 840 bhp, 2,750 rpm take off to 1,000 ft or one minute. All-out level flight (five minutes), +5 lb, 840 bhp, 2,750 rpm. Fuel 87 Octane (DTD 230).
Aircraft:
> Blackburn B-24 Skua I
> Bristol 146
> Bristol 148
> Gloster F.5/34 Gladiator II
> Gloster Sea Gladiator I
> Hawker Hind (Latvia)
> Westland Lysander prototype

MERCURY X, 820 hp, (1937). Compression ratio 6.25:1. Medium supercharged. Geared, epicyclic reduction .666:1. L.H. tractor-drive, ME-3M(a)66.

MERCURY XI, 820 hp, (1937). Compression ratio 6.25:1. Medium supercharged. Geared, epicyclic reduction .572:1. L.H. tractor-drive. ME-3M(a)57.
Aircraft:
> Hawker Hart

MERCURY XII, 820 hp, (1937). Compression ratio 6.25:1, medium supercharged. Geared, epicyclic reduction .5:1. L.H. tractor-drive, ME-3M(a)50. Power Curve at rated altitude 3,500 ft from A.& A.E.E., Martlesham, Report M.694, dated 27.7.36. Boost, rated +3.5 lb/sq inch. Max 3.5 lb/sq inch., 2,650 rpm.

RPM	2,750	2,650	2,500	2,400	2,200
BHP	905	868	820	786	689
BOOST	+5.3lb	+4.82lb	+4.35lb	+3.9lb	+2.89lb

Max boost +5.3 lb/sq inch. 905 bhp, 2,750 rpm take off to 1,000 ft or one minute. All-out level flight (five minutes), +3.5 lb, 905 bhp, 2,750 rpm. Fuel 87 Octane (DTD 230).
Aircraft:
> Westland Lysander I

MERCURY XV, 825 hp, (1938), developed from and similar to Mk VIII, compression ratio 6.25:1. Fully supercharged. Geared, epicyclic reduction .572:1. L.H. tractor-drive. (converted to 100 Octane fuel from 87 Octane).
Aircraft:

> Bristol 149 Blenheim IV
> Bristol 149 Bolingbroke IV
> Miles M.19 Master II
> Westland Lysander I

MERCURY XVI, 830 hp, compression ratio 5.3:1, Geared, epicyclic .572:1
Aircraft:

> Bristol 160 Bisley I

MERCURY XX, 810 hp, (1940), compression ratio 6.25:1, medium supercharged. Geared, epicyclic reduction .572:1. L.H. tractor-drive. ME-6M, developed from Mk XV with 8.25 inch impeller, 87 Octane fuel. Max 3,120 rpm for 20 seconds). Power Curve at rated altitude 2,500 ft from A.& A.E.E., Martlesham, Report M.694, dated 20.3.41. Boost, rated +4.25 lb/sq inch.

RPM	2,750	2,400
BHP	870	810
BOOST	+4.25lb	+4.25lb

Max boost +4.25 lb/sq inch. 870 bhp, 2,750 rpm take off to 1,000 ft or one minute. All-out level flight (five minutes), +4.25 lb, 870 bhp, 2,750 rpm, 4,500 ft. Max rpm 20 sec. 3,120. Fuel 87 Octane (DTD 230).
Aircraft:

> Bristol 149 Bolingbroke IV, IVT
> Miles M.19 Master II
> Miles M.25 Martinet I (12/41)
> Miles M.37 Martinet Trainer
> Miles M.50 Queen Martinet
> Westland Lysander III, IIIA

MERCURY 25, 825 hp, (1941), compression ratio 6.25:1, Fully supercharged. Geared, epicyclic reduction .572:1. L.H. tractor-drive. Was a Mk XV, with fixed crankpin sleeve and locked wrist pins. Converted to 100 Octane fuel.
Aircraft:

> Bristol 160 Blenheim V

MERCURY 26, 825 hp, compression ratio 6.25:1, fully supercharged. Geared, epicyclic reduction .572:1. L.H. tractor-drive, As Mercury 25, with single lever carburettor.

MERCURY 30, 810 hp, (1941), compression ratio 6.25:1, medium supercharged. Geared, epicyclic reduction .572:1. L.H. tractor-drive. Fuel 100 Octane. As Mercury XX, with fixed crankpin sleeve and locked wrist pins. ME-10M.
Aircraft:

> Boulton & Paul P.108 (T.7/45)
> Bristol 160 Blenheim V
> Miles M.25 Martinet I (12/41)
> Miles M.50 Queen Martinet
> Supermarine 309 Sea Otter
> Westland Lysander III, IIIA

MERCURY 31, 810 hp, (1945), compression ratio 6.25:1, medium supercharged. Geared, epicyclic reduction .572:1. L.H. tractor-drive. As Mercury 30 but with a single lever carburettor and fixed-pitch propeller.
Aircraft:

> General Aircraft Hamilcar X

PEGASUS.
The Bristol Pegasus started off as a long-stroke version of the Mercury, thereby reverting to the same internal dimensions as the earlier Jupiter, which had itself superseded by the Mercury, the displacement figure thus turning full circle.

Combinations of numbers and letters which follow the names of Pegasus (and Mercury) engines have a definite meaning, indicating the principal characteristics of the respective engines. At first, they may seem enormously complicated but, when studied, are logical. The first Roman numeral indicates the Series, or Mark of the engine. Difference of a major character result in a different Series, or Mark. This is followed by a letter showing whether the engine is naturally aspirated (unsupercharged) or supercharged and to what degree. Following this, the numeral 2, or 3 indicates the propeller reduction gear ratio.

Thus, I, II, III etc, is the Series.

F. Engine-speed Induction Fan.
U. Induction fan, geared 4.5:1, better mix, to about 500ft.
L. Low Duty fan, geared 5.7:1, supercharged to 1,500 ft.
M. Fan geared 7:1, Moderately Supercharged to 5-7,000 ft.
P. Pusher installation.
S. Fan geared 10:1, Fully Supercharged to 10-15,000 ft.
2. Airscrew Reduction Gear ratio .655:1.
2A. Airscrew Reduction Gear ratio .666:1.
3. Airscrew Reduction Gear ratio .5:1.
4. Airscrew Reduction Gear ratio .572:1.

NOTE: Where necessary, reduction gear ratios on Experimental PE-type engines were also denoted by the addition, to type symbols, of 50, for .500 gear; 57 for .572 gear; 66 for .666 gear; e.g. PE-6S57.

SINGLE-SPEED, SINGLE-STAGE SUPERCHARGED PEGASUS
PEGASUS I, II, III, LC, IV, V, VI, VII, VIII, IX, X, XI, XII, XIII, XV, XIX, XX, 21, 22, 23, 24, 25, 26, 27, 30, 38, LC

TWO-SPEED, SINGLE-STAGE SUPERCHARGED PEGASUS
PEGASUS XVII, XVIII, 48

Bristol Pegasus 9-cylinder, air-cooled single-row poppet-valve radial engines had the following in common:-
Bore/stroke 5.75 x 7.5 in. (146.0 x 190.0 mm)
Swept Volume 1,753.0 cu in. (28.7 litre)
Dimensions vary according to accessories.
Diameter 55.3 in; Length, two-speed supercharged, 61.0 in
Weights, where published — *see* Performance tables.

Compression ratio, supercharge and boost (*see* text). Epicyclic-geared — reduction ratio as in text, all having L.H. drive. Those from the Mk X onwards being provided for controllable-pitch propellers, the later Pegasus engines being equipped with constant-speed units or converted to them.

A sectioned early Bristol Pegasus

Fuel. The first Pegasus to be able to use DTD 230, (87 Octane) fuel was the Mk X of 1938. A strengthened engine was required for using this fuel. The first of these to enter service was the Mk XC for Imperial Airways 'Empire' flying-boats. After 100 Octane fuel became available, from early 1940, it was available for use in suitably modified Pegasus engines.

Dry weight and Dimensions. These varied from one Mark to another, variations of weight and length, depending on the type of engine and the accessories fitted, direct-drive or propeller reduction gear, unsupercharged or supercharged (single-speed, single-stage). Examples, as above, basically, were:-

UNSUPERCHARGED PEGASUS, Mk IF, IU and IIU series (with an engine-speed or a slightly-geared induction fan to improve mixing, instead of the early induction spiral).
Mk I, Dry Wt. 680 lb.

SUPERCHARGED PEGASUS, Mks II to 48.
Mk IV, Dry Wt. 940 lb.
Mk 38, Dry Wt. 1,180 lb.

Early Pegasus ran at around 2,250 rpm at take-off but, from the Mk X, standard Pegasus in service, ran at a maximum 2,600 rpm on take-off and had a 20-second peak limit, when diving, of 3,120 rpm.

PEGASUS IF, 546 hp, compression ratio 5.3:1. Geared, epicyclic reduction .5:1. L.H. tractor-drive.

PEGASUS IM, 590 hp, (1932), 9-cylinder, single-row radial air-cooled poppet-valve. Bore/stroke 5.75 x 7.5 in. Vol. 1,753 cu in. (146 x 190 mm. Vol. 28.7 litre). Compression ratio 5.3:1, medium supercharged. Geared, epicyclic .5:1. L.H. tractor-drive.

PEGASUS IM.2, 590 hp, (1933), compression ratio 6.25:1, medium supercharged. Geared, epicyclic reduction .655:1. L.H. tractor-drive. Was originally the long-stroke Mercury VIIA. Power Curve at rated altitude 4,500 ft from A.& A.E.E., Martlesham, Report M.512, dated 15.1.33. Boost, rated zero lb/sq inch.

RPM	2,300	2,000	1,800
BHP	695	586	526
BOOST	+1lb	zero	

Max boost +1 lb/sq inch. 695 bhp, 2,300 rpm take off to 1,000 ft or one minute. All-out level flight (five minutes), +1 lb, 695 bhp, 2,300 rpm. Fuel 73 Octane (DTD 134).
Aircraft:
> Boulton & Paul P.64 Mailplane
> Hawker Hart (Sweden)
> Westland Wallace I
> Westland Wapiti

PEGASUS IM.3, 590 hp, (1933). Compression ratio 6.25:1, medium supercharged. Geared, epicyclic reduction .5:1. L.H. tractor-drive. Was originally the long-stroke Mercury VIIB. Power Curve at rated altitude 4,500 ft from A.& A.E.E., Martlesham, Report M.593, dated 8.2.33. Boost, rated zero lb/sq inch. Max +1 lb/sq inch., 2,000 rpm.

RPM	2,300	2,000	1,800
BHP	665	540	529
BOOST	+1lb	zero	

Max boost +1 lb/sq inch. 600 bhp, rpm take off to 1,000 ft or one minute. All-out level flight (five minutes), zero lb, 552 bhp, 2,000 rpm. Fuel 73 Octane (DTD 134).
Aircraft:
> Blackburn B.5 Ripon V
> Blackburn B.5 Baffin
> Boulton & Paul P.29 Sidestrand III
> Boulton & Paul P.75 Overstrand I
> Bristol 120
> Handley Page H.P.43 (C.16/28)
> Hawker Hart
> Vickers 195, 255 Vanox (B.19/27)

> Vickers 212 Vellox
> Vickers 244 Vildebeest I
> Vickers 248 Victoria V
> Vickers 251 Vildebeest X
> Vickers 257 Vildebeest XII
> Vickers 259 Viastra X
> Vickers 263 Vildebeest T.S.R.
> Westland Wallace prototype
> Westland Wallace I

PEGASUS IS.2, 546 hp. Compression ratio 5.3:1, fully supercharged. L.H. tractor-drive, geared epicyclic reduction .656:1. Was previously the long-stroke Mercury VA, before becoming the Pegasus IS.2.

PEGASUS IS.3, 550 hp, (1933). Compression ratio 5.3:1. Geared, epicyclic reduction .5:1. Previously the long-stroke Mercury VB, this became the Pegasus IS.3. The Vespa VII gained World's Altitude Record in September, 1932.
Aircraft:
> Vickers 250 Vespa VII
> Westland-Houston PV-3

The Vickers Vespa VII, powered by a Pegasus IS.3, before a height record attempt in September, 1932. The engine has an early Townend cowling ring.

The Vickers Vespa VII, having attained the World's Altitude Record of 43,976 feet in September, 1932, powered by a Pegasus IS.3. Centre is the pilot, Captain C.F. Uwins, left — Roy Fedden, right Rex Pierson of Vickers Ltd, with barograph.

Westland Wallace

PEGASUS IU.2, previously the long-stroke Mercury VIA, 575 hp, (1928), compression ratio 5.3:1, geared, epicyclic reduction .656:1.
Aircraft:
> Hawker Hart

PEGASUS IU.2P, previously the long-stroke Mercury VIIIA, 535 hp, compression ratio 5.3:1. Geared, epicyclic .656:1. R.H. pusher-drive.

PEGASUS IU.3, previously the long-stroke Mercury VIB, 575 hp, (1928), geared, epicyclic .5:1.

PEGASUS IU.3P, previously the long-stroke Mercury VIIIB, 535 hp, compression ratio 5.3:1. Geared, epicyclic .5:1.

PEGASUS IIL.2, 625 hp, (1934), compression ratio 5.5:1, low supercharged. Geared, epicyclic reduction .655:1. L.H. tractor-drive.
Aircraft:
> Gloster Goring

PEGASUS IIL.2P, 625 hp, (1934), compression ratio 5.5:1 low supercharged. Geared, epicyclic reduction .655:1. R.H. pusher-drive.
Aircraft:
> Supermarine Seagull V

PEGASUS IIL.3, 625 hp, (1934), compression ratio 5.5:1, low supercharged. Geared, epicyclic reduction .5:1. L.H. tractor-drive.
Aircraft:
> Vickers 252 Vildebeest XI
> Vickers 259 Viastra X
> Vickers 260, 262, 269 Victoria VI (Valentia)

Vickers Valentia K2340, with Pegasus IIL.2 engines.

PEGASUS IIM, 620 hp, (1934), compression ratio 5.5:1, medium supercharged. Geared, epicyclic reduction .5:1. L.H. tractor-drive.
Aircraft:
> Fairey TSR I
> Hawker Audax (Persia)
> Hawker Hart (Persia)

PEGASUS IIM.2, 620 hp, (1934), compression ratio 5.5:1, medium supercharged. Geared, epicyclic reduction .5:1. L.H. tractor-drive.
Aircraft:
> Hawker Osprey
> Hawker Audax (Iraq)

PEGASUS IIM.2P, R.H. pusher-drive.
Aircraft:
> Supermarine Walrus I

PEGASUS IIM.3, 620 hp, (1934), compression ratio 5.5:1, medium supercharged. Geared, epicyclic reduction .5:1. L.H. tractor-drive. Power Curve at rated altitude 5,000 ft, from A.& A.E.E., Martlesham, Report M.665, dated 27.9.33. Boost, rated zero lb/sq inch.

RPM	2,300	2,200	2,100	2,000	1,900	1,800
BHP	674	643	610	576	536	515
BOOST	+1.5lb			zero		

Max boost +1.5 lb/sq inch. 674 bhp, rpm take off to 1,000 ft or one minute. All-out level flight (five minutes), +1.5 lb, 580 bhp, 2,300 rpm. Fuel 73 Octane (DTD 134).
Aircraft:
> Blackburn T.5 Ripon IIF
> Blackburn B-5 Baffin
> Boulton & Paul P.75 Overstrand I
> Fairey G.4/31
> Vickers 253 G.4/31 (Biplane)

Vickers 258 Vildebeest II
Vickers 264, 276, 278, 282, 283 Valentia
Vickers 266 Vincent
Vickers 267, 277 Vildebeest III
Vickers 268 Virginia X
Westland Wallace I, II

PEGASUS IIU, 595 hp, compression ratio 5.5:1. Geared, epicyclic reduction .655:1. L.H.tractor-drive,

PEGASUS LC, (previously called Pegasus III-LC), 595 hp, compression ratio 5.5:1, low supercharged. Geared, epicyclic reduction .5:1. L.H. tractor-drive. Commercial engine.

PEGASUS MC, (previously called Pegasus III-MC), 595 hp, compression ratio 5.5:1, medium supercharged. Geared, epicyclic reduction .5:1. L.H. tractor-drive. Commercial engine.

PEGASUS IIIM.2, 690 hp, 1935, compression ratio 6:1, became Pegasus VI, medium supercharged. Geared, epicyclic reduction .666:1. L.H. tractor-drive.
Aircraft:
> Bristol 130 (C.26/31) Bombay prototype
> Fairey Swordfish I (S.15/33)
> Handley Page 47 (G.4/31)
> Hawker Hart
> Vickers 266 Vincent

Hawker Hart, G-ABTN with a Bristol Pegasus IIIM.2

PEGASUS IIIM.3, 690 hp, (1935), compression ratio 6:1, medium supercharged. Geared, epicyclic reduction .5:1. L.H. tractor-drive. Previously called Pegasus III-M(3). Often abbreviated to Pegasus III. Power Curve at rated altitude 3,500 ft from A.& A.E.E., Martlesham, Report M.648, dated 3.1934. Medium supercharged. Boost, rated +0.5lb/sq inch. Max +2.0lb/sq inch, 2,525 rpm, 4,500 ft. Fuel 87 Octane (DTD 230).

RPM	2,525	2,400	2,300	2,200	2,100	2,000
BHP	777	744	705	677	646	612
BOOST	+2.0lb			+0.5lb		

Aircraft:
> Blackburn T.9A Shark II
> Blackburn T.9B Shark III
> Bristol 130 (C.26/31) Bombay prototype
> Fairey Seal
> Fairey TSR II
> Fairey Swordfish I
> Handley Page H.P.47
> Handley Page H.P.51
> Hawker Hart
> Hawker P.V.4 (G.4/31)
> Parnall G.4/31
> Saro A.27 London I
> Supermarine Stranraer
> Vickers 212 Vellox
> Vickers 246 G.4/31 Monoplane (Wellesley prototype)
> Vickers 266 Vincent
> Westland P.V.7 G.4/31 (Wallace prototype)

PEGASUS IIIS.2, 700 hp, 1935, similar to the Pegasus IV, Compression ratio 6:1, fully supercharged. Geared, epicyclic reduction .666:1. L.H. tractor-drive,

PEGASUS IV, 700 hp, (1933), compression ratio 6:1, fully supercharged. Geared, epicyclic reduction .5:1. L.H. tractor-drive. Previously called Pegasus III-S(3). Later renamed Pegasus VIII with altered reduction gear.
Aircraft:

    Boulton & Paul P.29 Sidestrand III
    Bristol 138A, 2/34
    Hawker P.V.4
    Koolhoven F.K.52
    Westland Wallace II

PEGASUS V, 690 hp, 1935, was the Pegasus IIIM.4. Compression ratio 6:1, medium supercharged. Geared, epicyclic reduction .572:1. L.H. tractor-drive,

PEGASUS VI, 690 hp, (1937), was Pegasus IIIM.2, compression ratio 6:1, medium supercharged. Geared, epicyclic reduction .666:1. L.H. tractor-drive.
Aircraft:

    Douglas DC-2
    Hawker Audax/Nisr Iraq (Avro 674)
    Junkers Ju 52/3m
    Junkers Ju 86

Pegasus VI trial installation in a Junkers Ju 52/3m, with a Hamilton bracket-type variable-pitch propeller.

The Bristol 138A high-altitude monoplane with a special Pegasus PE.6S. This drove a separate supercharger through a flexible shaft, feeding compressed air to the main supercharger through an intercooler.

PEGASUS PE.6S, 500 hp, a special high-altitude, fully-supercharged engine, with an extra second-stage supercharger driven by a flexible shaft and clutch, with an inter-cooler (mounted externally, below and behind the cowling). The auxiliary blower was engaged at about 35,000 feet. After initially successful flights, the engine's supercharger impeller and the propeller were both modified. The World's Altitude Record was attained at 53,937 feet, in a flight by Flt Lt M.J.Adam on 30 June 1937; a Record homologated by the F.A.I. the following November.
Aircraft:

    Bristol 138A

PEGASUS VIP, 690 hp, as Pegasus VI, compression ratio 6:1, medium supercharged. Geared, epicyclic reduction .666:1. L.H. pusher drive.
Aircraft:

    Supermarine Walrus I, II.

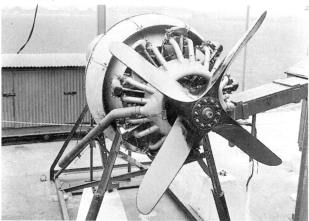

Pegasus VIP, a test of the pusher installation for the Supermarine Seagull V.

PEGASUS VII, 620 hp, Pegasus VI with a II-M rating. Compression ratio 5.5:1, medium supercharged. Geared, epicyclic reduction .5:1. L.H. tractor-drive.

PEGASUS VIII, 700 hp, compression ratio 6.0:1, fully supercharged. Geared, epicyclic reduction .666:1. L.H. tractor-drive. Was developed from Pegasus IIIS.2 and then IV, with .666 reduction gear ratio.

PEGASUS IX, 725 hp, (1934), compression ratio 6.55:1, medium supercharged. Geared, epicyclic reduction .5:1. L.H. tractor-drive. Was a Pegasus XXII, modified to give Pegasus III performance.
Aircraft:

    Blackburn T.9B Shark III

PEGASUS X, 980 hp, (1936), compression ratio 6.55:1, medium supercharged, 11 inch supercharger rotor. Geared, epicyclic reduction .5:1. L.H. tractor-drive. PE-5M50. Power Curve at rated altitude 4,000 ft from A.& A.E.E., Martlesham, Report M.703 dated 19.5.36. Boost, rated +2.25 lb/sq inch.

RPM	2,750	2,650	2,550	2,250	2,050
BHP	980	925	900	826	741
BOOST	+4.5lb	+3.75lb	+2.8lb		

Max boost +4.5 lb/sq inch. 915 bhp, 2,475 rpm take off to 1,000 ft or one minute. All-out level flight (five minutes), +2.5 lb, 915 bhp, 2,600 rpm, 6,250 ft. Fuel 87 Octane (DTD 230).
Aircraft:

    Bristol 130 (C.26/31) Bombay prototype
    Handley Page H.P.54 Harrow I
    Hawker Hart
    Hawker P.V.4 (G.4/31)
    Saro A.27 London II
    Supermarine Stranraer
    Vickers 271 B.9/32
    Vickers 281 Wellesley
    Vickers 285 Wellington prototype

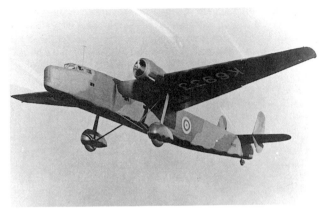

The prototype Handley Page Harrow K6933, with Pegasus X engines.

Handley Page Harrow II G-AFRG, converted for refuelling in Flight, over Canada. The original Pegasus Xs engines were changed to Pegasus XXs. The quilted effect of the lifting upper wing fabric is noticeable.

PEGASUS XC, 900 hp, (1936), (was originally called Pegasus X-C). Compression ratio 6.55:1, medium supercharged, 9.5 inch supercharger rotor. Geared, epicyclic reduction .5:1. L.H. tractor-drive. Lightened engine for Imperial Airways, PE-IM.
Aircraft:
> Short L.17 Syrinx
> Short S.23, S.33 Empire
> Short-Mayo S.21 Composite, *Maia*

PEGASUS XI, 850 hp, (1936), compression ratio 6.55:1, medium supercharged. Geared, epicyclic reduction .572:1. L.H. tractor-drive. PE-5M57.

PEGASUS XII, 850 hp, (1936), compression ratio 6.55:1, medium supercharged. Geared, epicyclic reduction .666:1. L.H. tractor-drive. PE-5M66

PEGASUS XIII, 960 hp, compression ratio 6.55:1, medium supercharged. Geared, epicyclic reduction .5:1. L.H. tractor-drive.

PEGASUS XV, 725 hp, (PE-5S(a)50), *see* Pegasus XX. Fully supercharged. Reduction gear ratio .5:1. Power Curve at rated altitude 16,000 ft, from A.& A.E.E., Martlesham, Report M.697, dated 5.1.37. Boost, rated +3.5 lb/sq inch.

RPM	2,600	2,475	2,250	2,150	2,050
BHP	894	866	764	696	628
BOOST	+6lb	+3.5lb			

Max boost +5 lb/sq inch. 894 bhp, 2,600 rpm take off to 1,000 ft or one minute. All-out level flight (five minutes), +5 lb, 2,600 rpm. Fuel 87 Octane (DTD 230).
Aircraft:
> Handley Page H.P.52 B.9/32 Hampden prototype

PEGASUS XVII, 815 hp, (1937), lightened engine, as Mk XVIII with two-speed supercharger but different reduction gear. Compression ratio 6.25:1. Geared, epicyclic reduction .572:1. L.H. tractor-drive. PE-5SM(a)57 and PE-5SM(c)57 (with Mk IV supercharger).

PEGASUS XVIII, 815 hp, (1937), lightened engine, previously known as PE-5SM(a & b), two-speed, fully/medium supercharged. PE-5SM(b)50 had a three-plate clutch type supercharger drive. Compression ratio 6.25:1. Geared, epicyclic reduction .5:1. L.H. tractor-drive. Pilot's Notes state 'Avoid rpm between 2,250 and 2,550' (Vibration). Fuel 87 Octane (DTD 230).
Aircraft:
> Bristol 120
> Handley Page H.P.52 B.9/32 Hampden prototype
> Short S.25 Sunderland II, III
> Vickers 287 Wellesley I
> Vickers 285, 290, 295-7, 403, 408-9, 412, 415 Wellington I, IA, IB, IC
> Vickers 418, 419 Wellington D.W.I. Mk I, II
> Vickers 429 Wellington VIII, C.XV, C.XVI

The Pegasus X was widely used and the Mk XC was a civil version.

The Pegasus XVIII, the first two-speed version of the engine, very widely used and developed into the Mks 38 and 48.

PEGASUS XIX, 835 hp, compression ratio .655:1, fully supercharged. Geared, epicyclic reduction .572:1. L.H. tractor-drive. Originally to be Pegasus XIV, PE-5S(a)57 but, as a lightened engine with reduced altitude Mercury supercharger, was redesignated PE-8S57, Pegasus XIX.

PEGASUS XX, 835 hp, (1937), compression ratio 6.55:1, fully supercharged. Geared, epicyclic reduction .5:1. L.H. tractor-drive. It was originally the Pegasus XV, PE-5S(a)50 but modified to have a reduced altitude rating with a Mercury supercharger. Became Pegasus XX, PE-8S50. Power Curve at rated altitude 9,000 ft from A.& A.E.E.,Martlesham, Report M.706, dated 27.8.37. Boost, rated +3 lb/sq inch.

RPM	2,600	2,475	2,250	2,050
BHP	921	878	785	684
BOOST	+5.17lb	+4.35lb	+3.07lb	+1.96lb

Max boost +4.25 lb/sq inch. 878 bhp, 2,475 rpm take off to 1,000 ft or one minute. All-out level flight (five minutes), +4.25 lb, 921 bhp, 2,600 rpm. Fuel 87 Octane (DTD 230).
Aircraft:

    Fokker C.X
    Handley Page H.P.53 Hampden (Sweden) prototype
    Handley Page H.P.54 Harrow II
    P.Z.L. P.37B Los B (Elk)
    Vickers 287, 291, 402 Wellesley I

PEGASUS 21, 835 hp, compression ratio 6.55:1, fully supercharged. Geared, epicyclic reduction .666:1. L.H. tractor-drive. Was PE-5S(a)66 with a reduced altitude rating using a Mercury supercharger, becoming a Pegasus 21, PE-8S66.

PEGASUS 22, (XXII) 835 hp, (1937), compression ratio 6.55:1, medium supercharged. Geared, epicyclic reduction .5:1. L.H. tractor-drive, this engine was a revised Mk X, with 100 mm propeller shaft, Rotol or D.H. propeller. Pilot's Notes: 'Avoid rpm between 2,250 and 2,550 as far as possible' (vibration). PE-9M50. Power Curve at rated altitude 4,000 ft from A.& A.E.E., Martlesham, Report M.684, dated 4.2.38. Boost, rated +2.5 lb/sq inch.

RPM	2,600	2,475	2,250	2,150	2,050
BHP	1,004	949	853	814	756
BOOST	+4.32lb	+3.82lb	+2.91lb	+2.56lb	+2.13lb

Max boost +4.35 lb/sq inch. 1,004 bhp, 2,600 rpm take off to 1,000 ft or one minute. All-out level flight (five minutes), +2.5 lb, 1,000 bhp, 2,600 rpm. Fuel 87 Octane (DTD 230).
Aircraft:

    Bristol 130A Bombay I C.26/31
    Handley Page H.P.52 Hampden I
    Short S.23, S.33 Empire
    Short S.25 Sunderland I, III

A Short Sunderland I, with Pegasus XXII engines howling at full bore on take-off.

A Short Sunderland I, L2160, powered by Pegasus XXII engines

PEGASUS 22 LR, 835 hp, (1937), similar to Mk 22. Geared, epicyclic .5:1, Rotol propeller. Pilot's Notes: 'Avoid rpm between 2,250 and 2,550 as far as possible' (vibration). For Wellesleys of Long Range Development Unit.
Aircraft:

    Vickers 292, 294 Wellesley (L.R.D.U.)

One of the Vickers Wellesleys of the Royal Air Force Long Range Development Unit being shown to King George VI by Rex Pierson, Chief Designer of Vickers Armstrongs Ltd.

One of the Vickers Wellesleys of the Royal Air Force Long Range Development Unit being prepared in 1937 at Ismailia, near Cairo, for its non-stop flight to Darwin.

PEGASUS 23, 800 hp, compression ratio 6.55:1, medium supercharged. As Pegasus XXII, geared, epicyclic reduction .572:1. L.H. tractor-drive. PE-9M57.

PEGASUS 24, 800 hp, compression ratio 6.55:1, medium supercharged. Pegasus 22, geared, epicyclic reduction .666:1. PE-9M66. L.H. tractor-drive.

PEGASUS 25, 1,010 hp, compression ratio 6.25:1, fully supercharged. Geared, epicyclic reduction .5:1. L.H. tractor-drive. Pegasus XXVI with .5 reduction gear.

PEGASUS 26, 1,010 hp, compression ratio 6.55:1, fully supercharged. Geared, epicyclic reduction .666:1. L.H. tractor-drive. Constant speed propeller rating.

PEGASUS 27, 1,010 hp, compression ratio 6.55:1, fully supercharged. Geared, epicyclic reduction .572:1. L.H. tractor-drive. Pegasus XXVI with .572 reduction gear.

PEGASUS 29, 1,010 hp, compression ratio 6.55:1, medium supercharged. Geared, epicyclic reduction .666:1. L.H. tractor-drive. Pegasus replacement and rating from Pegasus XX stock (XXA). AVT.85MB carburettor. PE-12M.

PEGASUS 30, 775 hp, compression ratio 6.0:1, medium supercharged. Geared, epicyclic reduction .5:1. L.H. tractor-drive. As Pegasus IIIM with sleeve crankpin-type big end.
Aircraft:
  Fairey Swordfish I, II, III.

PEGASUS 32, 890 hp, compression ratio 6.55:1, medium supercharged. Geared, epicyclic reduction .5:1. L.H. tractor-drive.

PEGASUS 38, 805 hp. Compression ratio 6.25:1, medium supercharged. Similar to two-speed Pegasus XVIII but locked in 'M' gear. Geared, epicyclic reduction .5:1, for Hydromatic-type. L.H. tractor-drive. A medium-altitude civil engine, with civil accessories.
Aircraft:
  Short S.25 Sunderland III
  Short S.25 Sandringham I

The two-speed Pegasus 38, a medium altitude civil development of the Mk XVIII, locked in M gear.

PEGASUS 48, 805 hp. Compression ratio 6.25:1, two-speed, fully/medium supercharged. Geared, epicyclic reduction .5:1, Hydromatic-type. L.H. tractor-drive. Similar to Pegasus XVIII but a high-altitude civil engine, with civil accessories.
Aircraft:
  Short S.25 Sunderland III
  Short S.25 Sandringham I

DRACO, 540 hp, 9-cylinder 1-row radial, air-cooled poppet-valve. Bore/stroke 5.75 x 7.5 in. Vol. 1,753 cu in. (146 x190 mm. Vol. 28.7 litre). Compression ratio 5.3:1. Medium supercharged 7:1. Fuel-injection into the induction elbows instead of normal carburettor. Developed from Pegasus IM.3. Geared, epicyclic .5:1 L.H. tractor-drive. Diameter 55.5 in; length 43.5 in.
Aircraft:
  Westland Wapiti

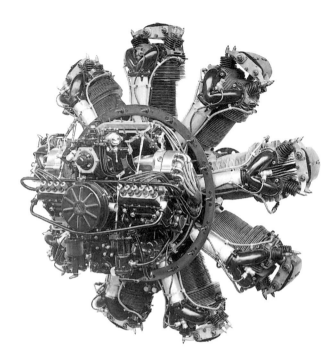

Bristol Draco, a direct-injection version of the Pegasus IM.3, showing the fuel injection into the induction elbows.

PHOENIX I, 470 hp, (1928), a diesel engine, similar to the Pegasus IF.2, the principal difference being its diesel system. The symbol 'F' indicated fan distribution. Bore/stroke 5.75 x 7.5 in. Vol. 1,753 cu in. (146 x 190 mm. Vol. 28.7 litre). Compression ratio 14:1. Geared, epicyclic .655:1, L.H. tractor-drive. Diameter 53.25 in; length 43.75 in.
Aircraft:
  Westland Wapiti I

PHOENIX IIM, 470 hp, (1932), a diesel engine similar to the Phoenix I, the principal difference being its medium supercharge, ratio 7:1. Developed from the Pegasus IM.3. Geared, epicyclic .5:1. L.H. tractor-drive. Diameter 54.36 in.
Aircraft:
  Westland Wapiti I, J9102 (World altitude record for
  diesel engines, 27,453 ft, 11 May 1932).

Bristol Phoenix IIM, one of two experimental diesel engines developed from the Pegasus IM.3, in this case medium-supercharged.

HYDRA — 'DOUBLE OCTAGON', 870 hp, (1931), 16-cylinder 2-row radial, air-cooled poppet-valve. Bore/stroke 5.0 x 5.0 in. Vol. 1,570 cu in. (127 x 127 mm. Vol. 25.7 litre). Compression ratio 6:1. Medium supercharged, 4.5:1. Geared epicyclic .424:1. L.H. tractor-drive. (H.101). Diameter 46.5 in; length 57.0 in. Fuel DTD 134.
Aircraft:
    Hawker Harrier

The Bristol 'Double Octagon', or Hydra. A two-row 16-cylinder air-cooled engine, one of Bristol's more adventurous engines, featuring opposed cylinders and overhead cam gear.

The Hawker Harrier, J8325 with a Hydra (Double Octagon) sixteen-cylinder engine.

The Hawker Harrier, J8325 with a Hydra (Double Octagon) sixteen-cylinder engine.

BRISTOL SLEEVE-VALVE FAMILY GROUP.
PERSEUS, AQUILA, TAURUS, HERCULES, CENTAURUS.
In 1927 Roy Fedden, determined as ever, believed that there was a future for the Burt-McCollum type of sleeve-valve, which he had first seen installed in an Argyll engine when he was working for Brazil Straker (*see* Bristol-Cosmos). This design, which he adopted, had a four-port sleeve and the cylinder barrel had five ports, three for inlet and two for exhaust. One sleeve port acted for both inlet and exhaust purposes. Despite formidable production problems, particularly with the emergence of 'shadow factories' run by the motor-car industry before and during the Second World War, he managed to create a successful series of light, powerful nine, fourteen and eighteen-cylinder engines, particularly noteworthy examples being the Hercules, another hard-slogging bomber engine of the Second World War and the big, compact and complicated Centaurus which emerged at the very end of the war. The civil Centaurus, together with civil versions of the Hercules in post-war air transport, big engines running at modest power, setting remarkable records for economy of operation.

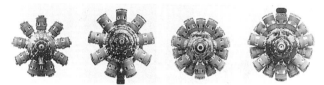

Sleeve-valve engines — Aquila, Perseus, Taurus, Hercules.

In all, one and a half million sleeves were turned out. The Bristol sleeve-valve took the form of a thin-walled tube, which slid within the cylinder, between the piston and the cylinder wall. The sleeve had apertures cut in it, whose shape and location were precisely defined. Their function was to operate as inlet and exhaust valves by being positioned opposite inlet and exhaust ports exactly at the required point in each stroke. Each cylinder had three inlet and two exhaust ports and each sleeve had four apertures, or ports, two acting as inlets and one exhaust and the fourth acting, alternately, as a combined inlet and exhaust port. Sliding to and fro, between the piston and the cylinder wall, it was attached at its lower skirt to a crank which not only gave it the required reciprocating movement but, at the same time gave it a wrist-like semi-rotary action. By carefully designing the location and shape of the sleeve's apertures with the combined reciprocating and rotary movements, the sleeve could be made to serve both its inlet and exhaust functions, so saving a considerable number of component parts by comparison with the poppet-valve. This effect, on a fourteen-cylinder or eighteen-cylinder engine was considerable, although the complications of design, manufacture, assembly and maintenance of the sleeve-valve were formidable.

By comparison, the well-established and relatively simple poppet-valve engine was perhaps better understood. This is not an appropriate place to debate the respective merits of the sleeve, as opposed to the poppet-valve system. There are of course powerful proponents of both. Distortion, caused by heat in the manufacture of the sleeves, aggravated by heat distortion in operation, gave some trouble due to piston seizure in the early days of the Bristol sleeve-valve engines. Any sort of distortion of the sleeves was unhelpful to reliable lubrication. The mass-production of these engines in wartime, particularly in 'shadow factories', away from the design offices when local management and skills were put to the test, had to be faced and the problem of satisfactory sleeve manufacture was solved in a curious manner. Sleeve forgings required boring and then grinding to very fine limits and distortions were repeatedly encountered. For the latter operation, an old and worn wheel was used for the initial grinding operation. Subsequently, a new wheel was used for the finishing process. The problem of distortion persisted but there came a day when a machinist, working on a batch of sleeves, forgot to change grinding wheels, starting with a new wheel and finishing with a worn one, with the unexpected result that the sleeve did not distort. Thus, and somewhat surprisingly, the problem was resolved and a generally similar process was subsequently adopted as well for all engine sleeves.

An equally unexpected result was that, when Napier also encountered piston seizure trouble with the sleeve-valve Sabre in the Hawker Typhoon it was decided that, as their cylinder dimensions and sleeves were similar to those of the Bristol Taurus (apart from the stroke), Taurus sleeves cut to the appropriate length should be tried out on the Sabre. Bristol made two sets of sleeves for Napier, with immediate results. Engine failures in Typhoons were reduced dramatically, after Napier adopted the Bristol method of sleeve manufacture. The Company obtained identical machine tools, including special grinders, which were rushed over from the United States in the great liner *Queen Mary*, by then a troopship.

BRISTOL PERSEUS.
This was the first production engine, to incorporate the Burt-McCollum sleeve valve system, put into production at Bristol.

NOTE: similar engine designations to those of the Mercury and Pegasus also referred to the Perseus.

The first production sleeve-valve aero-engine, the Bristol Perseus I.

PERSEUS I, II, VIII, X, XA, XI, XII, XIIC, XIVC, XVI

Bristol Perseus 9-cylinder, single-row air-cooled, sleeve-valve radial engines had the following in common:-
Bore/stroke 5.75 x 6.5 in. (146.0 x 165.0 mm)
Swept Volume 1,520.0 cu in (24.9 litres).
Dimensions vary according to accessories.
Diameter 55.3 in; length 49.0 in
Weights, where published — *see* Performance tables.

Compression ratio, supercharge and boost (see text). Epicyclic-geared — reduction ratio as in text, all having L.H. drive, the later Perseus being equipped with constant-speed units or converted to them.

Fuel. The production Perseus used DTD 230, (87 Octane) fuel. After 100 Octane fuel became available, from early 1940, it could be used in the modified Mk X, provided that an entry was made in the Tech. log and Form 700. Dry weights and dimensions which varied from one Mark to another, depended on the type of engine and the accessories fitted, all being supercharged (single-speed, single-stage). All Perseus ran at a maximum 2,650 rpm on take-off and, when diving, had a 20-second peak limit of 3,120 rpm.

PERSEUS I, 515 hp, (1932), compression ratio 6.2:1. Single-speed medium-supercharged. Geared, epicyclic .5:1. L.H. tractor-drive. Prototype only.

PERSEUS I.A, 515 hp, (1932), compression ratio 6.2:1, single-speed, medium supercharged. Perseus I, with a larger impeller. Geared, epicyclic reduction .5:1. L.H. tractor-drive.
Aircraft:
    Bristol 105A Bulldog IVA

Bristol Perseus in a Bristol Bulldog IVA.

PERSEUS II-L, 665 hp, (1932), compression ratio 6.75:1, single-speed, low supercharged. Geared, epicyclic reduction .5:1. L.H. tractor-drive. Imperial Airways prototype with low-level supercharger.
Aircraft:
    Gloster Goring
    Short L.17 Scylla
    Vickers 212 Vellox

PERSEUS III, 665 hp, (1932), compression ratio 6.75:1, single-speed, medium supercharged. Geared, epicyclic reduction .5:1. L.H. tractor-drive.
Aircraft:
    Hawker Hart

Perseus trial installation in Hart K3050.

PERSEUS VIII, 745 hp, (1936), compression ratio 6.75:1, single-speed, medium supercharged. Geared, epicyclic reduction .5:1. L.H. tractor-drive. PRE-4M50, was a de-rated PRE-3M with a high-speed impeller, which was not developed. Power Curve at rated altitude 5,000 ft from A.& A.E.E., Martlesham, Report M.510, dated 14.7.37. Boost, rated +2.5 lb/sq inch.

RPM	2,525	2,400	2,200	2,000
BHP	824	768	688	583
BOOST	+4lb		+2.5lb	

Max boost +4 lb/sq inch. 670 bhp, 2,200 rpm take off to 1,000 ft or one minute. All-out level flight (five minutes), +4 lb, bhp, 2,525 rpm. Fuel 87 Octane (DTD 230).
Aircraft:
    Vickers 286 Vildebeest IV

PERSEUS X, 750 hp, compression ratio 6.75:1, single-speed, fully supercharged with a 12 inch impeller. Geared, epicyclic reduction .5:1. L.H. tractor-drive. Accessory gearbox, 100 mm propeller shaft. Fuel 87 or 100 Octane. Power Curve at rated altitude 14,500 ft from A.& A.E.E., Martlesham, Report M.742, dated 14.6.39. Boost, rated +1.5 lb/sq inch.

RPM	2,750	2,650	2,500	2,400	2,200
BHP	890	848	773	710	597
BOOST	+3.99lb	+3.34lb	+2.68lb	+1.71lb	+0.46lb

Max boost +3 lb/sq inch. 880 bhp, 2,750 rpm take off to 1,000 ft or one minute. All-out level flight (five minutes), +3 lb, 880 bhp, 2,750 rpm. Fuel 87 Octane (DTD 230).
Aircraft:
    Blackburn B-26 Botha I

PERSEUS XA, 860 hp, (1939), basically Perseus X with a cropped 9.25 inch supercharger impeller, running at Perseus XII rating. Compression ratio 6.75:1, single-speed, medium supercharged. Geared, epicyclic reduction .5:1. L.H. tractor-drive. AVT.85 MB carburettor. 'Because of vibration and minimum rpm at which the generator will charge, cruising rpm is limited to 1,900-1,950 and 2,300-2,400 rpm'. Fuel DTD 230 (87 Octane, type-tested for 100 Octane but restricted use). PRE-13M.
Aircraft:
    Blackburn B-26 Botha I

PERSEUS XI, 745 hp, (1939), compression ratio 6.75:1, single-speed, medium supercharged. Geared, epicyclic reduction .572:1. Propeller shaft 100 mm and accessory gearbox. L.H. tractor-drive.

PERSEUS XII, 905 hp, (1939), compression ratio 675:1, single-speed, medium supercharged, 10 inch rotor. Geared, epicyclic reduction .5:1. L.H. tractor-drive. Propeller shaft 100 mm and accessory gearbox. Power Curve at rated altitude 6,500 ft from A.& A.E.E., Martlesham, Report M.694, dated 17.9.37. Boost, rated +1.25 lb/sq inch.

RPM	2,900	2,750	2,600	2,400	2,000
BHP	961	878	824	728	537
BOOST	+2.92lb	+2.44lb	+1.93lb	+1.29lb	+0.22lb

The Perseus XII in a Blackburn Skua I dive-bomber.

Max boost +2.5 lb/sq inch. 850 bhp, 2,650 rpm take off to 1,000 ft or one minute. All-out level flight (five minutes), +2.5 lb, 878 bhp, 2,750 rpm. Fuel 87 Octane (DTD 230).
Aircraft:
    Blackburn B-24 Skua I
    Blackburn B-25 Roc I
    Bristol 148
    Saro A.33
    Westland Lysander II

PERSEUS XIIC, 815 hp, (1939), civil-rated Perseus XII, compression ratio 6.75:1, single-speed, medium supercharged, 9.25 inch rotor. Geared, epicyclic reduction .5:1. L.H. tractor-drive. Imperial Airways type. Controllable-pitch propeller. PRE-2M50. Power Curve at rated altitude 4,000 ft from A.& A.E.E., Martlesham, Report M.745, dated 18.6.39. Boost, rated +3 lb/sq inch.

RPM	2,700	2,600	2,250
BHP	894	854	700
BOOST	+3lb	+1.25lb	

Max boost +3 lb/sq inch. 900 bhp, 2,700 rpm take off to 1,000 ft or one minute. All-out level flight (five minutes), +1.25 lb, 815 bhp, 2,600 rpm. Fuel 87 Octane (DTD 230).
Aircraft:
    de Havilland 95 Flamingo
    Short S.30 Empire (Flight Refuelling trials)

The civil Perseus XIIC.

The de Havilland D.H.95 Flamingo, powered by Bristol Perseus XIIC engines.

PERSEUS XII-C1, 8150 hp, (1939), civil-rated Perseus XII, compression ratio 6.75:1, single-speed, medium supercharged, 9.25 inch impeller. Geared, epicyclic reduction .5:1. L.H. tractor-drive. Similar to PERSEUS XII-C but with Hydromatic propeller.
Aircraft:

    de Havilland 95 Flamingo
    Short S.30 Empire

PERSEUS XIV-C, 710 hp, (1939), civil-rated, as Perseus XII-C, compression ratio 6.75:1, single-speed, medium supercharged with 9.25 inch rotor. Geared, epicyclic reduction .66:1. L.H. tractor-drive, with Hydromatic propeller.
Aircraft:

    British Burnelli/Cunliffe-Owen OA-1 Flying Wing.

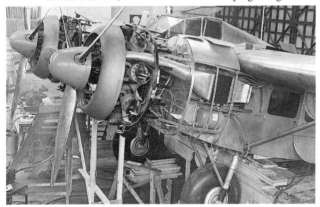

Bristol Perseus XIVC engines in the British Burnelli/Cunliffe-Owen OA-1 Flying Wing.

PERSEUS XIV-C Special, 710 hp, (1939), civil-rated Perseus X-A. Compression ratio 6.75:1, single-speed, medium supercharged, Perseus XIV-C rating. Supercharger impeller diameter 9.25 inches. Geared, epicyclic reduction .66:1. L.H. tractor-drive. AVT.85 MB carburettor.

PERSEUS XVI, 745 hp, (1939), civil-rated, compression ratio 6.75:1, single-speed, medium supercharged, with Perseus XII supercharger. Geared, epicyclic reduction .5:1. Hydromatic propeller. L.H. tractor-drive. Fuel 87 Octane. PRE-9M.
Aircraft:

    de Havilland 95 Flamingo
    de Havilland 95 Hertfordshire I

PERSEUS XVIC, 745 hp, (1939), civil-rated, compression ratio 6.75:1, single-speed, medium supercharged. Geared, epicyclic reduction .5:1. Hydromatic propeller. L.H. tractor-drive. As above but with fixed crankpin sleeve and fuel 100 Octane. PRE-17M.
Aircraft:

    de Havilland 95 Flamingo
    de Havilland 95 Hertfordshire I

AQUILA I, 600 hp, (1934), 9-cylinder, single-row radial air-cooled, sleeve-valve. Bore/stroke 5 x 5.375 in. Vol. 950 cu in. (127 x 136.5 mm. Vol. 15.6 l), compression ratio 7.3:1, medium supercharged. Geared, epicyclic .5:1. L.H. tractor-drive. V/P propeller. Fuel, initially was DTD 134 (73 Octane) but DTD 230 (87 Octane) was normally used in the few aircraft to use the engine. Diameter 46.0 in.
Aircraft:

    Bristol 105A Bulldog IIA
    Bristol 107 Bullpup
    Bristol 143
    Vickers 279 Venom

The little Vickers 279 Venom, powered by a Bristol Aquila I.

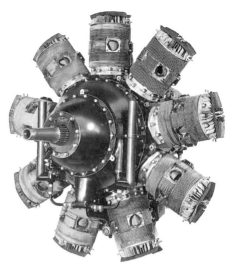

The Bristol Aquila I

BRISTOL TAURUS.

TAURUS II, III, VI, XII, XVI

Bristol Taurus 14-cylinder, two-row sleeve-valve, air-cooled radial engines had the following in common:-
Bore/stroke 5.0 x 5.625 in. (127.0 x 143.0 mm)
Swept Volume 1,550.0 cu in. (25.4 litres).
Compression Ratio 7.2:1.
Dimensions vary according to accessories.
Diameter 46.25 in; length 49.2 in
Weights, where published — *see* Performance tables.

TAURUS II, 1,060 hp, (1940), single-speed, medium supercharged. Geared, epicyclic .444:1 L.H. tractor-drive. (The basic Taurus sleeve was used in the Napier-Halford Sabre). Power Curve at rated altitude 5,000 ft from A.& A.E.E., Martlesham, Report M.740, dated 26.10.39. Boost, rated +2.75 lb/sq inch.

RPM	3,225	3,000	2,800	2,600	2,400
BHP	1,140	1,048	958	848	760
BOOST	+4.3lb	+3.51lb	+2.88lb	2.03lb	+1.47lb

Max boost +4.25 lb/sq inch. 1,140 bhp, 3,225 rpm take off to 1,000 ft or one minute. All-out level flight (five minutes), +4.25 lb, bhp, 3,225 rpm. Fuel 87 Octane (DTD 230).

Bristol Taurus II, fourteen-cylinder engine, used on the Fairey Albacore and Bristol Beaufort torpedo-bombers.

Aircraft:
> Bristol 148B
> Bristol 152 Beaufort I (10/36)
> Fairey Battle I
> Fairey Albacore I (41/36)
> Gloster F.9/37

TAURUS III, 935 hp. Compression ratio 7.2:1, single-speed, medium supercharged. Geared, epicyclic reduction .444:1. L.H. tractor-drive.
Aircraft:
> Bristol 152 Beaufort I (Australia)

TAURUS VI, 985 hp. Compression ratio 7.2:1, single-speed, medium supercharged. Geared, epicyclic reduction .444:1. L.H. tractor-drive.
Aircraft:
> Bristol 152 Beaufort I (Australia) (M.15/35 & G.24/35)

TAURUS XII, 985 hp, (1940), Compression ratio 7.2:1, single-speed, medium supercharged. Geared, epicyclic reduction .444:1. L.H. tractor-drive. Similar to Taurus XVI but with supercharger ratio 5.6:1, having impeller diameter of larger diameter so that engine output was maintained.
Aircraft:
> Bristol 152 Beaufort I
> Fairey Albacore II

TAURUS XVI, 985 hp, (1940), Compression ratio 7.2:1, single-speed, medium supercharged. Geared, epicyclic reduction .444:1. L.H. tractor-drive. Supercharger impeller drive ratio 7.5:1.
Aircraft:
> Bristol 152 Beaufort I

TAURUS XX, trials engine, one-off.
Aircraft:
> Bristol 152 Beaufort IV

BRISTOL HERCULES.
Similar guidance notes regarding the rather complex engine Specifications, referred to under the Mercury and Pegasus, also apply to the Hercules.

SINGLE-SPEED, SINGLE-STAGE SUPERCHARGED
HERCULES
HERCULES I, II, IV, VIII, XIV, XVII, XIX, 130, 230, 630srs, 670 srs, 730 srs

---

TWO-SPEED, SINGLE-STAGE SUPERCHARGED
HERCULES
HERCULES III, VI, VII, X, XI, XVI, XVII, XIX, XX, 36, 100, 120, 260, 600 srs, 760

SPECIAL HIGH-ALTITUDE HERCULES
HERCULES VIII, XV

Bristol Hercules 14-cylinder, two-row sleeve-valve, air- cooled radial engines had the following in common:-
Bore/stroke 5.75 x 6.5 in. (146.0 x 165.0 mm)
Swept Volume 2,360.0 cu in. (38.7 litres).
Dimensions vary according to accessories.
Mk I, Diameter 52 in. Mk 763, Diameter 55 in. As a power-egg, the extra diameter includes the cowling.
Weights, where published — *see* Performance tables.

Compression ratio, supercharge, boost, reduction gear ratio as in text, all having left-hand tractor propeller drive and V/P, C/S, propellers. All engines were for military applications, unless otherwise stated.

Fuel was initially 87 Octane but most engines in service ran on 100 Octane, which became available from early 1940, or later grades, in which case greater power output was available.

Dry weights, as in all installations, varied from one Mark to another, depending on accessories but, as examples, the single-speed Mk I weighed 1,845 lb. and the two-speed Mk 763 weighed 2,400 lb.

All early standard Hercules in service, ran at 2,800 rpm on take-off, late engines being increased to 2,900.

HERCULES I, 1,150 hp, (1936), compression ratio 6.75:1, single-speed, medium supercharged. Geared, epicyclic reduction .5:1. This single prototype Hercules first ran as a fully-supercharged engine, HE-1S50, running on DTD 230 fuel and, after initial runs, was converted to a medium-speed blower, as the HE-IM50. A two-speed development, the HE-ISMa was not proceeded with but see Hercules III.
Aircraft:
> Northrop 2-L Gamma Commercial.
> Short S.29 Stirling prototype
> Vickers 289 Wellesley

The clean lines of the sleeve-valve Bristol Hercules I.

The prototype Short Stirling, L7600, was flown first with Hercules I engines, the intended Mk III not then being available.

HERCULES II, 1,375 hp, (1938), compression ratio 6.75:1, single-speed, medium supercharged. Geared, epicyclic reduction .444:1. The Hercules II emerged from a development engine, as the HE-IM44, the first in the series to have accessories driven from a Bristol auxiliary gearbox, rather than being mounted on the rear cover. Units of this kind, fitted to all Bristol sleeve-valve engines, enabled rapid engine changes to be made in aircraft following wartime operations and were fitted to subsequent civil Hercules models. See Hercules IV, V, VIII and XV. Power Curve at rated altitude 5,000 ft from A.& A.E.E., Martlesham, Report M.754, dated 5.7.39. Medium supercharged. Boost, rated +1.75 lb/sq inch. Max 3.25 lb/sq inch., 2,750 rpm. HE.IM

RPM	2,800	2,600	2,500	2,400	2,200
BHP	1,375	1,255	1,201	1,139	1,018
BOOST	+3.31lb	+2.6lb	+2.33lb	+2.04lb	+1.46lb

Max boost +3.25lb/sq inch. 1,375 hp, 2,800 rpm take off, to 1,000 ft or one minute. All-out level flight (five minutes), +3.25lb, 1,375 hp, 2,750 rpm. Fuel 87 Octane (DTD 230).
Aircraft:
> Bristol 156 Beaufighter I F.17/39
> Fairey Battle I
> Fokker T.9
> Saro A.36 Lerwick I
> Short S.29 Stirling I srs I

The Bristol Hercules II in a Northrop 2-L. The long-chord cowling is seen with the cooling gills closed.

HERCULES III, 1,400 hp, (1939), compression ratio 6.75:1, two-speed, fully/medium supercharged. Geared, epicyclic reduction .444:1. The Mk III Hercules was the production version of a two-speed development of the Hercules I engine, (the HE-ISMb), and featured a Hydromatic propeller. It had a supercharger diffuser of 8.5 degrees. In service, it could be run on either 87 or 100 Octane fuel, subject to limitations. HE-ISM.
Aircraft:
      Armstrong Whitworth A.W.41 Albemarle I
      Bristol 156 Beaufighter I
      Short S.29 Stirling I srs I
      Vickers 299, 417 Wellington III

HERCULES IV, 1,380 hp, (1939), compression ratio 6.75:1, single-speed, medium supercharged. Geared, epicyclic reduction .444:1. A derivative of the Mk II with a cropped 12 in diameter supercharger impeller, the HE-4M became the production Hercules IV, running on 87 Octane fuel. HE-4M.
Aircraft:
      Saro A.36 Lerwick I
      Short S.26 'G' class flying-boat

A Hercules IV installed in a Saro Lerwick flying-boat of Coastal Command.

HERCULES IV HY, 1,380 hp, (1939), was the designation of the Hercules IV, equipped with a Hydromatic propeller.
Aircraft:
      Short S.26 'G' class flying-boat

HERCULES V, 1,380 hp, (1939), compression ratio 6.75:1, single-speed, medium supercharged. Geared, epicyclic reduction .444:1. This was a civil prototype, evolved from the Hercules IV but not developed.

HERCULES VI, 1,615 hp, (1941). After the initial production series, begun by the Hercules II, the Mk VI and its successors were of fundamental importance to the Hercules line. This originated with the HE-6SM, a development engine with a compression ratio of 7:1. It was a two-speed, fully/medium supercharged engine, geared, epicyclic reduction .444:1. As with the earlier versions, it had a gearbox for auxiliary drives and could be run on 87 or 100 Octane fuel, with suitable precautions. The production version of the HE-6SM was very widely used and evolved into a complex family tree of other versions, apart from the VIII, X, XI, XIV and XV, from the VII and XVI onwards.
Aircraft:
      Avro 683 Lancaster II
      Bristol 156 Beaufighter I, VIC, VIF, XTF
      Handley Page H.P.61 Halifax III
      Handley Page H.P.69 Halifax VII
      Short S.29 Stirling III, IV, V
      Vickers 454, 458 Wellington XI
      Vickers 455 Wellington XII

A Hercules VI installed in a Bristol 156 Beaufighter VIC.

HERCULES VII, as Hercules VI, compression ratio 7:1, two-speed, fully/medium supercharged but with a reduced 12 inch diameter impeller. Geared, epicyclic reduction .444:1. Production HE-7SM. See also Hercules XVII. (Similar Mks 27 and 37, with Bendix and R.A.E.-Hobson injector carburettors — production cancelled).

HERCULES VIII, 1,650 hp, a very high-altitude version of the Hercules II. This had a single-speed, medium supercharger and the Mk VIII remained basically medium-supercharged but had an auxiliary high-altitude single-speed 'S' supercharger, giving its maximum 1,100 hp at 32,000 feet. Geared, epicyclic reduction .444:1, it was designated the HE-8MAS (Medium supercharged, auxiliary 'S' blower). It was produced in a modified version (Mod 1, or Mk II), raising the maximum power level to 40,000 feet.
Aircraft:
      Folland Fo.108 43/37
      Vickers 407, 426 Wellington V

HERCULES X, 1,420 hp, (1941), As the Hercules III, developed from the HE-ISMb, with 10 degree supercharger diffuser. Compression ratio 6.75:1.

Aircraft:

Armstrong Whitworth A.W.41 Albemarle I, II, V, VI
Bristol 156 Beaufighter I
Short S.29 Stirling I
Vickers 417 Wellington III

HERCULES XI, 1,590 hp, (1941). Derived from the Hercules III, like the Hercules X, running on 100 Octane fuel. Compression 6.75:1

Aircraft:

Armstrong Whitworth A.W.41 Albemarle I, II, V, VI
Bristol 156 Beaufighter I
Fairey Battle I
Folland Fo.108 43/37
Short S.29 Stirling I srs II, srs III
Vickers 417 Wellington III
Vickers 428 Wellington D.W.I. Mk III
Vickers 440 Wellington X

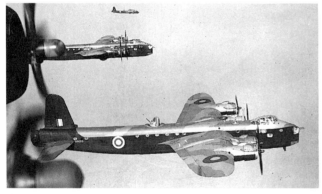

Short Stirlings on a training flight. The nearest, N6069 was lost on a raid on Hamburg in July, 1942 while operating with 1651 Heavy Conversion Unit.

HERCULES XII, as Hercules VI, with separate induction pipes. Compression ratio 7:1

HERCULES XIV, 1,500 hp, (1942), a civil development of the Hercules IV for B.O.A.C., running on 100 Octane fuel. compression ratio 7:1.

Aircraft:

Short S.26 'G' class flying-boat

HERCULES XVMT, 1,650 hp, like the Hercules VIII, was a very high-altitude development of the Hercules II, with a single auxiliary high-altitude turbo-supercharger. Basically, it remained, like the Mk VIII, a moderately-supercharged engine but, thus equipped, it became a two-speed, two-stage fully/medium supercharged engine, geared, epicyclic .444:1. producing a maximum of 1,230 hp at 38,000 feet.

Aircraft:

Folland Fo.108 43/37
Vickers Wellington V

HERCULES XVI, 1,615 hp, (1942). Similar to Hercules VI, with a Hobson single-lever carburettor. This originated with the HE-6SM, a development engine with a compression ratio of 7:1, a two-speed, fully/medium supercharged engine, geared, epicyclic reduction .444:1. It had a gearbox for auxiliary drives and could be run on 87 or 100 Octane fuel, with suitable precautions.

Aircraft:

Avro 683 Lancaster II
Avro 685 York II
Bristol 156 Beaufighter VIC, VIF, TFX
Handley Page H.P.61 Halifax III, VI
Handley Page H.P.69 Halifax VII
Handley Page H.P.71 Halifax IX
Short S.29 Stirling III, IV, V
Vickers 437 Wellington X
Vickers 439, 440 Wellington IX, X
Vickers 478, 487 etc Wellington X, XI, XII, XIII, XIV, XVII, XVIII

HERCULES XVII, 1,725 hp, (1943), (as Hercules VII, developed from the Hercules VI), compression ratio 7:1. Basically, two-speed,

fully/medium supercharged but with supercharger locked in 'M' gear, a reduced 12 inch diameter impeller and single-lever carburettor. Geared, epicyclic reduction .444:1. Production HE-7SM. (Similar Mks 27 and 37 but with Bendix and R.A.E.-Hobson injector carburettors — production cancelled). Production of a Marine version, locked in 'M' gear was also cancelled, as the HE-17MB.

Aircraft:

Bristol 156 Beaufighter TFX, XIC
Vickers 466 etc Wellington X, XI, XII, XIII, XIV, XVII, XVIII

HERCULES XVIII, low-level engine, developed from the Mk VI and similar to the Hercules XVI, with a cropped, 12 inch supercharger impeller.

Aircraft:

Bristol 156 Beaufighter TFX, XIC, 21

HERCULES XIX, 1,725 hp, (1943), developed from the Hercules XVII, with 'Long Tom' plugs and ignition harness, the Hercules XIX had a compression ratio of 7:1. Although basically a two-speed, fully/medium supercharged engine, with a reduced 12 inch diameter impeller and single-lever carburettor, it was operated locked in 'M' gear. Geared, epicyclic reduction .444:1.

Aircraft:

Short S.45 Sunderland IV (Seaford) R.8/42

308B A Short S.45 Sunderland IV (Seaford) with Hercules XIX engines.

HERCULES XX, similar to the Hercules XIX two-speed, fully/medium supercharged. Geared, epicyclic reduction .444:1.

Aircraft:

Short S.45 Solent I

HERCULES 36, initially a development engine from the Hercules VI and XVI which was to have had a Bendix injector carburettor and to be known as the Hercules 26. However, production of this was cancelled and a version with a Hobson-R.A.E. injector was substituted, as the HE-9SM. Thus modified, it was produced as the Hercules 36 with a compression ratio of 7:1, a two-speed, fully/medium supercharged engine, geared, epicyclic reduction .444:1 and a gearbox for auxiliary drives. It ran on 100 Octane fuel.

HERCULES 38, a development engine from the Hercules 36, the Mk 38 was locked in 'M' gear and employed a turbo-supercharger, designated HE-11MT (Medium/Turbo) and was in small-scale production as the Hercules 38. The basic supercharger was the Mk VI. A Hobson-R.A.E. injector was incorporated.

HERCULES 100, 1,675 hp. The Bristol Hercules 100 marked a major turning point in the development of Bristol sleeve-valve engines. With the likelihood of a successful conclusion of the war in Europe, the development of a new sub-family of engines with civil applications became a practical proposition. The Hercules 100 was the basis of this, with its exceptional reliability and economy, its time between overhauls at the time of its introduction in 1944 already approaching 2,000 hours.

There was to be a family of civil engines, developed in parallel with the military power plants (the direct civil variants, as a whole, having 500 added to the military type numbers) and the whole series was to be split, progressively as it developed, into those having the usual Bristol epicyclic reduction gearing and an entirely new concept, the torquemeter-type reduction gear. This enabled the pilot to select accurately what power he was taking from each engine, thus exercising the maximum fuel economy. From the Mk 100 onwards, to aid identification, engines with ordinary reduction gears were to be given type numbers ending with even numbers and those with torquemeters ending with odd numbers.

The **HERCULES 100** was designated HE-10SM, having a compression ratio of 7:1 and was geared, epicyclic .444:1. It had a turbine entry two-speed supercharger, with ratios 6.68 and 8.35:1.
Aircraft:

    Handley Page H.P.61 Halifax VI
    Handley Page H.P.67 Hastings C.1.
    Handley Page H.P.68 Hermes I
    Handley Page H.P.70 Halifax VIII
    Handley Page H.P.70 Halton I, II
    Nord 1400
    Vickers 478 Wellington X

HERCULES 101, 1,675 hp, as Hercules 100 'dressed' with 2 1/8 inch diameter rear-swept exhaust system. HE-10SM. Hercules 103 was a torquemeter version of the Hercules 101.
Aircraft:

    Handley Page H.P.67 Hastings C.1
    Handley Page H.P.68 Hermes I
    Sud Est S.E.1010

Bristol Hercules 101 series, with rear-swept exhausts. The civil versions of the 100 series of Hercules are usually identified by adding 500 to the type number.

HERCULES 105, 1,675 hp, as Hercules 101, with Mk 120 supercharger gears.
Aircraft:

    Handley Page H.P.67 Hastings C.1.

HERCULES 106, 1,675 hp, as Hercules 101 with modified injector and increased take-off boost. Hercules 107 was a torquemeter version of the Hercules 106.
Aircraft:

    Handley Page 67 Hastings C.2
    Handley Page H.P.74 Hermes II

HERCULES 110, as Hercules 101, with 150 hp accessory drive, submerged scavenge pump in sump and vertically mounted starter. HE-18SM.

HERCULES 120, 1,715 hp, as Hercules 101. modified for high altitude rating and 150 hp accessory drive. Submerged scavenge pump in sump and vertically mounted starter and drive for cabin supercharger. HE-18SM. Hercules 121 was a torquemeter version of the Hercules 120.
Aircraft:

    Avro 689 Tudor VII
    Handley Page H.P.74 Hermes II

The sole Avro 689 Tudor VII with Hercules 120 engines.

HERCULES 130, 1,600 hp, as the Hercules 100, with four-point mounting ring. Single-speed, medium supercharged. Geared, epicyclic reduction .444:1. HE-10M.
Aircraft:

    Bristol 156 Beaufighter VIC
    Handley Page H.P.74 Hermes II
    Vickers 401, 491, 495, 496 Viking I

HERCULES 134, as Hercules 130 with modified four-point mounting ring and 2 1/8 inch diameter rear-swept exhaust pipes to suit a rear manifold.
Aircraft:

    Vickers 498 Viking IA

HERCULES 200, as Hercules 120. Modified for high altitude rating and 150 hp accessory drive. Submerged scavenge pump in sump and vertically-mounted starter and drive for cabin supercharger. The basic engine for the 200 series, HE-18SM.

HERCULES 216, as Hercules 106 converted with Mk 230 power section and single-speed supercharger gears, with increased performance.
Aircraft:

    Handley Page H.P.67 Hastings C.2

HERCULES 230, 1,925 hp, as Hercules 130. Re-designed power section with 1 inch diameter bearing rollers enabling increased performance. Four-point mounting ring, 2⅛ inch diameter exhaust pipes for a rear manifold. Compression ratio 7:1, Geared, epicyclic .444:1. HE-20SM. Hercules 231 was a torquemeter version of the Hercules 230.
Aircraft:

    Vickers 637 Valetta C.1

HERCULES 232, as the Hercules 230 but with a six-point mounting. Small diameter ignition harness, modified magnetos and 3 inch diameter exhaust pipes. Master connecting rods in cylinders 6 and 7. Increased performance. Hercules 233 was a torquemeter version of the Hercules 232.
Aircraft:

    Short S.45 Solent I

HERCULES 234, as Hercules 232 with large diameter ignition harness. Modified rich mixture rating. Free exit cowling. Master connecting rods in cylinders 4 and 11. Hercules 235 was a torquemeter version of the Hercules 234.
Aircraft:

    Bristol 170 Freighter

HERCULES 238, a military engine, based on the Hercules 734, itself a civil 234, with special auxiliaries.
Aircraft:
 Bristol 170 Freighter

A Bristol 170 Freighter for the Royal New Zealand Air Force. The engines are Hercules 238s.

HERCULES 260, as the Hercules 230 but with 1 inch bearing rollers. Redesigned two-speed epicyclic supercharger drive. Six-point mounting ring, front cover and reduction gear to suit braking-type propeller. Submerged oil pipes and 150 hp accessory drive. Cylinder heads sealed to suit free exit cowling and 3 inch diameter pipes for a rear exhaust manifold. Hercules 261 was a torquemeter version of the Hercules 260.
Aircraft:
 Blackburn & G.A. 60 'Universal' Freighter I

HERCULES 264, 1,950 hp, as Hercules 260 with Mk 230 front cover and reduction gear. Cylinder heads sealed to suit 'clover leaf' cowling and 3 inch diameter exhaust pipes for rear manifold. Hercules 265 was a torquemeter version of the Hercules 264.
Aircraft:
 Vickers 668 Varsity T.1.

Bristol Hercules 264 in a Vickers Varsity T.1

HERCULES 268, as the Hercules 260 but with a Mk 230 front cover and reduction gear. Head seals to suit free exit cowling and rear-swept exhaust pipes. Increased climb rpm. Hercules 269, a torquemeter version of the Hercules 268.
Aircraft:
 Bristol 170 Freighter (R.I.A.F.).

HERCULES 270, as the Hercules 230 but with a redesigned rear cover having increased power accessory gearbox drive and provision for tachometer generator drive. Starter position modified. Hercules 271, a torquemeter version of the Hercules 270.
Aircraft:
 Vickers 637 Valetta C.1.

HERCULES 630, 1,675 hp, civil-series engine, as Hercules 100 and 230 single-speed, medium supercharged. Geared, epicyclic reduction .444:1. Four-point mounting ring and front exhaust system. Hercules 631, a torquemeter version of the Hercules 630.
Aircraft:
 Vickers 498 Viking I

HERCULES 632, 1,690 hp, a civil-series engine, compression ratio 7:1, Geared, epicyclic .444:1. As Hercules 630 with six-point mounting ring and 2 1/8 inch diameter rear-swept exhaust system. Hercules 633, a torquemeter version of the Hercules 632.
Aircraft:
 Bristol 170 Freighter I, IA, II, IIA, IIB, IIC, XI, XIA
 Bristol 170 Wayfarer

HERCULES 634, 1,690 hp, a civil-series engine, as the Hercules 630 with modified four-point mounting ring and exhaust pipes swept to suit rear manifold. Compression ratio 7:1, Geared, epicyclic .444:1. Hercules 635, a torquemeter version of the Hercules 634.
Aircraft:
 Vickers 610, 614, 616, 621, 623 Viking IA, B

Vickers Viking IB G-AIVH 'Vicinity' of British European Airways. The engine is a Bristol Hercules 634.

HERCULES 636, a civil-series engine, as the Hercules 630, with special mounting attachments for installation in a monocoque engine nacelle. Modified magnetos and master connecting rods in cylinders 6 and 7. Hercules 637, a torquemeter version of the Hercules 636 with front exhaust system.
Aircraft:
 Short S.45 Solent 2

HERCULES 637-2, a torquemeter version of the Hercules 636 with increased oil consumption limits and differences in piston ring assembly.
Aircraft:
 Short S.45 Solent 3 (Aquila Airways)

HERCULES 637-3, a torquemeter version of the Hercules 636 with copper-based cylinder heads, modified cylinder head baffles and a larger oil pump.
Aircraft:
 Short S.45 Solent 3 (Aquila Airways)

Short S.43 Solent, 'Somerset', with Hercules 636 engines arriving at Southampton Docks Air Terminal in 1952.

HERCULES 638, 1,690 hp, a civil-series engine, as the Hercules 632 with rear-swept exhaust pipes to suit rear manifold. Hercules 639, a torquemeter version of the Hercules 638.
Aircraft:

Bristol 170 Freighter
Bristol 170 Wayfarer

HERCULES 656, a civil-series engine, as the Hercules 636 with front cover and reduction gear to suit braking-type propeller. Hercules 657, a torquemeter version of the Hercules 656, with front exhaust system.
Aircraft:

Short S.45 Solent 3

HERCULES 672, 1,690 hp, a civil-series engine, as the Hercules 632, 'dressed' with equipment for free exit cowling and 3 inch diameter rear-swept exhaust pipes. Hercules 673, a torquemeter version of the Hercules 672.
Aircraft:

Bristol 170 Freighter 21, 21E, 21P

HERCULES 730, 2,040 hp, a civil-series engine, as the Hercules 230 and 630, with redesigned power section, 1 inch bearing rollers, and 6-point mounting ring. Dressed with free exit cowling equipment and 3 inch exhaust branch pipes to suit rear manifold. Small diameter ignition harness and modified magnetos. Master connecting rods in cylinders 4 and 11. Hercules 731, a torquemeter version of the Hercules 730.
Aircraft:

Blackburn & G.A. 60 Universal Freighter II
C.A.S.A. 207 prototype

A cut-away of the Hercules 730.

HERCULES 732, a civil-series engine, as the Hercules 730 with exhaust pipes to suit rear manifold. Small diameter ignition harness, modified magnetos and master connecting rods in cylinders 6 and 7. Hercules 733, a torquemeter version of the Hercules 732.
Aircraft:

Short S.45 Solent 4, (T.E.A.L.)

HERCULES 734, 1,980 hp, a civil-series engine, as the Hercules 730 with free exit cowling, equipment and exhaust branch pipes to suit rear-swept pipes. Large diameter ignition harness and standard magnetos. Master connecting rods in cylinders 4 and 11. Modified rich mixture rating. Hercules 735, a torquemeter version of the Hercules 734.
Aircraft:

Bristol 170 Freighter 31 srs, 32.

HERCULES 736, 2,040 hp, a civil-series engine, as the Hercules 730 with a modified six-point mounting. Parallel cowling, large diameter ignition harness, standard magnetos and master connecting rods in cylinders 4 and 11. Hercules 737, a torquemeter version of the Hercules 736.
Aircraft:

Handley Page H.P.94 Hastings C.4
Handley Page H.P.95 Hastings C.3.

HERCULES 738, a civil-series engine, as the Hercules 730, 'dressed' with free exit cowl equipment and exhaust branch pipes to suit rear-swept pipes. Large diameter ignition harness and standard magnetos. Master connecting rods in cylinders 4 and 11.
Aircraft:

Breguet 890H prototype

HERCULES 739, a torquemeter version of the Hercules 738.
Aircraft:

Nord 1401
Nord 2501 prototype

HERCULES 750, a civil-series engine, as the Hercules 730 with re-designed front cover and reduction gear to suit braking propeller. Six-point mounting ring and 3 inch diameter rear exhaust pipes. Hercules 751, a torquemeter version of the Hercules 750.

HERCULES 758, a civil-series engine, as the Hercules 750, 'dressed' with equipment for 'free exit' cowling and exhausts arranged for rear-swept pipes. Hercules 759, a torquemeter version of the Hercules 758.
Aircraft:

Nord 2501

HERCULES 760, a civil-series engine, as the Hercules 730, with two-speed epicyclic drive supercharger. Six-point mounting ring. Front cover and reduction gear for braking propeller. Submerged oil pumps, 150 hp accessory drive and 3 inch diameter rear manifold exhaust pipes.

HERCULES 762, 2,080 hp, a civil-series engine, as the Hercules 760, with modified supercharger to give a high altitude rating, using 115/145 grade fuel. Hercules 763, a torquemeter version of the Hercules 762.
Aircraft:

Handley Page H.P.74 Hermes II
Handley Page H.P.81 Hermes IV

A Hercules 763, showing a torquemeter fitted to the reduction gear casing.

HERCULES 772, 1,965 hp, a civil-series engine, as the Hercules 762, basically two-speed, supercharged but with the supercharger locked in 'M' gear. Supercharger impeller cropped to suit 100/130 grade fuel rating with methanol/water injection. Hercules 773, a torquemeter version of the Hercules 772, for Airwork Ltd.
Aircraft:

Handley Page 81A Hermes IVA

HERCULES 790, a civil-series engine, as the Hercules 758, with a re-designed rear cover, a modified starter, a 150 hp accessory gearbox drive and provision for a tachometer generator. Hercules 791, a torquemeter version of the Hercules 790.
Aircraft:

Nord Noratlas

CENTAURUS.

SINGLE-SPEED, SINGLE-STAGE SUPERCHARGED CENTAURUS
CENTAURUS 70, 71, 170, 171, 173, 373, 630, 631

TWO-SPEED, SINGLE-STAGE SUPERCHARGED CENTAURUS
CENTAURUS I, IV, V, VI, VII, VIII, IX, X, XI, XII, 14, 15, 16, 18, 20, 57, 58, 59, 160, 161, 165, 568, 660, 661, 662, 663

Bristol Centaurus 18-cylinder, two-row air-cooled sleeve-valve radial engines had the following in common:-
Bore/stroke 5.75 x 7.0 in. (146.0 x 178.0 mm)
Swept Volume 3,270.0 cu in. (53.6 litres).
Compression Ratio 7.2:1.
Dimensions vary according to accessories.
Diameter Mk XI 55.3 in; Mk 660 56.4 in (includes cowling as power egg).
Weights, where published — *see* Performance tables.

Supercharge, boost, reduction gear ratio or torquemeter, as in text, all having left-hand tractor propeller drive and V/P, C/S, propellers. All engines for military applications, unless otherwise stated.

Fuel was 100 Octane or later grades, as stated in Key. Dry weight. As in all installations, this varied from one Mark to another, depending on accessories but, as examples, the Mk XI weighed 2,695 lb and the Mk 660 weighed 3,300 lb. The Coupled Centaurus 20 installation weighed 8,390 lb.

Dimensions also varied slightly, particularly the length, according to accessories fitted. All standard Centaurus in service (except the 600 series) ran at 2,700 rpm on take-off. The latter ran at 2,900 rpm.

CENTAURUS I, 2,000 hp, compression ratio 7.2:1, two-speed, fully/medium supercharged. Geared, epicyclic reduction .4:1. L.H. tractor-drive, V/P, C/S, propeller. Fuel 100 Octane.
Aircraft:

Folland Fo.108 43/37

The first Bristol Centaurus I in 1938.

CENTAURUS IV, 2,300 hp, two-speed, fully/medium supercharged. Geared, epicyclic .4:1, rigid mounting. Single maneton bolt type crankshaft. CE-4SM. Retrospective conversion capability to Centaurus V or VII.
Aircraft:

Bristol 163 Buckingham I
Folland Fo.108 43/37
Hawker Tornado
Hawker Tempest II
Vickers 413 Warwick ASR.II
Vickers 484 Warwick C.IV

CENTAURUS V, 2,500 hp, similar to Mk IV with 2-bolt maneton, flexible mounting, cropped impeller and inter-connected throttle/propeller controls. Two-speed, fully/medium supercharged. Geared, epicyclic reduction .4:1. CE-7SM.
Aircraft:

Hawker Tempest II F.10/41

The Bristol Centaurus V which powered the Hawker Tempest II

CENTAURUS VI, 2,500 hp. As Mk V with master connecting rods in nos 7 & 8 cylinders. Two-speed, fully/medium supercharged. Geared, epicyclic reduction .4:1.
Aircraft:

Hawker Tempest II

CENTAURUS VII, 2,400 hp. As Mk V with single bolt maneton and rigid mounting but without inter-connected throttle/propeller controls. Two-speed, fully/medium supercharged. Geared, epicyclic reduction .4:1. CE-7SM.
Aircraft:

Blackburn B-45 Firebrand III
Bristol 163 Buckingham I
Bristol 166 Buckmaster I
Folland Fo.108 43/37
Hawker Tempest II
Short S.40 Shetland I
Vickers 462, 469, 473, 474 Warwick II, V

CENTAURUS VIII, 2,500 hp. As Mk VI, with methanol/water fittings and rating. Two-speed, fully/medium supercharged. Geared, epicyclic reduction .4:1.
Aircraft:

Hawker Tempest II

CENTAURUS IX, 2,500 hp. As Mk VII with 2 bolt maneton and inter-connected throttle/propeller controls. Two-speed, fully/ medium supercharged. Geared, epicyclic reduction .4:1. CE-7SM.
Aircraft:

Blackburn B-45 Firebrand III
Blackburn B-46 Firebrand IV, V, VA

CENTAURUS X, 2,500 hp. As Mk IX with methanol/water fittings and rating. Two-speed, fully/medium supercharged. Geared, epicyclic reduction .4:1.
Aircraft:

Blackburn B-47 Firebrand V

CENTAURUS XI, 2,500 hp. As Mk VII with 2 bolt maneton. Two-speed, fully/medium supercharged. Geared, epicyclic reduction .4:1. CE-8SM.
Aircraft:

> Blackburn B-47 Firebrand V
> Bristol 166 Buckmaster I
> Short S.40 Shetland II

CENTAURUS XII, 2,300 hp. Centaurus IV with redesigned .4:1 propeller reduction gear. Twin turbine entry supercharger. Hobson-R.A.E. injector. Vertically-mounted starter motor. Bomber-type rigid mounting. CE-12SM.
Aircraft:

> Hawker Tempest II
> Hawker F.2/43 Fury I prototype
> Hawker Sea Fury X prototype
> Vickers 600 Warwick (flight test)

Hawker Sea Fury prototype. with a Centaurus XII.

CENTAURUS XV, 2,300 hp. Developed from the proposed Centaurus 14, this was effectively a Mk XII, with a redesigned epicyclic propeller reduction gear, (.4:1 ratio), twin-turbine entry supercharger and Hobson-R.A.E. injector. It had a vertically-mounted starter motor. Instead of the proposed, rigid fighter-type mounting, the Mk 15 had a flexible mounting. Inter-connected throttle-propeller controls, two-speed, fully/medium supercharged. CE.12SM
Aircraft:

> Hawker Sea Fury X
> Hawker Tempest II

CENTAURUS XVIII, 2,470 hp. As Centaurus 15. Two-speed, fully/medium supercharged. Geared, epicyclic reduction .444:1. Centaurus 57 supercharger and rating. Master connecting rods in Nos. 7 & 8 cylinders.
Aircraft:

> Hawker Tempest II
> Hawker Fury F.1
> Hawker Sea Fury X

The Bristol Centaurus XVIII in a Hawker Sea Fury X

CENTAURUS XX, 2,360 hp. Dual installation engine. Two-speed Fully/medium supercharged. Basically, a pair of independent Centaurus 57s, less reduction gear, adapted for Brabazon dual installation, mounted at an included angle of 64 degrees. Torquemeter-type reduction gear, co-axial counter-rotating, feathering and reversing tractor propeller drive. CE-20SM.
Aircraft:

> Bristol 167 Brabazon I Mk I.

A dramatic view from the hangar roof of the trial wing installation of the Bristol Brabazon's Bristol Centaurus XX. This comprised a coupled pair of Centaurus 57s.

The trial wing installation of the Bristol Brabazon's Bristol Centaurus XX.

CENTAURUS 57, 2,470 hp. Centaurus XII with modified supercharger and injector for methanol/water rating. Two-speed, fully/medium supercharged. Geared, epicyclic reduction .4:1. CE-17SM.
Aircraft:

> Blackburn B-46 Firebrand IV, V, VA
> Bristol 164 Brigand I

CENTAURUS 58, 2,470 hp. Centaurus 57 with inter-connected throttle/propeller control. Two-speed, fully/medium supercharged. Geared, epicyclic reduction .444:1. CE-17SM.
Aircraft:

> Fairey Spearfish I

CENTAURUS 59, 2,470 hp. Centaurus 58 with flexible mounting. Two-speed, fully/medium supercharged. Geared, epicyclic reduction .444:1. CE-17SM.
Aircraft:

> Blackburn B-48 Firecrest S.28/43.

The Centaurus 57, a half of the coupled Centaurus XX.

CENTAURUS 70, 2,470 hp. Centaurus 57 with single-speed, medium supercharged. Lightened and shortened reduction gear, epicyclic reduction .4:1. 150 hp accessory drive.

CENTAURUS 71, 2,470 hp. Centaurus 70 with single-speed, medium supercharged. Lightened, with torquemeter-type reduction gear and 150 hp accessory drive.

CENTAURUS 100, 2,470 hp. As Centaurus 57, with modified supercharger and injector for methanol/water rating. Two-speed, fully/medium supercharged. Geared, epicyclic reduction .4:1. CE-22SM

CENTAURUS 130, 2,470 hp. Civil engine, as Centaurus 100. Single-speed, medium supercharged. Geared, epicyclic reduction .4:1. CE-22SM
Aircraft:
Airspeed A.S.57 Ambassador prototype

Installation of Centaurus 130 with a geared cooling fan drive in the prototype Airspeed A.S.57 Ambassador.

CENTAURUS 160, 2,625 hp, two-speed, fully/medium supercharged. Geared, epicyclic reduction .40:1, with front cover to suit braking propeller. Dynamic suspension mounting. Front ignition system, 150 hp accessory drive and improved sleeve timing.

CENTAURUS 161, 2,625 hp. As Centaurus 160. two-speed, fully/medium supercharged. Equipped with torquemeter-type reduction gear. Front cover to suit braking propeller. Dynamic suspension mounting. Front ignition system, 150 hp accessory drive and improved sleeve timing.

CENTAURUS 165, 2,625 hp. As Centaurus 161 with stiffened power section and two-speed, fully/medium supercharger. Equipped with torquemeter-type reduction gear. Front cover to suit braking propeller. Dynamic suspension mounting. Cylinder head

seals to suit free exit cowling. Methanol/water injection equipment fitted enabling increased take-off power to be obtained. Front ignition system, 150 hp accessory drive and improved sleeve timing.
Aircraft:
Blackburn & General Aircraft B-101 Beverley prototype

CENTAURUS 170, 2,625 hp. As Centaurus 160, single-speed, medium supercharged. Geared, epicyclic reduction .40:1. Centaurus 171, as Centaurus 170, 1-speed, medium supercharged, with torquemeter-type reduction gear.

CENTAURUS 173, 2,625 hp. As Centaurus 160, single-speed, medium supercharged. Torquemeter-type reduction gear. Front cover with single drive for combined propeller C.S.U. and braking pump. Cylinder head seals to suit free exit cowling. Methanol/water injection equipment and accessory drive with shear coupling.
Aircraft:
Blackburn & G.A. B-101 Beverley C.1

Blackburn Beverley C.1 transports of the Royal Air Force were powered by Bristol Centaurus engines of the 170 and 370 series.

CENTAURUS 175, as Mk 173 but with modified valve port timing and boost reduced by 1 lb to +13, giving the same power but longer time between overhauls.
Aircraft:
Blackburn & G.A. B-101 Beverley C.1

CENTAURUS 373, 2,370 hp. As Centaurus 173, single-speed, medium supercharged. Torquemeter-type reduction gear. Front cover with single drive for combined propeller C.S.U. and braking pump. Cylinder head seals to suit free exit cowling. D.P.I. and Methanol/water injection equipment and accessory drive with shear coupling.
Aircraft:
Blackburn B-101 Beverley C.1

CENTAURUS 568, 2,470 hp. Civil engine, two-speed, fully/medium supercharged. Geared, epicyclic reduction .444:1. As Centaurus 58, with flexible mounting, throttle and propeller controls not inter-connected.
Aircraft:
Breda-Zappata BZ.308

CENTAURUS 630, 2,450 hp. Civil engine, equivalent of proposed Centaurus 130. single-speed, medium supercharged. Geared, epicyclic reduction .40:1, front cover to suit braking propeller. Dynamic suspension mounting (Dynafocal). Front ignition system and 150 hp accessory drive.

CENTAURUS 631, 2,450 hp. Civil engine, similar to Centaurus 630. single-speed, medium supercharged. Torquemeter-type reduction gear. Front cover to suit braking propeller. Dynamic suspension mounting. Front ignition system and 150 hp accessory drive.
Aircraft:
Airspeed A.S.57 Ambassador prototype

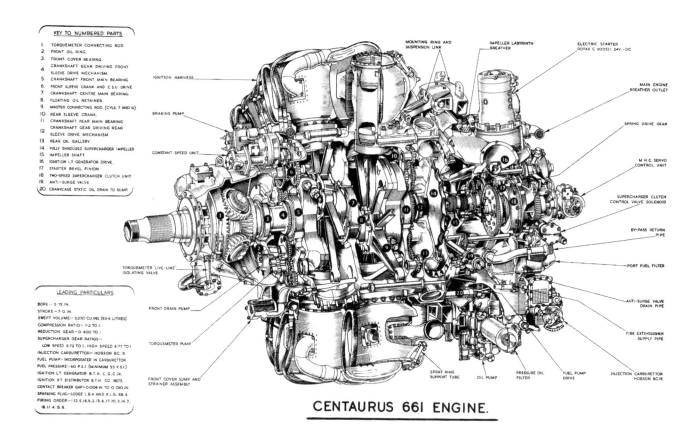

KEY TO NUMBERED PARTS

1. TORQUEMETER CONNECTING ROD.
2. FRONT OIL RING.
3. FRONT COVER BEARING.
4. CRANKSHAFT GEAR DRIVING FRONT SLEEVE DRIVE MECHANISM.
5. CRANKSHAFT FRONT MAIN BEARING.
6. FRONT SLEEVE CRANK AND C.S.U. DRIVE.
7. CRANKSHAFT CENTRE MAIN BEARING.
8. FLOATING OIL RETAINER.
9. MASTER CONNECTING ROD. (CYLS. 7 AND 16)
10. REAR SLEEVE CRANK.
11. CRANKSHAFT REAR MAIN BEARING.
12. CRANKSHAFT GEAR DRIVING REAR SLEEVE DRIVE MECHANISM.
13. REAR OIL GALLERY.
14. FULLY SHROUDED SUPERCHARGER IMPELLER.
15. IMPELLER SHAFT.
16. IGNITION L.T. GENERATOR DRIVE.
17. STARTER BEVEL PINION.
18. TWO-SPEED SUPERCHARGER CLUTCH UNIT.
19. ANTI-SURGE VALVE.
20. CRANKCASE STATIC OIL DRAIN TO SUMP.

LEADING PARTICULARS

BORE:- 5·75 IN.
STROKE:- 7·0 IN.
SWEPT VOLUME:- 3,270 CU INS. (53·6 LITRES)
COMPRESSION RATIO:- 7·2 TO I.
REDUCTION GEAR:- 0·400 TO I.
SUPERCHARGER GEAR RATIOS:-
   LOW SPEED 5·72 TO I. HIGH SPEED 6·77 TO I
INJECTION CARBURETTOR:- HOBSON BC.15
FUEL PUMP:- INCORPORATED IN CARBURETTOR.
FUEL PRESSURE:- 60 P.S.I. (MINIMUM 53 P.S.I.)
IGNITION L.T. GENERATOR B.T.H. C.G.C./4.
IGNITION H.T. DISTRIBUTOR B.T.H. CD. 18C/3.
CONTACT BREAKER GAP:- 0·008 IN. TO 0·010 IN.
SPARKING PLUG:- LODGE L.B.4 AND K.L.G. KB.4
FIRING ORDER:- 1,12,5,16,9,2,13,6,17,10,3,14,7, 18,11,4,15,8.

CENTAURUS 661 ENGINE.

A cut-away of the Centaurus 661, with torquemeter transmission.

CENTAURUS 660, 2,625 hp. Civil engine, two-speed, fully/medium supercharged. Geared, epicyclic reduction .40:1. Front cover to suit braking propeller and engine synchronizing gear. Front ignition and improved sleeve timing. Integral cylinder baffles. 150 hp accessory drive.
Aircraft:

> Airspeed A.S.57 Ambassador srs 2
> Short S.40 Shetland 2

Airspeed A.S.57 Ambassador srs 2 of British European Airways, by which it was known as the 'Elizabethan'.

CENTAURUS 661, 2,625 hp. Civil engine, two-speed, fully/medium supercharged. Centaurus 660 with torquemeter-type reduction gear. Front cover to suit braking propeller and engine synchronizing gear. Front ignition and improved sleeve timing. Integral cylinder baffles. 150 hp accessory drive.
Aircraft:

> Airspeed A.S.57 Ambassador srs 2

CENTAURUS 662, 2,625 hp. Civil engine, 2-speed, fully/medium supercharged with methanol/water injection equipment for increasing take-off power. As Centaurus 660, geared, epicyclic reduction .40:1. Front cover to suit braking propeller and engine synchronizing gear. Front ignition and improved sleeve timing. Integral cylinder baffles. 150 hp accessory drive.
Aircraft:

> Airspeed A.S.57 Ambassador srs 2

CENTAURUS 663, 2,405 hp. Civil engine, two-speed, fully/medium supercharged with methanol/water injection equipment for increasing take-off power. As Centaurus 662, with torquemeter-type reduction gear. Front cover to suit braking propeller and engine synchronizing gear. Front ignition and improved sleeve timing. Integral cylinder baffles. 150 hp accessory drive.
Aircraft:

> Airspeed A.S.57 Ambassador srs 2

BRITISH SALMSON

The British Salmson Company was formed in 1930, at New Malden, Surrey, to produce under licence the French Salmson air-cooled radial engines. This arrangement was distinct from that concerning the water-cooled radials built by the Dudbridge Iron Works during the First World War. By the beginning of 1936, the A.D.9, A.D.9R and A.C.9 were in production.

A.C.7, 105 hp, 7-cylinder, single-row radial air-cooled poppet-valve. Bore/stroke 100 x 130 mm. Vol. 7.15 litre. Compression ratio 5:1. Direct L.H. tractor-drive. Diameter 37.0 in; length 32.3 in.
Aircraft:

> Cierva C.18 Autogiro
> Surrey Flying Services A.L.1.

A.C.9, 135 hp, 9 cylinders, bore/stroke 100 x 130 mm. Vol. 9.2 litre. and compression ratio 5.6:1. Diameter 37.4 in; length 35.4 in.
Aircraft:

> Arpin A-1 'Safety-Pin'
> Comper C.L.A.7 Swift
> General Aircraft Monospar ST-3
> Henderson-Glenny HSF II Gadfly III

A.D.9, 54 hp, (1930), 9-cylinder, single-row radial air-cooled, poppet-valve. Compression ratio 6:1. Bore/stroke 70 x 86 mm. Vol. 2.97 litre. Direct L.H. tractor/pusher drive. Diameter 24.8 in; length 27.2 in.
Aircraft:

    Angus Aquila
    B.A. Swallow
    Boulton & Paul P.41 Phoenix II
    Comper C.L.A.7 Swift
    General Aircraft Monospar ST-3
    Hafner R.II Revoplane II helicopter
    Hinkler Ibis
    Klemm L.25
    Parmentier Wee Mite

The British Salmson A.D.9, a 54 hp nine-cylinder radial.

A.D.9R, srs III, 70 hp, (1934), Bore/stroke 73 x 86 mm. Vol. 197 cu in. Compression ratio 6:1. Reduction gear ratio .5:1. Diameter 28.5 in; length 31 in.
Aircraft:

    Arpin A-1 'Safety-Pin'
    British Klemm Swallow (See also B.A. — British Aircraft)

The British Salmson A.D.9R, a geared version of the A.D.9. developing about 70 hp.

A.D.9NG, 203 hp. Bore/stroke 100 x 140 mm. Vol. 10 l.
Aircraft:

    Cierva C.40 Rota II Autogiro

CARDEN. (1923), air-cooled, 750 cc two-stroke, vertical two-cylinder, direct-drive.
Aircraft:

    Gloucestershire Gannet

CARDEN AERO-ENGINES
(initially of Heston Airport, Middlesex).
Company formed in 1935 to build engines for ultra-light aeroplanes, in particular an adaptation of the Ford 10, Model C motor car-engine. It was first introduced for the 'Flying Flea', the Mignet 'Pou du Ciel'. The founder, Sir John Carden, was killed in an air accident on 10 December the same year, the Company being first taken over by Carden-Baynes Aircraft Ltd and, two years later, by Chilton Aircraft Ltd of Hungerford, Berkshire.

CARDEN-BAYNES AUXILIARY, 'outboard' engine for sailplane. 350 cc.
Aircraft:

    Scud III Auxiliary

CARDEN-FORD S.P.1, 40 hp, developed from the Carden-Ford, with several special features. These included a Centric supercharger, with a slight step-up gear ratio of 1.1:1. It was designed for an internal wing installation and had a splined propeller shaft extension from the crankshaft. The compression ratio was 6:1. It was mounted, via three-point attachments, on its side. 4-cylinder, in-line, water-cooled, poppet-valve. Bore/stroke 63.5 x 92.5 mm. Vol. 1.17 litre. Direct L.H. pusher drive. Dual magnetos.
Aircraft:

    Carden-Baynes Bee

The 31 hp Carden-Ford converted motor car engine in a Chilton D.W.1A.

The Carden-Ford powering a Mignet HM 14 Flying Flea.

CARDEN-FORD 31 hp, (1935). Generally similar to Ford 10 motor car engine, but much modified. 4-cylinder, upright in-line, water-cooled, poppet-valve. Compression ratio 6.6:1. Bore/stroke 63.5 x 92.5 mm. Vol. 1.17 litre. Direct R.H. tractor-drive. Dual magnetos.
Aircraft:

    B.A.C. Drone
    Broughton-Blayney Brawney
    Chilton D.W.1, D.W.1A

Kronfeld Monoplane
Mignet HM 14 Pou du Ciel
Perman Parasol (variation on Carden design)
Taylor Watkinson Dingbat

CAUNTER, C.F., FARNBOROUGH, HAMPSHIRE.

C.F. Caunter, who was a research engineer at the R.A.E., designed a series of two-stroke engines of novel design. There is no certain proof that any of them flew but they are included in case this is incorrect. (C.F. Caunter, together with S. Child, wrote *A Historical Summary of the Royal Aircraft Factory and its Antecedents: 1878-1918*. Report, Aero 2150, R.A.E., 1947).

CAUNTER 'B', 4-cylinder, upright in-line, air-cooled engine. It was generally similar to the Types C and D. Unsupercharged, its propeller drive was direct, L.H. tractor. Bore/stroke 90 x 82.5 mm. Vol. 2.1 l, compression ratio 7.5:1. Length 31.0 in; width 10.0 in; height 20.0 in.

A test-run of the Caunter 'B' four-cylinder two-stroke engine.

CAUNTER 'C', 4-cylinder, inverted in-line, air-cooled engine. It was generally similar to the Types B and D. Unsupercharged, its propeller drive was direct, L.H. tractor. Bore/stroke 82 x 100 mm. Vol. 2.3 l, compression ratio 7.5:1. Length 30.0 in; width 12.0 in; height 21.5 in.

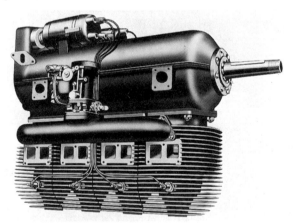

The inverted 'C' version of the Caunter engine.

CAUNTER 'D', 3-cylinder, inverted in-line, air-cooled engine. It was generally similar to the Types B and C. Unsupercharged, its propeller drive was direct, L.H. tractor. Bore/stroke 90 x 100 mm. Vol. 1.91 litre.

CIRRUS AERO-ENGINES (FORMERLY A.D.C. CIRRUS).

The Cirrus engine was devised by Major F.B.Halford, formerly head of the Aircraft Disposal Company (A.D.C.) formed in 1924, by laying-out on a bench the components of a 120 hp air-cooled Airdisco engine, an 80 hp Renault V-8 which had been greatly improved in design and power output. After designing a new

crankshaft and case, he used half of the components to make up a four-cylinder unit of 60 hp, known as the Cirrus. This was, therefore outwardly, half an 80 hp Renault. The Airdisco company soon ceased trading but Cirrus engines continued to be made by Cirrus Aero-Engines Ltd. In 1931, the Cirrus-Hermes Engineering Co took over trading in Cirrus engines. In February 1934, Phillips & Powis Aircraft (Reading) Ltd acquired the existing stocks of the Cirrus Mks I, II and III engines, together with their spare parts and rights to build. At about the same time, Blackburn Aircraft took the concern over and a new range of Blackburn Cirrus engines appeared.

CIRRUS I, 60 hp, (1925), 4-cylinder, upright in-line air-cooled poppet-valve. Bore/stroke 4.13 x 5.12 in. Vol. 274.36 cu in. (105 x 130 mm). Compression ratio 4.7:1. Cast-iron cylinder barrels, aluminium alloy heads, steel connecting rods. Direct R.H. tractor-drive. Single induction system. Length 45.8 in; width 18.26 in; height 34.3 in.

Aircraft:

Avro 543 Baby
Avro 581E Avian
de Havilland D.H.60 Moth
Short S.7 Mussel I
Westland Widgeon III

The original Cirrus I, half an 80 hp Renault, with improvements to increase power.

CIRRUS II, 85 hp, (1926). This was similar in many respects to the Cirrus I. In order to keep up with the increasing demand for more power without increasing weight in the new generation of light aircraft, Halford redesigned the cylinder head and valve gear and these modifications, together with a redesigned induction system, increasing the power originally developed by the Cirrus engine by some 30 per cent. Forged Duralumin connecting rods and pistons. Duplex Zenith or Claudel-Hobson exhaust-heated carburettor. Compression ratio 4.9:1. Bore/stroke 110 x 130 mm. Vol. 301.56 cu in., 4.939 litre. Length 45.8 in; width 18.26 in; height 34.3 in.

The Cirrus II, in a D.H.60 Moth. The induction manifold is improved.

Aircraft:
  Avro 594 Avian II, III
  de Havilland D.H.60 Moth
  de Havilland D.H.71 Tiger Moth
  Short S.7 Mussel I
  Westland Widgeon III

Bert Hinkler working on his Cirrus II Avro Avian G-EBOV.

CIRRUS III, 90 hp, (1929), similar to Cirrus II, with improved cylinder head cooling and valves. Compression ratio of 5.1:1. Length 46.0 in; width 18.9 in; height 35.6 in.

The Dudley Watt D.W.2 was powered by a Cirrus III.

Aircraft:
  Avro 594 Avian IV
  Avro 594, 605 Avian IIIA
  Avro 616 Avian IV, IVM
  Blackburn L.1B Bluebird III
  Blackburn L.1C Bluebird IV
  Cierva C.17 Mk I, II Autogiro (Avro 612)
  de Havilland D.H.60 Moth

  de Havilland D.H.71 Tiger Moth
  Dudley Watt D.W.2
  Klemm L.26a-III
  Klemm L.27aIII
  Short S.7 Mussel II
  Simmonds Spartan
  Spartan Arrow
  Westland IV (Wessex)
  Westland Widgeon III, IIIA

A German Klemm L.26a fitted with a Cirrus III.

A Curtiss-Reid Rambler was powered by an American Cirrus III.

CIRRUS IIIA, 90 hp, (1933). Compression ratio 5.4:1. Otherwise, similar to Mk III.
Aircraft:
  Miles M.2, M.2D Hawk.

CIRRUS-HERMES I, 105 hp, (1929). A slightly larger engine, to exchange for the Cirrus II and III. The valves were similar to those of the Cirrus III. The Hermes was a 4-cylinder, upright in-line air-cooled poppet-valve engine. Bore/stroke 4.48 x 5.51 in. Vol. 347.2 cu in, 5.717 litre. (114 x 140 mm). Direct R.H. tractor-drive. Length 38.5 in; width 18.97 in; height 36.06 in.
Aircraft:
  Avro 594 Avian IV
  Avro 616 Sports Avian IV/IVM
  Avro 625 Sports Avian (Monoplane)
  Blackburn L.1C Bluebird IV
  de Havilland D.H.60 Moth
  Desoutter I
  Hawker Tomtit
  Hendy 302
  Parnall Elf I
  Saro A.17 Cutty Sark
  Simmonds Spartan
  Southern (Miles) Martlet
  Westland IV (Wessex)
  Westland Widgeon IIIA

The 105 hp Cirrus-Hermes I, an improved and enlarged version of the Cirrus III.

The 105 hp Cirrus-Hermes I, an improved and enlarged version of the Cirrus III.

CIRRUS-HERMES II, 110 hp, (1930). An improved version of the Mk I, with the same capacity. Compression ratio 5.1:1. Bore/stroke 4.48 x 5.51 in. Vol. 347.2 cu in. (114 x 140 mm). Direct R.H. tractor-drive. Length 42.0 in; width 18.8 in; height 29.0 in.
Aircraft:

     Avro 594 Avian IV
     Avro 616 Avian IV/IVM
     Blackburn L.1C Bluebird IV
     Desoutter I
     Parnall Elf II
     Simmonds Spartan
     Spartan Arrow
     Spartan Three-Seater I
     Westland Widgeon IIIA

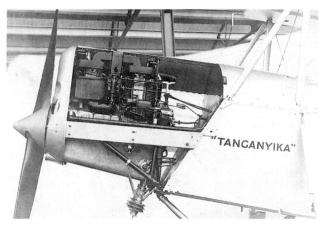

The Cirrus-Hermes II of 110 hp mounted in Avro 594 Avian IVM G-ABIC, exported to Tanganyika as VR-TAD.

CIRRUS-HERMES IIB, 115 hp, (1931), (Inverted Cirrus-Hermes II), 4-cylinder, inverted in-line air-cooled poppet-valve. Compression ratio 5.1:1. Bore/stroke 4.48 x 5.51 in. Vol. 347.2 cu in. (114 x 140 mm). Direct R.H. tractor-drive. Length 42.4 in; width 21.26 in; height 29.1 in.
Aircraft:

     Arrow Active I
     Klemm L.27a-VIII
     Spartan Three-Seater II

CIRRUS-HERMES IV, 120 hp, (1930), an improved Mk IIB.
Aircraft:

     Avro 640 Cadet Three-seater
     Hendy 302A
     Miles M.2B Hawk
     Percival D.1 Gull Four
     Spartan Cruiser II
     Spartan Three-Seater II

CIRRUS-HERMES IVA, 140 hp. Length 42.0 in; width 18.8 in; height 29.0 in.
Aircraft:

     Avro 638 Club Cadet
     Blackburn B-2
     Blackburn C.A.18 Segrave I

The inverted Cirrus-Hermes IVA developed 130 hp and led the way to the new generation of Blackburn Cirrus engines.

CLERGET BLIN et Cie

In 1913, there appeared the first of the 80–150 hp series of rotary engines, designed near Paris by Clerget, Blin et Cie, one of the best-known of the early pioneers. This introduced, for the first time in rotary engines, independently operated inlet and exhaust valves. Clerget engines were subsequently built in large numbers in Britain during the First World War. Like all rotaries, the Clerget tended to overheat and W.O. Bentley, on behalf of the Admiralty, introduced major modifications to the Clerget engine design to reduce this failing as far as possible. These included aluminium cylinder barrels with steel liners, with separate steel heads, with aluminium pistons.

CLERGET 7Z, 80 hp, (1916), 7-cylinder, single-row rotary air-cooled poppet-valve. Bore/stroke 4.72 x 5.91 in. Vol. 722.75 cu in. (120 x 150 mm). Compression ratio 4.3:1. Direct R.H. tractor/L.H. pusher-drive. Bloctube carburettor, one magneto. Diameter 36 in.
Production, 8/1914-12/1918, from:-
Gordon Watney & Co Ltd, Weybridge,
Ordered, 553;   Delivered, 300;   Cancelled/suspended, 253
Gwynnes Ltd, Hammersmith,
Ordered, 100;   Delivered, 47;   Cancelled/suspended, 53
Aircraft:
      Avro 504
      Beardmore W.B.III
      Bristol 1 Scout C
      Grahame-White 20
      Royal Aircraft Factory B.E.8a 'Bloater'
      Royal Aircraft Factory S.E.2
      Royal Aircraft Factory S.E.4a
      Sopwith Pup

CLERGET 9B, 130 hp, (1917), 9-cylinder, rotary air-cooled poppet-valve. Bore/stroke 120 x 160 mm. Vol. 16.29 litre. Compression ratio 4.56:1. Direct R.H. tractor/L.H pusher-drive. Bloctube carburettor, two magnetos. Diameter 40.2 in; length 43.5 in.
Production, 8/1914-12/1918, from:-
Ruston Proctor & Co Ltd, Lincoln,
Ordered, 1,300;   Delivered, 1,300; Cancelled/suspended, 0

A 130 hp Clerget 9B in an Avro 504C.

Aircraft:
      Armstrong Whitworth F.K.10
      Avro 504C, 504K, 504L
      Avro 531, 531A Spider
      Bristol 10 M.1A
      Bristol 11 M.1B
      Cierva C.6C Autogiro (Avro 574)
      Cierva C.6D Autogiro (Avro 575)
      Cierva C.8R Autogiro (Avro 587)
      Fairey Hamble Baby
      Nieuport 12 Fr
      Nieuport 17
      Nieuport 17bis
      Nieuport Triplane
      Sopwith Baby
      Sopwith Triplane
      Sopwith F.1 Camel
      Sopwith F.1/1 Taper Camel
      Sopwith 2F.1 (Ship) Camel
      Sopwith Scooter
      Sopwith Triplane
      Sopwith LCT 1½ Strutter

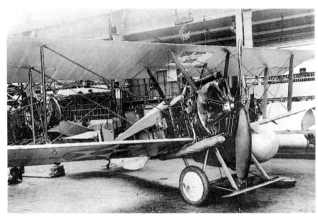

The U.S. Navy used Sopwith F.1 Camels towards the end of the first World War. This is powered by a 130 hp Clerget 9B.

CLERGET 9Bf, 140 hp, (1917), 9-cylinder, single-row rotary air-cooled, poppet-valve. Bore/stroke 4.72 x 6.77 in. Vol. 1,066.5 cu in. (120 x 172 mm), a long-stroke version of the engine. Compression ratio, Gwynnes, 5.14:1; Ruston Proctor 5.29:1. Direct R.H. tractor/L.H. pusher-drive. Bloctube carburettor, two magnetos. Diameter 40.2 in; length 43.5 in.
Production, 8/1914-12/1918, from:-
Gwynnes Ltd, Hammersmith,
Ordered, 1,750;   Delivered, 1,750; Cancelled/suspended, 0
Ruston Proctor & Co Ltd, Lincoln,
Ordered, 600;   Delivered, 600;   Cancelled/suspended, 0
Aircraft:
      Sopwith F.1 Camel

CLERGET 9Z, 110 hp, (1917), 9-cylinder, single-row rotary air-cooled, poppet-valve. Bore/stroke 4.72 x 6.3 in. Vol. 992.25 cu.in. (120 x 160 mm, Vol. 16.28 litre). Compression ratio 4.36:1. Direct R.H. tractor/L.H. pusher-drive. The chief differences from other rotary engines were that the pistons were of aluminium alloy, the connecting rods were of tubular section and the inlet and exhaust cams were mechanically operated by separate cams, tappets and rocker-arms. Bloctube carburettor, two magnetos.
Aircraft:
      Airco D.H.2
      Airco D.H.5
      Alcock Scout
      Armstrong Whitworth F.K.9
      Avro 521
      Blackburn Triplane
      Bristol 5 Scout D
      Bristol 8 S.2A
      Bristol 10 M.1A

Bristol 11 M.1B
Fairey Hamble Baby
Nieuport 12
Nieuport 17bis
Pemberton Billing P.B.25
Royal Aircraft Factory F.E.8
Royal Aircraft Factory S.E.2
Sopwith Baby
Sopwith Triplane
Sopwith F.1 Camel
Sopwith LCT 1½-Strutter
Vickers E.S.1, 2 Bullet
Vickers F.B.5 Gunbus.
Vickers F.B.19 Bullet Mk II

110 hp Clerget rotary.

CLERGET 11Eb, 200 hp, (1918), 11-cylinder, single-row rotary air-cooled poppet-valve. Bore/stroke 4.72 x 7.48 in. Vol. cu. in (120 x 190 mm). Compression ratio 5.1:1. Direct R.H. tractor/L.H. pusher-drive. Bloctube carburettor, two Nilmelior magnetos.

A 200 hp, eleven-cylinder Clerget 11Eb in a Sopwith Bulldog, an unlovely two-seater. It bristles with guns, two Vickers and two Lewis being visible.

Aircraft:
Sopwith 2FR.2 Bulldog
Sopwith 3F.2 Hippo
Sopwith T.F.2 Salamander

COVENTRY VICTOR MOTOR CO LTD, COVENTRY.

This company was engaged in making two-, four- and eight-cylinder horizontally-opposed engines from 1911, ranging in power up to 50 hp and used in several light aircraft.

NEPTUNE III, 40 hp, a 4-cylinder, horizontally-opposed air-cooled poppet-valve engine. It was generally similar to the 10 and 12 hp Mks I and II. It was unsupercharged, and its propeller drive was direct. Bore/stroke 85 x 80 mm. Vol. 1.82 litre. Compression ratio 6.7:1.
Aircraft:
Druine D.54 Turbi

CURTISS.

The American aviation pioneer Glenn H. Curtiss had built internal combustion engines before the first Wright Brothers flight in 1903. This engineering development provided a new outlet and, subsequently Curtiss aircraft and engines and, early in the 1914-1918 war, Curtiss Aeroplane and Motor Corporation built Curtiss engines to fill large contracts for the British Government. These included, initially, Curtiss OX engines. The OX was derived from a string of engines, being a development of the Vee-8 Model L, water-cooled engine. The Model O was an improved L, rated at 75 hp, at 1,100 rpm. This, in turn, was refined, as the 90 hp Model OX, of which there were several sub-variants, with varying types of equipment. The most significant of these was the OX-5, notable for powering the Curtiss JN series of training aircraft, which was very extensively used by the Allies during the First World War.

CURTISS OX-2, 90 hp, bore/stroke 4.0 x 5.0 in, 101.6 x 127 mm, compression ratio 5.4:1, similar to the Curtiss OX-5 but run at slightly higher rpm. Length 56.75 in; width 29.75 in; height 36.75 in.
Aircraft:
Curtiss H.4 Small America
Curtiss JN-4, 4A
Royal Aircraft Factory B.E.2c

CURTISS OX-5, 90 hp, (1915), 8-cylinder, upright 90-degree Vee engine, water-cooled poppet-valve, unsupercharged. Its propeller drive was direct and could be in either direction, with L.H. or R.H. tractor or pusher-drive. Bore/stroke 4.0 x 5.0 in. Vol. 502.4 cu in (101.6 x 127.0 mm). The cylinders were of cast-iron, with separate monel-metal water jackets. The iron cylinder head had single valves, operated by push and pull-rods operated by a camshaft running in the vee. Connecting rods of opposite cylinders lay side by side on a four-throw, five-bearing crankshaft, the cylinder rows therefore being slightly staggered. The pistons were of cast aluminium and the compression ratio was 5.4:1. One Claudel-Hobson or Zenith duplex carburettor and one magneto.

Regrettably, during the First World War there were numerous accidents in flying training which were caused by engine failure. This has long been attributed to the poor quality control and performance of the Curtiss OX-5 engines supplied from the United States and the British Government gave Brazil Straker in Bristol, under A.H.R. Fedden, the task of a virtual redesign of the engine, so as to make it safely usable. The figures quoted are as reconstructed. Length 56.75 in; width 29.75 in; height 36.75 in.
Aircraft:
Airco D.H.6
Avro 545
Curtiss JN-3

CURTISS OXX, 100 hp, (1917) similar in design to OX series but, with the bore increased to 4.25 in, 107.9 mm and the volume increased proportionately to 567.44 cu in, it developed marginally higher power. Compression ratio 5.4:1.
Aircraft:
Curtiss H.4 Small America

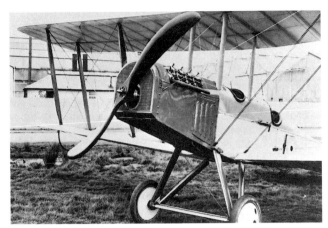

A B.E.2c, 1738, powered by the American Curtiss OX-5, as rebuilt by Brazil Straker at Bristol.

A Curtiss JN-3, powered by a Curtiss OX-5.

The Curtiss OX-5 was imported in some numbers from the United States during the early part of the first World War. It was not satisfactory and was extensively redesigned and rebuilt by Brazil Straker at Bristol. This is an example.

CURTISS VX, 160 hp, (1917), 8-cylinder, upright 90-degree Vee, water-cooled, unsupercharged poppet-valve engine. Its propeller drive was direct and could be in either direction, with L.H. or R.H. tractor or pusher-drive. Bore/stroke 5.0 x 7.0 in. Vol. 1,099.6 cu in

(127 x 177.8 mm). Compression ratio 4.71:1. Two Zenith carburettors, one magneto. Length 68 in; width 37 in; height 34 in.
Aircraft:
    Curtiss C
    Curtiss R-2, R-4

CURTISS D-12 — *See* Fairey Felix.

de HAVILLAND.

Geoffrey de Havilland, born in 1882, studied at the Crystal Palace Engineering School and, aged 21, undertook an extra term to complete a 500 cc motor-cycle engine which he had designed. This was an advanced design for its day and, in a frame also designed by de Havilland, was successful and de Havilland sold both pattern and manufacturing rights. In 1913, a 500 cc motor-cycle was announced by Burney and Blackburne Ltd 'until recently known as the de Havilland'. In 1908, de Havilland designed a small four-cylinder engine, intended to power an aeroplane which he also designed and built. This engine was built by the Iris Motor Company of Willesden (run by Geoffrey de Havilland's brother). The engine, of which some half-dozen were built, was first exhibited at the 1910 Aero Show at Olympia.

In 1910, Geoffrey (later Sir Geoffrey) de Havilland joined the staff at the Army Balloon Factory at Farnborough, later to become the Royal Aircraft Factory, as a designer and test pilot. He concentrated on airframe design and, in 1914, joined the new Aircraft Manufacturing Company, later to become known as 'Airco'. Commissioned into the Royal Flying Corps at the outbreak of war, he was posted back to industry shortly afterwards. His first important design was the famous D.H.4 of 1916, forerunner of the D.H.9 and 9A of 1917-18. The first chosen power plant of the D.H.4 was the 230 hp B.H.P., an engine designed by F.B.Halford and described at greater length in another part of the book. Although the engine itself was not a great success, its selection for the D.H.4 was noteworthy because it resulted in the collaboration between de Havilland and Halford. Thus, in 1916 began a business association and friendship which lasted for some forty years.

Following the end of the First World War, the Aircraft Manufacturing Co, 'Airco', of which de Havilland was Chief Designer, was bought by Birmingham Small Arms Ltd (B.S.A.). The company then promptly terminated the aviation side of its business. De Havilland, needing financial backing to start his own company, obtained it from a former Director of Airco, Holt Thomas, who had formed Air Transport and Travel Ltd, using D.H. aircraft, adapted as transports. The designs of de Havilland were released by B.S.A. and the de Havilland Aircraft Co was formed at Stag Lane, Edgware on 25 September 1920. De Havilland had a genius for matching his aeroplane designs with suitable engines, when available and, having made several tentative starts with interim transport aircraft, he produced the two-seat D.H.51, powered by an A.D.C. Airdisco (described under A.D.C.) and the little ultra-light D.H.53 Humming Bird monoplane, powered by a Bristol Cherub. Then, in 1925 came his quite brilliant idea, the D.H.60 Moth light two seater, a scaled-down D.H.51.

As related previously, the ideal engine was thought to be Halford's A.D.C. 4-cylinder Cirrus (half an Airdisco) but it was found to be too heavy for the competition for which it was intended and so the lighter Armstrong Siddeley Genet was at first substituted. Nevertheless, Cirrus-engined Moths subsequently became extremely popular. In October 1926 Halford, as a consultant in collaboration with de Havilland, designed a new engine somewhat similar to the Cirrus, but more powerful and using new and lighter parts. It was an upright four-cylinder engine, called Gipsy, following D.H.'s particular liking for Lepidoptera. Nominally of 100 hp, the Gipsy engine showed great promise. In order to establish what its potential might be and delivering 135 hp, it was tried out in a little single seat racing monoplane, the D.H.71 Tiger Moth. It was an immediate success, gaining a World's Speed Record for light aeroplanes in the process.

This was an auspicious start and, in derated form giving a maximum of 100 hp, it found fame as the engine for the de Havilland Gipsy Moth. Subsequently, it appeared in inverted form, to give a higher thrust line and improved pilot's view, as the Gipsy

III. Again, this was a success, leading directly to the similar Gipsy Major, which appeared in numerous versions and was, perhaps, the most successful 130–150 hp engine ever produced. With Halford's early help, the reliable little Gipsy I, II, III and Major four-cylinder and later 200 hp Gipsy Six and Queen six-cylinder engines for light aircraft, were the holders of endless records for speed and distance. The Gipsy Twelve, or King of 1936 was a double Six, an inverted, supercharged and geared Vee-12. Because of the outbreak of war in 1939 and the big building programme for the Gipsy Major, installed in Tiger Moth and Magister trainers, it did not achieve the success expected. But for the war, the neat little inverted Gipsy Minor might have been a winner as well.

Until 1930, construction of de Havilland airframes and engines was concentrated at Stag Lane, Edgware. As the outer London sprawl encroached, the Hatfield site was selected, airframe manufacture being transferred there and the last flight from Stag Lane took place in 1934. Engine and propeller work continued at Stag Lane and, in February 1944, the de Havilland Engine Company was formed there, from the Engine Division of the de Havilland Aircraft Company. F.B. Halford, who had been in charge of design at Napier until 1944, became Chairman and Technical Director of the de Havilland Engine Company upon its formation. In 1945, the Government leased the Leavesden aircraft factory, near Watford, to the D.H.Engine Company and, in 1946, the Gipsy production division moved into the Leavesden No 1 Factory, where the London Aircraft Production Group had built Halifax bombers during the Second World War. The No 2 factory, previously making Mosquitos, was then turned over to engine sheet metal fabrication.

IRIS, 45/52 hp, (1909–10), de Havilland's first engine design, built by the Iris Motor Company, was a 4-cylinder, horizontally opposed, water-cooled (thermo-syphon), poppet-valve. Bore/stroke 114 x 120 mm. (Vol. 4.94 litre). Cylinders were in pairs, held by one yoke and three bolts. Each tappet operated inlet and exhaust valves. It had a two-throw crankshaft and suffered from a weakness incurred by this design. The first engine, in 1909, had a pusher drive with fly-wheel and two geared propellers, reduction .5:1. After an accident, de Havilland redesigned both the engine and aircraft, eliminating the need for double bevel drives and shafts and, using one propeller, was driven direct from the crankshaft. This saved some 30 lb weight and tuning the engine improved its power output from the original 45 hp. Other figures quoted are for the improved Iris engine. The power/weight ratio was the remarkably low figure of 3.8 lb/hp, almost half that of the contemporary, 1910, Wright engine. About 6 were built and run.

Aircraft:
    de Havilland Biplane No 1, No 2
    Government Balloon Factory airship *Gamma*

De Havilland Gipsy engines are listed, in approximate order of appearance. After the upright four-cylinder Gipsy I, II and Vee-8 Ghost, all subsequent de Havilland engines were of the inverted four-cylinder, six-cylinder and twelve-cylinder pattern.

The first Gipsy was a high-compression racing version of what was to become known as the famous Gipsy I. It powered the first Tiger Moth, a single-seat racing monoplane, seen here piloted by Hubert Broad.

GIPSY 'R', 135 hp at 2,850 rpm, (1927). The first Gipsy, a racing engine, 4-cylinder, upright in-line air-cooled poppet-valve. Bore/stroke 114 x 128 mm. Vol. 5.226 litre. High compression ratio 5.5:1. Direct L.H. tractor-drive.

Aircraft:
    De Havilland D.H.71 Tiger Moth (a racing monoplane which, on 27 August 1927, broke the light aeroplane 100 km Closed Circuit Record, at 186.5 mph. Pilot Hubert Broad).

GIPSY I, (GIPSY ONE) 98 hp, (1926) de Havilland-Halford, 4-cylinder, upright in-line air-cooled poppet-valve. Cast-iron cylinders, with detachable two-valve aluminium heads and exposed valve gear. Slipper-type cast aluminium alloy pistons. Connecting rods were Y-alloy forgings. Bore/stroke 114 x 128 mm. Vol. 5.226 litre. Zenith carburettor with altitude control. Compression ratio 5:1. Direct L.H. tractor-drive. This was the production version of a derated Gipsy 'R'. Fuel — 'Any good grade No 1 petrol. It is not necessary to use Aviation petrol or benzole'. Total number built, 1,445.

Aircraft:
    Avro 594 Avian IV
    Avro 616 Sports Avian IV/IVM
    Blackburn L.1C Bluebird IV
    Breda 15
    de Havilland D.H.60G, D.H.60M Gipsy Moth
    de Havilland D.H.60T Gipsy Moth Trainer
    de Havilland D.H.71 Tiger Moth
    Simmonds Spartan
    Southern (Miles) Martlet
    Spartan Arrow
    Westland Widgeon III, IIIA

A D.H.60 Gipsy Moth G-EBTD, powered by a Gipsy I engine which was 'sealed' and flown for 600 hours on a reliability test, between 29 December, 1928 and 24 September 1929. It covered 51,000 miles with only routine attention.

The de Havilland Gipsy I engine, with exposed valve gear.

Blackburn Bluebird IVs under construction at Brough.

GHOST, 198 hp, (1928). Made up effectively of two upright Cirrus engines on a common crankcase. Generally similar in appearance to the 80 hp Renault from which it originated but with the Cirrus modifications, enabling it to develop over twice the power for a lower weight. It was an 8-cylinder, upright 90-degree Vee, air-cooled, poppet-valve engine. Bore/stroke 114 x 128 mm. Vol. 8.17 litre. Compression ratio 5:1. Geared, spur R.H. tractor-drive.
Aircraft:

    de Havilland D.H.75 Hawk Moth.

de Havilland's Ghost engine of 1928, mounted in a D.H.75 Hawk Moth, was a curious reversion to the design of the wartime 80 hp Renault. A geared Vee-8, it used Cirrus components which, in turn, were evolved originally from the Renault.

GIPSY II, (GIPSY TWO) 108 hp, (1930). Halford, together with Eric Moult redesigned the Gipsy Mk I. This engine was outwardly similar to the Gipsy One but had enclosed valve gear, forged steel cylinders, the stroke increased from 128 mm to 140 mm and a compression ratio of 5.2:1. Claudel Hobson carburettor. Total built, 309.
Aircraft:

    Airspeed A.S.4 Ferry
    Avro 594 Avian IV
    Avro 616 Avian IVA/IVM
    Blackburn L.1C Bluebird IV
    Bristol 20 M.1
    de Havilland D.H.60G, D.H.60M Gipsy Moth
    de Havilland D.H.60T Gipsy Moth Trainer
    Saro A.17 Cutty Sark
    Saro A.21 Windhover
    Short S.7 Mussel II
    Simmonds Spartan
    Southern (Miles) Martlet
    Spartan Arrow
    Spartan Three-Seater I

The de Havilland Gipsy II engine, with enclosed valve gear.

Inverted 4-cylinder engines, Gipsy III, Minor and Major

Year	Unleaded Fuel	Leaded Fuel	Note
1929	Gipsy III		Aluminium head
1931	Gipsy IV 'Minor'		
1932	Gipsy Major I		Bronze head
1934		Gipsy Major I srs II	V/P prop, Al. head
1934		Gipsy Major II	As srs II, Al. hd.
1936		Gipsy Major IC	For Canada
1937	Gipsy Minor		
1938		Gipsy Major III EX	As srs II Major IIA
1938		Gipsy Major IIA	Was Major IIIEX
1943		Gipsy Major III	Became Major 30
1944		Gipsy Major 30	Was Major III
1944		Gipsy Major ID	Modified Major IC
1944		Gipsy Major IIIS	Became Major 50
1944		Gipsy Major 50	Was Major IIIS
1946	Gipsy Major IF		Aluminium head
1946		Gipsy Major 5	Mod. Mk IC. No prod
1946		Gipsy Major 7	RAF mod of Major ID
1946		Gipsy Major 10-1	Civil Major 7/8
1948		Gipsy Major 10-2	Civil Major 8
1946		Gipsy Major 10-3(M)	Fixed-pitch prop
1946		Gipsy Major 10-4(M)	Manual V/P prop
1948		Gipsy Major 8	For RAF, manual V/P

GIPSY III, (GIPSY THREE) 110 hp, (1932, inverted GIPSY II). Bore/stroke 114 x 140 mm. LH tractor direct drive. Power Curve at rated altitude sea level to 2,000 ft, from A.& A.E.E., Martlesham, Report M.613, dated 6.5.32.

RPM	2,300	2,200	2,150	2,000	1,800
BHP	121	117	115	107.5	96.5

The Gipsy III was little more than an inverted Gipsy II, with a revised oil system. It bred one of the most successful light aircraft engines ever built.

Max 121 bhp, 2,300 rpm, all-out level flight (5 min). Total built 611.

Aircraft:

> Airspeed A.S.4 Ferry
> Arrow Active II
> Avro 616 Sports Avian IV/IVM
> Blackburn L.1C Bluebird IV
> Blackburn B-2
> Blackburn-Saro (Segrave) Meteor
> Breda 33
> Cierva/de Havilland C.24 Autogiro
> Comper C.L.A.7 Swift
> Darmstadt D.22
> de Havilland D.H.60G Gipsy Moth
> de Havilland D.H.60GIII Moth Major
> de Havilland D.H.80 Puss Moth
> de Havilland D.H.82A Tiger Moth I
> de Havilland D.H.83 Fox Moth
> de Havilland D.H.85 Leopard Moth
> de Havilland D.H.87 Hornet Moth
> de Havilland D.H. T.K.1
> Desoutter II
> Heinkel He 64C
> Klemm L.26a-X
> Klemm L.27a-IX
> Klemm L.32-X
> Miles M.2A, M.2C Hawk
> Miles M.2F Hawk Major
> Saro A.17 Cutty Sark
> Saro-Percival A.24 Mailplane
> Saro/Segrave A.22 Meteor
> Spartan Cruiser I
> Spartan A.24 Mailplane
> Westland-Hill Pterodactyl IV

A Gipsy III engine powered D.H.80A Puss Moth in which James Mollison made the first solo East-West Atlantic crossing, in 31 hours in August 1932. This and numerous other records proved the slogan 'You can rely on a Gipsy'.

GIPSY IV. (1931). This was the fore-runner of the Gipsy Minor (q.v.) and was unofficially known as such.

Aircraft:

> D.H.81, 81A Swallow Moth

GIPSY MAJOR. (1932). It differed little from the Gipsy III, apart from the cylinder bore, increased from 114 to 118 mm and was given the more military name after the adoption of the Tiger Moth as a Royal Air Force trainer. This was probably the most successful and widely-used light aeroplane engine ever built, at least on the European side of the Atlantic. It was much in demand for club, sports and racing aircraft before the Second World War. Thanks to the enormous production required for trainers during the war, principally for de Havilland Tiger Moths and Miles Magisters, in the peace which followed there was a great demand for the engine which was relatively cheap and of course easily available from Government surplus stock. It was thus very widely used in flying clubs. It was used for racing, several versions being available, designed to accept higher compression and leaded fuel, incorporating the modifications necessary because of these factors.

A simple, straightforward engine, the Gipsy Major could quickly be replaced, exchanging one version for another in a few hours, when required. In clubs, the famous Tiger Club for example where racing was a normal weekend activity, a high-compression engine could be installed before a race. This gave marginally more power and could be installed in proper time, so as to declare it and still hope for the extra half-knot in speed and the possibility to outwit the handicappers, with all their clever calculations. The frantic competition activity thus created in the air racing fraternity gave rise to the 'Throttle-benders Union' of the 1950s and 60s.

It says a great deal for the Gipsy Major I that, despite the thrashing which it continues to put up with, in the endless and tedious rounds of training flying, to say nothing of racing and sometimes insensitive handling by pilots who only had two speeds — flat out and stop — engine failure was extremely uncommon. This reliability contributed much to its popularity.

Because of the ease and frequency of changes between one version of the basic engine and another, there can be no absolute certainty about the combination of versions of aeroplanes and versions of engines. The following record is therefore offered, of aircraft powered by the Gipsy Major in all its versions and is therefore as accurate as published and available information permits (despite numerous contradictions), and no guarantees can be offered as to its completeness, nor even of its total accuracy at any particular point in the life of any aeroplane. It is more of a pointer to the light-hearted manner, (while staying fairly strictly within the Airworthiness Regulations) in which the light aviation business ran itself after the Second World War. With such a reliable and simple little engine, flying for fun really meant just that. In all, 14,615 Gipsy Major Is were built. In addition, because the Gipsy Major was very extensively used as a training engine during the Second World War, many were damaged in accidents and a massive Gipsy Engine Repair Department and several 'daughter' firms overhauled or repaired some 7,000 Gipsies of various kinds.

Gipsy Major engines, up to the Mk 10, had the following in common:-

> Bore/stroke 4.646 x 5.512 in. (118.0 x 140.0 mm)
> Swept Volume 6.124 litre.
> Compression Ratio 5.25:1 or 6:1 (*see* text)
> Dimensions vary according to accessories, see below.
> Weights, where published — *see* Performance tables.

Dimensions, approx:
All Gipsy Major Is, II and VII; length 1028.5 mm; width 508 mm; height 759.5 mm (II & VII, 777.5 mm).
Gipsy Major 30, 50; length 1,067 mm; width 416 mm; height 818 mm.

GIPSY MAJOR I srs I, 130 hp, (1934). The 'srs I' was intended for use with fixed-pitch propellers and had a modest compression ratio. Its normal output was 120 hp at 2,350 rpm. It was a 4-cylinder, inverted in-line, air-cooled, poppet-valve engine. Its cylinders were carbon steel forgings. There were three Royal Air Force versions of this engine. The Tiger Moth II and Queen Bee aircraft, fitted with floats, had special precautions to protect them from sea water corrosion and the Queen Bee, radio-controlled target version of the Tiger Moth, had screened ignition. Both were intended for catapulting and had the float chamber in front of the choke tube to

The Gipsy Major was an improved Gipsy III, originally intended for service with the Royal Air Force but soon to find its way into countless types of light aircraft, the World over.

prevent the fuel supply being interrupted when catapulting. Twin fuel pumps were fitted to Magister I aircraft only. Bore/stroke 118 x 140 mm. Vol. 6.124 litre. Compression ratio 5.25:1. Direct L.H. tractor-drive. Power Curve at rated altitude sea level to 2,000 ft, from A.& A.E.E., Martlesham, Report M.649, dated 14.10.35.

RPM	2,350	2,300	2,200	2,100	1,900
BHP	132	130.5	122.5	123.5	113

Max 130 bhp, 2,350 rpm, all-out level flight (5 min). Fuel, in 1937, 'Good grade automobile fuel', or non-leaded 73-77 Octane (DTD 134). The engine was also built in Australia, to Imperial measurements by General-Motors Holdens, where it was known originally as the Gipsy Trainer.

The Gipsy Major I chosen for the Miles Magister trainer was fitted with twin fuel pumps, as shown here.

Aircraft:

Airspeed A.S.4 Ferry
Arrow Active II
Auster (Taylorcraft F) III, VC
Auster 6A Tugmaster
Auster J/1 Autocrat
Auster J/1B Aiglet
Auster J/1N Alpha
Auster J/5B Autocar
Auster J/5F Aiglet Trainer
Avro 638 Club Cadet
B.A.Eagle II
B.A.III Cupid
B.A.IV Double Eagle
British Klemm Eagle
Blackburn B-2
Blackburn-Saro (Segrave) Meteor II
Boulton Paul P.92/2, F.11/37 (model)
Comper C.L.A.7 Swift
Comper Mouse
De Bruyne (Aero Research) Snark
de Havilland D.H.60GIII Moth Major

de Havilland D.H.80A Puss Moth
de Havilland D.H.82A Tiger Moth I
de Havilland D.H.82B, D.H.82C Tiger Moth II
de Havilland D.H.82B Queen Bee I (prototype)
de Havilland D.H.83 Fox Moth
de Havilland D.H.84 Dragon
de Havilland D.H.85 Leopard Moth
de Havilland D.H.87A, B Hornet Moth
de Havilland D.H.90 Dragonfly
de Havilland D.H. T.K.2
de Havilland D.H. T.K.5 (taxi only)
Foster Wickner G.M.1 Wicko
General Aircraft G.A.L.42 Cygnet Major
General Aircraft Monospar ST-11
General Aircraft Monospar ST-12
Hirtenberg H.S.9A
Miles M.2F, H, M, P, R Hawk Major
Miles M.2W, X, Y Hawk Trainer
Miles M.3, 3A Falcon Major
Miles M.5 Sparrowhawk
Miles M.11, 11A Whitney Straight
Miles M.14, 14A Hawk Trainer III (Magister I T.37/37)
Miles M.17 Monarch
Miles M.18 Mk I
Miles M.28 Mercury
Miles M.30X Minor
Miles M.35 Libellula
Miles M.38 Messenger IIC, IVA
Percival D.2 Gull Major
Reid & Sigrist R.S.3 Desford
Royal Aircraft Factory B.E.2c replica
(upright engine)
Rumpler C.IV (Slingsby 58) replica (upright engine)
Saunders-Roe Skeeter — see Cierva
Spartan Cruiser II, III
Stampe et Vertongen SV-4B
Taylorcraft F (Auster III)

Another mount for the Gipsy Major I was the Miles M.11 Whitney Straight.

GIPSY MAJOR I srs II, 138 hp, (1934), often referred to as the Gipsy Major II, was outwardly similar to the Mk I srs I but it differed from it considerably in design detail and materials employed in its construction. Having a higher compression ratio than the series I, at 6:1 and using minimum 77 Octane, leaded fuel (requiring stellited exhaust valves to resist corrosion), it was more of a competition engine and was available with either a fixed or a de Havilland two-position bracket-type variable-pitch propeller. It ran at slightly greater rpm and produced significantly greater power than the earlier engine. It was designed for longer hours between overhaul and improved accessibility for routine servicing. Later models with Elektron magnesium-alloy crankcase. Power Curve at rated altitude 2,000 ft, from A.& A.E.E., Martlesham, Report M.711, dated 23.6.37. Power Curve at rated altitude 2,000 ft.

There a few aircraft designed to take twin Gipsy Majors. This example was a de Havilland D.H.90 Dragonfly, G-AEWZ, was a pretty miniature version of the Rapide, which could carry five people. It was owned by Air Commodore G.J. Powell CBE, head of Silver City Airways.

RPM	2,400	2,300	2,200	2,100	2,000	1,900
BHP	137	133	128.5	124	119.5	114

Max 132/138 bhp, 2,400 rpm, all-out level flight (5 min). Total built 91.
Aircraft:

Comper Streak
de Havilland D.H.80A Puss Moth
de Havilland D.H. T.K.2
de Havilland D.H. T.K.4
Miles M.5, M.5A Sparrowhawk
Miles M.11, M.11A, M.11C Whitney Straight
Miles M.13 Hobby
Miles M.28 Mercury II, 4
Miles M.38 Messenger I
Miles M.65 Gemini 7

GIPSY MAJOR IC, similar to Mk I. Compression ratio 6:1. Initially for Canada, using leaded fuels, 80 Octane. Slightly higher max rpm. Unscreened ignition. Any of the above could be powered by the Mk IC for racing purposes.
Aircraft:

Auster J/1 Autocrat
de Havilland D.H. T.K.2
de Havilland D.H. T.K.5
de Havilland D.H.82A, C Tiger Moth II
de Havilland D.H.83, 83C Fox Moth
de Havilland D.H.87A, B Hornet Moth
Miles M.39B Libellula
Miles M.65 Gemini 3
Thruxton Jackaroo

Powered by a Gipsy Major, this D.H.82A Tiger Moth is in the handsome black and red livery of pre-war Brooklands Aviation Ltd. The pilot is the late Air Commodore Allen Wheeler CBE, formerly Director of the Shuttleworth Trust Museum of Historic Aircraft.

Another, rather special Gipsy Major C engined Tiger Moth, G-AOAA 'The Deacon' belonging to the Tiger Club. 'You can rely on a Gipsy' surely says it all.

GIPSY MAJOR ID, similar to Mk IC. Compression ratio 6:1. Similar except for fuel pump, priming and screened ignition harness. Any of the above could be powered by the Mk ID for racing purposes.
Aircraft:

Auster J/1 Autocrat
de Havilland D.H. T.K.2
de Havilland D.H. T.K.5 (taxi only)
de Havilland D.H.82A, C Tiger Moth II
de Havilland D.H.82B Queen Bee I
de Havilland D.H.83, 83C Fox Moth
de Havilland D.H.87A, B Hornet Moth
Miles M.39B Libellula
Miles M.65 Gemini 3
Taylorcraft F (Auster III), derated engine, c.r. 5.25:1
Thruxton Jackaroo

GIPSY MAJOR IF, aluminium heads, as Mk IC but with unleaded fuel. Compression ratio 5.25:1. Unscreened ignition.
Aircraft:

de Havilland D.H.82A Tiger Moth I
de Havilland D.H.87A, B Hornet Moth
Miles M.14, M.14A Magister, Hawk Trainer Mk III

GIPSY MAJOR 7, 145 hp, (1946), a service version of the Gipsy Major ID, increased continuous climb rpm. Compression ratio 6:1, similar fuel pump, priming and screened ignition harness.
Aircraft:

Auster A.O.P. VI, T.7
Auster 6A Tugmaster

GIPSY MAJOR 8, 145 hp, (1948), an engine developed from the Mk ID and VII, running on leaded fuel, with sodium-cooled exhaust valves and adapted for R.A.F equipment. A self-indexing cartridge starter is fitted to Royal Air Force Chipmunks and the propeller is of the two-blade, fixed pitch metal Fairey-Reed type. The engine drives two fuel pumps, a 500-watt generator and a vacuum pump. Total built 952.
Aircraft:

Bjorn Andreasson KZ VIII
Cierva W.14 Skeeter 3 (prototype)
de Havilland (Canada) D.H.C.1B Chipmunk T.10

The Chipmunk T.10, basic trainer in the Royal Air Force, powered by a de Havilland Gipsy Major 8.

GIPSY MAJOR 10 Mk 1, 145 hp, a more powerful post-war version of the Gipsy Major srs II, with a compression ratio of 6:1, incorporating all the advances which massive wartime production prevented. It ran on 80 Octane leaded fuel, featured an aluminium head, with improved and stellited valve seats and was available with a splined propeller shaft, generator and vacuum pump. An electric starter was available. Total of all Mk 10 versions built, 1,248.
Aircraft:

Auster 6A Tugmaster
Auster J/1S
Auster J/5P Autocar
Auster J/5R Alpine
Auster P Avis 1
Beagle A.61 Terrier

Chrislea CH.3 srs 2 Super Ace
Cierva W.14 Skeeter 2
Fairey Primer
Firth Helicopter
Miles M.38 Messenger 4, 4B
Miles M.57 Aerovan 5
Miles M.65 Gemini 3A, B, C, 7
Newbury A.P.4 Eon
Pfalz D.III replica (upright engine)
Reid & Sigrist R.S.3 Desford
Tipsy M

GIPSY MAJOR 10 Mk 2, (1948), 145 hp, a civil version of the service Mk 8, available with a manually-operated v/p propeller.
Aircraft:

Auster J/5L Aiglet Trainer
Cierva W.14 Skeeter II
de Havilland (Australia) D.H.A.3 Drover 2
de Havilland (Canada) D.H.C.1B Chipmunk T.10
Miles M.65 Gemini 3C
SAAB 91 Safir

GIPSY MAJOR 10 Mk 3, similar to Mk 2, adapted for the use of locally-produced accessories.
Aircraft:

de Havilland (Australia) D.H.3 Drover 2
de Havilland (Canada) D.H.C.1B Chipmunk T.10

GIPSY MAJOR 30, 160 hp, formerly the Gipsy Major 3. The Gipsy Major 30 was a major redesign of the basic engine, with the cylinders having a bore increased from 118 to 120 mm, which was as large as the crankcase would take. At the same time, the stroke was increased from 140 to 150 mm, the volume increased from 374 cu in (6.1l) to 415 cu in (6.8 l) and the power went up accordingly. At the same time, the compression ratio was increased from 6:1 to 6.5:1.

GIPSY MAJOR 50, 197 hp, formerly the Gipsy Major 3S (Supercharged). Developed from the major redesign of the Mk 30, the Gipsy Major 50 was a supercharged engine with a compression ratio 6.5:1. It was available with a conventional carburettor or with direct fuel injection. The prototype de Havilland Chipmunk CF-DIOX, (later registered G-AKEV), was handed over to the D.H. Engine Company on 16th August, 1949, as G-5-3 and fitted with a Gipsy Major 50. Height tests of the supercharged engine were made by R. Plenderleith and C. Capper on 3rd September and 17th October, 1949, reaching 22,000 and 25,500 feet respectively. A total of eight hours were flown and a further ten hours development flying were anticipated before attempting a World's altitude record in the class but the company abandoned the project.
Aircraft:

de Havilland (Canada) D.H.C.-1B Chipmunk

The Chipmunk with the supercharged Gipsy Major 50 engine.

GIPSY MAJOR 200, 200 hp, originally designed as a 'utility Major' the 200 series was intended to develop the maximum output that could be squeezed out of the long-suffering Gipsy Major. Using the cylinder heads and barrels of the Gipsy Queen 30/70 series, it was intended to be a light helicopter engine. Fuel 100/130 grade. Total of all Mk 200/215 versions built, 106.
Aircraft:

Cierva W.14 Skeeter 6

GIPSY MAJOR 215, 220 hp, cylinder and valve assemblies are as the Gipsy Queen 70. Exhaust-driven turbo-supercharged to 4,000 ft, automatic boost control. Fuel 100/130 grade. Electric or cartridge starter.
Aircraft:

Cierva W.14 Skeeter 7

GIPSY MINOR, 90 hp, 4-cylinder, inverted in-line, air-cooled poppet-valve. Bore/stroke 4.016 x 4.528 in. Vol. 229.29 cu in. (102 x 115 mm. Vol. 3.759 litre). Compression ratio 6:1. 'Any fuel not inferior to 70 Octane'. It was intended for the D.H.94 Moth Minor and was a very light and compact engine, featuring a single, dual output magneto. As the Second World War intervened before full production started, all drawings and parts of the aircraft and engine were shipped to Australia in 1940. Direct L.H. tractor-drive. Total built 171, including about 100 in Australia.
Aircraft:

de Havilland D.H.94 Moth Minor
Short S.16 Scion II

The de Havilland Chipmunk prototype, bearing B class serial G-5-3, which climbed to 25,500 ft in October, 1949, under the power of a supercharged Gipsy Major 50, flown by R. Plenderleith.

Gipsy Minor engined de Havilland Moth Minors under construction. The outbreak of the second World War prevented production of this little engine for private flying.

INVERTED 6- & 12-CYLINDER ENGINES, GIPSY SIX, QUEEN, TWELVE & KING

Year	Unleaded Fuel	Leaded Fuel	Note
1933	Gipsy Six I		Bronze head
1934	Gipsy Six R		V/P prop
1935		Gipsy Six Srs II	C/S prop, Al. head
1936	Gipsy Six IF		Aluminium head
1936		Gipsy Queen I	RAF Gipsy Six Srs II, modified to Queen II
1936		Gipsy Queen II	V/P prop
1936		Gipsy Twelve	Geared, supercharged
1937		Gipsy King	RAF Gipsy Twelve
1938		Gipsy Six 3 EX	V/P prop then Queen 30
1940	Gipsy Queen III		Detuned Gipsy Queen II
1940		Gipsy Six II	Wellington DWI A.G.P.
1941		Gipsy Queen IV	Gipsy III S, Queen 50
1944		Gipsy Six III S	Became Gipsy Queen 50
1944		Gipsy Queen 50	Was Queen IV, Six IIIS
1944		Gipsy Queen 70-1	Was Gipsy Six III SG
1944		Gipsy Queen 71	RAF Gipsy Queen 70-1
1945		Gipsy Queen 30	Was Gipsy Six 3 EX
1945		Gipsy Queen 32	RAF Gipsy Queen 30
1946		Gipsy Queen 70-2	Early production
1947		Gipsy Queen 33	As Queen 30, pusher 1947
		Gipsy Queen 34	As Queen 32, tractor
1947		Gipsy Queen 72	
1949		Gipsy Queen 70 Mk 2	Civil Gipsy Queen 72
1949		Gipsy Queen 70-3	Mod. Gipsy Queen 70-2
1950		Gipsy Queen 70-4	Mod. Gipsy Queen 70-3

GIPSY SIX.

The need of a 200 hp engine for a coming generation of light transport aircraft became apparent in 1933. Halford therefore designed a six-cylinder version of the Gipsy Major, with the same 5.25 compression ratio, using the same bore and stroke and many of the Major's components. Thus emerged the Gipsy Six, a well-proportioned engine in appearance but at first with some very unacceptable features in running. Six-throw crankshafts can produce difficult vibration characteristics, at critical rpm, leading to torsional vibration and eventual failure. When this was all-too apparent in the Gipsy Six, with the help of the R.A.E. at Farnborough, a different firing order from normal was devised, which quickly eliminated the problem. This was 1-2-4-6-5-3. The twin-carburettor system having been produced already, this resulted initially in a rather complex induction manifold. The de Havilland D.H.86 Express airliner was the first production aeroplane to be powered by the new engine, followed soon after by the D.H.89 Dragon Six, later named Dragon Rapide. Many of the detail comments about the Gipsy Major apply to its six-cylinder relative and the military version the, Gipsy Queen.

The single event which first really put the Gipsy Six on the map was the Melbourne Centenary Air Race, 11,700 miles long, starting at Mildenhall in Suffolk. For this, de Havilland built three special twin-engined, two-seat D.H.88 Comet racers and, to power them, a specially uprated Gipsy Six 'R' engine. The six-stop journey would have to be made at full-throttle, in the light of the inevitable American competition. In order to achieve a reasonable fuel economy over the necessary stage lengths at about 10,000 ft, a variable-pitch propeller was essential.

Fully controllable-pitch propellers were in their infancy and the only suitable unit available at short notice was French, made by Ratier. Unlike forthcoming constant-speed propellers, this was a two-pitch variant, take-off being achieved as usual in fine pitch, being changed to coarse pitch at climbing speed. The method of achieving this was ingenious and, these days almost defies belief, suggesting a bizarre form of black Gallic humour. Before starting the engine, to achieve fine pitch for take-off, a bicycle pump was attached to a valve in the propeller mechanism, so as to inflate a rubber 'sac' within. This then pressed upon the pitch-change mechanism, twisting the blades to fine pitch. The spinner had, at its

front, a flat circular disc. As flying speed built up to about 150 mph, the air pressure on the disc pressed on a bicycle-type valve, deflating the 'sac', thus changing the pitch to coarse. After landing, the pump routine changed the pitch back to fine, ready for the next take-off. One of the Comets, flown by Scott and Campbell Black was declared the winner. These remarkable aircraft set several records for speed and distance and the propellers were changed to de Havilland units, built under licence from Hamilton-Standard.

The Gipsy Six I srs I, the beginning of a long line.

The Gipsy Six series I was widely used in de Havilland Rapides, D.H.86s and numerous other civil aircraft. This D.H.86B, G-AEWR of Railway Air Services was photographed at Croydon in 1938.

The Gipsy Six series I was widely used in de Havilland Rapides, D.H.86s and numerous other civil aircraft. This shows the neat cowling of the starboard outer engine of a D.H.86A destined for Australia.

GIPSY SIX srs I, 200 hp, (1934), 6-cylinder, inverted in-line air-cooled poppet-valve. Bronze head. Bore/stroke 4.646 x 5.512 in. Vol. 560.6 cu in. (118 x 140 mm. Vol. 9.186 litre). Compression ratio 5.25:1. Direct L.H. tractor-drive. Power Curve at rated altitude sea level to 2,000 ft, from A.& A.E.E., Martlesham, Report M.691, dated 4.10.35.

The 90 hp de Havilland Gipsy Minor. A sectioned drawing by Max Millar.

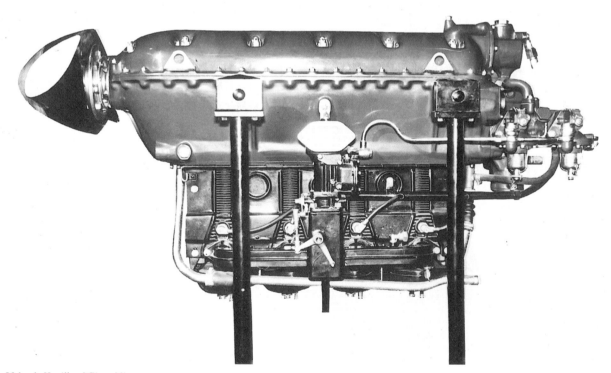

The 90 hp de Havilland Gipsy Minor

RPM	2,350	2,300	2,200	2,100	1,900
BHP	199.5	197.5	191.5	185	169

Max 199.5 bhp, 2,350 rpm, all-out level flight (5 min). 'Good grade automobile fuel', or non-leaded 73–77 Octane (DTD 134). Equivalent to Queen III, de-tuned Queen II. Total built 1,139.
Aircraft:

de Havilland D.H.86A, B Express
de Havilland D.H.89 D.H.89M Rapide
de Havilland D.H.89A Dominie I, II
Hendy 3308 Heck
Heston Phoenix I

Miles M.3B, C, D, E, F Falcon Six
Miles M.4, M.4A Merlin
Miles M.6 Hawcon
Miles M.7 Nighthawk
Miles M.15 Trainer
Miles M.16 Mentor
Parnall Heck 2C (ex Hendy)
Parnall 382 Heck III
Percival D.3 Gull
Percival E.1, E.2 Mew Gull
Percival Q.6 Petrel
Percival Vega Gull

The Gipsy Six series I was widely used in de Havilland Rapides, D.H.86s and numerous other civil aircraft. This Rapide was one of two ordered by the then Prince of Wales in 1935, finished in the colours of the Brigade of Guards.

The Gipsy Six series I in a Heston Phoenix I.

GIPSY SIX srs II, 205 hp, (1936). Aluminium alloy head. Compression ratio 6:1, designed for leaded fuel. Fixed or two-pitch propeller. Power Curve at rated altitude 2,000 ft from A.& A.E.E., Martlesham, Report M.636, dated 24.6.36, rated 165 hp, 2,100 rpm, -2.125 lb/sq inch.

RPM	2,400	2,300	2,200	2,100	2,000	1,900
BHP	209	203.5	196.5	188	179.5	170.5

Max 209 bhp, 2,400 rpm, all-out level flight (5 min). Fuel 77 Octane (+4 cc TEL/Imperial gallon). Queen I, converted to Queen II, equivalent. Total built 248.

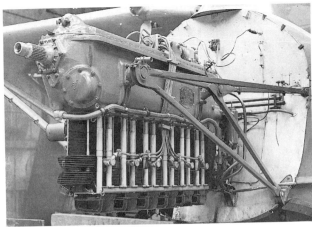

The Gipsy Six series II in a Heston Phoenix II.

Aircraft:
    B.A.IV Double Eagle
    de Havilland D.H.86A, B Express
    de Havilland D.H.89, 89M Rapide
    de Havilland D.H.89A Dominie I, II
    Heston Phoenix II

Heston T.1/37
Marendaz III
Miles M.2E, M.2L Hawk Speed Six
Miles M.7A Nighthawk
Miles M.8 Peregrine
Miles T.1/37
Parnall T.1/37
Percival Gull Six
Percival E.2, E.3H Mew Gull
Percival Vega Gull
Percival Q.6 Petrel
Reid & Sigrist R.S.1 'Snargasher'

The Gipsy Six series I, fitted in a Percival Vega Gull.

GIPSY SIX srs II, V/P propeller. As above, Queen II.
Aircraft:
    de Havilland D.H.88 Comet
    de Havilland D.H.92 Dolphin
    Miles M.7A Nighthawk
    Percival E.2, E.3H Mew Gull
    Percival Gull Six
    Percival Q.6 Petrel
    Percival Vega Gull

GIPSY SIX 'R', 220 hp, (1934), 6-cylinder, inverted in-line air-cooled poppet-valve. Racing engine with high-lift cams. Compression ratio 6.5:1. Direct L.H. tractor-drive. Fuel 77 Octane.
Aircraft:
    de Havilland D.H.85 Leopard Moth (test-bed)
    de Havilland D.H.88 Comet
    Miles M.2U Hawk Speed Six
    Percival E.2 Mew Gull

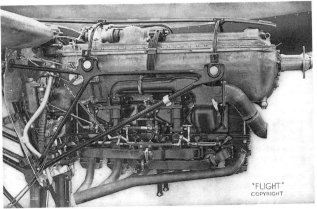

The Gipsy Six 'R', the racing version of the engine, as fitted to the D.H.88 Comet.

GIPSY QUEEN I, 205 h.p. (R.A.F. version of Gipsy Six srs II, usually modified to Queen II), 6-cylinder, inverted in-line air-cooled poppet-valve. Bore/stroke 118 x 140 mm. Vol. 9.186 litre. Compression ratio 6:1. Direct L.H. tractor-drive, fixed-pitch propeller. Power Curve at rated altitude 2,000 ft from A.& A.E.E., Martlesham, Report M.725, dated 26.11.37.

RPM	2,400	2,300	2,200	2,100	1,985	1,900
BHP	207.9	202.1	197.1	189.9	180.6	171.9

Max 210 bhp, 2,400 rpm, all-out level flight (5 min). Leaded or unleaded fuel, 77 Octane (DTD 224) or 87 Octane (DTD 230).
Aircraft:

Miles M.16 Mentor

GIPSY QUEEN II, 210 hp, (1939), a Gipsy Six srs II or modified Queen I, with v.p. propeller. Compression ratio 6:1. Power Curve at rated altitude 2,000 ft from A.& A.E.E., Martlesham, Report M.759, dated 2.12.39. Power Curve at rated altitude sea level to 2,000 ft, from A.& A.E.E., Martlesham, Report M.759, dated 2.12.39.

RPM	2,400	2,300	2,200	2,100	2,000
BHP	213.8	206.7	199.6	191.5	181.4

Max 210 bhp, 2,400 rpm, all-out level flight (5 min). Fuel 77 Octane (DTD 224) or 87 Octane (DTD 230). Total built 1,681.
Aircraft:

Cierva W.9, W.9A, W.9B
de Havilland D.H.89 Rapide
de Havilland D.H.89A Dominie
Percival Proctor I (T.20/38)
Percival Proctor II, III, IV (T.9/41), V

GIPSY QUEEN III, 200 hp, (1940), as Gipsy Six srs I, a de-tuned Queen II, compression ratio 5.25:1, non-leaded fuel DTD 134. Total built 1,358.
Aircraft:

de Havilland D.H.89 Rapide
de Havilland D.H.89A Dominie
Parnall/Hendy Heck

The neat cowling of the Gipsy Queen 30 in a spectacular light on the prototype D.H.114 Heron.

GIPSY QUEEN IV, (1941), a supercharged version, originally the Queen IIIS. Compression ratio 6.2:1. Name changed to Gipsy Queen 50 in June, 1944. Fuel 87 Octane (DTD 230).
Aircraft:

Airspeed A.S.40 Oxford IV

GIPSY QUEEN 30, 240 hp, (1946), Compression ratio 6.5:1. Fuel 87 Octane (DTD 230). Total of all versions built, 1,762.
Aircraft:

de Havilland D.H.114 Heron prototype
Miles M.71 Merchantman

GIPSY QUEEN 30-2, 240 hp, (1946), Compression ratio 6.5:1. Fuel 87 Octane (DTD 230).
Aircraft:

de Havilland D.H.114 Heron 2
de Havilland D.H.114 Sea Heron
Percival P.40 Prentice I

GIPSY QUEEN 30-3, 240 hp, (1946), Compression ratio 6.5:1. Fuel 87 Octane (DTD 230).
Aircraft:

de Havilland D.H.114 Heron prototype

GIPSY QUEEN 30-4, 240 hp, (1946), Compression ratio 6.5:1. Fuel 87 Octane (DTD 230).
Aircraft:

de Havilland D.H.114 Heron prototype

GIPSY QUEEN 32, 250 hp, (1946), Compression ratio 6.5:1. Fuel 87 Octane (DTD 230).
Aircraft:

Percival P.40 Prentice I
Planet Satellite
Scottish Aviation Pioneer I
Youngman-Baynes High-Lift

The Gipsy Queen 32 for the Percival Prentice I.

GIPSY QUEEN 33, as Queen 30, 240 hp, (1946). For a pusher installation. Compression ratio 6.3:1. Fuel 87 Octane (DTD 230).
Aircraft:

Heston A.2/45

GIPSY QUEEN 34, 250 hp, (1947), as Queen 30. Compression ratio 6.3:1. Fuel 87 Octane (DTD 230).
Aircraft:

Scottish Aviation Pioneer I

GIPSY QUEEN 50, 295 hp, (1944), formerly Gipsy Queen IV. A direct-drive supercharged version, originally the Queen IIIS. Single-speed, 1-stage supercharger ratio 11.6:1. Name changed to Gipsy Queen 50 in June, 1944. Fuel 87 Octane. Hydromatic propeller. Total built 14 approx.
Aircraft:

Airspeed A.S.40 Oxford IV

GIPSY QUEEN 51, 295 hp, compression ratio 6.5:1, as Queen 50.
Aircraft:

Percival Merganser

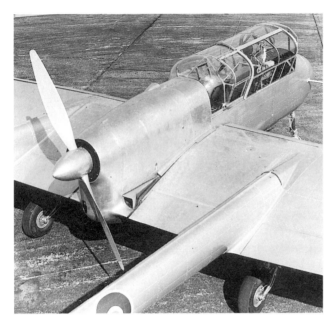

The Heston A.2/45 was a post-war attempt to produce a pusher-engined battlefield air observation aircraft. It was powered by a Gipsy Queen 33, a version of the 240 hp Queen 30.

The Gipsy Queen 34 fitted to the Scottish Aviation Pioneer I

A D.H.104 Dove supplied to the Arab Legion. The engines were Gipsy Queen 70 series.

de Havilland D.H.104 Dove 8, powered by the Gipsy Queen 70-3.

GIPSY QUEEN 70-1, (1946), formerly Gipsy Six S.G. Compression ratio 6.5:1. Single-speed, 1-stage medium supercharged, gear ratio 11.22:1. Geared, epicyclic .711:1, Hydromatic propeller. Fuel 100/130 grade. Total of all versions built 1,889.
Aircraft:
>de Havilland D.H.104 Dove prototype
>Percival Proctor (engine's first flight).

GIPSY QUEEN 70-2, 380 hp, Compression ratio 6.5:1, 1-speed, medium supercharged, ratio 11.206:1. Geared, .711:1 L.H. tractor-drive. Fuel 100/130 grade. Length 71.74 in; width 19.56 in; height 33.23 in.
Aircraft:
>de Havilland D.H.104 Dove 5, 6
>Short S.A.6 Sealand

GIPSY QUEEN 70-3, 380 hp, Compression ratio 6.5:1, 1-speed, medium supercharged, ratio 11.206:1. Geared, .711:1 L.H. tractor-drive. Fuel 100/130 grade. Length 71.74 in; width 19.56 in; height 33.23 in.
Aircraft:
>de Havilland D.H.104 Dove 1, 2, 7, 8
>Handley Page (Reading) H.P.R.1 Marathon 1, T.11
>Short S.A.6 Sealand

GIPSY QUEEN 70-4, 340 hp, Compression ratio 6.5:1, 1-speed, medium supercharged. Geared, .711:1 L.H. tractor-drive. Fuel 100/130 grade.
Aircraft:
>de Havilland D.H.104 Devon C.1
>de Havilland Sea Devon 20
>de Havilland D.H.104 Dove 1B, 2B
>Handley Page (Reading) H.P.R.1A Marathon 1A
>Short S.A.6 Sealand

GIPSY QUEEN 71, 330 hp, (1950), Compression ratio 6.5:1, Geared, epicyclic .71:1 L.H. tractor-drive. Fuel 100/130 grade.
Aircraft:
>de Havilland D.H.104 Devon C.1
>Miles M.60 Marathon

(Above and below) The de Havilland Albatross 'Frobisher' G-AFDI of B.O.A.C., showing the cooling air intakes in the wing leading edges. The airflow enters at the back, flowing forwards and discharging below.

The air-cooled inverted twelve-cylinder de Havilland Gipsy XII, or Gipsy King in its military version.

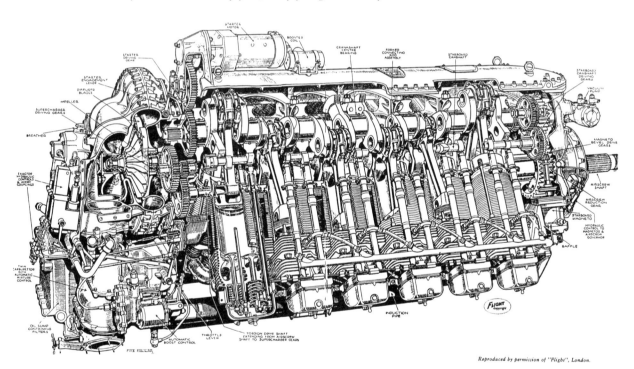

Reproduced by permission of "Flight", London.

The Gipsy XII drawn in section by Max Millar.

GIPSY KING I, 405/425 hp, (1937), 12-cylinder, inverted 60-degree Vee air-cooled poppet-valve. Bore/stroke 4.646 x 5.512 in. Vol. 560.6 cu in. (118 x 140 mm. Vol. 9.186 litre). Compression ratio 6:1, single-speed, medium supercharged. Geared drive, spur .667:1 L.H. tractor-drive. Power Curve at rated altitude 7,500 ft from A.& A.E.E., Martlesham, Report M.716, dated 2.5.38. Boost, rated zero lb/sq inch.

RPM	2,575	2,400	2,200	2,000	1,720
BHP	443.8	414	369.9	322.5	253.8
BOOST	+.706lb	+.1lb	-.446lb	-.89lb	-1.61lb

Max boost zero lb/sq inch. 425 bhp, 2,600 rpm take off to 1,000 ft or one minute. All-out level flight (five minutes), zero lb, 425 bhp,

2,450 rpm. Fuel 87 Octane (DTD 230). Length 82.6 in; width 31.5 in; height 37.4 in. Total of Gipsy XII/Kings built, 90 approx.
Aircraft:

de Havilland D.H.93 Don.

GIPSY XII (GIPSY TWELVE), 405/425 hp, (1938), similar to GIPSY KING. Power Curve at rated altitude 7,750 ft from A.& A.E.E., Martlesham, Report M.728, dated 20.4.38. Medium supercharged. Geared drive, spur .667:1 L.H. tractor-drive. Boost, rated zero lb/sq inch.

RPM	2,575	2,400	2,200	2,000
BHP	452.6	411.8	371.5	325.8
BOOST	+.71lb	+.121lb	-.36lb	-.98lb

Max boost +3.5 lb/sq inch. 425 bhp, 2,600 rpm take off to 1,000 ft or one minute. All-out level flight (five minutes), zero lb, 425 bhp, 2,450 rpm. Fuel 87 Octane (DTD 230). Length 82.6 in; width 31.5 in; height 37.4 in. Total of Gipsy XII/Kings built, 90 approx.
Aircraft:

      de Havilland D.H.91 Albatross (36/35)
      de Havilland D.H.93 Don 6/36

DOUGLAS (WILLIAM DOUGLAS (BRISTOL) LTD.).

Taken over by Aero Engines Ltd in 1935. *See* Aero Engines Ltd.

DOUGLAS 500 cc, 17 hp, (1922), 2-cylinder, horizontally-opposed air-cooled, poppet-valve. Vol. 500 cc. Direct R.H. tractor-drive.
Aircraft:

      Avro 558
      Parnall Pixie I, II
      R.A.E. Hurricane
      R.A.E. Zephyr
      Ward Gnome

DOUGLAS 736/750 cc, 6/6.5 hp.
Aircraft:

      de Havilland D.H.53 Humming Bird
      Parnall Pixie I, II

E.N.V. (en 'V').

The original E.N.V. engines were designed in England in 1908, when the company that came to be known as the London and Parisian Motor Co, an Anglo-French company was registered in London. With foundry facilities in the British steel centre, Sheffield, the major castings and forgings were exported to Courbevois, now part of the outskirts of Paris, where the French assembly was done. The first engine was exhibited at the 1908 Paris Salon de l'Aéronautique, as 'le Moteur en Vée'. Largely because of government opposition in France to the importation of such engines, the decision was made, initially, to manufacture the engine in that country. The following year, it was decided to make the engines in England and the works of the E.N.V. Motor Syndicate Ltd was built at Willesden, London. As a result, only the engines made in England are listed below, although many others, including Types A, C and FA were made only in France but imported into England. The firm virtually ceased to build engines in 1914.

E.N.V. TYPE D, 35-40 hp, (1909–1910), 8-cylinder, upright 90-degree Vee water-cooled, poppet side-valve. Bore/stroke 3.35 x 3.54 in. Vol. 249.6 cu in. (85 x 90 mm. Vol. 4.087 litre). Direct R.H. tractor/L.H. pusher-drive.
Aircraft:

      Avro (Roe) Tractor Biplane
      Blériot Type XII
      Duigan Biplane
      Eardley Billing Tractor Biplane
      Fritz Tractor Monoplane
      Lane Tractor Monoplane
      Piffard 1 & 2 Tractor Monoplanes
      Piffard 3 & 4 Hydro Biplanes
      Sopwith-Howard Wright 1910 Avis Monoplane
      Swan Pusher Biplane
      Swan Tractor Monoplane
      Weiss No 2 Tractor Monoplane

E.N.V. TYPE F, 60-80 hp, (1909–1911), 8-cylinder, upright 90-degree Vee water-cooled, poppet side-valve. Bore/stroke 105 x 110 mm. Vol. 7.623 litre. Single Zenith carburettor and single magneto. Direct R.H. tractor-drive.
Aircraft:

      Avro Types D & E Tractor Biplanes
      Blériot Type XII
      Bristol Boxkite
      Cody IIB
      Farman Pusher Biplane
      Grahame-White Pusher Biplane
      Howard Wright Pusher Biplane
      Royal Aircraft Factory B.E.2

      Royal Aircraft Factory S.E.1
      Sanders II Pusher Biplane
      Short S.27 Pusher Biplane
      Short S.29 Pusher Biplane
      Skinner Tractor Monoplane
      Voisin Boxkite Pusher Biplane

The 'en Vee' shape of the 60-80 hp E.N.V. Type F, water-cooled Vee-8 engine of 1911.

FAIREY AVIATION LTD, HAYES MIDDLESEX

C.R. Fairey became interested in aero engines, in addition to his aircraft work, after watching the Schneider Trophy Contest at Cowes in 1923. This was won by the U.S.Navy's Curtiss CR-3 biplane, powered by the compact and lightweight 465 hp Curtiss D-12A engine. Fairey agreed a licence for the use of design data and patents with Curtiss, without Air Ministry support for the venture, and negotiated the import of 50 Curtiss D-12 engines from the United States. These were delivered to the Fairey works at Hayes and named the Fairey Felix for use in Britain. They were never built under licence in Britain, as has been suggested. This engine immediately enabled Fairey's handsome Fox two-seat day bomber to outpace, by a useful margin, the fighters meant to intercept it. One D-12 was sent by the Air Ministry, with Fairey's knowledge, to Rolls-Royce at Derby for examination.

In 1931 Captain A. Graham Forsyth, a former R.F.C. pilot, joined Fairey Aviation, initially as 'Power Plant Specialist', becoming Chief Engine Designer. Before the First World War, he had worked with Wolseley Motors and with the Sage company on racing car design and, after the 1914–1918 war was, at first, responsible at the Air Ministry for liquid-cooled aero-engine development policy and of course was well-acquainted with the work of Napier and Rolls-Royce. He was then appointed by Fairey to design a new range of Fairey engines. He also pursued the company's well-established tradition of manufacturing metal propellers (to designs initially made under American licence and bought in 1924 from Curtiss-Reed) and began the design of a range of hydraulically-operated constant-speed propellers — in those days generally known as airscrews.

Graham Forsyth had come from a senior position in the Air Ministry's aero-engine hierarchy. It was curious therefore that, for whatever political reason was deemed convenient at the time in industry or Government circles, the Ministry subsequently refused to allocate any funds for engine development work to Fairey (who was not at the time universally popular) and did nothing whatever to promote the company's attempts to break into this field. Despite the lack of official encouragement, Forsyth proceeded with the design of three engines as private ventures, for which Fairey hoped eventually to gain Air Ministry support. This, unfortunately for both Fairey and Forsyth, was not forthcoming, due no doubt to the considerable weight of existing British companies. Despite this, Fairey continued with the development of new Fairey liquid-cooled engines, on which he is said to have spent a great deal of his own money. There were two basic types, concerning which there has for many years a great deal of confusion and it is hoped that the following may help to clarify the situation.

Fairey formed the habit of designating his engines after the number of cylinders and, in this context, he followed the custom of the Curtiss company, with which he had formerly been associated in the importation of the D-12, as the Felix. This in itself has led to confusion, as will be shown. The first real Fairey engine was designed in considerable secrecy. It was intended to be directly competitive with Rolls-Royce's highly-supercharged P.V.12 (later named Merlin), a conventional water-cooled vee-12 cylinder engine. It was designated the Fairey P.12 and given the name Prince. This was built and run in two versions, labelled according to the degree of supercharging (as was Rolls-Royce's Kestrel), the 670 hp Prince I and the 900 hp Prince II (or Super Prince). By the end of 1934, three engines had completed 550 hours of bench running, including ten hours at 420 h.p. and three hours at 700 hp. One Prince was flown in a Belgian-built Fox II.

If there was confusion (conceivably intentional on the part of the Company) about the Vee-12 engine, this was nothing by comparison with that which surrounded the second and radically new type of Fairey Prince, the 'double-engine'. Pursuing the Prince theme has been an intriguing exercise. Graham Forsyth had very ingenious ideas about a double engine in the shape of a vertical H. His idea was that each vertically-opposed half should operate quite independently, each driving a separate unit of a pair of co-axial counter-rotating and constant-speed feathering propellers, with independent reduction gears, on a common crankcase. (This antedated the idea of Armstrong Siddeley's Double Mamba turbo-prop by some two decades). For long and economical overseas patrols, this is an interesting solution, offering twin-engine reliability from a 'single-engine' installation, without inconvenient asymmetric characteristics. The Royal Navy was known to be interested and Fairey himself was well-known in the Admiralty. The idea of an H-shaped engine was of course not new at the time. Frank Halford's air-cooled 16-cylinder Napier Rapier and 24-cylinder Dagger, both of which had twin crankshafts geared together, were in Royal Air Force use and widely advertised.

Complete official company records have been hard to discover but, thanks to the researches and personal recollections of Sir Peter Masefield (a redoubtable historian who, in his early years worked at Fairey's 'Great West Aerodrome' headquarters at Hayes), some most revealing facts have emerged. Indeed, he himself made a number of flights in a Fairey Battle test-bed, behind a twenty-four cylinder Fairey P-24 'Double Prince'.

Almost at the end of frustrating searches into these little-known engines, an unpublished series of engine data sheets, dated 5 March, 1941, from Sir Roy Fedden's Bristol archives, came to light and included some unexpected information on the Fairey engines. As with so many long lost sources of information, total reliance on its accuracy at first seemed unwise, although the source of it is was as impeccable as it could be. And then, at the very last minute, some long-lost details of the Fairey P-24 Monarch were, thankfully, made available to the author.

The unique new layout, in accordance with the novel ideas of Graham Forsyth, was intended to appear in two versions, with 16 and 24 cylinders and used the same bore and stroke as the earlier Prince (5.25 x 6.0 in). In the Fairey system, the H-16 was to be a 16-cylinder engine, retaining the name Prince. However, the name 'Monarch' was adopted for the 24-cylinder H-shaped P-24 engine in the first drawing, dated 29 August, 1932.

Exactly what was the eventual outcome of the proposed 16-cylinder engine was still unclear at the time of writing but, happily, an engine called a 'Fairey Prince' is carefully preserved at the Fleet Air Arm Museum at Yeovilton. The engine was originally rescued from a scrap-yard in Kingston-upon-Thames after the Second World War. This unique engine is believed to be a P-24 Monarch. All the surviving Fairey drawings and data, signed out and authorised A.G. Forsyth call it so. It is a vertical, H-shaped engine with side-mounted superchargers (as adopted in Germany).

Therefore it is a rare, if not the uniquely surviving Fairey four-speed, two-stage engine. The photograph of a Prince-engined Battle, having one engine run-up also show four exhaust stubs top and bottom, suggesting a H-16. The drawings show however that the six exhausts in each bank were combined in four outlets, an arrangement also adopted by Rolls-Royce in certain instances.

Examination of the reverse side of these original photographs (which have previously appeared in print several times), also suggests a source of the confusion. They are both marked with the Fairey Aviation Company Photographic Department's rubber stamp. (The 1940 prints are post-dated 1951, when they first came to be reproduced). Both are hand-written 'P.24', rather than 'Monarch', perhaps leading to a misunderstanding which has persisted for over forty years.

The first Monarch to be built was installed in Fairey Battle K9370 in October, 1938 and had a civil Type Test in May and June 1939. It achieved 50 hours without incident, with fixed-pitch contra-rotating propellers, being first flown by Chris Staniland in June. Tests went so well that it was cleared for flight trials of 120 hours and it was delivered to R.A.E. Farnborough on 12 July 1941, having completed a 50-hour bench test and 87 hours flying in the Battle. While there, it was installed in the large wind-tunnel, for the study of contra-rotating propeller effects, together with thrust and propeller blade strain-gauge tests. It was submitted to 15 hours testing at take-off power, without trouble.

The H-24 engine, of 51.078 litres, was intended initially to develop 2,000 hp and, eventually, to achieve 3,200 hp. Early in the Second World War, in discussions at the Ministry of Aircraft Production under Lord Beaverbrook, a proposal was made that the H-24 should be built by Ford in the U.S.A., to power the Republic P-47 Thunderbolt. As a preliminary while development work was done on the H-24, the Battle test-bed was sent with a spare engine, by sea, to the U.S.A. on 15 January 1942 and, while at Wright Field, it flew 250 hours in 18 months, after which it was returned to Britain and is now probably the sole survivor. A second P-24 was installed in a Battle at the R.A.E., this time equipped with fully-feathering propellers.

Further development of the Prince was abandoned in 1943, while Sir Richard Fairey was in the United States. The P-24, had it been adopted as Fairey originally intended, would have given the Battle twice the power and a rather more adequate performance. What eventually happened to the H-24 is, as Sir Peter Masefield has recorded is, unfortunately, 'still lost in the mists of wartime affairs'. It is a sad reflection on wartime finances and politics that, with a limited amount of money to go round and the existence of a number of established aero-engine manufacturers, a very senior Government official was heard to express the view that 'Fairey would have to go it alone, or fold up'. This was a pity because, with real support, Fairey and Forsyth might well have achieved useful results. By that time, Fairey is said to have expended the enormous sum of over £100,000 of his own money on the development of the Prince engines, in 1992 terms amounting to a figure nearer to a million.

FELIX (CURTISS D.12), (1926), 465 hp, 12-cylinder, upright 60-degree Vee, water-cooled poppet-valve. Bore/stroke 4.5 x 6.0 in. Vol. 1,145 cu in. (18.8 litre). Compression ratio 6:1. Direct R.H. tractor-drive. It had a monobloc type of cylinder head, with basically individual water-cooled cylinders and poultice heads. Length 56.75 in; width 28.25 in; height 34.75 in.
Aircraft:
    Fairey Firefly I
    Fairey Fox I

FAIREY V-12 PRINCE I, 650/670 hp and SUPER PRINCE II, 720 hp, 12-cylinder, upright 60-degree Vee-shaped, poppet-valve water-cooled engine. It was built in two versions, unsupercharged and fully supercharged but exact details are few. Its propeller drive was spur-geared, R.H. tractor-drive. Bore/stroke 5.25 x 6.0 in. Vol. 1,558.62 cu in, 25.54 litre. The fully-supercharged version, designated V-12S, Prince II, (or, probably Super Prince) was intended to develop 720 hp at 2,500 rpm at 12,000 ft, for a modest dry weight of 1,150 lb.
Aircraft:
    Fairey Fox II (probably the Prince I but uncertain)

The Fairey Felix was a Curtiss D.12, imported from the United States and re-named. Its excellent performance in the Fairey Fox day bomber created much concern in official circles.

FAIREY H-16S PRINCE 3, 1,540 hp, (1939), 16-cylinder 'double' engine, in-line vertically-opposed H-shaped, poppet-valve liquid-cooled. Bore/stroke 5.25 x 6.0 in (133.35 x 152.4 mm), vol. 2,078 cu in, 34.05 litre. Two-speed, single-stage supercharged. Effectively, two independent engines, driving co-axial, counter-rotating L.H./R.H. propellers.

NOTE: certain figures have been obtained by Sir Peter Masefield, from Pilot's Notes still existing in the United States, dated March 1940.

Aircraft:
 Fairey Battle I

FAIREY P-24 MONARCH, (1939), 2,240 hp, a more powerful development of the Prince H-16, with greater capacity. 24-cylinder 'double' engine, in-line vertically-opposed monobloc castings, H-shaped, poppet-valve liquid-cooled. Bore/stroke 5.25 x 6.0 in (133.35 x 152.4 mm), vol. 3,117 cu in, 51.08 litre. Compression ratio 6:1. Four-speed, two-stage supercharged. Geared, spur .543:1. Independently controlled and synchronized, co-axial counter-rotating and feathering L.H. (front)/R.H. (rear) propeller drives. Length 86.25 in; width 43.0 in; height 52.5 in.
Aircraft:
 Fairey Battle I

The Fairey P-24 Monarch being ground run. Only half the unit is running, turning the front propeller, the other remaining stationary.

Believed to be the same engine as shown running is shown here on a stand and is probably the same unit as that taken to Wright Field and later returned to be intended for scrap.

FLETCHER EMPRESS, 50 hp, (1910). Five and nine hp engines were made, before this 7-cylinder, air-cooled single-row rotary poppet-valve engine. cast-iron cylinders. Connecting rods pivoting direct on crank pin, with no master rod. It was unsupercharged and its propeller drive was direct R.H. tractor/L.H. pusher-drive. Bore/stroke 110 x 130 mm. Vol. 8.65 litre. Diameter 36.0 in; length 15.0 in.
Aircraft:
 Macfie Biplane

The Fletcher Empress, a rare picture of a rotary engine which did not achieve success.

GALLOWAY ENGINEERING CO. LTD.
A subsidiary of Beardmore and based in Dumfries (Scotland) which built B.H.P. engines under the name of Galloway. *See* Beardmore.

GENERAL AIRCRAFT LTD, HANWORTH AIR PARK, FELTHAM, MIDDLESEX.

MONARCH, V.4, 85 hp (1935), an experimental, inverted Vee-4 air-cooled engine, designed by A.H. Caple, formerly Chief Designer for Cirrus-Hermes Engineering Co Ltd. A six-cylinder version was projected.
Aircraft:
 de Havilland D.H.60G Moth

The prototype General Aircraft inverted air-cooled V.4 engine of 85 hp, installed in a D.H.60 Moth.

GNOME ET RHONE

The origin of the name 'Gnome' has long been in dispute. In an article published in the noted German aviation magazine *Aerokurier* in 1983, the writer stated that, in 1900 the clever French engineer brothers Laurent and Louis Seguin began licence production of a single-cylinder, stationary internal combustion engine for industrial purposes, developed by the German Engine Factory Oberursel. This small and successful engine was to replace the large and cumbersome steam engine as a source of power and was called the 'Gnom' (a colloquial word signifying 'dwarf'). The Seguins adopted the name in its French version for their own industrial engine and, when they began to design their highly successful series of rotary aero-engines in 1907, they adopted the name Gnome for them. It was natural that, when Germany appreciated the virtues of these engines, the firm Oberursel reversed the process and acquired the licence to build them and used them to considerable effect, notably in the early Fokker fighters.

The first production type rotary engine to appear was the two-valve 50 hp Gnome. It featured an inlet valve in the piston head and a push-rod operated exhaust valve. It was followed by the 'Monosoupape' type engine, some five years later. The 50 hp seven-cylinder engine was designed by Laurent Seguin. It had a R.H. tractor/L.H. pusher-drive. Like all rotaries, it suffered from cooling problems and consequent distortion of the cylinders, particularly on their 'downwind' side. Seguin used the French-designed 'obturator' ring on the cast-iron pistons, made in very thin brass or aluminium alloy, in an attempt to ensure gas-tightness, despite the cylinder distortion. It was not a very efficient or reliable system and the obturators were very fragile. These rings had a life of about fifteen hours flying and, when they broke, the pistons seized at once.

GNOME 7 GAMMA, 70 hp, 7-cylinder, single-row rotary air-cooled, poppet-valve. Bore/stroke 120 x 130 mm. Vol. 679.84 cu in. Direct R.H. tractor/L.H. pusher-drive. Diameter 34.2 in; length 44.4 in.

A 70 hp Gnome Gamma in the Handley Page H.P.3, about 1911.

Aircraft:

    Blériot XXI
    Bristol Biplane Type T
    Bristol Prier-Dickson
    Henry Farman Biplane
    Grahame-White Passenger Biplane VIIc
    Grahame-White Pusher Biplane
    Handley Page H.P.3 F/70
    Morane-Borel seaplane
    Nieuport Monoplane
    Paulhan Biplane
    Royal Aircraft Factory B.E.3, B.E.4
    Short School Biplane
    Short S.32 Pusher Biplane
    Short S.36 Tractor Biplane
    Short S.38 'Long-Range' Biplane
    Short S.45 Tractor Biplane
    Sopwith D.1 'Three-seater'
    Vickers No 6 Monoplane
    Vickers No 8 Monoplane

Morane-Borel seaplane, 70 hp Gnome.

GNOME 7 LAMBDA, 80 hp, (1916), 7-cylinder, single-row rotary air-cooled, two poppet-valves. Bore/stroke 4.88 x 5.51 in. Vol. 721.2 cu in (124 x 140 mm). Compression ratio 3.75:1. (A long-stroke version had a stroke of 145 mm, and a compression ratio 3.87:1, producing marginally greater power). Cast-iron pistons with automatic inlet valves in the piston-head centres. Exhaust valves, in the cylinder heads, operated by hollow steel tappet rods and steel rocker arms. Direct R.H. tractor or L.H. pusher-drive. One carburettor, one magneto. Diameter 36.6 in; length 44.0 in.
Production, 8/1914-12/1918, from:-
Daimler Co Ltd, Coventry,
Ordered, 1,030;   Delivered, 967;   Cancelled/suspended, 63
Sopwith Aviation Co Ltd, Kingston-on-Thames,
Ordered, 12;   Delivered, 12;   Cancelled/suspended, 0

Avro 504C, 80 hp Gnome.

Aircraft:

Avro 504, 504A, B, C, D, G, H
Blackburn Type 1
Blériot Parasol
Blériot XI
Bristol Boxkite
Bristol Gordon England G.E.3
Bristol-Coanda Competition Monoplane
Bristol-Coanda Military Monoplane
Bristol-Coanda Hydro 120 Biplane
Bristol-Coanda T.B.8
Bristol 1 Scout A, B, C
Bristol 2 Scout D
Caudron G.III
Deperdussin Type B
Dunne D.8
Henry Farman F.20
Grahame-White G.W.15
L & P 4
Lowe H.L.(M).9 Marlburian
Nieuport IVG
Nieuport 10
Radley-England Waterplane
Royal Aircraft Factory B.E.3, B.E.4
Royal Aircraft Factory B.E.8, B.E.8a 'Bloater'
Royal Aircraft Factory B.S.1
Royal Aircraft Factory S.E.2
Royal Aircraft Factory S.E.4a
Short S.37 Tractor Biplane
Short S.38 'Long-Range' Biplane
Short S.41 Tractor Seaplane
Short S.60 Seaplane
Short S.70 Type
Sopwith Gordon Bennett Racer
Sopwith Pup
Sopwith Sociable
Sopwith Tabloid
Sopwith Three-Seater
Vickers No 8 Monoplane

Burga Monoplane
Duigan Biplane
Henry Farman Type Militaire
Grahame-White School Biplane
Nieuport Monoplane
Paulhan Biplane
Pemberton Billing P.B.9
Royal Aircraft Factory B.E.3
Royal Aircraft Factory B.E.4
Royal Aircraft Factory F.E.2
Short S.26 Pusher Biplane
Short SD.27 Tandem Twin
Short S.33 Pusher Biplane
Short S.34 'Long-Range' Biplane
Short S.35 Pusher Biplane
Short S.37 Tractor Monoplane
Short S.38 'Long-Range' Biplane
Short S.39 Triple Twin
Short S.43, S.44 Biplane
Short S.47 Triple Tractor
Short S.62
Sopwith Bee
Sopwith Sparrow
Valkyrie Type B (Aero. Syndic.)
Vickers No 6 Monoplane
Vickers No 8 Monoplane
Vickers Boxkite, School Biplane

(Above and below) The remarkable Short S.39 Triple Twin of 1911. It had two 50 h.p. Gnome 7 Omega rotaries in tandem, the front engine driving two tractor propellers via chains and the rear engine, behind its propeller, acting as a pusher.

Henry Farman F.20, 80 hp Gnome, after 'throwing a pot'. The crew were lucky in this instance. Losing a cylinder in a rotary was not uncommon and the results in a pusher were usually disastrous.

GNOME 7 OMEGA, 50 hp, 7-cylinder, single-row rotary air-cooled, poppet-valve. Bore/stroke 110 x 120 mm. Vol. 488.5 cu in. Direct R.H. tractor/L.H. pusher-drive. Diameter 33.0 in; length 31 in. Production, 8/1914-12/1918, from:-
Unknown manufacturer.
Aircraft:

Avro 500 Type E, Es
Blackburn Mercury 2, 3
Blackburn Single-Seat Monoplane
Blériot XI
Bristol Boxkite
Bristol Racing Biplane (1911)
Bristol Monoplane (1911)
Bristol-Prier P-1
Bristol-Coanda School Monoplane
Bristol-Coanda T.B.8

GNOME 9 DELTA, 100 hp, 9-cylinder, single-row rotary air-cooled, poppet-valve. Bore/stroke 124 x 150 mm. Vol. 993.23 cu in. Direct R.H. tractor/L.H. pusher-drive. Diameter 40.2 in; length 45.3 in.

Aircraft:

> Avro 500, 501
> Pemberton Billing P.B.25
> Royal Aircraft Factory S.E.2
> Vickers No 7 Monoplane
> Vickers Hydravion
> Vickers E.F.B.8
> Vickers F.B.9 Gunbus

GNOME 14 GAMMA-GAMMA, 140 hp, 14-cylinder, two-row Gamma, rotary air-cooled, poppet-valve. Bore/stroke 130 x 120 mm. Vol. 1,359.68 cu in. Direct R.H. tractor/L.H. pusher-drive.
Aircraft:

> Royal Aircraft Factory B.E.7
> Short S.41 Tractor Biplane

GNOME 14 LAMBDA-LAMBDA, 160 hp, (1916), 14-cylinder, 2-row Lambda, rotary air-cooled, two poppet-valves. Bore/stroke 124 x 140 mm. Vol. 23.7 litre. Cast-iron pistons with automatic inlet valves in the piston-head centres. Exhaust valves, in the cylinder heads, operated by hollow steel tappet rods and steel rocker arms. Direct R.H. tractor or L.H. pusher-drive. Diameter 36.7 in; Length 49.8 in.
Aircraft:

> Avro 510
> Royal Aircraft Factory S.E.4
> Short S.63, S.64 Folder Seaplanes
> Short S.70 Seaplane
> Short S.80 'Nile Seaplane'
> Short S.74 Admiralty Seaplane
> Short S.81 'Gun-bus' Seaplane
> Short S.82-S.85 Folder Seaplanes

A fourteen-cylinder two-row Gnome rotary. It is unidentified and can be of 100, 140 or 160 hp, all outwardly very similar to double-row versions of the Gamma, Lambda and Omega.

GNOME 14 OMEGA-OMEGA, 100 hp, 14-cylinder, 2-row Omega, rotary air-cooled, poppet-valve. Bore/stroke 110 x 120 mm. Vol. 973 cu in. Direct R.H. tractor/L.H. pusher drive. Diameter 32.5 in; length 49.5 in.
Aircraft:

> Bristol Gordon England G.E.2
> Coventry Ordnance Works Biplane 10
> Nieuport Monoplane
> Short S.41 Tractor Biplane
> Short S.57 Seaplane
> Short S.64 Folder Seaplane
> Short S.74 Admiralty Seaplane

GNOME MONOSOUPAPE 7 TYPE A, 80 hp, (1916), 7-cylinder, single-row rotary air-cooled poppet-valve. Bore/stroke 110 x 150 mm. Vol. 609.2 cu in. Direct R.H. tractor or L.H. pusher drive. The chief points of difference from other rotary engines were absence of a carburettor and inlet valves. The inlet ports were in the cylinder walls, there being a non-explosive mixture in the crankcase. The pistons were of cast-iron. As the name of the engine implies, there was only one valve per cylinder, mounted in the cylinder head. It performed the following dual functions. It acted as an exhaust valve, in doing so its temperature being raised. It then admitted to the cylinder sufficient air for combustion of the charge entering through ports at the base of the cylinder, so cooling it. Diameter 35.3 in; length 39.3 in.

Aircraft:

> Avro 504
> Avro 511
> Bristol-Coanda G.B.75
> Sopwith Pup

GNOME MONOSOUPAPE 9 TYPE B-2, 100 hp, (1916), 9-cylinder, single-row rotary air-cooled poppet-valve. Bore/stroke 4.33 x 5.9in. Vol. 781.63 cu in. (110 x 150 mm). Compression ratio 4.85:1. Direct R.H. tractor or L.H. pusher-drive. The chief points of difference from other rotary engines were absence of a carburettor and inlet valves. The inlet ports were in the cylinder walls, there being a non-explosive mixture in the crankcase. The pistons were of cast-iron. As the name of the engine implies, there was only one valve per cylinder, mounted in the cylinder head. It performed the following dual functions. It acted as an exhaust valve, in doing so its temperature was raised. It then admitted to the cylinder sufficient air for combustion of the charge entering through ports at the base of the cylinder, so cooling it. One magneto. Diameter 37.4 in; length 42.3 in.

Production, 8/1914-12/1918, from:-
Brazil Straker & Co Ltd, Bristol,
Ordered, 500;   Delivered, 0;   Cancelled/suspended, 500
W.S. Laycock Ltd, Millhouses, Sheffield,
Ordered, 1,000;   Delivered, 0;   Cancelled/suspended, 1,000
Peter Hooker Ltd.
Ordered, 4,115;   Delivered, 2,169;   Cancelled/suspended, 1,946
Vickers Ltd, London SW3,
Ordered, 19;   Delivered, 19;   Cancelled/suspended, 0

Possibly the most famous and important of the Gnome line, the 100 hp Monosoupape B-2.

Aircraft:

> A.D. Scout (Blackburn)
> Airco D.H.2
> Airco D.H.5
> Alcock Scout
> Avro 504E, J, K, M
> 504R Gosport
> B.A.T. F.K.23 Bantam II
> Blackburn T.B.
> Blackburn Triplane
> Bristol-Coanda T.B.8
> Bristol 4 Scout D
> Bristol 8 Scout S.2A
> Coventry Ordnance Works Biplane No 2
> F.B.A. C Flying boat (Franco-British Aviation)
> Nieuport 12
> Nieuport 28
> Royal Aircraft Factory B.E.8, B.E.8a 'Bloater'
> Royal Aircraft Factory F.E.8
> Short S.70
> Short S.80
> Short Type C (improved S.74)

The great training aeroplane, the Avro 504R Gosport, powered by a 100 hp Gnome Monosoupape B-2.

A F.E.8 of 41 Sqn, Royal Flying Corps, powered by a 100 hp Gnome 'Mono' pusher.

Sopwith 1914 Circuit Seaplane
Sopwith 'Gunbus'
Sopwith Tabloid
Sopwith Sociable, 'Tweenie'
Sopwith (Admiralty Type) 807 Folder Seaplane
Sopwith Two-Seat Scout 'Spinning Jenny'
Sopwith Schneider
Sopwith Pup
Sopwith F.1 Camel
Vickers E.F.B.2, 3, 5 'Gunbus'
Vickers F.B.5, 6 'Gunbus'
Vickers E.F.B.7

Vickers E.S.1 Bullet
Vickers F.B.12A
Vickers F.B.19 Bullet Mk I

The Vickers E.F.B.7 with twin, opposite-handed 100 hp Gnome Monosoupape 9B-2 engines.

GNOME MONOSOUPAPE 9 TYPE N, 150 hp, (1917), 9-cylinder, single-row rotary air-cooled poppet-valve. Bore/stroke 4.53 x 6.69 in. Vol. 970 cu in. (115 x 170 mm). Compression ratio 5.2:1. Direct R.H. tractor or L.H. pusher-drive. Two magnetos. Diameter 38.6 in.
Aircraft:
    Nieuport 28C.1
    Sopwith F.1 Camel.

GREEN ENGINE CO LTD, London.

The British aero-engine pioneer, Gustavus Green, like many aviation pioneers, was a bicycle maker and repairer in the late 1890s and undertook light engineering work locally in Sussex, where he had moved from London in 1897, while retaining a London office. In 1904, Green worked on motor-car and cycle patents, designing and building motor-cycles and engines, including a four-cylinder 26-30 hp car which was exhibited in chassis form at the 1906 motor show. It had a number of outstanding features which impressed the head of the Balloon Factory at Farnborough, Colonel Capper, who invited Green to design a developed version of the engine for use in the airship *Nulli Secundus*. This was a 80 hp vee-8 and a contract was signed in 1908, although the engine was transferred to a second airship the *Gamma* before the original was completed, this being the first British airship to fly powered by a British engine.

Gustavus Green was able to make almost every part of the engine in his works. Green transferred his work to a small factory at Twickenham, mainly for testing engines, the manufacture of which he had sub-contracted. When the 80 hp engine was being designed in 1908, he also made a 35 hp four-cylinder water-cooled upright engine, described as the 'first practicable motor that has yet appeared for aerial navigation'. This was in a brochure of Green's Motor Patents Syndicates Ltd, later to operate as the Green Engine Co. Green engines, which were water-cooled, incorporated numerous ingenious design features which were very advanced for their day, including closely-spaced one-piece cast steel cylinders and heads, with copper water-jackets and overhead camshafts. The operating valve mechanisms rested on removable cages, enclosed in aluminium castings.

Green exhibited at the first Olympia Aero Show and the Paris Salon in 1909, at which 30 and 50 hp engines were shown. The Short No 2 biplane, flown by J.T.C. Moore-Brabazon and powered by a 50/60 hp Green, became the first aeroplane to fly with a Green engine when 'Brab' won the *Daily Mail* Prize of £1,000 for a flight of one mile in a closed-circuit on 30 October 1909. Subsequently, Green engines became accepted for reliability and sound design, being used successfully in races and long-distance circuits, particularly by S.F. Cody, who constantly demanded more power. Of the seven British Empire Michelin Trophies and Prize contests flown from 1909 to 1913, Cody won four, using 60 and 100 hp Green engines, Moore-Brabazon and R.H. Carr winning two of the others. Other successful users of Green engines were A.V. Roe and

Harry Hawker. A 100 hp, six-cylinder Green won the 1914 £5,000 Naval and Military Aero-Engine Competition held at Farnborough.

Despite this success, Green engines played little part in the air war in the 1914-1918 period. Green engines increased in power, in twelve- and eighteen-cylinder form, up to 450 hp, although a 1,000 hp unit was designed. Many were used in high-speed motor launches, for which their comparatively heavy weight made them more suited than to aircraft. Nevertheless, a 260 hp engine was initially installed in a Porte 'Baby' flying-boat, until replaced by a Rolls-Royce engine. In 1920, Bert Hinkler made a remarkable 650 mile flight from Croydon to Turin, in 9½ hours, in an Avro Baby powered by a 35 hp Green. Gustavus Green died on 29 December 1964, within three weeks of his hundredth birthday.

GREEN 80–100 hp, (1908–1909), a 8-cylinder, upright 90-degree Vee, water-cooled poppet-valve engine. Unsupercharged, its propeller drive was direct R.H. tractor/L.H. pusher-drive. Bore/stroke 116 x 140 mm. Vol. 11.85 litre. Green engines had cast iron cylinders, spun copper water jackets and overhead camshafts. Pistons were of cast-iron. Crankshaft and connecting rods were of chrome vanadium steel and the crankcase was of aluminium alloy.

The justly famous 35 hp Green four-cylinder water-cooled engine of 1908.

GREEN C.4, 30–35 hp, (1908–10), 4-cylinder, upright in-line, water-cooled, poppet-valve. Bore/stroke 4.13 x 4.73 in, Vol. 253.44 cu in. (105 x 120 mm. Vol. 4.158 litre). Direct R.H. tractor/L.H. pusher-drive. Length 39.0 in; width 16.0 in; height 28.0 in.
Aircraft:

    Aero. Syndic. Valkyrie Type A
    Avro Types II-IV
    Avro Type D
    Avro 534, 543 Baby
    Blackburn Monoplane, 1
    Handley Page H.P.4 (Type D)
    Martin-Handasyde No 3
    Short S.26, 27, 28 Pusher Biplanes
    Sopwith Burgess-Wright
    and other pioneers

The Avro Type D, on floats lowered onto the water in the big airship hangar at Barrow-in-Furness.

The Roe III triplane, 35 hp Green, of 1909, A.V. Roe at the controls.

The Avro Type D, with a 35 hp Green C.4, as a landplane.

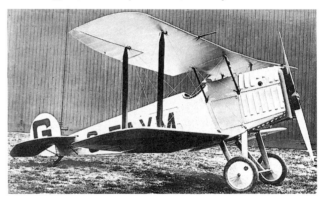

The Avro 534D Baby G-EAYM, powered by a 35 hp Green for use in India in 1921. Apart from a larger radiator, it is similar to that used by Bert Hinkler flying 800 miles, non-stop, from Sydney N.S.W. to Bundaberg in 1921.

GREEN D.4, 50–60 hp, (1909–10), 4-cylinder, upright in-line, water-cooled, poppet-valve. Bore/stroke 5.51 x 5.75 in, Vol. 548.78 cu in (140 x 146 mm. Vol. 8.99 litre). Direct R.H. tractor/L.H. pusher-drive. Zenith carburettor. (A long-stroke version of 152 mm but believed not to have flown — see E.6).
Aircraft:

    Aero. Syndic. No 2, Valkyrie Type C
    Avro Type G
    Blackburn Type E Single Seater
    Cody Type IIA, C, D
    Cody Type III, VC, VI
    Flanders F.3
    Grahame-White Type XV Boxkite
    Handley Page H.P.2 (Type B)
    Humphreys Nos 1 & 2 Tractor Monoplanes
    Northern Aircraft Co. P.B.1
    Royal Aircraft Factory F.E.2a
    Short No 2, S.26, S.28 Pusher Biplanes
    Sonoda Tractor Biplane.

GREEN E.6, 100–120 hp, (1912–16), 6-cylinder, upright in-line, water-cooled, poppet-valve. Bore/stroke 5.51 x 5.98 in, Vol. 855.54 cu in. (140 x 152 mm. Vol. 14.03 litre). Direct R.H. tractor-drive.
Production, 8/1914-12/1918, from:-
Mirrlees, Bickerton & Day Ltd, Stockport,
Ordered, 42;   Delivered, 42;   Cancelled/suspended, 0
Aircraft:

     Avro 504K
     Avro 523A
     Cody Types VC, VI
     Gnosspelius Hydro Tractor Biplane
     Grahame-White Charabancs Type 10
     Royal Aircraft Factory F.E.2a
     Short S.68 Seaplane
     Sopwith Three-Seater
     Sopwith Bat Boat 1A Amphibian
     Sopwith 1913 Circuit Seaplane

An experimental fitting of a six-cylinder Green E.6 in an Avro 504K.

GREEN 260–275 hp, (1914–15), 12-cylinder, upright 60-degree Vee water-cooled, poppet-valve. Bore/stroke 142 x 172 mm. Vol. 32.7 litre. Direct R.H. tractor-drive.
Production, 8/1914-12/1918, from:-
Mirrlees, Bickerton & Day Ltd, Stockport,
Ordered, 75;   Delivered, 21;   Cancelled/suspended, 54
Aircraft:

     Porte Baby

HART ENGINE COMPANY.

Based in Leeds it had, as a partner, the engineer C.B. Redrup. He started as an aero-engine designer in 1910, when he designed a 10-cylinder 50 hp air-cooled rotary engine, in which the cylinders and crankshaft rotated in opposite directions. By 1914 he had patented a seven-cylinder air-cooled radial engine of 150 hp. He had also begun work on five- (and later seven-) cylinder 'barrel' type engines *(see* **REDRUP**), the first of which was to appear some years later. Upon the outbreak of war in 1914, it was recognized that French demands were likely to dominate the aero-engine industry in that country and therefore British demands, for the Royal Flying Corps and the Royal Naval Air Service might not be able to be met.

At this time, there were few indigenous designs for aero-engines of about 150 hp in Britain and Vickers therefore began negotiations with the Hart Engine Co, which led to an agreement to finance the development of the proposed 150 hp engine designed by Redrup. At that time, the industry was in its infancy and things were liable to go wrong. The Hart engine was no exception and there were serious delays in developing it. Vickers persisted and obtained an order for fifty engines. In due course, a Vickers F.B.12A Scout was fitted with a Hart engine and on Christmas Eve 1916, it was flown to France for evaluation. The aircraft itself was unsatisfactory and a modified aircraft, a F.B.12B was flown shortly afterwards. The short life of the 150 hp Hart engine was terminated by a crash of the F.B.12B. This followed a string of engine troubles and Vickers then lost interest and abandoned further development of the engine. This led to a legal dispute between Redrup and Vickers, the former protesting that the aeroplane was an experimental type and that the engine should have been tested in a standard aeroplane. Curiously, the Vickers F.B.12 featured in another experimental and equally unsuccessful engine. *(see* **SMITH**)

HART 150 hp, (1916) seven-cylinder air-cooled radial.
Aircraft:

     Vickers F.B.12A, F.B.12B
     Vickers F.B.16 Hart Scout

The 150 hp Hart in the Vickers F.B.16 in its original form.

The 150 hp Hart in the Vickers F.B.16 in modified form.

HERMES — see Cirrus.

HISPANO-SUIZA

At Hispano-Suiza (whose Vee-8 engines were built under licence by Wolseley) Marc Birkigt had designed an aluminium block which employed dry screwed-in steel liners so as to ensure the best possible metal-to-metal contact, as mentioned above. To get around some of the acknowledged porosity problems, all blocks were enamelled inside and out. The 8-cylinder 90-degree Vee Hispano-Suiza engine in its many variations was used very widely and the British and French versions were virtually indistinguishable visually. The bore and stroke of all engines under 300 hp was the same at 120 mm x 130 mm. The low compression pistons measured 45 mm from gudgeon pin centre to the top of the crown, giving a ratio of 4.7:1. The high compression pistons similarly measured 50 mm, with a ratio of 5.3:1. The majority of early low compression pistons were removed and 5.3:1 pistons substituted. The makers stated that, as issued, the geared engines issued to England and all French 1170 engines were low compression. By September 1918, all Hispano-Suiza engines had been converted to high compression as they were overhauled. The direct-drive Wolseley Viper version (q.v.) was built as a high compression engine, as was the great majority of the French version known as the '1500 gear'.

Made in geared and ungeared (direct-drive) versions, three gear ratios were used, known respectively as 1500 gear, 1330 gear and 1170 or 1185 gear, the number being the approximate propeller revs. when the engine was turning at 2,000 rpm. A Ministry of Munitions Report stated that, by September 1918, there were no longer any 1330 geared engines in Service; most of the 1170 geared engines were installed in S.E.5 aircraft with four-bladed propellers. Most of the 1500 geared engines were in use in a number of machines with two-bladed propellers. All English geared engines were actually 1185, the number of teeth being 35 and 59. French 1170 geared engines had 24 and 41 teeth, whereas French 1500 geared engines had 21 and 28 teeth. A few English-made gears had 28 and 37 teeth, i.e. geared 1,513 to 2,000 rpm. Carburettors were of Claudel or Zenith design and manufacture and magnetos were made by B.T.H. or Dixie. The reduction gears in many Hispano engines were not of a satisfactory standard, many failing and some 200 hp Hispanos were de-geared, so as to give their propellers direct drive and, thereby, reversing their rotation. Sopwith Dolphins, modified to use these engines (*see* text and illustration), were named Dolphin IIIs. In *War in the Air*, Vol. VI, there is an alarming passage about Engine Log Book entries to the effect that geared Hispano engines were unsatisfactory but had been fitted to S.E.5as, in the absence of any suitable alternative. The effect on pilot morale, in the terrible circumstances of 1918, can well be imagined.

Maximum running times between overhauls of these Hispano-Suiza engines, involving complete dismantling for cleaning, was recommended as 60 hours, a very optimistic figure. The pure castor oil used as the lubricant was sticky when cold and, if allowed to accumulate dirt in the crankcase oilways, endangered the engine, which usually wrecked itself from this cause. The problems of such servicing in the field, in the appalling conditions experienced on the Western Front in 1917–18 may be imagined.

HISPANO-SUIZA 8, 140 hp, 8-cylinder, upright 90-degree Vee water-cooled poppet-valve. Bore/stroke 4.72 x 5.12 in. Vol. 716.69 cu in. (120 x 130 mm. Vol. 11.76 litre). Compression ratio 4.7:1. Unsupercharged. Direct R.H. tractor/L.H. pusher-drive. Length 48.4 in; width 33.1 in; height 31.5 in.
Aircraft:

Airco D.H.6

HISPANO-SUIZA 8Aa, 150 hp, (1917), 8-cylinder, upright 90-degree Vee water-cooled poppet-valve. Bore/stroke 4.72 x 5.12 in. Vol. 716.69 cu in. (120 x 130 mm. Vol. 11.76 litre). Compression ratio 4.7:1. Unsupercharged. Direct R.H. tractor/L.H. pusher-drive. Zenith Duplex carburettor. Only 150 ordered for England, all of which were converted, as occasion permitted, to Type 8Ab. Length 51.0 in; width 33.2 in; height 33.2 in.

Hispano-Suiza 8Aa, 150 hp (1917).

Aircraft:

A.D. Flying-boat (Admiralty Air Dept)
Bristol 12 F.2A Fighter
Bristol 13 M.R.1
Norman Thompson N.T.4
Royal Aircraft Factory B.E.2e
Royal Aircraft Factory S.E.5, S.E.5a
Sopwith Triplane
SPAD 7
Vickers F.B.16A
Vickers F.B.25

Direct Drive Hispano-Suiza 8a, for the Bristol F.2A Fighter.

HISPANO-SUIZA 8Ab, 180 hp, (1918). Generally similar to Type 8Aa. Ungeared (or Pousse model) but using high-compression pistons and carburettor and induction pipes from 200 hp engine. Compression ratio 5.3:1. Direct R.H. tractor/L.H. pusher drive. Production, 8/1914–12/1918, 150–180 hp engines from:-
Wolseley Motors Ltd, Birmingham,
Ordered, 4,350; Delivered, 1,853; Cancelled/suspended, 2,497
Aircraft:

Austin-Ball AFB.1
Beardmore W.B.II
Beardmore W.B.IV
Bristol F.2B Fighter
Royal Aircraft Factory S.E.5, S.E.5a
Sopwith 5F.1 Dolphin I
SPAD 7

HISPANO-SUIZA 8B, 200 hp, (1917), 8-cylinder, upright 90-degree Vee water-cooled engine, generally similar to 150 hp engine. Its propeller drive was geared, spur, reduction .75:1. L.H.tractor/R.H. pusher-drive. Bore/stroke 4.72 x 5.12 in. Vol. 716.8 cu in (120 x 130 mm). High compression ratio, 5.3:1. Length 53.4 in; width 33.9 in; height 35.3 in.
Aircraft:

Bristol 16 F.2B Fighter
Sopwith Triplane
Supermarine N.1B Baby

HISPANO-SUIZA 8Ba, 200 hp, (1917). Generally similar to Type 8Ab. 8-cylinder, upright 90-degree Vee water-cooled, poppet-valve. Bore/stroke 4.72 x 5.12 in. Vol. 716.8 cu in. (120 x 130 mm). Low compression ratio, 4.7:1. Geared, spur .585:1. L.H. tractor/R.H. pusher-drive.
Production, 8/1914–12/1918, 200 hp engines from:-
Wolseley Motors Ltd, Birmingham,
Ordered, 700; Delivered, 449; Cancelled/suspended, 251
Aircraft:

Avro 530
Beardmore W.B.IV
Bristol 16 F.2B Fighter
Martinsyde F.2
Martinsyde S.1
Royal Aircraft Factory B.E.12b
Royal Aircraft Factory F.E.9

Royal Aircraft Factory N.E.1
(Night Experimental, modified R.E.8)
Royal Aircraft Factory S.E.5a
Siddeley R.T.1
Sopwith B.1 Bomber
Sopwith T.1
Sopwith 5F.1 Dolphin I
Sopwith 5F.1 Dolphin III (degeared engine)
SPAD 13
Vickers F.B.16D
Vickers F.B.24A, B, D, E
Vickers F.B.26 Vampire I
Vickers F.B.27 Vimy prototype

The reduction gears of 200 hp Hispano-Suiza engines gave so much trouble that some of those in Sopwith Dolphins were de-geared and ran direct, as Dolphin IIIs.

The geared 200 h.p. Hispano-Suiza engine.

NOTE: These engines gave so much trouble that, those fitted to Sopwith Dolphin Is were de-geared, so becoming direct drive and thus rotating in the opposite direction. Dolphins so treated became Dolphin IIIs and are believed to be the only type to be regularly so treated, although this cannot be guaranteed.

HISPANO-SUIZA 8Bb, 200 hp. Low compression ratio 4.8:1. Geared, spur .75:1. L.H. tractor pusher drive. Few built
Aircraft:
    A.D. Flying-boat
    Handley Page H.P.14 R/200
    Norman Thompson N.T.4A
    Sopwith 5F.1 Dolphin I
    SPAD 13

HISPANO-SUIZA 8Bc, 220 hp. High compression ratio 5.3:1. Geared, spur .75:1 L.H. tractor/pusher-drive.
Aircraft:
    Avro 504K
    Royal Aircraft Factory S.E.5, S.E.5a
    SPAD 13

A Royal Aircraft Factory F.E.9, powered by a Hispano-Suiza 8Ba.

HISPANO-SUIZA 8Bd, 220 hp. High compression ratio 5.3:1. Geared, spur .75:1. L.H. tractor/pusher-drive.
Aircraft:
    SPAD 13

HISPANO-SUIZA 8Be, 220 hp. High compression ratio 5.3:1. Geared, spur .75:1. L.H. tractor/pusher-drive.
Aircraft:
    Royal Aircraft Factory S.E.5, S.E.5a
    Sopwith 5F.1 Dolphin I
    SPAD 13

HISPANO-SUIZA 8Cb.
Aircraft:
    SPAD 13

HISPANO-SUIZA 8F, 300 hp. Length 51.8 in; width 35.4 in; height 38.2 in.
Aircraft:
    Bristol 17, 17A, 17B F.2B Fighter
    Short 'Shrimp' Sporting Seaplane
    Supermarine Sea King II
    Westland Limousine II

A line-up of Sopwith Dolphin IIIs with de-geared Hispano-Suiza 8Ba engines.

HISPANO-SUIZA 8Fb, 'Type 42', 300 hp, (1918) 8-cylinder, upright 90-degree Vee water-cooled, poppet-valve. Bore/stroke 5.51 x 5.9 in. Vol. 1,125.2 cu in. (140 x 150 mm). Compression ratio 5.3:1. Direct R.H. tractor/L.H. pusher-drive. It closely resembled a Wolseley Viper, in having transverse magnetos and double oil pump. The gun gear fitted on the rear end of the engine and was not actuated from the propeller hub. An oil filter in the suction pipe was essential as there was no filter on the delivery side of the oil pump. Length 51.8 in; width 35.4 in; height 38.2 in.
Aircraft:

> Airco D.H.9 srs
> Alula Semiquaver (Martinsyde)
> Bristol 17 F.2B Fighter
> Martinsyde A.V.1
> Martinsyde F.3
> Martinsyde F.4, F.4A Buzzard
> Martinsyde F.6
> Martinsyde Type A Mk II
> Royal Aircraft Factory S.E.5a
> Sopwith 5F.1 Dolphin II

ISAACSON ENGINE (MOTOR SUPPLY CO).
R.J.Isaacson was designer to the Manning Wardle Engine Company, locomotive builders of Leeds.

ISAACSON 60 hp, (1910). R.J.Isaacson also designed a six-cylinder water-cooled radial engine of very unusual design. It weighed 245 lb and had six staggered cylinders which were bolted to a circular aluminium crankcase. The hollow crankshaft had two crankpins, each with three piston rods. Ahead of its time, the engine had aluminium cylinder heads and water jackets, overhead valves and a flywheel. Bore/stroke 120 x 125 mm. (Vol. 8.4 litre).
Aircraft:

> Avro Type D
> Blackburn Monoplane No 2
> Blackburn Mercury 1
> Blackburn Mercury 3
> Bristol Prier
> Flanders B.2
> Mersey Monoplane

The little 60 hp Isaacson radial on the nose of the Flanders B.2 biplane of 1910.

J.A.P. (J.A.PRESTWICH).
John Alfred Prestwich, born in 1874, became well-known for the Vee-twin, air-cooled motor-cycle engines which were made at his Tottenham (North London) factory. From about 1907, he began producing engines suitable for powering early aeroplanes, the first notable example of which is the little 9 hp twin. In September of that year, A.V. Roe used it in unsuccessful attempts at Brooklands to take-off solely under this power in his Roe I biplane. The engine was extremely heavy for its nominal horse-power (actually believed to develop nearer 10 hp) but, after the Roe I biplane was badly damaged in 1908, a triplane version was built and Roe persevered in his attempts to fly, using the same engine and experimenting with various propellers and drives.

At last, Roe managed (after several marginally successful hops) to make the first flight in Britain in a British aeroplane powered by

a British engine. On 13 July 1909 and again ten days later, Roe flew short distances at Lea Marshes, Essex, at about ten feet above the ground. Greatly encouraged by this success, Roe built a second Roe I triplane, powered by a more suitable, air-cooled four-cylinder J.A.P. engine of nominal 20 hp (in fact nearer 14–15 hp). Using this engine in the first of the two Roe I triplanes, he made a few short hops at the Blackpool Race Meeting in October 1909 and, two months later, in the second Roe I triplane, he made the first circular flight at Wembley, landing near the spot from where he had taken off.

J.A.P. 9 hp, (1909), a modified standard 2-cylinder air-cooled motor-cycle engine.
Aircraft:

> Roe I Triplane

J.A.P. 20 hp, (1909), a 4-cylinder, upright 90-degree Vee-shaped air-cooled poppet-valve engine. Bore/stroke 85 x 110 mm. Vol. 2.5 litre.
Aircraft:

> Roe I Triplane

The silhouette of the 90 degree, 20 hp J.A.P. used by A.V. Roe in his No 1 Triplane.

J.A.P. 40 hp, (1910), upright 90-degree Vee-shaped air-cooled poppet-valve engine. Single magneto. Bore/stroke 3.35 x 3.74 in, Vol. 263.68 cu in. (85 x 95 mm, vol 4.4 litre).
Aircraft:

> Martinsyde No 3 monoplane

The Martin-Handasyde No 3, powered by a 40 hp J.A.P. air-cooled engine.

J.A.P. made several other 8-cylinder air-cooled aero-engines, although they were not particularly noteworthy, the successful motor-cycle and light car business principally occupied the firm's time until, in the flourishing ultra-light aeroplane era of the 1930s, J.A.P. took out a licence to manufacture American Aeronca engines.

The Martin-Handasyde No 3, powered by a 40 hp J.A.P. air-cooled engine.

AERONCA-J.A.P. J-99, 36 hp, (1936), Aeronca E-113-C, built under licence by J.A.P., 2-cylinder, horizontally-opposed air-cooled poppet-valve. Bore/stroke 108 x 101.6 mm. Vol. 1.86 litre. Direct R.H. drive. Power Curve at rated altitude sea level to 2,000 ft, from A.& A.E.E., Martlesham, Report M.704, dated 7.4.37.

RPM	2,650	2,400	1,900
BHP	40.8	38.65	32.65

Max 40 bhp, 2,650 rpm, all-out level flight (5 min). Fuel Shell No 1.
Aircraft:

    Aeronca 100
    Britten Norman BN-1F
    Currie Wot
    Dart Kitten
    Hants & Sussex Herald
    Heath Parasol
    Hillson Praga
    Luton L.A.4A Minor
    Peterborough Ely
    Slingsby 29B Motor Tutor
    Taylor J.T.1
    Tipsy Junior

JAMESON AERO ENGINES LTD, EWELL, SURREY.
The Chief engineer of the company, A.E. Moser designed a four-cylinder four-stroke engine for light aircraft in 1943. It underwent a 100 hour Air Ministry Development Test in 1946. It was subjected to a Type-Test in 1948 but, owing to the failure of a valve spring, was only granted a 100 hour civil flight clearance. A gearbox was fitted in 1948 and it was used to power the Skeeter light helicopter.

JAMESON FF-1, 110 hp, (1948), a 4-cylinder, horizontally-opposed air-cooled poppet-valve engine. It was unsupercharged and its propeller drive was geared, spur, reduction .691:1. Bore/stroke 4.125 in x 3.75 in. Vol. 200.4 cu in (105 x 95 mm. Vol. 3.28 litre). Compression ratio 7.4:1. Length 33.0 in; width 34.0 in; height 23.5 in.
Aircraft:

    Cierva W.14 Skeeter I (prototype, Saro P.501)
    Miles M.18 Mk I

LE RHONE
The French Le Rhône rotary engine appeared in 1912, designed by Ingenieur Verdet, who had worked for Peugeot and for their drivers Giuppone and Boillot. Great numbers of Le Rhône rotary engines were built by the Société des Moteurs Gnome et Rhône, based in Paris. Large numbers were also built in Britain during the First World War, under an associated company, The Gnome and Le Rhône Engine Company in London, in a variety of models. They were basically two-valve engines, all of similar design but differing in mechanical detail and incorporating a single push-pull valve rod and rocker. The Gnome engine used a master big-end, with slave rods attached, whereas the Le Rhône had an unusual arrangement whereby the heels or slippers of the connecting rods in the nine-cylinder engines were assembled on a thrust block in three concentric grooves, giving them limited sliding or oscillating movement as the engine rotated. The engines had steel cylinders with cast-iron liners and pistons of steel (later aluminium). They were equipped with single magnetos and Bloctube carburettors.

LE RHONE 7, 50 hp, (1913). 7-cylinder, single-row rotary air-cooled poppet-valve. Bore/stroke 4.13 x 5.51 in. Vol. 516.67 cu in. (105 x 140 mm). Compression ratio 4.5:1. Direct R.H. tractor/L.H. pusher-drive.
Aircraft:

    Bristol 46A Babe III
    Bristol-Coanda T.B.8

LE RHONE 9C, 80 hp, (1916), 9-cylinder, single-row rotary air-cooled poppet-valve. Bore/stroke 4.13 x 5.51 in. Vol. 664.47 cu in. (105 x 140 mm). Compression ratio 4.5:1. Direct R.H. tractor/L.H. pusher-drive. The chief external difference between this and other rotaries is the set of nine curved copper induction pipes which carried the explosive mixture from the crankcase to the inlet valves which, with the exhaust valves, were operated by one tappet rod per cylinder. There was no master connecting rod. Diameter 37.2 in. Production, 8/1914–12/1918, from:-
W.H. Allen Son & Co Ltd, Bedford.
Ordered, 1,200;   Delivered, 339;   Cancelled/suspended 861;
F.W. Berwick & Co Ltd, Park Royal,
Ordered, 500;   Delivered, 400;   Cancelled/suspended, 100
Daimler Co Ltd, Coventry,
Ordered, 550;   Delivered, 349;   Cancelled/suspended, 201
Gordon Watney & Co Ltd, Weybridge,
Ordered, 200;   Delivered, 0 ;   Cancelled/suspended, 200
Peter Hooker Ltd.
Ordered, 400;   Delivered, 0;   Cancelled/suspended, 400

Nieuport Type 10 with a 80 hp Le Rhône 9C rotary, featuring a front mounting.

Aircraft:

    Avro 504, 504A, B, C, J
    Avro 554 Baby
    Beardmore W.B.III
    Bristol-Coanda T.B.8

Bristol 1 Scout C
Bristol 3 Scout D
Bristol 20 M.1C
Caudron G.III, IV
Henry Farman F.20
Grahame-White G.W.15
Grahame-White G.W.E.6 Bantam
Morane-Saulnier G, H
Morane-Saulnier L, LA
Morane-Saulnier N
Morane-Saulnier P
Nieuport 10, 11
Nieuport 21
Pemberton Billing P.B.23E Push-Proj
Royal Aircraft Factory S.E.4a
Sopwith Pup
Sopwith F.1 Camel
Sopwith Dove
Thomas Morse S-4
Vickers F.B.12

Production, 8/1914–12/1918, from:-
W.H.Allen Son & Co Ltd,
Ordered, 1,800;   Delivered, 953;   Cancelled/suspended, 847
Peter Hooker Ltd.
Ordered, 300;   Delivered, 0;   Cancelled/suspended, 300
Aircraft:
Airco D.H.2
Airco D.H.5
Armstrong Whitworth F.K.10
Avro 504K, L
Avro 531 Spider
Bristol 20 M.1C
Cierva C.6A, B Autogiro
Hanriot HD-1
Morane-Saulnier AC, BB, I, V, P
Nieuport 16
Nieuport 17, 17bis
Nieuport 20
Nieuport Triplane
Royal Aircraft Factory F.E.8
Sopwith Pup
Sopwith F.1 Camel
Sopwith LCT 1½ Strutter
Sopwith Gnu
Sopwith Swallow
Vickers E.S.1, E.S.2 Bullet
Vickers F.B.12C
Vickers F.B.19 Bullet Mk I, Mk II

A line-up of Avro 504Cs, powered by 80 hp Le Rhône 9Cs and having front mountings.

Rear view of a 110 hp Le Rhône 9J rotary.

A Nieuport Type 11, with a 80 hp Le Rhône 9C rotary, captured by Germans.

LE RHONE 9Ja, 110 hp, (1916), Note. There were two variants of this engine, of 130 hp, the 9Jb and 9Jby and 9Z, with slightly increased rotation. All were 9-cylinder, single-row rotary air-cooled poppet-valve. Bore/stroke 4.41 x 6.63 in. (112 x 170 mm). Vol. 911.4 cu in. Compression ratio 5:1. Direct R.H. tractor-drive. Diameter 39.6 in.

An Avro 504K single-seat night fighter, with a 110 hp Le Rhône 9Ja rotary.

LE RHONE 9Jb, 130 hp.
Aircraft:
> Morane-Saulnier AC
> Nieuport 23
> Nieuport 24, 24bis

LE RHONE 9Jby, 130 hp.
Aircraft:
> Nieuport 23, 24, 24bis
> Nieuport 27

LE RHONE 9R, 170 hp, (1916), 9-cylinder, single-row rotary air-cooled poppet-valve. Bore/stroke 115 x 170 mm. Compression ratio 5.65:1. Direct R.H. tractor-drive.
Aircraft:
> Bristol 3 Scout D
> Sopwith F.1 Camel

LIBERTY.

The justly famous Liberty 12-cylinder engine, though not built in Britain was, as indicated in the Introduction, used and overhauled in such great numbers in Britain that it cannot fairly be neglected. Its existence came about because of increasing demands, in the late stages of the First World War, for an engine of about 400 hp. Something, broadly similar, was urgently needed to augment the supply of Rolls-Royce Eagle VIIIs. Because of the incessant demands of war, and consequent drainage of resources, European designs were tending to stagnate or to become obsolete and no suitable standard engine then existed which could readily be produced in large numbers in the U.S.A., by American methods. The decision to develop a standard engine was made at a momentous five-day meeting at a Washington hotel, between British, French and American representatives, at the end of May 1917. Those present were Jesse G. Vincent of the Packard Company and Major G.E.J. Hall, of the Hall-Scott Company. The decision was made that both companies should collaborate to design and manufacture a 400 hp water-cooled engine.

Sketches of eight and twelve-cylinder engines, which could be mass-produced, were agreed at a meeting of the Joint Army and Navy Technical Board within five days. The U.S. Government requested five examples of each engine and the first eight-cylinder engine ran just a month later, being delivered to the Bureau of Standards on 3 July. However, reports from the Front suggested that the type was already obsolescent and should not be proceeded with and the twelve-cylinder derivative was put in hand. On 25 August 1917, the new engine had passed a fifty-hour test and an order for 1,000 was promptly cabled from England. The engine was to be called the Liberty. The speed with which it was produced was due to its design being based on well-known practices, proven in service and, in large measure, to the pooling of knowledge and consultations between experts in the enormous and varied engineering fields available in the States. Separate steel cylinders had water-jackets welded on to them. Pistons were of aluminium and there were dual carburettors and magnetos. Complete Liberty engines were made by Ford, Lincoln, Packard, Marmon and Buick.

The Liberty engine had several smaller variants, with four, six and eight cylinders but the 12A was the only engine in the series to be built in quantity. There were two main versions, which differed only in the 5:1 compression ratio of those for Naval use and the 5.42:1 ratio for the Army. Its production was a major wartime achievement for the United States. According to Packard's records, at the Armistice on 11 November 1918, America was turning out over 4,000 Liberty engines a month. Unfortunately there is no complete record of the total numbers built but it must have been in the region of 80,000. In February 1934, the U.S. Army ordered that no more Liberty engines were to be used, by then the Royal Air Force and several other Air Forces had already phased out what, by any standards, was a very remarkable engine.

LIBERTY 12A (Army), 400 hp, (1918), 12-cylinder, upright 45-degree Vee, water-cooled, poppet-valve. Bore/stroke 5.0 x 7.0 in. Vol. 1,648.8 cu in. (127.0 x 177.8 mm). Compression ratio 5.42:1. Direct R.H. tractor/L.H. pusher-drive. Delco magnetos, 2 duplex Claudel HC7 or 52 Zenith carburettors. Length 69.4 in; width 26.9 in; height 43.7 in.

Aircraft:
> Airco D.H.9A
> Bristol 25 Braemar II (double engine installation)
> Bristol 26 Pullman
> de Havilland D.H.10 Amiens
> de Havilland D.H.10A Amiens III, IIIA
> de Havilland D.H.16

The Liberty 12 engine was characterised by the very narrow angle of 45 degrees between the cylinder blocks.

The Liberty was a 400 hp direct-drive water-cooled vee-12.

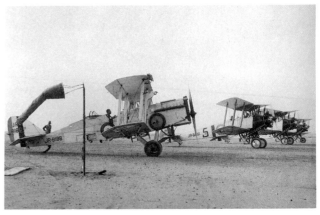

A Liberty-engined Airco D.H.9a in the Middle-East, with a spare wheel on the cowling. This and the Avro 504N have the 'JR' serial, indicating 'Rebuilt' aircraft. Wooden airframes suffered severely from shrinkage and consequent distortion, due to heat and lack of humidity.

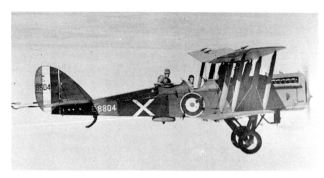

A Liberty-engined Airco D.H.9a in the Middle-East, complete with spare wheel, extra radiator and solar topees for the crew.

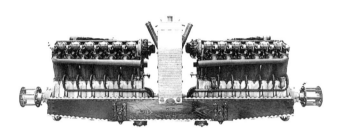

The unique double Liberty mounting of the big Bristol Braemar II transport.

LIBERTY 12N (Navy), 350 hp, Compression ratio 5:1, otherwise similar to 12A.
Aircraft:

    Airco D.H.4, (U.S.A., tests with various
    propellers, at McCook Field, Dayton, Ohio)
    Handley Page H.P.12 O/400
    Handley Page H.P.20 Type X/4B

LUTON ANZANI — see ANZANI (BRITISH/LUTON).

METEOR ENGINEERING CO, LONDON.
This somewhat obscure company, formed by W.J. Newman and H.J. Fenner in 1931, designed and built a small 110 hp eight-cylinder, air-cooled two-stroke radial engine. Called the Meteor Mk I, it explored a novel method of changing the reciprocating motion of the piston into the rotary motion of the crankshaft. Photographs exist of the engine's installation in an Avro aircraft but it is by no means certain that it actually flew.

A 40 hp four-cylinder, blown N.E.C. engine.

NEW ENGINE CO. (N.E.C.).
This company was based in Acton. West London, in 1910, the Managing Director and Works Manager, respectively, being J.C. and G.F. Mort. Their first aero-engine was a two-cylinder two-stroke. The engine was unusual in having a rotary valve which admitted mixture from a Roots blower and acted similarly for scavenging, the first supercharged engine used for aircraft use. They were successful in producing water-cooled, vertical in-line 40 and 50 hp, four-cylinder and 60 hp, 6-cylinder two-stroke engines. The bore/stroke of the 40 hp engine being 3.32 x 4.25 in and those of the 50 hp version being 3.69 x 4.5 in. Cast-iron cylinders had electrolytically-deposited copper on steel water jackets, cast-iron pistons, vanadium steel crankshaft and connecting rods. The crankcase was of aluminium.
Aircraft:

    Short-Wright Biplane

NAPIER.
The old-established firm of D.Napier & Son Limited, piston aero-engine makers of great distinction is now, sadly, little more than a memory. In the 1920s and 30s, vehicles driven or piloted by men bearing such famous names as Segrave, Campbell, Cobb and Scott-Paine, were breaking speed and distance records on land, sea and in the air. *Golden Arrow*, *Blue Bird*, *Miss England*, *Miss Britain* and *Napier-Railton* were rather better-known names, perhaps, than their common and rightly famous Napier Lion aero-engines. In the Lion's true setting, there were many other examples most importantly the winning of the Schneider Trophy Contests in 1922 and 1927, to say nothing of the Aerial Derbys of 1919–1923. Supermarine seaplanes, powered by Lion engines twice claimed the World's Absolute speed record in 1925 and 1929. Quite apart from the sheer speed which these compact and powerful engines made possible, there were numerous long-distance flights in which their reliability was of the utmost importance.

Robert Napier, of Levenside in Dunbartonshire, an Eighteenth Century blacksmith (a key trade in the Industrial Revolution) married Jean Denny, a member of the great shipbuilding family of Dumbarton. They had a large family and a grandson, David Napier born about 1785, after completing an apprenticeship in London under Henry Maudslay, set up a general engineering business at York Road, Lambeth, London. The work undertaken included the design and building of steam-operated printing machinery, notably for T.C.Hansard, the Parliamentary printer, in the 1820s. His Napier cousins were also engineers, one of whom helping Samuel Cunard to form the shipping line and build ships.

In addition to making printing machinery, for the Bible, bank notes and other important work, the firm progressed to the manufacture of rifle bullets and other machinery for the Board of Ordnance at Woolwich Arsenal. Lighter engineering included machinery for the weighing of coins, devised for the Bank of England while, amongst heavy engineering work at the other end of the scale, work was undertaken for I.K.Brunel in building the Great Western Railway. Napier was therefore a distinguished name, intimately associated with engineering and the works in Lambeth were known to be the best equipped and run in London, with machine tools to tackle almost any engineering job. The firm took great pride in its achievements, living up to an interpretation of the Scots origin of its name 'Nay Peer', or unequalled.

David Napier was succeeded by his son, J.M.Napier. Though a man of talent and imagination, under him the firm did not prosper. After he died in 1895, leaving the company in reduced circumstances, the youngest of his four sons, Montague Stanley Napier took it over. Among his friends was S.F.Edge, London sales representative of the Dunlop Tyre Co who, though not an engineer, saw the value in the new cause of 'automobilism'. In 1896, the Locomotives on The Roads' Act came into force, drawing public attention to the novel motor-car. Edge, inspired by French successes in motoring, inspired Montague Napier to enter the motor-car business by suggesting that he could improve the design of a Panhard-Levassor, as an interesting engineering problem. So, in 1899, started the long series of Napier engines for cars, boats and aircraft. Edge and his former boss at Dunlop, Harvey Du Cros set up the Motor Vehicle Company in London to sell cars and, in particular, all the cars that Napier could make, starting in 1900.

The story is similar to that of Rolls and Royce and roughly contemporary with it and, indeed, that year Edge drove a 16 hp Napier car in a race from Paris to Toulouse and back, with C.S.Rolls acting as his mechanic. Lack of success caused by ignition trouble, gave the impetus to Napier to design new and greatly improved cars for the nobility, as well as racing motor launches. A Napier 'Flying Machine', a steerable balloon, was also proposed but not proceeded with. The new motor car activity having outgrown the Lambeth site, land was bought for a new factory, west of London, at Acton in 1902 and 1904. In 1903, Edge suggested that Napier should produce a six-cylinder engine instead of the more usual two-, or four-cylinder variety, which he did most successfully. Napier and Edge eventually parted company when Napier bought out Edge's business in 1912 and continued in the private and commercial vehicle business.

The outbreak of war in 1914 brought much business to the Acton works, principally constructing vans, ambulances and lorries. A year later, the works became a 'controlled establishment' and was engaged in sub-contract work on the R.A.F.3a aero-engine for the Government. The company was also asked to build Sunbeam Arab engines. These were not satisfactory and Napier was convinced that he could design something better. In July 1916, he had begun the design of such an engine, to be of the twelve-cylinder, broad-arrow layout, probably inspired by a Royal Aircraft Factory proposal. Illness intervened, compelling him to retire in 1917 from active work at the age of 47, although he remained very firmly at the helm of policy. At a meeting in France in 1919, Montague Napier announced the proposal, in principle, to give up making cars in favour of the then risky business of making aero-engines.

The Company's Chief Designer was by then A.J.Rowledge and the new 12-cylinder engine was named the Lion. It was a very compact 450 hp engine in the 'broad-arrow' (W-shape) and became a very widely-used and reliable power unit. (Rowledge subsequently joined Rolls-Royce). The Lion turned out to be a trusty power unit, extensively used in bombers and flying-boats, operating over long distances and for record attempts, and was still in regular use, over twenty five years later. It is rightly famous in the aviation annals of the 1920s and 1930s as a reliable, hard-working engine, which propelled most Royal Air Force aircraft (except fighters), throughout the then British Empire and beyond.

In 1927, the monthly production rate was fifty Lions, although it had fallen to fewer than eighteen by the end of 1929, with the prospect of further reductions. Napier were in the difficult position of having only one major product, dependent largely on Air Ministry orders and which was nearing the extremity of its potential development. Against this were three other major engine manufacturers, competing for orders in the 450-500 hp range. Napier contemplated an amalgamation with one or other of them but nothing came of the idea. Montague Napier died on 22 January, 1931, being succeeded by H.T. Vane, a long-time employee of company and the first Chairman not to be a member of the Napier family. He resigned after about a year, in disagreement with the Board on policy and the firm passed effectively into the control of a City finance house.

NAPIER LION

Despite the Lion's well-recorded fame, its detailed history has been strangely obscure and there can have been few more frustrating tasks than trying to sort out the published designations of the earliest Napier Lions. Many articles and books are to be found which quote numerous aircraft as being powered variously (and sometimes contradictorily) by 'a 450 hp Napier Lion Mk I, IA, IAX, IB, IC', or a Mk II or IIB.

The exact differences between the various early Lions have been hard to discover, let alone define, with the only published common factor throughout being the output of 450 horse-power. A most experienced test pilot from the early 1920s onwards, and in a better position than most to know the facts was Norman Macmillan. He wrote, in an article in *Shell Aviation News* in 1968, 'Today, Napiers are unable to find any records showing the production dates of the different series of Lion aero-engines, in their manufacturing run from 1917 to 1932. But, from my Log-Books I have taken (the following) information recording first engine flights; if it does not establish the precise date of the first engine of a series, it must provide a fair approximation of series production'. Macmillan tested almost all the Napier Lion engines built, straight off the test bench, involving a total of 798 flights. His judgement deserves respect — even if some questions remain unanswered, the precise dates, of course, being relatively less important.

Macmillan stated categorically that the 425 hp Mk I Lion was only the prototype (suggesting that only two or three engines were built) and that the actual production run began with the 450 hp Mk II. The lack of other detailed records retained by the Company makes an assessment very difficult and dispute pointless. Adding to the general confusion is the fact that the Lion IIB was also quoted as a 450 hp engine. To what extent other published records were accurate, particularly in view of their many contradictions was, until research was seriously undertaken for this book, quite a problem. At least 59 types of aircraft of one sort or another have been listed as having various sub-types of 'Lion I', or simply '450 hp Lion'.

Then, unexpectedly out of the blue, the author was given, from private archives, faint copies of details of some of Napier's aero engines, just in time for some details to be included in this text. Even so, it needed a great deal of checking to ensure as much accuracy as possible at the time, as the new information conflicted with so much of the information previously published. Much was accurate and new though, tantalizingly, not really enough. A certain amount of conjecture, the 'educated guess' is therefore inevitable. All, or the great majority of aircraft powered by the engine have been listed in these documents although the exact early versions are not specified in any of them. No doubt, in time, research will reveal still further details, including more exact definitions of the various sub-types of the early engines. Fortunately, towards the end of the 1914-18 war, the Ministry of Munitions Aeronautical Inspection Department issued brief engine Specifications and rare copies of these survive, including that of the earliest Lion to enter service with the Royal Air Force. It is dated 4 October 1918 and it also has a power curve, dated 4 October the same year.

The Napier Lion had three rows of four cylinders and, for a 12-cylinder engine, was short and compact. It also benefited from an equally short and stiff crankshaft, resulting in uniform turning moment and good dynamic balance. Unlike Birkigt's earlier and Royce's later approaches to the subject of the water-cooled engine, Rowledge's Lion had individual cylinders. The liners were separate machined steel forgings, their flat-topped, poultice-type combustion heads being integral with the barrels and the four separate valve seats screwed in from within. The four liners in each row were screwed into a single cast aluminium head, the two faces having to be matched accurately with a good finish and, to ensure a good contact, an extra holding-down stud was added between each set of four valve ports and tightened after the main studs had been screwed up. This also required the valve-seatings at the closed top end of the liner to be machined in situ after it had been screwed tightly into position. The sparking plugs had to be screwed through the screw thread between the liner and the head, an adaptor needing to be inserted for each plug, sealing off any possible leaks. The replacement of a cylinder liner due to wear or damage was therefore an expensive operation. The pistons were flat-topped and of cast aluminium alloy.

The cylinder head was an aluminium alloy casting, containing induction and exhaust passages and bearings for twin overhead camshafts. The sheet steel water jackets were made in two halves, welded together. Cooling such a layout was complicated because each head and cooling jacket had to be fed individually, resulting in a rather heavy installed weight. The water pump fed the port side head block and also the centre and starboard side head blocks via double cast unions, each in turn feeding their own jackets and thence returning to the radiator. There was also a warming water feed to the carburettors. The port and centre induction pipes were fed from one Napier Claudel-Hobson duplex carburettor, mounted on the port side and the starboard induction pipe from a single unit, mounted on that side. Both H.C.7 carburettor units were installed in the front of the engine in early Lions and at the rear on later versions, Service engines being unsupercharged. Regrettably, as indicated previously, published details of the early Lions and their performance have varied to a considerable degree but the following have been abstracted from Ministry of Munitions and Napier sources and are as accurate as can be discovered.

NAPIER LION I, 468 hp, (1918). Several prototypes and a few special engines had direct drive but most production engines were spur-geared, with 44:29 teeth, or .659:1, L.H. tractor/R.H. pusher-drive. Two magnetos, B.T.H. A.V.12, or Rémy, battery-operated.
Initial production, 1917, from:-
D.Napier & Son Ltd, Acton,
Ordered, 100;   Delivered, 35;   Cancelled/suspended, 65.

One of the prototype geared Lions of 1919.

Bore/stroke 5.5 x 5.125in. (139.69 x 130.17 mm)
Swept Volume 1,461.6 cu in. (23.9 litres).
Compression Ratio 5.53:1.
Weight and Dimensions — *See* Performance Tables

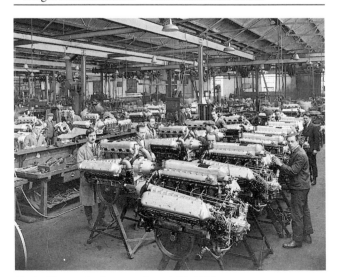

Napier Lion production was substantial in 1924.

First fitted to a D.H.9, the Lion gained an unofficial (not officially observed) British Altitude Record on 2 January 1919, reaching 30,500 feet in 68 minutes. Also fitted initially to the prototypes of the Fairey Pintail and Parnall Puffin. Apart from the quite small number of prototype and test engines referred to above, the true production version was the Mk II.

LION II, 480/500 hp, (1919), E64. 12-cylinder, upright W-shaped 'Broad Arrow', water-cooled, poppet-valve engine. It was generally similar to the Mk I. Operators' running instructions were that the full-throttle speed of the engine should be at least 1,850 rpm at ground level, with the machine standing. Full throttle should only be used for a few seconds, to test running order. In flight, full-throttle revolutions should not be at less than 1,950 rpm or over 2,200 rpm. When flying below 5,000 ft, except for getting off the ground or in emergencies, full-throttle should not be used for continuous running. Cruising rpm should be 1,800-1,850.

Early Napier Lions had twin carburettors on the port side and a single one on the other. This Airco D.H.9A had special intake pipes.

A Napier Lion II, showing the twin carburettors at the front.

Versions of the early Lions were interchangeable, to suit operators' requirements. Generally, low compression engines were for civil use. Apart from its widespread Service and civil use, this engine was the basis of several special racing engines and, as the Sea Lion was adapted for use in high-speed motor launches was still in use over forty years after the Lion's first appearance.

Bore/stroke 5.5 x 5.125in. (139.69 x 130.17 mm)
Swept Volume 1,461.6 cu in. (23.9 litres)
Compression Ratio; Military, 5.8:1; Civil, 5.0 or 5.55:1
Weights and Dimensions, liable to vary according to
accessories — See Performance Tables

Fuel: BS.121/23, 80/20 standard petrol/benzol. Length 57.5 in;
width 42.0 in; height 43.5 in.
Aircraft:

 Airco D.H.4A
 Airco D.H.9 srs
 Airco D.H.9R
 Airco D.H.9A srs
 Alliance P.2 Seabird
 Armstrong Whitworth Awana
 Avro 539B
 Avro 555 Bison I, II

Armstrong Whitworth Awana, with a Napier Lion II.

 Blackburn T.1 Swift I
 Blackburn T.1A Swift II
 Blackburn Pellet
 Boulton & Paul P.8 'Atlantic'
 Bristol 62 Ten Seater
 de Havilland D.H.14A
 de Havilland D.H.16
 de Havilland D.H.18A, B
 de Havilland D.H.29 Doncaster
 de Havilland D.H.34 (17/21)
 Dornier Do J Wal
 Fairey N.10
 Fairey IIIA
 Fairey Pintail
 Fairey Fawn I, II
 Felixstowe F.5
  Gloucestershire Mars I (Bamel)
 Gloster I (Seaplane)
 Grahame-White G.W.E.9 Ganymede

Winner of the 1922 Schneider Trophy contest and holder of World's records for speed and distance, the Supermarine Sea Lion II was powered by a direct-drive Napier Lion II. Seen here, under assembly with its financial backer, Hubert Scott-Paine and its young designer, R.J. Mitchell.

 Handley Page H.P.12 O/400
 Handley Page H.P.15 V/1500
 Parnall Possum (11/20)
 Parnall Puffin
 Supermarine Sea Lion I
 Supermarine Sea Lion II (Direct-drive racing engine)
 Supermarine Seal II
 Tarrant Tabor (6 engines)
 Vickers F.B.27 Vimy Ambulance
 Vickers 13 Vernon II, III
 Vickers 18 Viking III
 Vickers 54, 55, 58, 60, 64, 67, 84 Viking IV
 Vickers 56 Victoria I
 Vickers 57 Virginia I
 Vickers 59 Viking V
 Vickers 62 Vanguard
 Vickers 71 Vixen I
 Vickers 74 Vulcan
 Vickers 76 Virginia II
 Vickers 78 Vulture I (Viking VI)
 Vickers 79 Virginia III
 Vickers 81 Victoria II
 Vickers 83 Vanellus (Viking VII)
 Vickers 87 Vixen II
 Vickers 91 Vixen III
 Vickers 93 Valparaiso I
 Vickers 94 Venture I
 Vickers 99 Virginia IV
 Vickers 102 Valparaiso
 Vickers 108 Virginia VI
 Vickers 117, 138 Victoria III
 Westland Limousine III

LION IIB, 480 hp, (1925), E64. Mainly military engines, with a
compression ratio standardized at 5.8:1. Geared spur .659:1, similar
to the Lion II, except that the reduction gear was improved, having
41:27 teeth.

The Napier Lion (in this case the Mk IIB) was a neat, compact engine. Its installation and radiator in the Blackburn Dart were functional rather than artistic.

Aircraft:

 Blackburn Blackburn I
 Blackburn T.2 Dart
 Blackburn T.3 Velos
 English Electric M.3 Ayr (Taxi only)
 English Electric P.5 Kingston I, II, III
 Fairey Fawn I
 Fairey IIID

Handley Page H.P.18 W.8
Handley Page H.P.19 Hanley (Type T) (3/20)
Handley Page H.P.24 W.8d Hyderabad
Handley Page H.P.25 Hendon (Type Ta)
Handley Page H.P.30 W.10
Phoenix P.5 Cork III
Supermarine Swan
Supermarine Seagull I, II
Supermarine Southampton I
Vickers 158 Victoria IV
Westland Walrus
Westland Dreadnought

The Napier Lion (in this case the Mk IIB) was a neat, compact engine. Its installation and radiator in the Blackburn Dart were functional rather than artistic.

LION IV, 470 hp, (1927), one of the few fighter applications of the Lion. The engine fitted to the Gloster Guan was equipped with an exhaust-driven turbo-supercharger which maintained maximum power up to 15,000 feet. The supercharger gave much trouble and development was abandoned. Direct R.H. tractor-drive.
Aircraft:

Gloster Gorcock
Gloster Guan

LION V, 470 hp, (1925), E64. Compression ratio 5.8:1, Geared, spur .659:1. L.H.tractor.
Aircraft:

Avro 555 Bison
Blackburn T.2 Dart
Blackburn T.5 Ripon I
Blackburn T.3A Velos
Blackburn Blackburn II
Fairey Fawn I, II
Fairey Pintail
Fairey IIID
Fairey IIIF/I
Handley Page H.P.24 W.8d Hyderabad
Hawker Horsley
Parnall Pike
Supermarine Seagull III
Supermarine Sheldrake
Supermarine Southampton I
Vickers 100 Virginia V
Vickers 111, 112 Virginia VI, VII
Vickers 128, 129 Virginia VIII, IX
Vickers 106, 116, 148 Vixen III, V
Vickers 158 Victoria IV

LION V*, 500 hp, (1930). E64. Reconditioned engine, compression ratio 5.8:1, Geared, spur .659:1.
Aircraft:

Vickers 158 Victoria IV

LION VA, 500 hp, (1926). E64. Compression ratio 5.8:1, Geared, spur .659:1. L.H. tractor-drive.
Aircraft:

Avro 571 Buffalo I
Fairey IIID
Fairey IIIF Mk I
Gloster II (Seaplane), racing engine.
Handley Page H.P.31 Harrow I (Type E)
Saunders A.14 (Metal Hull)
Supermarine Southampton II
Vickers 122 Virginia VII
Vickers 130 Vivid (Vixen VII)

LION VI, 525 hp, (1926). E75. Compression ratio 5.8:1, direct-drive, R.H. tractor. Turbo-supercharged.
Aircraft:

Fairey Fawn III
Gloster Guan

LION VII, 680 hp, (1925), racing engine, high-compression ratio 8:1. Reduced depth cylinder blocks and reduced frontal area. Direct R.H. tractor-drive.
Aircraft:

Gloster III, IIIA, IIIB
Supermarine S.4

LION VIIA, 875 hp, (1927), E86, 91. Direct-drive high-compression racing engine similar to Mk VII, the principal difference being as above, but high-compression ratio 10:1. Direct R.H. tractor-drive.
Aircraft:

Gloster IV (6/26)
Gloster IVA (6/26) (World's speed record 226.75 mph)
Supermarine S.5 S.5/21

The direct-drive Napier Lion VIIA, of 1927.

The direct-drive Napier Lion VIIA installed in the 1927 Supermarine S.5 Schneider seaplane N219.

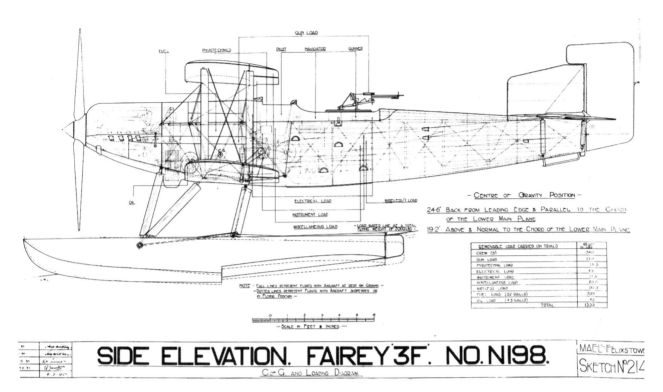

The Napier Lion V neatly fitted the nose of the Fairey IIIF, in this case the float seaplane.

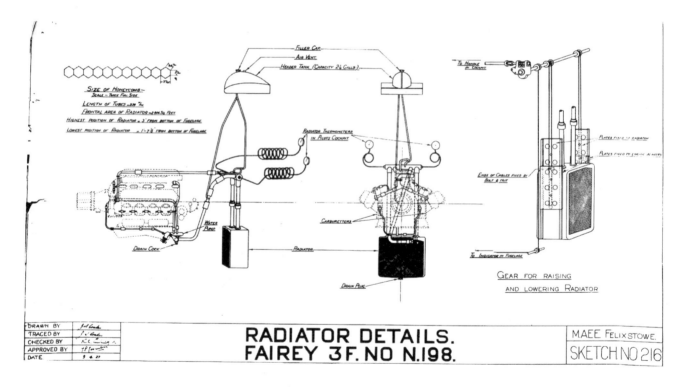

The cooling system devised for the Fairey IIIF was neat and the fore-runner of the 'Fairey Eversharp Nose', an allusion to a then-new type of pencil.

LION VIIB, 880 hp (1927). E.90. High-compression, geared racing engine, as Lion VIIA but with double-reduction gear through a layshaft, mounted over the airscrew shaft and a co-axial crankshaft. Special fuel was 25/75 per cent petrol/benzol with 10.75 cc/Imperial gallon TEL additive. Won the Schneider Trophy contest in Venice in 1927, and gained the World's Speed Record in 1928. Similar to VIIA, the principal difference being high-compression ratio 10:1, geared, co-axial double-reduction .766:1. R.H. tractor-drive. Length 66.3 in; width 38.4 in; height 34.5 in.
Aircraft:

    Gloster IVB (6/26)
    Supermarine S.5 (S.5/21)

LION VIID, (1929), 1,320 hp. E94. High-compression racing engine, as Lion VIIA but with double-reduction gear through layshaft, mounted over the airscrew shaft and a co-axial crankshaft. Special fuel, as in the Mk VIIB, was petrol/benzol with ethyl additive. Similar to VIIA, the principal difference being the rear-mounted, gear-driven supercharger and high-compression ratio 10:1. Geared, co-axial double-reduction .694:1. R.H. tractor-drive. Length 64.8 in; width 37.4 in; height 34.125 in.
Aircraft:

    Gloster VI Golden Arrow

The geared Napier Lion VIIB, as fitted to the Supermarine S.5s N220 & N221. The Winner of the 1927 Schneider contest at Venice was N220, flown by Flt Lt Webster.

The ultimate racing Lion, supercharged and geared, had a co-axial drive, via a layshaft, accounting for the 'hump' behind the propeller.

LION VIII, 535 hp, (1927). E83. Compression ratio 6.25:1. Direct R.H. tractor-drive. Carburettors removed to the rear of the engine.
Aircraft:

    Avro 566 Avenger I
    de Havilland D.H.65 Hound
    Gloster Gorcock

LION IX, 500 hp, Compression ratio 5.8:1, geared, spur .66:1, L.H tractor.
Aircraft:

    Avro 567 Avenger II

LION X, 460 hp, (1930), Compression ratio 5.8:1, geared, spur .66:1. L.H tractor.
Aircraft:

    Blackburn T.5 Ripon IIA

LION XA, 460 hp, (1929), Compression ratio 5.8:1, geared, spur .66:1.
Aircraft:

    de Havilland D.H.65 Hound

LION XI, 530/540 hp, (1930), E89. Compression ratio 6.25:1, geared, spur .531:1. L.H tractor.
Aircraft:

    Blackburn T.5 Ripon II, IIA
    de Havilland D.H.65A Hound
    Fairey IIIF, IIIF Mk II
    Fairey Seal
    Vickers 127 Wibault Scout
    Vickers 139, 140, 162 Virginia X
    Vickers 213 Victoria III
    Vickers 261, 274 Victoria V
    Vickers 146 Vivid

LION XIA, 530 hp, (1930), E89. Compression ratio 6:1, geared, spur .531:1. R.H. tractor. The Lion XIA was not altogether satisfactory in service particularly in the Middle East in Victorias of

No 70 (B.T.) Squadron, having replaced the Lion VA and VA*. It suffered from breakages of the modified master connecting rod big-end studs, reducing overhaul times to 250 hr. Length 61.0 in; width 42.0 in; height 39.0 in.
Aircraft:

    Avro 572 Buffalo II
    Blackburn T.5 Ripon IIA, IIC, III
    Fairey IIIF Mk IIIB (12/29), Mk IIIM
    Fairey IIIF Mk IVB (3/31), IVC, IVCM, IVM
    Fairey Long Range Monoplane I, II
    Handley Page H.P.31 Harrow II (Type E)
    Vickers 142 Vivid
    Vickers 169 Victoria V

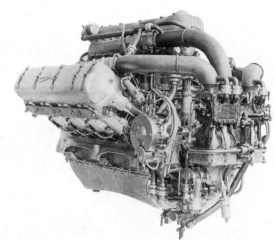

The Lion XI, had the carburettors mounted at the rear.

LION XIA (Special), 525 hp, (1930), E89. Compression ratio 5.8:1, geared, spur .531:1, L.H. tractor.
Aircraft:

    Fairey Long-Range Monoplane II

LION XV, 555 hp, (1932), geared, unsupercharged, compression ratio 6:1.

Surely one of the most extraordinarily-shaped engines ever built was the Napier Cub, comprising two superimposed Vees, with different included angles.

CUB, 1,000 hp, 1,800 rpm (1919), 16-cylinder, X-shaped (Upper angle is 52.5 deg., outer angles 90 deg.,lower angle 127.5 deg.) Single crankshaft. Described as a 'lop-sided St Andrew's Cross', with four banks of four cylinders. Between the two lower rows of cylinders, the crankcase protruded forwards to connect with the carburettors and downwards to form a sump. The carburettor bodies had a common float chamber and four jet chambers, one for each row of cylinders. The reduction gear was built-up on the front end of the crankcase, the valve drives, magnetos and pumps being at the rear. The cylinders were separate steel forgings with welded sheet steel water-cooling jackets. Four poppet-valves per cylinder were operated by rocker arms from a single camshaft for each bank of cylinders. Bore/stroke 6.25 x 7.5 in. Vol. 3,681 cu in. Compression ratio 5.3:1. Geared, spur .489:1 L.H. tractor-drive. Six ordered in 1919, designed and built in 22 months. First engine developed 1,057 hp on an early run. Dry wt 2,450 lb. First flown in Avro Aldershot, 15 December 1922.

Aircraft:

> Avro 549 Aldershot II
> Blackburn T.4 Cubaroo

One of the few applications of the massive 1,000 hp Napier Cub was the Avro 549 Aldershot II of 1923.

CULVERIN, (1934), E102, 720 hp. The Lion's sales had passed their peak in 1928, production having fallen to eighteen per month and likely to fall further to seven, from fifty the previous year, and there was a badly needed boost for Napier's flagging morale. In addition to the appointment of F.B.Halford to take the place of A.J. Rowledge who had departed to Rolls-Royce, another very different line of action taken was an agreement with Junkers Flugmotoren, to manufacture under licence the German company's diesel aero-engines. A trial British version was undertaken by Napier of the Junkers Jumo 204, 720 hp 2-stroke (diesel). It was a vertically-opposed, 6-cylinder engine. That is, it had two six-throw crankshafts (top and bottom) connected by a train of gears in the front of the engine, each shaft driven by a set of six pistons operating in opposition in the six cylinders.

The Blackburn Iris V flying-boat S1593, with three Napier Culverin engines, photographed at M.A.E.E., Felixstowe in November, 1938.

The Napier Culverin double-acting six-cylinder diesel, which was in effect a Junkers Jumo 204 under licence from Junkers Flugmotoren. The cylinders each had two pistons, driving crankshafts top and bottom.

The combined stroke was therefore unusually large, resulting in the name 'Culverin', a French word from which was derived the name of a very early form of cannon of great length. It was used in a Blackburn Iris V flying-boat at the M.A.E.E., Felixstowe, as a flying test-bed. As built by Napier, it had a body cast in Hiduminium. The inlet ports were controlled by the lower piston and the exhaust by the upper piston. Two fuel injection pumps were operated by camshafts and supplied by two gear-type pumps. Used particularly in Germany, it was economical in fuel but massive and heavy. It was water-cooled. Bore/stroke 4.75 x 8.25 in, vol. 1,737 cu in. Geared spur .6935:1. R.H. tractor-drive. Compressed-air starter. Power Curve at rated altitude sea level to 2,000 ft, from M.A.E.E., Felixstowe, Report F.93, dated 4.11.38.

RPM	2,050	2,000	1,900	1,800	1,700	1,600
BHP	821	815	791	770	745	721

Fuel: Shell Diesolene; length 83.5 in; width 23.0 in; height 67.0 in.

Aircraft:

> Blackburn R.B.1 Iris V
> Fairey IIIF

NOMAD 7, 3,037 shaft hp, (1951), N.Nm.7. This was a 'brochure', development of the basic E.145 Nomad Mk II. Almost defying description and probably the most complex aero-engine ever devised, the Nomad was a compound engine. It took the form of a twelve-cylinder horizontally opposed in-line, pressure liquid cooled, sleeve-valve compression ignition (diesel) engine, operating on a two-stroke cycle and supercharged by an axial flow compressor. The turbo-compressor unit was made up of a twelve-stage axial-flow compressor driven by a three-stage exhaust turbine. The turbine-compressor set was mechanically coupled to the compression ignition engine through variable speed gearing. The power developed by the compression ignition engine and the surplus power available from the exhaust turbine were absorbed by a common single-rotation feathering and braking propeller. To enable increased powers to be available for take-off or operational necessity, the engine had a 60 per cent methanol/40 per cent water internal coolant injection system, coupled with automatic fuel enrichment in the event of the water/methanol supply being exhausted.

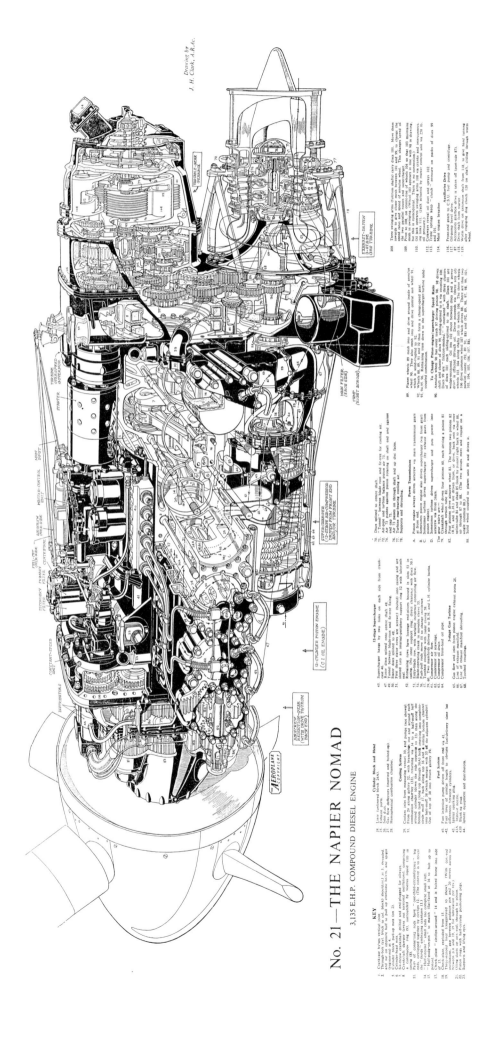

Drawing by J. H. Clark, A.R.Ac.

No. 21—THE NAPIER NOMAD

3,135 E.H.P. COMPOUND DIESEL ENGINE

The remarkable cut-away drawing by J.H. Clark of the very complicated Napier Nomad II compound engine.

The power plant, in spite of its interior complexity, was completely controlled by a single pilot's lever, the inter-connection including the turbo-compressor speed control, an automatic torque sensing device being fitted and arranged to move the propeller to coarse pitch in the event of engine or fuel failure. In order to achieve the lowest possible fuel consumption in any operating conditions, Napier devised the sleeve-valve, diesel-type engine to be capable of operating on a very wide range of fuels, said to be from margarine to creosote but actually from diesel fuel to kerosene or wide-cut petrol. It was a brave and imaginative attempt to produce a multi-fuel engine. Being a diesel, the Nomad operated at formidable manifold boost pressures (+86 lb/sq inch) and, although not quoted in the Performance tables for reasons of space, there were small amounts of residual jet thrust, amounting to 110–250 lb, according to conditions.

The Nomad was intended for use in the Avro Shackleton. The first installation, with the power delivered through a single four-bladed propeller, is recorded as having first run in 1949, following which, it was extensively redesigned. The only Nomad to fly (and therefore to qualify for inclusion here) was the developed Mk II, installed in the nose of an Avro Lincoln B.4 bomber, with three-blade contra-rotating propellers. Its only recorded appearance in public was at the Farnborough Air Display in September, 1951. This most interesting power unit was overtaken by events, in particular by the propeller-turbine, or turbo-prop.

The Avro 694 Lincoln B.4 SX973 with the Napier Nomad II in its nose as a test-bed, on public display at the Farnborough Air Display on 10 September, 1951

Diesel unit, 12-cylinder horizontally-opposed sleeve-valve. Bore/stroke 6.0 x 7.385 in. Vol. 2,505 cu in. (Vol. 41.1 litre). Fuel Avtur 100 or Wide-cut gasoline or 47 Cetane diesel fuel. Coolant 70 per cent water/30 per cent ethylene-glycol. Length 110 in; width 58.5 in; height 53 in.
Aircraft:
　　Avro 694 Lincoln 4

NAPIER-HALFORD.

In the 1920s, Napier had achieved considerable success with its Lion engine, in competition with the Bristol Jupiter, Armstrong Siddeley Jaguar and Rolls-Royce Kestrel. However, the water-cooled Lion (though far from dead) appeared to be approaching the peak of its success in 1927, when, in 1928, A.J.Rowledge, Napier's Chief Designer decided to go to Rolls-Royce. Napier, for the first time, decided to engage a designer who was not an employee of the company. This was F.B.Halford, whose name has appeared so often in this account. Montague Napier's insistence on personal control of his company was well-known, despite his retirement form active design work and the appointment of Halford, at the age of 34, eminent in his profession as an independent engine designer, marked a major turning point in Napier's policy. Halford would never have been happy in a salaried position and had been a successful engine consultant for some years. He was approached by Napier in 1928 and, after signing a consultancy agreement with the company, continued with his other work, particularly with de Havilland, with whom he had initiated the highly successful Gipsy range of engines culminating in the twelve-cylinder 525 hp, supercharged Gipsy XII. This had emerged in 1937, maintaining the air-cooled tradition which Halford had pursued from Airdisco and Cirrus days, a dozen years earlier.

Halford's agreement with Napier gave the company the right to make, to his designs, air-cooled engines having cylinder capacities between 404.09 and 718.39 cu in, a badly needed boost for Napier's flagging morale. Another very different line of action was an agreement with Junkers Flugmotoren to manufacture under licence the German company's diesel aero-engines (see Napier Culverin).

Halford started work and, by November 1929, according to Montague Napier's own account, the works had nothing in progress but Halford's novel and ingenious engines. Finances were very low and, to add to the company's troubles, Montague Napier died in January 1931.

What Halford initially proposed was a series of engines in a vertical 'H' configuration, with twin crankshafts geared together. There were to be two basic types, the first being called the Rapier, which was like four four-cylinder Gipsy engines, on a common crankcase. This engine, produced in small numbers, was adopted for the Short *Mercury* seaplane, the upper component of the Short-Mayo Composite which, in 1938 made the first commercial Atlantic crossing. In 1935, the Chairman of Napier, then Sir Harold Snagge, (with the inventive Major Mayo) had also become Chairman of Mayo Composite Aircraft Ltd.

The second engine, which followed the Rapier some five years later, was similar and comprised the elements of four six-cylinder engines. This was the Dagger. Both engines were of short stroke and therefore ran at substantially higher speeds than the Gipsies they resembled. The line of thought which led to the formidable wartime Sabre is clear, despite the change to liquid-cooling, horizontal 'H' configuration, sleeve-valves and all the problems which that eventually entailed.

After the initial appearance of the Rapiers, Halford briefly turned his attention to the upper end of the market for light aeroplane engines. This resulted in the 155 hp, inverted six-cylinder Javelin, which made a brief if rather unsuccessful appearance, filling a power gap between Halford's other and highly successful de Havilland designs, the Gipsy Major and Six. As it turned out, this was not really needed and it was discontinued in 1935, a market for the big military 24-cylinder Dagger by then being more clearly identifiable and was ordered in quantity by the Air Ministry. After seven years as a consultant to the Napier company, Halford joined the Board the same year. Also in 1935, Halford began the design of the Sabre, a single-cylinder prototype of which was tested in December of that year, amid great hopes and expectations of an engine potentially more powerful than anything previously visualized by Napier.

RAPIER I, 300 hp, (1929). E93, E94. Originally the Napier-Halford 'H' engine, this became the double-crankshaft Rapier I. It was a 16-cylinder, upright vertically-opposed H-shaped, air-cooled, poppet-valve engine. Bore/stroke 3.5 x 3.5 in. Vol. 538.78 cu in. (Vol. 8.55 litre). Single-speed medium supercharged. Geared, spur

.256:1. L.H. tractor-drive. Length 55.25 in; width 20.75 in; height 35.25 in.
Aircraft:
 Bristol 124 Bulldog TM
 de Havilland 77 (F.20/27)

RAPIER II, 305 hp, E95. Compression ratio 6:1. Fully-supercharged. Geared, spur .256:1. Length 55.25 in; width 20.75 in; height 35.25 in.
Aircraft:
 de Havilland 77

RAPIER IV, 340 hp, modified from Mk II, medium supercharged. Compression ratio 6:1, Geared, spur .256:1. Length 52.0 in; width 21.0 in; height 47.7 in.
Aircraft:
 Airspeed A.S.5C Courier
 Saro A.19 Cloud

RAPIER V, 360 hp, (1936), E100. Fully supercharged. Compression ratio 6:1, double crankshaft, geared spur .39:1. Power Curve at rated altitude 10,000 ft from M.A.E.E., Felixstowe, Report F.147, dated 1.7.36. Boost, rated +1.5 lb/sq inch, 305/315 hp, 3,500 rpm.

RPM	4,000	3,800	3,500	3,200	3,000
BHP	379	360	325	286	255
BOOST	+3.0lb		+1.5lb		

Supercharger ratio 6.33:1. Max boost +3 lb/sq inch. 380 bhp, 4,000 rpm take off to 1,000 ft or one minute. Fuel 87 Octane (DTD 230). Length 57.37 in; width 23.37 in; height 36.0 in.
Aircraft:
 Short-Mayo S.20 Composite *Mercury*

RAPIER VI, 365 hp. (1935). Compression ratio 7:1. Medium supercharged, ratio 5.27:1. Geared, spur 2.563:1. Length 56.6 in; width 22.4 in; height 36.0 in.
Aircraft:
 Blackburn H.S.T.10
 Fairey Seafox
 Short-Mayo S.20 Composite *Mercury*

The Napier-Halford Rapier VI, an air-cooled, medium-supercharged engine, here fitted to a Fairey Seafox Fleet-spotter seaplane.

The upper component of the Short-Mayo Composite aircraft, the long-range S.20 'Mercury', powered by Napier-Halford Rapier VI engines.

The 16-cylinder H-shaped Napier-Halford Rapier VI.

JAVELIN I, 155 hp (1932), E97. A 6-cylinder, inverted in-line air-cooled poppet-valve engine. It was unsupercharged and its propeller was direct, L.H. tractor-drive. Bore/stroke 4.5 x 5.25 in. Vol. 501 cu in. Compression ratio 5.3:1. Length 58.5 in; width 26.0 in; height 31.5 in.
Aircraft:
 Percival E.1 Mew Gull

The Napier-Halford Javelin, a six-cylinder air-cooled engine for light aircraft.

The Percival D.2 Gull Four was powered by this 160 hp Napier Javelin III. The carburettor intakes are on the far side.

JAVELIN III, 160 hp, long-stroke version of the Mk I. Bore/stroke 4.5 x 5.5 in. Vol. 524.83 cu in. Length 64.25 in; width 19.5 in; height 34.5 in.
Aircraft:

Percival D.2 Gull Four
Spartan Arrow

JAVELIN IIIA (1935). Mk III with generator, starter and other minor modifications.
Aircraft:

Martin Baker M.B.1

NAPIER-HALFORD DAGGER I, 650 hp approx (1934), E98, E104. 24-cylinder, double-crankshaft, upright, vertically-opposed H-shaped, air-cooled, poppet-valve engine. Bore/stroke 3.813 x 3.75 in. Vol. 1,027 cu in (16.8 litre). Compression ratio 7.75:1, single-speed, medium supercharged, geared, spur .372:1. L.H. tractor-drive.
Aircraft:

Hawker Hart

DAGGER II, 755 hp, (1938), uprated version of the Dagger I, with generator and air compressor. Supercharger ratio 6.47:1. Length 80.0 in; width 22.5 in; height 45.125 in.
Aircraft:

Hawker Hart

DAGGER IIIM, 725 hp, (1938), L.H. tractor-drive, gear ratio .372. Power Curve at rated altitude, 3,500 ft, from A.& A.E.E., Martlesham, Report M.690, dated 3.7.36. Medium supercharged. Boost, rated +2.25 lb/sq inch. Supercharger ratio 5.04:1.

RPM	4,000	3,800	3,500	3,200	3,000
BHP	829	780	709	635	584
BOOST	+3.5lb		+2.25lb		

The Napier-Halford Dagger IIIM in a Hawker Hector Army co-operation aircraft.

The Napier-Halford Dagger IIIM air-cooled 24-cylinder engine fitted to the Hawker Hector.

Max boost +3.5 lb/sq inch. 829 bhp, 4,000 rpm take off to 1,000 ft or one minute. All-out level flight (five minutes), +2.25 lb, bhp, rpm. Fuel 87 Octane (DTD 230). Length 80.0 in; width 23.0 in; height 45.125 in.
Aircraft:

Hawker Hart
Hawker Hector (14/35)
Martin-Baker M.B.2

The Napier-Halford Dagger IIIM was a medium-supercharged, air-cooled 24-cylinder engine.

The prototype Martin-Baker M.B.2 in its original form.

DAGGER VIII, 955 hp, (1938), E108. Developed from Dagger III, 24-cylinder, vertically-opposed H-shaped engine. Air-cooled poppet-valve engine. It was medium supercharged. Its propeller drive was geared, spur, reduction .308:1. L.H. tractor-drive, V/P propeller. Bore/stroke 3.813 x 3.75 in. Vol. 1,027 cu in. 16.8 litre. Compression ratio 7.5:1. This engine initially suffered from starting difficulties, cured by alteration to the priming system. The limited warm-up period which the cylinder heads would tolerate, could result in poor oil circulation. Length 73.9 in; width 26.8 in; height 47.7 in.
Aircraft:

Fairey Battle I
Handley Page H.P.52 Hereford I

The Napier-Halford Dagger VIII, a medium-supercharged, air-cooled 24-cylinder engine, fitted to the Handley Page Hereford, a variant of the Hampden. The engine was fitted with a spur reduction gear.

The big Folland Fo.108 engine test bed, built to Spec. 43/37, though not a particularly successful aeroplane, served a useful purpose and is here seen in February, 1941 with a Napier Sabre engine installed.

SABRE

When Frank Halford and his design team turned their attention to a really powerful engine, they made Napier's sparks fly in earnest. Originally proposed in 1935 and intended for high-altitude fighters, this was the horizontally-mounted, H-shaped Sabre, a liquid-cooled 24-cylinder sleeve-valve engine which eventually began life in the Royal Air Force in 1940, at just over 2,000 hp. It had two crankshafts geared together, as did the Rapier and Dagger before it. The Sabre differed by incorporating the Burt-McCollum sleeve-valve system, with a four-port sleeve and a cylinder barrel with five ports, the system using three for inlet and two for exhaust, one sleeve port acting for both inlet and exhaust purposes. This was the system on which Halford had worked with Harry Ricardo twenty years previously.

The engine passed its Type-Test in 1939 but, once in production, manufacturing problems with the chrome-molybdenum sleeves resulted in lubrication failures, engine seizures and a number of serious accidents to Hawker Typhoons in Squadron service. These troubles were all too common, leading to a serious lack of confidence in the engine, then the most powerful type in production by a considerable margin. Initially, it inhibited the success of the aircraft. Urgent action was needed to rectify or at least improve the Sabre's reliability.

The problem had arisen in the chosen method of sleeve manufacture, rather than in its design. Napier had tried in vain to achieve satisfactory sleeves on a production line basis but only partially succeeded, due to oval distortion of some .008 inch during manufacture. Lubrication, in the cat's cradle of a sleeve-valve system, is of critical importance and ovality in sleeves effectively made this a haphazard business, leading to seizures. Failures occurring, even in two-hour acceptance tests, resulted in delays to production schedules and engineless Typhoons awaiting delivery. Rod Banks, in his book *I Kept No Diary*, has recorded that he proposed to Napier and to Halford that they should ask Bristol (who had mastered the art of making satisfactory sleeves) for help. Banks eventually managed to obtain, through Bristol's Managing Director

Norman Rowbotham, a pair of Taurus nitrided austenitic steel sleeves for the Sabre two-cylinder test rig because, by good fortune, they were suitable in size for adaptation for use in the Sabre. Napier's own sleeves usually lasted for twenty to thirty hours before wear caused excessive oil consumption but the Bristol sleeves lasted 120 hours without trouble.

Two Sabre Type-Tests were completed satisfactorily. After contractual, manufacturing and other technical problems had been resolved, special machine tools were brought over from the United States, aboard the converted liner *Queen Mary*, with a Division of American troops. The tools were working on Sabre sleeves at Napier's Liverpool factory within a month.

After the sleeve redesign and other modifications to the Sabre, the Typhoon and Tempest powered by these engines became formidable low-level fighters in the last two years of the war. The Typhoon distinguishing itself in its cab-rank role, loitering over enemy territory, on call to attack anything that moved, from locomotives and their trains to tanks. The Tempest and Typhoon, in addition, were eventually more than a match for the fast-flying German V-1 'doodle-bug' flying-bombs which had become a considerable nuisance over southern Britain from mid-1944, causing Winston Churchill to demand the provision of standing air defence patrols against them. There were three important versions of the Sabre, the Mks II, V and VII.

F.B. Halford, continued in charge of design until 1944, when he became Chairman and Technical Director of the de Havilland Engine Company upon its formation.

SABRE I, 2,000 hp, (1939), Type E107, 24-cylinder, horizontally opposed, H-shaped, 70-30 per cent water/ethylene-glycol cooled, sleeve-valve. Bore/stroke 5.0 x 4.75 in. Vol. 2,240 cu in. (127 x 120 mm. Vol. 36.65 litre). Compression ratio 7:1. Two-speed, medium/fully supercharged, 4.68: and 5.83:1. Geared, spur .274:1. L.H. tractor-drive. Plessey Coffman cartridge starter. Power Curve at rated altitude 2,250 ft, from A.& A.E.E., Martlesham, Report M.761, dated 31.8.40. M Gear, boost, rated +6 lb/sq inch, 3,500 rpm.

RPM	3,700	3,500	3,300	3,150	3,000
BHP	2,041	1,914	1,805	1,693	1,588
BOOST	+7.02lb	+6.14lb	+5.51lb	+5lb	+4.62lb

Max boost +7 lb/sq inch. 2,041 bhp, 3,700 rpm take off to 1,000 ft or one minute. All-out level flight (five minutes), +7 lb, 2,000 bhp, 3,700 rpm. Max rpm 20 sec 4,000. Power Curve at rated altitude 14,500 ft. S Gear, boost, rated +6 lb/sq inch, 3,500 rpm.

RPM	3,700	3,500	3,300	3,150	3,000
BHP	1,868	1,735	1,570	1,442	1,308
BOOST	+7.95lb	+6.44lb	+5.27lb	+3.96lb	+2.96lb

All-out level flight (five minutes), +7 lb, 1,868 bhp, 3,700 rpm. S.U. carburettor. These figures are for 87 Octane (DTD 230) fuel, (initially), later 100 Octane. NS1.SMb
Aircraft:
　　Fairey Battle
　　Folland Fo.108 43/37
　　Hawker Typhoon F.18/37 prototype, Mk I
　　Heston Type 5 Racer ('Special', derated engine)

SABRE II, 2,300 hp, (1940), (experimental .322 reduction gear). E115. Plessey Coffman cartridge starter. Length 82.25 in; width 40 in; height 46.0 in.
Aircraft:
　　Fairey Battle I
　　Folland Fo.108 43/37
　　Hawker F.18/37 Typhoon prototype, Mk I, IA, IB
　　Hawker Typhoon II (Tempest I)
　　Hawker Tempest I

SABRE IIA, 2,235 hp, Sabre II modified for mixed matrix radiators. Similar to Mk VB. Altered ignition and plugs. Supercharger ratios 4.48:1 and 6.26:1. Reduction gear ratio .274:1.

Aircraft:

    Folland Fo.108 43/37
    Hawker Tempest V
    Hawker Typhoon I, IB

The Napier-Halford Sabre II series, a very powerful sleeve-valved engine, was the heart of the great Hawker Typhoon and Tempest fighter-bombers in the latter part of the second World War.

SABRE IIB, 2,400 hp, similar to Mk IIA, S.U carburettor.

Aircraft:

    Hawker Typhoon I, IB
    Hawker Tempest V

The pugnatious nose of a Hawker Typhoon. Here, a heating duct is inserted into the air intake of its Sabre IIA, in very cold weather to aid starting. The Sabre tended to be a difficult starter.

SABRE IIC, 2,065 hp, similar to Mk VII but with supercharger ratios 4.73:1 and 6.26:1. S.U. AQV carburettor.

Aircraft:

    Hawker Typhoon I, IB
    Hawker Tempest V

A Hawker Typhoon IB, powered by a Napier Sabre IIB

A Hawker Typhoon IB on the prowl, laden with 60 lb rockets. With wheels tucked away, it has a very purposeful look.

SABRE III, 2,250 hp, similar to IIA, to suit Firebrand. Higher rpm.

Aircraft:

    Blackburn B-37 Firebrand F.I, T.F.II
    Folland Fo.108 43/37

SABRE IV, 2,240 hp, (1943), as Mk VA with R.A.E.-Hobson fuel injector.

Aircraft:

    Hawker Typhoon I, II (Tempest I)
    Hawker Tempest V

SABRE V, 2,600 hp, (1944), E121. Development of Mk II. Increased boost, redesigned supercharger and induction system, supercharger ratios 4.68:1, 5.83:1. R.A.E. BI/NS2 fuel injection. Experimental annular radiator on Tempest V.

Aircraft:

    Hawker Tempest I, V, VI

A Hawker Tempest V, powered by a Sabre V and flown (hatless) by a Hawker test pilot, despite the Sabre's howl.

The Tempest V NV768 was used as a test-bed for the Sabre V with an annular radiator.

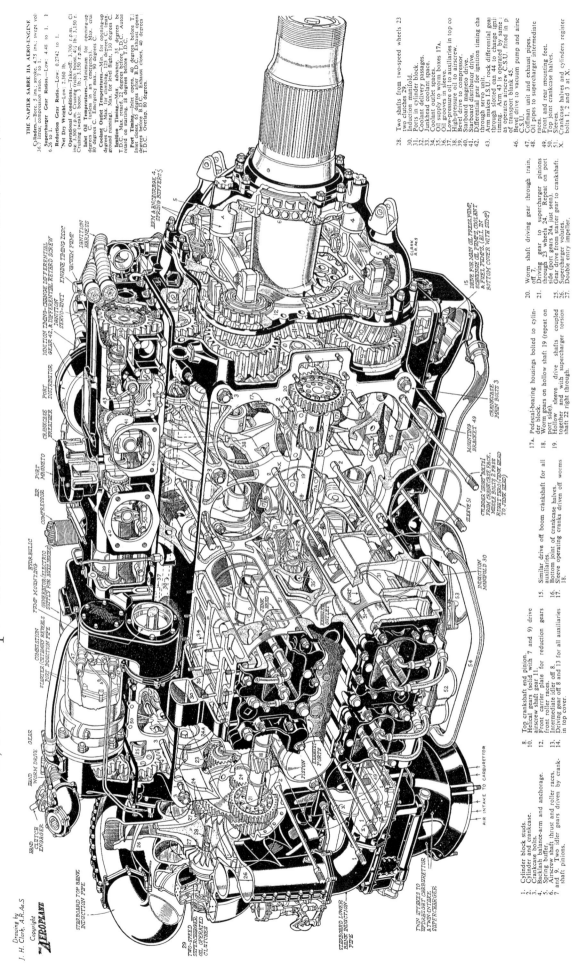

THE 2,400 b.h.p. NAPIER SABRE IIA AERO-ENGINE

Drawing by
J. H. Clark, A.R.Ae.S

Copyright
AEROPLANE

THE NAPIER SABRE IIA AERO-ENGINE

Cylinders.—Bore, 5 ins., stroke, 4.75 ins., swept vol., 36.7 litres, compression ratio, 7 to 1.

Supercharger Gear Ratios.—7 to 1.
6.26 to 1.

Reduction Gear Ratio.—Low: 0.2742 to 1.
4.48 to 1.

Net Dry Weight.—Low: 2,360 lb.

Operational Conditions.—Take-off, 3,700 r.p.m. Climbing, 3,500 r.p.m. Cruising (rich) boost, 4¼ lb.; 3,150 r.p.m. Cruising (weak) boost, 3 lb.; 3,150 r.p.m.

Inlet Oil Temperatures.—Minimum (or opening-up degrees C. Emergency max., 90 degrees C.

Coolant Outlet Temperatures.—Min. (for opening-up degrees C. Max. for climbing, 125 degrees. Max. for level flight, 110 degrees C. ground running). Max. for level flight, 110 degrees C.

Ignition Timing.—Max. advance, 35 degrees before T.D.C. Max. retard, 22 degrees before T.D.C. Autom. retard starting, 18 degrees before T.D.C.

Port Timing.—Inlet opens, 40 degrees before T.D.C. Inlet closes, 65 degrees after B.D.C. Exhaust opens, 80 degrees before B.D.C. Exhaust closes, 40 degrees before T.D.C. Overlap, 80 degrees.

1. Cylinder block studs.
2. Cylinder and crankcase.
3. Crankcase bolts.
4. Backlash balance-arm and anchorage.
5. Spring buffer.
6. Airscrew shaft thrust and roller races.
7 and 9. Two idler gears driven by crankshaft pinions.

8. Top crankshaft end pinion.
10. Helical gears (solid with 7 and 9) drive airscrew shaft gear 11.
12. Front carrier plate for reduction gears front roller races.
13. Intermediate idler off 8.
14. Driving gear off 8 and 13 for all auxiliaries in top cover.

15. Similar drive off boom crankshaft for all auxiliaries.
16. Bottom joint of crankcase halves.
17. Sleeve operating cranks driven off worms 18.

17A. Pedestal-bearing housings bolted to cylinder block.
18. Worm gears on hollow shaft 19 (repeat on port side).
19. Hollow sleeve drive shafts coupled together and with supercharger torsion shaft 22 right through.

20. Worm shaft driving gear through train, off 7.
21. Driving gear to supercharger pinions through 23 wheels 24. Repeat on port side (port gears 24A just seen).
25. Gear drive from starter gear to crankshaft.
26. Supercharger volutes.
27. Double entry impeller.

28. Two shafts from two-speed wheels 23 two clutches 29.
30. Induction manifold.
31. Ports in cylinder block.
32. Coolant delivery passages.
33. Combined coolant space.
34. Coolant outlet space.
35. Oil supply to worm boxes 17A.
36. Oil grooves in sleeve.
37. Low-pressure oil to auxiliaries in top cover.
38. High-pressure oil to airscrew.
39. Bevel drive to compressor.
40. Starboard magneto drive.
41. Starboard distributor drive.
42. Differential gear for ignition timing change through servo unit.
43. Arm makes I.S.U. rock differential gear through slotted can 44 to change ignition timing. Arm 43 is operated by same as it operates airscrew C.S.U. fitted in place of transport blank 45.
46. Bevel drive to vacuum pump and airscrew C.S.U.
47. Coffman unit and exhaust pipes.
48. Oil pipes to supercharger intermediate races.
49. Front and rear mounting feet.
50. Top joint crankcase halves.
X. Crankcase halves and cylinders register bolts 1, 2 and 3 at X.

A cut-away drawing of the Napier-Halford Sabre IIA by J.H. Clark.

SABRE VA, 2,600 hp, as Mk V with Hobson-R.A.E. NS4 fuel injector. Inter-connected, single-lever propeller and throttle controls. Length 82.25 in; width 40.0 in; height 46.0 in.
Aircraft:
>Folland Fo.108 43/37
>Hawker Tempest VI

SABRE VI, 2,310 hp, similar to Mk VA, with Rotol geared cooling fan and annular radiator.
Aircraft:
>Vickers 460 Warwick III (Research)

SABRE VII, 3,500 hp, E118, 122, generally similar to Mk VA, except for being strengthened to withstand higher powers available with water/methanol injection for take-off and combat power. Length 83.0 in; width 40.0 in; height 47.75 in.
Aircraft:
>Folland Fo.108 43/37
>Hawker Fury I

This Vickers Warwick III was used as a test-bed for the Sabre VI with an annular radiator.

SABRE VIII, 3,000 hp. Intended for Hawker Fury.
Aircraft:
>Folland Fo.108 43/37

SABRE E.118, (1941), three-speed, two-stage, contra-prop. No details published.
Aircraft:
>Folland Fo.108 43/37

PACKARD — *see* **ROLLS-ROYCE MERLIN V-1650**

POBJOY AIRMOTORS AND AIRCRAFT LTD, HOOTON PARK, CHESHIRE.

The designer of this series of engines, D.R. Pobjoy was born in Kent and worked under A.H.R. Fedden with the Cosmos Engineering Company. He set up Pobjoy Airmotors in Surrey and, in 1928, the firm became established at Hooton in the Wirral peninsular of Cheshire. Eventually, this small firm's wanderings came to rest back in Kent, at Rochester. In 1928, the first little P Type seven-cylinder air-cooled engine passed its Air Ministry Type-Test. It was followed by the well-known R type and the Niagara and Cataract. The last was intended to be a derated, cheaper and uncowled version of the Niagara, with simple baffles between cylinders, retaining the open valve gear of the R type. All three models were mechanically almost identical in their major components, differing only in detail, with minor variations in power. Sadly Pobjoy, who had worked in close collaboration with Short Brothers before the Second World War and at Rotol on auxiliary accessory gearboxes, was killed on 4 July 1948. Laconically, on 8 July *Flight* reported 'Aircraft collision 4 pm at Northolt. Mr D.R. Pobjoy killed, total death roll 38. Rained all day'.

POBJOY P-1, 67 hp (1928), 7-cylinder, single-row radial air-cooled, poppet-valve. Bore/stroke 2.385 x 3.425 in. Vol. 1.51.33 cu in (72 x 87 mm. Vol. 2.48 litre). Geared, spur .468:1, L.H. tractor-drive. Diameter 25.0 in.
Aircraft:
>Comper C.L.A.7 Swift.
>Parnall Imp

POBJOY R, 85 hp, (1933), 7-cylinder, single-row radial air-cooled, poppet-valve. Bore/stroke 3.03 x 3.43 in. Vol. 173.05 cu in. (77 x 87 mm. Vol. 2.84 litre). Geared, spur .47:1, L.H. tractor-drive. Diameter 25.5 in.
Aircraft:
>Cierva/Comper C-25 Autogiro
>Comper C.L.A.7 Swift
>Currie Super Wot
>General Aircraft Monospar ST-4
>General Aircraft Monospar ST-6
>Kay 33/1 Gyroplane
>Miles M.1 Satyr
>Short S.16 Scion
>Spartan Clipper

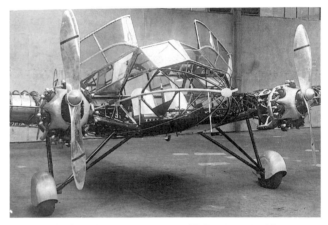

(Above and below) The Monospar series of light twin engined four-seaters were mostly powered by Pobjoy engines. These are the ST-4 and (with a retractable undercarriage) the ST-6. Both had Pobjoy 'R' engines.

The little seven-cylinder air-cooled Pobjoy engines, as the 'R' engines illustrated were, unusually for radials, spur-geared, here powering a Short Scion transport.

CATARACT I, 80 hp, (1934), 7-cylinder, single-row radial air-cooled, poppet-valve. Bore/stroke 3.03 x 3.43 in. Vol. 173.05 cu in. (77 x 87 mm. Vol. 2.84 litre). Geared, spur .47:1, L.H. tractor-drive. Diameter 25.5 in.
Aircraft:

    Hafner A.R.III Mk I Gyroplane
    Hendy 281 Hobo

CATARACT II, 90 hp, similar to Mk I:
Aircraft:

    British Klemm Swallow

CATARACT III, 98 hp, (1936), basically similar to Mks I & II, with minor differences.
Aircraft:

    B.A.Swallow
    Hendy 281 Hobo

NIAGARA I, 84 hp, (1936), 7-cylinder, single-row radial air-cooled, poppet-valve. Bore/stroke 77 x 87 mm. Vol. 2.835 l, 173 cu in. compression ratio 6.25:1. Geared, double-helical spur .47:1. L.H. tractor-drive. Enclosed valve gear and cowling provided as standard, together with vertical grid intended to ensure even cooling. Diameter 26.5 in.
Aircraft:

    General Aircraft Monospar ST-6
    General Aircraft Monospar ST-10
    Hafner A.R.III Mk II Gyroplane
    Shapley Kittiwake II
    Short S.16 Scion I

NIAGARA II, Compression ratio 6:1, geared, spur .39:1.
Aircraft:

    Short S.16 Scion I

NIAGARA III, 85 hp, (1937), geared spur .468:1. L.H. tractor-drive. Power Curve at rated altitude 2,000 ft from A.& A.E.E., Martlesham, Report M.713, dated 25.6.36.

RPM	3,625	3,300	2,900
BHP	91.6	87.3	79.4

Max 95 bhp, 3,625 rpm, all-out level flight (5 min). Fuel Shell No 1. Starting by hand lever in cabin or electric.

Similar to the others in the Pobjoy range, with minor differences,the Niagara was the most widely used.

Aircraft:

    C.L.W.Curlew
    Cierva/Westland CL.20 Autogiro
    Comper Kite
    General Aircraft Monospar ST-25 Universal
    Hafner A.R.III Gyroplane
    Moss M.A.I Mosscraft
    Pobjoy Pirate

    Saro A.37 Shrimp
    Shapley Kittiwake
    Short S.16 Scion II
    Short S.22 Scion Senior
    Spartan Clipper

NIAGARA IV, 98 hp, (1937), geared spur .468:1. L.H. tractor-drive. Minor differences from Mk III.
Aircraft:

    G.A.Monospar ST-25 Universal.

NIAGARA V, 130 hp, (1937), bore/stroke 3.19 x 3.43 in. (81 x 87 mm). Vol. 191.01 cu in, 3.13 litre. Compression ratio 8:1. Geared spur .468:1. L.H. tractor-drive. Fuel DTD 230, 87 Octane. Diameter 26.5 in.
Aircraft:

    Airspeed A.S.39 Fleet Shadower
    General Aircraft G.A.L.38 Night Shadower

Considerably more powerful than the earlier Pobjoy engines, the 130 hp Niagara V was intended for light four-engined aircraft, for fleet reconnaissance work.

R.E.P.

Named after Robert Esnault-Pelterie, a pioneer French engine designer, R.E.P. engines were upright fan-shaped. Vickers arranged to make and market them in Britain but little came of the plan.

R.E.P.-Vickers, 60 hp, (1910), five-cylinder, fan-shaped, air-cooled semi-radial. Bore/stroke 110 x 160 mm, Vol. 7.6 litre. Cast iron cylinders, both valves operated by a single rocker. Aluminium alloy crankcase.
Aircraft:

    Vickers Monoplanes 1-3

REDRUP FURY II 85 hp,(1929). This oddly-shaped engine was produced by The Aero Syndicate Ltd of London. It was an axial, 7-cylinder, barrel-type, lever-operated swashplate engine, air-cooled. Very little has been published about the actual use of engines of this type, although at least one is known to have flown. Redrup, the designer of the 150 hp Hart engine (q.v.) designed five- and seven-cylinder axial-type radial engines, ranging from 35 to 85 hp, of which the Fury II was the largest. If an axial radial seems to be a contradiction in terms, the cylinders (air-cooled in this case) lay parallel to the crankshaft. The cast aluminium cylinders had integral heads and steel liners and the pistons were also of cast aluminium. A star-shaped master big-end had universal joints at the extremities of the star, to receive auxiliary connecting rods of + section, which were symmetrical, having universal joints at each end. A forked torque rod slid in a universally-jointed housing in the crankcase and prevented the master big-end from rotating. The barrel-type crankcase was split vertically, just in front of the crank. A lobed eccentric on the crankshaft was rotated at half engine speed, the lobes actuating the valves, which were set at right-angles to the cylinder centre lines, by means of short tappets. It had a dry sump, two B.T.H. magnetos and a Claudel-Hobson carburettor. The overall diameter was very small, only 17.125 inches and the carburettor projected about 6.75 inches below this. The length was 39 inches, the weight was 200 lb. It was claimed to produce 85 hp at 2,000 normal rpm and 95 hp at 2,200 maximum rpm.

Aircraft:
Simmonds Spartan

(Above and below) The curious 95 hp Redrup Fury was a 'swash-plate' engine, the cylinders lying parallel to the crankshaft.

A 70 hp Renault WC. This was a widely-used air-cooled engine, here seen in its pusher form, with fan-cooling.

Maurice Farman Shorthorn, 70 hp Renault, after engine and propeller failure.

A Royal Aircraft Factory B.E.2, powered by a Renault 70 hp.

RENAULT LTD, West Brompton, London.

These engines were also built by Wolseley Motors in Birmingham. Moteurs Louis Renault Cie originated at Billancourt, Seine, France, where aero engines began to be made in 1907. They were all of the same basic air-cooled design, characterised by the large air-cooling scoop above the cylinder heads. The pusher versions had a deeply-shrouded cooling fan ahead of the cylinders.

RENAULT 60 hp, 8-cylinder, upright 90-degree Vee air-cooled, poppet-valve. Bore/stroke 3.54 x 4.72 in (90 x 120 mm). Vol. 371.68 cu in. Geared, spur .5:1 off the camshaft. L.H. tractor/R.H. pusher-drive, the pusher type having a cooling fan. Length 48.5 in; width 26.5 in; height 25.5 in.
Aircraft:
      Blackburn Mercury III
      Bristol Boxkite
      Royal Aircraft Factory B.E.1
      Royal Aircraft Factory B.E.2, B.E.2a, b

RENAULT TYPE WB, WC 70 hp, 8-cylinder, upright 90-degree Vee air-cooled, poppet-valve. Bore/stroke 3.78 x 4.72 in (96 x 120 mm). Vol. 423.76 cu in. Compression ratio 4.12:1. Type WB had the oil pump inside the sump and the Type WC had the pump outside as a separate unit. Geared, spur .5:1. L.H. tractor/R.H. pusher-drive, the pusher type having a cooling fan. Length 45.5 in; width 29.8 in; height 32.8 in.

B.E.2, 70 hp Renault. G. de Havilland in rear cockpit.

B.E.2c, 80 hp Renault.

Production, 8/1914–12/1918, from:-
Aircraft Mfg Co Ltd., Hendon.
Ordered, 42;   Delivered, 42;   Cancelled/suspended, 0
Renault Ltd, West Brompton, SW6
Ordered, 35;   Delivered, 35;   Cancelled/suspended, 0
Rolls-Royce Ltd, Derby,
Ordered, 50;   Delivered, 50;   Cancelled/suspended, 0
Wolseley Motors Ltd, Birmingham,
Ordered, 100;   Delivered, 100;   Cancelled/suspended, 0
Aircraft:
   Airco D.H.1
   Armstrong Whitworth F.K.2
   Blackburn Type E Two-Seater
   Caudron G.III
   Central Centaur IVA
   Maurice Farman Serie 11 Shorthorn
   Flanders F.4
   Royal Aircraft Factory B.E.2, 2a, b, c, d, e, f, g
   Royal Aircraft Factory F.E.2
   Royal Aircraft Factory R.E.1
   White & Thompson 'Bognor Bloater'

RENAULT TYPE WS, 80 hp, 8-cylinder, upright 90-degree Vee
air-cooled, poppet-valve. Bore/stroke 4.13 x 5.12 in. Vol. 548.9 cu
in. (105 x 130 mm). Compression ratio 4.16:1. Geared, spur .5:1.
L.H. tractor/R.H. pusher-drive. Single 32 mm Claudel-Hobson or
Zenith 42 R.A. carburettor. Single A.8 magneto. Length 50.6 in;
width 35.5 in; height 35.3 in.
   Production, 8/1914–12/1918, from:-
Brazil Straker & Co Ltd, Bristol,
Ordered, 650;   Delivered, 610;   Cancelled/suspended, 40
Rolls-Royce Ltd, Derby,
Ordered, 164;   Delivered, 164;   Cancelled/suspended, 0
Standard Motor Co Ltd, Coventry,
Ordered, 400;   Delivered, 0;   Cancelled/suspended, 400
Star Engineering Co, Wolverhampton,
Ordered, 400;   Delivered, 12;   Cancelled/suspended, 388
Swift Aeronautical Engineering Co, Kingston-on-Thames,
Ordered, 1,200;   Delivered, 1,090; Cancelled/suspended, 110
Vickers Ltd, London SW3,
Ordered, 36;   Delivered, 36;   Cancelled/suspended, 0
Wolseley Motors Ltd, Birmingham,
Ordered, 304;   Delivered, 304;   Cancelled/suspended, 0
Aircraft:
   Airco D.H.6
   Alliance P.1
   Avro 548
   Caudron G.III
   Maurice Farman Serie VII 'Longhorn'
   Maurice Farman Serie 11 'Shorthorn'
   Royal Aircraft Factory S.E.5a
   Vickers F.B.7A

RENAULT 160 hp.
Aircraft:
   Henry (Horace) Farman F.40

RENAULT 8Gd, 190 hp.

RENAULT 12Fe, 220 hp 12-cylinder, upright 50-degree Vee
water-cooled, poppet-valve. Bore/stroke 4.92 x 5.91 in. Vol.
1,345.9 cu in. (125 x 150 mm). Compression ratio 5.1:1. Direct R.H.
tractor/L.H. pusher-drive. Two Zenith 4B.DF duplex carburettors,
four S.E.V. magnetos.
Aircraft:
   Airco D.H.4
   Royal Aircraft Factory R.E.7
   Short (Admiralty Type) 184

RICARDO.

The name H.R. Ricardo appears repeatedly throughout British aero-
engine history. As recorded elsewhere in this book, Harry (later Sir
Harry) Ricardo was a remarkable engineering consultant, who
specialized in research into anti-knock fuel, combustion and
supercharging and much else besides, in advanced engine design,
including investigation of the possible uses of the Burt-McCollum
single-sleeve valve. Engine Patents Ltd, the name which Ricardo
first adopted for his firm in July 1917, later became Ricardo & Co.
Much of Ricardo's early work, following the First World War, was
done in association with F.B.Halford.
   One remarkable experimental type of single-cylinder sleeve
valve engine was the E5/1. Its purpose, as a trials unit, was to
evaluate the knock properties of various grades of fuel. It had a bore
of under three inches and a variable compression ratio which, if
required, could be altered from 3:1 to as much as 30:1, while
running. Though trouble-free over a long period, the engine was so
small that there was no room for instrumentation, nor indeed
anything but the sparking plug! Despite this, the E5s were
particularly interesting, several serving Ricardo's research work as
fuel rating engines for the Shell Company. Ricardo was particularly
interested in variable compression single-cylinder engines for test
purposes, so that he could accurately determine the compression
ratio which they could tolerate for a given quality of fuel,
collaborating in particular with Rolls-Royce.
   Several very advanced engine designs, projects and prototypes
have appeared over the years, bearing Ricardo's name but most of
them turned out to be really stepping-stones and aids towards other
firms' progress, and they have not strictly justified entries in their
own right. For example, the Ricardo supercharger (invented before
the First World War) was most unusual in concept. It involved, to
quote his own words, the use of the underside of his working pistons
to provide a top-up supercharge of pure air, admitted through ports
round the lower end of the cylinder liner, uncovered by the piston
at the bottom of its stroke. Thus, by varying the mixture strength
admitted in the normal manner, he could at will utilize the
supercharge air either to dilute and reduce the fuel consumption by
up to 10 per cent at cruising speeds or as a power boost, maintaining
ground-level conditions up to 10,000 feet. This idea, offered to the
War Office, was politely declined as of little use as the only use
which the Army had for aviation was low-level spotting for
artillery. The captive balloon, silent and still, was all that was
needed. As so often is the fate of a consulting engineer of the calibre
of Sir Harry Ricardo, such people seldom receive proper credit for
their work.

RICARDO-BURT S55/4, 65 hp, (1927). This was an intriguing
little four-cylinder water-cooled engine, about which practically
nothing has appeared until recently. With such an interesting
parentage, it was bound to have been innovative, to say the least. It
had as its purpose the evaluation of a small in-line sleeve valve
engine for light aircraft and was commissioned by the Air Ministry
in 1925. It was a 'square' engine, having both bore and stroke of 3.5
inches and a 2.2 litre capacity. Several were built and tested at the
Ricardo works and one was tested under R.A.E. supervision at the
Marine Aircraft Experimental Establishment, Felixstowe, mounted
in the bow of the little single-seat Parnall Prawn flying-boat. It had
a tiny four-blade propeller driven by a long shaft and, so as to raise
it as far as possible above the spray, the shaft or the combined
engine and propeller drive could be tilted upwards at about 20
degrees. Slightly modified engines were built for the purpose of
acting as starting engines for the great and tragic dirigible airship

R101. This engine was also used to try out the arrangement of spur gears to drive the sleeve cranks later used on the Rolls-Royce Kestrel sleeve valve experimental conversions. With the genius of Harry Ricardo, it is no surprise that a diesel version of the S55/4 engine was also built.

Aircraft:

Parnall Prawn

RICARDO-HALFORD-ARMSTRONG R.H.A.

This is an engine which has long been something of an enigma. Harry Ricardo, during the second half of the First World War, had recognized the need for and been experimenting with ideas on supercharging and combustion. He put them to test in a 230 B.H.P. engine which, using a Ricardo supercharger, did in fact fly in 1917 at Farnborough, although few details have so far emerged from dusty archives. He also designed engines which were built respectively by Armstrong Co. and Brotherhood. The former, called the R.H.A., designed with Frank Halford, was built and flown but, again, it has not yet been possible to prove whether the Brotherhood engine flew. After the Armistice in November 1918 Frank Halford, by now promoted to Major and released from active service, joined forces with Ricardo in a company initially called Engine Patents Ltd, in order to continue his work on engine design and combustion research. (In 1923, he formed an independent design Company, becoming well-known again for his design work with the Aircraft Disposal Company, A.D.C., q.v.). The R.H.A., of which six were ordered in 1917 and two were already completed by Armstrongs and tested by the Armistice of 1918, was a 45-degree upright Vee-12, 260 hp water-cooled engine. With a Ricardo supercharger it developed 300–360 hp and was flown at R.A.E., Farnborough.

Aircraft:

Airco D.H.4

The Ricardo-Halford-Armstrong, an experimental engine employing ingenious features of Ricardo design, including a supercharger.

ROLLASON AIRCRAFT AND ENGINES LTD, CROYDON, SURREY.

The Ardem 4CO2-2 was produced in France by Roger Druine from the standard Volkswagen motor-car power unit. It was intended for the little French Turbulent single-seater, also designed by Druine. Both airframe and engine were built under licence by Rollason from the end of the 1950s for several years.

ARDEM 4CO2, 30 hp, a 4-cylinder, horizontally-opposed, air-cooled poppet-valve engine. It was generally adapted to power ultra-light aircraft and was unsupercharged, its propeller having direct L.H. tractor-drive. Bore/stroke 3.03 x 2.52 in. Vol. 72.62 cu in (77 x 64 mm. Vol. 1.19 litre). Compression ratio 6.6:1. Fuel: 80 Octane. Rollason introduced a modification to the carburettor which made starting easier and also pre-heated the air entry, making the use of a separate carburettor heater box unnecessary. Rollason also introduced a version, the 4CO2 FH MOD, which had larger aluminium cylinders of 1,300 cc capacity, increasing the power to 40 hp.

Aircraft:

Evans VP-1 Volksplane
Luton LA 4A Minor
Rollason (Druine) Turbulent
Tipsy Nipper III

The author having a little fun in an Ardem-engined Rollason Turbulent, in the snow at Redhill, Surrey, in 1963.

ROLLS-ROYCE LIMITED, DERBY, CREWE and GLASGOW.

Most people refer to a Rolls-Royce motor-car as a 'Rolls' (or, unspeakably, worse) but few may realize that, in the Derby area, the works has for years been known as 'Royce's'. The epitome of perfection in the car industry, whatever the company's temporary financial troubles, the original conjugation of Rolls and Royce is about as improbable as can be imagined. Frederick Henry Royce was born in 1863, in circumstances of considerable poverty which was to be the cause of ill-health which would dominate the rest of his life. After only two years at school, with a brief railway apprenticeship behind him and practically no money, in 1884 he and a friend set up a company F.H.Royce & Co, in Manchester to make industrial electrical components. He then bought a second-hand car and, finding fault with almost everything in it, to his partner's dismay he decided to design and build a better one, with a small two-cylinder engine.

Seven years earlier, in 1877, the Hon Charles Stewart Rolls was born. A son of a wealthy peer and landowner, he bought his first car, a Peugeot, at the age of 17 and then graduated from Cambridge with a Degree in Mechanics and Applied Sciences. He went on to indulge a love of motor racing, taking part in a race in 1900 from Paris to Toulouse and return in a Napier car, acting as mechanic to S.F. Edge, subsequently gaining racing trophies and achieving the World's Speed Record on land. In 1901, having trouble with his car while passing through Reading, Rolls asked at a cycle shop for assistance, which was willingly and expertly given by a young man called Ernest Hives. Events happened unexpectedly and sometimes quickly in those days. Rolls invited Hives, there and then, to go to London with him and join his staff as a mechanic.

Rolls set up his own company, C.S. Rolls & Co, to sell cars to those who could afford them, most cars then being large, expensive and of foreign make, often requiring chauffeurs. A friend of Rolls told him of a small car being produced in Manchester by Royce's. Despite a prejudice against two, rather than four or six-cylinder engines, Rolls tried out the Royce car and was impressed by its smoothness and performance. With his partner and Company Secretary, Claude Johnson, Rolls arranged to take and sell all the three, four and six-cylinder cars that Royce could build, marketed and distributed under the name of Rolls-Royce Limited, which took over a new works in Derby in 1908. Hives left Rolls to join Napier and race for them, in one of the very early Brooklands meetings, before rejoining Rolls-Royce at Derby, where the Chief Tester was Eric Platford ('EP').

Royce, despite his ill-health, became Engineer-in-Chief and started to design and supervise the construction of the series of cars which, ever since, have been second to none in quality, performance and reliability. Rolls gave up his executive work in 1910 but remained on the Board. Having taken up flying, he bought a modified Wright Flyer and, on 2 June that year, made the first double-crossing of the English Channel. A month later, at the Bournemouth flying meeting, Rolls's aircraft broke up in the air and he was killed. Soon afterwards, Royce himself became extremely ill, his life being saved by Johnson who insisted that he recuperate in the south of France, where he was subsequently obliged to spend cold weather months. Otherwise, he lived by the sea in Kent or Sussex. Despite this, everything by way of drawings or new components were sent from Derby to him for approval. Arising out of this, he instituted the curious and unique designations, applicable to senior Rolls-Royce executives, ensuring unambiguous attribution of all correspondence and drawings, Royce himself being 'R', Hives 'Hs' and so on.

Shortly after the outbreak of war in August 1914, the Air Department of the Admiralty, faced with a delay in the production of 200 hp Sunbeam engines, requested Rolls-Royce to produce an engine of similar horse power. Royce, in his pursuit of excellence, wanted to create an aero engine designed (as were his motor cars) as nearly as possible, to perfection. He was persuaded to take a close look at a successful Mercedes racing car engine (*see* Historical Note) and made certain decisions in the light of what he saw. This came about in the following way.

Royce welcomed a look at the Mercedes, not for the main engine structure, because he very well understood high-performance, in terms of crankshaft, connecting rods and the materials used. All the same, he did not at that time fully understand the individual cylinder with its water jacket. This was a feature of the Mercedes racing car, whereas his 40/50 Silver Ghost had cast-iron blocks, which were heavy. What was wanted was a lightweight cylinder, so the whole concept was new to Royce. He therefore took a careful look at the Mercedes individually water-jacketed cylinders, before doing his own design work. He then took out a number of patents of his own, in the course of designing his aero-engine cylinder and the methods of making it. The principal reason for getting hold of a Mercedes was therefore justified. While he undoubtedly learned from it, rather as he did subsequently from the Curtiss D.12, neither example prevented him from following his own instincts when he came to doing his own design.

Of course, this stood the firm in very good stead until the 'F', or Kestrel came along. The great weakness of the individual cylinder, apart from the fact that individual jackets added to the length and breadth of the engine, the system tended to corrode and leak. It is worth recording that, during the Second World War, when Rolls-Royce had a Packard marine engine in the Experimental Department at Derby, it still used individual cylinder jackets. The inevitable leaks were cured by the simple process of placing a rubber pad over the leak and a large Jubilee clip round the cylinder to hold it in place.

Rolls accepted the suggestion by W.O. Bentley that forged aluminium, being a good deal lighter, would be a better material for pistons, rather than the customary cast-iron. Despite persuasion from the Royal Aircraft Factory that he should consider air cooling, Royce decided on a water-cooled Vee-12 engine, with separate steel cylinders and water jackets, set at sixty degrees. The result of this was the Eagle initially capable of delivering 300 hp at 2,000 rpm, Rolls-Royce's first and highly successful aero-engine. It was initially run at 1,600 rpm, giving the desired 200 hp, then rerated to 250 hp at 1,650 rpm while experience with it was built up and was thus officially known as the Mk I. The Eagle, so named in September 1917 like the subsequent Falcon, had an epicyclic propeller reduction gear. It was followed by the 75 hp six-cylinder Hawk, a small but reliable engine for coastal airships, and one of the very rare examples of the production of Rolls-Royce engines being 'farmed out' to a sub-contractor, Brazil Straker of Bristol, a firm which also contributed parts for the Eagle.

Next there appeared the equally successful 260 hp Falcon, a scaled-down and lighter Eagle, designed by R.W.Harvey-Bailey ('By'), the father of Alec Harvey-Bailey ('AHB') who has been a major contributor towards the compiling of this book. The Falcon was a fighter-type engine which was also built under sub-contract by Brazil Straker. Rolls-Royce ended the 1914–1918 war as the largest supplier of aero-engines in Britain, having produced, with Brazil Straker, in excess of 7,000, of which the great majority were Eagles and with the big Condor under development. Details of these and subsequent engines appear below. Royce continued to control very effectively the design and production of the company's engines although much design work was undertaken by A.J. Rowledge ('Rg'), from the Condor III onwards. He contributed in particular to the success of the 'R' racing engine which enabled

Mitchell's Supermarine S.6B seaplane to win outright the Schneider Trophy for Britain in 1931.

Royce (by then, Sir Henry) died two years later, in the spring of 1933, after much ill-health and was in due course succeeded by Ernest Hives. As head of that great company, E.W. Hives ('Hs') was supported by a team of engineers who individually gained fame in their own right. From 1936 initially as General Works Manager, Hives (later, Lord Hives), led the Rolls-Royce team with great energy, supported by such famous names as Elliott ('E'), Harvey-Bailey ('By'), Lovesey ('Lov'), Rubbra ('Rbr') and Hooker ('SGH'), and continued the great ideals and traditions of excellence and simplicity which their former chief had demanded.

NOTE: The piston aero-engines built by Rolls-Royce are listed as nearly as possible in order of appearance. For obvious reasons, where types overlap this is not always possible. The figures quoted for the numbers of new engines built and the duration of production are, as nearly as possible, Rolls-Royce's own figures for totals of new engines despatched, as summarized below. These figures do not therefore include considerable numbers of re-built and modified engines, such as the Kestrel XXX or 30, which was built typically from up-dated Mk V and Mk XVI components.

Totals of new engines Despatched

Eagle	4,681	(Early type)
Hawk	201	(Derby and Brazil Straker, Bristol)
Falcon	2,185	
Condor	327	
Kestrel	4,750	
Buzzard	100	
Goshawk	20	
'R' type	20	
Peregrine	301	
Vulture	538	
Merlin	149,659	(Derby, Crewe, Glasgow, Fords, Packard)
Griffon	8,108	(Derby, Crewe, Glasgow)
Eagle	15	(Late type)

ROLLS-ROYCE EAGLE.
The Eagle was the first production Rolls-Royce aero-engine to be used in Service. It was a 60-degree Vee-12, water-cooled engine, originating in 1915 from an Admiralty requirement of the previous year for an engine of about 250 hp. The first experimental engine was first run in February 1915, developing 225 hp at 1,650 rpm. Production, from Rolls-Royce Ltd, Derby, 4,681.

Eagle engines had the following in common:-
Bore/stroke 4.5 x 6.5 in. (114.3 x 165.1 mm)
Swept Volume 1,239 cu in. (20.32 litres).
Compression Ratios Mks I-II 4.53:1; III-IV 4.9:1;
Mk VIII 5.3:1
Dimensions vary according to accessories.
Length 72.6 in; Width 42.6 in; Height 46.4 in.
Weights, where published — *see* Performance tables.

EAGLE I, 225 hp. Officially called 'Rolls-Royce 250 hp, Mk I', was a 12-cylinder, upright 60-degree Vee with separate water-jacketed cylinders, poppet-valves, a two-valve engine with single overhead camshafts. Royce used the same 4.5 inch cylinder bore as the 40/50 motor car, of which he had great experience. The power assembly was of the master and articulated rod type. Geared, epicyclic .64:1, propeller rotation being the same as the crankshaft, which could turn in either direction. Two single 36 mm Claudel carburettors. Six-cylinder inlet manifolds. Two Bosch magnetos. L.H./R.H. tractor/pusher-drive. 104 built at Derby, 1915–1916.
Aircraft:
  Curtiss H.12 Large America
  Curtiss-Wanamaker Triplane
  Felixstowe F.2A
  Handley Page H.P.11 O/100 Type O
  Porte Baby
  Royal Aircraft Factory F.E.2d

Royal Aircraft Factory F.E.4
Sopwith L.R.T.Tr Triplane
Vickers F.B.11
N.S. 3 Admiralty North Sea Airship
R23, R26 (Vickers) Admiralty (23 class) dirigible airship, four engines fitted.
R24, (Beardmore) and R25 (Armstrong Whitworth), as above.

Aircraft:
Airco D.H.4
Royal Aircraft Factory R.E.7
R31, R32 (Short Bros) Admiralty dirigible airship, originally six, later five engines fitted. Alternatively, Eagle IV.

Handley Page O/100 after a forced landing behind German lines.

A Rolls-Royce Eagle I in the big Porte 'Baby' flying boat.

Eagle I in a Handley Page O/100, in an armoured installation

EAGLE II, 250 hp. 'Rolls-Royce 250 hp, Mk II', generally similar to Mk I, with modifications to suit particular installation. Compression ratio 4.53:1. Four Claudel-Hobson, 36 mm choke, carburettors, three-cylinder inlet manifolds. Two Dixie magnetos. 36 built at Derby, 1916.
Aircraft:
Short Bomber

EAGLE III, 250 hp. 'Rolls-Royce 250 hp, Mk III', generally similar to Mk II, with modifications to suit particular installations. Strengthened pistons, compression ratio 4.9:1. 36 mm choke carburettors. Two Watford or Dixie magnetos. Otherwise, similar to Mk II. 110 built at Derby, 1916–1917.

Royal Aircraft Factory F.E.2d, captured behind German lines by Fl Abt 292 in 1917.

EAGLE IV, 270/286 hp. 'Rolls-Royce 250 hp, Mk IV', Generally similar to earlier types, with modifications to suit particular installations. Compression ratio 4.9:1. Two 38 mm, duplex Claudel carburettors, replacing four single 36 mm choke carburettors in Series II and III Eagles. Otherwise, induction system unaltered. Two Dixie magnetos. 150 built at Derby, 1916-1917.
Aircraft:

> Fairey F.16 Campania
> Handley Page H.P.12 O/400
> Handley Page H.P.15 V/1500
> Short (Admiralty Type) 184D
> R27 (Beardmore), R29 (Armstrong Whitworth)
> Admiralty dirigible airship (23X class), four engines fitted.
> R31, R32 (Short Bros) Admiralty dirigible airship, originally six, later five engines fitted. Alternatively, Eagle III.

A Rolls-Royce Eagle IV.

EAGLE V, 275 hp. 'Rolls-Royce 275 hp, Mk.I', generally similar to Mk IV, with reversion to four single 38 mm choke Claudel-Hobson carburettors. Watford magnetos. Higher-lift camshaft. Compression ratio 4.9:1. 100 built at Derby, 1916–1917.
Aircraft:

> Airco D.H.4
> Fairey F.17 Campania
> Grahame-White G.W.E.7

The Grahame-White G.W.E.7 Ganymede limousine, with two Eagle Vs.

EAGLE VI, 275 hp. 'Rolls-Royce 275 hp, Mk II', similar to Mk V but with reduction gear .6:1 and four Watford magnetos. Two sparking plugs per cylinder were used for the first time. Compression ratio 4.9:1. 300 built at Derby, 1917.
Aircraft:

> Airco D.H.4
> Wight 'Converted' Seaplane

EAGLE VII, 275 hp. 'Rolls-Royce 275 hp, Mk III', similar to Mk VI, minor differences. 200 built at Derby, 1917–1918.
Aircraft:

> Airco D.H.4
> Curtiss H.12 Large America
> Fairey F.17 Campania
> Porte Baby

EAGLE VIII, 300 hp. Extensive modifications, though generally similar to Mk VII. High compression ratio 5.3:1, reduction gear .6:1. Four 42 mm-choke Rolls-Royce (Claudel-Hobson) carburettors, mounted in pairs at each end, attached to four redesigned three-cylinder inlet manifolds. L.H. tractor in all but F.E.2ds and H.P.V/1500, the former of which had R.H. tractors and the latter both pusher and tractor types in pairs. Four Watford magnetos. 3,302 built at Derby, 1917–1922, in approximately equal quantities, L.H. & R.H.. Length 72.5 in; width 42.6 in; height 44.5 in.
Aircraft:

> Airco D.H.4, 4A
> Airco D.H.9A srs
> ANEC III
> B.A.T. F.K.26
> Blackburn Blackbird
> Curtiss H.12, H.16 Large America
> de Havilland D.H.10C Amiens II, IIIC
> de Havilland D.H.16
> Fairey F.17 Campania
> Fairey IIIC, IIID
> Felixstowe F.2A
> Felixstowe F.3
> Felixstowe F.5

An Eagle VIII in a Handley Page O/400 bomber.

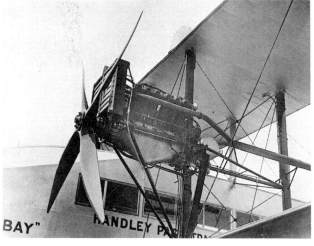

A civil application of the Eagle VIII, Handley Page W.8b G-EBBG, of Handley Page Transport, a forerunner of Imperial Airways.

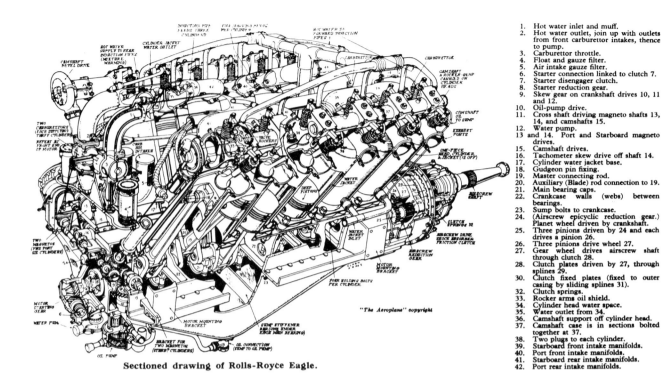

1. Hot water inlet and muff.
2. Hot water outlet, join up with outlets from front carburettor intakes, thence to pump.
3. Carburettor throttle.
4. Float and gauze filter.
5. Air intake gauze filter.
6. Starter connection linked to clutch 7.
7. Starter disengager clutch.
8. Starter reduction gear.
9. Skew gear on crankshaft drives 10, 11 and 12.
10. Oil-pump drive.
11. Cross shaft driving magneto shafts 13, 14, and camshafts 15.
12. Water pump.
13 and 14. Port and Starboard magneto drives.
15. Camshaft drives.
16. Tachometer skew drive off shaft 14.
17. Cylinder water jacket base.
18. Gudgeon pin fixing.
19. Master connecting rod.
20. Auxiliary (Blade) rod connection to 19.
21. Main bearing caps.
22. Crankcase walls (webs) between bearings.
23. Sump bolts to crankcase.
24. (Airscrew epicyclic reduction gear.) Planet wheel driven by crankshaft.
25. Three pinions driven by 24 and each drives a pinion 26.
26. Three pinions drive wheel 27.
27. Gear wheel drives airscrew shaft through clutch 28.
28. Clutch plates driven by 27, through splines 29.
30. Clutch fixed plates (fixed to outer casing by sliding splines 31).
32. Clutch springs.
33. Rocker arms oil shield.
34. Cylinder head water space.
35. Water outlet from 34.
36. Camshaft support off cylinder head.
37. Camshaft case is in sections bolted together at 37.
38. Two plugs to each cylinder.
39. Starboard front intake manifolds.
40. Port front intake manifolds.
41. Starboard rear intake manifolds.
42. Port rear intake manifolds.

Sectioned drawing of Rolls-Royce Eagle.

Rolls-Royce Eagle VIII cut-away drawing.

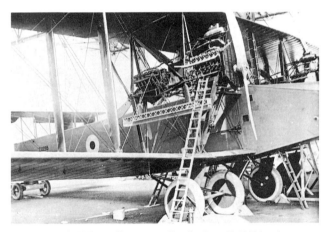

A double Eagle VIII installation, in a Handley Page V/1500 bomber.

The Vickers Vimy of Alcock and Brown, the first non-stop crossing of the Atlantic Ocean, powered by Rolls-Royce Eagle VIIIs.

EAGLE IX, 360 hp. Developed after the First World War as a civil engine, from the Mk VIII, compression ratio being slightly reduced to 5.22:1. The crankshaft was strengthened and camshaft-drive was improved, as was the design of cylinder water jackets and water pump. Ignition was via four magnetos and the two Rolls-Royce Claudel-Hobson carburettors were mounted low and centrally on either side of the crankcase. Long, water-jacketed air intake pipes extended from beyond the cowling up the sides and between cylinders 3 and 4 to the induction pipes within the Vee. This was to reduce fire risk. The altitude mixture control was improved. L.H. tractor, except for Dornier Wal, which had L.H. and R.H. propellers in tandem. 373 built at Derby, 1922–1928.
Aircraft:

Handasyde H.2
Handley Page H.P.12 O/400
Handley Page H.P.15 V/1500
Handley Page H.P.18 W.8b
Handley Page O/7
Handley Page O/10
Handley Page O/11
Hawker Horsley I
Porte Baby
Porte (Felixstowe) Fury
Royal Aircraft Factory F.E.2d
Short N.1B, N.2B Shirl
Sopwith Atlantic
Sopwith Wallaby
Supermarine Commercial Amphibian
Supermarine Sea Eagle
Vickers 12 Vernon I
Vickers VIM (Vickers Instructional Machine)
Vickers 17 Viking II
Vickers F.B.27 Vimy IV
Vickers 61, 63 Vulcan
Vickers 66 Vimy Commercial
Vickers 85 Viking IV
Vickers 92 Valparaiso II

Airco D.H.4
Airco D.H.9B
de Havilland D.H.16
Dornier Do J Wal
Fairey IIID
Felixstowe F.4, F.5
Handley Page H.P.12 O/400
Handley Page H.P.15 V/1500
Handley Page H.P.18 W.8c
Handley Page H.P.26 W.8e/f Hamilton (+ 2 Pumas)
Supermarine Scarab
Supermarine Sea Eagle
Supermarine Swan
Vickers F.B.27A Vimy Mk II
Vickers 61 Vulcan
Vickers 66 Vimy Commercial
Vickers 69, 73, 77 Viking IV
Vickers 95 Vulture II

The ultimate Eagle, the civil Mk IX.

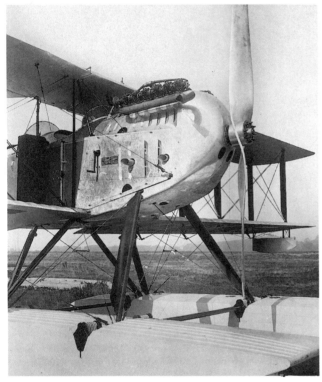

Fairey IIID seaplane with an Eagle IX.

A Handley Page W.8f built for SABENA, with one Eagle IX and a pair of Siddeley-Deasy Pumas.

EAGLE X, (1922), Generally similar to Mk IX except that two 12-cylinder B.T.H. magnetos were substituted for the four Watford 6-cylinder units.

EAGLE XV, (1924), Generally similar to Mk IX except that it was equipped with a two-speed epicyclic propeller reduction gear. L.H. tractor-drive. 6 built at Derby.

EAGLE XVI, 500 hp, (1925), 16-cylinder, 90-degree X-shaped water-cooled, poppet-valve. Bore/stroke 4.5 x 4.75 in. (Vol. 19.8 litre). Not completed.

HAWK I, 75 hp, (1916), 6-cylinder, upright in-line, water-cooled, poppet-valve. Bore/stroke 4.0 x 6.0 in. Vol. 452.3 cu in. (101.6 x 152.4 mm). Compression ratio 5.1:1. Direct L.H. tractor/R.H. pusher-drive. Single Dixie magneto ignition and twin 28 mm Claudel-Hobson FZR carburettors, each supplying three cylinders. 1 built at Derby and 205 by Brazil Straker, a very rare example of Rolls-Royce 'farming out' production. A Naval 'Blimp' coastal airship, powered by a Hawk, is recorded as having made a patrol lasting over 50 hours. Length 46.85 in; width 23.5 in; height 35.5 in.

Production, 8/1914–12/1918, from:-

Brazil Straker & Co Ltd, Bristol,

Ordered, 205;   Delivered, 205;   Cancelled/suspended, 0
Aircraft:

Avro 504F

Maurice Farman Serie VII 'Longhorn'

Royal Aircraft Factory B.E.2e

Sage III

otherwise, mostly used in R.N.A.S. S.S.E & Z airships.

The Rolls-Royce Hawk I.

A Hawk I installed as a pusher in a Maurice Farman Longhorn.

HAWK II, 90/100 hp, (1917), generally similar to Series I with higher rpm. One (and probably as many as ten more) experimental engines, built by Brazil Straker at Bristol.

FALCON was a very successful Vee-12 fighter-type engine, similar in design and construction to the Eagle but slightly scaled down in size and power. Designed by R.W.Harvey-Bailey, it also gained great respect for its reliability in service.

Twin Hawk installation in an SS E airship.

FALCON I, 230 hp, (1916-17), 'Rolls-Royce 190 hp, Mk I', 12-cylinder, upright 60-degree Vee water-cooled, poppet-valve (two-valve engine), Bore/stroke 4 x 5.75in (101.6 x 146.0 mm). Vol. 866.5 cu in. (14.2 litre). Compression ratio 5.15:1, geared, epicyclic .589:1, R.H./L.H. tractor-drive. (Engines with even serial numbers were L.H. tractor but the great majority built were R.H., with odd numbers). Two Watford magnetos, two Duplex 34 mm Claudel-Hobson carburettors, feeding three-cylinder inlet manifolds. 250 built at Derby and by Brazil Straker. Length 68.0 in; width 40.3 in; height 37.2 in.
Aircraft:

>   Avro 529
>   Blackburn G.P. Seaplane
>   Bristol 12 F.2A,
>   Bristol 14 F.2B Fighter
>   Fairey F.2
>   Fairey N.9
>   Martinsyde F.3
>   Martinsyde R.G.
>   Royal Aircraft Factory R.E.7
>   Vickers F.B.14B, F.B.14D

FALCON II, 253 hp, (1917), 'Rolls-Royce 190 hp, Mk II', similar to Mk I but carburettor size increased to 36 mm. R.H. tractor-drive. 250 built at Derby.
Aircraft:

>   Blackburn Kangaroo
>   Bristol 14 F.2B Fighter
>   Royal Aircraft Factory F.E.2d

FALCON III, 285 hp, (1917-27), 'Rolls-Royce 190 hp, Mk III', similar to Mk II, except for compression ratio 5.3:1 and larger three-cylinder inlet manifolds, fed by four single 38 mm Rolls-Royce/Claudel-Hobson carburettors. Two Watford magnetos. Length 65.2 in; width 38.4 in; height 42.0 in. 1,685 built at Derby.

The very successful Rolls-Royce Falcon III fighter engine, similar in design to the Eagle.

Aircraft:

>   Blackburn Kangaroo
>   Blackburn T.R.1 Sprat
>   Bristol 14 F.2B Fighter Mk II, III, IV
>   Bristol 27 F.2B Coupe
>   Bristol 86 Greek Tourer
>   Bristol 96, 96A
>   de Havilland D.H.37
>   Martinsyde F.3, F.4 Buzzard
>   Martinsyde Type A Mk I
>   Martinsyde R.G.
>   Parnall Perch
>   Vickers 16 Viking I
>   Vickers 120 Vendace I
>   Vickers 133 Vendace
>   Westland Limousine I, II
>   Westland Wizard I

A Bristol F.2B Fighter in India, Falcon III engine.

A Bristol F.2B Fighter, with a Falcon III modified to be evaporatively-cooled. It has condensers on top and bottom wings which are metal-covered and bi-convex, of R.A.F. 34 section.

ROLLS-ROYCE 'G', CONDOR.
The Condor was a large and very powerful engine developed by Rolls-Royce in 1918 for use in long-range heavy bombers, at the end of the First World War, principally for bombing Berlin. Design work was begun at the end of 1917 and retained the same cylinder construction of earlier types. Rolls-Royce Condors, of which a total of 327 is recorded as having been built, had the following in common:-

Bore/stroke 5.5 x 7.5 in. (139.7 x 190.5 mm)
Swept Volume 2,137.5 cu in.
Compression Ratio 5.1:1.
Dimensions vary according to accessories.
Length (Mk I) 88.4 in; Width 44.1 in; Height 44.45 in
Length (Mk IIIB) 69.3 in; Width 41.1 in; Height 43.2 in
Weights, where published — *see* Performance tables.

CONDOR I, 600 hp, (1920–21) was a 12-cylinder, upright 60-degree Vee, water-cooled, poppet-valve engine, with separate water-jacketed cylinders and four valves instead of two, as fitted to the Falcon and Eagle. Geared, epicyclic .666:1 or .554:1 L.H. tractor-drive. Two Rolls-Royce/Claudel-Hobson carburettors and two Watford magnetos. Provision was made for an electric starter

and dynamo (generator). Length 88.4 in; width 41.1 in; height 47.5 in. 72 built at Derby.
Aircraft:

Airco D.H.4
de Havilland D.H.14
Short N.3 Cromarty

The original Condor I. Though powerful, it was a somewhat heavy engine. The separate cylinders and the epicyclic reduction gear also made it lengthy.

CONDOR IA, *see below.*

CONDOR II, 650 hp, (1921), sometimes referred to as Mk IA, succeeded the generally similar Mk I, apart from the reduction gear ratio. Two Rolls-Royce Claudel-Hobson carburettors, mounted low on either side of the engine, supplied mixture through water-jacketed uptake pipes, passing between 3 and 4 cylinders to the induction pipes within the Vee. Compression ratio 5.17:1. Geared, epicyclic .5537:1. as Falcon and Eagle. L.H. tractor-drive. 34 built at Derby.
Aircraft:

Beardmore BeRo.1 Inflexible
Fairey N.4 Atalanta
Hawker Horsley

CONDOR III, 670 hp, (1924) prototype, a major redesign of the Mk IA/II and the first Condor to be fitted with spur reduction gears, 0.477:1, and carburettor at rear end. It did not incorporate the production Condor III crankcase and water circulation features. Provision for gas starting and C.C. gun fire control gear.

CONDOR III, 650/670 hp, (1923–1927), production version, similar in power to the Mk II. Compression ratio 6.5:1. The first production Rolls-Royce engine to feature a spur reduction drive, .477:1. Despite the need for a stiffer crankcase, it was considerably lighter. L.H. tractor-drive. Duplex Claudel-Hobson carburettor built by Rolls-Royce. Most major components were extensively redesigned, in particular the master and articulated connecting rods being replaced by the fork and blade type, subsequently used in Rolls-Royce engines. Provision for a gas starter. 196 built at Derby and many modified, as below. Length 69.3 in; width 31.0 in; height 45 in.
Aircraft:

Avro 549 Aldershot I, III
Avro 557 Ava
Avro 561 Andover
Blackburn R.B.1 Iris I
Bristol 90 Berkeley
de Havilland D.H.27 Derby
Fairey Fremantle
Handley Page H.P.28 Handcross
Hawker Horsley I
Short S.5 Singapore I
Vickers 96 Virginia I
Vickers 103, 170 Vanguard
Vickers 105 Vixen IV
Vickers 115 Virginia VIII
Westland Yeovil

CONDOR IIIA, 650/665 hp, (1925), similar to Mk III but modified so as to give a higher power, compression ratio 6.5:1. Improved main bearing design and materials. Geared .477:1 or .582:1.

Aircraft:

Avro 563 Andover
Blackburn R.B.1 Iris II
de Havilland D.H.54 Highclere
Fairey N.4 Titania
Hawker Horsley I, II
Saunders A.3 Valkyrie
Short S.5 Singapore I
Vickers 124 Vixen VI

The Condor III, modified with a spur reduction gear, thereby making it considerably more compact.

The Vickers Vanguard G-EBCP, with Condor III engines.

The Condor IIIA installed in a Hawker Horsley.

CONDOR IIIB, 650 hp, (1930), similar to Mk IIIA, modified with an entirely new and stronger crankcase, with a larger diameter crankshaft and longer main bearings. The crankcase join was lowered leaving the bearing caps in the top half. The compression ratio was 6.5:1, the spur-geared drive .477:1.

Aircraft:

      Blackburn R.B.1 Iris III

      Hawker Horsley II

      R100 (Airship Guarantee Co Ltd), H.M. dirigible airship, six engines installed

CONDOR IV, 750 hp, (1925), similar to Mk III and IIIA but with direct-drive and modified, 3-feet mounting. 6.5:1 compression ratio. 13 built at Derby.

Aircraft:

      Hawker Hornbill

      Saunders A.3 Valkyrie

CONDOR IVA, 750 hp, (1927), similar to Mk IIIA but with direct-drive and modified mounting. 9 built at Derby.

CONDOR V, (1925), similar to Mk IIIA but with an exhaust-driven two-stage turbo supercharger, running at 26,000 rpm at 20,000 ft and delivering +13.5 lb boost. The reason for the compact, two-stage design was to instal it between the cylinder blocks, the first stage impeller being 7.5 inches in diameter and the second stage 8.25 in. It was a joint design by A.J.Rowledge and J.E. Ellor and was run (but not flown) at R.A.E. Farnborough. One was built at Derby but development work was stopped on Air Ministry instructions.

CONDOR VII, similar to Mk IIIA but with direct-drive and modified mounting. 2 built at Derby, date unrecorded.

CONDOR C.I., 480 hp, (1932), compression ignition (Diesel) version of the Condor, compression ratio 12.5:1. Two diesel Condors were tested and flown, following research by Rolls-Royce and of H.R.Ricardo on high-compression combustion.

Aircraft:

      Hawker Horsley.

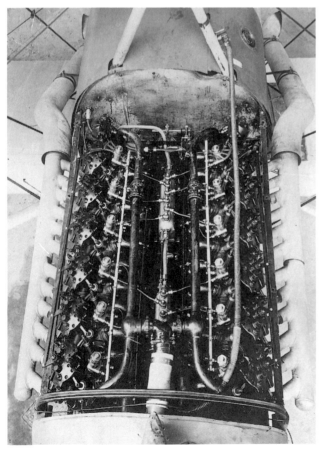

The Compression Ignition Condor was tested in a Hawker Horsley.

ROLLS-ROYCE 'F' X.

Developed from the Falcon range of V-12, water-cooled engines, the F.X was the only direct-drive, ungeared version in the series F.X — F.XIV (the 'unlucky' number being omitted). The 'F' X was the outcome of the proposed Rolls-Royce Falcon X. Similarly, the F.XI and F.XII were, at first referred to as Falcons but the series design incorporated new ideas to such an extent that it was appropriate to re-name it and thus it became known as the Kestrel.

The Kestrel broke new ground for Rolls-Royce, in particular, by being fitted with a 6-cylinder casting, an aluminium 'monobloc' derived from a type of construction introduced during the First World War but with wet-lined forged steel cylinder barrels, instead of the then more usual individual forged cylinders, each with its own cooling jacket (usually a welded sheet-steel shell).

With individual cylinders, six in a row, an engine tends to be long and heavy. Long before the advent of the wet-lined water-cooled cylinder block, at Hispano-Suiza (whose Vee-8 engines came to be built under licence by Wolseley), Marc Birkigt had designed an aluminium block which employed dry screwed-in steel liners so as to ensure the best possible metal to metal contact, as mentioned above. This resulted in a shorter, more compact and somewhat lighter engine. Comparing the Rolls-Royce Eagle with Hispano engines, the latter had the better power/weight ratio although the more robust Rolls engine had the edge in terms of power per litre.

Using individual cylinders, Royce had used a 4.5 inch bore on the Silver Ghost car engine with a bore/stroke ratio of 75 per cent, on the theory that a long stroke imposed the lowest cylinder side loads (a connecting-pod of infinite length imposing none). He worked on ways of making a shorter and lighter engine and came up with the Eagle XVI, an X-shaped 16-cylinder engine, with dry cylinder liners.

Royce also studied the design of the 12-cylinder Curtiss D-12 which C.R. Fairey had imported from the United States, following its two major successes in the Schneider Trophy contests. The D-12 was undoubtedly an initial success in its first application (as the Fairey Felix) in a British aircraft. The Fairey Fox light bomber, so powered, was rather faster than contemporary fighters intended to intercept it. Royce looked at the D-12 and, despite its success, smooth-running and, low-frontal area, he didn't care for it. It had monobloc-type poultice heads on basically individual cylinders, the coolant being fed from passages in the skirt into the head and then via two outlets to the radiator. Royce decided that many improvements could be made on a generally similar layout and that a wet liner monobloc was a practical solution to the problems of producing a more compact and lighter engine.

He therefore decided to go for a development of the Falcon, the Mk X, with a bore/stroke ratio of 90 per cent and which gave a shorter connecting rod. This resulted in the F.X (later the Kestrel), which was intended from the outset to be available in supercharged form if required and, in its production form, featured a spur-type reduction gear, raising the thrust line well above that of the Falcon's low-set epicyclic gear. This also resulted in both a shorter engine and reduced frontal area. The seven-bearing crankshaft was driven by fork and blade-ended connecting rods, which Royce had first introduced in the Condor III and used on subsequent engines.

Royce designed his 'F' (Kestrel) engine with a one-piece cylinder block consisting of the head and skirt, into which were fitted six individual cylinder liners. He employed the monobloc cylinder layout in order to stiffen the whole engine as well as to contain the cylinder side loads. Initially he used dry cylinder liners, inserted with an interference fit and, to assist coring the jacket, provided openings at the side which were closed with sheet aluminium covers. These proved to be leaky and piston seizures were attributed to poor cooling caused by the use of dry liners.

When Royce learnt that Curtiss had experienced similar problems, he decided to produce what A.A. Rubbra called a 'rather daring design' and to alter the F.X to incorporate open-ended wet cylinder-liners. Having appreciated the advantages, partial or otherwise, of wet liners, he stayed with them thereafter. This arrangement left the jacket space open, without the need for separate covers. The wet liners were inserted into the cylinder block through the base of the skirt, each cylinder liner's top flange making a joint with the cylinder head through a soft aluminium joint ring at the top end, the bottom flange sitting on the crankcase deck. From Kestrel manuals, it can be seen that great care had to be taken in getting a consistent height of each cylinder liner. To maintain the top joint, the compression loads were held by long cylinder holding-down studs, tapped deeply into the crankcase. These studs of course had to carry both the compression and firing loads of the engine. It was very difficult to get a reliable and consistent top joint and, although it was never entirely satisfactory, it worked quite well. Rolls-Royce also devised a range of high-strength light alloys, production of which was licensed to High Duty Alloys Ltd, under the name of Hiduminium and bearing 'RR' reference numbers.

There can have been few, if any families of engines as complex as the Kestrels, of which 4,750 were built. The variants were very numerous and there has been much uncertainty in the past, as to exactly what Kestrel designations implied. Despite this apparent complication, each variant could be identified by observance of a coded string of letters which logically followed the name and saved a lot of time and space. Kestrels (which were only built by Rolls-Royce) are listed alpha/numerically. In view of the variety and complexity of the Kestrel family, it is here broken down into groups, the divisions being determined by the propeller reduction gear ratios, the compression ratios and the degrees of supercharging. Hopefully, readers who are unfamiliar with the pattern of Kestrel development may thus more easily locate the type looked for. The system worked as follows.

Initially, there were only three basic types of Kestrel, the Rolls-Royce F.XI (or Kestrel I), the F.XII (Kestrel II) and the F.XIV (Kestrel III). All had spur-type reduction gears, with right-hand tractor propeller drives. (A few engines were provided with pusher thrust drives, for aircraft such as the Short Singapore II and III flying boats). All but the Kestrel XXX, or 30, normally drove fixed-pitch propellers, although several other marks were available for variable-pitch propellers, notably the Mk XVI which powered to the Miles 'Kestrel', forerunner of the Master I trainer, this in turn being the only user of the Kestrel XXX (sometimes called the Mk 30). The F.XI, Kestrel I had a propeller reduction gear of .632:1. The F.XII, Kestrel II had a reduction gear of .552:1 and the F.XIV (Kestrel III) a reduction gear of .475:1.

These three early Kestrels first appeared in unsupercharged form and each was produced in 'A' and 'B' versions, the Kestrel IA, IIA and IIIA, all having a compression ratio of 6:1. At the same time, high-compression 'B' versions of them also appeared, having a ratio of 7:1. The early unsupercharged Kestrels being available with these two different compression ratios, the choice depended on the use for which they were supplied and on the quality of fuel they needed to use. The engine naturally responded to whatever fuel it was given and high-compression engines had to be guarded against the detonation inherent with unsuitable fuel and, as recorded elsewhere, were equipped with gated throttles to protect them from attempting to deliver more power at low altitudes than they were able to withstand.

As well as the low and high compression, unsupercharged, 'A' and 'B' variants, from the outset the Kestrel was designed to be able to take a gear-driven supercharger and all three of the early engines became available in supercharged variations. Early 'blown' versions of the Kestrels I, II and III, each engine were either moderately supercharged (MS, with their impellers driven at 5.5 times crankshaft speed), or fully supercharged (S, driven at 10 times crankshaft speed). Reverting to compression ratios, the MS engines had a third compression ratio, slightly lower than that of the 'A' versions, at 5.5:1, while the fully supercharged units reverted to the 6:1 compression of the 'A' engines.

All of these engines developed very similar, if not quite identical power outputs, but in different conditions and it is important to appreciate the significance of the relationship between the compression ratios and the heights at which maximum power was developed. The 'A' engines, each with a different propeller gear ratio but with a compression ratio of 6:1, developed 490 horse-power at the normal 2,250 rpm at take-off.

The 'B' series engines, with their increased compression ratio of 7:1 were unsupercharged but, like even moderately supercharged engines at similar rpm, were capable of developing rather greater power at sea-level than was good for them. If allowed to do so, other

than briefly on take-off, they would suffer damage and therefore required a 'gated' throttle or a boost gauge (or both) to enable the pilot accurately to restrict its opening until a specified (Rated) Altitude was reached. On take-off, some of the early Kestrels were capable of developing 546 hp and so, when an engine was quoted as capable of delivering 'Normal bhp, at an altitude (other than Sea Level, Take-off)', a gated throttle or a boost control needed to be used below that altitude. The gate restricted the continuous power output of the 'B' engines to 480 hp, which the engine would maintain up to 3,000 feet, upon reaching which the engine could safely deliver full throttle power, at normal rpm.

The gated throttle was not always the most convenient way of restricting throttle openings and the important aneroid-operated automatic boost control was soon developed as standard equipment on British supercharged engines. Supercharged Kestrels were therefore provided with automatic boost controls which would maintain the throttle opening set by the pilot, up to the engine's rated altitude. (The author, trained on Kestrels, once came perilously close to blowing-up a Wright Cyclone, by momentarily forgetting this on take-off, an all too easy mistake to make).

The 525 hp, moderately supercharged Kestrels, most of which only had the relatively modest compression ratio of 5.5:1, still required a boost gauge because they could deliver 500 hp, up to 2,000 feet at 2,250 normal rpm, their impellers running at a modest 5.5:1 ratio, relative to the crankshaft speed. The fully supercharged Kestrel IS, IIS and IIIs, with the same compression ratio of 6:1 as the 'A' series engines, would give 480 hp, on take-off and could maintain this power up to a Rated Altitude of 11,500 feet. Rolls-Royce were therefore able to offer a very useful choice of Kestrels, capable of providing constant power over a wide spectrum of rated altitudes, depending upon the user's requirements. In all, Rolls-Royce recorded a manufacture of 4,750 Kestrels.

A most important factor was the quality of the available fuel, a factor particularly significant to the Royal Air Force because of the enormous area of the Middle and Far East in which it had to operate in the 1930s. Consistent fuel quality control was not as certain as it is today. A high-powered engine, rather like a highly-bred racehorse, sometimes required restraint and, as previously mentioned, a high-compression engine had to be restricted in its throttle opening and the fuel it could use (or both), without risking detonation at the highest power of which it was capable.

As an example of this, a note from Rolls-Royce's 'Instructions for the installation, running and maintenance of Rolls-Royce 'F' Aero-engines' states: 'The maximum permissible speed of the engine is 2,700 rpm. Full throttle must never be used at altitudes less than the following:- 3,000 feet with a high-compression unsupercharged engine; 2,000 feet with a moderately supercharged engine; or 11,500 feet with a fully supercharged engine. The best cruising speed for the engine is in the neighbourhood of 2,000 to 2,100 rpm, depending on the type of machine and the propeller being used. The normal speed is 2,250 rpm, which should not normally be exceeded...'.

Following the initial sequence of F.XI, F.XII and F.XIV (or Kestrel I, II and III) engines, there followed a further bewildering number of variants, after the basic engine had been strengthened and increased in performance. At the same time (after the Kestrel III and from the Mk IV onwards) the 'MS and 'S' supercharge qualifications (for alternative versions of the same engine) were dropped because they were unnecessary. There remains the 'Kestrel VS' designation, which has often been repeated in books. This may originated in a long-distant printing error because, in Rolls-Royce terminology, all Kestrel IV, V and VI engines were fully supercharged in any case and the 'S' in such a context would therefore have been superfluous. There were, however, numerous 'Special' variants of Kestrel which were used to develop greater power and improve its cooling. The 'VS' is believed to be a misprint of 'V Spl' which, like its derivatives the Kestrel VI Spl and XVI Spl were specially modified versions of the basic engine. For example the Kestrel V and its derivatives, as fitted to variants of the Hawker Hart and Fury, were engines used for evaporative-cooling and coil-ignition trials in the course of development testing, in a manner similar to the Goshawk. In such circumstances, with modified engines repeatedly being substituted it is impossible to be precise with a picture caption.

The Kestrel IV (which became the Goshawk), V and VI comprised a group of high-performance, fully-supercharged engines, rated at 11,000 feet, developing 600 hp, thanks to a normal rpm which was increased to 2,500 when using 87 Octane fuel. In this group, all the superchargers ran at 8.8 times crankshaft speed. The main difference between them all was simply the reduction gear ratio.

The next group, Kestrels VII, VIII and IX were medium altitude supercharged engines, rated at 675 hp at normal rpm at 3,000 feet and were used, for example, on maritime reconnaissance flying-boats. Each group of three engines had reduction gear ratios of .632, .533 and .477:1 respectively. The moderately supercharged engines in this group drove their impellers at 6.9 times crankshaft speed.

Then there were three final groups of engines, the first group comprising the Mks X, XI and XII, all of which were unsupercharged high-compression (7:1) engines capable of delivering 585 hp, at sea level. The second group, Kestrels XIV, XV and XVI, with corresponding propeller reduction gear ratios, were even higher rated than the Mks IV, V and VI, their normal rpm being increased to 2,600, enabling them to develop 690 hp, maintained to 11,000 ft., their superchargers running at 9.4 times crankshaft speed. Fuel Octane rating of 87 (DTD 230) was of course mandatory in most circumstances with these late, high-powered Kestrels, to avoid the risk of detonation. The exception was the case of engines which were de-rated, that is reduced in power output by reducing their throttle opening and, therefore, their rpm in conditions where damage could be caused. This was usually due either to the unavailability of suitable high-Octane fuel or where, in the interests of economy (such as in training aircraft) the use of expensive 87 Octane petrol (still a rather advanced fuel) was not regarded as strictly necessary. The ultimate Kestrel variant was the Mk XXX, which had a compression ratio raised slightly to 6.2:1. These engines were not new, being rebuilt and uprated from earlier engines, mostly Mk Vs.

All Kestrels, apart from an experimental sleeve-valve engine, had similar design features, apart from the obvious technical advances to be expected in the development life of an engine which served the Royal Air Force for some eighteen years. The matching of engine and airframe and therefore the selection of the appropriate engine for its duties was very much a matter of 'horses for courses' and it is hoped that the foregoing will throw some light on this very involved subject.

THE KESTREL FAMILY GROUPS.

UNSUPERCHARGED (NORMALLY ASPIRATED) ROLLS-ROYCE KESTRELS.
F.X, KESTREL IA (F.XIA), IIA (F.XIIA), IIIA (F.XIVA), IB (F.XIB), IB3 (F.XIB3), IB4 (F.XIB4), IB5 (F.XIB5), IIB (F.XIIB), IIIB (F.XIVB), X, XDR, XI, XII.

MEDIUM SUPERCHARGED KESTRELS.
KESTREL IMS (F.XIMS), IIMS (F.XIIMS), IIMS (F.XIIMS) (pusher), IIMS.2 (F.XIIMS.2), IIMS.5 (F.XIIMS.5), IIMS.6 (F.XIIMS.6), IIIMS (F.XIVMS), IIIMS.2 (F.XIVMS.2), IIIMS.4 (F.XIVMS.4), IIIMS.6 (F.XIVMS.6), VII, VIII (Pusher), IX (Tractor).

FULLY SUPERCHARGED KESTRELS.
KESTREL IS (F.XIS), IIS (F.XIIS), IIS (F.XIIS) (pusher), IIIS (F.XIVS), IIIS.3 (F.XIVS.3), IV, V, VDR, VI, XIV, XV, XVI, XVI(DR), XVI(Spl), XVI(VP), XXX.

The Rolls-Royce Kestrel was a 12-cylinder, upright 60-degree Vee, water-cooled, poppet-valve engine. It appeared in numerous versions, all of which had the following in common:-

Bore/stroke 5.0 x 5.5 in. (127.0 x 140.0 mm)
Swept Volume 1,295.88 cu in. (21.25 litres).
Compression Ratio varies, 5.5:1, 6:1, 7:1.
Dimensions vary according to accessories, see below.
Weights, where published — *see* Performance tables.

Fuel, initially, was unleaded 73 Octane (DTD 134) or 77 Octane (DTD 224) but, when leaded 87 Octane (DTD 230) became available, Kestrels (except those which were de-rated) were modified or adapted to run on this fuel.

Dry weight. As in all installations, this varied from one Mark to another, depending on accessories but, for example:

Unsupercharged Kestrel I (F.XI)	884 lb.
Moderately supercharged Mk IIMS (F.XIIMS)	950 lb.
Fully supercharged Mk XVI	970 lb.

Dimensions. These also varied slightly, particularly the length according to accessories fitted but, basically were:-
Unsupercharged   L. 66.72 in;   W. 24.4 in;   H. 39.40 in.
Supercharged   L. 69.82 in;   W. 24.4 in;   H. 37.53 in.

Most Kestrels in service, ran at maximum 2,750 rpm and, when diving, had a 20-second peak limit of 3,000 rpm The Kestrel XXX peaked at 3,300 rpm

Rolls-Royce test fleet at Hucknall.

ROLLS-ROYCE F.X, 460 hp, (1927–28), 12-cylinder, upright 60-degree Vee water-cooled, poppet-valve. Bore/stroke 5 x 5.5 in. Vol. 1,295.88 cu in. (127 x 140 mm. Vol. 21.25 litre). Compression ratio 6:1. Direct (ungeared) L.H. tractor-drive. Length 66.7 in; width 24.4 in; height 39.4 in.

The progressive cleaning-up of the 60-degree Rolls-Royce layout. L-R Condor IIIA; Buzzard; Kestrel.

KESTREL IA, F.XIA, 490 hp, (1927–1928). Compression ratio 6:1. Geared, spur .632:1. R.H. tractor-drive. 18 built at Derby. *Aircraft:*

Fairey Fleetwing
Fairey Fox IA
Handley Page H.P.30 W.10
Hawker Hart
Parnall Pipit
Westland Wizard I

KESTREL IB, F.XIB, 480 hp, (1929–34), similar to Mk IA, except High compression, ratio 7:1. Geared .632:1. 580 built at Derby. Power Curve at rated 2,250 rpm, altitude 3,000 ft from A.& A.E.E., Martlesham, Report M.610, dated 26.8.30.

An unsupercharged Kestrel, the twin air intakes emerging above the centrally-mounted carburettors.

A Hawker Hart with an unsupercharged Kestrel, the carburettor intakes being visible as 'nostrils' above the cowling.

A Hawker Hart Trainer. Kestrels cannot be identified exactly by type with any certainty, except that the carburettor intakes of unsupercharged engines are visible above the cowling, whereas supercharged engines have intakes low on each side.

RPM	2,700	2,500	2,250	2,050	1,950	1,850
BHP	616	588	546	499	476	452

Max 600 bhp, 2,700 rpm, all-out level flight (5 min). Fuel 77 Octane (DTD 134). 580 built at Derby.
Aircraft:
> Avro 604 Antelope
> Hawker Audax I, Audax (India)
> Hawker Hardy (GP) I (de-rated engine on DTD 224 fuel, giving 543 hp at 2,700 rpm, 3,000 ft)
> Hawker Hart I, II, Hart (T)

KESTREL IB3, F.XIB3, 480 hp, (1934), similar to Mk I. High compression, ratio 7:1. Geared .632:1, 92 built at Derby.

KESTREL IB4, F.XIB4, 480 hp, (1934), similar to Mk I. High compression, ratio 7:1. Geared .632:1. 5 built at Derby.

KESTREL IB5, F.XIB5, 480 hp, (1934), similar to Mk I. High compression, ratio 7:1. Geared .632:1. 34 built at Derby.

KESTREL IMS, F.XIMS, 525/535 hp, (1929), similar to Mk I Compression ratio 6:1, medium supercharged, geared .632:1. 1 built at Derby.

KESTREL IS, F.XIS, 480 hp, (1928-33), similar to Mk I. Compression ratio 6:1. fully-supercharged, geared .632:1. 9 built at Derby.
Aircraft:
> Fairey Firefly II, III
> Fairey Fox IIM
> Hawker Fury I
> Hawker Hornet
> Saro A.10
> Vickers 141 Scout F.21/26
> Westland Wizard II

KESTREL IIA, F.XIIA, 490 hp, (1927–1929), similar to Mk I. Kestrel II and IIA, 31 built at Derby.
Aircraft:
> Fairey Fox IA
> Handley Page H.P.26 W.8g Hamilton
> Handley Page H.P.30 W.10

The Handley Page W.10 G-EBIX, temporarily fitted with two Rolls-Royce F.XIIAs, later known as Kestrel IIAs, thus redesignated W.8g.

KESTREL IIB, F.XIIB, 480 hp, (1933), similar to Mk II. High compression, ratio 7:1. Geared drive .553:1. 20 built at Derby.
Aircraft:
> Airco D.H.9A
> Fairey IIIF Mk IV
> Fairey Fox II
> Hawker Demon I

KESTREL IIMS, F.XIIMS, 525/535 hp, (1928–35), similar to Mk II, Compression ratio 5.5:1. Medium supercharged, geared drive .553:1. 82 built at Derby. Power Curve at rated altitude 2,000 ft from M.A.E.E., Felixstowe, Report F.114, dated 20.11.30.

RPM	2,700	2,500	2,250	2,050	1,950	1,850
BHP	620/660	603	525	471	443	415
BOOST	+1.5		+1.375			

Max boost +1.5 lb/sq inch. 558 bhp, 2,500 rpm take off to 1,000 ft or one minute. All-out level flight (five minutes), 660 bhp, 2,700 rpm. Fuel 77 Octane (DTD 134). 82 built at Derby.
Aircraft:
> Blackburn 2F.1 Nautilus
> Blackburn R.B.2 Sydney
> Fairey Fox II, III, IIIM
> Fairey S.9/30
> Fairey TSR.38
> Fairey Fleetwing
> Hawker Hart (Naval), prototype of Osprey
> Hawker Osprey I, II

Short S.10 Gurnard II
Short S.12 Singapore III (Tractor Engine)
Supermarine Southampton IV

Short S.12 Singapore II, N246, wearing the Royal Air Force Ensign at Bahrain, with awnings to protect the crew in the metal hull a little from the searing heat. The paired engines were Kestrel IIMS and IIIMS. (See text).

KESTREL IIMS, F.XIIMS (Pusher), 525/535 hp, (1928–35), similar to Mk II, Compression ratio 5.5:1. Medium supercharged, geared drive .553:1. The installation in the Singapore II was a reconditioned standard engine, except for being a pusher, with a 9 in smaller diameter propeller. M.A.E.E. Report F.73.
Aircraft:
> Short S.12 Singapore II

KESTREL IIMS.2, F.XIIMS.2, 525/535 hp, (1933–34), similar to Mk IIMS. Compression ratio 6:1. Medium supercharged, geared drive .553:1. 64 built at Derby.
Aircraft:
> Hawker Hart
> Hawker Osprey

KESTREL IIMS.5, F.IIMS.5, 525/535 hp, (1934), similar to Mk IIMS. Compression ratio 6:1. Medium supercharged, geared drive .553:1. 5 built at Derby. Power Curve at rated altitude 2,000 ft from A.& A.E.E., Martlesham, Report M.644, dated 25.1.34.

RPM	2,700	2,250	1,950
BHP	656	547	463

Fuel 77 Octane (DTD 224).
Aircraft:
> Hawker Osprey III

KESTREL IIMS.6, F.IIMS.6, 525/535 hp, (1935), similar to Mk IIMS. Compression ratio 6:1. Medium supercharged, geared drive .553:1. 16 built at Derby. Fuel 87 Octane (DTD 230).
Aircraft:
> Supermarine Scapa

KESTREL IIS, F.XIIS, 480 hp, (1928–38), similar to Mk IIMS. Compression ratio 6:1. Fully supercharged, geared drive .552:1. 605 built at Derby. The installation in the Gloster TC.33 was evaporatively-cooled and a pusher but, otherwise similar to standard Kestrel IIS engines. Power Curve at rated altitude 11,500 ft from A.& A.E.E., Martlesham, Report M.587, dated 12.6.33. Boost, rated -.5 lb/sq inch.

RPM	2,700	2,250	1,950
BHP	581	476	380
BOOST	+1.75	-.5	

Max boost +1.75 lb/sq inch. 480 bhp, 2,250 rpm take off to 1,000 ft or one minute. All-out level flight (five minutes), +1.75 lb, 550 bhp, 2,750 rpm. Fuel 77 Octane (DTD 134).
Aircraft:
> Avro 604 Antelope
> Fairey Firefly II, III
> Fairey Fox II, IIS, IIIS
> Gloster Gnatsnapper II

Gloster TC.33 C.16/28 (Pusher Engine, A. & A.E.E. Report M.618)
Hawker Demon (Hart Fighter)
Hawker Fury I
Hawker Hart
Hawker Nimrod I (originally 'Norn')

KESTREL IIIB, F.XIVB, 480 hp, similar to Mk XIVA. High compression, ratio 7:1, geared drive .475:1

KESTREL IIIMS, F.XIVMS, 515/535 hp, (1933–35), similar to Mk III. Compression ratio 5.5:1. Medium supercharged, geared drive .475:1. The installation in the Singapore III was a standard Kestrel III engine, except for being a pusher, with a reduction gear of .447:1.
Aircraft:
> Short S.12 Singapore II (Tractor — M.A.E.E. Report F.73)
> Short S.12 Singapore III (Pusher Engine)
> Supermarine Scapa

KESTREL IIIMS.2, F.XIVMS.2, 515/535 hp, (1933–34), similar to Mk III. Compression ratio 6:1. Medium supercharged, geared drive .475:1. 20 built at Derby.

KESTREL IIIMS.4, F.XIVMS.4, 515/535 hp, (1934), similar to Mk III. Compression ratio 6:1. Medium supercharged, geared drive .475:1. 16 built at Derby.

KESTREL IIIMS.6, F.XIVMS.6, 515/535 hp, (1935), similar to Mk III. Compression ratio 6:1. Medium supercharged, geared drive .475:1. 16 built at Derby. Power Curve at rated altitude 2,000 ft from M.A.E.E., Felixstowe, Report F.139, dated 25.3.30.

RPM	2,700	2,500	2,350	2,250	2,100
BHP	650	604	570	545	501
BOOST	+1.5		zero		

Max boost +1.5 lb/sq inch. 650 bhp, 2,700 rpm take off to 1,000 ft or one minute. Fuel 77 Octane (DTD 224).
Aircraft:
> Supermarine Scapa

KESTREL IIIS, F.XIVS, 480 hp, (1930–38), similar to Mk IIIMS. Compression ratio 6:1. Fully supercharged geared drive .475:1. 71 built at Derby. The installations in the Gloster TC.33, the Vickers 150 and 163 were evaporatively-cooled but, otherwise similar to standard Kestrel IIIS engines. Power Curve at rated altitude 11,500 ft, from A.& A.E.E., Martlesham, Reports M.607, M.618, dated 10.33 & 9.32. Boost, rated -.5 lb/sq inch.

RPM	2,700	2,250	2,150	2,050	1,950	1,850
BHP	581	476	447	420	389	360
BOOST	+1.75	-.5				

Max boost +1.75 lb/sq inch. 580 bhp, 2,700 rpm take off to 1,000 ft or one minute. Fuel 77 Octane (DTD 224).
Aircraft:
> Fairey B.19/27 Hendon I
> Gloster TC.33 C.16/28 (Tractor Engine, A.& A.E.E. Report M.618)
> Handley Page H.P.50 Heyford I, IA
> Hawker Hart
> Hawker Nimrod (Denmark)
> Supermarine Scapa
> Vickers 150 B.19/27
> Vickers 163 P.V. Bomber

KESTREL IIIS.3, F.XIVS.3, 480 hp, (1934), similar to Mk IIIMS. Compression ratio 6:1. Fully supercharged geared drive .475:1. 48 built at Derby.

KESTREL IV, 665/695 hp, (1935), compression ratio 6:1. Fully supercharged, geared drive .632:1 tractor-drive. 1 built at Derby. (The prototype of the Goshawk, q.v.).

The Handley Page Heyford prototype J9130, powered by Kestrel IIIS engines. Note the unusual exhausts to clear the upper wing surface.

KESTREL V, V Spl., 665/695 hp, (1933–38), compression ratio 6:1. Fully supercharged, geared drive .553:1. 1,178 built at Derby. Power Curve at rated altitude 11,000 ft, from A.& A.E.E., Martlesham, Report M.594, dated 22.2.35. Boost, rated +1.5 lb/sq inch. Max +3.5 lb/sq inch., 2,900 rpm

A Hawker Osprey IV fleet fighter, with a Kestrel V and 'kidney' exhausts.

RPM	2,900	2,700	2,500	2,300	2,100
BHP	742	677	608	532	455
BOOST	+3.5		+1.5		-.43

Fuel 87 Octane (DTD 230).
Aircraft:
    Fairey Fox III, IIIC
    Hawker Demon I, II (Turret)
    Hawker Fury
    Hawker Hart (Kestrel V Spl, evaporative cooling)
    Hawker Hart I, Hart (India)
    Hawker Hart Fighter (Demon)
    Hawker Hartbees
    Hawker Hind I, Hind (T)
    Hawker Nimrod I
    Hawker Osprey IV
    Heinkel He 70G
    Junkers Ju 87 prototype
    Messerschmitt Bf 109a(V1) prototype

KESTREL VDR, 492 hp, (1937), de-rated version, similar to Mk V. Compression ratio 6:1. Fully supercharged, geared drive .553:1. Power Curve at rated altitude 11,000 ft, from A.& A.E.E., Martlesham, Report M.587, dated 31.7.37.

RPM	2,350	2,350	2,010
BHP	566	473	492
BOOST	+2.25	zero	+2.25

Max boost +2.25 lb/sq inch. 492 bhp, 2,010 rpm take off to 1,000 ft or one minute. All-out level flight (five minutes), -.35 lb, 508 bhp, 2,350 rpm, 12,000 ft. Fuel 77 Octane (DTD 224).
Aircraft:
    Hawker Demon I, Turret
    Hawker Hart
    Hawker Hind I

KESTREL VI, 665/695 hp, (1934–1936). Compression ratio 6:1. Fully supercharged, geared drive .477:1. 258 built at Derby. Power Curve at rated altitude 11,000 ft from A.& A.E.E., Martlesham, Report M.607, dated 9.5.35.

RPM	2,900	2,700	2,500	2,300	2,100
BHP	740	679	608	533	455
BOOST	+6		+1.5		

Max boost +6 lb/sq inch. 740 bhp, 2,700 rpm take off to 1,000 ft or one minute. All-out level flight (five minutes), +1.5 lb, 640 bhp, 2,900 rpm. Fuel 87 Octane (DTD 230).
Aircraft:
    Fairey Hendon II
    Handley Page H.P.50 Heyford II, III
    Hawker Demon I, II (Turret)
    Hawker Fury II
    Hawker Hart

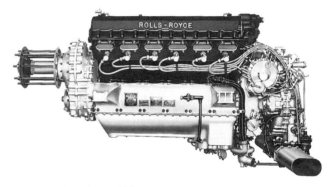

The supercharged Kestrel VI.

Production line of Hawker Furies, supercharged Kestrels installed.

The Handley Page Heyford III, powered by Kestrel VI engines. The engine cowlings may be compared with the Kestrel IIIS installation.

Hawker High-Speed Fury K3586, with tapered wings, and a Kestrel VI.

KESTREL VII, 675/700 hp, Compression ratio 6:1. Medium supercharged, geared drive .632:1

KESTREL VIII, 675/700 hp, (1935–36). Compression ratio 6:1. Medium supercharged, geared drive .553:1 pusher drive. 133 built at Derby.
Aircraft:
        Short S. Singapore III (Pusher Engine)

KESTREL IX, 675/700 hp, (1934–36), similar to Mk VIII. Compression ratio 6:1. Medium supercharged geared drive .477:1. 136 built at Derby.
Aircraft:
        Short S. Singapore III (Tractor Engine)

KESTREL X, 520/545, (1934–36), high compression, ratio 7:1. Geared drive .632:1. 1,161 built at Derby. Power Curve at rated altitude sea level to 2,000 ft, from A.& A.E.E., Martlesham, Report M.669, dated 15.6.36.

RPM	2,900	2,700	2,500	2,300	2,100
BHP	636	617	581	541	493

Max 636 bhp, 2,900 rpm, all-out level flight (5 min). Fuel 87 Octane (DTD 230).
Aircraft:
        Hawker Audax I, Audax (India)
        Hawker Hardy
        Hawker Hart, Hart (T)

KESTREL XDR, 500/525 hp, (1937), de-rated version, similar to Mk X. High compression, ratio 7:1. Geared drive .632:1.
Aircraft:
        Hawker Audax I
        Hawker Hardy
        Hawker Hart, Hart (T)

KESTREL XI, 520/545 hp, (1935–36). High compression, ratio 7:1. Geared drive .553:1. 55 built at Derby.

KESTREL XII, 520/545 hp, high compression, ratio 7:1. Geared drive .477:1

KESTREL XIV, 640/670 hp, higher rated than Mks IV, V and VI, with single-entry to the supercharger. Compression ratio 6:1. Fully supercharged, geared drive .632:1

KESTREL XV, 640/670 hp, Similar to Mk XIV. Compression ratio 6:1. Fully supercharged geared drive .553:1

KESTREL XVI, XVI Spl., 640/670 hp, (1936–38), a developed Mk V, similar to Mk XIV. Compression ratio 6:1. Fully supercharged and with geared drive .477:1. 95 built at Derby.
Aircraft:
        Hawker Fury II
        Hawker Hart, Hart (T)
        Hawker Hind (Jugoslav)
        Heinkel He 70G
        Junkers Ju 86 (Civil version, S.A.Airways)

KESTREL XVI(DR), 640/670 hp, (1937), de-rated version, similar to Mk XVI. Compression ratio 6:1. Fully supercharged. Geared drive .477:1
Aircraft:
        Hawker Audax I
        Hawker Hart

KESTREL XVI(VP), 640/670 hp, converted from Mk V. Compression ratio 6:1. V/P prop. Fully supercharged geared drive .477:1. Power Curve at rated altitude 12,250 ft from A.& A.E.E., Martlesham, Report M.719, dated 1.3.37.

RPM	3,000	2,750	2,600	2,400	2,200
BHP	773	690	642	566	496
BOOST	+3.25	+3.25	+2.25		

Max boost +6 lb/sq inch. 670 bhp, 2,750 rpm take off to 1,000 ft or one minute. All-out level flight (five minutes), +3.25 lb, 715 bhp, 3,000 rpm. Fuel 87 Octane (DTD 230).
Aircraft:
        Miles M.9 'Kestrel'

Heinkel He 70G used by Rolls-Royce at Hucknall, from its arrival 1936 with a Kestrel V, as a test-bed for Kestrel XVI and Peregrine engines. In this case a Kestrel XVI(VP).

The prototype Miles M.9 'Kestrel' trainer, with Kestrel XVI(VP).

KESTREL XXX, 720 hp, (1938), compression ratio 6.2:1. Fully supercharged, geared drive .553:1 V/P C/S prop. Power Curve at rated altitude 12,500 ft from A.& A.E.E., Martlesham, Report M.719, dated 18.1.39.

RPM	2,750	2,600	2,400	2,200	2,000
BHP	647	599	529	454	382
BOOST	+1.6	+.85	zero	-.45	-1.75

Max boost +5 lb/sq inch. 720 bhp, 2,750 rpm take off to 1,000 ft or one minute. All-out level flight (five minutes), +.5 lb, 585 bhp, 2,750 rpm. Fuel 87 Octane (DTD 230).
Aircraft:
        Miles M.9A Master I
        Miles M.24 Master Fighter

The Kestrel XXX, the ultimate Kestrel fitted to the Miles M.9A Master I.

It will be noted that the seemingly endless variants of the basic Hawker Hart airframe were used as test-beds for almost the whole Kestrel range, as well as for other makes of engine, thanks to its remarkable adaptability. To identify supercharged Kestrels with their twin-choke updraught carburettors, the two air intakes could easily be identified by small 'nostrils', low down on each side of the cowling. Unsupercharged engines had twin 'nostrils' side by side on the upper cowling panel, feeding a pair of separate Duplex carburettors mounted between the cylinder blocks.

GOSHAWK, (1933).

This was an experimental series of twenty engines, evolved from the Kestrel IV. Its purpose was to investigate the possibilities and the properties of evaporative-cooling (sometimes called 'steam-cooling', a rather misleading term), thereby reducing the size of the radiator and cooling drag, even the possible elimination of the radiator altogether. Looking at the principle of latent heat, when water boils the process of producing steam takes in a very large amount of heat. Therefore, if the water in the cylinder heads is allowed to boil and the resultant steam is piped to a condenser mounted in the air stream so as to convert it back to water before returning it to the engine, it can be a very much more efficient cooling system than a normal air-cooled water radiator, or heat exchanger and can be made virtually drag-free. Unfortunately, the operative word is 'can' and there were problems.

In the Goshawk installation, the coolant in the jackets was allowed to boil and the mixture of steam and water separated in the header tank. The hot water was immediately returned to the inlet side of the circulating pump. The steam, after passing through a condenser, returned to the water state and was returned to the circuit by means of a gear-type pump. This system caused difficulties which compounded those inherent with the pressures which the steam itself generated. A great deal of work was done in collaboration with aircraft manufacturers, notably Hawker, to produce a satisfactory installation. A notable example was the High Speed Fury which had a trial installation with condensers installed flush with the leading edge of the upper wing surface and eliminated the radiator altogether. The system was excellent in theory and worked adequately but steam separation was a difficult problem, with the risk of vapour-locking. It eliminated drag but resulted in a slightly heavier installation. Experience with these engines showed that, in addition to the great difficulty in preventing plumbing leaks in the pressurised cooling system, the large area of the condensers made it much more vulnerable to enemy attack than the conventional radiator. A total of twenty Goshawks were built in 1933 and, although it was dropped, much was learned from it in the development of later pressure-cooled systems, notably in the Merlin.

GOSHAWK I, (1932). Experimental engine developed from the prototype (and only) Kestrel IV. 12-cylinder, upright 60-degree Vee, evaporatively-cooled, poppet-valve. Bore/stroke 5.0 x 5.5 in. (127 x 140 mm. Vol. 21.25 litre). Compression ratio 6:1, fully

supercharged, geared, spur .632:1. R.H. tractor-drive. 20 built at Derby, most converted to other Marks.
Aircraft:
Westland-Hill Pterodactyl V F.7/30

GOSHAWK II, (Experimental engine), 600 hp, (1935), similar to Mk I, fully supercharged. Geared, spur, .553:1 (on extended shaft in Westland F.7/30). Power Curve at rated altitude 12,000 ft from A.& A.E.E., Martlesham, Report M.676, dated 9.6.34. Boost, rated +1.5 lb/sq inch.

RPM	3,000	2,800	2,600	2,400	2,200
BHP	722	664	602	524	450
BOOST	+3.0		+1.5		

Max boost +3.0 lb/sq inch. 722 bhp, 3,000 rpm take off to 1,000 ft or one minute. Fuel 77 Octane (DTD 224).
Aircraft:
Supermarine 224 F.7/30 'Spitfire'
Westland-Hill Pterodactyl V F.7/30

The experimental Supermarine F.7/30 with a Goshawk evaporatively-cooled engine.

GOSHAWK III, 600 hp, (1935), fully supercharged, similar to Mk II. Geared, spur .477:1.
Aircraft:
Blackburn F.3 (Taxi only)
Bristol 123
Gloster Gnatsnapper III
Gloster TSR.38
Hawker P.V.3
Hawker 'High Speed' Fury

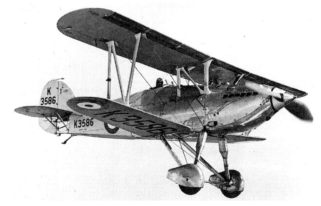

The Hawker High-Speed Fury with a Goshawk III, an experimental engine intended to make use of evaporative cooling to eliminate the drag of a conventional radiator. Steam condensers are mounted in the upper wing leading edges.

GOSHAWK VI, 660 hp, medium supercharged. Geared, spur, .632:1.

GOSHAWK VII, 660 hp, medium supercharged. Geared, spur, .553:1

GOSHAWK VIII Special (Experimental engine), 660 hp, medium supercharged, 7.4:1. Evaporative cooling. Geared, spur, .477:1. Power Curve at rated altitude 3,000 ft from M.A.E.E., Felixstowe Report F.130, dated 8.9.34. Boost, rated +3.75 lb/sq inch.

RPM	3,000	2,800	2,600	2,400	2,200
BHP	837	779	720	650	578
BOOST	+5.75		+3.75		

Max boost +5.75 lb/sq inch., 837 bhp, 3,000 rpm, take off to 1,000 ft or one minute. Fuel 87 Octane (DTD 230).
Aircraft:

 Short S.18 'Knuckleduster' R.24/31.

Experimental Goshawk VIII evaporatively-cooled engines in the Short S.18, built to Specification R.24/31. Though a handsome flying boat, it is inelegantly shown on a beaching chassis at Felixstowe, betraying its nickname 'Knuckleduster'.

PEREGRINE I, 880 hp, (1938–1942) single speed, medium supercharged. +9 lb, 3,000 rpm A medium-level engine, the ultimate development of the Kestrel, using many components from the Mks V and XVI. The design used the early experience with the Merlin, auxiliaries and a new supercharger. A downdraught carburettor was employed. 12-cylinder, upright 60-degree Vee, 70-30 per cent water/ethylene-glycol pressure-cooled, poppet-valve. Bore/stroke 5.0 x 5.5 in, Vol. 1,296 cu in. (127 x 139.7 mm. Vol. 21.24 l.). Compression ratio 6:1, Geared, spur .477:1. R.H. tractor-drive. Length 73.6 in; width 27.1 in; height 41.0 in. 301 built at Derby.
Aircraft:

 Gloster F.9/37
 Heinkel He 70G
 Westland Whirlwind I

The Rolls-Royce Peregrine, developed from the Kestrel but showing its down-draught carburettor.

The black prototype Westland Whirlwind, looking menacing even without its four cannon, was powered by the Rolls-Royce Peregrine.

ROLLS-ROYCE 'H' BUZZARD.

Following the successful testing of the ungeared version of the 'F' engine (to be named Kestrel), in 1927 Royce saw the imminent need for a much more powerful engine and, using the same basic design but scaled up by over 70 per cent in cubic capacity, the 'H' engine was produced. It was moderately supercharged to 5,000 feet, delivering 825 hp at a normal rpm of 2,000 and a maximum of 920 at 2,300 and it was, at Royce's express instruction, considerably strengthened. To his great pleasure, the new engine, to be named Buzzard, was test run as early as June 1928.

BUZZARD IMS, H.XIMS, (1927), 12-cylinder, upright 60-degree Vee, water-cooled, poppet-valve. The general design was similar to that of the 'F' type, or Kestrel and had the following in common:-

Bore/stroke 6.0 x 6.6 in.
Swept Volume 2,239.3 cu in. (36.7 litres).
Compression Ratio 5.5:1; 5.53:1.
Approximate dimensions;
length 75.7 in; width 30.6 in; height 44.4 in.
Weights, where published — *see* Performance tables.

Compression ratio 5:1, single-speed, medium supercharged 5.59:1 impeller ratio. Geared, spur .632:1. R.H. tractor-drive, 9 built at Derby.
Aircraft:

 Hawker Horsley
 Short S.5 Singapore I
 Short-Kawanishi S.15 K.F.1

BUZZARD IIMS, H.XIIMS, 825 hp, (1932–33), similar to Mk I note compression ratio 5.53:1. Medium supercharged, geared .553:1. R.H. tractor-drive. 69 built at Derby.
Aircraft:

 Blackburn R.B.1 Iris V
 Blackburn R.B.3A Perth

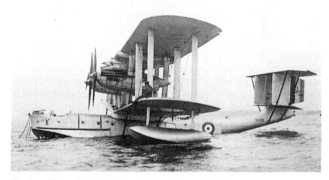

The Blackburn R.B.1 Iris V, with three Buzzard IIMS.

The Rolls-Royce Buzzard IIMS.

BUZZARD IIIMS, H.XIVMS, 825 hp, (1931-33), similar to Mk IIMS note compression ratio 5.5:1. Medium supercharge, impeller ratio 5.59:1. Geared drive .477:1 R.H. tractor-drive. 22 built at Derby. Power Curve at rated altitude S/L, from A.& A.E.E., Martlesham, Report M.621, dated 7.6.32. Medium supercharged, boost not quoted.

RPM	2.300	2,100	2,000	1,900	1,800	1,600
BHP	937	863	825	784	742	642

Aircraft:

> Blackburn B.3, M.1/30, M.1/30A
> Handley Page H.P.46
> Hawker Horsley
> Short S.14 Sarafand R.6/28
> Vickers 207 M.1/30

'R'-TYPE RACING ENGINE, 1929–1931. Although in failing health, Royce continued to control the design and manufacture of the company's engines and, in particular, building racing engines for the Schneider Trophy contests. In the contests before 1929, Napier Lion engines, had dominated the British challenges. By 1927 the Lion, which won it that year, had clearly reached the peak of its potential performance and the Italian challenge needed to be taken very seriously. Royce decided to go ahead with the development of a new engine to take the racing Lion's place and chose the Buzzard design as a basis for the new project. Much of the design work was undertaken by A.J. Rowledge ('Rg'), who had earlier joined Rolls from Napier. Although the moving parts had a great deal in common, it amounted to a new engine. Royce clearly had something up his sleeve when he directed the strengthening to be built into the Buzzard. In the event, for example, the two additional holding-down saddle studs per cylinder, enabled the engine's structure to withstand the enormous stress when its power output was almost trebled as a racing engine.

The go-ahead for the new engine was not given until February 1929, with the contest just over six months away. The requirement was for an engine delivering 1,500 hp, weighing 1lb/hp. The effort required from Derby was phenomenal, including the design of a new and bigger double-sided supercharger impeller, redesigned cylinders, improved valve-cooling and valve covers which were angled so as to reduce drag. Tests showed that the forked connecting rods required strengthening. Enormous efforts were made by the development team led by Hives and Lovesey. On its first run, the 'R' engine delivered 1,545 hp at 2,750 rpm and, for the race, it delivered 1,900 hp at 3,000 rpm and +13.5 lb boost continuously. It is hard to realize that this remarkable engine, designed for sustained high power, idled happily at 450 rpm.

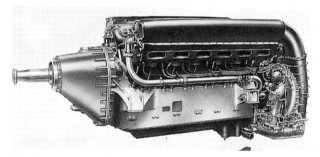

The Supermarine S.6 seaplane's 'R' racing engine, which won the Schneider Trophy contest of 1929.

R.J. Mitchell's Supermarine S.6, flown by Waghorn, won the Schneider Contest in 1929 at 328.65 mph, a clear 42 mph faster than the nearest competitor. That was two in a row and, to win it outright, a third successive win was required. Inexplicably, the British Government decided not to enter for the next contest in 1931. Then, private intervention by Lady Houston who put up the then enormous sum of £100,000, finally shamed the Government into action and, with barely six months to go before the 1931 race, Royce and Mitchell were able to pursue the proven combination of engine and seaplane. Hives and his team managed to increase the power of the 'R' engine to 2,350 hp with 17.5 lb boost and 3,100 rpm, thereby enabling Flt. Lt. J.N. Boothman in the S.6B to gain the Trophy for the third time and outright for Britain, at 340 mph average.

What was not apparent to most people was the huge job of redesign work involved, in particular a reversion to the master and articulated connecting rod assembly, instead of fork and blade, to take account of the enormous loads involved, as well as a redesigned crankshaft and, for the first time, sodium-cooled exhaust valves. The 'R' engine, which had enabled Mitchell's Supermarine S.6B seaplane to claim the Schneider Trophy outright for Britain on 13 September 1931, this remarkable seaplane, with a sprint 'R' engine and with some very exotic fuel, immediately went on to gain, briefly, the World's Speed Record at 407.5 mph on 29 September 1931, before losing it to Italy. The development of the fuel which made this possible is a story in itself and it was largely due to the genius of Rod Banks. Using his famous 'cocktail', a witch's brew comprising methanol, benzol, acetone and tetra-ethyl-lead (TEL) the special engine on the Record flight delivered 2,530 hp at 3,200 rpm. It was cleared for a special sprint rating of 2,783 hp at 3,400 rpm. This was three times the power of the Buzzard, although this capability was not, in the end, used because of doubts of whether the airframe could usefully absorb such enormous power.

The 'R' engine was a 12-cylinder, upright, 60-degree Vee, water-cooled, poppet-valve. Bore/stroke 6.0 x 6.6 in. Vol. 2,239 cu in. (152.4 x 167.6 mm, Vol. 36.7 litre). Compression ratio 6:1, with a single speed, double-sided supercharger, four Duplex updraught RR-Claudel-Hobson carburettors. Exhaust valves with hollow stems were filled with metallic sodium for rapid heat transfer. The propeller was geared, spur .6:1. R.H. tractor-drive. Fixed-pitch Fairey-Reed type propeller.

For the 1929 and 1931 Contests (as well as air, land and water speed record-breaking events) a total of 20 engines were built at Derby. The 1929 engines had a supercharger ratio of 7.034:1 and ran on fuel comprising 22 per cent Romanian petrol and 78 per cent benzol, with 3 cc/Imperial gallon TEL.

The 1931 Schneider engines developed 2,350 hp at 3,200 rpm and +17.5 lb boost, the supercharger drive ratio being 7.47:1. The fuel 'Cocktail' devised by R.R. Banks, comprised 20 per cent Californian petrol, 70 per cent benzol, 10 per cent methanol plus 4 cc TEL, about 92 Octane.

The 407 mph Speed Record was achieved on 29 September, 1931 using an engine still further improved in power output. This increase was not achieved without difficulty and a few mechanical failures but, on the twelfth run, a 60 minute full-throttle run was achieved and the engine cleared for a safe life of five hours. The additional power was achieved thanks largely to a very exotic and potent mixture devised by Banks, which allowed a slight increase in boost, at greater rpm, while retaining the same supercharger ratio. In this case, the fuel comprised 30 per cent benzol, 60 per cent methanol and 10 per cent acetone plus 5 cc/Imperial gallon TEL. Apart from its great toxicity from handling and breathing, the use of TEL had to be carefully watched because of its harmful effects on sparking plugs. The methanol content was in effect a consumable inter-cooler. Approx. dimensions; length 100 in; width 32 in; height 42 in.

Aircraft:

> Supermarine S.6 (N247), 1929
> S.6A, S.6B (S1595), 1931

The final 1931 version of the 'R' engine whose huge power output enabled the Supermarine S.6B to win the Schneider Trophy outright and gain, if briefly, the World's Speed Record in 1931.

Supermarine S.6B, S1596 at Calshot, one of the pair which between them, on 13 September 1931, won the Schneider Trophy outright and, in this case, also broke the World's Absolute speed record, both aircraft powered by the 'R' racing engine.

VULTURE I, 1,800 hp, (1939), resembled two Kestrel-sized Vee-12 units with a common crankshaft mounted on a common crankcase, with a two-speed, single-stage supercharger. A 24-cylinder, 90-degree X-shaped engine. Virtually two Peregrines, one above the other on a single crankcase and with all four banks of connecting rods operating on a single crankshaft. In order to avoid different cylinder spacings on upper and lower halves, keeping all four pistons on the same centre line, the usual Rolls-Royce fork and blade arrangement was impractical and it was decided to anchor all four big-ends on a single crankpin. This arrangement led to many development troubles, fatigue and other failures, including lubrication in the lower cylinders, connecting rod and big-end bearings. Some cylinder blocks were damaged as a result of failure of the coolant system. There were two coolant pumps in parallel but one pump could suffer a breakdown in flow due to cavitation at the inlet, while the other maintained full flow.

The troubled 24-cylinder Vulture engine, in X formation and a direct descendant of the Kestrel/Peregrine series.

The solution lay in introducing a balance pipe between the two inlets. Although the engine eventually achieved about 3,000 hp, it was finally abandoned in favour of the Merlin. The engine was 70/30 per cent water/ethylene-glycol cooled, poppet-valve. Bore/stroke 5.0 x 5.5 in, Vol. 25.92 cu in. (127 x 139.7 mm. Vol. 42.47 litre). Compression ratio 6:1 Two-speed, single-stage supercharged, 5.5:1, 7.3:1, with a downdraught S.U. carburettor. Geared, spur with four layshafts, reduction .35:1. L.H. tractor-drive. Fuel 87 Octane (DTD 230). The total number built was 538.
Aircraft:

> Avro 679 Manchester I, IA
> Hawker Henley

VULTURE II, similar to the Vulture I, a two-speed, single-stage supercharger. A 24-cylinder, 90-degree X-shaped 70/30 per cent water/ethylene-glycol cooled poppet-valve engine. Bore/stroke 5.0 x 5.5 in, Vol. 25.92 cu in. (127 x 139.7 mm. Vol. 42.47 litre). Compression ratio 6:1. Two-speed, single-stage supercharged. L.H. tractor-drive. Fuel 100 Octane.

Aircraft:

> Avro 679 Manchester I, IA
> Blackburn B-20
> Hawker Henley
> Hawker Tornado I F.18/37
> Vickers 284 Warwick B.1/35

The prototype Hawker Henley L5115 used as a flying test bed for the Vulture II. The intake for the down-draught carburettor stands rather untidily above the cowling.

Avro 679 Manchester I (L7432), of 207 Squadron with two Rolls-Royce Vulture II engines. Troubled development of the Vulture led to the redesign of the Manchester as the very successful Lancaster, with four Merlins.

The Hawker Tornado, similar to the early-type Typhoon but with, in this case, a Rolls-Royce Vulture V engine. The air intake has been moved forward to improve the ram-effect to the carburettor and supercharger.

VULTURE V, the ultimate development of the Vulture which, had it had the chance, could have been a successful engine. However, pressure of Merlin production led to its abandonment. It had a two-speed, single-stage supercharger. As the previous models, it was a 24-cylinder, 90-degree X-shaped 70/30 per cent water /ethylene-glycol cooled poppet-valve engine. Bore/stroke 5.0 x 5.5 in, Vol. 25.92 cu in. (127 x 139.7 mm. Vol. 42.47 litre). Compression ratio 6:1. It was two-speed, single-stage supercharged. Geared, layshaft spur, reduction .35:1. L.H. tractor-drive.
Aircraft:
    Hawker Tornado I

EXE, 1,150 hp/4,200 rpm, (1936), originally to be named Boreas but the name was dropped because it infringed Bristol's Greek mythology names. It differed in many ways from the traditional Rolls-Royce design, in having master and articulated connecting rods in a 24-cylinder, 90-degree X-shaped, layout. It was efficiently pressure air-cooled with very low-drag, sleeve-valve. Bore/stroke 4.2 x 4.0 in. Vol. 1,348 cu in. (Vol. 22.1 litre). Compression ratio 8:1, two-speed .4265:1, 5.6:1, single-stage supercharged. Geared, spur .358:1. L.H. tractor-drive, V/P, C/S propeller. 100 Octane fuel. Originally intended for the Fairey Barracuda but dropped in favour of Merlin production. It featured coil ignition instead of magnetos. It ran with little trouble in a Fairey Battle but consumed unusually large amounts of oil. First flown 30.11.38. RB.1SM. Fuel 100 Octane.
Aircraft:
    Fairey Battle I.

The pressure air-cooled Rolls-Royce Exe, development of which was overtaken by the urgency of wartime Merlin production. It flew happily in Rolls-Royce's Fairey Battle but suffered from a formidable rate of oil consumption.

ROLLS-ROYCE P.V.12 MERLIN, (Private Venture, 12-cylinder). It is worthy of note here that A.C.Lovesey, Deputy Director of Engineering at Derby said, in a Sir Henry Royce Memorial Lecture, before the Royal Aeronautical Society in 1966, that one of the early design investigations, leading to the P.V.12 was an inverted engine. The general idea was to give a pilot a better view ahead, with the bonus of better cylinder head cooling. He also recalled, somewhat wryly, that a mockup of the engine was on display in 1933 on the occasion of a high level visit to Derby by German Government representatives and engineers, some from Junkers and Daimler-Benz, who showed a particular interest in it. To what extent this was mischievously intended to mislead or indeed had any effect on subsequent engines built by those two firms is not recorded but the fact is that the Merlin was built 'the right way up' and the roughly comparable German engines, inverted.

NOTE: In the interest of consistency throughout the book, Merlins, built by Rolls-Royce and Packard, referred to in the text and data pages are listed, like other engines, alpha/numerically. In view of the great variety and complexity of the Merlin family, in the following tables they have also been broken down into family groups, the divisions being determined by the three major variations

in the methods and degrees of supercharging. Readers unfamiliar with the pattern of Merlin development can more easily locate the type looked for.

THE MERLIN FAMILY GROUPS COMPARED.

SINGLE-SPEED, SINGLE-STAGE SUPERCHARGED MERLINS.
P.V.12 Prototype. Merlin B, C, E, F, G. Merlin I, II, II (Special), III, IV, V, VIII, XII, 30, 32, 35, 38, 45, 45M, 46, 47, 50, 50A, 50M, 55, 55A,

TWO-SPEED, SINGLE-STAGE SUPERCHARGED MERLINS.
Merlin X, XX, 21, 22, 22A, 23, 23A, 24, T.24/2, T.24/4, 25, 27, 28, 29, 29, 31, 33, T.34, 38, 224, 225, 228, 500, 500/29, 500/45, 501.
PACKARD (Merlin) V-1650-1.

TWO-SPEED, TWO-STAGE SUPERCHARGED MERLINS.
Merlin 60, 61, 63, 63A, 64, 65, 66, 67, 68, 6 A, 69, 70, 71, 72, 73, 76, 77, 85, 85B, 102, 102A, 104, 110, 112, 113, 113A, 114, 114A, 130, 131, 132, 133, 134, 135, 140, 150, 266, 300, 301, 600, 604, 620, 621, 622, 623, 624, 626-1, 626-12, 722, 724-1, 724-1C, 724-10.
PACKARD (Merlin) V-1650-3, V-1650-5, V-1650-7, V-1650-9, V-1650-9A, V-1650-11, V-1650-21, V-1650-23, V-1650-25.

British and American-built Merlins and Packard V-1650s compared.

British Built Rolls-Royce Merlins	Equivalent American-Built Engines	
	Packard Merlin	Packard V-1650
Mks I-XX, 21, 22, 22A	28, 29, 31, 33, 38	V-1650-1
23, 23A, 24/T.24, 25, 27	224, 225, 228	
30, 32, 35, 45-55MA		
60		
61-67	69, 266, 300, 301	V-1650-3
70-77	V-1650-5	
85, 85B	68, 68A, 69, 300	V-1650-7
86-150		V-1650-9/9A
		V-1650-11, 21
		V-1650-23, 25
500, 600, 700 srs.		

The Merlin appeared in many variants and was built in enormous numbers. Instead of joining the aircraft industry's Shadow Factory scheme run by the motor car industry, Rolls-Royce chose to build their own factories, first at Crewe, with a conveniently direct rail and road link with Derby. This was started in May 1938 and came into production in 1939, the Derby works itself being considerably expanded. Shortly afterwards, a new factory was begun near Glasgow, at Hillington, production starting in 1941. Ernest Hives (later Lord Hives), on the outbreak of war, expressed the fervent belief that Britain had to win — there was little point in coming a good second. By the time of the Munich crisis, 1,700 Merlins had already been built, although only 400 were installed. The Crewe factory was started in May 1938 but, by the start of the Battle of Britain, 2,000 Merlins had been produced. The Ford Motor Co was asked to join in and, after some delay caused by a perceived need on the part of Ford to re-tool the Merlin for mass-production, from 1941 the Ford works at Trafford Park, Manchester began to produce Merlins reaching a rate of over 200 per week. In 1943, the factories at Derby, Crewe and Glasgow were jointly turning out engines at a rate of 18,000 a year.

There were not really major differences between British and American Merlins. The supercharger drive was different and so were the carburettors and magnetos. Otherwise, the engines were very similar and collaboration between Derby, Glasgow and Packard was very close. On the outbreak of the Second World War, the Government asked Rolls-Royce to send a set of Merlin drawings to the U.S. Government for safe-keeping. In June 1940 just before the Battle of Britain, the U.S. Commissioner for Industrial Production asked Packard if the company would undertake the production of 9,000 Merlin XXs, 6,000 for Britain and 3,000 for the U.S. Government. Henry Ford had turned down a similar request because he had little confidence in Britain's chances of survival and also because of the difficulties of modifying production techniques. Within two days, a memorandum was agreed to produce the engines, the only modifications required being those enabling the engine to accept U.S. approved standardized carburettors, propellers, magnetos etc.

Within one month, Packard had set up an engineering organization at Detroit and a month later, a team from Derby arrived. The exchange of information and drawings between Packard and Rolls-Royce became a flood, as did the flow of engines for the Royal Air Force and the Commonwealth Air Forces, as well as the U.S.A.A.F.

The first crucial question immediately following concerned the type of cylinder block to be produced. The existing one-piece block was difficult to produce and prone to coolant leaks. It was decided that Packard should build Rolls-Royce's newly-designed two-piece block as it was not possible to change Rolls's production lines quickly. Packard was therefore asked to proceed at once with the new two-piece blocks and, in fact, the first British engine fitted with a two-piece block was delivered shortly after Packard. It was a Merlin 61, despatched from Derby's Nightingale Road works, on Christmas Day 1941.

Packard did their own block design on the Merlin 28, with a different form of coolant transfer between the head and skirt, taking the form of an external transfer. From the Merlin 38 onwards, however, Packard engines used a British type design of block, with conventional transfer ferrules. This was considered to be a better solution to the problem. Packard-built engines were therefore the first to have them and, after a very rapid re-drawing of the Merlin to conform to American practice, the first two Packard-built Merlin XXs were run in August 1941 and the engine was in full production in 1942. Packard engines all had British screw threads and not American ones. They continued the use of Whitworth and B.S.F. threads, previously almost unknown in U.S. industry. In addition, Packard instituted cadmium plating to reduce corrosion of bolts and contributed major design changes. These included the introduction of the Bendix-Stromberg carburettor; an automatic Farman-type two-speed supercharger drive with a friction clutch; the use, in a few late Merlin versions, of water-methanol injection for charge-cooling; an improved coolant pump; an oil separator to reduce foaming and a new magneto capable of operating at over 50,000 feet. It is sad to relate that, production having already ceased, the day after Japan's surrender, the Packard gates were locked and Merlin crankshafts were flung from upper windows into waiting trucks for scrap.

Although there are fine distinctions between the Rolls-Royce Merlin, the Packard-built Merlin and the Packard V-1650 engines, visually and aurally, they were effectively all Merlins and those engines built by Packard for the Royal Air Force were still called Merlins. The engines built specifically for use in American aircraft, were properly called V-1650s and all Mustangs built for the Royal Air Force were powered by these engines. (The figure related to the cubic capacity, U.S.-built engines being quoted to the nearest 5 cu in, rather than in the European style of cc or litres). Such engines had American propeller splines, whereas those with Merlin Mark numbers had SBAC propeller splines.

All Packard-built engines, whether with Merlin numbers or V-1650s, had Bendix-Stromberg carburettors (unless of the very late types of two-stage, fuel-injected engines) and, although they had an epicyclic-geared supercharger drive, the ratios were the same as used by Rolls-Royce. This latter was essentially a friction-clutch operated mechanism, with a camshaft to enable change of gear to take place by placing or relieving load on the clutch weight fingers. (The epicyclic gearbox works just as a conventional epicyclic drive does, by putting a brake on a gear). In addition, the Packard engines had American magnetos, although they were built to suit the Merlin pattern. The quality of the American engines was very high and, comparing like with like and accepting that all engines, especially

when first introduced present problems, there was nothing to choose between them.

Confusion has existed ever since as to exactly how each British Merlin related to its American equivalent and has been the source of much work and research, amid endless contradictions in articles and books published in the past fifty years. To record every detail of every variation would take several volumes and, in this book, it is possible to select only a few as pointers to the reasons for their adoption and use. Alec Harvey-Bailey, who was Head of the Merlin Defect Investigation Department and the possessor of a phenomenal memory, has provided the majority of the details of the Merlin, despite ill-health and it is entirely thanks to him and to the back-up information provided by the Rolls-Royce Heritage Trust, headed by Mike Evans, that the figures can be regarded as authentic. Details of the output of new Merlins from the several factories (and of the Griffon which followed it) are taken from contemporary Company records. It should be stressed that there were numerous sub-variants of particular models which were modified after despatch from the works and their numbers, therefore, will be included in the parent heading, not necessarily appearing under the precise heading.

The output of Merlins was enormous. It is worth mentioning that the Merlin was produced in larger numbers than any other piston engine the World has seen and this includes all the big American radials. This, of course, has to be put into the proper context of the environment in which the engine was intended to exist. Quite apart from the large number of single-engine fighters and twin-engined Mosquitos, the majority of Lancasters and Halifaxes had four of them and it was not uncommon therefore for at least 80–100 engines to be lost in a single night's raid and sometimes rather a lot more. By March 1944 the British factories, plus Packard in the United States, had turned out 100,000 Merlins and, by the end of the European War in 1945 over 165,000 Merlins had been completed. Rolls-Royce, at Derby built 32,377, Crewe built 26,065 and Glasgow 23,647. Ford built 30,428 Merlins at the big Trafford Park works. The output in the United States, from Packard, was 55,523 of which 37,143 were Merlins and 18,380 were V-1650s. The eventual total reached a phenomenal 168,040.

The Merlin engine was a 12-cylinder, upright 60-degree Vee, liquid-cooled, poppet-valve engine. All Merlins had the following in common:-

---

Bore/stroke 5.4 x 6.0 in. (137.0 x 152.0 mm)
Swept Volume 1,637.0 cu in. (27.0 litres).
Compression Ratio 6.0:1.
Dimensions, (inches approx), according to accessories.

	Length	Width	Height
Single-speed supercharger	69.0	29.8	41.2
Two-speed supercharger	71.0	29.8	43.0
Two-speed, two-stage supercharger	88.7	30.7	40.0

Weights, where published — *see* Performance tables.

Spur-geared, reduction ratio varied, as in text, all having right-hand tractor-drive. All had variable-pitch propellers, (exceptions being prototype engine installations and the earliest Squadron Hurricanes and Spitfires as well as the 'sprint' installation in the high-speed Spitfire), and all but the early Merlin Is and IIs were equipped with constant-speed units or were converted to them. Fuel, initially, was DTD 230, (87 Octane) but 100 Octane became available from early 1940. From then on, most Merlins ran on this fuel or later grades. All standard Merlins, in service, ran at 3,000 rpm on take-off and, when diving, had a 20-second peak limit of 3,600 rpm

The original Merlin had a plain crankcase with hand-turning crank handles for starting. Subsequently, in most versions, an electric starter was mounted on the wheelcase. As an alternative, first on the Merlin VIII in the Fairey Fulmar and on the contemporary Merlin XII in the Spitfire Mk II, the Coffman cartridge starter was used, starting the engine by turning it over through the reduction gear. Later in its development, a universal crankcase was introduced, redesigned so as to provide the availability of a drive which could be used, either to the reduction gear when there was a Coffman starter, or from it in high-altitude aircraft when a cabin blower was needed, the same facing that took the Coffman starter mounting the cabin blower. The reason for this arrangement was that this was the kind of drive that could not be taken from any other accessory. The oil relief valves were also placed there and not as a separate unit bolted on to the side of the crankcase which was therefore known as the universal crankcase because it provided a number of options.

Early Rolls-Royce engines had separate liners and individual water-jackets. Royce looked at the Curtiss D-12 engine, with monobloc-type poultice heads on basically individual cylinders and didn't care for it. He therefore designed his 'F' (Kestrel) engine with a one-piece cylinder block consisting of the head and skirt, cast in one piece, into which were fitted six individual wet cylinder liners.

When the P.V.12 came along in 1933, like the Kestrel it had a single-speed, single-stage supercharger. Rolls-Royce adopted a single big casting for the crankcase with integral cylinder blocks and detachable heads. Although this provided a very rigid carcase to contain the Merlin's potential 1,000 hp, the big casting tended to crack while on test. This could have been remedied but it was decided instead to revert to a removable single-piece cylinder block, in order to assist maintenance and field repair. After this decision was taken, Elliott noted the promising results of single-cylinder combustion chamber tests on a ramp, or semi-penthouse cylinder head (with normal exhaust and inclined inlet valves) and it was at first decided to adopt this form of head.

Subsequently, on full engine testing, it was found that neither the expected performance nor reliability were realized. The ramp head unfortunately suffered from cracking in manufacture and in service, the cracking occurring between the combustion chambers and the coolant spaces, probably due both to detonation and to the lack of symmetry. The design therefore had to be abandoned but not before the Merlin F and 172 production ramp head engines had already been built and installed as Merlin Is.

Hives decided to revert to the best standard of one-piece block that the Company knew, the most satisfactory block for the Merlin at that time. It followed well-established Kestrel practice, with a single-plane combustion chamber (flat-head), except that it had liner clamp-bolts at each cylinder liner so that there was an additional clamping force created by a bolt, or stud, in the cylinder which had to be nutted-up from an external window when tightened up the cylinder assembly before putting it on the engine. This very much improved the engine which became the Merlin G and went into service as the Mk II. It was the Merlin G which demonstrated the engine's reliability in a Horsley, by flying 100 hours in under a week.

Critics of the Merlin have talked about the top joint problem, particularly because it allowed either a direct gas-coolant or coolant-gas leak. This was because it was only the joint-ring which protected the system against such a problem. In fact, cylinder internal coolant leaks were about fourth on our list of engine removals in early Lancasters. Therefore, it cannot be regarded by any means as being the major problem. Plenty of engines went through to time-expiry. The cylinder assembly was very much improved by Mod 155, the Shrouded Joint-ring. The other problem with the one-piece block is that the block was maintaining the sealing of the liner, principally by means of the main cylinder holding-down studs. Thus, the cylinders had to cope with the dynamic distortions of the crankcase as well as the combustion pressures. Boost pressure and engine power output were constantly being increased as wartime uses demanded and these factors tended to make the problem worse. To enable the Merlin to achieve its great potential, the solution lay in the two-piece block.

When the two-piece block Merlin was designed, there was a flange liner trapped between the head and the cylinder skirt, coolant being transferred between head and skirt by transfer ferrules. These were in brass or Tungum and had rubber seals on either end. Later engines had double rubber on each end of the ferrules and this gave complete reliability. Thus, there was no contact of coolant to combustion chamber via the cylinder joint and this was the great advantage of the two-piece block. Also, because the joint was trapped between the head and skirt and the bottom of the liner was just located in the cylinder skirt, with no compression on it, it produced a very much more reliable assembly. In the early days of

two-piece blocks, one occasionally found cracked cylinder liners, adjacent to the upper flange and this was cured by Mod 674, the Taper Fillet Liner which reduced the stress at the flange. For later engines, Rolls-Royce increased the area of the top joint on which were called Wide-Flange Liners, these being very reliable. The two-piece block was introduced in Britain with the delivery of the first Mk 61 on Christmas Day 1941 (the Packard-designed block in the Mk 28, built in the U.S.A., beating it by a short head) and in America in Packard V-1650s.

MERLIN PROTOTYPE, two built. As previously indicated, this was a departure from usual R-R practice, by having the crankcase and cylinder blocks cast as one large unit. It was fully supercharged, spur-geared .477:1 and was first run on 15 October 1933. There were difficulties with making double-helical reduction gears and these were replaced by plain spur-type; the big casting suffered from cracking and coolant leaks. The coolant system was of the 'composite' type, combining water and steam, with both radiator and condenser. A Type-Test was passed in July 1934, first flown 21 Feb 1935.
Aircraft:

       Hawker Hart K3586
       Hawker Horsley

MERLIN B. Two were built at Derby, similar to the prototypes, with a single-speed supercharger. First run in February 1935, the flat cylinder heads were replaced by 'ramp' or 'semi-penthouse' shaped heads with the inlet and exhaust valves set at an angle of about 45 degrees. The combustion chamber, thus shaped, was intended to improve the performance but, ultimately, did not fulfil its promise. After continued cracks in water jackets it was decided, in the next version of the Merlin, to replace the big casting with aluminium monobloc cylinder castings and a separate upper crankcase. A major redesign to this effect, the Merlin C, was made by A.G. Elliott.
Aircraft:

       Hawker Hart

MERLIN C, 890 hp. Like the Merlin B, it was spur-geared .477:1, with ramp-type detachable heads. The first two were on test in April 1935. Both Hawker and Supermarine chose this variant for new fighter projects, despite the lack of official Air Ministry approval. The first flight was in the Hawker Hurricane prototype, powered initially by the 11th Merlin C, this being replaced by three subsequent engines after various mechanical failures. Mechanical troubles, including exhaust-valve failures persisted, cracking occurring in the ramp heads and performance was below expectations. It failed a 50-hour civil type-test and the decision was made to replace the composite cooling system, using pure ethylene-glycol, without the need for boiling and condensing. Power Curve at rated altitude 11,000 ft from A.& A.E.E., Martlesham, Report M.689, dated 22.2.36. Fully supercharged. Boost, rated +6lb/sq inch. Max 6lb/sq inch., 3,000 rpm. 4 built at Derby, 1935-1936.

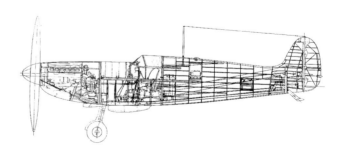

Supermarine Spitfire prototype drawing, showing the installation of the early Merlin 'C'.

RPM	3,000	2,800	2,600	2,400	2,200
BHP	1,189	1,129	1,029	905	780
BOOST	+6lb		+6lb		

Fuel 87 Octane (DTD 230).
Aircraft:
>   Hawker Hart
>   Hawker Horsley
>   Hawker Hurricane prototype
>   Supermarine Spitfire prototype

MERLIN E, 890 hp. A development of the Merlin C, it passed a civil type-test in December 1935 but failed a 100-hour military test in March 1936. The Horsley flew with a Hamilton-Standard bracket-type V/P propeller. 100 per cent ethylene-glycol cooled, boost +6.25 lb.
Aircraft:
>   Hawker Hart
>   Hawker Horsley
>   Supermarine Spitfire prototype

MERLIN F. A number of minor modifications from the Merlin E. Single-speed supercharger. This first flew in a Fairey Battle on 10 March 1936 and became the Merlin I, still retaining the ramp or semi-penthouse head. It was decided to redesign the cylinder head but meanwhile, from July 1936, because of the urgency of impending confrontation with Germany, a small number of engines were delivered at this stage of development, redesignated Merlin I. In November 1936, the engine successfully passed a reduced type test. It was cooled by 100 per cent ethylene-glycol, with a maximum boost of +5.75 lb/sq inch. Power Curve at rated altitude 12,250 ft, from A.& A.E.E., Martlesham, Report M.700, dated 10.5.37. Fully supercharged. Boost, rated +5.75lb/sq inch.

RPM	3,000	2,800	2,600	2,400	2,200
BHP	1,212	1,110	980	846	708
BOOST	+10.21	+8.08	+6.01	+4.22	+2.32

The Merlin 'F' at a development stage still retaining the ramp-head, becoming the Merlin I.

Max boost +6lb/sq inch. 3,000 rpm take off to 1,000 ft or one minute. All-out level flight (five minutes), +6lb, 1,030 bhp, 3,000 rpm. Fuel 87 Octane (DTD 230). 25 built at Derby, 1935-1937.

Servicing a Merlin I in a Fairey Battle in 1937.

Aircraft:
>   Fairey Battle I
>   Hawker Hart
>   Hawker Henley
>   Hawker Horsley
>   Hawker Hurricane prototype

MERLIN G. Single-speed supercharger. It was a redesigned Merlin F, incorporating a one-piece cylinder block, with a flat head and parallel valves and, in this form, it passed a type test in October 1936, so becoming the Merlin II. 100 per cent ethylene-glycol cooled, boost +6.25 lb. An efficient flame trap was a safeguard against backfires.
Aircraft:
>   Hawker Horsley

MERLIN I, 1,030 hp, (1937). Like all Merlins prior to the Mk X, it had a single-speed supercharger. It was 100 per cent ethylene-glycol cooled, with a boost +5.75 lb. Propeller reduction gear .477:1. Previously called the Merlin F, it had a ramp head cylinder block. It passed a reduced Type-Test in November 1936. Power Curve at rated altitude 12,500 ft from A.& A.E.E., Martlesham, Report M.700, dated 10.5.37. Fully supercharged. Boost, rated +5.75lb/sq inch.

RPM	3,000	2,800	2,600	2,400	2,200
BHP	1,212	1,110	980	846	708
BOOST	+10.21	+8.08	+6.01	+4.22	+2.32

Max boost +6lb/sq inch. 890 bhp, 3,000 rpm take off to 1,000 ft or one minute. All-out level flight (5 min) +6lb, 1,030 bhp, 3,000 rpm. Fuel 87 Octane (DTD 230). Rated RM.IS, supercharger rotor diameter 10.25 inches; gear ratio 8.58:1. Max boost, 5.75lb. 172 built at Derby, 1935–1937.
Aircraft:
>   Fairey Battle I
>   Fairey P.4/34
>   Hawker Henley

MERLIN II, 1,030 hp, (1937). With a one-piece, flat head cylinder block and a full diameter propeller shaft, it was originally the Merlin G design. It was 100 per cent ethylene-glycol cooled and had a maximum boost +6.25 lb and a propeller reduction gear of .477:1. These and other early Merlins tended to suffer from piston ring flutter at maximum supercharge, leading to rings breaking up, seizure and rapid total engine failure. Rolls-Royce successfully used 4K6 as a piston ring material on the Merlin at very high powers until later in the war, when DTD 485 was adopted, behaving more like steel than cast-iron. This was a special alloy for piston rings developed by the firm of Wellworthy Ltd, granted DTD approval and adopted for future engines. Power Curve at rated altitude 12,250 feet, from A.& A.E.E., Martlesham, Report M.689, dated 30.8.37.

RPM	3,000	2,800	2,600	2,400	2,200
BHP	1,225	1,101	979	847	703
BOOST	+10.1	+7.99	+6.21	+4.44	+2.46

Rolls-Royce Merlin II.

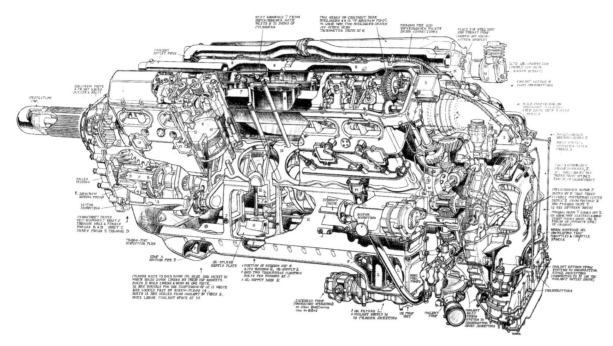

Rolls-Royce Merlin III drawn by A.J. Clark.

111 Sqn Hurricane Is being serviced at Northolt.

Max boost +6.25lb/sq inch. 890 bhp, 3,000 rpm take off to 1,000 ft or one minute. All-out level flight (five minutes), +6.25lb, 1,030 bhp, 3,000 rpm, 16,500 ft. Fuel 87 Octane (DTD 230). Rated RM.1S, supercharger rotor diameter 10.25 inches; gear ratio 8.58:1. 1,283 built at Derby, 1937–1939.

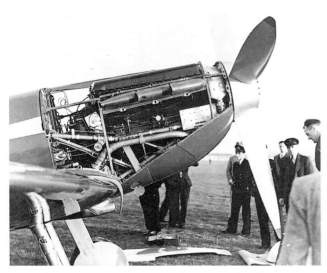

The Merlin II (special), fitted to the Spitfire registered N-17 and intended for an attack on the World's speed record.

Aircraft:

> Armstrong Whitworth A.W.38 Whitley I (experimental)
> Boulton Paul P.82 Defiant I
> Fairey Battle I
> Hawker Henley I
> Hawker Horsley
> Hawker Hotspur
> Hawker Hurricane I, Sea Hurricane I
> Supermarine Spitfire prototype
> Supermarine Spitfire I

MERLIN II (SPECIAL), 2,160 hp, (1939), similar to Mk II, but specially strengthened and modified for possible World's Speed Record attempt. Using special fuel, it produced 2,160 hp, at 3,200 rpm, +27 lb boost at S/L. 100 per cent ethylene-glycol cooled. Fixed-pitch 4-blade propeller, reduction gear .477:1.

Aircraft:

> Supermarine Spitfire (High-Speed K9834, 'N-17')

MERLIN III, 1,030 hp, (1939), single-speed supercharge, similar to Mk II. A necked-down propeller shaft, together with a smaller retaining nut were adopted for this and subsequent production Merlins. This modification protected the shaft threads when changing propellers and was adopted as a universal shaft for accepting either D.H. or Rotol propellers. The Merlin III was 100 per cent ethylene-glycol cooled and gave a boost of +6.25 lb. Propeller reduction gear .477:1. Power Curve at rated altitude 12,250 ft from A.& A.E.E., Martlesham, Report M.689, dated 27.1.39. Fully supercharged.

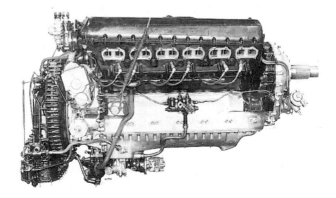

Rolls-Royce Merlin III.

RPM	3,000	2,800	2,600	2,400	2,200
BHP	1,209	1,099	963	821	687
BOOST	+9.8	+7.9	+5.85	+3.8	+2.15

Max boost +6.25lb/sq inch. 890 bhp, 3,000 rpm take off to 1,000 ft or one minute. All-out level flight (five minutes), +6.25lb, 1,030 bhp, 3,000 rpm, 16,250 ft. Fuel 87 Octane (DTD 230). Rated RM.1S, supercharger rotor diameter 10.5 inches; gear ratio 8.58:1. 6,444 built at Derby and 2,012 at Crewe, 1938–1941.

Aircraft:

    Boulton & Paul P.82 Defiant I, II
    Fairey Battle I
    Hawker Henley
    Hawker Hurricane I, Sea Hurricane I
    Renard R.38
    Supermarine Spitfire prototype
    Supermarine Spitfire I

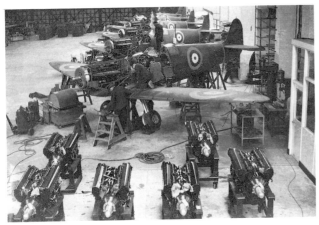

Supermarine Spitfire Is, with Merlin III engines on the assembly line.

MERLIN IV, 1,030 hp, (1939), single-speed supercharge. This was the first of the pressure-cooled engines with 70/30 per cent water/glycol cooling and had a similar rating to the Mk III, boost +6.25 lb. Propeller reduction gear .477:1, necked-down propeller shaft. Rated RM.1S, supercharger rotor diameter 10.25 inches; gear ratio 8.58:1. 73 built at Derby, 1938.

Aircraft:

    Armstrong Whitworth A.W.38 Whitley IV.

MERLIN V, 1,030 hp, single-speed supercharge. A converted Merlin III, similar to Mk IV, with a necked-down propeller shaft but not a universal shaft (the bore was different) so it could only take certain types of propeller, that being the only significant difference. Glycol-cooled. Boost +6.25 lb. Propeller reduction gear.477:1. Rated RM.1S, supercharger rotor diameter 10.25 inches; gear ratio 8.58:1.

Aircraft:

    Hawker Henley

MERLIN VIII, 1,275 hp This was a single-speed supercharged engine, similar to the Mk V, intended for the Royal Navy and, in particular, for the first British naval monoplane fighter, the Fairey Fulmar. A low-level Merlin, it was moderately supercharged and also had the first of the Merlin crankcases, provided with a mounting plate to take a cartridge-operated Coffman starter. The boost was increased to +9 lb. Propeller reduction gear .477:1. Power Curve at rated altitude 6,500 ft from A.& A.E.E., Martlesham, Report M.757, dated 27.10.38.

RPM	3,000	2,850	2,600	2,400	2,200
BHP	1,078	1,016	896	793	686
BOOST	+4.56lb	+3.75lb	+2.83lb	+1.87lb	+1.03lb

Max boost +5.75lb/sq inch. 1,275 bhp, 3,000 rpm take off to 1,000 ft or one minute. All-out level flight (five minutes), +4 lb,

1,060 bhp, 3,000 rpm. Fuel 87 Octane (DTD 230). Rated RM.3M, supercharger rotor diameter 10.25 inches; gear ratio 6.313:1. 184 built at Derby, 1939-1940.

Aircraft:

    Fairey Fulmar I

MERLIN X, 1,145 hp, this was the first of the two-speed engines, with a propeller reduction gear of .42:1. (This gear ratio was adopted for bomber engines involved in long-distance cruising). Pressure water-glycol cooled. Power Curve at rated altitude 2,250 ft from A.& A.E.E., Martlesham, Report M.699, dated 1939. Medium supercharged M Gear, boost rated +5.75lb/sq inch. Max take-off 5.75lb/sq inch., 3,000 rpm. All out level flight +5.75lb/sq inch, 1,150 hp, 3,000 rpm.

RPM	3,000	2,800	2,600	2,400	2,200
BHP	1,227	1,145	1,033	914	803
BOOST	+7.9	+6.95	+5.9	+4.85	+3.9

Power Curve at rated altitude 13,000 ft. Fully supercharged S Gear. Boost, rated +5.75lb/sq inch.

RPM	3,000	2,800	2.600	2,400	2,200
BHP	1,174	1,058	941	805	676
BOOST	+9.9	+7.9	+6.05	+4.15	+2.35

All-out level flight (five minutes), +5.75 lb, 1,010 bhp, 3,000 rpm. Fuel 87 Octane. Rated RM.1SM, supercharger rotor diameter 10.25 in; gear ratios 6.39/8.75:1. 312 built at Derby and 4,589 at Crewe, 1938-1942.

Aircraft:

    Armstrong Whitworth A.W.38 Whitley V, VII
    Avro 679 Manchester III
    Handley Page H.P. 57 Halifax I
    Hawker Horsley
    Supermarine Spitfire III
    Vickers 298, 406 Wellington II

The first two-speed Merlin X, showing the extra length of supercharger.

The Merlin XII, the power unit for the Spitfire II. The Coffman cartridge starter can be seen at the side of the crankcase, working directly on the reduction gear.

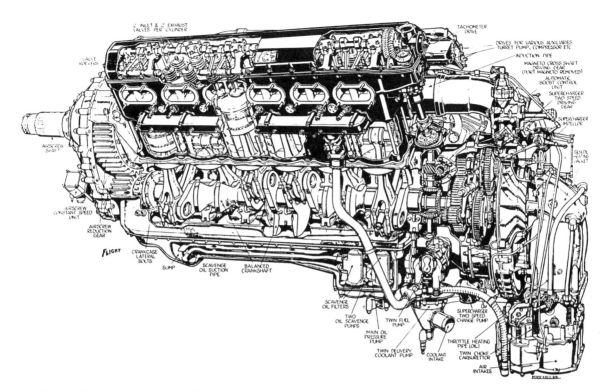

A cutaway drawing of the Merlin XX by Max Millar

MERLIN XII, 1,175 hp, (1940), single-speed supercharge, similar to Mk III but 70-30 per cent pressure water/ethylene-glycol cooled. Boost +12 lb. Propeller reduction gear.477:1. Like the Merlin VIII, it had the crankcase-mounted Coffman starter. Rated RM.3S, supercharger rotor diameter 10.25 in; gear ratio 9.09:1. 1,104 built at Derby, 1939-1941.

Aircraft:

  Fairey Battle I
  Supermarine Spitfire II

MERLIN XX, 1,390 hp, (1940), two-speed supercharger, designed as to replace the Mk X, from which it was modified, this was an engine with 70–30 per cent ethylene-glycol pressure cooling. It had a 10.25 in diameter supercharger rotor and gear ratios of 8.15:1 and 9.49:1 and a propeller reduction gear of .42:1. It gave 1,150 hp, at around 18,500 ft., at +12 lb boost, 3,000 rpm. Power Curve at rated altitude 9,500 ft from A.& A.E.E., Martlesham, Report M.720, dated 3.4.40. M Gear; Boost, rated +9 lb/sq inch.

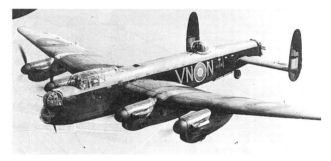

Perhaps the greatest heavy bomber of them all, capable of carrying a ten-ton bomb. An Avro Lancaster Mk I, R5689 of 50 Squadron R.A.F., powered by Merlin XX series engines. It succeeded its stablemate, the twin Vulture-powered Manchester.

RPM	3,000	2,850	2,650	2,400	2,200
BHP	1,373	1,251	1,075	885	749
BOOST	+11.44	+9.35	+7.0	+4.52	+2.89

Max boost +12lb/sq inch. 1,280 hp, 3,000 rpm take off to 1,000 ft or one minute. All-out level flight (five minutes), +9 lb, 1,270 bhp, 3,000 rpm. Fuel 100 Octane. Power Curve at rated altitude 18,500 ft, S Gear; Boost, rated +9 lb/sq inch.

One of the great trio of four-engined heavy bombers used in the second World War, the Handley Page H.P.57 Halifax V srs I Special, powered by two-speed supercharged Merlin XXs. Earlier Halifaxes had the first two-speed Merlin Xs.

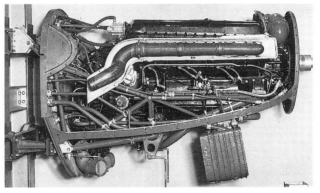

There were numerous sub-types based on the two-speed supercharged Merlin XX, the installations varying mostly in minor degrees. This and the following picture are of the installation in the Bristol Beaufighter II.

RPM	3,000	2,850	2,650	2,400	2,200
BHP	1,272	1,147	956	731	587
BOOST	+11.64	+9.35	+5.97	+2.45	+0.87

All-out level flight (five minutes), +9 lb, 1,185 hp, 3,000 rpm. Fuel 100 Octane. RM.3SM. 2,592 built at Derby, 3,391 at Crewe, 9,500 at Glasgow, 12,538 by Ford. Total 28,021, 1940-1944.
Aircraft:

> Avro 683 Lancaster I, III, VII
> Boulton & Paul P.82 Defiant II
> Bristol 156 Beaufighter II
> Handley Page H.P.59 Halifax II
> Handley Page H.P.63 Halifax V
> Hawker Hurricane IIA, IIB, IIC, IID, IV
> Hawker Sea Hurricane II
> Miles M.20, (2nd prototype, N.1/41)
> Supermarine Spitfire III

The two-speed supercharged Merlin XX in the Bristol Beaufighter II.

MERLIN 21, 1,390 hp, (1940), two-speed supercharger, similar to the Mk XX, developed from the Mk X, with 'reversed-flow cooling'. Note — reversed-flow cooling requires some explanation. Despite its name, it was not truly a reversed-flow system. With a conventional cooling system, (in aircraft with chin-type radiators, such as the Beaufighter, Lancaster and Halifax) the water comes out of the cylinder heads, into the header tank, down through the radiator where it is drawn by the coolant pump and then passed back up to the cylinder blocks, via the two horn-pipes, as Rolls-Royce calls them, one on each side of the block. On the Mosquito-type system, for efficient cooling with high-placed wing-mounted radiators, the coolant is drawn from the header tank by the coolant pump and is then taken by the conventional coolant pump outlets which normally feed the cylinder blocks, to the radiator and, from there, the radiator then feeds the coolant back, through a splitter pipe to the cylinder blocks. It is therefore not a truly reversed-flow system. Propeller reduction gear .42:1. Rating RM.3SM. 3 built at Derby and 2,026 at Crewe, 1941–1943.
Aircraft:

> de Havilland D.H.98 Mosquito I, F.II, T.III, B.IV, F.VI, NF.XII, NF.XIII, NF.XVII, NF.XIX

The prototype de Havilland D.H.98 Mosquito, powered by Merlin 21s.

The de Havilland D.H.98 Mosquito required a different coolant-flow from others in the Merlin series. The prototype was powered by Merlin 21s.

MERLIN 22, 1,390 hp, a two-speed supercharger, modified from Mks XX and 21. Propeller reduction gear.42:1. The engine was rated at +14 lb boost in MS gear, and +16 lb in FS gear. This gave about 1,400 hp, for take-off in MS and the full-throttle height in MS gear 1,480 hp, at about 5,500 ft. and 1,420 hp, at 12,000 ft. Rating RM.3SM. 1,478 Mk 22s and eight Mk 22Ys built at Derby, 1,387 at Crewe, 2,164 at Glasgow, 5,590 by Ford. Total 10,627, 1942–1943.
Aircraft:

> Avro 683 Lancaster I, VII
> Avro 685 York I
> Handley Page H.P.59 Halifax II
> Handley Page H.P.63 Halifax V

MERLIN 22A, 1,390 hp, with a two-speed supercharger was similar to the Mk 22, itself a Mk XX, but had a two-piece cylinder block. The Merlin 22A came in after the Mk 22, consisting of high modification standard Merlin XXs, built by Ford which originally had single-piece blocks and were converted to two-piece blocks. They were called 22As because Rolls-Royce retained the 3.5 per cent nickel-steel cylinder holding-down studs, instead of going to chrome-vanadium. They had different torque-loadings to allow for this, which accounts for the 22A. Rating RM.3SM
Aircraft:

> As Mk XX

MERLIN 23, 1,390 hp, two-speed supercharger, similar to Mk 22, but with reverse-flow coolant modification. An engine for the Mosquito only, it was rated at +14 lb boost in MS gear, and +16 lb in FS gear. This gave about 1,400 hp, for take-off in MS and, at the full-throttle height in MS gear, 1,480 hp, at 5,500 ft. and 1,420 hp, at 12,000 ft in FS gear. Rating RM.3SM. 758 built at Crewe, 836 at Glasgow, 1942–1943.
Aircraft:

> de Havilland D.H.98 Mosquito I, F.II, IV, F.VI, NF.XII, NF.XIII, NF.XVII, NF.XIX

MERLIN 23A, 1,390 hp, two-speed supercharged, like the Mk 21 but converted to have a two-piece block. Reversed-flow coolant system. Rating RM.3SM

MERLIN 24, 1,610 hp, two-speed supercharged, as the Mks XX and 22, but had an R.A.E. anti-G carburettor. It differed from the Merlin XX because, apart from having 2-piece blocks, it also had a strengthened supercharger drive, with an increased-capacity MS

clutch and a stiffer torsion shaft. The engine also had double girder pistons and was capable of operating at +18 lb boost. This gave 1,620 hp, at about 2,500 ft in MS gear and just over 1,500 hp, at about 9,000 ft. Rating RM.3SM. 542 built at Derby, 229 at Crewe, 2,550 at Glasgow and 10,400 by Ford, 1944–1945.
Aircraft:

> Avro 683 Lancaster I, VII
> Avro 685 York I
> Avro 691 Lancastrian I
> Cierva W.11 Air Horse
> Handley Page H.P.59 Halifax II

MERLIN T.24-1 & 2, 1,610 hp, two-speed supercharged, as the Mk 24 but modified to improve its service life, a Royal Air Force Transport Command modification. The same powers apply as in the Mk 24. The civil version became the Merlin 500 (q.v.). See also Merlin Mk 34.T. Rating RM.3SM. 35 built at Glasgow, 903 at Derby and 1,000 by Ford, 1944-1945.
Aircraft:

> Avro 683 Lancaster I
> Avro 685 York I
> Avro 691 Lancastrian I

MERLIN T.24/4, 1,610 hp, a similar engine to the Mk. T.24/2 with after-heater. The same powers apply as the Mk 24. The civil version became the Merlin 501 (q.v.). Rating RM.3SM
Aircraft:

> Avro 691 Lancastrian I

MERLIN 25, 1,610 hp, two-speed, single-stage supercharged, like the Mk 24 but with reversed coolant-flow, particularly for the Mosquito. The same powers as the Mk 24. RM.3SM. 176 built at Derby, 3,274 at Glasgow, 2,900 by Ford, 1943–1947.
Aircraft:

> de Havilland D.H.98 Mosquito F.VI, NF.XII, NF.XIII, NF.XVII, NF.XIX, T.R.33, T.R.37
> Hawker Hurricane XII (Canada)

MERLIN 27, 1,390 hp, a similar engine to the Mk 25, without reversed coolant flow. Rating RM.3SM. 141 built at Glasgow, 1943–44.
Aircraft:

> Hawker Hurricane II, V

MERLIN 28, 1,390 hp, (1941), a two-speed, single-stage supercharged engine, similar to the Mk 22A, a Packard-built Rolls-Royce engine for use by the Royal Air Force, with a British propeller shaft etc., and a two-piece block of Packard design (equivalent of V-1650-1). It was introduced as an interim, because Rolls-Royce recognized it would take them time to change over from the single-piece to the two-piece block in England and they told Packard to proceed with a design of their own, introduced on the Merlin 28. All Packard Merlins had Bendix carburettors except for the very late, injected engines. They also used an epicyclic supercharger drive, although the ratios were the same as used by Rolls-Royce with the Farman drive. This is essentially a friction-clutch operated drive, with a camshaft to enable change of gear to take place by placing or relieving load on the clutch weight fingers. The epicyclic gearbox works like a conventional epicyclic drive, putting a brake on a gear. The Americans also used American magnetos on the Packard engines, although they were built to suit the Merlin pattern. The propeller reduction gear remained at .42:1, for use by the Royal Air Force, with a British S.B.A.C. propeller shaft. Rating RM.3SM.
Aircraft:

> Avro 683 Lancaster III & X (Canada)
> Curtiss P-40F Kittyhawk II
> Hawker Hurricane X (Canada)

MERLIN 29, 1,390 hp, (1941). A two-speed, single-stage supercharger, not a production engine but modified from and similar to the Mk 28. Packard-built with U.S.-splined propeller shaft. Propeller reduction gear .477:1. Rating RM.3SM.
Aircraft:

> Curtiss P-40F Kittyhawk II
> Hawker Hurricane XI, XII (Canada)

MERLIN 30, 1,300 hp, a low level engine, single-speed medium supercharged, giving 1,300 hp, but with a smaller diameter supercharger rotor and a higher gear ratio than the Merlin VIII had but still giving a low-level performance. It was used in a few Barracudas and Fulmar IIs, an engine for Royal Navy use, with a Coffman starter. Geared drive .477:1. Rated RM.5M, supercharger rotor diameter 9.75 in; gear ratio 8.58:1. 660 built at Derby, 1940–1942.
Aircraft:

> Fairey Barracuda I (S.24/37)
> Fairey Fulmar II
> Supermarine 322, S.24/37 'Dumbo'

MERLIN 31, 1,390 hp, (1941), two-speed, single-stage supercharged, a version of the Merlin 21, with reversed coolant-flow, used in Canadian and Australian-built Mosquitos. Also built for the Royal Air Force for use principally in the Mosquito, Packard-built. Propeller reduction gear.420:1. Rating RM.3SM.
Aircraft:

> Curtiss P-40F Kittyhawk II, P-40L Kittyhawk II
> de Havilland D.H.98 Mosquito XX (Canada),
> de Havilland D.H.98 Mosquito 40 (Australia)

MERLIN 32, 1,620 hp, a low-level engine for Royal Navy use, Coffman starter, similar to the Mk 30 with two-piece blocks. Single-speed medium supercharged. Propeller reduction gear .477:1. Mk 34 similar, with electric starter. Rating RM.5M. 3,500 built at Derby, 1942–1945.
Aircraft:

> Fairey Barracuda II, III
> Supermarine Seafire I, II, LF.IIC, III, PR.XIII
> Supermarine S.24/37 'Dumbo'

The medium-supercharged Merlin 32 for the Fairey Barracuda. Its two-piece cylinder blocks can be seen.

MERLIN 33, 1,390 hp, a two-speed, single-stage supercharged engine, similar to the Mk 23, Packard-built for the Canadian and Australian Mosquitos. Reversed coolant-flow. Propeller reduction gear .42:1. Rated RM.3SM, supercharger rotor diameter 10.25 in; gear ratios 8.15:1 and 9.49:1.
Aircraft:

> de Havilland D.H.98 Mosquito XX (Canada),
> de Havilland D.H.98 Mosquito 40 (Australia)

MERLIN T.34, 1,390 hp, two-speed, single-stage supercharged, a modified T.24/2 with an R.A.E. anti-G carburettor. Geared drive .42:1. Rating RM.3SM.

MERLIN 35, 1,390 hp, a T24-2 single-speed, medium-supercharged engine for training purposes. Rated RM.5M, supercharger rotor diameter 9.75 in; gear ratio 8.58:1. Propeller reduction gear ratio .471:1.
Aircraft:

> Avro 701 Athena prototype, Athena T.2
> Boulton & Paul P.108 Balliol (T.14/47)

MERLIN 38, 1,390 hp, a two-speed, single-stage supercharged, Packard-built Mk.22. Some were modified to give +14lb boost at

sea level (through the gate) and, using boost control cut-out, +14lb in M gear and +16lb in S gear. (Also applied to Mks 22 and 28). Geared drive .42:1. Rated RM.3SM, supercharger rotor diameter 10.25 in; gear ratios 8.15:1 and 9.49:1.
Aircraft:

Avro 683 Lancaster III, X (Canada)

MERLIN 45, 1,230 hp, single-speed supercharger, about 1,210 hp, at 3,000 rpm, +9 lb boost at 18,000 ft. Propeller reduction gear .477:1. Rated RM.5S, supercharger rotor diameter 9.09 in. 2,000 built at Derby, 1,574 at Crewe, 1941–1943.
Aircraft:

Hawker Hurricane I
Supermarine Seafire I, II, III
Supermarine Spitfire PR.IV, F.VA, B, C, PR.VI

The Merlin 45, a modified Mk III, used for medium level Spitfire Vs.

MERLIN 45M, 1,580 hp, single-speed, medium supercharged, a low-level engine similar to the Merlin 45 but with a cropped supercharger rotor. Maximum power was 1,580 hp, at 2,600 ft. Propeller reduction gear .477:1. Rating RM.5M.
Aircraft:

Supermarine Spitfire LF.VA, B, C

MERLIN 46, 1,190 hp, single-speed supercharger. An engine with true circular arc rotating guide vanes and slightly larger impeller of 10.85 diameter, to give a little more altitude performance. Used in Spitfires and Seafires, interchangeable with the Merlin 45, it was not popular because it did not give the same amount of power low down. R.M.6S rating. Propeller reduction gear .477:1. 2,372 built at Derby, 1,297 at Crewe, 1941–1943.
Aircraft:

Supermarine Seafire IB, IIC
Supermarine Spitfire PR.IV, F.VA, B, C

MERLIN 47, 1,100 hp. This high-altitude engine delivered the same power as the Merlin 46 but had a cabin blower drive. It featured the universal crankcase, with a mounting plate capable of mounting either a cabin blower or a Coffman starter. A single-speed supercharger. Propeller reduction gear .477:1. Rating RM.6S. 120 built at Derby, 1941–1942.
Aircraft:

Supermarine Spitfire H.F.VI

MERLIN 50, 1,230 hp, single-speed supercharger, purely a Service Trials engine. It was a modified Mk 46, with a diaphragm-controlled fuel feed. Later, this was deleted in favour, first of Miss Shilling's 'restrictor' and then the R.A.E. anti-G device. Rolls-Royce had done much work on a diaphragm type of negative-G carburettor which was flown in two squadrons of Spitfire Vs with Merlin 50 engines at North Weald. It was found to be unsatisfactory because it could not sense zero-G and was therefore rejected, being later changed as above. These trials resulted in a retrospective modification on all Merlins fitted with S.U.-carburettors. Rated RM.5S, supercharger rotor diameter 10.25 in; gear ratio 9.09:1. Propeller reduction gear ratio .477:1. 629 built at Crewe, 1943.
Aircraft:

Supermarine Spitfire VA, B, C.

MERLIN 50A, 1,100 hp, gave the same power as the Merlin 45. It had the Merlin 46 rotor and guide vanes, thus becoming a Merlin 46, in practice. Single-speed supercharged. Propeller reduction gear.477:1. Rating RM.6S. 100 built at Derby, 1942.
Aircraft:

Supermarine Spitfire VA, B, C.

MERLIN 50M, 1,230 hp, a modified Mk 50. This was a low-level engine delivering the same power as the Merlin 45M. Similar to Merlin 50 but with a cropped supercharger rotor. Propeller reduction gear.477:1. Rated RM.5M, supercharger rotor diameter 9.5 in; gear ratio 9.09:1.
Aircraft:

Supermarine Seafire I, II, III
Supermarine Spitfire LF.VA, B, C

MERLIN 55, a modified Mk 50 (itself a modified Mk 45, with anti-G carburettor) but with two-piece cylinder blocks. Propeller reduction gear.477:1. Rating RM.5S. 472 built at Crewe, 1943.
Aircraft:

Supermarine Seafire I, II, III

MERLIN 55A, 1,230 hp, a similar engine to the Mk 45 but to a lower modification standard. Propeller reduction gear.477:1. RM.5S
Aircraft:

Supermarine Spitfire V

MERLIN 55M, 1,580 hp, a low-level engine similar to the Mk 50 but with a cropped supercharger rotor, giving the same powers as the Merlin 45M. Propeller reduction gear.477:1. Rating RM.5S. 1,428 built at Crewe, 1943–1944.
Aircraft:

Supermarine Seafire I, II, III
Supermarine Spitfire LF.VA, B, C

MERLIN 55MA, 1,580 hp, a similar engine to the Mk 45M (itself a Mk 45 with a cropped supercharger rotor) but with two-piece cylinder blocks. Propeller reduction gear .477:1. Rating RM.5S.
Aircraft:

Supermarine Spitfire V

MERLIN 56, 1,580 hp, modified Mk 55, as Mk 46 with diaphragm fuel feed in carburettor. Rating RM.6S. 28 built at Derby 1942.

MERLIN 60, 1,280 hp, the first Merlin with a two-speed, two-stage supercharger and intercooler (also known by Rolls-Royce as an aftercooler). It had a high-altitude performance and a different supercharger rotor from the Merlin 61. It was intended as an engine, with cabin supercharger, for the Wellington VI. Although some production engines were made, it never saw regular operational Squadron service. No performance curves appear to have survived for this engine. It had single-piece cylinder blocks and therefore did not give much more than a maximum 1,200–1,280 hp. Rated RM.6SM, supercharger rotor diameters 11.5 and 10.1 in; gear ratios 5.52:1 and 8.41:1. Propeller reduction gear ratio .42:1. 75 built at Derby, 1941–1942.
Aircraft:

Vickers 431, 442 Wellington VI

NOTE ON 150 GRADE FUEL.

From this point onwards in the development of the two-speed, two-stage Merlin, reference is made to the possibility of using 150 grade fuel in certain engines. This was a super-grade fuel which became available in 1944, used particularly for the high-speed pursuit of German V-1 flying bombs and enabled the use of +25 lb cleared for +30 lb, had the war not finished.

MERLIN 61, 1,280 hp, (1942), the first of the two-speed, two-stage supercharged Merlins for fighters. It was similar to the Mk 60, with a propeller reduction gear of .420:1 and featured a cabin supercharger. The Merlin 61 was the first Merlin with two-piece cylinder blocks to be built by Derby. The MS supercharger gear ratio was 6.39:1 and the FS ratio 8.03:1. Using 100 Octane fuel, it was rated at +15 lb boost and, at 3,000 rpm, this gave 1,560 hp, at about 15,000 ft and 1,300 hp, at about 23,000 ft, in MS and FS gear respectively. Rating RM8.SM. 734 built at Derby, 1942–1943.

Aircraft:

Bristol 156 Beaufighter II
Supermarine Spitfire H.F.VII, F.VIII, IX, PR.XI
Vickers 432 F.7/41

A Merlin 60 series engine, showing the big inter-cooler or heat-exchanger box which kept the supercharged mixture temperature within limits.

MERLIN 62, a special test version of the Mk 60 engine, with two-piece blocks. 95 built at Derby, 1942.

Aircraft:

Vickers 470 Wellington II (Jet engine test-bed)

MERLIN 63, 1,280 hp, a two-speed, two-stage supercharged engine, similar to the Mk 61 but with a stronger supercharger drive-shaft and without provision for a cabin blower. It had a S.U. carburettor and was cleared potentially for +21 lb. boost on 150 grade fuel. At +21 lb boost, this mark would give 1,800 hp, at around 6,000 ft. and about 1,580 hp, at 18,000 ft. On 100 Octane fuel, 1,690 hp, would be available in MS gear at 9,000 ft and 1,450 hp, at 21,000 ft. Propeller reduction gear .477:1. Rated RM.8SM, supercharger rotor diameters 11.5 and 10.1 in; gear ratios 6.39:1 and 8.03:1. 375 built at Derby, 950 at Crewe, 1942–1944.

Aircraft:

Supermarine Spitfire F.VIII, F.IX, PR.XI

MERLIN 63A, 1,280 hp, a modified Mk 63, with Mk 64 crankcase and no cabin supercharger. It had a S.U. carburettor and was cleared potentially for +21lb boost on 150 grade fuel. At +21 lb boost, this gave 1,800 hp, at around 6,000 ft. and about 1,580 hp, at 18,000 ft. On 100 Octane fuel, 1,690 hp, was available in MS gear at 9,000 ft and 1,450 hp, at 21,000 ft. Propeller reduction gear .477:1. Rating RM.8SM. 143 built at Derby 1943.

Aircraft:

Supermarine Spitfire VIII, IX

MERLIN 64, 1,280 hp, similar to the Mk 63, with cabin supercharger and S.U. carburettor. It was also cleared potentially for +21 lb. boost on 150 grade fuel, at +21 lb boost, giving 1,800 hp, at around 6,000 ft. and about 1,450 hp, at 21,000 ft. On 100 Octane fuel, 1,690 hp, would be available in MS gear at 9,000 ft and 1,450 hp, at 21,000 ft. Propeller reduction gear .477:1. Rating RM.8SM. 182 built at Derby, 1943–1944.

Aircraft:

Supermarine Spitfire F.VII, PR.X

MERLIN 65, 1,315 hp, like its predecessors having a two-speed, two-stage supercharger, similar to the Mk 63 but with an increased supercharger rotor diameter. Propeller reduction gear .42:1. It was developed to test Mustangs converted in U.K. in the development flying programme and did not have inter-connected controls. Using 150 grade fuel, these engines gave just over 2,000 hp, at sea level at 3,000 rpm, using +25 lb boost, and 1,880 hp, at just over 10,000 ft in FS gear. At +18 lb, 3,000 rpm, 100 Octane fuel, the engine would give about 1,780 hp, in MS gear at just over 5,000 ft and 1,610 hp, at 15,000 ft in FS gear. Rated RM.10SM, supercharger rotor

diameters 12.0 and 10.1 in; gear ratios 5.79:1 and 7.06:1. 2 built at Derby 1943.

Aircraft:

Avro 683 Lancaster I
North American Mustang X

MERLIN 66, 1,315 hp. A two-speed, two-stage supercharged low-altitude engine, similar to Mk 63 and 65 but with interconnected engine controls and a Stromberg injection carburettor. The Merlin 66 was the most effective engine in the Spitfire in regular operation and it flew consistently at +25 lb boost at over 2,000 hp, both on anti-flying bomb operations and against the Luftwaffe. RM.10SM Rating. Propeller reduction gear .477:1. RM10.SM. 2,992 built at Derby, 2,588 at Crewe, 816 at Glasgow, 1943–1945.

Aircraft:

Supermarine Spitfire F.VIII, LF.IX, T.8, T.9

The Merlin 66, probably the best Merlin in fighter operations. The joint in the two-piece cylinder block can be seen at the end.

MERLIN 67, 1,315 hp, the first version of the 60 series Merlin to have a reversed coolant-flow. Propeller reduction gear .420:1. Rating RM.10SM. 2 built at Derby, 35 at Crewe, 34 at Glasgow, 1943–1944.

MERLIN 68, 1,315 hp, a two-speed, two-stage supercharged engine with similar ratings to the Merlin 66, apart from certain modifications around the intercooler header tank which was of an integral type. Propeller reduction gear.420:1. This engine, the Packard-built version of the Merlin 85, used in Lincolns, post-war, were the first production engines to have a 30 hp, auxiliary gearbox drive connected to the aircraft's own auxiliary gearbox. It had the usual Packard characteristics of an epicyclic supercharger drive and Bendix carburettor. Supercharger rotor diameters 12.0 and 10.1 in; gear ratios 5.802:1 and 7.349:1.

Aircraft:

Avro 694 Lincoln II

MERLIN 68A, 1,315 hp, a Packard-built two-speed, two-stage supercharged engine, similar to the Mk 68 but with a charge-temperature control scheme. As the Merlin 68, it was a Packard version of the Merlin 85, used in production versions of the Avro Lincoln II, post-war. It had the usual Packard characteristics of epicyclic supercharger drive and a Bendix carburettor. Propeller reduction gear .420:1.

Aircraft:

Avro 694 Lincoln II

MERLIN 69, 1,315 hp, a two-speed Mk 67 engine, built by Packard, with a different reduction-gear drive, .42:1, similar to the V-1650-7. It corresponded to the Mks 65, 66-68, and, in particular to the Mk 67, with reversed coolant-flow.

Aircraft:

North American P-51C Mustang III
North American P-51D, P-51F, P-51K Mustang IV

MERLIN 70, 1,250 hp, a two-speed, two-stage supercharged engine, broadly similar to Merlin 66. The difference between this and the Mk 66 was that it had the higher supercharger gear ratios of 6.39:1 and 8.03:1, which improved the altitude performance. It was

used in high-altitude Spitfires. The maximum power on +25 lb boost at 3,000 rpm was about 1,950 hp, at 5,000 ft, in MS gear and 1,700 hp, at 18,000 ft in FS gear. On 100 Octane fuel the engine would give 1,700 hp, at just over 10,000 ft in MS gear and 1,450 hp, at just over 22,000 ft in FS. It had an injection carburettor. Propeller reduction gear .477:1. Rating RM.11SM. 1,000 built at Crewe, 1944–1945.
Aircraft:

Supermarine Spitfire HF.VIII, HF.IX, PR.XI

MERLIN 71, 1,250 hp, a similar engine to the Mk 70, with a cabin supercharger. Propeller reduction gear .477:1. Rating RM.11SM. 16 built at Derby 1944.
Aircraft:

Supermarine Spitfire H.F.VII, PR.X

MERLIN 72, 1,280 hp, a two-speed, two-stage supercharged engine, similar to Mks 63 and 70 but with reversed coolant-flow. It had an S.U. carburettor and was cleared, potentially, for +21 lb. boost on 150 grade fuel. At +21 lb boost, this engine would give 1,800 hp, at around 6,000 ft. and about 1,580 hp, at 18,000 ft. On 100 Octane fuel, 1,690 hp, would be available in MS gear at 9,000 ft and 1,450 hp, at 21,000 ft. It gave similar powers to Merlin 61. A Mosquito engine. Propeller reduction gear.420:1. Rated RM.8SM, supercharger rotor diameter 11.5 and 10.1 in; gear ratios 6.39:1 and 8.03:1. Propeller reduction gear ratio 42:1. 500 built at Derby, 500 at Crewe, 1943–1944.
Aircraft:

de Havilland D.H.98 Mosquito B.IX, PR.IX,
de Havilland D.H.98 Mosquito B.XVI, B.30
Westland Welkin I

MERLIN 73, 1,280 hp, a similar engine to the Mk 72, with similar powers to Merlin 63. With reversed coolant-flow, it was a Mosquito engine and had a cabin supercharger and S.U. carburettor, and was cleared potentially for +21lb. boost on 150 grade fuel. At +21 lb boost, this mark would give 1,800 hp, at around 6,000 ft. and about 1,580 hp, at 18,000 ft. On 100 Octane fuel, 1,690 hp, would be available in MS gear at 9,000 ft and 1,450 hp, at 21,000 ft. Propeller reduction gear .420:1. Rating RM.8SM. 700 built at Derby 1942–1944.
Aircraft:

de Havilland D.H.98 Mosquito XVI, T.39
Westland Welkin I

A de Havilland D.H.98 Mosquito P.R.XVI, with many others awaiting test and delivery at Hatfield in 1944. The engines are Merlins in the 70 series.

MERLIN 76, 1,280 hp, a two-speed, two-stage engine, broadly similar to the Merlin 66. The difference between this and the Merlin 66 was that it had the higher supercharger gear ratios of 6.39:1 and 8.03:1, which improved altitude performance. It was used in high-altitude versions of the Mosquito and the then new Welkin. Bendix carburettor. It was also similar to the Mks 72 & 73 with reversed coolant-flow and cabin supercharge. Propeller reduction gear.420:1. Rating RM.11SM. 1,200 built at Crewe, 600 built at Crewe, 1944–1945.
Aircraft:

de Havilland D.H.98 Mosquito XVI, 30, T.T.39
Westland Welkin II

MERLIN 77, 1,250 hp, another engine broadly similar to Merlin 66 but having the higher supercharger gear ratios of 6.39:1 and 8.03:1, which improved altitude performance. Used in high-altitude versions of the Mosquito and Spitfire, with cabin blower drive. Rating RM.11SM. 584 built at Derby, 1944–1945.
Aircraft:

de Havilland D.H.98 Mosquito XVI, T.T.39
Supermarine Spitfire PR.X
Westland Welkin II

MERLIN 85, 1,635 hp, a two-speed, two-stage supercharged engine, with similar ratings to the Merlin 66 and Merlin 68, apart from certain modifications around the intercooler header tank which was of an integral type. This engine was the equivalent of the Packard-built Merlin 68 for the Lincoln II. The 85 used in the Lancaster VI was the first production engine to have a 30 hp, auxiliary gearbox drive to the aircraft's own auxiliary gearbox. Propeller reduction gear .420:1. Rating RM.10SM. 34 built at Derby, 1,400 at Glasgow, 1944–1945.
Aircraft:

Avro 683 Lancaster VI
Avro 694 Lincoln I, II, IV
Vickers 480 Windsor

MERLIN 85B, 1,635 hp, a two-speed, two-stage engine, similar to Mk 85, with an American constant-speed unit. Propeller reduction gear .420:1. Rating RM.10SM

MERLIN 86, as Mk 85A with anti-surge diffusers. Equivalent of the Packard V-1650-9.
Aircraft:

Avro 694 Lincoln II
Avro 695 Lincolnian

MERLIN 100, 101, 18 test engines built at Glasgow, 1944-1945. Rated RM.14SM, supercharger rotor diameter 12.0 and 10.1 in; gear ratios 5.79:1 and 7.06:1. Propeller reduction gear ratio .42:1.

MERLIN 102, 1,635 hp, An experimental type, the first civil two-speed, two-stage Merlin leading to a series of engines for post-war commercial aircraft. A strengthened engine, with end-feed lubrication. 169 built at Glasgow, 1944–1946. Rating RM.14SM.
Aircraft:

Avro 688 Tudor prototype
Avro 689 Tudor II
Avro 691 Lancastrian I

MERLIN 102A, 1,635 hp, an experimental civil engine, similar to the Mk 102 but with an after-heater.
Aircraft:

Avro 688 Tudor I
Avro 691 Lancastrian I

MERLIN 104, 1,635 hp, a two-speed, two-stage engine with reversed-flow cooling and cabin supercharger. Similar to Mk 114, with lower drive ratios. 102 built at Glasgow 1945.

MERLIN 110 and 112, 1,225 hp, two-speed, two-stage supercharge, geared drive .4707:1. Rating RM.16SM

MERLIN 113/113A, 1,535 hp, a two-speed, two-stage engine, similar to the Mks 110 and 112 but with reversed coolant-flow, an anti-surge supercharger diffuser and altered reduction gear ratio. It was a 100 series engine, a sub-family of the two-stage engines with end-feed lubrication and a new supercharger with the overhung first-stage impeller and single-point fuel injection. Propeller reduction gear .42:1. Rating RM.16SM. 650 built at Glasgow, 1944–1945.
Aircraft:

de Havilland D.H.98 Mosquito 34

MERLIN 114/114A, 1,535 hp, another engine similar to the Mk 113 but with reversed coolant-flow, cabin supercharger and an anti-surge supercharger diffuser. Propeller reduction gear .42:1. Rating RM.16SM. 1 built at Derby, 1,198 built at Glasgow, 1944–1945.
Aircraft:

de Havilland D.H.98 Mosquito 34

MERLIN 130, 1,670 hp, a two-speed, two-stage engine designed to power the de Havilland Hornet, with a down-draught air intake and reversed coolant-flow. For this installation, it had a side-mounted coolant pump and a considerably neater, cleaned-up profile. R.H. tractor. Propeller reduction gear .42:1. Rating RM.14SM. 254 built at Derby, 80 at Glasgow, 1945–1951.
Aircraft:

de Havilland D.H.103 Hornet I, Sea Hornet XX

The Merlin 130 series, with a down-draught intake for de Havilland Hornet/Sea Hornet installation.

MERLIN 131, 1,670 hp, a two-speed, two-stage engine similar to the Mk 130 with a down-draught air intake and reversed coolant-flow for the Hornet, with a side-mounted coolant pump and cleaned-up profile. It differed from the 130 in having a reversed L.H. tractor propeller drive, thus giving the Hornet 'handed' propellers, with a .42:1 reduction gear. Rating RM.14SM. 256 built at Derby, 80 at Glasgow, 1945–1951.
Aircraft:

de Havilland D.H.103 Hornet I, Sea Hornet XX

de Havilland D.H.103 Sea Hornet F.20 with Merlin 130 series engines.

MERLIN 132, 133, 1,670 hp, similar engines to the Mks 130 and 131, with airscrew-braking (reverse-pitch). Rating RM.14SM. 11 of each type built at Derby 1946.

A de Havilland D.H.103 Sea Hornet N.F.21 with opposite-rotating Merlins Mk 134/135.

MERLIN 134, a two-speed, two-stage engine, which the Hornet had installed latterly in its career. This engine was similar to the earlier Merlin 130-series but had a Corliss throttle. This is a steam engine-type throttle and it has the effect of providing an unrestricted air-intake when the throttle is fully open. The other factor about it is that it reduces the torque on the throttle levers when flying the aircraft. A plate throttle tends to snap open as it is moved. A Corliss throttle is composed of two cylindrical ends with a sector blanked in, which rotates in the throttle body, having the effect of an unrestricted intake and a very low opening torque on the throttle levers. Rating RM.14SM. 25 built at Derby, 1950.
Aircraft:

de Havilland D.H.103 Hornet F.III, Sea Hornet 21

MERLIN 135, similar to the Merlin 134 but an opposite-handed L.H. tractor propeller drive. Like the 134, the Merlin 135 had Corliss throttles. 45 built at Derby 1949–1950.
Aircraft:

de Havilland D.H.103 Hornet F.III, Sea Hornet 21.

MERLIN 140, 1,725 hp. This was a special, two-speed, two-stage Merlin, designed for the Short Sturgeon. It featured a shunt-flow and a Coffman starter. It had a L.H./R.H. counter-rotating propeller drive with a reduction gear ratio of .512:1. Rating RM.14SM. 57 built at Derby 1947–1948.
Aircraft:

Short S.A.1 Sturgeon I

MERLIN 100-series, RM.17SM rating. A Merlin which was flown in prototype form but was not allocated a Mark number. The RM.17SM does meet the qualification of having flown. As a 100-series engine, with larger-diameter supercharger rotors, it was cleared for +30 lb boost and was flight-cleared at 2,340 hp. It was type-tested at 2,200 hp, and flew from Hucknall in a Mustang X but was never taken any further because of the end of the war.
Aircraft:

North American P-51 Mustang X

MERLIN 150, 1,740 hp, a commercial engine, two-speed, two-stage which was given a revised Mark Number, changed to Merlin 620, q.v.

MERLIN 224, 1,610 hp, a two-speed, single-stage supercharged, Packard-built Mk 24 for the Lancaster. This was similar to Mks XX and 22 Merlins and therefore had a Merlin Mark number. It did not have the R.A.E. anti-G carburettor but, like all Packard engines (unless they were of the later type with Simmonds injectors) had a Bendix carburettor. Propeller reduction gear .420:1. Rating RM.3SM.
Aircraft:

Avro 683 Lancaster I, III

MERLIN 225, 1,610 hp, a two-speed, single-stage supercharged, Packard-built engine, equivalent to the Mk 25 (a Mk 24 with reversed coolant-flow). It was a similar engine to the Merlin 224, built for the Mosquito. Propeller reduction gear .420:1. Rating RM.3SM.
Aircraft:

de Havilland D.H.98 Mosquito 25, 26 (Canada)

MERLIN 228, 1,320 hp, a two-speed, single-stage supercharged engine, similar to the Mk 28. It was Packard-built, similar to the V-1650-1. Propeller reduction gear .420:1.

MERLIN 266, 1,315 hp. This two-speed, two-stage engine was a Mk 66 with the same ratings but built by Packard. With the same ratings, it was a low-altitude engine. It had the usual Packard features, interconnected engine controls and Stromberg injection carburettor. Propeller reduction gear.479:1. Rating RM.10SM.
Aircraft:

Supermarine Spitfire LF.XVI

MERLIN 300, 1,660 hp. This engine had a two-speed, two-stage supercharger and was built by Packard, to replace the Merlin 68. With a different reduction-gear drive, it was also known as the V-1650-7 and was similar to the Mks 65, 66 & 69. An American Mk 100. Rating RM.14SM.

MERLIN 301, 1,660 hp, an American-built two-speed, two-stage supercharged engine, to replace the Mk 69. This engine, built by Packard and with a different reduction-gear drive, was also known as the V-1650-7. Similar to Mks 65-68, and, in particular to the Mk 67 with reversed coolant-flow. Propeller reduction gear .479:1. As Mk 101.

MERLIN 500, 1,660 hp, a two-speed, single-stage supercharged engine was a civil version of the Mk T.24/2. This was, in turn, similar to the Mk 24 but with several sub-variants with various modifications, mainly to suit Royal Air Force Transport Command. Propeller reduction gear.42:1. RM.3SM. 500-3, 10 built; 500-4, 2 built; 500-5, 20 built; 500-6, 1 built; 500-20, 2 built, all at Derby 1947–1949.
Aircraft:
> Avro 685 York I
> Avro 691 Lancastrian I

MERLIN 500/29, 1,610 hp, a two-speed, single-stage supercharged engine which was a version of the Mk T.24/2, similar to the Mk 24 but with modifications to suit the Spanish version of the Heinkel He 111 built by C.A.S.A. and designated C2111-D. Propeller reduction gear.42:1. RM.3SM
Aircraft:
> C.A.S.A. C2111-D (Heinkel He 111H-16).

A Spanish-built C.A.S.A. C2111-D (Heinkel He 111H-16) powered by Rolls-Royce Merlin 500/29s.

MERLIN 500/45, 1,660 hp, two-speed, single-stage supercharged, similar to the 500/29 but with modifications to suit the Spanish versions of the Messerschmitt Bf 109. Propeller reduction gear .42:1. RM.3SM
Aircraft:
> Hispano Aviacion HA-1109-M1L, -M2L
> Hispano Aviacion HA-1112-M1L Buchon

MERLIN 501, 1,660 hp, a two-speed, single-stage supercharged engine. It was based on the civil Merlin T.24/4 but with an after-heater, to prevent plug-leading at cruising power. RM.3SM
Aircraft:
> Avro 685 York I
> Avro 691 Lancastrian I

MERLIN 502, RM.3SM, as Mk 500 but with climb boost increased to +12 lb.
Aircraft:
> Avro 685 York I

MERLIN 600, 1,725 hp. Two-speed, two-stage supercharged engines, the 600 and 700 series of Merlin engines were designed with the post-war civil market in mind. They were mechanically similar to the 100 series having, among other things, end-feed lubrication, single-point fuel injection and an overhung first-stage impeller. The first of these, the 600 was basically a civil Mk 102A, which in turn was similar to the Mk 102 but with an after-heater. Maximum Boost was +20 lb. Propeller reduction gear .420:1. Rated RM.14SM, supercharger rotor diameter 12.0 in and 10.1 in; gear ratios 5.79:1 and 7.06:1.
Aircraft:
> Avro 688 Tudor I

MERLIN 600A, similar to Mk 600.
Aircraft:
> Avro 689 Tudor II

MERLIN 604, 1,720 hp. A two-speed, two-stage supercharged engine which was a military version of the 621, and was used by the Argentine Government in their Lincoln bombers. Supercharger rotor diameter 12.0 and 10.1 in; gear ratios 5.59:1 and 7.06:1. Propeller reduction gear ratio .420:1.
Aircraft:
> Avro 694 Lincoln II

MERLIN 620, 1,725 hp. This was the two-speed, two-stage Mk 150, re-designated. The series which started with the Merlin 620, goes through to the 724-1C. These were all commercial engines, the new 600 series breed being strongly influenced by the requirements of Trans-Canada Airlines who were to use the engines in the DC-4M, the commercial development of the Douglas C-54 military transport. Among the airline's requirements was an 'all-white' engine, finished in bare aluminium, with stainless-steel piping. External nuts and studs were to be cadmium plated. To obviate plug-leading at cruising power, charge-heating was required. This led to the redefinition of the function of what had started as an inter-cooler and had in effect become a two-way heat-exchanger. In addition, the 620 had U.S. splines for its 4-blade propeller. Maximum boost was +20 lb and the propeller reduction gear .4707:1. Rated RM.14SM. 242 built at Derby 1946–1948.
Aircraft:

> Canadair DC-4M.1 North Star

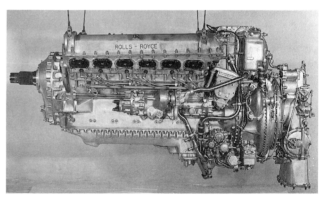

A two-stage Merlin in the 620 series.

MERLIN 621, 1,610 hp. A renamed Merlin 151, two-speed, two-stage supercharged engine, similar to the Mk 620 and, like it, nearing its power limit on take-off because of the risk of detonation. The Merlin 621 had a half-depth intercooler and charge heating. TMH power plant. Maximum boost was +20 lb and the propeller reduction gear .420:1, with British SBAC splines. Rated RM.14SM. 621, 416 built; 621 (S) 3 built; 621-5, 24 built; 621-15, 72 built, all at Derby 1946–1948.
Aircraft:
> Avro 689 Tudor I, II, III, IV, IVB, V

MERLIN 622, 1,725 hp, a two-speed, two-stage supercharged, TML power plant capable of full or no intercooling. Boost was increased slightly to +20.5 lb. It had U.S. propeller splines, a 4-blade propeller with electric de-icing and a reduction gear of .4707:1.
Aircraft:

    Canadair DC-4M.1, DC-4M.2, DC-4M.3 North Star(TCA)

MERLIN 623, 1,610 hp, a two-speed, two-stage supercharged engine, similar to the Merlin 622 but with British propeller splines. It featured half-depth intercooling and charge heating. It was a TMH power plant, maximum boost +20.5 lb and a propeller reduction gear ratio of .420:1.
Aircraft:

    Avro 689 Tudor I, III, IV, IVB, V

MERLIN 624, 1,610 hp, a very similar engine to the Merlin 622, with U.S. propeller splines but with a 3-blade propeller and electric de-icing. It was a TML power plant with full or no intercooling, maximum boost of +20.5 lb and a propeller reduction gear of .420:1. 624-10, 20 built, 1948.
Aircraft:

    Canadair DC-4M.2
    Canadair DC-4M.4 North Star (TCA)

MERLIN 626-1, 1,760 hp, a two-speed, two stage supercharged engine with U.S. propeller splines. The Merlin 626 series used full-depth intercooling on take-off, together with charge-heating at cruise as required, or no intercooling. In service, the system gave trouble due to intercooler pump leaks. Investigation into how to rectify the fault showed that the engine could be run with full intercooling for take-off and climb and, by introducing a stop-valve in the system, zero intercooling at cruise would maintain adequate charge temperature, with no linking of main and intercooling systems. Engines so modified therefore became the 724 series (q.v.). It was a TML power plant, with a maximum boost of +20.5 lb, electric propeller de-icing and a reduction gear ratio of .420:1. 204 built, 1948–1950.
Aircraft:

    Canadair C-4 (Argonaut, BOAC)

MERLIN 626-12, 1,760 hp. A two-speed, two-stage supercharged engine, similar to the Merlin 626-1. It had U.S. propeller splines and electric propeller de-icing. It was a TML power plant, with either full or ½ charge cooling or charge heating. Maximum boost was +20.5 lb and the propeller reduction gear .420:1. 26 built, 1949.
Aircraft:

    Canadair 4 DC-4M.2 (CPA)

A Canadair 4, DC-4M.2 of Canadian Pacific Airlines, powered by Merlin 626-12 engines, attended by a Silver Wraith.

MERLIN 631 (S) 5 built at Derby, 1947. Compression ratio 7:1.

MERLIN 641 (S) 5 built at Derby, 1947. Compression ratio 6.3:1.

MERLIN 722, a two-speed, two-stage supercharged engine for Trans-Canada Airlines, similar to the Merlin 724-1. Maximum boost +20.5 lb.
Aircraft:

    Canadair 4 DC-4M.2 North Star (TCA)

MERLIN 724-1. Two-speed, two-stage supercharged engines in the 724 series were similar to the 626 but incorporated the ability to run with full intercooling for take-off and climb. By introducing a stop-valve in the system, zero intercooling at cruise maintained adequate charge temperature, with no linking of main and intercooling systems. Maximum boost was 20.5 lb.

MERLIN 724-1C. The ultimate civil Merlin layout, the two-speed, two-stage supercharged Merlin 724-1C was similar to the 724-1 but had a crossover exhaust system. This ingenious arrangement discharged the inboard exhaust outboard and somewhat reduced aircraft cabin noise, a perpetual problem with civil Merlins. Maximum boost was +20.5 lb.
Aircraft:

    Canadair 4 DC-4M.2 North Star (TCA)

A Canadair 4, DC-4M.2 of Trans-Canada Air Lines with Merlin 724-1C engines. The exhausts from the inner sides cross over the engines, to join the outer outlets.

MERLIN 724-10, the end of the long Merlin line, this two-speed, two-stage engine was similar to the 724-1 and was intended for Trans-Canada Airlines. It used a slightly different intercooler system, to enable the airline to use the afterheater matrix partly as an intercooler. Maximum boost was +20.5 lb. Propeller reduction gear .42:1.
Aircraft:

    Canadair C-4 (Argonaut, BOAC)

PACKARD V-1650s (American Merlins)

V-1650-1, 1,390 hp, (1941), a two-speed, single-stage supercharged engine, similar to the Merlin 22A/28, with two-piece cylinder blocks. Propeller reduction gear.477:1. Rated RM.3SM, supercharger rotor diameter 10.25 in; gear ratios 8.15:1 and 9.25:1.
Aircraft:

    Curtiss P-40E Kittyhawk
    Curtiss XP-60.

V-1650-3, 1,280 hp, (1942), a two-speed, two-stage supercharged engine, with a different reduction-gear drive, was the Packard equivalent of the Merlin 63. Propeller reduction gear.479:1. Supercharger rotor diameters 12.0 and 10.1 in; gear ratios 6.39:1 and 8.095:1.

Aircraft:

> Curtiss P-40E Kittyhawk
> Curtiss XP-60
> North American P-51B/C Mustang III. (P-51C as the P-51B but built in Dallas)
> North American XP-78

V-1650-5, 1,400 hp, an experimental two-speed, two-stage supercharged engine. Supercharger rotor diameter 12.0 and 10.1 in; gear ratios 6.39:1 and 8.095:1.
Aircraft:

> Bell XP-63B

V-1650-7, 1,315 hp, two-speed, two-stage supercharged, this engine, with a different reduction-gear drive, was similar to the Merlin Mks 65, 66, 68 & 69. As in the V-1650-3, it was almost the equivalent of the Merlin 66 in terms of power. Propeller reduction gear.479:1. Rated RM.10SM, supercharger rotor diameter 12.0 and 10.1 in; gear ratios 5.8:1 and 7.34:1.
Aircraft:

> Commonwealth CA-17 Mustang
> Curtiss P-40E Kittyhawk
> North American P-51B, C, D, F, K Mustang III, IV

A late-series North American P-51 Mustang, powered by a Packard V-1650-7 Merlin.

V-1650-9, 1,380 hp. A two-speed, two-stage supercharged engine, similar to the Merlin 100 series, with an overhung impeller and end-feed lubrication system. It also featured, (for American Mustangs only), water-methanol injection and Simmonds power control. Propeller reduction gear.479:1. Rated RM.16SM, supercharger rotor diameter 12.0 and 10.1 in; gear ratios 6.39:1 and 8.095:1.
Aircraft:

> North American P-51D, G, H Mustang

V-1650-9A, 1,380 hp, an engine similar to the V-1650-9, as the Merlin 100, with detail differences but without water-methanol injection.
Aircraft:

> North American P-82B Twin Mustang

V-1650-11, 1,380 hp, another two-speed, two-stage variant of the V-1650-9 and -9A but with detail changes in the fuel system. It incorporated water-methanol injection and Simmonds power control. Propeller drive geared .479:1.
Aircraft:

> North American P-51H, L Mustang

V-1650-21, a two-speed, two-stage supercharged engine similar to the V-1650-9 or -11 but with opposite LHT rotation for handed mounting in the Twin Mustang.
Aircraft:

> North American P-82B Twin Mustang

V-1650-23, a two-speed, two-stage supercharged engine, similar to the V-1650-21 but with RHT propeller.
Aircraft:

> North American XP-82B Twin Mustang

V-1650-25, the ultimate V-1650 engine, similar to the V-1650-21, L.H. tractor-drive.
Aircraft:

> North American XP-82B Twin Mustang

ROLLS-ROYCE GRIFFON.

The Griffon was another development of the Buzzard and the racing 'R' engine. It was very much like a big Merlin, incorporating many of the features of that engine but turning the other way. It very successfully powered the later Spitfires and, aided by some very advanced fuel, enabled them to catch the small and elusive, very fast-flying German V-1 flying bomb. It was an engine which, when fitted in the relatively small Spitfire airframe was brutal in its power and, in one of its contra-prop versions, has also ground its reliable but noisy way into Royal Air Force history, powering the 'ten thousand rivets flying in close formation', the four-engined maritime reconnaissance Avro Shackleton.

THE GRIFFON FAMILY GROUPS.

TWO-SPEED, SINGLE-STAGE SUPERCHARGED GRIFFONS.
Griffon I, II, IIB, III, IV, VI, VIII, XII, 26, 29, 35, 36, 37, 56, 57, 57A.

TWO-SPEED, TWO-STAGE SUPERCHARGED GRIFFONS.
Griffon 61, 62, 64, 65, 66, 67, 68, 69, 70, 71, 72, 73, 74, 83, 85, 86, 87, 88, 89, 90, 91, 92, 94.

THREE-SPEED, TWO-STAGE SUPERCHARGED GRIFFONS.
Griffon 101, 102, 105, 121, 122, 130.

The Rolls-Royce Griffon was a 12-cylinder, upright 60-degree vee, liquid-cooled, poppet-valve engine. All Griffons had the following in common:

> Bore/stroke 6.0 x 6.6 in. (152.5 x 167.6 mm)
> Swept Volume 2,240.0 cu in. (36.7 litres).
> Compression Ratio 6.0:1.
> Dimensions vary according to accessories.
> Length 72.0-81.0 in; Width 30.3 in; Height 46.0 in.
> Weights, where published — *see* Performance tables.

Supercharge and boost (*see* text and tables). Spur-geared, reduction ratio as in text, all having left-hand tractor-drive. All had variable-pitch, constant-speed propellers. Fuel, normally, was 100/130 grade but 115/145 became available from early 1944 and, from then on, many Griffons ran on it, using +25 lb boost for the low-level pursuit of German V-1 flying-bombs and examples of the use of this fuel are included under the Griffon 70 and 80 series in the Performance Tables. Starting, in most Griffons, was by means of a Coffman cartridge starter.

Dry weight, as in all installations, varied from one Mark to another, depending on accessories. All standard Griffons, in service, ran at 2,750 rpm on take-off and, when diving, had a 20-second peak limit of 3,000 rpm

GRIFFON I.

This engine originated from the 1925 Buzzard, whose enormous potential was finally realized in the 1931 'R' racing engine. It was natural that the engine was in line for development into the upper bracket of military power units, even more potent than the P.V.12 (Merlin) already planned. A de-rated version of the 'R', to be called Griffon, was first run in 1933. The Griffon I never flew. There was considerable pressure to get on with the smaller engine, already planned for the new Hawker and Supermarine fighters and so active development did not continue until 1939. It was then extensively changed and made far more compact, as the Griffon II.

THE **GRIFFON II** was a major redesign of the original engine, first ran in November, 1939. It was generally similar to the earlier Rolls-Royce engines and the Merlin in particular, although of considerably larger capacity. It was necessary to keep its size and weight within the limits already imposed by the size and shapes of existing fighter aircraft. In order to do so, much thought went into redesigning the components so as to keep the engine's dimensions, particularly the overall length, to a minimum. As a result, the camshaft drives and the first part of the step-up of the supercharger drive were removed from the rear of the engine to the front. The crankshaft driving them via a pinion and shafts. The supercharger drive was a long shaft running to the rear, in bearings beneath the crankshaft; the second part of the step-up drive was completed at the rear of the engine through the usual moderate and full supercharge clutches. At first, it was thought that the small diameter of this drive was adequate for the spring drive.

The clutches at first used were of a type introduced by the Bristol Aeroplane Company, being engaged by oil pressure. The system was subsequently modified to be operated by revolving bob-weights which could apply load to either clutch, release or engagement being obtained by oil pressure on a piston. The original type of supercharger drive was not altogether satisfactory and in subsequent Griffons it was changed so that both step-up gears reverted to the rear. The real trouble, in its original form, was that it was expensive to make, hence the reversion to the drive at the back of the engine. It did not affect its operating reliability. In order to keep the engine's length to a minimum, a single magneto was used, mounted on the reduction gear casing, with two separate magnetic circuits to ensure the reliability formerly obtained with two separate instruments. These compact arrangements thus made it possible for the Griffon to be squeezed into the Spitfire, even with two-stage supercharging, after-cooling and ultimately a third supercharger drive. The Griffon turned in the opposite direction from that of earlier engines and at a rather lower speed, having a different firing order from that of the Merlin and producing a harsher exhaust note. An official total of 8,108 Griffons was built, 5,800 at Derby, 2,229 at Crewe and 79 at Glasgow. There were also a small number of additional experimental three-speed supercharged engines in the 101 series at the end of the production run, about which exact details are uncertain.

The Griffon was a 12-cylinder, upright 60-degree Vee, 70–30 per cent ethylene-glycol cooled, poppet-valve. Bore/stroke 6.0 x 6.6 in. Vol. 36.7 litre. Compression ratio 6:1; initially it was two-speed, single-stage fully/medium supercharged. Geared, spur .451:1, L.H. tractor-drive.

GRIFFON II, of 1,735 hp, was similar to Griffon VI. Single-stage supercharge, and the first production version. Auxiliary gearbox drive. Pedestal-type crankcase feet. Coffman starter. S.U. float feed and R.A.E. anti-G carburation. Compression ratio 6:1, geared drive .451:1. Rated RG.2SM, supercharger rotor diameter 10.1 in; gear ratios 7.85:1 and 10.68:1. 767 built at Derby, 1942–1945.
Aircraft:

    Fairey Firefly prototype
    Fairey Firefly Trainer I, II, III

GRIFFON IIB, 1,720 hp, (1939), two-speed, 7.85:1, 10.68:1, single-stage supercharge, similar to Mk II, compression ratio 6:1. Injection-type carburettor. Geared drive .451:1. Rated RG.2SM.
Aircraft:

    Bristol 156 Beaufighter II
    Fairey Firefly I
    Hawker Henley
    Hawker Tempest III
    Supermarine Spitfire IV, XX

Fairey Firefly F.1 carrier-borne fleet fighter, with a Griffon IIB.

GRIFFON III, 1,720 hp, Rated RG.2SM, supercharger rotor diameter 10.1 in; gear ratios two-speed, 7.85:1/10.68:1, single-stage supercharge, similar to Mk IIB with crankcase boom mounting. Geared drive .451:1. Rated RG.2SM. 101 built at Derby, 1942–1944.
Aircraft:

    Supermarine Spitfire XII

GRIFFON IV, 1,720 hp, as Mk III with two-speed supercharger ratios, 7.85:1 and 10.68:1, single-stage, similar to Mk III but geared drive .510:1. Rated RG.2SM. 25 built at Derby, 1942–1943.
Aircraft:

    Supermarine Spitfire XII

GRIFFON VI, 1,815 hp, similar to Griffon IV, with injection carburettor, two-speed, single-stage supercharge, automatic or manual gear change. Rated RG.14SM, supercharger rotor diameter 9.75 in; gear ratios 9.0:1 and 11.07:1. Propeller reduction gear ratio .510:1. Geared drive .51:1. 860 built at Derby, 1944–1945.
Aircraft:

    Supermarine Seafire XV, XVII, XVIII
    Supermarine Spitfire XII

The Rolls-Royce Griffon VI. The magneto mounted at the front of the engine (just appearing above the cylinder blocks) accounts for the slight bubble on the upper cowling of the Spitfire XII.

Spitfire XII, MB882, a low-level clipped-wing version, of 41 Squadron, powered by a Griffon VI. The magneto bubble on the cowling behind the propeller identifies it. Other Griffon Spitfires lacked this feature.

GRIFFON VIII, two-speed, single-stage supercharge, as Griffon VI with R-R fuel injection pump. Rated RG.14SM, supercharger rotor diameter 9.75 in; gear ratios 9.0:1 and 11.07:1. Propeller reduction gear ratio .510:1. 30 built at Derby, 1945–1946.
Aircraft:

    Fairey Barracuda V

GRIFFON XII, 1,815 hp, two-speed, single-stage supercharge, similar to Mk VI but with strengthened supercharger gear. Rated RG.2SM, supercharger rotor diameter 10.1 in; gear ratios 7.85:1 and 10.68:1. Geared drive .451:1. 410 built at Derby, 1945–1947.

Aircraft:
>   Fairey Firefly I, II
>   Fairey Firefly T.III Trainer

GRIFFON 26, two-speed, single-stage supercharge, Geared drive .4423:1. RG.14.SM
Aircraft:
>   Supermarine Seafire XV

GRIFFON 29, 1,815 hp, basically a Mk 21 and similar to Griffon 57. Rated RG.14SM, supercharger rotor diameter 9.75 in; gear ratios 9.0/11.7:1, single-stage supercharge. Geared, spur .59:1, with L.H./R.H. counter-rotating tractor-drive. Coffman starter Type 15. R-R fuel injection pump.
Aircraft:
>   Supermarine Seagull ASR 1.

The Supermarine Seagull ASR I, powered by a Griffon 29.

GRIFFON 35, two-speed, single-stage supercharge.

GRIFFON 36, two-speed, single-stage supercharge, RG.23SM

GRIFFON 37, 1,960 hp, similar to Griffon 57 but with single propeller shaft-drive. Pedestal-type crankcase feet. Fuel injection pump. Rated RG.23SM, supercharger rotor diameter 13.8 in; gear ratios 6.615:1 and 7.7:1. Single-stage supercharge. Spur-geared drive .510:1. 45 built at Derby, 1946.
Aircraft:
>   Fairey Barracuda V

GRIFFON 56, 2,000 hp, RG30SM, two-speed, single-stage supercharge, similar to Griffon 57 but without water-methanol injection.
Aircraft:
>   Blackburn B-54/Y.A.- 7, -8

GRIFFON 57, 2,500 hp, two-speed, 6.615:1 and 7.7:1, single-stage supercharge, geared .4423:1, L.H./R.H. counter-rotating tractor-drive. The various Griffon 50-series engines were electric started and not cartridge started, for Shackleton aircraft. The Griffon 57 was unique in that it was operated in the Shackleton in taking-off (wet) in FS gear and cruised in MS gear. This was because of the need of 150 grade fuel for getting +25 lb boost for take-off or, when 150 grade fuel was not available, +25 lb boost in conjunction with water-methanol injection. It had a Rolls-Royce fuel injection pump. Rated RG.30SM-2, supercharger rotor diameter 13.8 in; gear ratios 6.61:1 and 7.7:1. Propeller reduction gear ratio .442:1. 891 built at Derby, 1947–1953.
Aircraft:
>   Avro 696 Shackleton prototype
>   Avro 696 Shackleton MR.1 (mounted outboard)

GRIFFON 57A, two-speed, single-stage supercharge, similar to Mk 57 geared drive .4423:1 L.H./R.H. counter-rotating tractor-drive. 227 built at Derby, 1953-1955.
Aircraft:
>   Avro 696 Shackleton prototype
>   Avro 696 Shackleton MR.1, MR.1A, III

Rolls-Royce Griffon 57/58 series.

An Avro 696 Shackleton MR.3 powered by Rolls-Royce Griffon 57/58 series engines.

GRIFFON 59, Rated RG.30SM, supercharger rotor diameter 13.8 in; gear ratios 6.615:1 and 7.7:1. Propeller reduction gear ratio .51:1. Water-methanol in FS gear. Pedestal crankcase feet. 217 built at Derby, 1951–1953.
Aircraft:
>   Fairey Firefly VII, VIII

GRIFFON 61, 1,540 hp, a two-speed, two-stage engine, with two-piece cylinder blocks. Glycol-cooled auxiliary gearbox drive. Boom-mounted gearbox. Coarse pitch or inter-connected propeller controls. Bendix-Stromberg type carburettor. Rated RG.4SM, supercharger rotors diameter 13.4 and 11.3 in; gear ratios 5.84:1 and 7.58:1. Propeller reduction gear ratio .451:1. Geared, spur .451:1. 434 built at Derby, 700 at Crewe, 1942–1945.

Rolls-Royce Griffon 60 series engine, with intercooler.

Aircraft:

> Fairey Firefly III, IV
> Hawker Tempest IV
> Supermarine Seafire 45, 46, 47
> Supermarine Spitfire VIII (converted), XIV
> Supermarine Spitfire 21, 22 23, 24

GRIFFON 62, 1,540 hp, as Mk 61, with R-R fuel injection pump. Rated RG.4SM, two-stage supercharger rotors diameter 13.4 and 11.3 in; gear ratios 5.84:1 and 7.58:1. Propeller reduction geared drive .451:1. Fuel 115/150 grade (allows +25 lb boost).
Aircraft:

> Supermarine Seafire 46
> Supermarine Spitfire 21

GRIFFON 64, two-speed, two-stage supercharge, similar to Mks 61, 62 & 69, geared propeller drive .451:1. As Griffon 69. Rating RG.4SM. Fuel 115/150 grade. 200 built at Crewe, 1945.
Aircraft:

> Supermarine Seafire 46
> Supermarine Spitfire 21, 22

GRIFFON 65, as Mk 61 with two-speed, two-stage supercharge, geared drive .51:1. Triple choke RR-Bendix-Stromberg carburettor. Rated RG.4SM, supercharger rotors diameter 13.4 and 11.3 in; gear ratios 5.84:1 and 7.58:1. Propeller reduction gear ratio .51:1. 525 built at Derby, 950 at Crewe, 1943–1948.
Aircraft:

> Supermarine Spitfire VIII (converted) XIV, XVIII, XIX

A Spitfire XIV, RM619 of 130 Sqn, at an advanced airfield in Belgium in 1944.

Supermarine Spitfire PR.XIX

GRIFFON 66, as Mk 65, two-speed, two-stage supercharge, similar to Mks 65 & 69, with cabin blower drive. Geared drive .51:1. Rated RG.4SM. 260 built at Derby, 100 at Crewe, 1944–1945.
Aircraft:

> Supermarine Spitfire XIV, PR XIX (pressure cabin).

A Spitfire PR.XIX, powered by a Griffon 66, somewhat out of its element in a low-level beat-up.

GRIFFON 67, two-speed, two-stage supercharge, similar to Mk 65 & 69, no cabin blower drive fitted. Geared drive .51:1. Rated RG.4SM. Fuel 115/150 grade (allows +25 lb boost). 150 built at Crewe, 1945.
Aircraft:

> Supermarine Spitfire XIV, XVIII

GRIFFON 68, two-speed, two-stage supercharge, geared drive .51:1

GRIFFON 69, as Mk 64 but modified crankcase feet. Two-speed 5.84/7.58:1, two-stage supercharge. RR-Bendix Stromberg injection carburettor. Geared drive .51:1. Rated RG.4SM. Supercharger rotors diameter 13.4 and 11.3 in; gear ratios 5.84:1 and 7.58:1. Propeller reduction gear ratio .451:1. 130 built at Derby, 30 at Crewe, 1945.
Aircraft:

> Supermarine Spiteful XIV

GRIFFON 70, two-speed, two-stage supercharge, geared drive .451:1. Rating RG.4SM.

GRIFFON 71, 1,765 hp, two-speed, two-stage supercharge, to the requirements of the Royal Navy. Similar to Mks VI and 69 but with lower supercharger gear ratios, 5.16:1 and 6.79:1. Rating RG.10SM. 3 built at Derby, 1943.
Aircraft:

> Fairey Firefly IV prototype

GRIFFON 72, 2,100 hp, two-speed, two-stage supercharge, basically Mk 69, similar to Griffon 74, but with Stromberg carburettor. RG.10SM
Aircraft:

> Fairey Firefly III, IV

GRIFFON 73, 1,765 hp, two-speed, two-stage supercharge, similar to Mk VI but with lower supercharger gear ratios.
Aircraft:

> Fairey Firefly I, II

GRIFFON 74, 2,245 hp, two-speed 5.16:1, 6.79:1, two-stage supercharge, to requirements of Royal Navy. Rolls-Royce fuel injection pump. Fuel 100/130 grade but boost in S gear could be +25 lb when using 115/145 grade fuel. Geared drive .451:1. RG.10SM. 772 built at Derby, 30 at Glasgow, 1946–1952.
Aircraft:

> Fairey Firefly IV, V, VI

GRIFFON 83, 1,935 hp, (1944), rated RG.4SM, two-stage supercharger rotors diameter 13.4 and 11.3 in; gear ratios 5.84:1 and 7.58:1. Propeller reduction gear ratio .4423:1. Bendix-Stromberg Injection carburettor. L.H./R.H. counter-rotating props geared drive .442:1.
Aircraft:

> Martin-Baker M.B.5
> Supermarine Spitfire VIII converted to XIV

GRIFFON 85, two-speed 5.84:1/7.58:1, two-stage supercharge, similar to Mk 65 with Bendix-Stromberg, injection carburettor. L.H./R.H. counter-rotating props. geared .4423 L.H./R.H. tractor-drive. RG.4SM. 100 built at Derby, 1944–1945.
Aircraft:

> Hawker F.2/43 Fury I
> Supermarine Seafire 46
> Supermarine Spitfire XIV, 21

GRIFFON 86, as Mk85, with L.H./R.H. counter-rotating props. geared drive .4423:1. Rating RG.4SM. Cabin blower drive. Interconnected controls deleted.
Aircraft:

> Supermarine Spitfire XIV, 21

GRIFFON 87, 1,765 hp, two-speed 5.84:1 and 7.58:1, two-stage supercharge, similar to 85 but +25 lb boost operation, with Bendix-Stromberg Injection carburettor. L.H./R.H. counter-rotating props, geared drive .4423:1. Rating RG.4SM. 74 built at Crewe, 1945.
Aircraft:

> Supermarine Seafire 46, 47
> Supermarine Spitfire XIV, 21

THE 2,080 b.h.p. ROLLS-ROYCE GRIFFON 65 AERO-ENGINE

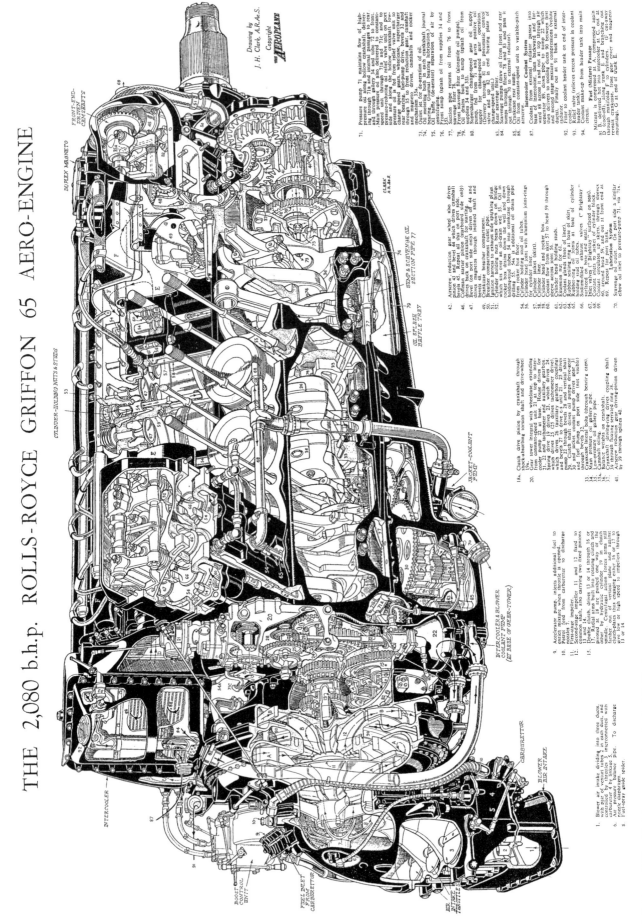

The Rolls-Royce Griffon 65. A fine cut-away drawing by J.H. Clark.

GRIFFON 88, 1,765 hp, as Mk 87, two-speed 5.84:1 and 7.58:1, two-stage supercharge, RR Mk IIC fuel-injection pump in place of carburettor with L.H/.R.H. counter-rotating props, geared drive 4423:1. Rating RG.4SM.
Aircraft:
>Supermarine Seafire 47
>Supermarine Spitfire XIV, 21

GRIFFON 89, 1,765 hp. Rated RG.4SM,, two-stage supercharger rotors diameter 13.4/11.3 in; gear ratios 5.84/7.58:1. Bendix-Stromberg Injection pump. LH/RH counter-rotating props geared drive .4423:1. 25 built at Crewe, 1945.
Aircraft:
>Supermarine Seafang 32

GRIFFON 90, 1,765 hp, as Mk 89, with R-R fuel injection pump, two-speed, two-stage supercharge, L.H./R.H. counter-rotating props geared drive .4423:1. Rating RG.4SM.
Aircraft:
>Supermarine Seafire 47

GRIFFON 91, two-speed, two-stage supercharge, basically a Mk 71, with LH/RH counter-rotating props. Rating RG.10SM

GRIFFON 92, RG.10SM. Basically a Mk 72 with contra-props. Rating RG.10SM.

GRIFFON 94, Basically a Mk 72 with contra-props and R-R fuel injection pump. Rating RG.10SM.

GRIFFON 100 series. As Griffon two-stage series, except for three-speed superchargers. Rated RG.3SML. Supercharger rotors diameter 14.3 and 12.25 in; gear ratios LS 5.72:1, MS 6.735:1, FS 7.703:1.

GRIFFON 101, 2,440 hp, two-stage supercharged. As Griffon 121 but geared, spur .451:1, single L.H. tractor-drive. RG.3SML.

Power Ratings:-

Normal Climb,	low-supercharge	1,515 hp,	2,600 rpm,	17,750 ft
Normal Climb,	medium-supercharge	1,430 hp,	2,600 rpm,	26,500 ft
Normal Climb,	high-supercharge	1,305 hp,	2,600 rpm,	33,075 ft
Maximum Climb,	low-supercharge	2,440 hp,	2,750 rpm,	6,000 ft
Maximum Climb,	medium-supercharge	2,300 hp,	2,750 rpm,	15,750 ft
Maximum Climb,	high-supercharge	2,085 hp,	2,750 rpm,	23,000 ft

Aircraft:
>Supermarine Spitfire XIV (at Hucknall)
>Supermarine Seafang XVI

A three-speed, two-stage Griffon 101. Most other engines in the Griffon 100 series had contra-props.

GRIFFON 102, 2,440 hp, three-speed 5.72:1, 6.735:1, 7.703:1, two-stage supercharged. Geared drive .450:1. L.H. R.H. counter-rotating props. Cabin blower drive. Power Ratings, as Griffon 101. Rating RG.3SML
Aircraft:
>Supermarine Spiteful
>Supermarine Spitfire 21

GRIFFON 105, 2,440 hp, three-speed 5.72:1, 6.735:1, 7.703:1, two-stage supercharged. Geared drive .510:1, L.H./R.H. counter-rotating props. Power Ratings, as Griffon 101.
Aircraft:
>Supermarine Spitfire 21

GRIFFON 121, 2,440 hp, three-speed 5.72:1, 6.735:1, 7.703:1, two-stage supercharged. Geared drive .4423:1, L.H./R.H. counter-rotating props. Power Ratings, as Griffon 101. RG.3SML
Aircraft:
>Supermarine Spitfire 21

GRIFFON 122, 2,440 hp, three-speed 5.72:1, 6.735:1, 7.703:1, two-stage supercharged. Cabin blower fitted. Geared drive .442:1, L.H./R.H. counter-rotating props. Power Ratings, as Griffon 101. Rated RG.3SML
Aircraft:
>Supermarine Seafire 46
>Supermarine Spitfire 21

GRIFFON 130, 2,440 hp, three-speed 5.72:1, 6.735:1, 7.703:1, two-stage supercharged. No cabin blower. Geared drive .4423:1, L.H./R.H. counter-rotating props. Power Ratings, as Griffon 101.

ROLLS-ROYCE 46H EAGLE I, (1944), 24-cylinder, horizontally opposed H-shaped, 70-30 per cent water, ethylene-glycol pressure-cooled, sleeve-valve. Bore/stroke 5.4 x 5.125 in. Vol. 2,807 cu in. (137 x 130 mm. Vol. 46 litre). Compression ratio 6.5:1, two-speed, two-stage supercharged, geared, spur .2985:1. L.H./R.H. tractor-drive. Coffman starter. Fuel 115/145 grade, DERD 2476.

EAGLE 46H EAGLE II, (1944), Generally similar to the Eagle I, with modifications. 24-cylinder, horizontally-opposed H-shaped, 70–30 per cent water, ethylene-glycol pressure-cooled, sleeve-valve. Bore/stroke 5.4 x 5.125 in. Vol. 2,807 cu in (137 x 130 mm. Vol. 46 litre). Compression ratio 6.5:1, two-speed, two-stage supercharged, geared, spur .2985:1. L.H./R.H. counter-rotating tractor-drive. Coffman starter. Fuel 115/145 grade, DERD 2476.

EAGLE 46H (20 srs) 22, (1947–49), 3,500 hp/3,500 rpm, +28 lb boost 24-cylinder, horizontally-opposed H-shaped, 70-30 per cent water, ethylene-glycol pressure-cooled, sleeve-valve. Bore/stroke 5.0 x 5.125 in. Vol. 2,807 cu in. (137 x 130 mm. Vol. 46 litre). Compression ratio 7:1, two-speed, 3:1, 3.67:1, two-stage supercharged, geared, spur .2985:1. L.H./R.H. counter-rotating tractor-drive. Coffman starter. Fuel 115/150 grade, DERD 2476. 15 built at Derby up to 1949. First flown in a Wyvern (W.35) 16.12.46. Length 135.5 in; width 43.4 in; height 50.0 in.
Aircraft:
>Westland Wyvern I (flying on 100 Octane fuel, derated).

The ultimate production Rolls-Royce piston engine, the big Eagle 22 which powered the first Westland Wyvern I.

ROYAL AIRCRAFT FACTORY.

Up to about the end of 1916, the Royal Aircraft Factory at Farnborough, in addition to designing and building aeroplanes, had designed a number of engines, mostly adaptations or redesigns of French engines and built some, although the large majority were put out to Industry. About 7,000 engines of Royal Aircraft Factory design were built, the majority being of R.A.F.1b and 4a types. A number of rather over-stated complaints were made in Parliament

THE 3,500 h.p. ROLLS-ROYCE EAGLE Mk. 22 AERO-ENGINE

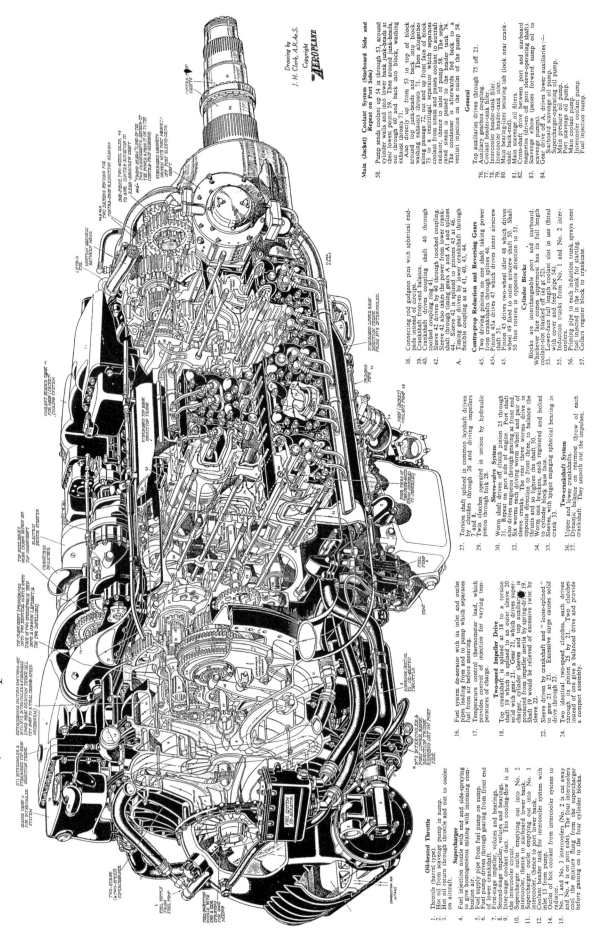

Drawing by
J. H. Clark, A.R.Ae.S.
Copyright *Aeroplane*

Oil-heated Throttle

1. Throttle (barrel type).
2. Hot oil from scavenge pump in sump.
3. Hot oil return through throttle and out to cooler on aircraft.

Supercharger

4. Fuel injection nozzle with end and side-spraying to give homogeneous mixing with incoming combustion air.
5. Fuel supply pipe from fuel pump on sump.
6. Fuel pump driven through gearing from front end of lower crankshaft.
7. First-stage impeller.
8. Second-stage impeller, volutes and bearings.
9. Inter-stage coolant duct. This cooling-flow is in the intercooler circuit.
10. Supercharger outlet emptying out into No. 2 intercooler, thence to starboard lower bank.
11. Supercharger outlet emptying out into No. 3 intercooler, thence to port lower bank.
12. Coolant header tank for intercooler system with inlet 13 from pump.
14. Outlet of hot coolant from intercooler system to radiator.
15. No. 1 and No. 3 intercoolers (No. 2 is cut away and No. 4 is on port side). The four intercoolers cool the mixture flung from the supercharger before passing on to the four cylinder blocks.

16. Fuel system de-aerator with its inlet and outlet pipes leading from and to pump which separates fuel from air before metering.
17. Temperature control thermometer lead, which provides control of injection for varying temperatures of charge.

Two-speed Impeller Drive

18. Top crankshaft is splined at 18 to a torsion shaft 19 which is splined to an outer sleeve 20 solid with gear 21. Gear 21, which drives supercharger, cylinder sleeves and top auxiliary is protected from impeller inertia by spring-drive 19. Shaft 19 would be relieved of excessive twist by sleeve 22.
22. Sleeve driven by crankshaft and "loose-splined" to 21 at 23. Excessive surge causes solid drive through 23.
24. Two identical two-speed clutches, each driven through its pinion 25 by 21. Two clutches instead of one give a balanced drive and provide a compact assembly.

27. Torsion shaft splined in common layshaft driven by clutches through 26 and driving impellers.
29. Twin clutches operated in unison by hydraulic piston through 6 at 28.

Sleeve-valve System

30. Worm shaft driven off clutch pinion 25 through 31. Repeat on port side of engine. Port shaft also drives magnetos through gearing at front end.
32. Six worms each driving worm wheel and pair of sleeve cranks. The rear three worms drive in opposite direction to front three, to balance the thrusts and so lighten the shaft 30.
34. Worm unit brackets, each registered and bolted to cylinder block base face.
35. Sleeves, with spigot engaging spherical bearing in crank 33.

Two-crankshaft System

36. Upper and lower crankshafts.
37. Dynamic balance on rearmost throw of each crankshaft. They smooth out the impulses.

38. Connecting rod gudgeon pins with spherical end-pads instead of circlips.
39. Crankshaft front-end balance.
40. Crankshaft coupling ring.
42. Sleeve 42 driven by 40 through toothed coupling. Sleeve 42 also takes the power from lower crankshaft through timing gears A and A1 and splines 44. Sleeve 42 is splined to pinions 45 at 46.
A. Timing gear driven by lower crankshaft through flexible coupling as at 41, 40, 43, 44.

Contra-prop Reduction and Reversing Gears

45. Two driving pinions on one shaft taking power from crankshafts through splines 46.
45A. Pinion 45A drives 47 which drives inner airscrew shaft 51.
45. Pinion 45 drives two-wheel idler 48 which drives wheel 49 fixed to outer airscrew shaft 50. Shaft 50 thus rotates in opposite direction to 51.

Cylinder Blocks

Blocks are interchangeable port and starboard. Whichever face comes uppermost has its full length coolant-slot blanked off (as at 52).
53. Lower-face full length coolant slot in use (fitted with cover and feed pipe 54).
55. Induction trunks from No. 1 and No. 2 intercoolers.
56. Induction pipe to each induction trunk sprays neat fuel injected in the trunk for starting.
57. Collars register block to crankcase.

Main (Jacket) Coolant System (Starboard Side and Repeat on Port Side)

58. Pump sends coolant up 54 in through 53, around cylinder walls and into lower bank junk-heads at their lowest points 59. Then around junk-heads, out through 60 and back into block, washing exhaust throats 71.
Also directly up from 53 to top of block around top junk-heads and back into block, washing exhaust throats 71. Then altogether along passage 72, out and up front face of block 73 to a centrifugal separator which separates coolant from steam and passes coolant to aircraft radiator, thence to inlet of pump 58. The separated steam is passed to the header tank 74. The condensate is afterwards fed back to a venturi injection on the outlet of the pump 58.

General

75. Top auxiliaries driven through 75 off 21.
76. Auxiliary gearbox coupling.
77. Coolant header-tank coupling.
78. Intercooler header-tank filler.
79. Coolant header-tank filler.
80. Main bearing-liner securing tab (look near crankshaft back-end).
81. Main scavenge oil filters.
82. Cross-shaft drive between port and starboard magnetos (driven off port sleeve-operating shaft).
83. Scavenge elbow (passes forward sump oil to scavenge pumps).
84. Gearing drive drives lower auxiliaries:—
Starboard scavenge oil pump.
Supercharger-operating oil pump.
Main pressure oil pump.
Port scavenge oil pump.
Main coolant pump.
Intercooler-coolant pump.
Fuel injection pump.

The Eagle 22, featured in one of J.H. Clark's famous cut-away drawings.

by Noel Pemberton Billing MP, that both the Royal Flying Corps and the Factory were inefficiently organized, the latter taking business from the aircraft industry. (The average pay of the Factory work force at the time was £3·00 per week). The Burbidge Committee considered the matter and the manufacturing side of the Factory was shut down soon after. It thus became the Royal Aircraft Establishment specializing, as it has ever since, in aeronautical research.

The designations of both engines and aircraft designed or built at the Factory are quoted in this book in accordance with preserved contemporary records. Unfortunately, the origins of some of the dimensions quoted are in Imperial measure and some in metric and they do not all correspond. Exact accuracy is as close as possible but cannot be guaranteed.

R.A.F.1, 90 hp, (prototype, 1913). An engine based on the 80 hp Renault. 8-cylinder, upright 90-degree Vee, air-cooled poppet-valve. Bore/stroke 3.94 x 5.51 in., Vol. 537.4 cu. in. (100 x 140 mm, Vol. 8.8 l.). Compression ratio 4.3:1, based on the 90 hp Renault. Geared, spur 5:1, L.H. tractor-drive.

A Royal Aircraft Factory B.E.2e, with a R.A.F.1a engine.

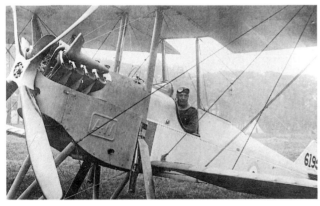

An Armstrong Whitworth F.K.3 powered by an R.A.F.1a.

In 1915, this geared supercharger was fitted to a B.E.2c at farnborough. The engine was a R.A.F.1a.

R.A.F.1a, 90 hp, (1914, an improved R.A.F.1), based on the 80 hp Renault, 8-cylinder, upright 90-degree Vee, air-cooled poppet-valve. Bore/stroke 3.94 x 5.51 in., Vol. 537.4 cu in. (100 x 140 mm., Vol. 8.8 l.). Compression ratio 4.3:1, geared spur .5:1, L.H. tractor-drive. This turned out to be a somewhat unreliable engine, low in power for its weight. Cast-iron cylinders. Camshaft in the vee, operating inlet valves by tappets and exhaust valves by push rods and rockers. Pistons were originally of cast-iron and later of aluminium. Claudel-Hobson dual Mk 1A carburettor and single magneto. Flywheel-operated oil pump. An experimental gear-driven supercharger was added at the rear of an engine in a B.E.2c in 1915.

Production, 8/1914–12/1918, from:-
Austin Motor Co Ltd, Birmingham,
Ordered, 1,425;   Delivered, 1,400; Cancelled/suspended,   25
Daimler Co Ltd, Coventry,
Ordered, 600;   Delivered, 600;   Cancelled/suspended, 0
Lanchester Motor Co, Birmingham,
Ordered, 650;   Delivered, 650;   Cancelled/suspended, 0
Rolls-Royce Ltd, Derby,
Ordered, 35;   Delivered, 35;   Cancelled/suspended, 0
Siddeley-Deasy Co Ltd, Coventry,
Ordered, 100;   Delivered, 25;   Cancelled/suspended, 75
Wolseley Motors Ltd, Birmingham,
Ordered, 150;   Delivered, 150;   Cancelled/suspended, 0
Aircraft:
>Airco D.H.6
>Armstrong Whitworth F.K.2, F.K.3
>Avro 504K
>Boulton & Paul P.6
>Boulton & Paul P.9
>de Havilland D.H.51
>Royal Aircraft Factory B.E.2c, d, e
>Royal Aircraft Factory B.E.9
>Royal Aircraft Factory S.E.5

R.A.F.1b, 105 hp, (1915, improved, large-bore R.A.F.1a), 8-cylinder, upright 90-degree Vee, air-cooled poppet-valve. Bore/stroke 4.13 x 5.51 in., Vol. 590.64 cu.in. (105 x 140 mm., Vol. 9.7 l.). Compression ratio 4.24:1, geared, spur .5:1, L.H. tractor-drive.
Production, 8/1914–12/1918, from:-
Rolls-Royce Ltd, Derby,
Ordered, 65;   Delivered, 65;   Cancelled/suspended, 0
Wolseley Motors Ltd, Birmingham,
Ordered, 50;   Delivered, 49;   Cancelled/suspended, 1
Aircraft:
>Armstrong Whitworth F.K.3
>Royal Aircraft Factory B.E.2e

R.A.F.1c, 105 hp, (1915), as R.A.F.1b with aluminium cylinders and steel shrunk-in liners. Bore either 100 or 105 mm, stroke 140 mm. Compression ratio 4.5:1.

R.A.F.1d, 150 hp, (1915), a R.A.F.1b with o.h.v., aluminium cylinders, as used in R.A.F.4D. Compression ratio 4.7:1.

R.A.F.1e, 150 hp, (1915), a R.A.F.1d with improved cy!inders.

R.A.F.2, 120 hp, (1913), 9-cylinder, single-row radial, air-cooled poppet-valve. Bore/stroke 3.94 x 5.51 in., Vol. 604.6 cu in. (100 x 140 mm., Vol. 9.9 l.). Geared epicyclic .563:1 R.H. tractor-drive.
Aircraft:
>Royal Aircraft Factory B.E.8a 'Bloater'

R.A.F.3, 200 hp, (1914), 12-cylinder, upright 60-degree Vee, water-cooled, poppet-valve. Bore/stroke 4.3 x 5.51 in., Vol. 960.2 cu. in. (109 x 140 mm., Vol. 15.67 l.). Compression ratio 5.3:1, geared, spur .5:1 L.H. tractor-drive.

R.A.F.3a, 200 hp, (large-bore R.A.F.3), 12-cylinder, upright 60-degree Vee, water-cooled, poppet-valve. Bore/stroke 4.5 x 5.5 in. Vol. 1,049.4 cu.in. (114.3 x 140 mm., Vol. 17.24 l.) Compression ratio 5.3:1, geared spur .5:1 L.H. tractor/R.H. pusher-drive. Forged steel cylinders. Inlet and exhaust valves for each cylinder were operated by one tappet rod. Slightly convex-crowned aluminium

alloy pistons. Welded steel water jacket. Claudel-Hobson 34 Mk 1A duplex carburettors. Dual A.65 magnetos. Length 65.6 in; width 37.5 in; height 35.3 in.
Production, 8/1914-12/1918, from:-
Armstrong Whitworth & Co Ltd, Gosforth.
Ordered, 30;   Delivered, 29;   Cancelled/suspended, 1
D.Napier & Son Ltd, Acton,
Ordered, 260;   Delivered, 260;   Cancelled/suspended, 0
Aircraft:
　　　　Airco D.H.4
　　　　Royal Aircraft Factory R.E.7

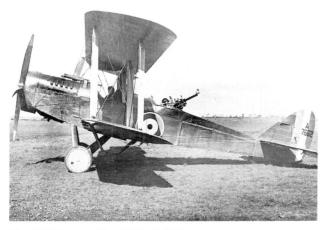

Airco D.H.4 powered by a 200 hp R.A.F.3a

R.A.F.4, 140 hp, (1915), a derivative of R.A.F.1A, designed by A.J. Rowledge at the request of the War Office and based on the R.A.F.3. With flywheel oil pump. A 12-cylinder, upright 60-degree Vee, air-cooled poppet-valve engine. Bore/stroke 3.94 x 5.51 in. Vol. 806.15 cu in. (100 x 140 mm., Vol. 13.2 l.). Geared, spur .5:1, L.H. tractor-drive.

R.A.F.4a, 150 hp, (1917, improved R.A.F.4, with side-valves and cast-iron cylinders), 12-cylinder, upright 60-degree Vee, air-cooled poppet-valve. Bore/stroke 3.94 x 5.51 in. Vol. 806.15 cu in. (100 x 140 mm., Vol. 13.2 l.). Compression ratio 5.3:1. Geared, spur .5:1 R.H. tractor-drive. Gear-operated oil pump. Dual A6.S magnetos, dual Claudel Hobson Mk 1A carburettors.
Production, 8/1914-12/1918, from:-
Daimler Co Ltd, Coventry,
Ordered, 2,300;   Delivered, 2,298; Cancelled/suspended, 2
Siddeley-Deasy Co Ltd, Coventry,
Ordered, 1,310;   Delivered, 1,310; Cancelled/suspended, 0
Aircraft:
　　　　Armstrong Whitworth F.K.8
　　　　Royal Aircraft Factory B.E.12, B.E.12a
　　　　Royal Aircraft Factory R.E.7
　　　　Royal Aircraft Factory R.E.8
　　　　Siddeley R.T.1
　　　　Vickers F.B.14F

A B.E.12, powered by a R.A.F.4a.

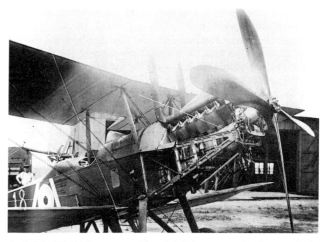

An R.E.8 of No 34 Sqn, powered by a R.A.F.4a, captured by Germans in the Spring of 1917.

Early type cooling baffles on a R.A.F.4a engine of a R.E.8.

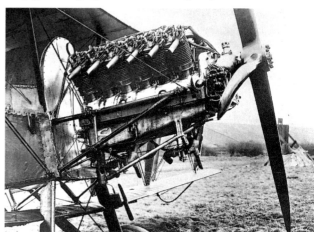

A Bristol F.2B Fighter, with an experimental R.A.F.4d installed.

R.A.F.4d, 180 hp, (1916), as R.A.F.4a but with redesigned cylinders in aluminium with liners shrunk-in under steam and O.H. Valves. 12-cylinder, upright 60-degree Vee, air-cooled poppet-valve. Bore/stroke 3.94 x 5.51 in. Vol. 806.15 cu. in. (100 x 140 mm. Vol. 13.2 l.), compression ratio 4.7:1. Geared, spur .5:1. L.H. tractor-drive. Dual A6.S magnetos, dual Claudel carburettors. A particularly interesting installation was made in 1918, with a French Rateau exhaust-driven supercharger connected directly to the blower wheel and mounted in an R.E.8 at Farnborough (with an enormous cooling-air scoop). This was to eliminate the supercharger gear drive, previously the subject of Farnborough experiments. Equally interesting was the variable-pitch propeller which was also designed and made there, in order to control the

power output. Had the turbine not failed at 26,500 rpm, it was calculated that ground pressure could have been maintained up to 17,000 feet.
Production, 8/1914-12/1918, from:-
Daimler Co Ltd, Coventry,
Ordered, 500; Delivered, 16; Cancelled/suspended, 484
Aircraft:
>Bristol F.2B Fighter
>Royal Aircraft Factory R.E.8

R.A.F.4e, 240 hp, (1917), R.A.F.4d with improved and strengthened cylinders and larger valves.

R.A.F.5, 150 hp, (1915), 12-cylinder, upright 60-degree Vee, air-cooled poppet-valve. Bore/stroke 3.94 x 5.51 in. Vol. 806.15 cu in. (100 x 140 mm. Vol. 13.2 l.). Compression ratio 4.3:1. Geared, spur .5:1 L.H. pusher version of the R.A.F.4A, with fan-cooling. Two Claudel-Hobson C.H.36.1 carburettors, two A.6S magnetos.
Aircraft:
>Royal Aircraft Factory F.E.2b, F.E.2c.
>Royal Aircraft Factory F.E.4

The R.A.F.5 was a pusher version of the air-cooled R.A.F.4a, seen here mounted on an F.E.2b.

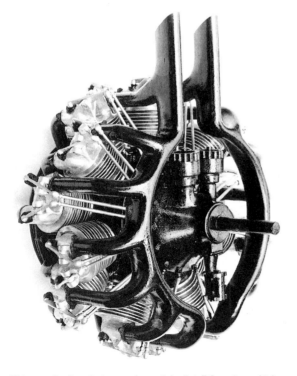

This was the first design mock-up of the R.A.F.8 engine, which was never built at the Factory but was destined eventually to appear as the Armstrong Siddeley Jaguar.

R.A.F.5b, 170 hp (aluminium or cast-iron cylinders, side-valves), 12-cylinder, upright 60-degree Vee, air-cooled poppet-valve. Bore/stroke 4.13 x 5.51 in. Vol. 885.77 cu.in. (105 x 140 mm. Vol. 14.55 l.). Geared, spur .5:1 L.H. pusher drive, fan-cooled.

R.A.F.7, 300 hp, a high-compression R.A.F.3A, with high-lift cams and outside exhaust valves.

R.A.F.8, 300 hp. In 1916, there were allegations in Parliament of shortcomings on the part of the Royal Aircraft Factory at Farnborough. In 1917, following the ensuing Report by the Burbidge Committee of Inquiry, the Factory's substantial design and construction capability was dismantled, its function changing to one principally of research, as the Royal Aircraft Establishment. This change led to some very experienced, senior designers leaving the Factory and joining other aircraft constructors. Among those to leave were Major F.M.Green, who had been in charge of design, John Lloyd, head of the Stress Department and S.D.Heron, the engine designer.

While at Farnborough, Green and Heron had been responsible for developing the proposed 300 hp, R.A.F.8, a fourteen-cylinder, 22.4 litre air-cooled radial engine. Together, they joined The Siddeley-Deasy Motor Car Co. at Coventry, a Company headed by John Siddeley who was determined to remain in the aircraft and engine industry, the upheaval providing the opportunity for the team to continue their development work and, particularly, on the new engine. *See* Armstrong Siddeley, Siddeley-Deasy.

SALMSON (CANTON-UNNE).
The French firm Sté des Moteurs Salmson, of Billancourt, Seine, produced in France, under Canton-Unné Patents in the unusual radial water-cooled form, engines of 85, 100, 110, 135, 150 & 160 hp, in 7 & 9-cylinder layouts, single and two-row. English licensees for the types below were the Dudbridge Ironworks Ltd., sub-contracted to Willans & Robinson Ltd, Rugby (French designations apparently reversed). All had steel cylinders with copper water jackets.

SALMSON (CANTON-UNNE) B.9, 140 hp (1913-14), 9-cylinder, single-row radial, water-cooled, poppet-valve. Bore/stroke 4.3 x 5.5 in. (122 x 140 mm). Compression ratio 5.16:1. Direct L.H. tractor/R.H. pusher drive. 106 B.9s and M.9s built at Rugby. One Zenith carburettor and magneto.
Production, 8/1914-12/1918, from:-
Willans & Robinson Ltd, Rugby,
Ordered, 106; Delivered, 106; Cancelled/suspended, 0
Aircraft:
>Henry Farman F.27
>Short S.87 Admiralty Type 135 Seaplane
>Short Type C (Improved S.74)
>Short 830 (Admiralty Type 830)
>Voisin LA.S

A rarity among radials was the Salmson water-cooled engine, built under French Canton-Unné patents. This was the first built by Willans & Robinson at Rugby and was mounted in a R.F.C. Henri Farman in India in 1916.

SALMSON (CANTON-UNNE) M.9, 120 hp, (1914-15), 9-cylinder, single-row horizontal radial water-cooled, poppet-valve. Bore/stroke 4.8 x 5.51 in. Vol. 897.03 cu in. (122 x 140 mm). Geared, spur at right-angle 1:1. L.H. tractor/R.H. pusher drive. Two Zenith 48 carburettors, one magneto.
Aircraft:

>   Blackburn Type L
>   Breguet U2
>   Voisin LA

SALMSON (CANTON-UNNE) R.9 160 hp/1,300 rpm, as B.9. Bore/stroke 125 x 140 mm. Diameter 42.5 in.
Aircraft:

>   Henry Farman F.27

SALMSON (CANTON-UNNE) 2M.7, 200 hp/1,300 rpm, was a 14-cylinder, water-cooled two-row radial poppet-valve engine. Bore/stroke 122 x 140 mm. Diameter 41.3 in.
Aircraft:

>   Kennedy Giant
>   Short Type A S.90 Admiralty Type 166
>   Sopwith Bat Boat II
>   Sopwith Special Seaplane, Admiralty Type C
>   Sopwith Admiralty Type 860 Seaplane
>   Wight A.1 Navyplane

SALMSON (CANTON-UNNE) 9ZM, 250 hp, (1917–18), 9-cylinder, single-row radial water-cooled, poppet-valve. Bore/stroke 4.92 x 6.69 in. Vol. 1,144.6 cu in. (125 x 170 mm). Early engines had 165 mm stroke. Compression ratio 5.4:1. Direct L.H. tractor/R.H pusher drive. Two Zenith carburettors, two Salmson magnetos.
Production, 8/1914-12/1918, from:-
Willans & Robinson, Rugby,
Ordered, 36;   Delivered, 36;   Cancelled/suspended, 0
Aircraft:

>   Vickers F.B.27 Vimy prototype

SCOTT MOTOR CYCLE COMPANY LTD, SHIPLEY, YORKSHIRE.

Following many years experience with motor cycle engines, the company has developed this engine for ultra-light aircraft.

FLYING SQUIRREL, A.2S, Mk II, 28 hp, (1935), 2-cylinder, inverted in-line, air-cooled, two-stroke, having only five main moving parts. Bore/stroke 2.87 x 3.07 in. Vol. cu 42.11in. (75 x 78 mm). Vol. 652 cc). Compression ratio 6.8:1. It had a spur-type reduction, L.H. tractor-drive.
Aircraft:

>   Barnwell B.S.W. Mk I
>   Dart Flittermouse
>   De Bruyne-Maas Ladybird
>   Howitt Monoplane
>   Luton L.A.4A Minor
>   Mignet HM 14 Pou du Ciel
>   Wren Goldcrest

SIDDELEY-DEASY — See Armstrong Siddeley and Beardmore.

SMITH STATIC.

This unorthodox engine was designed and originally built by John W. Smith, an American. He brought it to England in 1915 and, at first the Admiralty was interested in it. In appearance, it was a single-row 10-cylinder air-cooled radial but its connecting rods were offset and worked alternately on a two-throw crankshaft. It also featured an impeller, mounted as a fan on the tail of the crankshaft so as to improve mixture distribution, rather than to increase its pressure. It worked, in effect, as a double five-cylinder engine, with its cylinders set in a single row. The Admiralty, attracted to the idea of air-cooling rather than the winter problems of frozen radiators and the associated plumbing of simple water cooling, tested the engine for a reported 2,000 hours, on the bench and in the air. Believing that the engine could be as efficient as successful rotaries, a small manufacturing contract was given by the Ministry of Munitions to Heenan and Froude Ltd of Worcester, who built about six of them, together with a number of spares.

The little two-stroke Scott Flying Squirrel, which powered, among other ultra-lights, the Flying Flea.

A picture of the 150 hp Smith Static engine is a rarity, justifying its inclusion despite the poor quality of the print.

A few were tested experimentally by the Admiralty but the Smith Static turned out not to be a success, when fitted in the A.D Navyplane and a modified Vickers F.B.5. The Admiralty then turned the engine down and, on 13 September 1917, the progress and Allocation Committee, at the suggestion of General Sefton Brancker, decided that it could not be released for operational flying, but should be tried out on a Home Defence aircraft. It was proposed to be fitted to a Vickers F.B.12C but this turned out to involve numerous modifications and, although an aircraft is believed to have been sent to Martlesham, it probably was not fitted.

SMITH STATIC, 140/150 hp, (1915) was a 10-cylinder, single row radial, air-cooled, poppet-valve. Vol. 875 cu in. Direct R.H. tractor/L.H. pusher drive.
Aircraft:
> A.D.Navyplane (Pemberton Billing)
> Vickers F.B.5

Originally ordered by the R.N.A.S., the 150 hp Smith Static was not a success but is seen here in a Vickers F.B.5.

STATAX ENGINE CO. LTD, LONDON.
In 1914, this company announced a British engine of an entirely new type. It was to appear in at least three versions, a 5-cylinder engine delivering 40-45 hp at 1,200 rpm, as well as 80 hp 7-cylinder and 100 hp 10-cylinder engines. These were in fact 'barrel-type' engines, with their cylinders mounted axially, lying parallel with the propeller shaft. This layout was different from other types of barrel engine and it was claimed that it had '..no crankshaft, no wobble gear and centrifugal force entirely counteracted'. It was an extremely compact engine but little has been heard or printed about it, except that it was an air-cooled rotary. It was clearly a form of swash-plate engine, the plate being adjustable rather than having the slightly more normal 'wobble gear'. The 40 hp engine was claimed to have great fuel and oil economy, small diameter and low head resistance. Apart from having twin magnetos, about the only other published details are 'single piston valves', the gas inlet through the central shaft and the weight of 172 lb. Bore/stroke 3.94 x 4.73 in.

Nothing more has yet to come to light about any of these engines but the 40 hp version, at least, is believed to have flown. It was entered by a Dr F.Hansen for the 1914 Aerial Derby, which was postponed for bad weather perhaps to the good fortune of Dr Hansen. An interesting engine, it then seems to have disappeared without trace.
Aircraft:
> Caudron G.III

The unusual and very slim swash-plate Statax engine in a Caudron G.III.

SUNBEAM MOTOR CAR CO, LTD., Wolverhampton.
This company originated about 1899 as John Marston & Sons, bicycle manufacturers, later turning to the production of touring and racing motor cars. This happened when Louis Coatalen joined the firm from France in 1909, as Chief Engineer. After a Sunbeam car won the French Coupe des Voiturettes and the Coupe de l'Auto at Dieppe three years later, Coatalen turned his attention to the first of a large number of aero-engines. He based the design of the first on his successful 3-litre racing car engine. He adopted the aluminium alloy piston, on the recommendation of W.O. Bentley. Cylinders were mostly of cast aluminium, except for the Maori and Cossack, which were of cast-iron. Many of his engines were designed and built to order of the Admiralty, for the Royal Naval Air Service and a number were exported, notably to Russia (before the revolution). There has been much confusion about the exact identity of some of the early engines, which were initially identified by their theoretical horse powers and were then retrospectively named. They are listed here in approximate order of appearance, although as so often occurred, engine types overlapped. The large and powerful Sikh series of airship engines are not dealt with in detail. At first, Sunbeam engines were referred to as 'Sunbeam-Coatalens'.

The 150 hp Sunbeam Crusader, showing its inside exhausts.

CRUSADER, 150 hp, (1913), 8-cylinder, upright 90-degree Vee water-cooled. Two poppet side-valves, inside exhausts. Cylinders were cast 'en-bloc' in pairs, of cast-iron with electrolytically deposited copper. Opposing rows of cylinders were staggered, allowing two connecting rods to operate each crankpin. Claudel Hobson carburettors were attached to the inlet manifolds, on the outside of the blocks, the exhausts being on the inside. Bore/stroke 90 x 150 mm. Vol. 7.6 litre. Geared, spur .5:1. L.H. tractor-drive.
Production, 8/1914–12/1918, from:-
Sunbeam Motor Car Co Ltd, Wolverhampton.
Ordered, 224;   Delivered, 224;   Cancelled/suspended, 0
Aircraft:

    Curtiss C
    Short 827
    Sikorsky Il'ya Muromets
    Sikorsky S-19

MOHAWK, 225 hp, (1914), 12-cylinder upright 60-degree Vee water-cooled, two poppet side-valves. Bore/stroke 90 x 150 mm, Vol. 11.8 litre. Cylinders en-bloc threes, cast-iron. Geared, spur .5:1. L.H. tractor/R.H. pusher drive.
Production, 8/1914-12/1918, from:-
Sunbeam Motor Car Co Ltd, Wolverhampton.
Ordered, 287;   Delivered, 287;   Cancelled/suspended, 0
Aircraft:

    Avro 528
    Royal Aircraft Factory R.E.7
    Short (Admiralty Type) 184
    Short Bomber
    Sikorsky Il'ya Muromets
    Sopwith (Admiralty Type) 860 Seaplane
    Wight (Admiralty Type) 840 Seaplane

Captured German pictures of the Sunbeam Mohawk mounted in a Short 184 seaplane. The two carburettor intakes are mounted on the crankcase.

AMAZON, 160 hp, (1916), 6-cylinder upright in-line, water-cooled cast blocks of three, four poppet-valves, operated by twin camshafts. Bore/stroke 4.33 x 6.3 in, Vol. 556.44 cu in. (110 x 160 mm. Vol. 11.2 litre). Geared, spur .63:1. L.H. tractor/pusher drive. Mk I, 2 magnetos; Mk II, 1 magneto. Two 42 mm Claudel-Hobson B.Z.S. carburettors. Length 56.29 in; width 19.1 in; height 38.6 in.
Production, 8/1914-12/1918, from:-
Sunbeam Motor Car Co Ltd, Wolverhampton.
Ordered, 100;   Delivered, 77;   Cancelled/suspended, 23.
Aircraft:

    H.M. Airship C.14 (Coastal)

COSSACK, 320 hp, (1916), a 12-cylinder development of the Amazon, upright 60-degree Vee, water-cooled, four poppet-valves. Bore/stroke 4.33 x 6.3 in. Vol. 1,112 cu in. (110 x 160 mm. Vol. 22.4 litre). Compression ratio 5:1. Geared, spur .5:1. L.H. tractor/R.H. pusher drive. Cossack I, two magnetos. Mk II, four magnetos. Four Claudel-Hobson C.Z.S.42 carburettors. As two rows of a Viking. One version, Cossack III used for Admiralty dirigible airships R36, R38 (and intended for R39-41, all of which

were cancelled). The engine had features similar to the Maori 4. Length 61.8 in; width 37.8 in; height 38.9 in.
Production, 8/1914–12/1918, from:-
Sunbeam Motor Car Co Ltd, Wolverhampton.
Ordered, 382;   Delivered, 350;   Cancelled/suspended, 32
Aircraft:

    Handley Page H.P.11 O/100 Type O
    Short 310-A4
    Short 310-B North Sea Scout
    R36 (Beardmore) Admiralty dirigible airship, three Cossack engines installed, in addition to two German Maybach MbIVa six-cylinder engines.
    R38 (Royal Airship Works) Admiralty dirigible airship, six engines installed.

An engine nacelle for one of the interim batch of six Handley Page O/100 bombers ordered by the R.N.A.S. in 1916.

VIKING, 450 hp, 18-cylinder 60-degree W-shaped development of the Amazon and Cossack, water-cooled, four poppet-valves. Bore/stroke 110 x 160 mm. Vol. 33.6 litre. Compression ratio 5:1, Geared, spur reduction .5:1. L.H. tractor-drive. Length 63.0 in; width 46.5 in; height 44.5 in.
Production, 8/1914-12/1918, from:-
Sunbeam Motor Car Co Ltd, Wolverhampton.
Ordered, 50;   Delivered, 9;   Cancelled/suspended, 41

AFRIDI, 200 hp, (1916), 12-cylinder, upright 60-degree Vee. Water-cooled, four poppet-valves, inside exhaust valves. Four magnetos. Bore/stroke 3.62 x 5.31 in. Vol. 660 cu in. (92 x 135 mm. Vol. 10.8 litre). Compression ratio 5:1. Geared, spur reduction .5:1. L.H. tractor-drive. Length 55.9 in; width 33.5 in; height 33.9 in.
Production, 8/1914-12/1918, from:-
Sunbeam Motor Car Co Ltd, Wolverhampton.
Ordered, 300;   Delivered, 299;   Cancelled/suspended, 1
Aircraft:

    Short N.2A

DYAK 100 hp, 6-cylinder, upright in-line, water-cooled, two poppet-valves. Bore/stroke 4.72 x 5.12 in. Vol. 538.26 cu in. (120 x 130 mm. Vol. 8.8 litre). Compression ratio 5:1. Direct L.H. tractor-drive. Monobloc cylinders, two-valve engine with an overhead camshaft.
Production, 8/1914-12/1918, from:-
Sunbeam Motor Car Co Ltd, Wolverhampton.
Ordered, 160;   Delivered, 0;   Cancelled/suspended, 160
Aircraft:

    Avro 504K

The 100 hp Sunbeam Dyak fitted to an Avro 504K.

ARAB I, 200 hp, (1917), 8-cylinder, upright 90-degree Vee, water-cooled, three poppet-valves (one inlet, two exhaust). Bore/stroke 4.72 x 5.12 in. Vol. 717.65 cu in. (120 x 130 mm. Vol. 11.77 l.), compression ratio 5.3:1. Geared spur .6:1. L.H. tractor/R.H. pusher-drive, outside exhausts, one Claudel-Hobson H.C.7 carburettor, two A.V.8 or Dixie magnetos. Cast aluminium blocks with pressed-in steel liners. The Arab engine was put into production without sufficient preliminary testing and suffered severely from vibration troubles. The first Bristol Fighter powered by an Arab I suffered so badly from this that, on delivery across the Channel, it lost its exhaust stubs. It turned out to be a very unsatisfactory engine in service. Length 43.5 in; width 31.9 in; height 35.5 in.
Production, 8/1914-12/1918, from:-
Sunbeam Motor Car Co Ltd, Wolverhampton.
Ordered, 2,110;   Delivered, 590;   Cancelled/suspended, 1,520

The 200 hp Sunbeam-Coatalen Arab I, an engine which suffered severely from vibration.

The Arab I powered this Sopwith T.1 Cuckoo torpedo-dropper.

Aircraft:
    Avro 530
    Bristol 15 F.2B Fighter
    Bristol 21 Scout F
    Curtiss R-2, R-4
    Mann Egerton B
    Royal Aircraft Factory S.E.5, S.E.5a
    Sopwith T.1 Cuckoo
    Sunbeam Bomber

ARAB II, 200 hp, (1918), 8-cylinder, upright 90-degree Vee, water-cooled, three poppet-valves. Bore/stroke 4.72 x 5.12 in. Vol. 718.25 cu in. (120 x 130 mm. Vol. 11.77 l.), compression ratio 5.3:1. Direct drive version of the Arab I. R.H. tractor/L.H. pusher-drive, one inlet and two outside exhaust valves, two magnetos. Cast aluminium blocks, in fours. Length 40.9 in; width 31.9 in; height 35.5 in.
Production, 8/1914-12/1918, from:-
Austin Motor Co Ltd, Birmingham,
Ordered, 2,000;   Delivered, 411;   Cancelled/suspended, 1,589
Lanchester Motor Co, Birmingham,
Ordered, 600;   Delivered, 83;   Cancelled/suspended, 517
D.Napier & Son Ltd, Acton,
Ordered, 450;   Delivered, 111;   Cancelled/suspended, 339
Aircraft:
    Bristol 21 Scout F
    Grain (Port Victoria) Griffin
    Royal Aircraft Factory S.E.5, S.E.5a

MAORI I, 250 hp, (1918), 12-cylinder, upright 60-degree Vee water-cooled, four poppet-valves. Bore/stroke 3.94 x 5.31 in. Vol. 776.76 cu. in. (100 x 135 mm), compression ratio 5.3:1. Geared spur .5:1. L.H. tractor/R.H. pusher drive. Four 38 mm Claudel-Hobson CZS carburettors, 4 magnetos, inside exhaust valves. Length 63.5 in; width 33.5 in; height 34.4 in.
Production, 8/1914–12/1918, from:-
Sunbeam Motor Car Co Ltd, Wolverhampton.
Ordered, 1,063;   Delivered, 974;   Cancelled/suspended, 89
Aircraft:
    Short (Admiralty Type) 184
    Short N.2B

MAORI II, as Maori I, with inside exhaust valves.
Aircraft:
    Fairey F.22 Campania
    Fairey N.9
    Fairey N.10
    Fairey IIIA, IIIB
    Grahame-White Ganymede
    Handley Page H.P.12 O/400 Type O
    Parnall Scout ('Zepp-Chaser')
    Vickers F.B.27 Vimy prototype
    Wight 'Converted' Seaplane

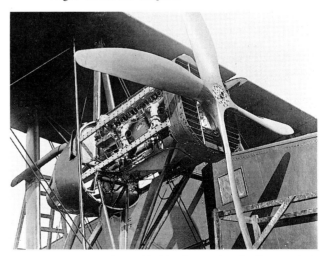

The Sunbeam Maori II featured inside exhaust valves, leading to a single outlet. Here seen in the starboard mounting of a Handley Page O/400 bomber.

Fairey F.22 Campania

MAORI III, as Maori II, compression ratio 5.2:1, with 2 Claudel-Hobson H.C.7 carburettors and four magnetos, outside exhaust valves. Length 65.5 in; width 33.5 in; height 34.4 in.
Aircraft:

    Short (Admiralty Type) 184
    Vickers F.B.27 Vimy prototype

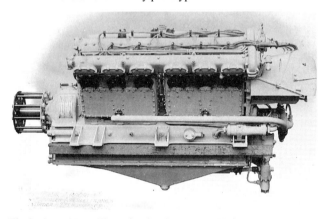

The Sunbeam Maori III was fitted to the prototype Vickers Vimy.

MAORI IV, 250 h.p. (1919) airship version of the engine. Geared, spur-drive .5:1, governed with fly-wheel, water-cooled exhaust. Twin camshafts, four valves.
Aircraft:

    R33 (Armstrong Whitworth) and R34 (Beardmore)
    Admiralty dirigible (33 class) airships (five engines on each).

MATABELE, 400 hp, virtually a double Amazon, rated at 420 hp, 12-cylinder, upright 60-degree Vee-12, water-cooled, poppet-valve. Cast aluminium blocks, in threes. Bore/stroke 4.8 x 6.3 in. (122 x 160 mm. Vol. 22.4 litre). Geared, spur .63:1. L.H. tractor-drive. Mk I, 2 magnetos; Mk II, 4 magnetos.
Aircraft:

    Airco D.H.4

GURKHA, 240 hp, (1914), 12-cylinder, upright 60-degree Vee water-cooled, two poppet side-valves. Bore/stroke 100 x 150 mm. Vol. 14.14 litre. Geared, spur .5:1. L.H. tractor-drive. Production, 8/1914-12/1918, from:-
Sunbeam Motor Car Co Ltd, Wolverhampton.
Ordered, 83;   Delivered, 83;   Cancelled/suspended, 0

MANITOU, 300 hp, (1917), 12-cylinder, upright 60-degree Vee water-cooled, four poppet-valves. Bore/stroke 4.33 x 5.3 in. Cast aluminium blocks with pressed steel liners. Features similar to Maori 4. Bore/stroke 110 x 135 mm, Vol. 15.4 litre. Compression ratio 5:1. Two Claudel-Hobson H.C.7 carburettors. Two B.T.H. A.V.12 magnetos. Geared, spur 28/44, .636:1. L.H. tractor/R.H. pusher drive. Outside exhaust valves. Length 65.2 in; width 33.6 in; height 35.2 in.

Production, 8/1914–12/1918, from:-
Sunbeam Motor Car Co Ltd, Wolverhampton.
Ordered, 840;   Delivered, 13;   Cancelled/suspended, 827

NUBIAN, 155 hp, 8-cylinder, upright 90-degree Vee water-cooled, poppet-valve. Bore/stroke 95 x 135 mm. Vol. 7.65 litre. Compression ratio 5:1. Geared, spur .615:1. Either rotation, L.H./R.H. tractor/pusher drive. Length; width 41.5 in; height 30.1 in.
Production, 8/1914–12/1918, from:-
Sunbeam Motor Car Co Ltd, Wolverhampton.
Ordered, 50;   Delivered, 36;   Cancelled/suspended, 14
Aircraft:

    A.D. Flying-boat (Admiralty Air Dept)
    Avro 510
    Avro 523 Pike
    Avro 527, 527A
    Blackburn G.P. Seaplane
    Curtiss C
    Curtiss H.4 Small America
    Saunders T.1
    Short Type C (Admiralty Type) 827
    Sopwith (Admiralty Type) 806 'Gunbus'

ZULU, 160 hp, (1915), 8-cylinder, upright 60-degree Vee water-cooled, two poppet side-valves. Bore/stroke Vol. 100 x 150 mm. Vol. 9.42 litre. Direct L.H. tractor-drive.
Production, 8/1914–12/1918, from:-
Sunbeam Motor Car Co Ltd, Wolverhampton,
Ordered, 75;   Delivered, 75;   Cancelled/suspended, 0
Aircraft:

    Sikorsky Il'ya Muromets

SIKH I and III were large, low-revving engines of between 850 and 1,000 hp, intended for airship use but no known use.

VIALE.

An interesting but neglected engine designer, Spirito Mario Viale was born in Turin on 7 February 1882. Not inclined to follow in his father's distinguished military footsteps, he was more interested in mathematics and engineering. The latter followed his leaving home for Paris where he believed, wrongly, that the outlet for his talents lay. In considerable poverty and too proud to return home, he survived, partly, by doing technical translation work. It was not until he was about 28 years of age that he was able to establish his own business at Boulogne-sur-Seine. Until 1914, Viale designed and built a small number of three, five and seven-cylinder star and fan-shaped engines and was an associate of Francesco Santarini, Alessandro Anzani's mechanic and, of course, fellow countryman. There was clearly an amicable association between Viale and Anzani, exemplified by Anzani's adoption of Viale patents, the design of Louis Blériot's little three-cylinder fan-shaped Anzani was influenced by Viale's ideas. Later, Viale's experiments with air-cooling came to the attention of H.P. Boot, the Royal Aircraft Factory's Chief Designer in 1915, with the approval of the Chief Engineer, Major F.M.Green.

As early as 1910, a 35-50 hp five-cylinder Viale engine powered a Blériot aeroplane which visited Brooklands. After being removed from the Blériot and overhauled, the engine was sold to A.V. Roe who used it in his Type D biplane in 1912. He transferred it to his Type F monoplane in the same year. Although the aircraft was wrecked soon afterwards, the engine survived and, after storage during the First World War is said to have been installed in F.S. Barnwell's little Bristol Babe. It has to be said that, although neither of the two Viale engines referred to below were built in Britain and do not strictly qualify for inclusion in this book, the work which Viale did while in this country, both before the First World War and during it when, in 1917, he was sent by the Italian Government to England to work as an engine adviser to Vickers, make their designer well worthy of inclusion. Following the dispersal, at the end of 1917, of the talented staff of the Royal Aircraft Factory at Farnborough, and the abandonment of engine development by Vickers, Viale joined Major F.M. Green at Siddeley-Deasy in 1919 and its successor Armstrong Siddeley

With that company, after Sam Heron had devised the sodium-cooled valve stem, Viale worked on a satisfactory method of operating it, with considerable success. Viale was subsequently involved in the design of the Armstrong Siddeley Lynx and the subsequent Cheetah engines. After designs left the drawing board, he tended to lose interest and, in 1932, returned to Italy. In 1938, disillusioned with Italian politics, he returned to England, at the invitation of A.G. Elliott of Rolls-Royce, to head the firm's Armament Division and lead in the design of its 40 mm gun.

The 30-50hp Viale engine in the first enclosed cabin aeroplane, Avro Type F.

The 35-50 hp Viale radial of 1910, whose power is arguable and depended very much on a variety of circumstances, not least the suitability of the propeller fitted, had a direct R.H. tractor-drive. It was fitted to the Avro Type D, Type F and the Bristol 30 Babe I. A Viale 70 hp seven-cylinder radial of 1912 was fitted to the Vickers No.6 monoplane.

VILLIERS-HAY DEVELOPMENT LTD, *London.*
The Villiers 4-L-318 Maya I engine was designed by Amherst Villiers and has been described as a very pleasant, smooth-running 120 hp power unit. Unfortunately, it was a contemporary of the inverted de Havilland Gipsy III and the competition was overwhelming.

The Villiers-Hay Maya, mounted in Miles M.11B Whitney Straight G-AERC.

VILLIERS 4-L-318 MAYA I, 130 hp, (1936), 4-cylinder, inverted in-line air-cooled poppet-valve engine. It was unsupercharged and its propeller was direct, tractor-drive. It featured 'radial' cylinder heads, with widely splayed valves for efficient cooling. As result of carefully balanced design, the Maya was notable for its smooth-running. The onset of war in 1939 prevented the production of a more powerful Mk II version. Bore/stroke 4.75 x 4.5 in. Vol. 319 cu in. Compression ratio, initially 5.5:1, later raised to 6:1, when the maximum power increased from 130 to 135 hp. Direct, R.H. tractor-drive. Length 43.88 in; width 15.75 in; height 22.75 in.
Aircraft:

Miles M.11B Whitney Straight

The 130-135 hp Villiers-Hay Maya, a smooth-running engine of 1936, which did not achieve success because of competition and the onset of the second World War.

WEIR PIXIE, 40 hp. (1936, Became Aero Engines Pixie, q.v.).

WICKO F, (a modified Ford V-8 motor car engine). Little known about this engine, about 40 hp and rather heavy.
Aircraft:

Foster Wickner F.W.1 Wicko

WOLSELEY MOTORS LTD, BIRMINGHAM.
In 1907, well before the First World War, the Wolseley Tool and Motor Car Co Ltd became interested in the design of aero-engines, initially for dirigible airships. The firm at first produced two types of engine, one being a 30 hp upright 4-cylinder water-cooled unit, bore/stroke being 3.75 x 5.5 in, appearing in 1908. This was too low-powered and was followed by an 8-cylinder 90 degree vee-type, effectively a double version, of 50 hp, geared .5:1. It was fitted to a Voisin biplane in 1909. There was also an air-cooled version, with water-cooled exhaust valves, about which little has previously been published.

During the First World War, the reconstituted Wolseley Motors Ltd built a large number of aero-engines, particularly Renault and Royal Aircraft Factory air-cooled types. In addition, all English-built Hispano-Suiza water-cooled engines were made by Wolseley. After the war, no further Wolseley aero-engines were built. However, with the formation of Wolseley Motors (1927) Ltd, after being acquired by Sir William Morris, in 1931, the nine-cylinder geared air-cooled A.R. radial was produced. It was at first known as the Morris engine because the idea for it was first that of William Morris, (later Sir William and, later still, Lord Nuffield), then the owner of the Wolseley company.

WOLSELEY 60 hp, (1911), Type C, 8-cylinder, upright 90-degree Vee, air-cooled with water-cooled exhausts, poppet-valve. Bore/stroke 95 x 140 mm. (Vol. 7.9 litre). Direct L.H. tractor-drive, with a 20 lb flywheel. Central camshaft. In an official continuous four-hour test, the engine developed an average 55 hp.
Aircraft:

Royal Aircraft Factory B.E.1

The early 60 hp Wolseley engine.

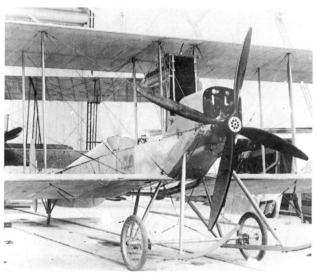

B.E.2 with a 60 hp Wolseley.

WOLSELEY 80 hp, (1911), Type B, geared spur .5:1. 8-cylinder, upright 90-degree Vee, combined air and water cooling (for exhausts). Steel cylinders, cast-iron heads. Aluminium jacket. Camshaft in crankcase, push rods and rockers. Drawn steel pistons. Nickel chrome steel crankshaft and connecting rods. Aluminium alloy crankcase.Bore/stroke 102 x 140 mm (Vol. 9.2 l.).
Aircraft:

    Vickers E.F.B.1 'Destroyer'

WOLSELEY 160 hp, (1912), a 120 h.p., 8-cylinder upright, 90-degree Vee, water-cooled poppet-valve airship engine. Its propeller drive was direct, L.H. tractor or R.H. pusher-drive. Bore/stroke 5.0 x 7.0 in. Vol. 1,100 cu in. Rated at 120 hp at 1,150 rpm. Maximum 147 hp at 1,400 rpm 'for short periods'.
Aircraft:

    H.M. Airship No 1 *Mayfly* (but did not fly, having broken its back on leaving shed, 24.9.11), Vickers-built, two engines.

W.4A PYTHON I, 150 hp, (1917, the 150 hp, Hispano-Suiza with minor structural changes). 8-cylinder, upright 90-degree Vee water-cooled, poppet-valve. Bore/stroke 4.72 x 5.12 in. Vol. 716.72 cu. in. (120 x 130 mm. Vol. 11.76 l.). Compression ratio initially 4.7:1, subsequently converted to high-compression (5.3:1), with 200 hp, engine's inlet pipes and carburettor, redesignated Python II. Direct R.H. tractor/L.H. pusher-drive. Length 46.7 in; width 33.5 in; height 35.4 in. Only 100 built.
Aircraft:

    Royal Aircraft Factory S.E.5, S.E.5a
    SPAD 7

W.4A PYTHON II, 180 hp, high compression version of the Python I, ratio 5.3:1. Direct R.H. tractor-drive.
Aircraft:

    Royal Aircraft Factory S.E.5, S.E.5a
    SPAD 7

W.4A* VIPER, 200 hp, (1918), 8-cylinder, upright 90-degree Vee water-cooled, poppet-valve. Bore/stroke 4.72 x 5.12 in. Vol. 716.8 cu. in. (120 x 130 mm). Compression ratio 5.3:1, although 19 early engines were at first fitted with 5.6:1 compression ratio pistons. Direct R.H. tractor/L.H. pusher-drive. Almost the equivalent of the French 180 hp, Hispano-Suiza 8Ab, with transverse magnetos and double oil pumps. All but the first eight engines had balanced crankshafts and all took the 200 hp, English Hispano propeller hub. Two Zenith Duplex carburettors, two magnetos.
Aircraft:

    Airco D.H.9 'Mantis'
    Avro 552
    Bristol 13 M.R.1
    Bristol 88 Bulgarian Tourer 1, 2
    Cierva C.8V Autogiro (Avro 586)
    Martinsyde F.6
    Royal Aircraft Factory S.E.5, S.E.5a
    Sopwith T.1 Cuckoo
    Sopwith Antelope

An Argentine Avro 504K with a Wolseley Viper engine.

W.4B ADDER I, 200 hp, Wolseley-built, modified version of the Hispano-Suiza 8B. (Apart from reduction gear, identical to the Python). 8-cylinder, upright 90-degree Vee water-cooled, poppet-valve. Bore/stroke 4.72 x 5.12 in. Vol. cu in. (120 x 130 mm. Vol. l.). Compression ratio 4.8:1. Geared, spur .593:1, L.H. tractor/R.H. pusher-drive. Adder I made to standard drawings. Two magnetos, one Zenith Duplex 58 DC carburettor.
Aircraft:

    Royal Aircraft Factory S.E.5, S.E.5a
    Sopwith 5F.1 Dolphin I

W.4B* ADDER II, 200 hp, Wolseley-built, modified version of the Adder I with stronger 19 mm crankshaft webs. Geared, spur .593:1. L.H. tractor-drive.
Aircraft:

    Royal Aircraft Factory S.E.5, S.E.5a

W.4B* ADDER III, 200 hp, Wolseley-built, modified version of the Adder II with balanced crankshaft. Geared, spur .593:1. L.H. tractor-drive.
Aircraft:

    Royal Aircraft Factory S.E.5, S.E.5a

AQUARIUS I, A.R.7, 155 hp, 7-cylinder, single-row radial air-cooled poppet-valve. Bore/stroke 4.188 x 4.75 in. Vol. 458 cu in. Compression ratio 5.35:1. Direct R.H. tractor-drive. Most parts interchangeable with Aries engines. Diameter 40.25 in; length 36.4 in.
Aircraft:

    Hawker Tomtit

A.R.9 Mk I, 203 hp, (1934), 9-cylinder, single-row radial, air-cooled poppet-valve engine. Bore/stroke 4.19 x 4.75 in, 106 x 120 mm. Vol. 588.6 cu in, 9.654 litre. It was unsupercharged, and its propeller drive was spur-geared, reduction .63:1. R.H. tractor-drive. Compression ratio 5.3:1. Diameter 41.25 in; length 38.25 in.

Aircraft:
  Airspeed A.S.6 Envoy I
  Hawker Tomtit

The seven-cylinder Wolseley direct-drive A.R.7 Aquarius.

The geared Wolseley A.R.9 Mk I, as fitted to the Airspeed Envoy I.

A.R.9 Mk II, 205 hp. Direct drive, minor variation of Mk I, higher rpm.
Aircraft:
  Hawker Tomtit

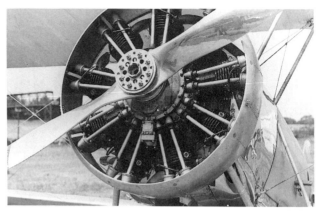

Direct-drive Wolseley A.R.9 Mk II in a Hawker Tomtit.

A.R.9 ARIES Mk III, 225 hp, (1935), 9-cylinder, single-row radial air-cooled, poppet-valve. Bore/stroke 4.198 x 4.75in. Vol. 588.6 cu in. Compression ratio 5.35:1. Single-speed, geared induction fan, for improved distribution with slight positive pressure at 3.8 times engine speed, giving a rated altitude of 5,000 ft. Geared, spur epicyclic .629:1, R.H. tractor-drive. Diameter 41.25 in; length 42.0 in.
Aircraft:
  Airspeed A.S.6H Envoy

SCORPIO I, 250 hp, 9-cylinder, single-row radial air-cooled poppet-valve. Bore/stroke 4.375 x 4.75 in. Vol. 643 cu in. Compression ratio 6.5:1, single-speed geared induction fan. Geared, spur epicyclic .629:1. R.H. tractor-drive. A slightly enlarged version of the Aries. Diameter 42.25 in; length 42.2 in.
Aircraft:
  Airspeed A.S.6G Envoy I

SCORPIO II, III, 250 hp, minor variations of Mk I but designed for 87 Octane fuel.
Aircraft:
  Airspeed A.S.6 Envoy II
  Airspeed A.S.6J Envoy III

PART 3

Aircraft and their Engines

A.B.C. Robin	A.B.C. Scorpion II
A.D.1 Navyplane (Pemberton Billing)	Bentley B.R.1 (A.R.1) 150 hp
A.D. Flying Boat (Admiralty Air Dept)	Hispano-Suiza 8Aa 150 hp
A.D. Flying Boat (Admiralty Air Dept)	Hispano-Suiza 8Bb 200 hp
A.D. Flying Boat (Admiralty Air Dept)	Sunbeam Nubian 150 hp
A.D. Navyplane (Pemberton Billing)	Smith Static 140/150 hp
A.D. Scout (Blackburn)	Gnome Monosoupape 9B-2 100 hp
Aeronca 100	J.A.P. J-99 (Aeronca E-113-C)
Aero. Syndic. No 1 Valkyrie Type A	Green C4 30-35 hp
Aero. Syndic. Valkyrie Type B	Gnome 7 Omega 50 hp
Aero. Syndic. No 2 Valkyrie Type C	Green D4 50-60 hp
Airco D.H.1	Renault WB, WC 70 hp
Airco D.H.1A	Beardmore 120 hp
Airco D.H.2	Clerget 9Z 110 hp
Airco D.H.2	Gnome Monosoupape 9B-2 100 hp
Airco D.H.2	Le Rhone 9Ja 110 hp
Airco D.H.3	Beardmore 120 hp
Airco D.H.3A	Beardmore 160 hp
Airco D.H.4	Armstrong Siddeley Jaguar I
Airco D.H.4	Armstrong Siddeley Jaguar II
Airco D.H.4	B.H.P. 200 hp
Airco D.H.4	B.H.P. 230 hp, Galloway Adriatic
Airco D.H.4	Liberty 12N 350 hp
Airco D.H.4	Renault 12Fe 220 hp
Airco D.H.4	Ricardo-Halford-Armstrong, R.H.A.
Airco D.H.4	Rolls-Royce Condor I
Airco D.H.4	Rolls-Royce Eagle III 284 hp
Airco D.H.4	Rolls-Royce Eagle V 322 hp
Airco D.H.4	Rolls-Royce Eagle VI 322 hp
Airco D.H.4	Rolls-Royce Eagle VII 322 hp
Airco D.H.4	Rolls-Royce Eagle IX 360 hp
Airco D.H.4	R.A.F.3a 200 hp
Airco D.H.4	Siddeley-Deasy Puma 236 hp
Airco D.H.4	Sunbeam Matabele 400 hp
Airco D.H.4A	Napier Lion II
Airco D.H.4A	Rolls-Royce Eagle VIII 375 hp
Airco D.H.5	Clerget 9Z 110 hp
Airco D.H.5	Gnome Monosoupape 9B-2 100 hp
Airco D.H.5	Le Rhone 9Ja 110 hp
Airco D.H.6	Curtiss OX-5 90 hp
Airco D.H.6	Hispano-Suiza 8 140 hp
Airco D.H.6	Renault WS 80 hp
Airco D.H.6	R.A.F.1a 90 hp
Airco D.H.6 (Alula)	Bentley B.R.2 230 hp
Airco D.H.9	Napier Lion I
Airco D.H.9 srs	A.D.C. Nimbus 300 hp
Airco D.H.9 srs	B.H.P. 230 hp, Galloway Adriatic
Airco D.H.9 srs	Hispano-Suiza 8Fb 300 hp
Airco D.H.9 srs	Napier Lion II
Airco D.H.9 srs	Siddeley-Deasy Puma 236 hp
Airco D.H.9 srs	Siddeley-Deasy Puma HC 290 hp
Airco D.H.9 ('Mantis')	Wolseley W.4A* Viper 200 hp
Airco D.H.9 ('M'pala I')	Bristol Jupiter VI

Airco D.H.9 ('M'pala II')	Bristol Jupiter VIII
Airco D.H.9A	Liberty 12A 400 hp
Airco D.H.9A	Rolls-Royce Kestrel IIB
Airco D.H.9A srs	Napier Lion II
Airco D.H.9A srs	Rolls-Royce Eagle VIII 375 hp
Airco D.H.9AJ Stag	Bristol Jupiter VI
Airco D.H.9B	Rolls-Royce Eagle IX 360 hp
Airco D.H.9J	Armstrong Siddeley Jaguar III
Airco D.H.9J	Armstrong Siddeley Jaguar IVC
Airco D.H.9J	Armstrong Siddeley Serval IV
Airco D.H.9R	Napier Lion II
Airspeed A.S.4 Ferry	de Havilland Gipsy II
Airspeed A.S.4 Ferry	de Havilland Gipsy III
Airspeed A.S.4 Ferry	de Havilland Gipsy Major I srs I
Airspeed A.S.5, 5A Courier	Armstrong Siddeley Lynx IVC
Airspeed A.S.5 Courier	Armstrong Siddeley Lynx IV*
Airspeed A.S.5B Courier	Armstrong Siddeley Cheetah V
Airspeed A.S.5C Courier	Napier-Halford Rapier IV
Airspeed A.S.5J Courier	Armstrong Siddeley Cheetah IX
Airspeed A.S.6 Envoy	Armstrong Siddeley Cheetah VI
Airspeed A.S.6 Envoy I	Armstrong Siddeley Cheetah V
Airspeed A.S.6 Envoy I	Wolseley A.R.9 Mk I
Airspeed A.S.6 Envoy II	Wolseley Scorpio II
Airspeed A.S.6A Envoy II	Armstrong Siddeley Lynx IVC
Airspeed A.S.6G Envoy I	Wolseley Scorpio I
Airspeed A.S.6H Envoy	Wolseley A.R.9 Aries III
Airspeed A.S.6J Envoy III	Wolseley Scorpio III
Airspeed A.S.6JM/C Envoy III	Armstrong Siddeley Cheetah IX
Airspeed A.S.8 Viceroy	Armstrong Siddeley Cheetah VIA
Airspeed A.S.10 Oxford I, II	Armstrong Siddeley Cheetah X
Airspeed A.S.10 Oxford III	Armstrong Siddeley Cheetah XV
Airspeed A.S.30 Queen Wasp	Armstrong Siddeley Cheetah X
Airspeed A.S.30 Queen Wasp	Armstrong Siddeley Cheetah XII
Airspeed A.S.39 Fleet Shadower	Pobjoy Niagara V
Airspeed A.S.40 Oxford IV	de Havilland Gipsy Queen IV
Airspeed A.S.40 Oxford IV	de Havilland Gipsy Queen 50
Airspeed A.S.41 Oxford	Alvis Leonides 501/4
Airspeed A.S.45 Cambridge	Bristol Mercury VIII
Airspeed A.S.57 Ambassador prot	Bristol Centaurus 130
Airspeed A.S.57 Ambassador prot	Bristol Centaurus 631
Airspeed A.S.57 Ambassador srs 2	Bristol Centaurus 660
Airspeed A.S.57 Ambassador srs 2	Bristol Centaurus 661
Airspeed A.S.57 Ambassador srs 2	Bristol Centaurus 662
Airspeed A.S.57 Ambassador srs 2	Bristol Centaurus 663
Airspeed A.S.65 Consul	Alvis Leonides 502/4
Airspeed A.S.65 Consul	Armstrong Siddeley Cheetah X
Alcock Scout	Clerget 9Z 110 hp
Alcock Scout	Gnome Monosoupape 9B-2 100 hp
Any aircraft powered by Jaguars	Armstrong Siddeley Jaguar IV*
Alliance P.1	Renault WS 80 hp
Alliance P.2 Seabird	Napier Lion II
Alula Semiquaver (Martinsyde)	Hispano-Suiza 8Fb 300 hp
ANEC I	Blackburne Tomtit 690 c.c. (inverted)
ANEC I, IA, II	Anzani (British) 35 hp 1,100 c.c.
ANEC II	Bristol Cherub III
ANEC III	Rolls-Royce Eagle VIII 375 hp
ANEC IV Missel Thrush	Armstrong Siddeley Genet II
ANEC IV Missel Thrush	Blackburne Thrush 35 hp
Angus Aquila	British Salmson A.D.9
Any powered by Gipsy Major I	de Havilland Gipsy Major IC
Any powered by Gipsy Major I	de Havilland Gipsy Major ID
Armstrong Whitworth A.W.XIV Starling I	Armstrong Siddeley Jaguar VIIA
Armstrong Whitworth A.W.XIV Starling II	Armstrong Siddeley Jaguar IV
Armstrong Whitworth A.W.XV Atalanta	Armstrong Siddeley Serval III
Armstrong Whitworth A.W.XV Atalanta	Armstrong Siddeley Serval IIIB
Armstrong Whitworth A.W.XVI	Armstrong Siddeley Hyena
Armstrong Whitworth A W XVI 9/26	Armstrong Siddeley Panther IIIA
Armstrong Whitworth A.W.XVI 9/26	Armstrong Siddeley Panther VII
Armstrong Whitworth A.W.XVII Aries	Armstrong Siddeley Jaguar IVA
Armstrong Whitworth A.W.19	Armstrong Siddeley Tiger VI
Armstrong Whitworth A.W.23 C.26/31	Armstrong Siddeley Tiger VI
Armstrong Whitworth A.W.23 C.26/31	Armstrong Siddeley Tiger VIII
Armstrong Whitworth A.W.27 Ensign I	Armstrong Siddeley Tiger IX
Armstrong Whitworth A.W.27 Ensign I	Armstrong Siddeley Tiger IXC
Armstrong Whitworth A.W.29	Armstrong Siddeley Tiger VIII
Armstrong Whitworth A.W.35 Scimitar	Armstrong Siddeley Panther VII
Armstrong Whitworth A.W.35 Scimitar	Armstrong Siddeley Panther IXA
Armstrong Whitworth A.W.35 Scimitar	Armstrong Siddeley Panther XI
Armstrong Whitworth A.W.38 Whitley I	Rolls-Royce Merlin II
Armstrong Whitworth A.W.38 Whitley I, III	Armstrong Siddeley Tiger IX
Armstrong Whitworth A.W.38 Whitley I, III	Armstrong Siddeley Tiger X

Armstrong Whitworth A.W.38 Whitley II	Armstrong Siddeley Deerhound I
Armstrong Whitworth A.W.38 Whitley II, III	Armstrong Siddeley Tiger VIII
Armstrong Whitworth A.W.38 Whitley IV	Rolls-Royce Merlin IV
Armstrong Whitworth A.W.38 Whitley V, VII	Rolls-Royce Merlin X
Armstrong Whitworth A.W.41 Albemarle I	Bristol Hercules III
Armstrong Whitworth A.W.41 Albemarle I, II	Bristol Hercules X
Armstrong Whitworth A.W.41 Albemarle I, II	Bristol Hercules XI
Armstrong Whitworth A.W.41 Albemarle V, VI	Bristol Hercules X
Armstrong Whitworth A.W.41 Albemarle V, VI	Bristol Hercules XI
Armstrong Whitworth Ajax	Armstrong Siddeley Jaguar III
Armstrong Whitworth Ape	Armstrong Siddeley Lynx III
Armstrong Whitworth Ara	A.B.C. Dragonfly I 320 hp
Armstrong Whitworth Argosy I	Armstrong Siddeley Jaguar III
Armstrong Whitworth Argosy I	Armstrong Siddeley Jaguar IIIA
Armstrong Whitworth Argosy II	Armstrong Siddeley Jaguar IVA
Armstrong Whitworth Atlas I, DC	Armstrong Siddeley Jaguar III
Armstrong Whitworth Atlas I	Armstrong Siddeley Jaguar VI
Armstrong Whitworth Atlas I	Armstrong Siddeley Jaguar VIC
Armstrong Whitworth Atlas I, DC	Armstrong Siddeley Jaguar IVC
Armstrong Whitworth Atlas I, DC.	Armstrong Siddeley Jaguar IV
Armstrong Whitworth Atlas II	Armstrong Siddeley Panther IIA (GF)
Armstrong Whitworth Atlas II	Armstrong Siddeley Panther III
Armstrong Whitworth Atlas II	Armstrong Siddeley Panther IIIA
Armstrong Whitworth Atlas DC	Armstrong Siddeley Jaguar IVA
Armstrong Whitworth Awana	Napier Lion II
Armstrong Whitworth F.K.2	Renault WB, WC 70 hp
Armstrong Whitworth F.K.2	R.A.F.1a 90 hp
Armstrong Whitworth F.K.3	Beardmore 120 hp
Armstrong Whitworth F.K.3	R.A.F.1a 90 hp
Armstrong Whitworth F.K.3	R.A.F.1b 105 hp
Armstrong Whitworth F.K.7, F.K.8	Beardmore 160 hp
Armstrong Whitworth F.K.8	Beardmore 120 hp
Armstrong Whitworth F.K.8	R.A.F.4a 140 hp
Armstrong Whitworth F.K.9	Clerget 9Z 110 hp
Armstrong Whitworth F.K.10	Clerget 9B 130 hp
Armstrong Whitworth F.K.10	Le Rhone 9Ja 110 hp
Armstrong Whitworth F.M.4 Armadillo	Bentley B.R.2 230 hp
Armstrong Whitworth G.4/31	Armstrong Siddeley Tiger IV
Armstrong Whitworth G.4/31	Armstrong Siddeley Tiger VI
Armstrong Whitworth Siskin II	Armstrong Siddeley Jaguar II
Armstrong Whitworth Siskin II, III, IIIA, IIIDC	Armstrong Siddeley Jaguar III
Armstrong Whitworth Siskin IIIA, IIIB, V	Armstrong Siddeley Jaguar IV (S)
Armstrong Whitworth Siskin IIIB	Armstrong Siddeley Jaguar VIII
Armstrong Whitworth Siskin III, IIIA	Armstrong Siddeley Jaguar IV
Armstrong Whitworth Siskin IV, V	Armstrong Siddeley Jaguar III
Armstrong Whitworth Starling	Armstrong Siddeley Panther IIA (GF)
Armstrong Whitworth Wolf	Armstrong Siddeley Jaguar III
Armstrong Whitworth Wolf	Armstrong Siddeley Jaguar IV
Armst Whit/Siddeley S.R.1 Siskin I	Armstrong Siddeley Jaguar I
Arpin A-1 'Safety-Pin'	British Salmson A.C.9
Arpin A-1 'Safety-Pin'	British Salmson A.D.9R srs III
Arpin A-1 Mk 2	Blackburn Cirrus Minor I
Arrow Active I	Cirrus Hermes IIB
Arrow Active II	de Havilland Gipsy III
Arrow Active II	de Havilland Gipsy Major I srs I
Auster - see Taylorcraft	
Auster (Taylorcraft F) III, VC	de Havilland Gipsy Major I srs I
Auster 6A Tugmaster	de Havilland Gipsy Major I srs I
Auster 6A Tugmaster	de Havilland Gipsy Major 7
Auster 6A Tugmaster	de Havilland Gipsy Major 10/1
Auster A.O.P. VI, T.7	de Havilland Gipsy Major I srs I
Auster A.O.P.9	de Havilland Gipsy Major 7
Auster B.4	Blackburn Cirrus Bombardier 203
Auster B.5	Blackburn Cirrus Bombardier 702
Auster J/1 Autocrat	Blackburn Cirrus Bombardier 203
Auster J/1 Autocrat	Blackburn Cirrus Minor II
Auster J/1 Autocrat	de Havilland Gipsy Major I srs I
Auster J/1 Autocrat	de Havilland Gipsy Major IC
Auster J/1B Aiglet	de Havilland Gipsy Major ID
Auster J/1N Alpha	de Havilland Gipsy Major I srs I
Auster J/1S	de Havilland Gipsy Major I srs I
Auster J/3A Adventurer	de Havilland Gipsy Major 10/1
Auster J/4	Blackburn Cirrus Minor I
Auster J/5B Autocar	Blackburn Cirrus Minor I
Auster J/5F Aiglet Trainer	de Havilland Gipsy Major I srs I
Auster J/5G Cirrus Autocar	de Havilland Gipsy Major I srs I
Auster J/5H Autocar	Blackburn Cirrus Major III
Auster J/5K Aiglet	Blackburn Cirrus Major II
Auster J/5L Aiglet Trainer	Blackburn Cirrus Major III
Auster J/5P Autocar	de Havilland Gipsy Major 10/2
Auster J/5R Alpine	de Havilland Gipsy Major 10/1
	de Havilland Gipsy Major 10/1

Auster P Avis 1	de Havilland Gipsy Major 10/1
Austin Greyhound	A.B.C. Dragonfly I 320 hp
Austin Greyhound	A.B.C. Dragonfly IA 330/360 hp
Austin Kestrel	Beardmore 160 hp
Austin Triplane	Bentley B.R.2 230 hp
Austin Whippet	Anzani (British) 45 hp
Austin Whippet	Anzani (British) 60 hp
Austin-Ball AFB.1	Hispano-Suiza 8Ab 180 hp
Avro (Roe) Tractor Biplane	E.N.V. Type D 35-40 hp
Avro Types II-IV	Green C4 30-35 hp
Avro Types D & E Tractor Biplanes	E.N.V. Type F 60-80 hp
Avro Type D	Green C4 30-35 hp
Avro Type D	Isaacson 40-50 hp
Avro Type D	Viale 35 hp
Avro Type E	A.B.C. 60 h.p.
Avro Type F	Viale 35 hp
Avro Type G	Green D4 50-60 hp
Avro 500	Gnome 9 Delta 100 hp
Avro 500 Type E, Es	Gnome 7 Omega 50 hp
Avro 501	Gnome 9 Delta 100 hp
Avro 504	Clerget 7Z 80 hp
Avro 504	Gnome Monosoupape 7 Type A 75 hp
Avro 504E, J, K, M	Gnome Monosoupape 9B-2 100 hp
Avro 504F	Rolls-Royce Hawk I 85 hp
Avro 504K	A.B.C. Wasp I
Avro 504K	A.B.C. Wasp II
Avro 504K	Armstrong Siddeley Lynx I
Avro 504K	Bentley B.R.1 (A.R.1) 150 hp
Avro 504K	Clerget 9B 130 hp
Avro 504K	Green E6 100-120 hp
Avro 504K	Hispano-Suiza 8Bc 220 hp
Avro 504K	Le Rhone 9Ja 110 hp
Avro 504K	R.A.F.1a 90 hp
Avro 504K	Sunbeam Dyak 100 hp
Avro 504K Lucifer	Cosmos Lucifer I
Avro 504L	Bentley B.R.1 (A.R.1) 150 hp
Avro 504L	Clerget 9B 130 hp
Avro 504L	Le Rhone 9Ja 110 hp
Avro 504N	Armstrong Siddeley Lynx III
Avro 504N	Armstrong Siddeley Lynx IV MOD
Avro 504N	Armstrong Siddeley Lynx IV*
Avro 504N	Armstrong Siddeley Lynx IVC
Avro 504N	Armstrong Siddeley Mongoose IIIC
Avro 504N	Bristol Lucifer II
Avro 504N	Bristol Lucifer IV
Avro 504N	Bristol Titan I Direct drive
Avro 504N, Q	Armstrong Siddeley Lynx II
Avro 504N, R	Armstrong Siddeley Mongoose IIIA
Avro 504N, R Gosport	Armstrong Siddeley Lynx IV
Avro 504O	Armstrong Siddeley Lynx IVC
Avro 504R Gosport	Armstrong Siddeley Mongoose I
Avro 504R Gosport	Avro Alpha 90 hp
Avro 504R Gosport	Gnome Monosoupape 9B-2 100 hp
Avro 504, 504A	A.B.C. 100 h.p.
Avro 504, 504A, B, C, D, G, H	Gnome 7 Lambda 80 hp
Avro 504, 504A, B, J	Le Rhone 9C 80 hp
Avro 510	Gnome 14 Lambda-Lambda 160 hp
Avro 510	Sunbeam Nubian 155 hp
Avro 511	Gnome Monosoupape 7 Type A 75 hp
Avro 521	Clerget 9Z 110 hp
Avro 523 Pike	Sunbeam Nubian 150 hp
Avro 523A	Green E6 100-120 hp
Avro 527, 527A	Sunbeam Nubian 150 hp
Avro 528	Sunbeam Mohawk 225 hp
Avro 529	Rolls-Royce Falcon I 190 hp
Avro 529A	B.H.P. 230 hp, Galloway Adriatic
Avro 530	Hispano-Suiza 8Ba 200 hp
Avro 530	Sunbeam Arab I 200 hp
Avro 531 Spider	Le Rhone 9Ja 110 hp
Avro 531, 531A Spider	Clerget 9B 130 hp
Avro 533 Manchester I	A.B.C. Dragonfly I 320 hp
Avro 533 Manchester II	Siddeley-Deasy Puma HC 290 hp
Avro 534 Baby	Green C4 30-35 hp
Avro 536	Bentley B.R.1 (A.R.1) 150 hp
Avro 538	Bentley B.R.1 (A.R.1) 150 hp
Avro 539A	Siddeley-Deasy Puma HC 290 hp
Avro 539B	Napier Lion II
Avro 539, 539A	Siddeley-Deasy Puma 236 hp
Avro 543 Baby	Cirrus I
Avro 543 Baby	Green C4 30-35 hp
Avro 545	Curtiss OX-5 90 hp

Avro 546	Bentley B.R.1 (A.R.1) 150 hp
Avro 547	Beardmore 160 hp
Avro 547A	Siddeley-Deasy Puma 236 hp
Avro 547A	Siddeley-Deasy Puma HC 290 hp
Avro 548	Renault WS 80 hp
Avro 548A	A.D.C. Airdisco
Avro 549 Aldershot I, III	Rolls-Royce Condor III
Avro 549 Aldershot II	Napier Cub
Avro 549 Aldershot IV	Beardmore Typhoon I
Avro 552	Wolseley W.4A* Viper 200 hp
Avro 554 Baby	Le Rhone 9C 80 hp
Avro 555 Bison	Napier Lion V
Avro 555 Bison I, II	Napier Lion II
Avro 557 Ava	Rolls-Royce Condor III
Avro 558	Blackburne Tomtit 690 c.c. (inverted)
Avro 558	Douglas 500 c.c. 3.5 hp
Avro 560	Blackburne Tomtit 690 c.c. (inverted)
Avro 560	Blackburne Tomtit 690 c.c. (upright)
Avro 561 Andover	Rolls-Royce Condor III
Avro 562 Avis	Blackburne Thrush 35 hp
Avro 562 Avis	Bristol Cherub I
Avro 562 Avis	Bristol Cherub II
Avro 563 Andover	Rolls-Royce Condor IIIA
Avro 566 Avenger I	Napier Lion VIII
Avro 567 Avenger II	Napier Lion IX
Avro 571 Buffalo I	Napier Lion VA
Avro 572 Buffalo II	Napier Lion XIA
Avro 581 Avian prot	Armstrong Siddeley Genet I
Avro 581E Avian	Cirrus I
Avro 584 Avocet	Armstrong Siddeley Lynx IV S
Avro 594 Avian II, III	Cirrus II
Avro 594 Avian IV	Cirrus III
Avro 594 Avian IV	Cirrus Hermes I
Avro 594 Avian IV	Cirrus Hermes II
Avro 594 Avian IV	de Havilland Gipsy I
Avro 594 Avian IV	de Havilland Gipsy II
Avro 594A Avian II (Alpha)	Avro Alpha 90 hp
Avro 594B Avian II	Armstrong Siddeley Genet II
Avro 594, 605 Avian IIIA	Cirrus III
Avro 604 Antelope	Rolls-Royce Kestrel IB
Avro 604 Antelope	Rolls-Royce Kestrel IIS
Avro 616 Avian IV, IVM	Cirrus III
Avro 616 Avian IVM	Armstrong Siddeley Genet Ma I
Avro 616 Avian IVM	Armstrong Siddeley Genet Ma IA
Avro 616 Sports Avian IV, IVM	Cirrus Hermes I
Avro 616 Sports Avian IV, IVM	Cirrus Hermes II
Avro 616 Sports Avian IV, IVM	de Havilland Gipsy I
Avro 616 Sports Avian IV/IVM	de Havilland Gipsy III
Avro 616 Sports Avian IVA, IVM	de Havilland Gipsy II
Avro 618 Ten	Armstrong Siddeley Lynx IVC
Avro 619 Five	Armstrong Siddeley Genet Ma I
Avro 621 Trainer	Armstrong Siddeley Mongoose IIIC
Avro 621 Tutor	Armstrong Siddeley Lynx IV
Avro 621 Tutor	Armstrong Siddeley Lynx IV MOD
Avro 621 Tutor	Armstrong Siddeley Lynx IV*
Avro 621 Tutor	Armstrong Siddeley Lynx IVC
Avro 621 Tutor	Armstrong Siddeley Mongoose IIIA
Avro 624 Six	Armstrong Siddeley Genet Ma I
Avro 625 Sports Avian (monoplane)	Armstrong Siddeley Genet Ma I
Avro 625 Sports Avian (monoplane)	Cirrus Hermes I
Avro 626 Prefect	Armstrong Siddeley Cheetah V
Avro 626 Prefect	Armstrong Siddeley Lynx IVC
Avro 627 Mailplane	Armstrong Siddeley Panther IIA (GF)
Avro 631 Cadet	Armstrong Siddeley Genet Ma IA
Avro 631 Cadet	Armstrong Siddeley Genet Ma III
Avro 636	Armstrong Siddeley Jaguar IV
Avro 636A	Armstrong Siddeley Panther XI
Avro 637 Trainer	Armstrong Siddeley Cheetah V
Avro 638 Club Cadet	Armstrong Siddeley Genet Ma I
Avro 638 Club Cadet	Cirrus Hermes IVA
Avro 638 Club Cadet	de Havilland Gipsy Major I srs I
Avro 639 Cabin Cadet	Armstrong Siddeley Genet Ma IA
Avro 640 Cadet Three-seater	Cirrus Hermes IV
Avro 640 Cadet Three-Seater	Armstrong Siddeley Genet Ma IA
Avro 641 Commodore	Armstrong Siddeley Lynx IVC
Avro 642/2m	Armstrong Siddeley Jaguar VID
Avro 642/4m	Armstrong Siddeley Lynx IVC
Avro 643 Cadet Mk II	Armstrong Siddeley Genet Ma IA
Avro 646 Sea Tutor	Armstrong Siddeley Lynx IVC
Avro 652	Armstrong Siddeley Cheetah V
Avro 652, 652A	Armstrong Siddeley Cheetah VI

Avro 652 Anson I	Armstrong Siddeley Cheetah VIA
Avro 652 Mk II	Armstrong Siddeley Cheetah IX
Avro 652A Anson I, X, XI	Armstrong Siddeley Cheetah XIX
Avro 652A Anson I, Anson X	Armstrong Siddeley Cheetah IX
Avro 652A Anson XII, XVIII	Armstrong Siddeley Cheetah XVII
Avro 652A Anson XII, XVIIIC, Nineteen	Armstrong Siddeley Cheetah XV
Avro 652A Anson XX, T.21, T.22	Armstrong Siddeley Cheetah XV
Avro 654	Armstrong Siddeley Tiger IV
Avro 667	Armstrong Siddeley Jaguar VIC
Avro 679 Manchester I, IA	Rolls-Royce Vulture I
Avro 679 Manchester I, IA	Rolls-Royce Vulture II
Avro 679 Manchester III	Rolls-Royce Merlin X
Avro 683 Lancaster I	Rolls-Royce Merlin T.24/2
Avro 683 Lancaster I	Rolls-Royce Merlin 65
Avro 683 Lancaster I, III	Rolls-Royce Merlin 224
Avro 683 Lancaster I, III, VII	Rolls-Royce Merlin XX
Avro 683 Lancaster I, VII	Rolls-Royce Merlin 22
Avro 683 Lancaster I, VII	Rolls-Royce Merlin 24
Avro 683 Lancaster II	Bristol Hercules VI
Avro 683 Lancaster II	Bristol Hercules XVI
Avro 683 Lancaster III, X (Canada)	Rolls-Royce Merlin 28 (V-1650-1)
Avro 683 Lancaster III, X (Canada)	Rolls-Royce Merlin 38
Avro 683 Lancaster VI	Rolls-Royce Merlin 85
Avro 685 York I	Rolls-Royce Merlin 22
Avro 685 York I	Rolls-Royce Merlin 24
Avro 685 York I	Rolls-Royce Merlin T.24/2
Avro 685 York I	Rolls-Royce Merlin 500
Avro 685 York I	Rolls-Royce Merlin 501
Avro 685 York I	Rolls-Royce Merlin 502
Avro 685 York II	Bristol Hercules XVI
Avro 688 Tudor I	Rolls-Royce Merlin 102A
Avro 688 Tudor I	Rolls-Royce Merlin 600
Avro 689 Tudor I, II, III, IV, IVB, V	Rolls-Royce Merlin 621
Avro 689 Tudor I, III, IV, IVB	Rolls-Royce Merlin 623
Avro 688 Tudor prot	Rolls-Royce Merlin 102
Avro 689 Tudor II	Rolls-Royce Merlin 102
Avro 689 Tudor II	Rolls-Royce Merlin 600A
Avro 689 Tudor VII	Bristol Hercules 120
Avro 691 Lancastrian I	Rolls-Royce Merlin 24
Avro 691 Lancastrian I	Rolls-Royce Merlin T.24/4
Avro 691 Lancastrian I	Rolls-Royce Merlin 102
Avro 691 Lancastrian I	Rolls-Royce Merlin 102A
Avro 691 Lancastrian I	Rolls-Royce Merlin 500
Avro 691 Lancastrian I	Rolls-Royce Merlin 501
Avro 694 Lincoln	Napier Nomad 7
Avro 694 Lincoln I, II, IV	Rolls-Royce Merlin 85
Avro 694 Lincoln II	Rolls-Royce Merlin 68
Avro 694 Lincoln II	Rolls-Royce Merlin 68A
Avro 694 Lincoln II	Rolls-Royce Merlin 86
Avro 694 Lincoln II	Rolls-Royce Merlin 604
Avro 695 Lincolnian	Rolls-Royce Merlin 86
Avro 696 Shackleton prot, MR.1	Rolls-Royce Griffon 57
Avro 696 Shackleton MR.1	Rolls-Royce Griffon 57
Avro 696 Shackleton prot, MR.1, 1A, III	Rolls-Royce Griffon 57A
Avro 701 Athena prot, Athena T.2	Rolls-Royce Merlin 35
B.A.Eagle II	de Havilland Gipsy Major I srs I
B.A.III Cupid	de Havilland Gipsy Major I srs I
B.A.IV Double Eagle	de Havilland Gipsy Major I srs I
B.A.IV Double Eagle	de Havilland Gipsy Six srs II
B.A.C. Drone	Bristol Cherub III
B.A.C. Drone	Carden-Ford 31 hp
B.A.C. Super Drone	Aero Engines Sprite I
B.A. Swallow	British Salmson A.D.9
B.A.Swallow	Pobjoy Cataract III
B.A.Swallow II	Blackburn Cirrus Minor I
B.A.T. F.K.22	A.B.C. Mosquito
B.A.T. F.K.23 Bantam	A.B.C. Wasp I
B.A.T. F.K.23 Bantam	A.B.C. Wasp II
B.A.T. F.K.23 Bantam II	Gnome Monosoupape 9B-2 100 hp
B.A.T. F.K.24 Baboon	A.B.C. Wasp I
B.A.T. F.K.25 Basilisk	A.B.C. Dragonfly IA 330/360 hp
B.A.T. F.K.26	Rolls-Royce Eagle VIII 375 hp
B.A.T. F.K.27	A.B.C. Wasp II
B.A.T. F.K.28 Crow	A.B.C. Gnat I 35 hp
B.K.Eagle I	de Havilland Gipsy Major I srs I
Barnwell B.S.W. Mk I	Scott Flying Squirrel
Beagle A.61 Terrier	de Havilland Gipsy Major 10/1
Beardmore BeRo.1 Inflexible	Rolls-Royce Condor II
Beardmore W.B.II	Hispano-Suiza 8Ab 180 hp
Beardmore W.B.IIB	Beardmore 160 hp
Beardmore W.B.III	Clerget 7Z 80 hp

Beardmore W.B.III	Le Rhone 9C 80 hp
Beardmore W.B.IV	Hispano-Suiza 8Ab 180 hp
Beardmore W.B.IV	Hispano-Suiza 8Ba 200 hp
Beardmore W.B.X	Beardmore 160 hp
Beardmore W.B.XXIV Wee Bee	Bristol Cherub I
Beardmore W.B.XXIV Wee Bee	Bristol Cherub III
Beatty-Wright	Beatty 50 hp
Bell XP-63B	Rolls-Royce/Packard V-1650-5 Merlin
Bjorn Andreasson KZ VIII	de Havilland Gipsy Major 8
Blackburn Monoplane, 1	Green C4 30-35 hp
Blackburn Monoplane No 2	Isaacson 40-50 hp
Blackburn Mercury 1	Isaacson 40-50 hp
Blackburn Mercury 2	Gnome 7 Omega 50 hp
Blackburn Mercury III	Anzani (British) 45 hp
Blackburn Mercury 3	Gnome 7 Omega 50 hp
Blackburn Mercury 3	Isaacson 40-50 hp
Blackburn Mercury III	Renault 60 hp
Blackburn Type E Single seater	Green D4 50-60 hp
Blackburn Type E Two-seater	Renault WB, WC 70 hp
Blackburn Single-Seat monoplane	Gnome 7 Omega 50 hp
Blackburn Type 1	Gnome 7 Lambda 80 hp
Blackburn Land/Sea	Anzani (British) 100 hp
Blackburn Type L	Salmson (Canton-Unne) M.9 120 hp
Blackburn T.B.	Gnome Monosoupape 9B-2 100 hp
Blackburn Triplane	Clerget 9Z 110 hp
Blackburn Triplane	Gnome Monosoupape 9B-2 100 hp
Blackburn White Falcon	Anzani (British) 100 hp
Blackburn G.P. Seaplane	Rolls-Royce Falcon I 190 hp
Blackburn G.P. Seaplane	Sunbeam Nubian 150 hp
Blackburn Kangaroo	Rolls-Royce Falcon II 220 hp
Blackburn Kangaroo	Rolls-Royce Falcon III 275 hp
Blackburn Blackburd	Rolls-Royce Eagle VIII 375 hp
Blackburn Sidecar	A.B.C. Gnat I 35 hp
Blackburn T.1 Swift I	Napier Lion II
Blackburn T.1A Swift II	Napier Lion II
Blackburn T.2 Dart	Napier Lion IIB
Blackburn T.2 Dart	Napier Lion V
Blackburn Blackburn I	Napier Lion IIB
Blackburn Blackburn II	Napier Lion V
Blackburn Pellet	Napier Lion II
Blackburn T.3 Velos	Napier Lion IIB
Blackburn T.3A Velos	Napier Lion V
Blackburn T.4 Cubaroo	Beardmore Simoon I
Blackburn T.4 Cubaroo	Napier Cub
Blackburn L.1 Bluebird I	Armstrong Siddeley Genet I
Blackburn L.1 Bluebird I	Blackburne Thrush 35 hp
Blackburn R.B.1 Iris I	Rolls-Royce Condor III
Blackburn R.B.1 Iris II	Rolls-Royce Condor IIIA
Blackburn R.B.1 Iris III	Rolls-Royce Condor IIIB
Blackburn R.B.1 Iris IV	Armstrong Siddeley Leopard III
Blackburn R.B.1 Iris V	Napier Culverin I
Blackburn R.B.1 Iris V	Rolls-Royce Buzzard IIMS
Blackburn R.2 Airedale	Armstrong Siddeley Jaguar III
Blackburn T.5 Ripon I	Napier Lion V
Blackburn T.5 Ripon IIA	Napier Lion X
Blackburn T.5 Ripon IIA, IIC, III	Napier Lion XIA
Blackburn T.5 Ripon IIF	Armstrong Siddeley Panther IIA (GF)
Blackburn T.5 Ripon IIF	Armstrong Siddeley Tiger I
Blackburn T.5 Ripon IIF	Bristol Jupiter VIII
Blackburn T.5 Ripon IIF	Bristol Pegasus IIM.3
Blackburn T.5 Ripon II, IIA	Napier Lion XI
Blackburn T.R.1 Sprat	Rolls-Royce Falcon III 275 hp
Blackburn F.1 Turcock	Armstrong Siddeley Jaguar VI
Blackburn 2F.1 Nautilus	Rolls-Royce Kestrel IIMS
Blackburn B.T.1 Beagle	Bristol Jupiter VIIIF
Blackburn B.T.1 Beagle	Bristol Jupiter XF
Blackburn L.1A Bluebird II	Armstrong Siddeley Genet II
Blackburn L.1B Bluebird III	Cirrus III
Blackburn F.2 Lincock I	Armstrong Siddeley Lynx IV
Blackburn F.2 Lincock I	Armstrong Siddeley Lynx IVC
Blackburn F.2 Lincock II	Armstrong Siddeley Lynx IV G
Blackburn F.2 Lincock III	Armstrong Siddeley Lynx V (Major, Cheetah)
Blackburn R.B.2 Sydney	Rolls-Royce Kestrel IIMS
Blackburn L.1C Bluebird IV	Armstrong Siddeley Genet Ma I
Blackburn L.1C Bluebird IV	Cirrus III
Blackburn L.1C Bluebird IV	Cirrus Hermes I
Blackburn L.1C Bluebird IV	Cirrus Hermes II
Blackburn L.1C Bluebird IV	de Havilland Gipsy I
Blackburn L.1C Bluebird IV	de Havilland Gipsy II
Blackburn L.1C Bluebird IV	de Havilland Gipsy III
Blackburn C.6/29 Biplane	Armstrong Siddeley Jaguar IVC

Blackburn C.6/29 Monoplane	Armstrong Siddeley Jaguar IVC
Blackburn F.3	Rolls-Royce Goshawk III
Blackburn R.B.3A Perth	Rolls-Royce Buzzard IIMS
Blackburn-Saro (Segrave) Meteor	de Havilland Gipsy III
Blackburn-Saro (Segrave) Meteor II	de Havilland Gipsy Major I srs I
Blackburn B-2	Blackburn Cirrus Major I
Blackburn B-2	Blackburn Cirrus Major III
Blackburn B-2	Cirrus Hermes IVA
Blackburn B-2	de Havilland Gipsy III
Blackburn B-2	de Havilland Gipsy Major I srs I
Blackburn B-3, M.1/30, M.1/30A	Rolls-Royce Buzzard IIIMS
Blackburn B.5 Ripon V	Armstrong Siddeley Tiger I
Blackburn B.5 Ripon V	Bristol Pegasus IM.3
Blackburn B-5 Baffin	Bristol Pegasus IM.3
Blackburn B-5 Baffin	Bristol Pegasus IIM.3
Blackburn B.6	Armstrong Siddeley Tiger IV
Blackburn T.9 Shark I	Armstrong Siddeley Tiger IV
Blackburn T.9A Shark II	Bristol Pegasus IIIM.3
Blackburn T.9A Shark IIA	Armstrong Siddeley Tiger VIC
Blackburn T.9A Shark II, IIA	Armstrong Siddeley Tiger VI
Blackburn T.9B Shark III	Armstrong Siddeley Tiger VI
Blackburn T.9B Shark III	Bristol Pegasus IIIM.3
Blackburn T.9B Shark III	Bristol Pegasus IX
Blackburn B-7, G.4/31	Armstrong Siddeley Tiger IV
Blackburn H.S.T.10	Napier-Halford Rapier VI
Blackburn B-20	Rolls-Royce Vulture II
Blackburn B-24 Skua I	Bristol Mercury IX
Blackburn B-24 Skua I	Bristol Perseus XII
Blackburn B-25 Roc I	Bristol Perseus XII
Blackburn B-26 Botha I	Bristol Perseus X
Blackburn B-26 Botha I	Bristol Perseus XA
Blackburn B-37 Firebrand F.I, T.F.II	Napier-Halford Sabre III
Blackburn B-47 Firebrand V	Bristol Centaurus X
Blackburn B-47 Firebrand V	Bristol Centaurus XI
Blackburn B-45 Firebrand III	Bristol Centaurus VII
Blackburn B-45 Firebrand III	Bristol Centaurus IX
Blackburn B-46 Firebrand IV, V, VA	Bristol Centaurus IX
Blackburn B-46 Firebrand IV, V, VA	Bristol Centaurus 57
Blackburn B-48 'Firecrest' S.28/43	Bristol Centaurus 59
Blackburn B-54/YA-7, -8	Rolls-Royce Griffon 56
Blackburn & G.A.60 Universal Freighter I	Bristol Hercules 260
Blackburn & G.A.60 Universal Freighter II	Bristol Hercules 730
Blackburn & G.A. B-101 Beverley C.1	Bristol Centaurus 165
Blackburn & G.A. B-101 Beverley C.1	Bristol Centaurus 173
Blackburn & G.A. B-101 Beverley C.1	Bristol Centaurus 175
Blackburn & G.A. B-101 Beverley C.1	Bristol Centaurus 373
Bleriot Parasol	Gnome 7 Lambda 80 hp
Bleriot Type XII	E.N.V. Type D 35-40 hp
Bleriot Type XII	E.N.V. Type F 60-80 hp
Bleriot XI	Gnome 7 Lambda 80 hp
Bleriot XI	Gnome 7 Omega 50 hp
Bleriot XXI	Gnome 7 Gamma 70 hp
Boulton Paul P.82 Defiant I	Rolls-Royce Merlin II
Boulton Paul P.82 Defiant I, II	Rolls-Royce Merlin III
Boulton Paul P.82 Defiant II	Rolls-Royce Merlin XX
Boulton Paul P.92/2	de Havilland Gipsy Major I srs I
Boulton Paul P.108 T.7/45	Bristol Mercury 30
Boulton Paul P.108 Balliol T.14/47	Rolls-Royce Merlin 35
Boulton & Paul Bobolink	Bentley B.R.2 230 hp
Boulton & Paul P.6	R.A.F.1a 90 hp
Boulton & Paul P.7 Bourges I	Bentley B.R.1 (A.R.1) 150 hp
Boulton & Paul P.7 Bourges IA	A.B.C. Dragonfly I 320 hp
Boulton & Paul P.7 Bourges IA	A.B.C. Dragonfly IA 330/360 hp
Boulton & Paul P.8 'Atlantic'	Napier Lion II
Boulton & Paul P.9	R.A.F.1a 90 hp
Boulton & Paul P.10	Cosmos Lucifer I
Boulton & Paul P.25 Bugle I	Bristol Jupiter II
Boulton & Paul P.25 Bugle I	Bristol Jupiter III
Boulton & Paul P.29 Sidestrand I	Bristol Jupiter VI
Boulton & Paul P.29 Sidestrand I	Bristol Jupiter VIII
Boulton & Paul P.29 Sidestrand III	Bristol Jupiter VIIIF
Boulton & Paul P.29 Sidestrand III	Bristol Pegasus IM.3
Boulton & Paul P.29 Sidestrand III	Bristol Pegasus IV
Boulton & Paul P.31 Bittern	Armstrong Siddeley Lynx IV
Boulton & Paul P.32	Bristol Jupiter XF
Boulton & Paul P.32	Bristol Jupiter XFBM
Boulton & Paul P.33 Partridge	Bristol Jupiter VII
Boulton & Paul P.41 Phoenix I	A.B.C. Scorpion I
Boulton & Paul P.41 Phoenix II	British Salmson A.D.9
Boulton & Paul P.64 Mailplane	Bristol Pegasus IM.2
Boulton & Paul P.71A Mailplane	Armstrong Siddeley Jaguar VI

Boulton & Paul P.71A-1 Mailplane	Armstrong Siddeley Jaguar VI
Boulton & Paul P.75 Overstrand I	Bristol Pegasus IM.3
Boulton & Paul P.75 Overstrand I	Bristol Pegasus IIM.3
Breda 15	de Havilland Gipsy I
Breda 33	de Havilland Gipsy III
Breda-Zappata BZ.308	Bristol Centaurus 568
Breguet 890H prot	Bristol Hercules 738
Breguet U2	Salmson (Canton-Unne) M.9 120 hp
Bristol Boxkite	E.N.V. Type F 60-80 hp
Bristol Boxkite	Gnome 7 Lambda 80 hp
Bristol Boxkite	Gnome 7 Omega 50 hp
Bristol Boxkite	Renault 60 hp
Bristol Racing Biplane (1911)	Gnome 7 Omega 50 hp
Bristol Monoplane (1911)	Gnome 7 Omega 50 hp
Bristol Biplane Type T	Gnome 7 Gamma 70 hp
Bristol-Prier P-1	Gnome 7 Omega 50 hp
Bristol Prier-Dickson	Gnome 7 Gamma 70 hp
Bristol Prier-Dickson	Anzani (British) 35 hp, 1,100 c.c.
Bristol Prier	Isaacson 40-50 hp
Bristol Gordon England G.E.2	Gnome 14 Omega-Omega 100 hp
Bristol Gordon England G.E.3	Gnome 7 Lambda 80 hp
Bristol-Coanda School Monoplane	Gnome 7 Omega 50 hp
Bristol-Coanda Competition Monoplane	Gnome 7 Lambda 80 hp
Bristol-Coanda Military Monoplane	Gnome 7 Lambda 80 hp
Bristol-Coanda Hydro 120 Biplane	Gnome 7 Lambda 80 hp
Bristol-Coanda T.B.8	Gnome Monosoupape 9B-2 100 hp
Bristol-Coanda T.B.8	Gnome 7 Lambda 80 hp
Bristol-Coanda T.B.8	Le Rhone 9C 80 hp
Bristol-Coanda T.B.8	Gnome 7 Omega 50 hp
Bristol-Coanda T.B.8	Le Rhone 9 60 hp
Bristol-Coanda G.B.75	Gnome Monosoupape 7 Type A 75 hp
Bristol 1 Scout A, B, C	Gnome 7 Lambda 80 hp
Bristol 1 Scout C	Clerget 7Z 80 hp
Bristol 1 Scout C	Le Rhone 9C 80 hp
Bristol 2 Scout D	Gnome 7 Lambda 80 hp
Bristol 3 Scout D	Le Rhone 9C 80 hp
Bristol 3 Scout D	Le Rhone 9R 110 hp
Bristol 5 Scout D	Clerget 9Z 110 hp
Bristol 4 Scout D	Gnome Monosoupape 9B-2 100 hp
Bristol 6 T.T.A	Beardmore 120 hp
Bristol 8 S.2A	Clerget 9Z 110 hp
Bristol 8 S.2A	Gnome Monosoupape 9B-2 100 hp
Bristol 10 M.1A	Bentley B.R.1 (A.R.1) 150 hp
Bristol 10 M.1A	Clerget 9B 130 hp
Bristol 10 M.1A	Clerget 9Z 110 hp
Bristol 11 M.1B	Clerget 9B 130 hp
Bristol 11 M.1B	Clerget 9Z 110 hp
Bristol 12 F.2A Fighter	Rolls-Royce Falcon I 190 hp
Bristol 13 M.R.1	Hispano-Suiza 8Aa 150 hp
Bristol 13 M.R.1	Wolseley W.4A* Viper 200 hp
Bristol 14 F.2B Fighter	Rolls-Royce Falcon I 190 hp
Bristol 14 F.2B Fighter	Rolls-Royce Falcon II 220 hp
Bristol 14 F.2B Fighter II, III, IV	Rolls-Royce Falcon III 275 hp
Bristol 14 F.2B Fighter	R.A.F.4d 200 hp
Bristol 15 F.2B Fighter	Sunbeam Arab I 200 hp
Bristol 16 F.2B Fighter	Hispano-Suiza 8Ab 180 hp
Bristol 16 F.2B Fighter	Hispano-Suiza 8B 200 hp
Bristol 16 F.2B Fighter	Hispano-Suiza 8Ba 200 hp
Bristol 17 F.2B Fighter	Hispano-Suiza 8Fb 300 hp
Bristol 17, 17A, 17B F.2B Fighter	Hispano-Suiza 8F 300 hp
Bristol 20	de Havilland Gipsy II
Bristol 20 M.1C	Le Rhone 9C 80 hp
Bristol 20 M.1C	Le Rhone 9Ja 110 hp
Bristol 21 Scout F	Sunbeam Arab I 200 hp
Bristol 21 Scout F	Sunbeam Arab II 200 hp
Bristol 21A Scout F.1	Cosmos Mercury
Bristol 23 Badger I	A.B.C. Dragonfly IA 330/360 hp
Bristol 23A Badger II	Cosmos Jupiter I
Bristol 23X Badger	Siddeley-Deasy Puma 236 hp
Bristol 24 Braemar I	Siddeley-Deasy Puma HC 290 hp
Bristol 25 Braemar II	Liberty 12A 400 hp
Bristol 26 Pullman	Liberty 12A 400 hp
Bristol 27 F.2B Coupe	Rolls-Royce Falcon III 275 hp
Bristol 28	Siddeley-Deasy Puma 236 hp
Bristol 29	Siddeley-Deasy Puma 236 hp
Bristol 30 Babe I	Viale 45 hp
Bristol 32 Bullet	Cosmos Jupiter I
Bristol 32A Bullet	Bristol Jupiter II
Bristol 34 Seaplane	Siddeley-Deasy Puma 236 hp
Bristol 36 Seely (S)	Bristol Jupiter IIIS
Bristol 36 Seely	Siddeley-Deasy Puma 236 hp

Bristol 40 F.2B Fighter	Siddeley-Deasy Puma HC 290 hp
Bristol 46 Babe	A.B.C. Gadfly
Bristol 46 Babe II	Armstrong Siddeley Ounce 40 hp
Bristol 46A Babe III	Le Rhone 9 60 hp
Bristol 47	Siddeley-Deasy Puma 236 hp
Bristol 52 MFA Bullfinch I	Bristol Jupiter III
Bristol 52 MFA Bullfinch I	Bristol Jupiter IV
Bristol 53 MFB Bullfinch II	Bristol Jupiter III
Bristol 53 MFB Bullfinch II	Bristol Jupiter IV
Bristol 62 Ten-seater	Napier Lion II
Bristol 72 Racer	Bristol Jupiter IV
Bristol 72 Racer	Bristol Jupiter IV (Special)
Bristol 73 Taxiplane	Bristol Lucifer II
Bristol 73 Taxiplane	Bristol Lucifer III
Bristol 75 Ten-seater	Bristol Jupiter IV
Bristol 75A Express Freighter	Bristol Jupiter IV
Bristol 76 Jupiter Fighter	Bristol Jupiter IV
Bristol 77 M.1D	Bristol Lucifer IV Special
Bristol 79 Brandon	Bristol Jupiter IV
Bristol 81 Puma Trainer	Siddeley-Deasy Puma 236 hp
Bristol 83 School Machine	Bristol Lucifer II
Bristol 83 School Machine	Bristol Lucifer III
Bristol 83 School Machine	Bristol Lucifer IV
Bristol 83 Trainer	Bristol Titan I Direct drive
Bristol 83E Trainer	Bristol Titan IV Geared drive
Bristol 84 Bloodhound	Bristol Jupiter IV
Bristol 84 Bloodhound	Bristol Jupiter V
Bristol 84 Bloodhound	Bristol Jupiter VI (DR)
Bristol 84 Bloodhound	Bristol Jupiter VI
Bristol 84 Bloodhound	Bristol Jupiter VIII
Bristol 84A Bloodhound	Bristol Jupiter IV (VT)
Bristol 84A Bloodhound	Bristol Jupiter IV
Bristol 84B Bloodhound	Bristol Jupiter IV (TS)
Bristol 84B Bloodhound	Bristol Jupiter IV
Bristol 86 Greek Tourer	Rolls-Royce Falcon III 275 hp
Bristol 86 Greek Tourer	Siddeley-Deasy Puma 236 hp
Bristol 88 Bulgarian Tourer (1, 2)	Wolseley W.4A* Viper 200 hp
Bristol 89	Bristol Jupiter III
Bristol 89 Advanced Trainer	Bristol Jupiter IV (DR)
Bristol 89, 89A	Bristol Jupiter IV
Bristol 89, 89A	Bristol Jupiter IV (DR)
Bristol 89, 89A	Bristol Jupiter VI (DR)
Bristol 89, 89A	Bristol Jupiter VI
Bristol 90 Berkeley	Rolls-Royce Condor III
Bristol 91 Brownie I	Bristol Cherub I
Bristol 91A Brownie I	Bristol Cherub III
Bristol 91B Brownie II	Bristol Cherub III
Bristol 92 'Laboratory'	Bristol Jupiter VI
Bristol 93 Boarhound I	Bristol Jupiter IV
Bristol 93A Beaver	Bristol Jupiter IV
Bristol 93A Beaver	Bristol Jupiter VI
Bristol 93B Boarhound II	Bristol Jupiter IV
Bristol 93B Boarhound II	Bristol Jupiter VI
Bristol 95 Bagshot	Bristol Jupiter VI
Bristol 96, 96A	Rolls-Royce Falcon III 275 hp
Bristol 98 Brownie III	Bristol Cherub III
Bristol 99 Badminton	Bristol Jupiter VII
Bristol 99, 99A Badminton	Bristol Jupiter VI
Bristol 99A Badminton	Bristol Jupiter VI Short Stroke
Bristol 101	Bristol Jupiter VI
Bristol 101	Bristol Jupiter VIA
Bristol 101	Bristol Mercury II
Bristol 105 Bulldog I	Bristol Jupiter VII
Bristol 105A Bulldog II	Bristol Jupiter VIA
Bristol 105A Bulldog IIA	Bristol Aquila I
Bristol 105A Bulldog IIA	Bristol Jupiter VIFH
Bristol 105A Bulldog IIA	Bristol Jupiter VIIF
Bristol 105A Bulldog IIA	Bristol Jupiter VIIF.P.
Bristol 105A Bulldog III	Bristol Mercury III
Bristol 105A Bulldog IIIA	Bristol Mercury IV
Bristol 105A Bulldog IIIA	Bristol Mercury IVA
Bristol 105A Bulldog IV	Bristol Mercury IVS.2
Bristol 105A Bulldog IVA	Bristol Mercury VIS.2
Bristol 105A Bulldog IVA	Bristol Perseus I.A
Bristol 107 Bullpup	Bristol Aquila I
Bristol 107 Bullpup	Bristol Jupiter VI
Bristol 107 Bullpup	Bristol Mercury IIA
Bristol 107 Bullpup	Bristol Mercury (short stroke)
Bristol 109	Bristol Jupiter VIII
Bristol 109	Bristol Jupiter XIF
Bristol 110A	Bristol Neptune I

Bristol 110A	Bristol Titan I Direct drive
Bristol 118	Bristol Jupiter XF
Bristol 118	Bristol Jupiter XFA
Bristol 118A	Bristol Mercury V
Bristol 120	Bristol Pegasus IM.3
Bristol 120	Bristol Pegasus XVIII
Bristol 123	Rolls-Royce Goshawk III
Bristol 124 Bulldog TM	Alvis 9ARS (Leonides)
Bristol 124 Bulldog TM	Armstrong Siddeley Cheetah IX
Bristol 124 Bulldog TM	Bristol Jupiter VI
Bristol 124 Bulldog TM	Bristol Jupiter VIFH
Bristol 124 Bulldog TM	Napier-Halford Rapier I
Bristol 130 C.26/31 (Bombay prot)	Bristol Pegasus IIIM.2
Bristol 130 C.26/31 (Bombay prot)	Bristol Pegasus IIIM.3
Bristol 130 (Bombay prot)	Bristol Pegasus X
Bristol 130A Bombay I C.26/31	Bristol Pegasus 22
Bristol 133	Bristol Mercury VIS.2
Bristol 138A 2/34	Bristol Pegasus IV
Bristol 138A	Bristol Pegasus PE.6S
Bristol 142 'Britain First'	Bristol Mercury VIS.2
Bristol 142M Blenheim I	Bristol Mercury VIII
Bristol 143	Bristol Aquila I
Bristol 146	Bristol Mercury IX
Bristol 148	Bristol Mercury IX
Bristol 148	Bristol Perseus XII
Bristol 148B	Bristol Taurus II
Bristol 149M Blenheim IV	Bristol Mercury XV
Bristol 149M Bolingbroke I, III	Bristol Mercury VIII
Bristol 149M Bolingbroke IV	Bristol Mercury XV
Bristol 149M Bolingbroke IV, IVT	Bristol Mercury XX
Bristol 152 Beaufort I	Bristol Taurus II
Bristol 152 Beaufort I	Bristol Taurus III
Bristol 152 Beaufort I (Australia)	Bristol Taurus VI
Bristol 152 Beaufort I	Bristol Taurus XII
Bristol 152 Beaufort I	Bristol Taurus XVI
Bristol 152 Beaufort IV	Bristol Taurus XX
Bristol 156 Beaufighter I	Bristol Hercules III
Bristol 156 Beaufighter I	Bristol Hercules X
Bristol 156 Beaufighter I	Bristol Hercules XI
Bristol 156 Beaufighter I F.17/39	Bristol Hercules II
Bristol 156 Beaufighter II	Rolls-Royce Griffon IIB
Bristol 156 Beaufighter II	Rolls-Royce Merlin XX
Bristol 156 Beaufighter II	Rolls-Royce Merlin 61
Bristol 156 Beaufighter VIC	Bristol Hercules 130
Bristol 156 Beaufighter VIC, VIF	Bristol Hercules XVI
Bristol 156 Beaufighter VIC, VIF	Bristol Hercules VI
Bristol 156 Beaufighter TF.X, XIC	Bristol Hercules XVII
Bristol 156 Beaufighter 21	Bristol Hercules XVIII
Bristol 156 Beaufighter TF.X, XIC	Bristol Hercules XVIII
Bristol 160 Bisley I	Bristol Mercury XVI
Bristol 160 Blenheim V	Bristol Mercury 25
Bristol 160 Blenheim V	Bristol Mercury 30
Bristol 163 Buckingham I	Bristol Centaurus IV
Bristol 163 Buckingham I	Bristol Centaurus VII
Bristol 164 Brigand I	Bristol Centaurus 57
Bristol 166 Buckmaster I	Bristol Centaurus VII
Bristol 166 Buckmaster I	Bristol Centaurus XI
Bristol 167 Brabazon I Mk I	Bristol Centaurus 20
Bristol 170 Freighter	Bristol Hercules 234
Bristol 170 Freighter	Bristol Hercules 238
Bristol 170 Freighter, Wayfarer	Bristol Hercules 638
Bristol 170 Freighter	Bristol Hercules 268
Bristol 170 Freighter I, IA, II srs, XI, XIA	Bristol Hercules 632
Bristol 170 Freighter 21, 21E, 21P	Bristol Hercules 672
Bristol 170 Freighter 31 srs, 32	Bristol Hercules 734
Bristol 170 Wayfarer	Bristol Hercules 632
Bristol 171 Sycamore 3, 4, H.C.14	Alvis Leonides 524/1 Mk 173
Bristol 173 prot	Alvis Leonides 525/1 Mk 173
Bristol 173 Mk III	Alvis Leonides Ma. 755/1 Mk 155
Bristol 173 Mk III	Alvis Leonides Ma. 755/2 Mk 160
Bristol 191 Belvedere	Alvis Leonides Ma. 755/2 Mk 160
British Burnelli - see Cunliffe Owen	
British Klemm Swallow	British Salmson A.D.9R
British Klemm Swallow	Pobjoy Cataract II
British Taylorcraft - see Auster	
Britten Norman BN-1F	J.A.P. J-99 (Aeronca E-113-C)
Broughton-Blayney Brawney	Carden-Ford 31 hp
Burga Monoplane	Gnome 7 Omega 50 hp
Burgess-Wright	A.B.C. 30 h.p.
C.A.S.A. 207 prot	Bristol Hercules 730
C.A.S.A. C2111-D	Rolls-Royce Merlin 500/29

C.L.W. Curlew	Pobjoy Niagara III
C.O.W. Biplane No 2	Gnome Monosoupape 9B-2 100 hp
C.W. Cygnet	Blackburn Cirrus Minor I
Canadair 4 DC-4M.2 North Star	Rolls-Royce Merlin 624
Canadair 4 DC-4M.2 North Star (TCA)	Rolls-Royce Merlin 722
Canadair 4 DC-4M.2 North Star (TCA)	Rolls-Royce Merlin 724-1C
Canadair 4 DC-4M.2 (CPA)	Rolls-Royce Merlin 626-12
Canadair C-4 Argonaut (BOAC)	Rolls-Royce Merlin 626-1
Canadair C-4 Argonaut (BOAC)	Rolls-Royce Merlin 724-10
Canadair C-54-M North Star	Rolls-Royce Merlin 620
Canadair DC-4M.1 North Star (TCA)	Rolls-Royce Merlin 622
Canadair DC-4M.1, 2, 3 North Star (TCA)	Rolls-Royce Merlin 622
Canadair DC-4M.2/4 North Star (TCA)	Rolls-Royce Merlin 624
Carden-Baynes Bee	Carden-Ford S.P.1 40 hp
Carden-Baynes Scud III Auxiliary	Carden-Baynes 350 c.c. Auxiliary
Caudron Biplane 45 h.p.	Anzani (British) 45 hp
Caudron G.III	Gnome 7 Lambda 80 hp
Caudron G.III	Renault WB, WC 70 hp
Caudron G.III	Renault WS 80 hp
Caudron G.III	Statax 40 hp
Caudron G.III, IV	Anzani (British) 100 hp
Caudron G.III, IV	Le Rhone 9C 80 hp
Central Centaur IIA	Beardmore 160 hp
Central Centaur IVA, IVB	Anzani (British) 100 hp
Central Centaur IVA	Renault WB, WC 70 hp
Chilton D.W.1	Carden-Ford 31 hp
Chilton Monoplane	Blackburn Cirrus Midget
Chrislea CH.3 srs 2 Super Ace	de Havilland Gipsy Major 10/1
Chrislea CH.3 srs 4 Skyjeep	Blackburn Cirrus Major III
Cierva C.6A, B Autogiro	Le Rhone 9Ja 110 hp
Cierva C.6C Autogiro (Avro 574)	Clerget 9B 130 hp
Cierva C.6D Autogiro (Avro 575)	Clerget 9B 130 hp
Cierva C.8L Mk I Autogiro	Armstrong Siddeley Lynx II
Cierva C.8L Mk II, III (Avro 617)	Armstrong Siddeley Lynx IV
Cierva C.8R Autogiro (Avro 587)	Clerget 9B 130 hp
Cierva C.8V Autogiro (Avro 586)	Wolseley W.4A* Viper 200 hp
Cierva C.9 Autogiro (Avro 576)	Armstrong Siddeley Genet I
Cierva C.10 Autogiro	Armstrong Siddeley Genet I
Cierva C.11 Parnall Gyroplane	A.D.C. Airdisco
Cierva C.12 Autogiro	Avro Alpha 90 hp
Cierva C.17 Mk I, II (Avro 612)	Cirrus III
Cierva C.17 Mk II Autogiro	Avro Alpha 90 hp
Cierva C.18 Autogiro	British Salmson A.C.7
Cierva C.19 Mk I Autogiro	Armstrong Siddeley Genet II
Cierva C.19 Mk II, IIA, III Autogiros	Armstrong Siddeley Genet Ma I
Cierva C.19 Mk IV, IVP Autogiros	Armstrong Siddeley Genet Ma I
Cierva/Westland CL.20 Autogiro	Pobjoy Niagara III
Cierva/de Havilland C.24 Autogiro	de Havilland Gipsy III
Cierva/Comper C-25 Autogiro	Pobjoy R
Cierva C.30 prot Autogiro	Armstrong Siddeley Genet Ma I
Cierva C.30A (Avro 671) Autogiro (Rota I)	Armstrong Siddeley Genet Ma IA
Cierva C.30A (Avro 671) Rota I Autogiro	Armstrong Siddeley Civet I
Cierva C.30P Autogiro	Armstrong Siddeley Genet Ma IA
Cierva C.40 Rota II Autogiro	British Salmson 9NG
Cierva W.9, W.9A, W.9B	de Havilland Gipsy Queen II
Cierva W.11 Air Horse	Rolls-Royce Merlin 24
Cierva W.14 Skeeter 3 prot	de Havilland Gipsy Major 8
Cierva W.14 Skeeter I (Saro P.501)	Jameson FF-1 110 hp
Cierva W.14 Skeeter 2	de Havilland Gipsy Major 10/1
Cierva W.14 Skeeter II	de Havilland Gipsy Major 10/2
Cierva W.14 Skeeter IIIB prot, V	Blackburn Cirrus Bombardier 702
Cierva W.14 Skeeter 6	de Havilland Gipsy Major 200
Cierva W.14 Skeeter 7	de Havilland Gipsy Major 215
Civilian Coupe I	A.B.C. Hornet
Civilian Coupe II	Armstrong Siddeley Genet Ma I
Clarke Cheetah (monoplane & biplane)	Blackburne Thrush 35 hp
Cody Types IIA, C, D	Green D4 50-60 hp
Cody IIB	E.N.V. Type F 60-80 hp
Cody Types III, VC, VI	Green D4 50-60 hp
Cody V	Beardmore 120 hp
Cody Types VC, VI	Green E6 100-120 hp
Commonwealth CA-17 Mustang	Rolls-Royce/Packard V-1650-7 Merlin 266
Comper C.L.A.7 Swift	A.B.C. Scorpion II
Comper C.L.A.7 Swift	British Salmson A.C.9
Comper C.L.A.7 Swift	British Salmson A.D.9
Comper C.L.A.7 Swift	de Havilland Gipsy III
Comper C.L.A.7 Swift	de Havilland Gipsy Major I srs I
Comper C.L.A.7 Swift	Pobjoy P1
Comper C.L.A.7 Swift	Pobjoy R
Comper C.L.A.7 Swift	Pobjoy Niagara III
Comper Kite	de Havilland Gipsy Major I srs I
Comper Mouse	

Comper Streak	de Havilland Gipsy Major I srs II
Coventry Ordnance Works Biplane 10	Gnome 14 Omega-Omega 100 hp
Cranwell C.L.A.2, 3	Bristol Cherub I
Cranwell C.L.A.4, 4A	Bristol Cherub III
Cunliffe-Owen Concordia	Alvis Leonides 501/4
Cunliffe-Owen OA-1 Flying Wing	Bristol Perseus XIV-C
Currie Super Wot	Pobjoy R
Currie Wot	J.A.P. J-99 (Aeronca E-113-C)
Curtiss C	Curtiss VX 160 hp
Curtiss C	Sunbeam Crusader 150 hp
Curtiss C	Sunbeam Nubian 150 hp
Curtiss H.4 Small America	Curtiss OXX 100 hp
Curtiss H.12 Large America	Rolls-Royce Eagle I 250 hp
Curtiss H.12 Large America	Rolls-Royce Eagle VII 322 hp
Curtiss H.12 Large America	Rolls-Royce Eagle VIII 375 hp
Curtiss H.16 Large America	Rolls-Royce Eagle VIII 375 hp
Curtiss H.4 Small America	Anzani (British) 100 hp
Curtiss H.4 Small America	Curtiss OX-2 90 hp
Curtiss H.4 Small America	Sunbeam Nubian 150 hp
Curtiss JN-3	Curtiss OX-5 90 hp
Curtiss JN-4, 4A	Curtiss OX-2 90 hp
Curtiss P-40E Kittyhawk	Rolls-Royce/Packard V-1650-1 Merlin 28
Curtiss P-40E Kittyhawk	Rolls-Royce/Packard V-1650-3 Merlin 61, 63
Curtiss P-40E Kittyhawk	Rolls-Royce/Packard V-1650-7 Merlin 266
Curtiss P-40F Kittyhawk II	Rolls-Royce Merlin 28 (V-1650-1)
Curtiss P-40F Kittyhawk II	Rolls-Royce Merlin 29
Curtiss P-40F, P-40L Kittyhawk II	Rolls-Royce Merlin 31
Curtiss R-2, R-4	Curtiss VX 160 hp
Curtiss R-2, R-4	Sunbeam Arab I 200 hp
Curtiss XP-60	Rolls-Royce/Packard V-1650-1 Merlin 28
Curtiss XP-60	Rolls-Royce/Packard V-1650-3 Merlin 61, 63
Curtiss-Wanamaker Triplane	Rolls-Royce Eagle I 250 hp
Darmstadt D.22	de Havilland Gipsy III
Dart Flittermouse	Scott Flying Squirrel
Dart Kitten	J.A.P. J-99 (Aeronca E-113-C)
De Bruyne (Aero Research) Snark	de Havilland Gipsy Major I srs I
De Bruyne-Maas Ladybird	Bristol Cherub III
De Bruyne-Maas Ladybird	Scott Flying Squirrel
de Havilland Biplane No 1	de Havilland 'Iris' 40 hp
de Havilland Biplane No 2	de Havilland 'Iris' 40 hp
de Havilland D.H. T.K.1	de Havilland Gipsy III
de Havilland D.H. T.K.2	de Havilland Gipsy Major I srs I
de Havilland D.H. T.K.2	de Havilland Gipsy Major I srs II
de Havilland D.H. T.K.2	de Havilland Gipsy Major IC
de Havilland D.H. T.K.2	de Havilland Gipsy Major ID
de Havilland D.H. T.K.4	de Havilland Gipsy Major I srs II
de Havilland D.H. T.K.5	de Havilland Gipsy Major I srs I
de Havilland D.H. T.K.5	de Havilland Gipsy Major IC
de Havilland D.H. T.K.5	de Havilland Gipsy Major ID
de Havilland D.H.10 Amiens	Liberty 12A 400 hp
de Havilland D.H.10 Amiens	Siddeley-Deasy Puma 236 hp
de Havilland D.H.10 Amiens I	B.H.P. 230 hp, Galloway Adriatic
de Havilland D.H.10C Amiens II, IIIC	Rolls-Royce Eagle VIII 375 hp
de Havilland D.H.10A Amiens III, IIIA	Liberty 12A 400 hp
de Havilland D.H.11 Oxford I	A.B.C. Dragonfly I 320 hp
de Havilland D.H.14	Rolls-Royce Condor I
de Havilland D.H.14A	Napier Lion II
de Havilland D.H.15 Gazelle	B.H.P. 500 hp, Galloway Atlantic
de Havilland D.H.16	Liberty 12A 400 hp
de Havilland D.H.16	Napier Lion II
de Havilland D.H.16	Rolls-Royce Eagle VIII 375 hp
de Havilland D.H.16	Rolls-Royce Eagle IX 360 hp
de Havilland D.H.18A, B	Napier Lion II
de Havilland D.H.27 Derby	Rolls-Royce Condor III
de Havilland D.H.29 Doncaster	Napier Lion II
de Havilland D.H.34 17/21	Napier Lion II
de Havilland D.H.37	Rolls-Royce Falcon III 275 hp
de Havilland D.H.37A	A.D.C. Nimbus 300 hp
de Havilland D.H.42 Dormouse	Armstrong Siddeley Jaguar IV
de Havilland D.H.42A Dingo I	Bristol Jupiter III
de Havilland D.H.42B Dingo II	Bristol Jupiter IV
de Havilland D.H.50	A.D.C. Nimbus 300 hp
de Havilland D.H.50	Bristol Jupiter IV
de Havilland D.H.50	Bristol Jupiter VI
de Havilland D.H.50	Bristol Jupiter XI
de Havilland D.H.50	Siddeley-Deasy Puma 236 hp
de Havilland D.H.50J	Armstrong Siddeley Jaguar III
de Havilland D.H.51	A.D.C. Airdisco
de Havilland D.H.51	R.A.F.1a 90 hp
de Havilland D.H.53 Humming Bird	A.B.C. Scorpion I
de Havilland D.H.53 Humming Bird	Blackburne Tomtit 690 c.c. (inverted)

de Havilland D.H.53 Humming Bird	Bristol Cherub III
de Havilland D.H.53 Humming Bird	Douglas 750 c.c., 6.5 hp
de Havilland D.H.54 Highclere	Rolls-Royce Condor IIIA
de Havilland D.H.56 Hyena	Armstrong Siddeley Jaguar III
de Havilland D.H.56 Hyena	Armstrong Siddeley Jaguar IV
de Havilland D.H.60 Moth	Armstrong Siddeley Genet I
de Havilland D.H.60 Moth	Armstrong Siddeley Genet II
de Havilland D.H.60 Moth	Cirrus I
de Havilland D.H.60 Moth	Cirrus II
de Havilland D.H.60 Moth	Cirrus III
de Havilland D.H.60 Moth	Cirrus Hermes I
de Havilland D.H.60G Gipsy Moth	de Havilland Gipsy I
de Havilland D.H.60G Gipsy Moth	de Havilland Gipsy II
de Havilland D.H.60G Gipsy Moth	de Havilland Gipsy III
de Havilland D.H.60G Gipsy Moth	General Aircraft V.4
de Havilland D.H.60M Gipsy Moth	de Havilland Gipsy I
de Havilland D.H.60M Gipsy Moth	de Havilland Gipsy II
de Havilland D.H.60T Moth Trainer	de Havilland Gipsy I
de Havilland D.H.60T Moth Trainer	de Havilland Gipsy II
de Havilland D.H.60GIII Moth Major	de Havilland Gipsy III
de Havilland D.H.60GIII Moth Major	de Havilland Gipsy Major I srs I
de Havilland D.H.61 Giant Moth	Armstrong Siddeley Jaguar VIC
de Havilland D.H.61 Giant Moth	Bristol Jupiter VI
de Havilland D.H.61 Giant Moth	Bristol Jupiter XIF
de Havilland D.H.65 Hound	Napier Lion VIII
de Havilland D.H.65A Hound	Napier Lion XA
de Havilland D.H.65A Hound	Napier Lion XI
de Havilland D.H.65J Hound	Bristol Jupiter VIIIF.P.
de Havilland D.H.66 Hercules	Bristol Jupiter VI
de Havilland D.H.67 Survey (Gloster A.S.31)	Bristol Jupiter VI
de Havilland D.H.67B Survey (Gloster A.S.31)	Bristol Jupiter VIII
de Havilland D.H.71 Tiger Moth	Cirrus II
de Havilland D.H.71 Tiger Moth	Cirrus III
de Havilland D.H.71 Tiger Moth	de Havilland Gipsy I
de Havilland D.H.71 Tiger Moth	de Havilland Gipsy 'R'
de Havilland D.H.72	Bristol Jupiter XFS
de Havilland D.H.75 Hawk Moth	Armstrong Siddeley Cheetah IX
de Havilland D.H.75 Hawk Moth	Armstrong Siddeley Lynx IVA
de Havilland D.H.75 Hawk Moth	de Havilland Ghost
de Havilland D.H.77	Napier-Halford Rapier I
de Havilland D.H.77	Napier-Halford Rapier II
de Havilland D.H.80 Puss Moth	de Havilland Gipsy III
de Havilland D.H.80A Puss Moth	de Havilland Gipsy Major I srs I
de Havilland D.H.80A Puss Moth	de Havilland Gipsy Major I srs II
de Havilland D.H.81, 81A Swallow Moth	de Havilland Gipsy IV
de Havilland D.H.82A Tiger Moth I	de Havilland Gipsy III
de Havilland D.H.82A Tiger Moth I	de Havilland Gipsy Major I srs I
de Havilland D.H.82A Tiger Moth I	de Havilland Gipsy Major IF
de Havilland D.H.82B, C Tiger Moth II	de Havilland Gipsy Major I srs I
de Havilland D.H.82A, C Tiger Moth II	de Havilland Gipsy Major IC
de Havilland D.H.82A, C Tiger Moth II	de Havilland Gipsy Major ID
de Havilland D.H.82B Queen Bee I prot	de Havilland Gipsy Major I srs I
de Havilland D.H.82B Queen Bee I	de Havilland Gipsy Major ID
de Havilland D.H.83 Fox Moth	de Havilland Gipsy III
de Havilland D.H.83 Fox Moth	de Havilland Gipsy Major I srs I
de Havilland D.H.83, 83C Fox Moth	de Havilland Gipsy Major IC
de Havilland D.H.83, 83C Fox Moth	de Havilland Gipsy Major ID
de Havilland D.H.84 Dragon	de Havilland Gipsy Major I srs I
de Havilland D.H.85 Leopard Moth	de Havilland Gipsy III
de Havilland D.H.85 Leopard Moth	de Havilland Gipsy Major I srs I
de Havilland D.H.85A Leopard Moth	de Havilland Gipsy Six 'R'
de Havilland D.H.86A, B Express	de Havilland Gipsy Six srs I
de Havilland D.H.86A, B Express	de Havilland Gipsy Six srs II
de Havilland D.H.87 Hornet Moth	de Havilland Gipsy III
de Havilland D.H.87A, B Hornet Moth	de Havilland Gipsy Major I srs I
de Havilland D.H.87A, B Hornet Moth	de Havilland Gipsy Major IC
de Havilland D.H.87A, B Hornet Moth	de Havilland Gipsy Major ID
de Havilland D.H.87A, B Hornet Moth	de Havilland Gipsy Major IF
de Havilland D.H.88 Comet	de Havilland Gipsy Six 'R'
de Havilland D.H.88 Comet	de Havilland Gipsy Six srs II V.P.
de Havilland D.H.89 Rapide	de Havilland Gipsy Queen II
de Havilland D.H.89 Rapide	de Havilland Gipsy Queen III
de Havilland D.H.89A Dominie	de Havilland Gipsy Queen II
de Havilland D.H.89A Dominie	de Havilland Gipsy Queen III
de Havilland D.H.89, 89M Rapide	de Havilland Gipsy Six srs I
de Havilland D.H.89, 89M Rapide	de Havilland Gipsy Six srs II
de Havilland D.H.90 Dragonfly	de Havilland Gipsy Major I srs I
de Havilland D.H.91 Albatross 36/35	de Havilland Gipsy XII Twelve
de Havilland D.H.92 Dolphin	de Havilland Gipsy Six srs II V.P.
de Havilland D.H.93 Don 6/36	de Havilland Gipsy XII Twelve
de Havilland D.H.93 Don 6/36	de Havilland Gipsy King I

de Havilland D.H.94 Moth Minor	de Havilland Gipsy Minor
de Havilland D.H.95 Flamingo	Bristol Perseus XIIC
de Havilland D.H.95 Flamingo	Bristol Perseus XIIC1
de Havilland D.H.95 Flamingo	Bristol Perseus XVI
de Havilland D.H.95 Flamingo	Bristol Perseus XVIC
de Havilland D.H.95 Hertfordshire I	Bristol Perseus XVI
de Havilland D.H.95 Hertfordshire I	Bristol Perseus XVIC
de Havilland D.H.98 Mosquito I, II	Rolls-Royce Merlin 23
de Havilland D.H.98 Mosquito I, II, III	Rolls-Royce Merlin 21
de Havilland D.H.98 Mosquito IV, VI	Rolls-Royce Merlin 21
de Havilland D.H.98 Mosquito IV, VI	Rolls-Royce Merlin 23
de Havilland D.H.98 Mosquito VI, XII	Rolls-Royce Merlin 25
de Havilland D.H.98 Mosquito IX, XVI, 30	Rolls-Royce Merlin 72
de Havilland D.H.98 Mosquito XII, XIII	Rolls-Royce Merlin 21
de Havilland D.H.98 Mosquito XII, XIII	Rolls-Royce Merlin 23
de Havilland D.H.98 Mosquito XIII, XVII	Rolls-Royce Merlin 25
de Havilland D.H.98 Mosquito XVI	Rolls-Royce Merlin 73
de Havilland D.H.98 Mosquito XVI	Rolls-Royce Merlin 77
de Havilland D.H.98 Mosquito XVI, 30	Rolls-Royce Merlin 76
de Havilland D.H.98 Mosquito XVII, XIX	Rolls-Royce Merlin 21
de Havilland D.H.98 Mosquito XVII, XIX	Rolls-Royce Merlin 23
de Havilland D.H.98 Mosquito XIX	Rolls-Royce Merlin 25
de Havilland D.H.98 Mosquito XX, 40	Rolls-Royce Merlin 31
de Havilland D.H.98 Mosquito XX, 40	Rolls-Royce Merlin 33
de Havilland D.H.98 Mosquito 25, 26	Rolls-Royce Merlin 225
de Havilland D.H.98 Mosquito T.R.33	Rolls-Royce Merlin 25
de Havilland D.H.98 Mosquito 34	Rolls-Royce Merlin 113/113A
de Havilland D.H.98 Mosquito 34	Rolls-Royce Merlin 114/114A
de Havilland D.H.98 Mosquito T.R.37	Rolls-Royce Merlin 25
de Havilland D.H.98 Mosquito T.T.39	Rolls-Royce Merlin 76
de Havilland D.H.98 Mosquito T.T.39	Rolls-Royce Merlin 77
de Havilland D.H.98 Mosquito T.T.39	Rolls-Royce Merlin 73
de Havilland D.H.103 Hornet F.I	Rolls-Royce Merlin 130
de Havilland D.H.103 Hornet F.I	Rolls-Royce Merlin 131
de Havilland D.H.103 Hornet F.III	Rolls-Royce Merlin 134
de Havilland D.H.103 Hornet F.III	Rolls-Royce Merlin 135
de Havilland D.H.103 Sea Hornet XX	Rolls-Royce Merlin 130
de Havilland D.H.103 Sea Hornet XX	Rolls-Royce Merlin 131
de Havilland D.H.103 Sea Hornet 21	Rolls-Royce Merlin 134
de Havilland D.H.103 Sea Hornet 21	Rolls-Royce Merlin 135
de Havilland D.H.104 Devon C.1	de Havilland Gipsy Queen 70-4
de Havilland D.H.104 Devon C.1	de Havilland Gipsy Queen 71
de Havilland D.H.104 Dove prot	de Havilland Gipsy Queen 70-1
de Havilland D.H.104 Dove 1B, 2B	de Havilland Gipsy Queen 70-4
de Havilland D.H.104 Dove 1, 2, 7, 8	de Havilland Gipsy Queen 70-3
de Havilland D.H.104 Dove 5, 6	de Havilland Gipsy Queen 70-2
de Havilland D.H.104 Sea Devon 20	de Havilland Gipsy Queen 70-4
de Havilland D.H.114 Heron prot	de Havilland Gipsy Queen 30
de Havilland D.H.114 Heron prot	de Havilland Gipsy Queen 30-3
de Havilland D.H.114 Heron prot	de Havilland Gipsy Queen 30-4
de Havilland D.H.114 Heron 2	de Havilland Gipsy Queen 30-2
de Havilland D.H.114 Sea Heron	de Havilland Gipsy Queen 30-2
de Havilland D.H.89A Dominie I, II	de Havilland Gipsy Six srs I
de Havilland D.H.89A Dominie I, II	de Havilland Gipsy Six srs II
de Havilland (Australia) D.H.A.3.Drover 2	de Havilland Gipsy Major 10/2
de Havilland (Australia) D.H.A.3.Drover 2	de Havilland Gipsy Major 10/3
de Havilland (Canada) D.H.C.1 Chipmunk	de Havilland Gipsy Major 50
de Havilland (Canada) D.H.C.1B Chipmunk T.10	de Havilland Gipsy Major 8
de Havilland (Canada) D.H.C.1B Chipmunk T.10	de Havilland Gipsy Major 10/2
de Havilland (Canada) D.H.C.1B Chipmunk	de Havilland Gipsy Major 10/3
de Havilland (Canada) D.H.C.2 Beaver 2	Alvis Leonides 502/4
Deekay Knight	Blackburn Cirrus Minor I
Deperdussin Type B	Gnome 7 Lambda 80 hp
Desoutter I	Cirrus Hermes I
Desoutter I	Cirrus Hermes II
Desoutter II	de Havilland Gipsy III
Dornier Do J Wal	Napier Lion II
Dornier Do J Wal	Rolls-Royce Eagle IX 360 hp
Douglas DC-2	Bristol Pegasus VI
Druine D.54 Turbi	Coventry Victor Neptune
Dudley Watt D.W.2	Cirrus III
Duigan Biplane	E.N.V. Type D 35-40 hp
Duigan Biplane	Gnome 7 Omega 50 hp
Dunne D.8	Gnome 7 Lambda 80 hp
Eardley Billing Tractor Biplane	E.N.V. Type D 35-40 hp
Edgar Percival Prospector	Armstrong Siddeley Cheetah X
English Electric M.3 Ayr (Taxy only)	Napier Lion IIB
English Electric P.5 Kingston I, II, III	Napier Lion IIB
English Electric S.1 Wren	A.B.C. 8 h.p.
Evans VP-1 Volksplane	Rollason Ardem 4CO2-1
F.B.A. C Flying Boat	Gnome Monosoupape 9B-2 100 hp

Fairey F.2	Rolls-Royce Falcon I 190 hp
Fairey F.16 Campania	Rolls-Royce Eagle IV 284 hp
Fairey F.17 Campania	Rolls-Royce Eagle V 322 hp
Fairey F.17 Campania	Rolls-Royce Eagle VII 322 hp
Fairey F.17 Campania	Rolls-Royce Eagle VIII 375 hp
Fairey F.22 Campania	Sunbeam Maori II 260/275 hp
Fairey Hamble Baby	Clerget 9B 130 hp
Fairey Hamble Baby	Clerget 9Z 110 hp
Fairey N.9	Rolls-Royce Falcon I 190 hp
Fairey N.9	Sunbeam Maori II 260/275 hp
Fairey N.10	Napier Lion II
Fairey N.10	Sunbeam Maori II 260/275 hp
Fairey IIIA	Napier Lion II
Fairey IIIA, IIIB	Sunbeam Maori II 260/275 hp
Fairey N.4 Atalanta	Rolls-Royce Condor II
Fairey N.4 Titania	Rolls-Royce Condor IIIA
Fairey IIIC	Rolls-Royce Eagle VIII 375 hp
Fairey Pintail	Napier Lion I
Fairey Pintail	Napier Lion II
Fairey Pintail	Napier Lion V
Fairey IIID	Napier Lion IIB
Fairey IIID	Napier Lion V
Fairey IIID	Napier Lion VA
Fairey IIID	Rolls-Royce Eagle VIII 375 hp
Fairey IIID	Rolls-Royce Eagle IX 360 hp
Fairey Fawn I	Napier Lion IIB
Fairey Fawn I, II	Napier Lion II
Fairey Fawn I, II	Napier Lion V
Fairey Fawn III	Napier Lion VI
Fairey Flycatcher prot	Armstrong Siddeley Jaguar II
Fairey Flycatcher	Armstrong Siddeley Jaguar IVC
Fairey Flycatcher I	Bristol Jupiter IV
Fairey Flycatcher I, III	Armstrong Siddeley Jaguar IV
Fairey Flycatcher II	Bristol Mercury IIA
Fairey Fremantle	Rolls-Royce Condor III
Fairey Ferret I	Armstrong Siddeley Jaguar IV
Fairey Ferret II, III	Bristol Jupiter VI
Fairey Fox I	Fairey Felix (Curtiss D.12)
Fairey Fox IA	Rolls-Royce Kestrel IA
Fairey Fox IA	Rolls-Royce Kestrel IIA
Fairey IIIF	Armstrong Siddeley Jaguar VI (S)
Fairey IIIF	Armstrong Siddeley Panther IIA (GF)
Fairey IIIF/IIIM	Armstrong Siddeley Panther VI
Fairey IIIF	Bristol Jupiter VIII
Fairey IIIF	Napier Culverin I
Fairey IIIF/I	Napier Lion V
Fairey IIIF/I	Napier Lion VA
Fairey IIIF/II	Napier Lion XI
Fairey IIIF/IIIB, IIIM, IVC, IVCM	Napier Lion XIA
Fairey IIIF/IV	Rolls-Royce Kestrel IIB
Fairey Firefly I	Fairey Felix (Curtiss D.12)
Fairey Firefly II, III	Rolls-Royce Kestrel IS
Fairey Firefly II, III	Rolls-Royce Kestrel IIS
Fairey Firefly II, III, IIIM	Rolls-Royce Kestrel IIMS
Fairey Long-range Monoplane I, II	Napier Lion XIA
Fairey Fleetwing	Rolls-Royce Kestrel IA
Fairey Fleetwing	Rolls-Royce Kestrel IIMS
Fairey Fox II	Armstrong Siddeley Serval V
Fairey Fox II	Rolls-Royce Kestrel IIB
Fairey Fox IIM	Rolls-Royce Kestrel IS
Fairey Fox II, IIS, IIIS	Rolls-Royce Kestrel IIS
Fairey Fox III, IIIC	Rolls-Royce Kestrel V
Fairey Hendon prot	Bristol Jupiter XF
Fairey Hendon I	Rolls-Royce Kestrel IIIS
Fairey Hendon II	Rolls-Royce Kestrel VI
Fairey Gordon I, II	Armstrong Siddeley Panther IIA (GF)
Fairey Seal	Armstrong Siddeley Panther IIA (GF)
Fairey Seal	Armstrong Siddeley Panther VI
Fairey Seal	Bristol Pegasus IIIM.3
Fairey Seal	Napier Lion XI
Fairey G.4/31	Armstrong Siddeley Tiger VI
Fairey G.4/31	Bristol Pegasus IIM.3
Fairey G.4/31 Mk II	Armstrong Siddeley Tiger IV
Fairey S.9/30	Rolls-Royce Kestrel IIMS
Fairey TSR I	Armstrong Siddeley Panther VI
Fairey TSR I	Bristol Pegasus IIM
Fairey TSR II	Bristol Pegasus IIIM.3
Fairey Swordfish I S.15/33	Bristol Pegasus IIIM.2
Fairey Swordfish I	Bristol Pegasus IIIM.3
Fairey Swordfish I, II, III	Bristol Pegasus 30
Fairey Battle I	Bristol Hercules II

Fairey Battle I	Bristol Hercules XI
Fairey Battle I	Bristol Taurus II
Fairey Battle I	Fairey P-24 Monarch
Fairey Battle I	Napier-Halford Dagger VIII
Fairey Battle I	Napier-Halford Sabre I
Fairey Battle I	Napier-Halford Sabre II
Fairey Battle I	Rolls-Royce Exe
Fairey Battle I	Rolls-Royce Merlin F
Fairey Battle I	Rolls-Royce Merlin I
Fairey Battle I	Rolls-Royce Merlin II
Fairey Battle I	Rolls-Royce Merlin III
Fairey Battle I	Rolls-Royce Merlin XII
Fairey Seafox	Napier-Halford Rapier VI
Fairey Albacore I	Bristol Taurus II
Fairey Albacore II	Bristol Taurus XII
Fairey P.4/34	Rolls-Royce Merlin I
Fairey Fulmar I	Rolls-Royce Merlin VIII
Fairey Fulmar II	Rolls-Royce Merlin 30
Fairey Barracuda I	Rolls-Royce Merlin 30
Fairey Barracuda II, III	Rolls-Royce Merlin 32
Fairey Barracuda V	Rolls-Royce Griffon VIII
Fairey Barracuda V	Rolls-Royce Griffon 37
Fairey Firefly prot	Rolls-Royce Griffon II
Fairey Firefly I	Rolls-Royce Griffon IIB
Fairey Firefly I, II	Rolls-Royce Griffon XII
Fairey Firefly I, II	Rolls-Royce Griffon 73
Fairey Firefly T.III Trainer	Rolls-Royce Griffon XII
Fairey Firefly III, IV	Rolls-Royce Griffon 61
Fairey Firefly III, IV	Rolls-Royce Griffon 72
Fairey Firefly IV prot	Rolls-Royce Griffon 71
Fairey Firefly IV, V, VI	Rolls-Royce Griffon 74
Fairey Firefly VII, VIII	Rolls-Royce Griffon 59
Fairey Firefly Trainer I, II, III	Rolls-Royce Griffon II
Fairey Spearfish I	Bristol Centaurus 58
Fairey Gyrodyne	Alvis Leonides 522/2
Fairey Primer	Blackburn Cirrus Major III
Fairey Primer	de Havilland Gipsy Major 10/1
Fairey Fox II	Fairey P.12
Fairey Long-range Monoplane 02	Napier Lion XIA (Special)
Farman Pusher Biplane	E.N.V. Type F 60-80 hp
Henry Farman Biplane	Gnome 7 Gamma 70 hp
Henry Farman F.20	Gnome 7 Lambda 80 hp
Henry Farman F.20	Le Rhone 9C 80 hp
Henry Farman F.27	Salmson (Canton-Unne) B.9 140 hp
Henry Farman F.27	Salmson (Canton-Unne) R.9 160 hp
Henry 'Horace' Farman F.40	Renault 160 hp
Henry Farman Type Militaire	Gnome 7 Omega 50 hp
Maurice Farman Serie VII Longhorn	Renault WB, WC 70 hp
Maurice Farman Serie VII Longhorn	Renault WS 80 hp
Maurice Farman Serie 11 Shorthorn	Renault WS 80 hp
Felixstowe F.2A	Rolls-Royce Eagle I 250 hp
Felixstowe F.2A	Rolls-Royce Eagle VIII 375 hp
Felixstowe F.3	Rolls-Royce Eagle VIII 375 hp
Felixstowe F.4, F.5	Rolls-Royce Eagle IX 360 hp
Felixstowe F.5	Napier Lion II
Felixstowe F.5	Rolls-Royce Eagle VIII 375 hp
Firth Helicopter	de Havilland Gipsy Major 10/1
Flanders Biplane	A.B.C. 100 h.p.
Flanders B.2	Isaacson 40-50 hp
Flanders F.3	Green D4 50-60 hp
Flanders F.4	Renault WB, WC 70 hp
Flanders Monoplane	Isaacson 40-50 hp
Fleet F.7D-2	Armstrong Siddeley Genet Ma IA
Fokker C.X	Bristol Pegasus XX
Fokker F.III	Siddeley-Deasy Puma 236 hp
Bristol Jupiter XI	Bristol Jupiter XI
Fokker F.VIIA/3m	Armstrong Siddeley Lynx IVC
Fokker G.1	Bristol Mercury VIIA
Fokker T.9	Bristol Hercules II
Folland Fo.108 43/37	Bristol Centaurus I
Folland Fo.108 43/37	Bristol Centaurus IV
Folland Fo.108 43/37	Bristol Centaurus VII
Folland Fo.108 43/37	Bristol Hercules VIII
Folland Fo.108 43/37	Bristol Hercules VIII (MOD)
Folland Fo.108 43/37	Bristol Hercules XI
Folland Fo.108 43/37	Bristol Hercules XVMT
Folland Fo.108 43/37	Napier-Halford Sabre I
Folland Fo.108 43/37	Napier-Halford Sabre II
Folland Fo.108 43/37	Napier-Halford Sabre IIA
Folland Fo.108 43/37	Napier-Halford Sabre III
Folland Fo.108 43/37	Napier-Halford Sabre VA

Folland Fo.108 43/37	Napier-Halford Sabre VII
Folland Fo.108 43/37	Napier-Halford Sabre VIII
Folland Fo.108 43/37	Napier-Halford Sabre E.118
Foster Wickner F.W.1 Wicko	Wicko F (mod Ford V-8)
Foster Wickner F.W.2 Wicko	Blackburn Cirrus Minor I
Foster Wickner F.W.3 Wicko	Blackburn Cirrus Major III
Foster Wickner G.M.1 Wicko	de Havilland Gipsy Major I srs I
Fritz Tractor Monoplane	E.N.V. Type D 35-40 hp
General Aircraft G.A.L.26	Blackburn Cirrus Minor I
General Aircraft G.A.L.38 Night Shadower	Pobjoy Niagara V
General Aircraft G.A.L.42 Cygnet II	Blackburn Cirrus Major II
General Aircraft G.A.L.42 Cygnet Major	de Havilland Gipsy Major I srs I
General Aircraft G.A.L.42 Cygnet Minor	Blackburn Cirrus Minor I
General Aircraft G.A.L.45 Owlet	Blackburn Cirrus Major II
General Aircraft G.A.L.47	Blackburn Cirrus Minor I
General Aircraft Hamilcar X	Bristol Mercury 31
General Aircraft Monospar ST-3	British Salmson A.C.9
General Aircraft Monospar ST-3	British Salmson A.D.9
General Aircraft Monospar ST-4	Pobjoy R
General Aircraft Monospar ST-6	Pobjoy Niagara I
General Aircraft Monospar ST-6	Pobjoy R
General Aircraft Monospar ST-10	Pobjoy Niagara I
General Aircraft Monospar ST-11	de Havilland Gipsy Major I srs I
General Aircraft Monospar ST-12	de Havilland Gipsy Major I srs I
General Aircraft Monospar ST-25 Universal	Pobjoy Niagara III
General Aircraft Monospar ST-25 Universal	Pobjoy Niagara IV
Gloucestershire Mars I (Bamel)	Napier Lion II
Gloucestershire I (Seaplane)	Napier Lion II
Gloucestershire II (Seaplane)	Napier Lion VA
Gloster III, IIIA, IIIB	Napier Lion VII
Gloucestershire Mars III Sparrowhawk I, II, III	Bentley B.R.2 230 hp
Gloucestershire Mars VI Nighthawk	Armstrong Siddeley Jaguar II
Gloucestershire Mars VI Nighthawk	Bristol Jupiter III
Gloucestershire Mars VI Nighthawk	Bristol Jupiter IV
Gloucestershire Mars X Nightjar	Bentley B.R.2 230 hp
Gloucestershire Grouse I	Bentley B.R.2 230 hp
Gloucestershire Grouse II	Armstrong Siddeley Lynx II
Gloucestershire Gannet	Blackburne Tomtit 690 c.c. (inverted)
Gloucestershire Gannet	Carden 750 c.c.
Gloucestershire Grebe I	Armstrong Siddeley Jaguar III
Gloucestershire Grebe I	Armstrong Siddeley Jaguar IIIA
Gloucestershire Grebe I	Bristol Jupiter IV
Gloucestershire Grebe II	Armstrong Siddeley Jaguar IV
Gloucestershire Gamecock I	Bristol Jupiter IV
Gloucestershire Gamecock I	Bristol Mercury IIA
Gloucestershire Gamecock II	Bristol Jupiter VI
Gloucestershire Gamecock (Special)	Bristol Jupiter VIIF.P.
Gloster Gorcock	Napier Lion IV
Gloster Gorcock	Napier Lion VIII
Gloster Guan	Napier Lion IV
Gloster Guan	Napier Lion VI
Gloster Goral	Bristol Jupiter VIA
Gloster Goring	Bristol Jupiter V
Gloster Goring	Bristol Jupiter VI
Gloster Goring	Bristol Jupiter VIIIF.P.
Gloster Goring	Bristol Jupiter XF
Gloster Goring	Bristol Mercury VIIA
Gloster Goring	Bristol Pegasus IIL.2
Gloster Goring	Bristol Perseus II-L
Gloster Gamecock I	Bristol Orion
Gloster Gamecock (Special)	Bristol Jupiter VII
Gloster Goldfinch	Bristol Jupiter VIIF
Gloster IV	Napier Lion VIIA
Gloster IVA	Napier Lion VIIA
Gloster IVB	Napier Lion VIIB
Gloster Gambet	Bristol Jupiter VI
Gloster Gnatsnapper I	Bristol Jupiter VII
Gloster Gnatsnapper I	Bristol Mercury IIA
Gloster Gnatsnapper II	Armstrong Siddeley Jaguar VIII
Gloster Gnatsnapper II	Rolls-Royce Kestrel IIS
Gloster Gnatsnapper III	Rolls-Royce Goshawk III
Gloster A.S.31 Survey	Bristol Jupiter XIF
Gloster S.S.18	Bristol Mercury IIA
Gloster S.S.18A	Bristol Jupiter VIIF
Gloster S.S.18B	Armstrong Siddeley Panther IIIA
Gloster S.S.19	Bristol Jupiter VIIF
Gloster S.S.19B	Bristol Mercury VIS
Gloster Gauntlet I, II	Bristol Mercury VIS
Gloster VI Golden Arrow	Napier Lion VIID
Gloster TC.33 C.16/28 (Pusher)	Rolls-Royce Kestrel IIS
Gloster TC.33 C.16/28 Tractor	Rolls-Royce Kestrel IIIS

Gloster TSR.38	Rolls-Royce Goshawk III
Gloster TSR.38	Rolls-Royce Kestrel IIMS
Gloster S.S.37 Gladiator prot	Bristol Mercury IV
Gloster S.S.37 Gladiator prot F.7/30	Bristol Mercury VIS.2
Gloster Gladiator I	Bristol Mercury VIIIA
Gloster F.5/34	Bristol Mercury VIII
Gloster F.5/34 Gladiator II	Bristol Mercury IX
Gloster Sea Gladiator I	Bristol Mercury VIIIA
Gloster Sea Gladiator I	Bristol Mercury IX
Gloster F.9/37	Bristol Taurus II
Gloster F.9/37	Rolls-Royce Peregrine I
Glster Goring	Bristol Orion
Gnosspelius Gull	Blackburne Tomtit 690 c.c. (upright)
Gnosspelius Hydro Tractor Biplane	Green E6 100-120 hp
Gordon Dove	Aero Engines Sprite I
Grahame-White VIII	Anzani (British) 60 hp
Grahame-White 20	Clerget 7Z 80 hp
Grahame-White Charabancs Type 10	Green E6 100-120 hp
Grahame-White G.W.15	Gnome 7 Lambda 80 hp
Grahame-White G.W.15	Le Rhone 9C 80 hp
Grahame-White G.W.E.6 Bantam	Le Rhone 9C 80 hp
Grahame-White G.W.E.7	Rolls-Royce Eagle V 322 hp
Grahame-White G.W.E.9 Ganymede	Napier Lion II
Grahame-White Passenger Biplane VIIc	Gnome 7 Gamma 70 hp
Grahame-White Pusher Biplane	E.N.V. Type F 60-80 hp
Grahame-White Pusher Biplane	Gnome 7 Gamma 70 hp
Grahame-White School Biplane	Gnome 7 Omega 50 hp
Grahame-White Type XV Boxkite	Green D4 50-60 hp
Grain (Pt.Vict.7) Kitten	A.B.C. Gnat I 35 hp
Grain (Pt. Vict.) Griffin	Bentley B.R.2 230 hp
Grain (Pt. Vict.) Griffin	Sunbeam Arab II 200 hp
Granger Archaeopteryx	Bristol Cherub I
Hafner A.R.III Gyroplane	Pobjoy Niagara III
Hafner A.R.III Mk I Gyroplane	Pobjoy Cataract I
Hafner A.R.III Mk II Gyroplane	Pobjoy Niagara I
Hafner R.II Revoplane II Helicopter	British Salmson A.D.9
Halton H.A.C.I Mayfly	Bristol Cherub III
Handasyde H.2	Rolls-Royce Eagle VIII 375 hp
Handley Page Type G	Anzani (British) 100 hp
Handley Page H.P.2 Type B	Green D4 50-60 hp
Handley Page H.P.3 F/70	Gnome 7 Gamma 70 hp
Handley Page H.P.4 Type D	Green C4 30-35 hp
Handley Page H.P.11 O/100	Rolls-Royce Eagle I 250 hp
Handley Page H.P.11 O/100	Sunbeam Cossack 310/320 hp
Handley Page H.P.12 O/400	Bristol Jupiter III
Handley Page H.P.12 O/400	Bristol Jupiter IV
Handley Page H.P.12 O/400	Liberty 12N 350 hp
Handley Page H.P.12 O/400	Napier Lion II
Handley Page H.P.12 O/400	Rolls-Royce Eagle IV 284 hp
Handley Page H.P.12 O/400	Rolls-Royce Eagle VIII 375 hp
Handley Page H.P.12 O/400	Rolls-Royce Eagle IX 360 hp
Handley Page H.P.12 O/400	Sunbeam Maori II 260/275 hp
Handley Page H.P.15 V/1500	B.H.P. 500 hp, Galloway Atlantic
Handley Page H.P.15 V/1500	Napier Lion II
Handley Page H.P.15 V/1500	Rolls-Royce Eagle IV 284 hp
Handley Page H.P.15 V/1500	Rolls-Royce Eagle VIII 375 hp
Handley Page H.P.15 V/1500	Rolls-Royce Eagle IX 360 hp
Handley Page H.P.17	Siddeley-Deasy Puma 236 hp
Handley Page H.P.18 W.8	Napier Lion IIB
Handley Page H.P.18 W.8b	Rolls-Royce Eagle VIII 375 hp
Handley Page H.P.18 W.8c	Rolls-Royce Eagle IX 360 hp
Handley Page H.P.19 Hanley (Type T)	Napier Lion IIB
Handley Page H.P.20 Type X/4B	Liberty 12N 350 hp
Handley Page H.P.21 Type S	Bentley B.R.2 230 hp
Handley Page H.P.22	A.B.C. 8 h.p.
Handley Page H.P.23	Blackburne Tomtit 690 c.c. (inverted)
Handley Page H.P.24 W.8d Hyderabad	Napier Lion IIB
Handley Page H.P.24 W.8d Hyderabad	Napier Lion V
Handley Page H.P.25 Hendon (Type Ta)	Napier Lion IIB
Handley Page H.P.26 W.8e/f Hamilton	Rolls-Royce Eagle IX 360 hp
Handley Page H.P.26 W.8e/f Hamilton	Siddeley-Deasy Puma 236 hp
Handley Page H.P.26 W.8g	Rolls-Royce Kestrel IIA
Handley Page H.P.27 W.9a Hampstead	Armstrong Siddeley Jaguar IV
Handley Page H.P.27 W.9a Hampstead	Bristol Jupiter VI
Handley Page H.P.28 Handcross	Rolls-Royce Condor III
Handley Page H.P.30 W.10	Napier Lion IIB
Handley Page H.P.30 W.10	Rolls-Royce Kestrel IA
Handley Page H.P.30 W.10	Rolls-Royce Kestrel IIA
Handley Page H.P.31 Harrow I Type E	Napier Lion VA
Handley Page H.P.31 Harrow II Type E	Napier Lion XIA
Handley Page H.P.32 Hamlet Type D	Armstrong Siddeley Lynx IVC

Handley Page H.P.32 Hamlet Type D	Armstrong Siddeley Mongoose II
Handley Page H.P.32 Hamlet Type D	Bristol Lucifer IV
Handley Page H.P.33 Clive I	Bristol Jupiter VIIIF
Handley Page H.P.33 Clive I	Bristol Jupiter VIIIF.P.
Handley Page H.P.33 Hinaidi I	Bristol Jupiter VIIF
Handley Page H.P.33 Hinaidi I	Bristol Jupiter VIII
Handley Page H.P.34 Hare Type H	Armstrong Siddeley Panther II (PF)
Handley Page H.P.34 Hare Type H	Armstrong Siddeley Panther IIA (GF)
Handley Page H.P.34 Hare Type H	Bristol Jupiter VIII
Handley Page H.P.34 Hare Type H	Bristol Jupiter XF
Handley Page H.P.35 Clive II, III	Bristol Jupiter IX
Handley Page H.P.36 Hinaidi II Type M	Bristol Jupiter IXF
Handley Page H.P.39 Gugnunc	Armstrong Siddeley Mongoose II
Handley Page H.P.39 Gugnunc	Armstrong Siddeley Mongoose III
Handley Page H.P.42E (H.P.45) Hannibal	Bristol Jupiter XIF
Handley Page H.P.42W Heracles	Bristol Jupiter XFBM
Handley Page H.P.43 C.16/28	Bristol Pegasus IM.3
Handley Page H.P.46	Rolls-Royce Buzzard IIIMS
Handley Page H.P.47 G.4/31	Bristol Pegasus IIIM.2
Handley Page H.P.50 Heyford I, IA	Rolls-Royce Kestrel IIIS
Handley Page H.P.50 Heyford II, III	Rolls-Royce Kestrel VI
Handley Page H.P.51	Armstrong Siddeley Tiger IV
Handley Page H.P.51	Bristol Pegasus III
Handley Page H.P.52 Hampden I	Bristol Pegasus 22
Handley Page H.P.52 B.9/32 Hampden prot	Bristol Pegasus XV
Handley Page H.P.52 B.9/32 Hampden prot	Bristol Pegasus XVIII
Handley Page H.P.52 Hereford I	Napier-Halford Dagger VIII
Handley Page H.P.53 Hampden (Sweden)	Bristol Pegasus XX
Handley Page H.P.54 Harrow I	Bristol Pegasus X
Handley Page H.P.54 Harrow II	Bristol Pegasus XX
Handley Page H.P.57 Halifax I	Rolls-Royce Merlin X
Handley Page H.P.59 Halifax II	Rolls-Royce Merlin XX
Handley Page H.P.59 Halifax II	Rolls-Royce Merlin 22
Handley Page H.P.59 Halifax II	Rolls-Royce Merlin 24
Handley Page H.P.61 Halifax III	Bristol Hercules VI
Handley Page H.P.61 Halifax III, VI	Bristol Hercules XVI
Handley Page H.P.61 Halifax VI	Bristol Hercules 100
Handley Page H.P.63 Halifax V	Rolls-Royce Merlin XX
Handley Page H.P.63 Halifax V	Rolls-Royce Merlin 22
Handley Page H.P.67 Hastings C.1	Bristol Hercules 100
Handley Page H.P.67 Hastings C.1	Bristol Hercules 101
Handley Page H.P.67 Hastings C.1	Bristol Hercules 105
Handley Page H.P.67 Hastings C.2	Bristol Hercules 106
Handley Page H.P.67 Hastings C.2	Bristol Hercules 216
Handley Page H.P.68 Hermes I	Bristol Hercules 100
Handley Page H.P.68 Hermes I	Bristol Hercules 101
Handley Page H.P.69 Halifax VII	Bristol Hercules VI
Handley Page H.P.69 Halifax VII	Bristol Hercules XVI
Handley Page H.P.70 Halifax VIII	Bristol Hercules 100
Handley Page H.P.70 Halton I, II	Bristol Hercules 100
Handley Page H.P.71 Halifax IX	Bristol Hercules XVI
Handley Page H.P.74 Hermes II	Bristol Hercules 106
Handley Page H.P.74 Hermes II	Bristol Hercules 120
Handley Page H.P.74 Hermes II	Bristol Hercules 121
Handley Page H.P.74 Hermes II	Bristol Hercules 130
Handley Page H.P.74 Hermes II	Bristol Hercules 762
Handley Page H.P.81 Hermes IV	Bristol Hercules 762
Handley Page H.P.81A Hermes IVA	Bristol Hercules 772
Handley Page H.P.94 Hastings C.4	Bristol Hercules 737
Handley Page H.P.95 Hastings C.3	Bristol Hercules 737
Handley Page O/7	Rolls-Royce Eagle VIII 375 hp
Handley Page O/10	Rolls-Royce Eagle VIII 375 hp
Handley Page O/11	Rolls-Royce Eagle VIII 375 hp
Handley Page (Reading) 1 Marathon I, T.11	de Havilland Gipsy Queen 70-3
Handley Page (Reading) 1A Marathon IA, T.11	de Havilland Gipsy Queen 70-4
Handley Page (Reading) H.P.R.2	Alvis Leonides 501/4
Handley Page (Reading) H.P.R.2	Armstrong Siddeley Cheetah XVII
Handley Page (Reading) H.P.R.2	Armstrong Siddeley Cheetah XVIII
Handley Page (Reading) H.P.R.5 Herald	Alvis Leonides Ma. 702/1
Hanriot HD-1	Le Rhone 9Ja 110 hp
Hants & Sussex Herald	J.A.P. J-99 (Aeronca E-113-C)
Hawker Duiker 7/22	Bristol Jupiter IV
Hawker Woodcock I	Armstrong Siddeley Jaguar II
Hawker Woodcock II	Bristol Jupiter IV
Hawker Cygnet	A.B.C. Scorpion I
Hawker Cygnet	Anzani (British) 35 hp 1,100 c.c.
Hawker Cygnet	Bristol Cherub III
Hawker Hedgehog	Bristol Jupiter IV
Hawker Hornbill	Rolls-Royce Condor IV
Hawker Danecock (Dankok)	Armstrong Siddeley Jaguar IV
Hawker Heron	Bristol Jupiter VI

Hawker Horsley	Armstrong Siddeley Leopard I
Hawker Horsley	Armstrong Siddeley Leopard II
Hawker Horsley	Armstrong Siddeley Leopard III
Hawker Horsley	Armstrong Siddeley Leopard IIIA
Hawker Horsley	Napier Lion V
Hawker Horsley	Rolls-Royce Buzzard IMS
Hawker Horsley	Rolls-Royce Buzzard IIIMS
Hawker Horsley	Rolls-Royce Condor C.I.
Hawker Horsley	Rolls-Royce Merlin Prot P.V. 12
Hawker Horsley	Rolls-Royce Merlin C
Hawker Horsley	Rolls-Royce Merlin E
Hawker Horsley	Rolls-Royce Merlin F
Hawker Horsley	Rolls-Royce Merlin G
Hawker Horsley	Rolls-Royce Merlin II
Hawker Horsley	Rolls-Royce Merlin X
Hawker Horsley	Rolls-Royce Condor II
Hawker Horsley I	Rolls-Royce Condor III
Hawker Horsley I	Rolls-Royce Eagle VIII 375 hp
Hawker Horsley II	Rolls-Royce Condor IIIA
Hawker Horsley II	Rolls-Royce Condor IIIB
Hawker Dantorp	Armstrong Siddeley Leopard II
Hawker Dantorp	Armstrong Siddeley Leopard IIIA
Hawker Hawfinch	Armstrong Siddeley Jaguar V
Hawker Hawfinch	Bristol Jupiter VI
Hawker Hawfinch	Bristol Jupiter VIIF
Hawker Harrier	Bristol Hydra
Hawker Harrier	Bristol Jupiter VIII
Hawker Hart	Armstrong Siddeley Panther IIA (GF)
Hawker Hart	Bristol Jupiter VIII
Hawker Hart	Bristol Jupiter XF
Hawker Hart	Bristol Jupiter XFAM
Hawker Hart	Bristol Mercury VIA
Hawker Hart	Bristol Mercury VIII
Hawker Hart	Bristol Mercury XI
Hawker Hart (Sweden)	Bristol Pegasus IM.2
Hawker Hart	Bristol Pegasus IM.3
Hawker Hart	Bristol Pegasus IU.2
Hawker Hart (Persia)	Bristol Pegasus IIM
Hawker Hart	Bristol Pegasus IIIM.2
Hawker Hart	Bristol Pegasus IIIM.3
Hawker Hart	Bristol Pegasus X
Hawker Hart	Bristol Perseus III
Hawker Hart	Napier-Halford Dagger I
Hawker Hart	Napier-Halford Dagger II
Hawker Hart	Napier-Halford Dagger IIIM
Hawker Hart	Rolls-Royce Kestrel IA
Hawker Hart I	Rolls-Royce Kestrel IB
Hawker Hart	Rolls-Royce Kestrel IIMS.2
Hawker Hart	Rolls-Royce Kestrel IIS
Hawker Hart	Rolls-Royce Kestrel IIIS
Hawker Hart I, Hart (India)	Rolls-Royce Kestrel V
Hawker Hart	Rolls-Royce Kestrel V Spl
Hawker Hart	Rolls-Royce Kestrel VDR
Hawker Hart	Rolls-Royce Kestrel VI
Hawker Hart	Rolls-Royce Kestrel X
Hawker Hart, Hart (T)	Rolls-Royce Kestrel XDR
Hawker Hart, Hart (T)	Rolls-Royce Kestrel XVI
Hawker Hart	Rolls-Royce Kestrel XVIDR
Hawker Hart	Rolls-Royce Merlin Prot P.V. 12
Hawker Hart	Rolls-Royce Merlin B
Hawker Hart	Rolls-Royce Merlin C
Hawker Hart	Rolls-Royce Merlin E
Hawker Hart	Rolls-Royce Merlin F
Hawker Tomtit	Armstrong Siddeley Mongoose II
Hawker Tomtit	Armstrong Siddeley Mongoose IIIA
Hawker Tomtit	Armstrong Siddeley Mongoose IIIC
Hawker Tomtit	Cirrus Hermes I
Hawker Tomtit	Wolseley Aquarius I
Hawker Tomtit	Wolseley A.R.9 Mk I
Hawker Tomtit	Wolseley A.R.9 Mk II
Hawker F.20/27	Bristol Mercury VIA
Hawker Hoopoe	Armstrong Siddeley Jaguar V
Hawker Hoopoe	Armstrong Siddeley Panther IIA (GF)
Hawker Hoopoe	Armstrong Siddeley Panther III
Hawker Hoopoe	Bristol Mercury IIA
Hawker Hoopoe	Bristol Mercury VIA
Hawker Hornet	Rolls-Royce Kestrel IS
Hawker Fury I	Rolls-Royce Kestrel IS
Hawker Fury I	Rolls-Royce Kestrel IIS
Hawker Fury II	Rolls-Royce Kestrel VI
Hawker Fury II	Rolls-Royce Kestrel XVI

Hawker Fury (Norway)	Armstrong Siddeley Panther IIIA
Hawker Fury (Norway)	Armstrong Siddeley Panther XI
Hawker Fury (Persia)	Bristol Mercury VISP
Hawker Nimrod I ('Norn')	Rolls-Royce Kestrel IIS
Hawker Nimrod I	Rolls-Royce Kestrel V
Hawker Nimrod (Denmark)	Rolls-Royce Kestrel IIIS
Hawker Demon (Hart Fighter)	Rolls-Royce Kestrel IIS
Hawker Demon I	Rolls-Royce Kestrel IIB
Hawker Hart Fighter (Demon)	Rolls-Royce Kestrel V
Hawker Demon I	Rolls-Royce Kestrel VDR
Hawker Demon I, II (Turret)	Rolls-Royce Kestrel V
Hawker Demon I, II (Turret)	Rolls-Royce Kestrel VI
Hawker Naval Hart	Rolls-Royce Kestrel IIMS
Hawker Osprey	Bristol Pegasus IIM.2
Hawker Osprey	Rolls-Royce Kestrel IIMS.2
Hawker Osprey I, II	Rolls-Royce Kestrel IIMS
Hawker Osprey III	Rolls-Royce Kestrel IIMS.5
Hawker Osprey IV	Rolls-Royce Kestrel V
Hawker Audax	Bristol Mercury IV
Hawker Audax I, Audax (India)	Rolls-Royce Kestrel IB
Hawker Audax I	Rolls-Royce Kestrel XDR
Hawker Audax I	Rolls-Royce Kestrel XVIDR
Hawker Audax (Iraq)	Bristol Pegasus IIM.2
Hawker Audax	Armstrong Siddeley Panther X
Hawker Audax I, Audax (India)	Rolls-Royce Kestrel X
Hawker Audax/Nisr Iraq (Avro 674)	Bristol Pegasus VI
Hawker Audax/Nisr, Egypt	Armstrong Siddeley Panther VIA
Hawker Audax (Persia)	Bristol Pegasus IIM
Hawker Hardy GP	Rolls-Royce Kestrel IB
Hawker Hardy	Rolls-Royce Kestrel X
Hawker Hardy	Rolls-Royce Kestrel XDR
Hawker 'High Speed' Fury	Rolls-Royce Goshawk III
Hawker P.V.3	Rolls-Royce Goshawk III
Hawker P.V.4 G.4/31	Bristol Pegasus IIIM.3
Hawker P.V.4	Bristol Pegasus IV
Hawker P.V.4 G.4/31	Bristol Pegasus X
Hawker Hartbees	Rolls-Royce Kestrel V
Hawker Hind I, Hind (T)	Rolls-Royce Kestrel V
Hawker Hind I	Rolls-Royce Kestrel VDR
Hawker Hind (Jugoslav)	Rolls-Royce Kestrel XVI
Hawker Hind (Latvia)	Bristol Mercury IX
Hawker Hind (Persia)	Bristol Mercury VIII
Hawker Hector	Napier-Halford Dagger IIIM
Hawker Hurricane prot	Rolls-Royce Merlin C
Hawker Hurricane prot	Rolls-Royce Merlin F
Hawker Hurricane I	Rolls-Royce Merlin II
Hawker Hurricane I	Rolls-Royce Merlin III
Hawker Hurricane I	Rolls-Royce Merlin 45
Hawker Hurricane II, IV	Rolls-Royce Merlin XX
Hawker Hurricane II, V	Rolls-Royce Merlin 27
Hawker Hurricane X (Canada)	Rolls-Royce Merlin 28 (V-1650-1)
Hawker Hurricane XI, XII (Canada)	Rolls-Royce Merlin 29
Hawker Hurricane XII (Canada)	Rolls-Royce Merlin 25
Hawker Sea Hurricane I	Rolls-Royce Merlin II
Hawker Sea Hurricane I	Rolls-Royce Merlin III
Hawker Sea Hurricane II	Rolls-Royce Merlin XX
Hawker Henley	Rolls-Royce Griffon IIB
Hawker Henley	Rolls-Royce Merlin F
Hawker Henley	Rolls-Royce Merlin I
Hawker Henley	Rolls-Royce Merlin II
Hawker Henley	Rolls-Royce Merlin III
Hawker Henley	Rolls-Royce Merlin V
Hawker Henley	Rolls-Royce Vulture I
Hawker Henley	Rolls-Royce Vulture II
Hawker Hotspur	Rolls-Royce Merlin II
Hawker F.18/37 Tornado	Rolls-Royce Vulture II
Hawker Tornado I	Rolls-Royce Vulture II
Hawker Tornado I	Rolls-Royce Vulture V
Hawker Tornado I	Bristol Centaurus IV
Hawker F.18/37 Typhoon	Napier-Halford Sabre I
Hawker Typhoon prot, I, IA, IB	Napier-Halford Sabre II
Hawker Typhoon I	Napier-Halford Sabre IIA
Hawker Typhoon I, IB	Napier-Halford Sabre IIB
Hawker Typhoon I	Napier-Halford Sabre IIC
Hawker Typhoon I, II (Tempest I)	Napier-Halford Sabre IV
Hawker Tempest I	Napier-Halford Sabre II
Hawker Tempest V	Napier-Halford Sabre IIA
Hawker Tempest V	Napier-Halford Sabre IIB
Hawker Tempest V	Napier-Halford Sabre IIC
Hawker Typhoon II	Napier-Halford Sabre II
Hawker Tempest II	Bristol Centaurus IV

Hawker Tempest II	Bristol Centaurus V
Hawker Tempest II	Bristol Centaurus VI
Hawker Tempest II	Bristol Centaurus VII
Hawker Tempest II	Bristol Centaurus VIII
Hawker Tempest II	Bristol Centaurus XII
Hawker Tempest II	Bristol Centaurus 15
Hawker Tempest II	Bristol Centaurus 18
Hawker Tempest III	Rolls-Royce Griffon IIB
Hawker Tempest IV	Rolls-Royce Griffon 61
Hawker Tempest I	Napier-Halford Sabre V
Hawker Tempest V	Napier-Halford Sabre IV
Hawker Tempest V	Napier-Halford Sabre V
Hawker Tempest VI	Napier-Halford Sabre V
Hawker Tempest VI	Napier-Halford Sabre VA
Hawker F.2/43 Fury I	Rolls-Royce Griffon 85
Hawker F.2/43 Fury prot, I	Bristol Centaurus XII
Hawker Fury F.1	Napier-Halford Sabre VII
Hawker Fury F.1	Bristol Centaurus 18
Hawker Sea Fury X prot	Bristol Centaurus XII
Hawker Sea Fury X	Bristol Centaurus 15
Hawker Sea Fury X	Bristol Centaurus 18
Heath Parasol	A.B.C. Scorpion II
Heath Parasol	Blackburne Tomtit 690 c.c. (inverted)
Heath Parasol	Bristol Cherub III
Heath Parasol	J.A.P. J-99 (Aeronca E-113-C)
Heinkel He 46	Armstrong Siddeley Panther IIA (GF)
Heinkel He 64C	de Havilland Gipsy III
Heinkel He 70G	Rolls-Royce Kestrel V
Heinkel He 70G	Rolls-Royce Kestrel XVI
Heinkel He 70G	Rolls-Royce Peregrine I
Helmy Aerogypt I, II, III	Aero Engines Sprite I
Henderson H.S.F.1	Siddeley-Deasy Puma 236 hp
Henderson-Glenny HSF II Gadfly I & II	A.B.C. Scorpion II
Henderson-Glenny HSF II Gadfly III	British Salmson A.C.9
Hendy 281 Hobo	A.B.C. Scorpion II
Hendy 281 Hobo	Pobjoy Cataract I
Hendy 281 Hobo	Pobjoy Cataract III
Hendy 302	Cirrus Hermes I
Hendy 302A	Blackburn Cirrus Major II
Hendy 302A	Cirrus Hermes IV
Hendy 3308 Heck - see also Parnall	de Havilland Gipsy Six srs I
Heston A.2/45	de Havilland Gipsy Queen 33
Heston Phoenix I	de Havilland Gipsy Six srs I
Heston Phoenix II	de Havilland Gipsy Six srs II
Heston Type 5 Racer (derated engine)	Napier-Halford Sabre I
Heston T.1/37	de Havilland Gipsy Six srs II
Hillson Helvellyn	Blackburn Cirrus Minor I
Hillson Praga	J.A.P. J-99 (Aeronca E-113-C)
Hinkler Ibis	British Salmson A.D.9
Hirtenberg H.S.9A	de Havilland Gipsy Major I srs I
Hispano Aviacion HA-1109-M1L, -M2L	Rolls-Royce Merlin 500/45
Hispano Aviacion HA-1112-M1L Buchon	Rolls-Royce Merlin 500/45
Howitt Monoplane	Scott Flying Squirrel
Humphreys Nos 1, 2 Tractor Monoplanes	Green D4 50-60 hp
H.M. Airship, No 1 'Mayfly'	Wolseley 160 hp
H.M. Airship 'Gamma'	de Havilland 'Iris' 40 hp
H.M. Airship C class (Coastal)	Sunbeam Amazon 170 hp
H.M. Airship NS class (North Sea)	Rolls-Royce Eagle I 250 hp
H.M. Airship R23, R26	Rolls-Royce Eagle I 250 hp
H.M. Airship R24	Rolls-Royce Eagle I 250 hp
H.M. Airship R27, R29	Rolls-Royce Eagle IV 284 hp
H.M. Airship R31, R32	Rolls-Royce Eagle III 284 hp
H.M. Airship R31, R32	Rolls-Royce Eagle IV 284 hp
H.M. Airship R33, R34	Sunbeam Maori IV 275 hp
H.M. Airship R36, R38	Sunbeam Cossack 310/320 hp
H.M. Airship R100	Rolls-Royce Condor IIIB
H.M. Airship R101	Beardmore Tordado III
H.M. Airship SS class (Submarine)	Rolls-Royce Hawk I 85 hp
I Ae D1 22C (Argentine)	Armstrong Siddeley Cheetah 25
Junkers A.50 Junior	Armstrong Siddeley Genet I
Junkers A.50 Junior	Armstrong Siddeley Genet II
Junkers F.13	Bristol Jupiter VI
Junkers Ju 52/3m	Bristol Jupiter VI
Junkers Ju 86	Bristol Pegasus VI
Junkers Ju 86	Rolls-Royce Kestrel XVI
Junkers Ju 87 prot	Rolls-Royce Kestrel V
Junkers W.34	Bristol Jupiter VII
Kay 32/1 Gyroplane	A.B.C. Scorpion I
Kay 33/1 Gyroplane	Pobjoy R
Kennedy Giant	Salmson (Canton-Unne) 200 hp
Klemm L.25	Armstrong Siddeley Genet II

Klemm L.25	British Salmson A.D.9
Klemm L.26a-III	Cirrus III
Klemm L.26a-X	de Havilland Gipsy III
Klemm L.27a-VIII	Cirrus Hermes IIB
Klemm L.27aIII	Cirrus III
Klemm L.27a-IX	de Havilland Gipsy III
Klemm L.32-X	de Havilland Gipsy III
Koolhoven F.K.52	Bristol Pegasus IV
Kronfeld Monoplane	Carden-Ford 31 hp
L & P 4	Anzani (British) 100 hp
L & P 4	Gnome 7 Lambda 80 hp
Lane Tractor Monoplane	E.N.V. Type D 35-40 hp
Larkin (L.A.S. Co) Lascoter	Siddeley-Deasy Puma 236 hp
Larkin (Lasco) Lascowl (ANEC III)	Armstrong Siddeley Jaguar IV
Leopoldoff L.7 Colibri	Anzani (British) 45 hp
Lowe H.L.(M).9 Marlburian	Gnome 7 Lambda 80 hp
Luton Buzzard I, II	Anzani (Brit. Luton) 35 hp
Luton L.A.4A Minor	Anzani (Brit. Luton) 35 hp
Luton L.A.4A Minor	J.A.P. J-99 (Aeronca E-113-C)
Luton L.A.4A Minor	Rollason Ardem 4CO2-1
Luton L.A.4A Minor	Scott Flying Squirrel
Macfie Biplane	Fletcher Empress
Mann Egerton B	Sunbeam Arab I 200 hp
Mann & Grimmer M.1	Anzani (British) 100 hp
Marendaz III	de Havilland Gipsy Six srs II
Marendaz Trainer	Blackburn Cirrus Minor I
Martin Monoplane	Bristol Cherub III
Martin-Baker M.B.1	Napier-Halford Javelin IIIA
Martin-Baker M.B.2	Napier-Halford Dagger IIIM
Martin-Baker M.B.5	Rolls-Royce Griffon 83
Martin-Handasyde No 3	Green C4 30-35 hp
Martinsyde A.D.C.1	Armstrong Siddeley Jaguar III
Martinsyde A.V.1	Hispano-Suiza 8Fb 300 hp
Martinsyde F.2	Hispano-Suiza 8Ba 200 hp
Martinsyde F.3	Rolls-Royce Falcon I 190 hp
Martinsyde F.3	Rolls-Royce Falcon III 275 hp
Martinsyde F.3	Hispano-Suiza 8Fb 300 hp
Martinsyde F.4 Buzzard	Rolls-Royce Falcon III 275 hp
Martinsyde F.4 Buzzard, 4A	Hispano-Suiza 8Fb 300 hp
Martinsyde F.6	Hispano-Suiza 8Fb 300 hp
Martinsyde F.6	Wolseley W.4A* Viper 200 hp
Martinsyde G.100 Elephant	Beardmore 120 hp
Martinsyde G.102	Beardmore 160 hp
Martinsyde No 3 Monoplane	J.A.P. 40 hp
Martinsyde R.G.	Rolls-Royce Falcon I 190 hp
Martinsyde R.G.	Rolls-Royce Falcon III 275 hp
Martinsyde S.1	Hispano-Suiza 8Ba 200 hp
Martinsyde Type A Mk I	Rolls-Royce Falcon III 275 hp
Martinsyde Type A Mk II	Hispano-Suiza 8Fb 300 hp
Martinsyde (Nimbus)	A.D.C. Nimbus 300 hp
Maurice Farman Serie VII Longhorn	Rolls-Royce Hawk I 85 hp
Mersey Monoplane	Isaacson 40-50 hp
Messerschmitt Bf 109a (V1) prot	Rolls-Royce Kestrel V
Messerschmitt M.17	Bristol Cherub I
Mignet HM 14 Pou du Ciel	Anzani (Brit. Luton) 35 hp
Mignet HM 14 Pou du Ciel	Bristol Cherub III
Mignet HM 14 Pou du Ciel	Carden-Ford 31 hp
Mignet HM 14 Pou du Ciel	Scott Flying Squirrel
Mignet HM 14N Pou du Ciel	A.B.C. Scorpion II
Mignet HM 14N Pou du Ciel	Aero Engines Sprite I
Miles M.1 Satyr	Pobjoy R
Miles M.14, M.14A Magister Hawk Tr III	de Havilland Gipsy Major IF
Miles M.2 Hawk	Cirrus IIIA
Miles M.2A, M.2C Hawk	de Havilland Gipsy III
Miles M.2B Hawk	Cirrus Hermes IV
Miles M.2D Hawk	Cirrus IIIA
Miles M.2E, 2L Speed Six	de Havilland Gipsy Six srs II
Miles M.2F Hawk Major	de Havilland Gipsy III
Miles M.2F, H, M, P, R Hawk Major	de Havilland Gipsy Major I srs I
Miles M.2S Hawk Major	Blackburn Cirrus Major II
Miles M.2S Hawk Major	Blackburn Cirrus Major III
Miles M.2U Hawk Speed Six	de Havilland Gipsy Six 'R'
Miles M.2W, X, Y Hawk Trainer	de Havilland Gipsy Major I srs I
Miles M.3B, C, D, E, F Falcon Six	de Havilland Gipsy Six srs I
Miles M.3, 3A Falcon Major	de Havilland Gipsy Major I srs I
Miles M.4, 4A Merlin	de Havilland Gipsy Six srs I
Miles M.5 Sparrowhawk	de Havilland Gipsy Major I srs I
Miles M.5 Sparrowhawk	de Havilland Gipsy Major I srs II
Miles M.6 Hawcon	de Havilland Gipsy Six srs I
Miles M.7 Nighthawk	de Havilland Gipsy Six srs I
Miles M.7A Nighthawk	de Havilland Gipsy Six srs II

Miles M.7A Nighthawk	de Havilland Gipsy Six srs II V.P.
Miles M.8 Peregrine	de Havilland Gipsy Six srs II
Miles M.9 'Kestrel'	Rolls-Royce Kestrel XVI(VP)
Miles M.9A Master I	Rolls-Royce Kestrel XXX
Miles M.11B Whitney Straight	Villiers Maya I
Miles M.11, 11A Whitney Straight	de Havilland Gipsy Major I srs I
Miles M.11, 11A, 11C Whitney Straight	de Havilland Gipsy Major I srs II
Miles M.13 Hobby	de Havilland Gipsy Major I srs II
Miles M.14A Hawk Trainer	Blackburn Cirrus Major III
Miles M.14A, B, Hawk Trainer	Blackburn Cirrus Major II
Miles M.14, 14A Hawk Trainer III	de Havilland Gipsy Major I srs I
Miles M.14, 14A Magister I	de Havilland Gipsy Major I srs I
Miles M.15 Trainer	de Havilland Gipsy Six srs I
Miles M.16 Mentor	de Havilland Gipsy Queen I
Miles M.16 Mentor	de Havilland Gipsy Six srs I
Miles M.17 Monarch	de Havilland Gipsy Major I srs I
Miles M.18 Mk I	de Havilland Gipsy Major I srs I
Miles M.18 Mk I	Jameson FF-1 110 hp
Miles M.18 Mk II, III	Blackburn Cirrus Major III
Miles M.19 Master II	Bristol Mercury XV
Miles M.19 Master II	Bristol Mercury XX
Miles M.20	Rolls-Royce Merlin XX
Miles M.24 Master Fighter	Rolls-Royce Kestrel XXX
Miles M.25 Martinet I	Bristol Mercury XX
Miles M.25 Martinet I 12/41	Bristol Mercury 30
Miles M.28 Mercury	de Havilland Gipsy Major I srs I
Miles M.28 Mercury II	Blackburn Cirrus Major II
Miles M.28 Mercury II, III, V, VI	Blackburn Cirrus Major III
Miles M.28 Mercury II, 4	de Havilland Gipsy Major I srs II
Miles M.30X Minor	de Havilland Gipsy Major I srs I
Miles M.35 Libellula	de Havilland Gipsy Major I srs I
Miles M.37 Martinet Trainer	Bristol Mercury XX
Miles M.38 Messenger I	de Havilland Gipsy Major I srs II
Miles M.38 Messenger IIA, IIB, III	Blackburn Cirrus Major III
Miles M.38 Messenger IIC, IVA	de Havilland Gipsy Major I srs I
Miles M.38 Messenger 4, 4B	de Havilland Gipsy Major 10/1
Miles M.38 Messenger 5	Blackburn Cirrus Bombardier 702
Miles M.39B Libellula	de Havilland Gipsy Major IC
Miles M.39B Libellula	de Havilland Gipsy Major ID
Miles M.48 Messenger	Blackburn Cirrus Major III
Miles M.50 Queen Martinet	Bristol Mercury XX
Miles M.50 Queen Martinet	Bristol Mercury 30
Miles M.57 Aerovan 1, 2, 3, 4	Blackburn Cirrus Major III
Miles M.57 Aerovan 5	de Havilland Gipsy Major 10/1
Miles M.60 Marathon	de Havilland Gipsy Queen 71
Miles M.65 Gemini 7	de Havilland Gipsy Major I srs II
Miles M.65 Gemini 8	Blackburn Cirrus Major III
Miles M.65 Gemini 1, 1A, 1B, 4	Blackburn Cirrus Minor II
Miles M.65 Gemini 3	de Havilland Gipsy Major IC
Miles M.65 Gemini 3	de Havilland Gipsy Major ID
Miles M.65 Gemini 3A, B, C, 7	de Havilland Gipsy Major 10/1
Miles M.65 Gemini 3C	de Havilland Gipsy Major 10/2
Miles M.68 'Boxcar'	Blackburn Cirrus Minor II
Miles M.71 Merchantman	de Havilland Gipsy Queen 30
Miles M.75 Aries	Blackburn Cirrus Major III
Miles T.1/37	de Havilland Gipsy Six srs II
Miles (Hurel Dubois) H.D.M.105	Blackburn Cirrus Major III
Morane-Borel seaplane	Gnome 7 Gamma 70 hp
Morane-Saulnier AC	Le Rhone 9Ja 110 hp
Morane-Saulnier AC	Le Rhone 9Jb 120 hp
Morane-Saulnier BB	Le Rhone 9Ja 110 hp
Morane-Saulnier G, H	Le Rhone 9C 80 hp
Morane-Saulnier I, V	Le Rhone 9Ja 110 hp
Morane-Saulnier L	Le Rhone 9C 80 hp
Morane-Saulnier LA	Le Rhone 9C 80 hp
Morane-Saulnier N	Le Rhone 9C 80 hp
Morane-Saulnier P	Le Rhone 9C 80 hp
Morane-Saulnier P	Le Rhone 9Ja 110 hp
Moss M.A.1 Mosscraft	Pobjoy Niagara III
Moss M.A.2	Blackburn Cirrus Minor I
Newbury A.P.4 Eon	Blackburn Cirrus Minor II
Newbury A.P.4 Eon	de Havilland Gipsy Major 10/1
Nieuport IVG	Gnome 7 Lambda 80 hp
Nieuport 10	Gnome 7 Lambda 80 hp
Nieuport 10	Le Rhone 9C 80 hp
Nieuport 11	Le Rhone 9C 80 hp
Nieuport 12	Clerget 9Z 110 hp
Nieuport 12	Gnome Monosoupape 9B-2 100 hp
Nieuport 12 Fr	Clerget 9B 130 hp
Nieuport 16	Le Rhone 9Ja 110 hp
Nieuport 17	Clerget 9B 130 hp

Nieuport 17	Le Rhone 9Ja 110 hp
Nieuport 17bis	Clerget 9B 130 hp
Nieuport 17bis	Clerget 9Z 110 hp
Nieuport 17bis	Le Rhone 9Ja 110 hp
Nieuport 20	Le Rhone 9Ja 110 hp
Nieuport 21	Le Rhone 9C 80 hp
Nieuport 23	Le Rhone 9Jb 120 hp
Nieuport 24, 24bis	Le Rhone 9Jb 120 hp
Nieuport 24, 24bis	Le Rhone 9Jby 130 hp
Nieuport 27	Le Rhone 9Jby 130 hp
Nieuport 28	Gnome Monosoupape 9B-2 100 hp
Nieuport B.N.1	Bentley B.R.2 230 hp
Nieuport Goshawk	A.B.C. Dragonfly IA 330/360 hp
Nieuport Monoplane	Gnome 7 Gamma 70 hp
Nieuport Monoplane	Gnome 7 Omega 50 hp
Nieuport Monoplane	Gnome 14 Omega-Omega 100 hp
Nieuport Nieuhawk	A.B.C. Dragonfly IA 330/360 hp
Nieuport Nighthawk	A.B.C. Dragonfly IA 330/360 hp
Nieuport Nighthawk	Armstrong Siddeley Jaguar I
Nieuport Nighthawk	Armstrong Siddeley Jaguar II
Nieuport Nightjar	Bentley B.R.2 230 hp
Nieuport Triplane	Clerget 9B 130 hp
Nieuport Triplane	Le Rhone 9Ja 110 hp
Nord 1400	Bristol Hercules 100
Nord 1401	Bristol Hercules 739
Nord 2501	Bristol Hercules 758
Nord 2501 prot	Bristol Hercules 739
Nord Noratlas	Bristol Hercules 790
Norman Thompson N.T.2B	Beardmore 160 hp
Norman Thompson N.T.4	Hispano-Suiza 8Aa 150 hp
Norman Thompson N.T.4A	Hispano-Suiza 8Bb 200 hp
North American Mustang X	Rolls-Royce Merlin 65
North American P-51 Mustang X	Rolls-Royce 100 srs (No number)
North American P-51 Mustang X	Rolls-Royce Merlin 100 srs
North American P-51B, C Mustang III	Rolls-Royce/Packard V-1650-7 Merlin 266
North American P-51B/C Mustang III	Rolls-Royce/Packard V-1650-3 Merlin 61, 63
North American P-51C Mustang III	Rolls-Royce Merlin 69
North American P-51D, F, K Mustang IV	Rolls-Royce Merlin 69
North American P-51D, F, K Mustang IV	Rolls-Royce/Packard V-1650-7 Merlin 266
North American P-51D, G, H Mustang	Rolls-Royce/Packard V-1650-9 Merlin 100
North American P-51H, L Mustang	Rolls-Royce/Packard V-1650-11 Merlin
North American P-82B Twin Mustang	Rolls-Royce/Packard V-1650-9A Merlin 100
North American XP-78	Rolls-Royce/Packard V-1650-3 Merlin 61, 63
North American XP-82B Twin Mustang	Rolls-Royce/Packard V-1650-21 Merlin
North American XP-82B Twin Mustang	Rolls-Royce/Packard V-1650-23 Merlin
North American XP-82B Twin Mustang	Rolls-Royce/Packard V-1650-25 Merlin
Northern Aircraft Co P.B.1	Green D4 50-60 hp
Northrop 2-L Gamma (Commercial)	Bristol Hercules I
Parmentier Wee Mite	A.B.C. Scorpion I
Parmentier Wee Mite	A.B.C. Scorpion II
Parmentier Wee Mite	British Salmson A.D.9
Parnall 382 Heck III	de Havilland Gipsy Six srs I
Parnall Elf I	Cirrus Hermes I
Parnall Elf II	Cirrus Hermes II
Parnall G.4/31	Bristol Pegasus IIIM.3
Parnall Heck 2C (ex Hendy)	de Havilland Gipsy Six srs I
Parnall Imp	Armstrong Siddeley Genet II
Parnall Imp	Pobjoy P1
Parnall N.2A Panther	Bentley B.R.2 230 hp
Parnall Parasol	Armstrong Siddeley Lynx IV (S)
Parnall Perch	Rolls-Royce Falcon III 275 hp
Parnall Peto	Armstrong Siddeley Mongoose I
Parnall Peto	Armstrong Siddeley Mongoose II
Parnall Peto	Armstrong Siddeley Mongoose IIIC
Parnall Peto	Bristol Lucifer III
Parnall Peto	Bristol Lucifer IV
Parnall Pike	Napier Lion V
Parnall Pipit	Rolls-Royce Kestrel IA
Parnall Pixie I, II	Douglas 500 c.c., 3.5 hp
Parnall Pixie I, II	Douglas 736 c.c., 6 hp
Parnall Pixie II	Blackburne Tomtit 690 c.c. (inverted)
Parnall Pixie III	Blackburne Thrush 35 hp
Parnall Pixie III, IIIA	Bristol Cherub III
Parnall Plover	Armstrong Siddeley Jaguar I
Parnall Plover	Bristol Jupiter IV
Parnall Possum 11/20	Napier Lion II
Parnall Prawn	Ricardo-Burt S55/4 65 hp
Parnall Puffin	Napier Lion I
Parnall Puffin	Napier Lion II
Parnall Scout (Zepp-Chaser)	Sunbeam Maori II 260/275 hp
Parnall T.1/37	de Havilland Gipsy Six srs II

Parnall/Hendy Heck	de Havilland Gipsy Queen III
Paulhan Biplane	Gnome 7 Gamma 70 hp
Paulhan Biplane	Gnome 7 Omega 50 hp
Pemberton Billing P.B.9	Gnome 7 Omega 50 hp
Pemberton Billing P.B.23E Push-Proj	Le Rhone 9C 80 hp
Pemberton Billing P.B.25	Clerget 9Z 110 hp
Pemberton Billing P.B.25	Gnome 9 Delta 100 hp
Pemberton Billing P.B.29E Nighthawk	Austro-Daimler 90 hp
Pemberton Billing P.B.31E Nighthawk	Anzani (British) 100 hp
Percival D.1 Gull Four	Cirrus Hermes IV
Percival D.2 Gull Four	Napier-Halford Javelin III
Percival D.2 Gull Major	de Havilland Gipsy Major I srs I
Percival D.3 Gull	de Havilland Gipsy Six srs I
Percival E.2, E.3H Mew Gull	de Havilland Gipsy Six srs II
Percival E.1 Mew Gull	de Havilland Gipsy Six srs I
Percival E.1 Mew Gull	Napier-Halford Javelin I
Percival E.2 Mew Gull	de Havilland Gipsy Six 'R'
Percival E.2 Mew Gull	de Havilland Gipsy Six srs I
Percival E.2, E.3H Mew Gull	de Havilland Gipsy Six srs II V.P.
Percival Gull Six	de Havilland Gipsy Six srs II
Percival Gull Six	de Havilland Gipsy Six srs II V.P.
Percival Merganser	de Havilland Gipsy Queen 51
Percival P.66 Pembroke C.C.1	Alvis Leonides 503/7 Mk 130
Percival President 1	Alvis Leonides 503/5 Mk 125
Percival President 1	Alvis Leonides 503/7A Mk 127
Percival President 1	Alvis Leonides 504/5
Percival President 2	Alvis Leonides 514/5A
Percival Prince 1, 2	Alvis Leonides 501/3
Percival Prince 1, 2	Alvis Leonides 501/4
Percival Prince 3B, 3D	Alvis Leonides 502/5
Percival Prince 3, 3A, 3E	Alvis Leonides 502/4
Percival Prince 4, 4E	Alvis Leonides 503/4 Mk 24
Percival Prince 4. 4D	Alvis Leonides 503/5 Mk 125
Percival Prince 6B	Alvis Leonides 504/5
Percival Proctor	de Havilland Gipsy Queen 70-1
Percival Proctor I, II, III, IV, V	de Havilland Gipsy Queen II
Percival P.40 Prentice I	de Havilland Gipsy Queen 30-2
Percival P.40 Prentice I	de Havilland Gipsy Queen 32
Percival P.54	Alvis Leonides 501/3
Percival P.54	Alvis Leonides 501/4
Percival Provost prot	Armstrong Siddeley Cheetah XVII
Percival P.56 Provost T.1, T.51	Alvis Leonides 503/6A Mk 126
Percival P.66 Pembroke C.1, C(PR) Mk 1	Alvis Leonides 503/7A Mk 127
Percival P.66 Sea Prince T.1	Alvis Leonides 503/5 Mk 125
Percival Q.6 Petrel	de Havilland Gipsy Six srs I
Percival Q.6 Petrel	de Havilland Gipsy Six srs II
Percival Q.6 Petrel	de Havilland Gipsy Six srs II V.P.
Percival Vega Gull	de Havilland Gipsy Six srs I
Percival Vega Gull	de Havilland Gipsy Six srs II
Percival Vega Gull	de Havilland Gipsy Six srs II V.P.
Perman Parasol	Carden-Ford 31 hp
Peterborough Ely	J.A.P. J-99 (Aeronca E-113-C)
Pfalz D.III replica (upright engine)	de Havilland Gipsy Major 10/1
Phoenix P.5 Cork III	Napier Lion IIB
Piffard 1 & 2 Tractor Monoplanes	E.N.V. Type D 35-40 hp
Piffard 3 & 4 Hydro Biplanes	E.N.V. Type D 35-40 hp
Planet Satellite	de Havilland Gipsy Queen 32
Pobjoy Pirate	Pobjoy Niagara III
Porte Baby	Green 260 hp
Porte Baby	Rolls-Royce Eagle I 250 hp
Porte Baby	Rolls-Royce Eagle VII 322 hp
Porte Baby	Rolls-Royce Eagle VIII 375 hp
Porte (Felixstowe) Fury	Rolls-Royce Eagle VIII 375 hp
Portsmouth Aerocar Major	Blackburn Cirrus Major III
P.Z.L. P.37B Los B	Bristol Pegasus XX
Radley-England Waterplane	Gnome 7 Lambda 80 hp
Reid & Sigrist R.S.1 'Snargasher'	de Havilland Gipsy Six srs II
Reid & Sigrist R.S.3 Desford	de Havilland Gipsy Major I srs I
Reid & Sigrist R.S.3 Desford	de Havilland Gipsy Major 10/1
Renard R.38	Rolls-Royce Merlin III
Robinson Redwing I	A.B.C. Hornet
Robinson Redwing I	Armstrong Siddeley Genet II
Robinson Redwing II, III	Armstrong Siddeley Genet IIA
Roe I Triplane	J.A.P. 9 hp
Roe I Triplane	J.A.P. 20 hp
Rollason (Druine) Turbulent	Rollason Ardem 4CO2-1
Rumpler C.IV replica (upright engine)	de Havilland Gipsy Major I srs I
R.A.E. Aerial Target	Armstrong Siddeley Ounce 40 hp
R.A.E. Hurricane	Bristol Cherub III
R.A.E. Hurricane	Douglas 500 c.c., 3.5 hp
R.A.E. Zephyr	Douglas 500 c.c., 3.5 hp

R.A.E. (P.B.) Scarab	Bristol Cherub III
R.A.F. B.E.1	Renault 60 hp
R.A.F. B.E.1	Wolseley 60 hp
R.A.F. B.E.2	E.N.V. Type F 60-80 hp
R.A.F. B.E.2c replica (upright engine)	de Havilland Gipsy Major I srs I
R.A.F. B.E.2c, d, e	R.A.F.1a 90 hp
R.A.F. B.E.2e	Hispano-Suiza 8Aa 150 hp
R.A.F. B.E.2e	Rolls-Royce Hawk I 85 hp
R.A.F. B.E.2e	R.A.F.1b 105 hp
R.A.F. B.E.2, 2a, b, c, d, e, f, g	Renault WB, WC 70 hp
R.A.F. B.E.2, 2a, 2b	Renault 60 hp
R.A.F. B.E.3	Gnome 7 Gamma 70 hp
R.A.F. B.E.3	Gnome 7 Lambda 80 hp
R.A.F. B.E.3	Gnome 7 Omega 50 hp
R.A.F. B.E.4	Gnome 7 Gamma 70 hp
R.A.F. B.E.4	Gnome 7 Lambda 80 hp
R.A.F. B.E.4	Gnome 7 Omega 50 hp
R.A.F. B.E.7	Gnome 14 Gamma-Gamma 140 hp
R.A.F. B.E.8a 'Bloater'	Clerget 7Z 80 hp
R.A.F. B.E.8a 'Bloater'	R.A.F.2 120 hp
R.A.F. B.E.8, B.E.8a 'Bloater'	Gnome Monosoupape 9B-2 100 hp
R.A.F. B.E.8, B.E.8a 'Bloater'	Gnome 7 Lambda 80 hp
R.A.F. B.E.9	R.A.F.1a 90 hp
R.A.F. B.E.12b	Hispano-Suiza 8Ba 200 hp
R.A.F. B.E.12, B.E.12a	R.A.F.4a 140 hp
R.A.F. B.S.1	Gnome 7 Lambda 80 hp
R.A.F. F.E.2	Gnome 7 Omega 50 hp
R.A.F. F.E.2	Renault WB, WC 70 hp
R.A.F. F.E.2a	Green D4 50-60 hp
R.A.F. F.E.2a	Green E6 100-120 hp
R.A.F. F.E.2a, b, c	Beardmore 120 hp
R.A.F. F.E.2b, c	Beardmore 160 hp
R.A.F. F.E.2b, F.E.2c	R.A.F.5 150 hp
R.A.F. F.E.2d	Rolls-Royce Eagle I 250 hp
R.A.F. F.E.2d	Rolls-Royce Eagle VIII 375 hp
R.A.F. F.E.2d	Rolls-Royce Falcon II 220 hp
R.A.F. F.E.2h	Siddeley-Deasy Puma 236 hp
R.A.F. F.E.4	Rolls-Royce Eagle I 250 hp
R.A.F. F.E.4	R.A.F.5 150 hp
R.A.F. F.E.8	Clerget 9Z 110 hp
R.A.F. F.E.8	Gnome Monosoupape 9B-2 100 hp
R.A.F. F.E.8	Le Rhone 9Ja 110 hp
R.A.F. F.E.9	Hispano-Suiza 8Ba 200 hp
R.A.F. N.E.1	Hispano-Suiza 8Ba 200 hp
R.A.F. R.E.7	Austro-Daimler 120 hp
R.A.F. R.E.1	Renault WB, WC 70 hp
R.A.F. R.E.5	Beardmore 120 hp
R.A.F. R.E.7	Beardmore 120 hp
R.A.F. R.E.7	Beardmore 160 hp
R.A.F. R.E.7	Renault 12Fe 220 hp
R.A.F. R.E.7	Rolls-Royce Eagle III 284 hp
R.A.F. R.E.7	Rolls-Royce Falcon I 190 hp
R.A.F. R.E.7	R.A.F.3a 200 hp
R.A.F. R.E.7	R.A.F.4a 140 hp
R.A.F. R.E.7	Sunbeam Mohawk 225 hp
R.A.F. R.E.8	R.A.F.1d (Supercharged)
R.A.F. R.E.8	R.A.F.4a 140 hp
R.A.F. R.E.08	R.A.F.4d 200 hp
R.A.F. S.E.2	Gnome 9 Delta 100 hp
R.A.F. S.E.1 Pusher Biplane	E.N.V. Type F 60-80 hp
R.A.F. S.E.2	Clerget 7Z 80 hp
R.A.F. S.E.2	Clerget 9Z 110 hp
R.A.F. S.E.2	Gnome 7 Lambda 80 hp
R.A.F. S.E.4	Gnome 14 Lambda-Lambda 160 hp
R.A.F. S.E.4a	Clerget 7Z 80 hp
R.A.F. S.E.4a	Gnome 7 Lambda 80 hp
R.A.F. S.E.4a	Le Rhone 9C 80 hp
R.A.F. S.E.5	R.A.F.1a 90 hp
R.A.F. S.E.5a	A.D.C. Airdisco
R.A.F. S.E.5a	Hispano-Suiza 8Ba 200 hp
R.A.F. S.E.5a	Hispano-Suiza 8Fb 300 hp
R.A.F. S.E.5a	Renault WS 80 hp
R.A.F. S.E.5, S.E.5a	Wolseley W.4B Adder I 200 hp
R.A.F. S.E.5, S.E.5a	Wolseley W.4B* Adder II 200 hp
R.A.F. S.E.5, S.E.5a	Wolseley W.4B* Adder III 200 hp
R.A.F. S.E.5, S.E.5a	Hispano-Suiza 8Aa 150 hp
R.A.F. S.E.5, S.E.5a	Hispano-Suiza 8Ab 180 hp
R.A.F. S.E.5, S.E.5a	Hispano-Suiza 8Bc 220 hp
R.A.F. S.E.5, S.E.5a	Hispano-Suiza 8Be 220 hp
R.A.F. S.E.5, S.E.5a	Sunbeam Arab I 200 hp
R.A.F. S.E.5, S.E.5a	Sunbeam Arab II 200 hp

R.A.F. S.E.5, S.E.5a	Wolseley W.4A Python I 150 hp
R.A.F. S.E.5, S.E.5a	Wolseley W.4A Python II 180 hp
R.A.F. S.E.5, S.E.5a	Wolseley W.4A* Viper 200 hp
SAAB 91 Safir	de Havilland Gipsy Major 10/2
Sage III	Rolls-Royce Hawk I 85 hp
Sanders II Pusher Biplane	E.N.V. Type F 60-80 hp
Saro A.7 Severn	Bristol Jupiter XIF.P.
Saro A.17 Cutty Sark	Armstrong Siddeley Genet Ma I
Saro A.17 Cutty Sark	Armstrong Siddeley Lynx IVC
Saro A.17 Cutty Sark	Cirrus Hermes I
Saro A.17 Cutty Sark	de Havilland Gipsy II
Saro A.17 Cutty Sark	de Havilland Gipsy III
Saro A.19 Cloud	Armstrong Siddeley Lynx IVC
Saro A.19 Cloud	Armstrong Siddeley Serval I
Saro A.19 Cloud	Armstrong Siddeley Serval III
Saro A.19 Cloud	Napier-Halford Rapier IV
Saro A.21 Windhover	de Havilland Gipsy II
Saro/Segrave A.22 Meteor see Blackburn	de Havilland Gipsy III
Saro-Percival A.24 Mailplane - see Spartan	de Havilland Gipsy III
Saro A.27 London I	Bristol Pegasus IIIM.3
Saro A.27 London II	Bristol Pegasus X
Saro A.33	Bristol Perseus XII
Saro A.37 Shrimp	Pobjoy Niagara III
Saro A.36 Lerwick I	Bristol Hercules II
Saro A.36 Lerwick I	Bristol Hercules IV
Saunders A.3 Valkyrie	Rolls-Royce Condor IIIA
Saunders A.3 Valkyrie	Rolls-Royce Condor IV
Saunders A.4 Medina	Bristol Jupiter VI
Saro A.10	Rolls-Royce Kestrel IS
Saunders A.14 (Metal Hull)	Napier Lion VA
Saunders Kittiwake	A.B.C. Wasp II
Saunders T.1	Sunbeam Nubian 150 hp
Saunders-Roe - see also Saro	
Saunders-Roe Skeeter - see Cierva	
Saunders/Saro - see also Saro	de Havilland Gipsy Major I srs I
Scottish Aviation Pioneer I	
Scottish Aviation Pioneer I	Alvis Leonides 501/3
Scottish Aviation Pioneer I	Alvis Leonides 501/4
Scottish Aviation Pioneer I	de Havilland Gipsy Queen 32
Scottish Aviation Pioneer C.C.1	de Havilland Gipsy Queen 34
Scottish Aviation Pioneer C.C.1	Alvis Leonides 502/4
Scottish Aviation Pioneer C.C.1	Alvis Leonides 502/7
Scottish Aviation Pioneer C.C.1	Alvis Leonides 503/7A Mk 127
Scottish Aviation Pioneer C.C.1	Alvis Leonides 514
Scottish Aviation Pioneer C.C.1	Alvis Leonides 514/8
Scottish Aviation Twin Pioneer prot	Alvis Leonides 514/8A
Scottish Aviation Twin Pioneer C.C.1, 2	Alvis Leonides 503/8
Scottish Aviation Twin Pioneer C.C.2, 3	Alvis Leonides 504/8B Mk 128
Shapley Kittiwake	Alvis Leonides 531/8B Mk 138
Shapley Kittiwake II	Pobjoy Niagara III
Short-Wright Biplane	Pobjoy Niagara I
Short S.26 Pusher Biplane	N.E.C. 50 hp
Short S.27 Pusher Biplane	Green C4 30-35 hp
Short S.28 Pusher Biplane	Green C4 30-35 hp
Short S.26 Pusher Biplane	Green C4 30-35 hp
Short S.27 type Pusher Biplane	Gnome 7 Omega 50 hp
Short School Biplane	E.N.V. Type F 60-80 hp
Short S.26 Pusher Biplane	Gnome 7 Gamma 70 hp
Short S.28 Pusher Biplane	Green D4 50-60 hp
Short SD.27 Tandem Twin	Green D4 50-60 hp
Short S.29 Pusher Biplane	Gnome 7 Omega 50 hp
Short S.33 Pusher Biplane	E.N.V. Type F 60-80 hp
Short S.32 Pusher Biplane	Gnome 7 Omega 50 hp
Short S.34 'Long-Range' Biplane	Gnome 7 Gamma 70 hp
Short S.35 Pusher Biplane	Gnome 7 Omega 50 hp
Short S.36 Tractor Biplane	Gnome 7 Omega 50 hp
Short S.37 Tractor Biplane	Gnome 7 Gamma 70 hp
Short S.37 Tractor Monoplane	Gnome 7 Lambda 80 hp
Short S.38 'Long-Range' Biplane	Gnome 7 Omega 50 hp
Short S.38 'Long-Range' Biplane	Gnome 7 Gamma 70 hp
Short S.38 'Long-Range' Biplane	Gnome 7 Lambda 80 hp
Short S.39 Triple Twin	Gnome 7 Omega 50 hp
Short S.41 Tractor Biplane	Gnome 7 Omega 50 hp
Short S.41 Tractor Biplane	Gnome 14 Gamma-Gamma 140 hp
Short S.41 Tractor Seaplane	Gnome 14 Omega-Omega 100 hp
Short S.43 Biplane	Gnome 7 Lambda 80 hp
Short S.44 Biplane	Gnome 7 Omega 50 hp
Short S.45 Tractor Biplane	Gnome 7 Omega 50 hp
Short S.47 Triple Tractor	Gnome 7 Gamma 70 hp
Short S.57 Seaplane	Gnome 7 Omega 50 hp
Short S.60 Seaplane	Gnome 14 Omega-Omega 100 hp
	Gnome 7 Lambda 80 hp

Short S.62	Gnome 7 Omega 50 hp
Short S.68 Seaplane	Green E6 100-120 hp
Short S.63 Folder Seaplane	Gnome 14 Lambda-Lambda 160 hp
Short S.64 Folder Seaplane	Gnome 14 Lambda-Lambda 160 hp
Short S.64 Folder Seaplane	Gnome 14 Omega-Omega 100 hp
Short S.70	Gnome Monosoupape 9B-2 100 hp
Short S.70 Seaplane	Gnome 14 Lambda-Lambda 160 hp
Short S.70 Type	Gnome 7 Lambda 80 hp
Short S.80	Gnome Monosoupape 9B-2 100 hp
Short S.80 'Nile Seaplane'	Gnome 14 Lambda-Lambda 160 hp
Short S.74 Admiralty Seaplane	Gnome 14 Lambda-Lambda 160 hp
Short S.74 Admiralty Seaplane	Gnome 14 Omega-Omega 100 hp
Short S.81 'Gun-bus' Seaplane	Gnome 14 Lambda-Lambda 160 hp
Short S.82-85 Folder Seaplanes	Gnome 14 Lambda-Lambda 160 hp
Short S.87 Admiralty Type 135 Seaplane	Salmson (Canton-Unne) B.9 140 hp
Short Type A S.90 Admiralty Type 166	Salmson (Canton-Unne) 200 hp
Short Type C (Improved S.74)	Gnome Monosoupape 9B-2 100 hp
Short Type C (Improved S.74)	Salmson (Canton-Unne) B.9 140 hp
Short Type C (Admiralty Type) 827	Sunbeam Nubian 150 hp
Short 830 (Admiralty Type 830)	Salmson (Canton-Unne) B.9 140 hp
Short (Admiralty Type) 184	Renault 12Fe 220 hp
Short (Admiralty Type) 184	Sunbeam Maori I 260/275 hp
Short (Admiralty Type) 184	Sunbeam Maori III 260/275 hp
Short (Admiralty Type) 184	Sunbeam Mohawk 225 hp
Short (Admiralty Type) 184D	Rolls-Royce Eagle IV 284 hp
Short 310-A4	Sunbeam Cossack 310/320 hp
Short 310-B North Sea Scout	Sunbeam Cossack 310/320 hp
Short Bomber	Rolls-Royce Eagle II 266 hp
Short Bomber	Sunbeam Mohawk 225 hp
Short N.2A	Sunbeam Afridi 200 hp
Short N.2B	Rolls-Royce Eagle VIII 375 hp
Short N.2B	Sunbeam Maori I 260/275 hp
Short N.1B Shirl	Rolls-Royce Eagle VIII 375 hp
Short N.3 Cromarty	Rolls-Royce Condor I
Short 'Shrimp' Sporting Seaplane	Beardmore 160 hp
Short 'Shrimp' Sporting Seaplane	Hispano-Suiza 8F 300 hp
Short 'Shrimp' Sporting Seaplane	Siddeley-Deasy Puma 236 hp
Short Silver Streak	Siddeley-Deasy Puma 236 hp
Short 827	Sunbeam Crusader 150 hp
Short L.17 Scylla	Bristol Perseus II-L
Short S.1 Cockle	Bristol Cherub II
Short S.1 Cockle (Stellite)	Blackburne Tomtit 690 c.c. (upright)
Short S.3 Springbok I, II	Bristol Jupiter IV
Short S.3b Chamois	Bristol Jupiter IV
Short S.4 Satellite	A.B.C. Scorpion II
Short S.4 Satellite	Bristol Cherub I
Short S.4 Satellite	Bristol Cherub II
Short S.5 Singapore I	Rolls-Royce Buzzard IMS
Short S.5 Singapore I	Rolls-Royce Condor III
Short S.5 Singapore I	Rolls-Royce Condor IIIA
Short S.6 Sturgeon I	Bristol Jupiter VI
Short S.7 Mussel I	Cirrus I
Short S.7 Mussel I	Cirrus II
Short S.7 Mussel II	Cirrus III
Short S.7 Mussel II	de Havilland Gipsy II
Short S.8 Calcutta	Armstrong Siddeley Tiger VI
Short S.8 Calcutta	Bristol Jupiter IXF
Short S.8 Calcutta	Bristol Jupiter XFBM
Short S.8 Calcutta	Bristol Jupiter XIF
Short S.8/8 Rangoon	Bristol Jupiter IXF
Short S.8/8 Rangoon	Bristol Jupiter XIF
Short S.10 Gurnard I	Bristol Jupiter X
Short S.10 Gurnard II	Rolls-Royce Kestrel IIMS
Short S.11 Valetta	Bristol Jupiter XIF
Short S.11 Valetta	Bristol Jupiter XIF P
Short S.12 Singapore II (Tractor)	Rolls-Royce Kestrel IIIMS
Short S.12 Singapore II (Pusher)	Rolls-Royce Kestrel IIMS
Short S.12 Singapore III (Tractor)	Rolls-Royce Kestrel IIMS
Short S.12 Singapore III (Pusher)	Rolls-Royce Kestrel IIIMS
Short S.14 Sarafand R.6/28	Rolls-Royce Buzzard IIIMS
Short S.16 Scion	Pobjoy R
Short S.16 Scion I	Pobjoy Niagara I
Short S.16 Scion I	Pobjoy Niagara II
Short S.16 Scion II	de Havilland Gipsy Minor
Short S.16 Scion II	Pobjoy Niagara III
Short S.17 Kent	Bristol Jupiter XFBM
Short L.17 Scylla	Bristol Jupiter XFBM
Short L.17 Syrinx	Bristol Pegasus XC
Short S.18 'Knuckleduster' R.24/31	Rolls-Royce Goshawk VIII
Short S.19 Singapore III Pusher	Rolls-Royce Kestrel VIII
Short S.19 Singapore III Tractor	Rolls-Royce Kestrel IX

Short S.22 Scion Senior	Pobjoy Niagara III
Short S.23 Empire	Bristol Pegasus XC
Short S.23 Empire	Bristol Pegasus 22
Short S.25 Sandringham I	Bristol Pegasus 38
Short S.25 Sandringham I	Bristol Pegasus 48
Short S.25 Sunderland I, III	Bristol Pegasus 22
Short S.25 Sunderland II, III	Bristol Pegasus XVIII
Short S.25 Sunderland III	Bristol Pegasus 38
Short S.25 Sunderland III	Bristol Pegasus 48
Short S.26 'G' class boat	Bristol Hercules IV
Short S.26 'G' class boat	Bristol Hercules IVHY
Short S.26 'G' class boat	Bristol Hercules XIV
Short S.29 Stirling I	Bristol Hercules X
Short S.29 Stirling I srs I	Bristol Hercules II
Short S.29 Stirling I srs I	Bristol Hercules III
Short S.29 Stirling I srs II, srs III	Bristol Hercules XI
Short S.29 Stirling III, IV, V	Bristol Hercules VI
Short S.29 Stirling III, IV, V	Bristol Hercules XVI
Short S.29 Stirling prot	
Short S.30 Empire	Bristol Perseus XIIC
Short S.30 Empire	Bristol Perseus XIIC1
Short S.33 Empire	Bristol Pegasus XC
Short S.33 Empire	Bristol Pegasus 22
Short S.40 Shetland I	Bristol Centaurus VII
Short S.40 Shetland II	Bristol Centaurus XI
Short S.40 Shetland 2	Bristol Centaurus 660
Short S.45 Solent I	Bristol Hercules XX
Short S.45 Solent I	Bristol Hercules 232
Short S.45 Solent 2	Bristol Hercules 636
Short S.45 Solent 3	Bristol Hercules 637-3
Short S.45 Solent 3	Bristol Hercules 657
Short S.45 Solent 3 (Seaford 1)	Bristol Hercules 637-2
Short S.45 Solent 4	Bristol Hercules 732
Short S.45 Sunderland IV (Seaford)	Bristol Hercules XIX
Short S.A.1 Sturgeon I	Rolls-Royce Merlin 140
Short S.A.6 Sealand	de Havilland Gipsy Queen 70-2
Short S.A.6 Sealand	de Havilland Gipsy Queen 70-3
Short S.A.6 Sealand	de Havilland Gipsy Queen 70-4
Short-Bristow Crusader	Bristol Mercury I
Short-Kawanishi S.15 K.F.1	Rolls-Royce Buzzard IMS
Short-Mayo S.20 Composite 'Mercury'	Napier-Halford Rapier VI
Short-Mayo S.20 Composite 'Mercury'	Napier-Halford Rapier V
Short-Mayo S.21 Composite, 'Maia'	Bristol Pegasus XC
Siddeley R.T.1	Hispano-Suiza 8Ba 200 hp
Siddeley R.T.1	R.A.F.4a 140 hp
Siddeley Sinaia I	Siddeley-Deasy Tiger 500 hp
Siddeley S.R.2 Siskin	A.B.C. Dragonfly IA 330/360 hp
Sikorsky Il'ya Muromets	Sunbeam Crusader 150 hp
Sikorsky Il'ya Muromets	Sunbeam Mohawk 225 hp
Sikorsky Il'ya Muromets	Sunbeam Zulu 160 hp
Sikorsky S-19	Sunbeam Crusader 150 hp
Simmonds - see Saro, Spartan	
Simmonds Spartan	Cirrus III
Simmonds Spartan	Cirrus Hermes I
Simmonds Spartan	Cirrus Hermes II
Simmonds Spartan	de Havilland Gipsy I
Simmonds Spartan	de Havilland Gipsy II
Simmonds Spartan	Redrup Fury II 85 hp
Skinner Tractor Monoplane	E.N.V. Type F 60-80 hp
Slingsby 29B Motor Tutor	J.A.P. J-99 (Aeronca E-113-C)
Sonoda Tractor Biplane	Green D4 50-60 hp
Sopwith-Howard Wright 1910 Avis Monoplane	E.N.V. Type D 35-40 hp
Sopwith Burgess-Wright	Green C4 30-35 hp
Sopwith Howard Wright Pusher Biplane	E.N.V. Type F 60-80 hp
Sopwith Three-Seater	Gnome 7 Lambda 80 hp
Sopwith Three-Seater	Green E6 100-120 hp
Sopwith Anzani Tractor Seaplane	Anzani (British) 100 hp
Sopwith Bat Boat I	Austro-Daimler 90 hp
Sopwith Bat Boat II	Salmson (Canton-Unne) 200 hp
Sopwith Bat Boat 1A Amhibian	Green E6 100-120 hp
Sopwith 1913 Circuit Seaplane	Green E6 100-120 hp
Sopwith 1914 Circuit Seaplane	Gnome Monosoupape 9B-2 100 hp
Sopwith (Admiralty Type) 806 'Gunbus'	Sunbeam Nubian 150 hp
Sopwith 'Gunbus'	Gnome Monosoupape 9B-2 100 hp
Sopwith Tabloid	Gnome 7 Lambda 80 hp
Sopwith Tabloid	Gnome Monosoupape 9B-2 100 hp
Sopwith Sociable	Gnome 7 Lambda 80 hp
Sopwith Gordon Bennett Racer	Gnome 7 Lambda 80 hp
Sopwith Sociable, 'Tweenie'	Gnome Monosoupape 9B-2 100 hp
Sopwith Special Seaplane Type C	Salmson (Canton-Unne) 200 hp
Sopwith (Admiralty Type) 807 Folder Seaplane	Gnome Monosoupape 9B-2 100 hp

Sopwith (Admiralty Type) 860 Seaplane	Salmson (Canton-Unne) 200 hp
Sopwith (Admiralty Type) 860 Seaplane	Sunbeam Mohawk 225 hp
Sopwith Two-Seater Scout 'Spinning Jenny'	Gnome Monosoupape 9B-2 100 hp
Sopwith Schneider	Gnome Monosoupape 9B-2 100 hp
Sopwith Baby	Clerget 9B 130 hp
Sopwith Baby	Clerget 9Z 110 hp
Sopwith Pup	Clerget 7Z 80 hp
Sopwith Pup	Gnome 7 Lambda 80 hp
Sopwith Pup	Gnome Monosoupape 7 Type A 75 hp
Sopwith Pup	Gnome Monosoupape 9B-2 100 hp
Sopwith Pup	Le Rhone 9C 80 hp
Sopwith Pup	Le Rhone 9Ja 110 hp
Sopwith Triplane	Clerget 9B 130 hp
Sopwith Triplane	Clerget 9Z 110 hp
Sopwith Triplane	Hispano-Suiza 8Aa 150 hp
Sopwith Triplane	Hispano-Suiza 8B 200 hp
Sopwith L.R.T.Tr Triplane	Rolls-Royce Eagle I 250 hp
Sopwith F.1 Camel	Bentley B.R.1 (A.R.1) 150 hp
Sopwith F.1 Camel	Bentley B.R.2 200 hp
Sopwith F.1 Camel	Clerget 9B 130 hp
Sopwith F.1 Camel	Clerget 9Bf 140 hp
Sopwith F.1 Camel	Clerget 9Z 110 hp
Sopwith F.1 Camel	Gnome Monosoupape 9B-2 100 hp
Sopwith F.1 Camel	Gnome Monosoupape 9N 150 hp
Sopwith F.1 Camel	Le Rhone 9C 80 hp
Sopwith F.1 Camel	Le Rhone 9Ja 110 hp
Sopwith F.1 Camel	Le Rhone 9R 110 hp
Sopwith 2F.1 (Ship) Camel	Bentley B.R.1 (A.R.1) 150 hp
Sopwith 2F.1 (Ship) Camel	Clerget 9B 130 hp
Sopwith LCT 1 1/2 Strutter	Clerget 9B 130 hp
Sopwith LCT 1 1/2 Strutter	Clerget 9Z 110 hp
Sopwith LCT 1 1/2 Strutter	Le Rhone 9Ja 110 hp
Sopwith Bee	Gnome 7 Omega 50 hp
Sopwith B.1 Bomber	Hispano-Suiza 8Ba 200 hp
Sopwith T.1	Hispano-Suiza 8Ba 200 hp
Sopwith T.1 Cuckoo	Sunbeam Arab I 200 hp
Sopwith T.1 Cuckoo	Wolseley W.4A* Viper 200 hp
Sopwith 5F.1 Dolphin I	Hispano-Suiza 8Ab 180 hp
Sopwith 5F.1 Dolphin I	Hispano-Suiza 8Ba 200 hp
Sopwith 5F.1 Dolphin I	Hispano-Suiza 8Bb 200 hp
Sopwith 5F.1 Dolphin I	Hispano-Suiza 8Be 220 hp
Sopwith 5F.1 Dolphin I	Wolseley W.4B Adder I 200 hp
Sopwith 5F.1 Dolphin III	Hispano-Suiza 8Ba 200 hp
Sopwith 5F.1 Dolphin II	Hispano-Suiza 8Fb 300 hp
Sopwith 3F.2 Hippo	Clerget 11Eb 200 hp
Sopwith Rainbow	A.B.C. Dragonfly I 320 hp
Sopwith 2FR.2 Bulldog	A.B.C. Dragonfly I 320 hp
Sopwith 2FR.2 Bulldog	Clerget 11Eb 200 hp
Sopwith 2B.2 Rhino	B.H.P. 230 hp, Galloway Adriatic
Sopwith Bee/Tadpole/Sparrow	A.B.C. Gnat I 35 hp
Sopwith Sparrow	Gnome 7 Omega 50 hp
Sopwith 7F.1 Snipe	Bentley B.R.2 230 hp
Sopwith 7F.1 Snipe	Bentley B.R.2 245 hp
Sopwith 7F.1 Snipe prot	Bentley B.R.1 (A.R.1) 150 hp
Sopwith 7F.1a Snipe (LR)	Bentley B.R.2 245 hp
Sopwith T.F.2 Salamander	Bentley B.R.2 230 hp
Sopwith T.F.2 Salamander	Clerget 11Eb 200 hp
Sopwith 8F.1 Snail	A.B.C. Wasp I
Sopwith 8F.1 Snail	A.B.C. Wasp II
Sopwith Buffalo	Bentley B.R.2 230 hp
Sopwith Scooter	Clerget 9B 130 hp
Sopwith Swallow	Le Rhone 9Ja 110 hp
Sopwith Dragon	A.B.C. Dragonfly IA 330/360 hp
Sopwith Snark	A.B.C. Dragonfly IA 330/360 hp
Sopwith R.M.1 Snapper	A.B.C. Dragonfly IA 330/360 hp
Sopwith Cobham I	A.B.C. Dragonfly IA 330/360 hp
Sopwith Cobham II	Siddeley-Deasy Puma HC 290 hp
Sopwith Atlantic	Rolls-Royce Eagle VIII 375 hp
Sopwith Wallaby	Rolls-Royce Eagle VIII 375 hp
Sopwith Dove	Le Rhone 9C 80 hp
Sopwith Gnu	Bentley B.R.2 230 hp
Sopwith Gnu	Le Rhone 9Ja 110 hp
Sopwith Antelope	Wolseley W.4A* Viper 200 hp
Sopwith Schneider	Cosmos Jupiter I
Sopwith Grasshopper	Anzani (British) 100 hp
Sopwith D.1 'Three-Seater'	Gnome 7 Gamma 70 hp
Southern (Miles) Martlet	A.B.C. Hornet
Southern (Miles) Martlet	Armstrong Siddeley Genet II
Southern (Miles) Martlet	Armstrong Siddeley Genet Ma I
Southern (Miles) Martlet	Cirrus Hermes I
Southern (Miles) Martlet	de Havilland Gipsy I

Southern (Miles) Martlet	de Havilland Gipsy II
SPAD 7	Hispano-Suiza 8Aa 150 hp
SPAD 7	Hispano-Suiza 8Ab 180 hp
SPAD 7	Wolseley W.4A Python I 150 hp
SPAD 7	Wolseley W.4A Python II 180 hp
SPAD 13	Hispano-Suiza 8Ba 200 hp
SPAD 13	Hispano-Suiza 8Bb 200 hp
SPAD 13	Hispano-Suiza 8Bc 220 hp
SPAD 13	Hispano-Suiza 8Bd 200 hp
SPAD 13	Hispano-Suiza 8Be 220 hp
SPAD 13	Hispano-Suiza 8Cb 220 hp
Spartan - see Saro, Simmonds	
Spartan Arrow	Cirrus III
Spartan Arrow	Cirrus Hermes II
Spartan Arrow	de Havilland Gipsy I
Spartan Arrow	de Havilland Gipsy II
Spartan Arrow	Napier-Halford Javelin III
Spartan A.24 Mailplane - see Saro-Percival	de Havilland Gipsy III
Spartan Clipper	Pobjoy Niagara III
Spartan Clipper	Pobjoy R
Spartan Cruiser I	de Havilland Gipsy III
Spartan Cruiser II	Cirrus Hermes IV
Spartan Cruiser II, III	de Havilland Gipsy Major I srs I
Spartan Three-seater I	Cirrus Hermes II
Spartan Three-seater I	de Havilland Gipsy II
Spartan Three-seater II	Cirrus Hermes IIB
Spartan Three-seater II	Cirrus Hermes IV
Stampe et Vertongen SV-4B	de Havilland Gipsy Major I srs I
Sud Est S.E.1010	Bristol Hercules 101
Sunbeam Bomber	Sunbeam Arab I 200 hp
Supermarine N.1B Baby	Hispano-Suiza 8B 200 hp
Supermarine Channel I	Beardmore 160 hp
Supermarine Channel II	Siddeley-Deasy Puma 236 hp
Supermarine Commercial Amphibian	Rolls-Royce Eagle VIII 375 hp
Supermarine Sea Eagle	Rolls-Royce Eagle VIII 375 hp
Supermarine Sea King I	Beardmore 160 hp
Supermarine Sea King I	Siddeley-Deasy Puma 236 hp
Supermarine Sea King II	Hispano-Suiza 8F 300 hp
Supermarine Sea Lion I	Napier Lion II
Supermarine Sea Lion II	Napier Lion II
Supermarine S.4	Napier Lion VII
Supermarine S.5	Napier Lion VIIA
Supermarine S.5	Napier Lion VIIB
Supermarine S.6	Rolls-Royce 'R' Type
Supermarine S.6A, S.6B	Rolls-Royce 'R' Type
Supermarine Seal II	Napier Lion II
Supermarine Swan	Rolls-Royce Eagle IX 360 hp
Supermarine Swan	Napier Lion IIB
Supermarine Seagull I, II	Napier Lion IIB
Supermarine Seagull II	Bristol Jupiter IX
Supermarine Seagull III	Napier Lion V
Supermarine Sparrow I	Blackburne Thrush 35 hp
Supermarine Sparrow I	Bristol Cherub I
Supermarine Sparrow II	Bristol Cherub III
Supermarine Sheldrake	Napier Lion V
Supermarine Scarab	Rolls-Royce Eagle IX 360 hp
Supermarine Seamew	Armstrong Siddeley Lynx IV
Supermarine Air Yacht	Armstrong Siddeley Jaguar VI
Supermarine Air Yacht	Armstrong Siddeley Panther IIA (GF)
Supermarine Southampton I	Napier Lion IIB
Supermarine Southampton I	Napier Lion V
Supermarine Southampton II	Napier Lion VA
Supermarine Southampton IV	Rolls-Royce Kestrel IIMS
Supermarine Nanok	Armstrong Siddeley Jaguar IV
Supermarine Solent	Armstrong Siddeley Jaguar IV
Supermarine Solent	Bristol Jupiter IXF
Supermarine Southampton X	Armstrong Siddeley Jaguar VIC
Supermarine Southampton X	Armstrong Siddeley Panther IIA (GF)
Supermarine Southampton X	Bristol Jupiter XFBM
Supermarine Scapa	Rolls-Royce Kestrel IIMS.6
Supermarine Scapa	Rolls-Royce Kestrel IIIMS
Supermarine Scapa	Rolls-Royce Kestrel IIIMS.6
Supermarine Scapa	Rolls-Royce Kestrel IIIS
Supermarine Stranraer	Bristol Pegasus X
Supermarine Stranraer	Bristol Pegasus IIIM
Supermarine Seagull V	Bristol Pegasus IIL.2P
Supermarine Walrus I	Bristol Pegasus IIM.2P
Supermarine Walrus I, II	Bristol Pegasus VIP
Supermarine 309 Sea Otter	Bristol Mercury 30
Supermarine S.24/37 'Dumbo'	Rolls-Royce Merlin 32
Supermarine S.24/37 'Dumbo'	Rolls-Royce Merlin 30

Supermarine 224 F.7/30 'Spitfire'	Rolls-Royce Goshawk IIS
Supermarine Seagull ASR 1	Rolls-Royce Griffon 29
Supermarine Spitfire prot	Rolls-Royce Merlin C
Supermarine Spitfire prot	Rolls-Royce Merlin E
Supermarine Spitfire prot	Rolls-Royce Merlin II
Supermarine Spitfire prot	Rolls-Royce Merlin III
Supermarine Spitfire I	Rolls-Royce Merlin II
Supermarine Spitfire I	Rolls-Royce Merlin III
Supermarine Spitfire, High-Speed	Rolls-Royce Merlin II Spl
Supermarine Spitfire II	Rolls-Royce Merlin XII
Supermarine Spitfire III	Rolls-Royce Merlin XX
Supermarine Spitfire IV	Rolls-Royce Griffon IIB
Supermarine Spitfire IV, V	Rolls-Royce Merlin 46
Supermarine Spitfire IV, V, VI	Rolls-Royce Merlin 45
Supermarine Spitfire V	Rolls-Royce Merlin 50
Supermarine Spitfire V	Rolls-Royce Merlin 50A
Supermarine Spitfire V	Rolls-Royce Merlin 50M
Supermarine Spitfire V	Rolls-Royce Merlin 55A
Supermarine Spitfire V	Rolls-Royce Merlin 55M
Supermarine Spitfire VA, B, C	Rolls-Royce Merlin 55MA
Supermarine Spitfire VI	Rolls-Royce Merlin 45M
Supermarine Spitfire VII, VIII, IX, XI	Rolls-Royce Merlin 47
Supermarine Spitfire VII, X	Rolls-Royce Merlin 61
Supermarine Spitfire VII, X	Rolls-Royce Merlin 64
Supermarine Spitfire VIII, IX	Rolls-Royce Merlin 71
Supermarine Spitfire VIII, IX, XI	Rolls-Royce Merlin 63A
Supermarine Spitfire VIII, IX, XI	Rolls-Royce Merlin 63
Supermarine Spitfire VIII, IX, T.8, 9	Rolls-Royce Merlin 70
Supermarine Spitfire VIII, XIV	Rolls-Royce Merlin 66
Supermarine Spitfire VIII, XIV	Rolls-Royce Griffon 65
Supermarine Spitfire VIII, XIV, 21	Rolls-Royce Griffon 83
Supermarine Spitfire X	Rolls-Royce Griffon 61
Supermarine Spitfire XII	Rolls-Royce Merlin 77
Supermarine Spitfire XII	Rolls-Royce Griffon III
Supermarine Spitfire XII	Rolls-Royce Griffon IV
Supermarine Spitfire XIV	Rolls-Royce Griffon VI
Supermarine Spitfire XIV, XVIII	Rolls-Royce Griffon 101
Supermarine Spitfire XIV, XIX	Rolls-Royce Griffon 67
Supermarine Spitfire XIV, 21	Rolls-Royce Griffon 66
Supermarine Spitfire XIV, 21	Rolls-Royce Griffon 85
Supermarine Spitfire XIV, 21	Rolls-Royce Griffon 86
Supermarine Spitfire XIV, 21	Rolls-Royce Griffon 87
Supermarine Spitfire XVI	Rolls-Royce Griffon 88
Supermarine Spitfire XVIII, XIX	Rolls-Royce Merlin 266
Supermarine Spitfire XX	Rolls-Royce Griffon 65
Supermarine Spitfire 21	Rolls-Royce Griffon IIB
Supermarine Spitfire 21	Rolls-Royce Griffon 62
Supermarine Spitfire 21	Rolls-Royce Griffon 102
Supermarine Spitfire 21	Rolls-Royce Griffon 105
Supermarine Spitfire 21	Rolls-Royce Griffon 121
Supermarine Spitfire 21, 22	Rolls-Royce Griffon 122
Supermarine Spitfire 22, 23, 24	Rolls-Royce Griffon 64
Supermarine Spiteful	Rolls-Royce Griffon 61
Supermarine Spiteful XIV	Rolls-Royce Griffon 102
Supermarine Seafire I, II	Rolls-Royce Griffon 69
Supermarine Seafire I, II, III	Rolls-Royce Merlin 46
Supermarine Seafire I, II, III	Rolls-Royce Merlin 45
Supermarine Seafire I, II, III	Rolls-Royce Merlin 50M
Supermarine Seafire I, II, III	Rolls-Royce Merlin 55
Supermarine Seafire I, II, III, XIII	Rolls-Royce Merlin 55M
Supermarine Seafire XV	Rolls-Royce Merlin 32
Supermarine Seafire XV, XVII	Rolls-Royce Griffon 26
Supermarine Seafire 45, 46, 47	Rolls-Royce Griffon VI
Supermarine Seafire 46	Rolls-Royce Griffon 61
Supermarine Seafire 46	Rolls-Royce Griffon 62
Supermarine Seafire 46	Rolls-Royce Griffon 64
Supermarine Seafire 46	Rolls-Royce Griffon 85
Supermarine Seafire 46, 47	Rolls-Royce Griffon 122
Supermarine Seafire 47	Rolls-Royce Griffon 87
Supermarine Seafire 47	Rolls-Royce Griffon 88
Supermarine Seafang XVI	Rolls-Royce Griffon 90
Supermarine Seafang 32	Rolls-Royce Griffon 101
Surrey Flying Services A.L.1	Rolls-Royce Griffon 89
Swan Pusher Biplane	British Salmson A.C.7
Swan Tractor Monoplane	E.N.V. Type D 35-40 hp
Tarrant Tabor	E.N.V. Type D 35-40 hp
Taylor Experimental	Napier Lion II
Taylor J.T.1	Blackburn Cirrus Minor I
Taylorcraft - see Auster	J.A.P. J-99 (Aeronca E-113-C)
Taylorcraft D Auster I	Blackburn Cirrus Minor I

Taylorcraft F (Auster III)	de Havilland Gipsy Major I srs I
Taylorcraft F (Auster III)	de Havilland Gipsy Major ID
Taylorcraft Plus C.2	Blackburn Cirrus Minor I
Taylorcraft Plus D	Blackburn Cirrus Minor I
Thomas Morse S-4	Le Rhone 9C 80 hp
Thruxton Jackaroo	de Havilland Gipsy Major IC
Thruxton Jackaroo	de Havilland Gipsy Major ID
Tipsy Junior	J.A.P. J-99 (Aeronca E-113-C)
Tipsy M	de Havilland Gipsy Major 10/1
Tipsy Nipper III	Rollason Ardem 4CO2-1
Tipsy S.2	Aero Engines Sprite I
Vickers Monoplanes 1-3	R.E.P.-Vickers 60 hp
Vickers No 6 Monoplane	Gnome 7 Omega 50 hp
Vickers No 6 Monoplane	Gnome 7 Gamma 70 hp
Vickers No 6 Monoplane	Viale 70 hp
Vickers No 7 Monoplane	Gnome 9 Delta 100 hp
Vickers No 8 Monoplane	Gnome 7 Gamma 70 hp
Vickers No 8 Monoplane	Gnome 7 Lambda 80 hp
Vickers No 8 Monoplane	Gnome 7 Omega 50 hp
Vickers Boxkite, School Biplane	Gnome 7 Omega 50 hp
Vickers Hydravion	Gnome 9 Delta 100 hp
Vickers E.F.B.1 ('Destroyer')	Wolseley 80 hp
Vickers E.F.B.2, 3, 5 Gunbus	Gnome Monosoupape 9B-2 100 hp
Vickers F.B.5 Gunbus	Clerget 9Z 110 hp
Vickers F.B.5	Smith Static 140/150 hp
Vickers F.B.5, 6 Gunbus	Gnome Monosoupape 9B-2 100 hp
Vickers E.F.B.7	Gnome 9 Delta 100 hp
Vickers F.B.7A	Renault WS 80 hp
Vickers E.F.B.8	Gnome 9 Delta 100 hp
Vickers F.B.9 Gunbus	Gnome 9 Delta 100 hp
Vickers F.B.9 Gunbus	Le Rhone 9Ja 110 hp
Vickers E.S.1 Bullet	Clerget 9Z 110 hp
Vickers E.S.1 Bullet	Gnome Monosoupape 9B-2 100 hp
Vickers E.S.1 Bullet	Le Rhone 9Ja 110 hp
Vickers E.S.2 Bullet	Clerget 9Z 110 hp
Vickers E.S.2 Bullet	Le Rhone 9Ja 110 hp
Vickers F.B.11	Rolls-Royce Eagle I 250 hp
Vickers F.B.12	Le Rhone 9C 80 hp
Vickers F.B.12A	Gnome Monosoupape 9B-2 100 hp
Vickers F.B.12A	Hart 150 hp
Vickers F.B.12B	Hart 150 hp
Vickers F.B.12C	Anzani (British) 100 hp
Vickers F.B.12C	Le Rhone 9Ja 110 hp
Vickers F.B.14	Beardmore 120 hp
Vickers F.B.14	Beardmore 160 hp
Vickers F.B.14B	Rolls-Royce Falcon I 190 hp
Vickers F.B.14D	Rolls-Royce Falcon I 190 hp
Vickers F.B.14F	R.A.F.4a 140 hp
Vickers F.B.16 Hart Scout	Hart 150 hp
Vickers F.B.16A	Hispano-Suiza 8Aa 150 hp
Vickers F.B.16D	Hispano-Suiza 8Ba 200 hp
Vickers F.B.19 Bullet Mk I	Gnome Monosoupape 9B-2 100 hp
Vickers F.B.19 Bullet Mk I, Mk II	Le Rhone 9Ja 110 hp
Vickers F.B.19 Bullet Mk II	Clerget 9Z 110 hp
Vickers F.B.24A, B, D, E	Hispano-Suiza 8Ba 200 hp
Vickers F.B.25	Hispano-Suiza 8Aa 150 hp
Vickers F.B.26 Vampire I	Hispano-Suiza 8Ba 200 hp
Vickers F.B.26A Vampire II	Bentley B.R.2 230 hp
Vickers F.B.27 Vimy	Bristol Jupiter IV
Vickers F.B.27 Vimy IV	Rolls-Royce Eagle VIII 375 hp
Vickers F.B.27 Vimy Ambulance	Napier Lion II
Vickers F.B.27 Vimy prot	Hispano-Suiza 8Ba 200 hp
Vickers F.B.27 Vimy prot	Salmson (Canton-Unne) Z.9m 260 hp
Vickers F.B.27 Vimy prot	Sunbeam Maori II 260/275 hp
Vickers F.B.27 Vimy prot	Sunbeam Maori III 260/275 hp
Vickers F.B.27A Vimy Mk II	Rolls-Royce Eagle IX 360 hp
Vickers Vernon I	Rolls-Royce Eagle VIII 375 hp
Vickers Vernon II, III	Napier Lion II
Vickers VIM (Vickers Instructional Machine)	Rolls-Royce Eagle VIII 375 hp
Vickers Viking I	Rolls-Royce Falcon III 275 hp
Vickers Viking II	Rolls-Royce Eagle VIII 375 hp
Vickers Viking III	Napier Lion II
Vickers 54, 55, 58, 60, 64, 67 Viking IV	Napier Lion II
Vickers 56 Victoria I	Napier Lion II
Vickers 57 Virginia I	Napier Lion II
Vickers 59 Viking V	Napier Lion II
Vickers 61 Vulcan	Rolls-Royce Eagle IX 360 hp
Vickers 61, 63 Vulcan	Rolls-Royce Eagle VIII 375 hp
Vickers 62 Vanguard	Napier Lion II
Vickers 66 Vimy Commercial	Rolls-Royce Eagle VIII 375 hp
Vickers 69, 73, 77 Viking IV	Rolls-Royce Eagle IX 360 hp

Vickers 71 Vixen I	Napier Lion II
Vickers 74 Vulcan	Napier Lion II
Vickers 76 Virginia II	Napier Lion II
Vickers 78 Vulture I (Viking VI)	Napier Lion II
Vickers 79 Virginia III	Napier Lion II
Vickers 81 Victoria II	Napier Lion II
Vickers 83 Vanellus (Viking VII)	Napier Lion II
Vickers 85 Viking IV	Rolls-Royce Eagle VIII 375 hp
Vickers 87 Vixen II	Napier Lion II
Vickers 89 Viget	Aero Engines Sprite I
Vickers 89 Viget	Blackburne Thrush 35 hp
Vickers 91 Vixen III	Napier Lion II
Vickers 92 Valparaiso II	Rolls-Royce Eagle VIII 375 hp
Vickers 93 Valparaiso I	Napier Lion II
Vickers 94 Venture I	Napier Lion II
Vickers 95 Vulture II	Rolls-Royce Eagle IX 360 hp
Vickers 96 Virginia I	Rolls-Royce Condor III
Vickers 98 Vagabond	Blackburne Thrush 35 hp
Vickers 98 Vagabond	Bristol Cherub III
Vickers 99 Virginia IV	Napier Lion II
Vickers 100 Virginia V	Napier Lion V
Vickers 102 Valparaiso	Napier Lion II
Vickers 103, 170 Vanguard	Rolls-Royce Condor III
Vickers 105 Vixen IV	Rolls-Royce Condor III
Vickers 106, 116 Vixen III, V	Napier Lion V
Vickers 108 Virginia VI	Napier Lion II
Vickers 111 Virginia VI	Napier Lion V
Vickers 112 Virginia VII	Napier Lion V
Vickers 113 Vespa I	Bristol Jupiter IV
Vickers 113 Vespa I	Bristol Jupiter VI
Vickers 115 Virginia VIII	Rolls-Royce Condor III
Vickers 116 Vixen V	Napier Lion V
Vickers 117, 138 Victoria III	Napier Lion II
Vickers 119 Vespa II	Bristol Jupiter VI
Vickers 120 Vendace I	Rolls-Royce Falcon III 275 hp
Vickers 121 Wibault Scout	Bristol Jupiter VI
Vickers 122 Virginia VII	Napier Lion VA
Vickers 124 Vixen VI	Rolls-Royce Condor IIIA
Vickers 125 Vireo	Armstrong Siddeley Lynx IV (S)
Vickers 127 Wibault Scout	Napier Lion XI
Vickers 128 Virginia IX	Napier Lion V
Vickers 129 Virginia VIII	Napier Lion V
Vickers 130 Vivid (Vixen VII)	Napier Lion VA
Vickers 131 Valiant	Bristol Jupiter VI
Vickers 132 Vildebeest I	Bristol Jupiter VIII
Vickers 133 Vendace	Rolls-Royce Falcon III 275 hp
Vickers 133 Vendace II	A.D.C. Nimbus 300 hp
Vickers 134 Vellore I	Armstrong Siddeley Jaguar IV
Vickers 134, 166 Vellore I	Bristol Jupiter IX
Vickers 139, 140, 162 Virginia X	Napier Lion XI
Vickers 141 F.21/26 Scout	Rolls-Royce Kestrel IS
Vickers 142 Vivid	Napier Lion XIA
Vickers 143 Bolivian Scout	Bristol Jupiter VIA
Vickers 143 Bolivian Scout	Bristol Jupiter VII
Vickers 144 Vimy Trainer	Bristol Jupiter IV
Vickers 145 Victoria	Bristol Jupiter IX
Vickers 146 Vivid	Napier Lion XI
Vickers 147 Valiant	Bristol Jupiter XI
Vickers 148 Vixen III	Napier Lion V
Vickers 149 Vespa III	Bristol Jupiter VI
Vickers 150 B.19/27	Bristol Jupiter VIII
Vickers 150 B.19/27	Rolls-Royce Kestrel IIIS
Vickers 151 Jockey F.20/27	Bristol Mercury IIA
Vickers 156 Vimy Trainer	Armstrong Siddeley Jaguar IV
Vickers 157 Vendace II	A.D.C. Nimbus II 300 hp
Vickers 158 Victoria IV	Napier Lion IIB
Vickers 158 Victoria IV	Napier Lion V
Vickers 158 Victoria IV	Napier Lion V*
Vickers 159 Vimy Trainer	BRistol Jupiter VI
Vickers 160 Viastra I	Armstrong Siddeley Lynx V (Major, Cheetah)
Vickers 161 F.29/27 C.O.W. Gun Fighter	Bristol Jupiter VIIF
Vickers 163	Rolls-Royce Kestrel IIIS
Vickers 166 Vellore I	Armstrong Siddeley Jaguar VI
Vickers 167 Virginia X	Bristol Jupiter IXF
Vickers 169 Victoria V	Napier Lion XIB
Vickers 171, 196 Jockey	Bristol Jupiter VIIF
Vickers 172 Vellore III	Bristol Jupiter XIF
Vickers 173 Vellore IV	Bristol Jupiter IX
Vickers 177 F.21/26 Fighter	Bristol Jupiter XFS
Vickers 192 Vildebeest	Bristol Jupiter VIIIF
Vickers 192 Vildebeest	Bristol Jupiter X

Vickers 192 Vildebeest	Bristol Jupiter XF
Vickers 193 Vespa IV	Armstrong Siddeley Jaguar VIC
Vickers 195, 255 Vanox (B.19/27)	Bristol Pegasus IM.3
Vickers 198 Viastra II	Bristol Jupiter XIF
Vickers 199 Viastra III	Armstrong Siddeley Jaguar VIC
Vickers 203 Viastra VI	Bristol Jupiter IXF
Vickers 204 Vildebeest IV	Armstrong Siddeley Panther IIA (GF)
Vickers 206 Vildebeest VI	Armstrong Siddeley Panther IIA (GF)
Vickers 207 M.1/30	Rolls-Royce Buzzard IIIMS
Vickers 208 Vespa V	Armstrong Siddeley Jaguar VIC
Vickers 209 Vildebeest III	Bristol Jupiter XIF
Vickers 210 Vespa VI	Bristol Jupiter VIIF
Vickers 212 Vellox	Bristol Pegasus IM.3
Vickers 212 Vellox	Bristol Pegasus III
Vickers 212 Vellox	Bristol Perseus II-L
Vickers 213 Victoria III	Napier Lion XI
Vickers 214 Vildebeest IV	Bristol Jupiter XFBM
Vickers 216 Vildebeest VII	Armstrong Siddeley Panther IIA (GF)
Vickers 220 Viastra VIII	Bristol Jupiter VIFM
Vickers 241 Victoria V	Bristol Jupiter XFBM
Vickers 242 Viastra IX	Bristol Jupiter IXF
Vickers 244 Vildebeest I	Bristol Pegasus IM.3
Vickers 246 G.4/31 Monoplane	Bristol Pegasus IIIM.3
Vickers 248 Victoria V	Bristol Pegasus IM.3
Vickers 250 Vespa VII	Bristol Pegasus IS.3
Vickers 251 Vildebeest X	Bristol Pegasus IM.3
Vickers 252 Vildebeest IX	Bristol Pegasus IIL.3
Vickers 253 G.4/31 (Biplane)	Bristol Pegasus IIM.3
Vickers 257 Vildebeest XII	Bristol Pegasus IM.3
Vickers 258 Vildebeest II	Bristol Pegasus IIM.3
Vickers 259 Viastra X	Bristol Pegasus IM.3
Vickers 259 Viastra X	Bristol Pegasus IIL.3
Vickers 260, 262, 269 Victoria VI	Bristol Pegasus IIL.3
Vickers 261, 274 Victoria V	Napier Lion XI
Vickers 262 Valentia	Bristol Pegasus IIL.3
Vickers 263 Vildebeest T.S.R.	Bristol Pegasus IM.3
Vickers 264 Valentia	Bristol Pegasus IIM.3
Vickers 266 Vincent	Bristol Pegasus IIIM.2
Vickers 266 Vincent	Bristol Pegasus IIIM.3
Vickers 266 Vincent	Bristol Pegasus IIIM.3
Vickers 267, 277 Vildebeest III	Bristol Pegasus IIM.3
Vickers 268 Virginia X	Bristol Pegasus IIM.3
Vickers 271 B.9/32 (Wellington prot)	Bristol Pegasus X
Vickers 276, 278, 282, 283 Valentia	Bristol Pegasus IIM.3
Vickers 279 Venom	Bristol Aquila I
Vickers 281 Wellesley	Bristol Pegasus X
Vickers 284 Warwick B.1/35	Rolls-Royce Vulture II
Vickers 285, 403 Wellington I, IA	Bristol Pegasus XVIII
Vickers 286 Vildebeest IV	Bristol Perseus VIII
Vickers 287 Wellesley I	Bristol Pegasus XVIII
Vickers 287, 291, 402 Wellesley I	Bristol Pegasus XX
Vickers 289 Wellesley	Bristol Hercules I
Vickers 285, 290 Wellington I	Bristol Pegasus XVIII
Vickers 292, 294 Wellesley L.R.D.U.	Bristol Pegasus 22 LR
Vickers 298, 406 Wellington II	Rolls-Royce Merlin X
Vickers 299 Wellington III	Bristol Hercules III
Vickers 408, 409 Wellington IA, IB	Bristol Pegasus XVIII
Vickers 412, 415 Wellington IA, IC	Bristol Pegasus XVIII
Vickers 413 Warwick ASR II	Bristol Centaurus IV
Vickers 417 Wellington III	Bristol Hercules X
Vickers 417 Wellington III	Bristol Hercules XI
Vickers 418 Wellington D.W.I. Mk I	Bristol Pegasus XVIII
Vickers 419 Wellington D.W.I. Mk II	Bristol Pegasus XVIII
Vickers 407, 426 Wellington V	Bristol Hercules VIII HE8MAS
Vickers 428 Wellington D.W.I. Mk III	Bristol Hercules XI
Vickers 429 Wellington VIII	Bristol Pegasus XVIII
Vickers 431, 442 Wellington VI	Rolls-Royce Merlin 60
Vickers 432 F.7/41	Rolls-Royce Merlin 61
Vickers 436 Wellington V	Bristol Hercules VIII (MOD)
Vickers 437 Wellington V	Bristol Hercules XVMT
Vickers 440 Wellington X	Bristol Hercules VI
Vickers 440 Wellington X	Bristol Hercules XVI
Vickers 460 Warwick III (Conversion)	Napier-Halford Sabre VI
Vickers 462, 473 Warwick II, V	Bristol Centaurus VII
Vickers 466 Wellington XIII	Bristol Hercules XVII
Vickers 469, 473, 474 Warwick II, V	Bristol Centaurus VII
Vickers 470 Wellington II (Jet test-bed)	Rolls-Royce Merlin 62
Vickers 478, 487 etc Wellington X, XI	Bristol Hercules VI
Vickers 478, 487 etc Wellington X, XI	Bristol Hercules XVII
Vickers 478, 487 etc Wellington X, XI, XII, XIII	Bristol Hercules XVI
Vickers 478, 487 etc Wellington XII, XIII	Bristol Hercules VI

Vickers 478, 487 etc Wellington XII, XIII	Bristol Hercules XVII
Vickers 480 Windsor	Rolls-Royce Merlin 85
Vickers 484 Warwick C.IV	Bristol Centaurus IV
Vickers 401, 491, 495, 496 Viking I	Bristol Hercules 130
Vickers 498 Viking I	Bristol Hercules 630
Vickers 498 Viking IA	Bristol Hercules 134
Vickers 600 Warwick	Bristol Centaurus XII
Vickers 610, 614, etc Viking IA, B	Bristol Hercules 634
Vickers 637 Valetta C.1	Bristol Hercules 270
Vickers 637 Valetta C.1	Bristol Hercules 230
Vickers 668 Varsity T.1	Bristol Hercules 264
Vickers (Canada) Vedette	Armstrong Siddeley Lynx II
Voisin Boxkite Pusher Biplane	E.N.V. Type F 60-80 hp
Voisin LA	Salmson (Canton-Unne) M.9 120 hp
Voisin LA.S	Salmson (Canton-Unne) B.9 140 hp
Ward Gnome	Douglas 500 c.c., 3.5 hp
Watkinson Dingbat	Carden-Ford 31 hp
Weir C.28 W.1, W.2 Autogiro	Aero Engines Dryad
Weir W.3, W.4 Autogiro	Aero Engines Pixie
Weir W.5 Helicopter	Aero Engines Pixie
Weiss No 2 Tractor Monoplane	E.N.V. Type D 35-40 hp
Westland 1N.1B	Bentley B.R.1 (A.R.1) 150 hp
Westland Wagtail	A.B.C. Wasp I
Westland Wagtail	A.B.C. Wasp II
Westland Wagtail	Armstrong Siddeley Lynx I
Westland Wagtail	Armstrong Siddeley Lynx II
Westland Weasel	A.B.C. Dragonfly IA 330/360 hp
Westland Weasel	Armstrong Siddeley Jaguar II
Westland Weasel	Bristol Jupiter II
Westland Limousine II	Cosmos Jupiter II (geared)
Westland Limousine I, II	Rolls-Royce Falcon III 275 hp
Westland Limousine II	Hispano-Suiza 8F 300 hp
Westland Limousine III	Napier Lion II
Westland Walrus	Napier Lion IIB
Westland Dreadnaught	Napier Lion IIB
Westland Woodpigeon	A.B.C. Scorpion I
Westland Woodpigeon I	Bristol Cherub III
Westland Woodpigeon II	Anzani (British) 60 hp
Westland Widgeon I	Blackburne Thrush 35 hp
Westland Widgeon II	Armstrong Siddeley Genet I
Westland Widgeon III	A.B.C. Hornet
Westland Widgeon III	Armstrong Siddeley Genet II
Westland Widgeon III	Cirrus I
Westland Widgeon III	Cirrus II
Westland Widgeon III	Cirrus III
Westland Widgeon III, IIIA	Cirrus Hermes I
Westland Widgeon IIIA	Cirrus Hermes II
Westland Widgeon IIIA	de Havilland Gipsy I
Westland Widgeon III, IIIA	Rolls-Royce Condor III
Westland Yeovil	Rolls-Royce Falcon III 275 hp
Westland Wizard I	Rolls-Royce Kestrel IA
Westland Wizard I	Rolls-Royce Kestrel IS
Westland Wizard II	Bristol Jupiter VI
Westland Westbury	Bristol Jupiter VIII
Westland Westbury	Bristol Jupiter VI
Westland Wapiti prot	Bristol Jupiter VI
Westland Wapiti I	Armstrong Siddeley Jaguar VI
Westland Wapiti III	Armstrong Siddeley Jaguar VIII
Westland Wapiti	Armstrong Siddeley Panther VII
Westland Wapiti	Bristol Draco
Westland Wapiti	Bristol Jupiter VIII
Westland Wapiti I, IA, II, IIA	Bristol Jupiter VIIIF
Westland Wapiti I, IA, II, IIA	Bristol Jupiter VIIIF.P.
Westland Wapiti I, IA, II, IIA	Bristol Jupiter IXF
Westland Wapiti VI	Bristol Jupiter XFA
Westland Wapiti IIA, III, V	Armstrong Siddeley Panther IIA (GF)
Westland Wapiti III, V, VIII	Armstrong Siddeley Jaguar IVC
Westland Wapiti IV	Armstrong Siddeley Panther II (PF)
Westland Wapiti V	Bristol Phoenix I
Westland Wapiti I	Bristol Phoenix IIM
Westland Wapiti I	Bristol Jupiter VIII
Westland Witch	Bristol Jupiter VI
Westland Witch I	Bristol Jupiter VIIIF.P.
Westland Witch II	Bristol Cherub I
Westland-Hill Pterodactyl I	Bristol Cherub III
Westland-Hill Pterodactyl IA	Armstrong Siddeley Genet I
Westland-Hill Pterodactyl IB, IC	Bristol Jupiter VII
Westland Interceptor F.20/27	Bristol Mercury IIA
Westland Interceptor F.20/27	Bristol Mercury III
Westland Interceptor F.20/27	Cirrus III
Westland IV (Wessex)	Cirrus Hermes I
Westland IV (Wessex)	

Westland Wessex	Armstrong Siddeley Genet Ma I
Westland Wessex	Armstrong Siddeley Genet Ma IA
Westland C.O.W. Gun F.29/27	Bristol Mercury IIIA
Westland-Hill Pterodactyl IV	de Havilland Gipsy III
Westland-Houston P.V.3	Bristol Jupiter XFA
Westland-Houston P.V.3	Bristol Pegasus IS.3
Westland Wallace prot	Bristol Pegasus IM.3
Westland Wallace I	Bristol Pegasus IM.2
Westland Wallace I	Bristol Pegasus IM.3
Westland Wallace	Bristol Pegasus IS.3
Westland Wallace I, II	Bristol Pegasus IIM.3
Westland Wallace II	Bristol Pegasus IV
Westland P.V.7 G.4/31 (Wallace prot)	Bristol Pegasus IIIM.3
Westland-Hill Pterodactyl V F.7/30	Rolls-Royce Goshawk I
Westland-Hill Pterodactyl V F.7/30	Rolls-Royce Goshawk IIS
Westland Lysander prot	Bristol Mercury IX
Westland Lysander I	Bristol Mercury XII
Westland Lysander I	Bristol Mercury XV
Westland Lysander II	Bristol Perseus XII
Westland Lysander III, IIIA	Bristol Mercury XX
Westland Lysander III, IIIA	Bristol Mercury 30
Westland Whirlwind I	Rolls-Royce Peregrine I
Westland Welkin I	Rolls-Royce Merlin 72
Westland Welkin I	Rolls-Royce Merlin 73
Westland Welkin II	Rolls-Royce Merlin 76
Westland Welkin II	Rolls-Royce Merlin 77
Westland Wyvern I	Rolls-Royce 46H Eagle Srs 22
Westland WS-51 Dragonfly H.R.1, 3, H.C.4	Alvis Leonides 521/1 Mk 50
Westland WS-51 Dragonfly H.R.5	Alvis Leonides 523/1 Mk 70
Westland WS-51 Mk 1A Dragonfly	Alvis Leonides 521/1 Mk 50
Westland WS-51 srs 2 Widgeon	Alvis Leonides 521/2
Westland S-55/2 Whirlwind H.A.S.5, 6, 7	Alvis Leonides Ma. 755/2 Mk 160
Westland S-55/2 Whirlwind H.A.S.7, 8	Alvis Leonides Ma. 755/1 Mk 155
Westland S-55/2 Whirlwind H.C.C.8	Alvis Leonides Ma. 755/2 Mk 160
Wheeler Slymph	A.B.C. Scorpion II
Wheeler Slymph	Blackburne Tomtit 690 c.c. (inverted)
White & Thompson 'Bognor Bloater'	Renault WB, WC 70 hp
White & Thompson No 3	Beardmore 120 hp
Wight (Admiralty Type) 840 Seaplane	Sunbeam Mohawk 225 hp
Wight A.1 Navyplane	Salmson (Canton-Unne) 200 hp
Wight 'Converted' Seaplane	Rolls-Royce Eagle VI 322 hp
Wight 'Converted' Seaplane	Sunbeam Maori II 260/275 hp
Wren Goldcrest	Scott Flying Squirrel
Youngman-Baynes High-Lift	De Havilland Gipsy Queen 32

N.R.	A.D.C. Airsix
N.R.	Alvis Leonides 501/1
N.R.	Alvis Leonides 501/2
N.R.	Alvis Leonides 502/1
N.R.	Alvis Leonides 502/2
N.R.	Alvis Leonides 502/3
N.R.	Alvis Leonides 503/2 Mk 22
N.R.	Alvis Leonides 514/2A
N.R.	Alvis Leonides 514/4A
N.R.	Alvis Leonides 514/6A
N.R.	Alvis Leonides 514/7A
N.R.	Alvis Leonides 522/1
N.R.	Alvis Leonides 531/8
N.R.	Alvis Leonides 532
N.R.	Alvis Pelides
N.R.	Armstrong Siddeley Cheetah VA
N.R.	Armstrong Siddeley Cheetah XI
N.R.	Armstrong Siddeley Cheetah 26
N.R.	Armstrong Siddeley Cheetah 27
N.R.	Armstrong Siddeley Genet Ma IV
N.R.	Armstrong Siddeley Tiger III
N.R.	Aspin Flat-Four
N.R.	Bristol Hercules VII
N.R.	Bristol Jupiter VIFL
N.R.	Bristol Jupiter VIFS
N.R.	Bristol Pegasus XVII
N.R.	Bristol Perseus XI
N.R.	Bristol Perseus XIVC Spl
N.R.	Bristol Titan IIF
N.R.	Caunter B
N.R.	Caunter C
N.R.	Caunter D
N.R.	de Havilland Gipsy Major 30
N.R.	Hart 35 hp
N.R.	Napier Lion XV
N.R.	Renault 190 hp 8Gd
N.R.	Rolls-Royce Condor III prot
N.R.	Rolls-Royce Condor IVA
N.R.	Rolls-Royce Condor V
N.R.	Rolls-Royce Condor VII
N.R.	Rolls-Royce Eagle X
N.R.	Rolls-Royce Eagle XV
N.R.	Rolls-Royce Eagle XVI
N.R.	Rolls-Royce 46H Eagle I
N.R.	Rolls-Royce 46H Eagle II
N.R.	Rolls-Royce Griffon I
N.R.	Rolls-Royce Griffon VIII
N.R.	Rolls-Royce Griffon 35
N.R.	Rolls-Royce Griffon 36
N.R.	Rolls-Royce Griffon 68
N.R.	Rolls-Royce Griffon 70
N.R.	Rolls-Royce Griffon 91
N.R.	Rolls-Royce Griffon 92
N.R.	Rolls-Royce Griffon 94
N.R.	Rolls-Royce Griffon 130
N.R.	Rolls-Royce Hawk II 100 hp
N.R.	Rolls-Royce Kestrel IB3
N.R.	Rolls-Royce Kestrel IB4
N.R.	Rolls-Royce Kestrel IB5
N.R.	Rolls-Royce Kestrel IMS
N.R.	Rolls-Royce Kestrel IIIMS.2
N.R.	Rolls-Royce Kestrel IIIMS.4
N.R.	Rolls-Royce Kestrel VII
N.R.	Rolls-Royce Kestrel XI
N.R.	Rolls-Royce Kestrel XII
N.R.	Rolls-Royce Kestrel XIV
N.R.	Rolls-Royce Kestrel XV
N.R.	Rolls-Royce Kestrel XVI(Spl)
N.R.	Rolls-Royce Merlin 22A
N.R.	Rolls-Royce Merlin 23A
N.R.	Rolls-Royce Merlin T.34
N.R.	Rolls-Royce Merlin 56
N.R.	Rolls-Royce Merlin 67
N.R.	Rolls-Royce Merlin 85B
N.R.	Rolls-Royce Merlin 104
N.R.	Rolls-Royce Merlin 110
N.R.	Rolls-Royce Merlin 112
N.R.	Rolls-Royce Merlin 132/133
N.R.	Rolls-Royce Merlin 150

N.R.	Rolls-Royce Merlin 228
N.R.	Rolls-Royce Merlin 300
N.R.	Rolls-Royce Merlin 301
N.R.	Rolls-Royce Merlin 724-1
N.R.	R.A.F.1
N.R.	R.A.F.1c
N.R.	R.A.F.1e
N.R.	R.A.F.3 200 hp
N.R.	R.A.F.4 140 hp
N.R.	R.A.F.4e 240 hp
N.R.	R.A.F.5b 170 hp
N.R.	R.A.F.7 300 hp
N.R.	Sunbeam Gurkha 240 hp
N.R.	Sunbeam Manitou 300 hp
N.R.	Sunbeam Viking 450 hp

PART 4

Engine Performance Figures

NOTE: Numbers in brackets refer to horsepower

Engine. Nominal/Rated BHP — N.R. = Engine Built, Not Flown Or Use in Flight Uncertain	Fuel Spec. – Where Stated (n/l = non-leaded) (TEL = Tetra-ethyl-lead)	Take-Off, S/L BHP, RPM, Max Boost	Normal, Continuous Climb (Rated) Power — Unsupercharged	Medium Supercharged	Fully Supercharged	Maximum Power (Emergency, Combat, 5 Minutes) — Unsupercharged	Medium Supercharged	Fully Supercharged	DRY WT LB
A.B.C. (30)	A. Pre-1923, 40-50 octane	30, 1,450	30, 1,450						155
A.B.C. (60)	A. Pre-1923, 40-50 octane	60, 1,450	60, 1,450						231
A.B.C. (100)	A. Pre-1923, 40-50 octane	115, 1,400	115, 1,400			140, 1,700			375
A.B.C. Gnat I (30)	A. Pre-1923, 40-50 octane	45, 1,920	45, 1,920			52, 2,200			115
A.B.C. Mosquito	A. Pre-1923, 40-50 octane	120,							180
A.B.C. Wasp I (160)	A. Pre-1923, 40-50 octane	170, 1,800	170, 1,800			185, 1,900			290
A.B.C. Wasp II	A. Pre-1923, 40-50 octane	176, 1,650	350						
A.B.C. Dragonfly I (320)	A. Pre-1923, 40-50 octane	320, 1,650	320, 1,650			340, 1,750			662
A.B.C. Dragonfly IA	A. Pre-1923, 40-50 octane	360, 1,650	360, 1,650						660
A.B.C. Gadfly	A. Pre-1923, 40-50 octane	65,							
A.B.C. (8)	B. BS.121/23, 74 oct, n/l	8, 4,500	3.75, 2,000			7-8, 4,500			41
A.B.C. Scorpion I	B. BS.121/23, 74 oct, n/l	30, 2,500	34, 2,300			30, 2,750			90
A.B.C. Scorpion II	B. BS.121/23, 74 oct, n/l	40, 2,750	34, 2,300			40, 2,750			109
A.B.C. Hornet	B. BS.121/23, 74 oct, n/l	75, 1,875	82, 2,175			81, 2,175			225
A.D.C. Airdisco	B. BS.121/23, 74 oct, n/l	120, 1800	120			140, 2,000			
A.D.C. Airsix (N.R.)	B. BS.121/23, 74 oct, n/l								
A.D.C Cirrus - see Cirrus	B. BS.121/23, 74 oct, n/l								
A.D.C. Nimbus	B. BS.121/23, 74 oct, n/l	305, 1,450	315, 1,450			332, 1,600			670
A.R.1 see Bentley B.R.1		150	150						
Aero Engines Dryad		40, 4,000	40, 4,000			52, 4,500			108
Aero Engines Pixie Was Weir	C. DTD 134, 73-77 oct, n/l	45, 2,300	45, 2,300			50, 2,550			112
Aero Engines Sprite I Was Douglas	C. DTD 134, 73-77 oct, n/l	22.7, 2,850	22.7, 2,850			24.3, 3,150			77
Aeronca-J.A.P., see J.A.P.	C. DTD 134, 73-77 oct, n/l								
Alvis 9ARS	D. DTD 224, 77 min oct n/l	430/450,							708
Alvis Leonides 501/1 (N.R.)	J. 100 oct, 100/130 grade	480/500 3,000, +6.5	440, 2,900, +2, 8,750			540, 3,000,	4,250		
Alvis Leonides 501/2 (N.R.)	J. 100 oct, 100/130 grade	480/500 3,000, +6.5	440, 2,900, +2, 8,750			540, 3,000,	4,250		742
Alvis Leonides 501/3	J. 100 oct, 100/130 grade	480/500 3,000, +6.5	440, 2,900, +2, 8,750			540, 3,000,	4,250		

Engine. Nominal/Rated BHP N.R. = Engine Built, Not Flown Or Use in Flight Uncertain	Fuel Spec. – Where Stated (n/l = non-leaded) (TEL = Tetra-ethyl-lead)	Take-Off, S/L BHP, RPM, Max Boost	Normal, Continuous Climb (Rated) Power. BHP, RPM, Max. Boost, Rated Alt.			Maximum Power (Emergency, Combat, 5 Minutes) BHP, RPM, Max. Boost, Altitude			DRY WT LB
			Unsupercharged	Medium Supercharged	Fully Supercharged	Unsupercharged	Medium Supercharged	Fully Supercharged	
Alvis Leonides 501/4	J. 100 oct, 100/130 grade	480/500 3,000, +6.5	440, 2,900, +2, 8,750				540, 3,000, 4,250		
Alvis Leonides 502/1 (N.R.)	J. 100 oct, 100/130 grade	520/540, 3,000, +8	460, 2,900, +3.5, 7,250				570, 3,000, +8, 2,000		770
Alvis Leonides 502/2 (N.R.)	J. 100 oct, 100/130 grade	520/540, 3,000, +8	460, 2,900, +3.5, 7,250				570, 3,000, +8, 2,000		
Alvis Leonides 502/3 (N.R.)	J. 100 oct, 100/130 grade	520/540, 3,000, +8	460, 2,900, +3.5, 7,250				570, 3,000, +8, 2,000		
Alvis Leonides 502/4	J. 100 oct, 100/130 grade	520/540, 3,000, +8	460, 2,900, +3.5, 7,250				570, 3,000, +8, 2,000		
Alvis Leonides 502/5	J. 100 oct, 100/130 grade	520/540, 3,000, +8	460, 2,900, +3.5, 7,250				570, 3,000, +8, 2,000		795
Alvis Leonides 502/7	J. 100 oct, 100/130 grade	520/540, 3,000, +8	460, 2,900, +3.5, 7,250				570, 3,000, +8, 2,000		
Alvis Leonides 503/2 (N.R.)	J. 100 oct, 100/130 grade	520/540, 3,000, +8	460, 2,900, +4.5, 6,000				545, 3,000, +8, 1,750		
Alvis Leonides 503/4	J. 100 oct, 100/130 grade	520/540, 3,000, +8	460, 2,900, +4.5, 6,000				545, 3,000, +8, 1,750		
Alvis Leonides 503/5	J. 100 oct, 100/130 grade	520/540, 3,000, +8	460, 2,900, +4.5, 6,000				545, 3,000, +8, 1,750		
Alvis Leonides 503/6A	J. 100 oct, 100/130 grade	520/540, 3,000, +8	460, 2,900, +4.5, 6,000				545, 3,000, +8, 1,750		
Alvis Leonides 503/7	J. 100 oct, 100/130 grade	500/520, 3,000, +8	460, 2,900, +4.5, 6,000				545, 3,000, +8, 1,750		810
Alvis Leonides 503/7A	J. 100 oct, 100/130 grade	540/560, 3,000, +8	460, 2,900, +4.5, 6,000				545, 3,000, +8, 1,750		
Alvis Leonides 503/8	J. 100 oct, 100/130 grade	540, 3,000, +8	460, 2,900, +4.5, 6,000				545, 3,000, +8, 1,750		
Alvis Leonides 504/5	J. 100 oct, 100/130 grade	540, 3,000, +8	495, 2,900, +6, 3,750				560, 3,000, +8, 1,750		
Alvis Leonides 504/8B	J. 100 oct, 100/130 grade	520/540, 3,000, +8	495, 2,900, +6, 3,750				560, 3,000, +8, 1,750		
Alvis Leonides 514	J. 100 oct, 100/130 grade	560, 3,000, +8	495, 2,900, +6, 3,750				560, 3,000, +8, 1,750		
Alvis Leonides 514/2A (N.R.)	J. 100 oct, 100/130 grade	560, 3,000, +8	495, 2,900, +6, 3,750				560, 3,000, +8, 1,750		
Alvis Leonides 514/4A (N.R.)	J. 100 oct, 100/130 grade	560, 3,000, +8	495, 2,900, +6, 3,750				560, 3,000, +8, 1,750		
Alvis Leonides 514/5A	J. 100 oct, 100/130 grade	560, 3,000, +8	495, 2,900, +6, 3,750				560, 3,000, +8, 1,750		
Alvis Leonides 514/6A (N.R.)	J. 100 oct, 100/130 grade	560, 3,000, +8	495, 2,900, +6, 3,750				560, 3,000, +8, 1,750		
Alvis Leonides 514/7A (N.R.)	J. 100 oct, 100/130 grade	560, 3,000, +8	495, 2,900, +6, 3,750				560, 3,000, +8, 1,750		
Alvis Leonides 514/8	J. 100 oct, 100/130 grade	560, 3,000, +8	495, 2,900, +6, 3,750				560, 3,000, +8, 1,750		
Alvis Leonides 514/8A	J. 100 oct, 100/130 grade	560, 3,000, +8	495, 2,900, +6, 3,750				560, 3,000, +8, 1,750		795
Alvis Leonides 521/1	J. 100 oct, 100/130 grade	500 3,000, +6.5	400, 2,800, +2.5, 7,750				515, 3,000, +6.5, 3,250		790
Alvis Leonides 521/2	J. 100 oct, 100/130 grade	500 3,000, +6.5	400, 2,800, +2.5, 7,750				515, 3,000, +6.5, 3,250		
Alvis Leonides 522/1 (N.R.)	J. 100 oct, 100/130 grade	500 3,000, +6.5	400, 2,800, +2.5, 7,750				515, 3,000, +6.5, 3,250		690
Alvis Leonides 522/2	J. 100 oct, 100/130 grade	500 3,000, +6.5	400, 2,800, +2.5, 7,750				515, 3,000, +6.5, 3,250		

Engine, Nominal/Rated BHP. N.R. = Engine Built, Not Flown Or Use in Flight Uncertain	Fuel Spec. – Where Stated (n/l = non-leaded) (TEL = Tetra-ethyl-lead)	Take-Off, S/L BHP, RPM. Max Boost	Normal, Continuous Climb (Rated) Power. BHP, RPM, Max. Boost, Rated Alt. Unsupercharged	Medium Supercharged	Fully Supercharged	Maximum Power (Emergency, Combat, 5 Minutes) BHP, RPM, Max. Boost, Altitude Unsupercharged	Medium Supercharged	Fully Supercharged	DRY WT LB
Alvis Leonides 523/1	J. 100 oct, 100/130 grade	520/540 3,000, +8		460, 2,900, +4.5, 6,000			545, 3,000, +8, 1,750		
Alvis Leonides 524/1	J. 100 oct, 100/130 grade	500/520, 3,200, +7		390, 2,800, +2, 9,250			540, 3,200, +7-8, 4,750		730
Alvis Leonides 525/1	J. 100 oct, 100/130 grade	500/520, 3,200, +7		390, 2,800, +2, 9,250			540, 3,200, +7-8, 4,750		790
Alvis Leonides 531/8 (N.R.)	J. 100 oct, 100/130 grade	640, 3,200, +8		590, 3,000, +6.5, 2,750			650, 3,200, +8, 2,000		850
Alvis Leonides 531/8B	J. 100 oct, 100/130 grade	625, 3,200, +8		585, 3,000, +6.5, 2,750			635, 3,200, +8, 2,000		
Alvis Leonides 532 (N.R.)	J. 100 oct, 100/130 grade	620, 3,200, +8,		565, 3,000, +6.5, 7,000			655, 3,200, +8, 7,000		
Alvis Leonides Ma.702/1	J. 100 oct, 100/130 grade	850, 3,000, +9.25		635, 2,900, +3.5, 8,500			870, 3,000, +9.25, 1,750		1,200
Alvis Leonides Ma.755/1	J. 100 oct, 100/130 grade	770, 2,900, +6.5		695, 2,900, +3.5, 8,500			795, 2,900, +6.5, 3,250		1,065
Alvis Leonides Ma.755/2	J. 100 oct, 100/130 grade	770, 2,900, +6.5		695, 2,900, +3.5, 8,500			795, 2,900, +6.5, 3,250		1,050
Anzani (British) (35)		26, 2,500	26, 2,500			34, 3,000			99
Anzani (British) (45)	A. Pre-1923, 40-50 octane	41, 1,200	41, 1,200			45, 1,300			154
Anzani (British) (60)	A. Pre-1923, 40-50 octane	54.6, 1,200	54.6, 1,200			60, 1,300			200
Anzani (British) (100)	A. Pre-1923, 40-50 octane	100, 1,200	100, 1,200			105, 1,300			398
Anzani (Brit. Luton) (35)	A. Pre-1923, 40-50 octane	35, 3,000	23, 2,700			35, 3,000			110
Armst Sidd Cheetah V	D. DTD 224, 77 min oct n/l	262, 1,995	275, 2,100			303, 2,400			566
Armst Sidd Cheetah VA (N.R.)	D. DTD 224, 77 min oct n/l	270, 2,100	285, 2,100			326, 2,400			596
Armst Sidd Cheetah VI	D. DTD 224, 77 min oct n/l	307, 2,100, +1.5		295, 2,100, +.5, 6,000			313, 2,300, +1.5, 7,000		592
Armst Sidd Cheetah VIA	D. DTD 224, 77 min oct n/l	307, 2,100, +1.5		295, 2,100, +.5, 6,000			313, 2,300, +1.5, 7,000		592
Armst Sidd Cheetah IX	H. 87 oct, higher with 100	340, 2,100 F/T +1.5		310, 2,100, +.5, 6,000			360, 2,425, +2.5, 7,300		635
Armst Sidd Cheetah X	H. 87 oct, higher with 100	360, 2,300 F/T		340, 2,300, +2.25, 6,750			375, 2,425, +2.25, 7,000		720
Armst Sidd Cheetah XI (N.R.)	H. 87 oct, higher with 100	460, 2,825		415, 2,650, +??, 7,500			435, 2,825, 8,750		750
Armst Sidd Cheetah XII	H. 87 oct, higher with 100								720
Armst Sidd Cheetah XV	H. 87 oct, higher with 1004	20, 2,550, +4		385, 2,300, +2.75, 3,600			405, 2,425, +2.75, 4,000		805
Armst Sidd Cheetah XVII	H. 87 oct, higher with 1004	20, 2,550		385, 2,300, +??, 3,600			405, 2,425, +2.75, 4,000		805
Armst Sidd Cheetah XVIII	H. 87 oct, higher with 1004	20, 2,550		385, 2,300, +??, 3,600			405, 2,425, +2.75, 4,000		805
Armst Sidd Cheetah XIX	H. 87 oct, higher with 1003	20, 2,300, F/T		310, 2,300, +2.25, 6,000			355, 2,425, +2.25, 7,000		705
Armst Sidd Cheetah 25	H. 87 oct, higher with 100	475, 2,700, +6 F/T		385, 2,300, +2.75, 3,500			405, 2,425, +2.75, 4,000		805
Armst Sidd Cheetah 26 (N.R.)	H. 87 oct, higher with 100	475, 2,700, +6 F/T		385, 2,300, +2.75, 3,500			405, 2,425, +2.75, 4,000		805

Engine, Nominal/Rated BHP N.R. = Engine Built, Not Flown Or Use in Flight Uncertain	Fuel Spec. – Where Stated (n/l = non-leaded) (TEL = Tetra-ethyl-lead)	Take-Off, S/L BHP, RPM, Max Boost	Normal, Continuous Climb (Rated) Power. BHP, RPM, Max. Boost, Rated Alt. — Unsupercharged	Medium Supercharged	Fully Supercharged	Maximum Power (Emergency, Combat, 5 Minutes) BHP, RPM, Max. Boost, Altitude — Unsupercharged	Medium Supercharged	Fully Supercharged	DRY WT LB
Armst Sidd Cheetah 27 (N.R.)	H. 87 oct, higher with 100	475, 2,700, +6 F/T		385, 2,300, +2.75, 3,500			405, 2,425, +2.75, 4,000		805
Armst Sidd Civet I	D. DTD 224, 77 min oct n/l	145, 2,090	150, 2,200			165, 2,425 S/L			327
Armst Sidd Deerhound I	G. DTD 230, 87 oct	1,115, 1,500							
Armst Sidd Genet I	C. DTD 134, 73-77 oct, n/l	65, 1,850	60, 1,800			80, 2,200 S/L			168
Armst Sidd Genet II	C. DTD 134, 73-77 oct, n/l	80, 2,000	80, 2,200			88, 2,200 S/L			210
Armst Sidd Genet IIA	C. DTD 134, 73-77 oct, n/l	80, 2,200							
Armst Sidd Genet Ma I	D. DTD 224, 77 min oct n/l	105, 2,200	106, 2,200			113, 2,420, S/L			242
Armst Sidd Genet Ma IA	D. DTD 224, 77 min oct n/l	145, 2,090	150, 2,200						327
Armst Sidd Genet Ma III	D. DTD 224, 77 min oct n/l	145, 2,090	150, 2,200			165, 2,425 S/L			360
Armst Sidd Genet Ma IV	(N.R.)D. DTD 224, 77 min oct n/l	160, 2,400	160, 2,400			180, 2,700, 2,000			367
Armst Sidd Hyena	D. DTD 224, 77 min oct n/l	618, 2,000		615, 2,250					
Armst Sidd Jaguar I	C. DTD 134, 73-77 oct, n/l	680							
Armst Sidd Jaguar II	C. DTD 134, 73-77 oct, n/l	360, 1,650	320, 1,500			360, 1,650, 2,000			710
Armst Sidd Jaguar III	C. DTD 134, 73-77 oct, n/l	385, 1,620	385, 1,620			425, 1,700, 2,000			798
Armst Sidd Jaguar IIIA	C. DTD 134, 73-77 oct, n/l	380, 1,620	380, 1,620			412, 1,780, 2,000			798
Armst Sidd Jaguar IV	C. DTD 134, 73-77 oct, n/l	385, 1,700	420, 1,870, 2,000			420, 1,870, 2,000			786
Armst Sidd Jaguar IVA	C. DTD 134, 73-77 oct, n/l	385, 1,800	445, 1,870, 2,000			440, 1,870, 2,000			812
Armst Sidd Jaguar IV*	C. DTD 134, 73-77 oct, n/l	385, 1,700	420, 1,870, 2,000			420, 1,870, 2,000			786
Armst Sidd Jaguar IVC	C. DTD 134, 73-77 oct, n/l	432, 1,800	449, 1,870, 2,000			440, 2,000, 2,000			822
Armst Sidd Jaguar IV(S)		365, 1,700			385, 1,870, 9,500			380, 2,000, S/L	1,048
Armst Sidd Jaguar IV(G)		440, 2,000	480, 2,200, 2,000			510, 2,200, 2,000			
Armst Sidd Jaguar IV(GS)	360, 2,000	400, 2,200, 15,000	400, 2,200, 15,000		400, 2,200, 15,000			380, 2,200, 15,000	910
Armst Sidd Jaguar V									
Armst Sidd Jaguar VI									
Armst Sidd Jaguar VI(S)									
Armst Sidd Jaguar VIC		490, 1,850	470, 2,000						910
Armst Sidd Jaguar VID									
Armst Sidd Jaguar VIIA		370, 2,000, +1.1lb			400, 2,000, +62lb, 14,500			457, 2,200, +1.1, S/L	910

Engine, Nominal/Rated BHP. N.R. = Engine Built, Not Flown Or Use in Flight Uncertain	Fuel Spec. – Where Stated (nil = non-leaded) (TEL = Tetra-ethyl-lead)	Take-Off, S/L BHP, RPM, Max Boost	Normal, Continuous Climb (Rated) Power. BHP, RPM, Max. Boost, Rated Alt.			Maximum Power (Emergency, Combat, 5 Minutes) BHP, RPM, Max. Boost, Altitude			DRY WT LB
			Fully Supercharged	Medium Supercharged	Unsupercharged	Fully Supercharged	Medium Supercharged	Unsupercharged	
Armst Sidd Jaguar VIII		370, 2,000, +1.1lb	400, 2,000, +62lb, 14,500			455, 2,200 +??, 15,000			958
Armst Sidd Leopard I		700, 1,500					770, 1,650		1,465
Armst Sidd Leopard II		700, 1,500			800, 1,700				1,650
Armst Sidd Leopard III		800, 1,700			800, 1,700				1,703
Armst Sidd Leopard IIIA		800, 1,700			800, 1,700			855, 1,870	1,615
Armst Sidd Lynx I	C. DTD 134, 73-77 oct, n/l	145, 1,500						150, 1,620	390
Armst Sidd Lynx II	C. DTD 134, 73-77 oct, n/l	184, 1,620			1,620			200, 2,000	512
Armst Sidd Lynx III	C. DTD 134, 73-77 oct, n/l	188, 1,620			184, 1,620			215, 2,000	
Armst Sidd Lynx IV	C. DTD 134, 73-77 oct, n/l	188, 1,620			170/180, 1,620			185/195, 1,780	610
Armst Sidd Lynx IV (G)	C. DTD 134, 73-77 oct, n/l								
Armst Sidd Lynx IV (MOD)	C. DTD 134, 73-77 oct, n/l	188, 1,620			187/195, 1,700			200/210, 1,870	
Armst Sidd Lynx IV (S)	C. DTD 134, 73-77 oct, n/l					200, 1,900, 11,500			540
Armst Sidd Lynx IVA	C. DTD 134, 73-77 oct, n/l	188, 1,620			187/195, 1,700				
Armst Sidd Lynx IVC	C. DTD 134, 73-77 oct, n/l	208/225, 1,805			215, 1,900			240, 2,090	515
Armst Sidd Lynx IV*	C. DTD 134, 73-77 oct, n/l	188, 1,620			205/215, 1,900			220/230, 2,090	
Armst Sidd Lynx V (Major) See Cheetah		230,							540
Armst Sidd Mongoose I	B. BS.121/23, 74 oct, n/l	125, 1,620						138, 1,780	340
Armst Sidd Mongoose II	B. BS.121/23, 74 oct, n/l	155, 1,850			155, 1,850			165, 2,035	370
Armst Sidd Mongoose III	B. BS.121/23, 74 oct, n/l	155, 1,850							360
Armst Sidd Mongoose IIIA	B. BS.121/23, 74 oct, n/l	150, 1,850						165, 2,035	360
Armst Sidd Mongoose IIIC	B. BS.121/23, 74 oct, n/l	158, 1,850			158, 1,850			170, 2,035	360
Armst Sidd Ounce	B. BS.121/23, 74 oct, n/l	45, 1,500			45, 1,600			50, 1,800	170
Armst Sidd Panther II (PF)	D. DTD 224, 77 min oct n/l	525, 2,000, -625			535, 2,000, +625, 3,000			600, 2,300, +0, 3,000	915
Armst Sidd Panther IIA (GF)	D. DTD 224, 77 min oct n/l					973			
Armst Sidd Panther III	D. DTD 224, 77 min oct n/l	450, 2,000,	510, 2,000, 12,000			565, 2,300, 12,000			990
Armst Sidd Panther IIIA	D. DTD 224, 77 min oct n/l	460, 2,000, -0.5	502, 2,000, -.5, 12,000			565, 2,300, 12,000			
Armst Sidd Panther VI	D. DTD 224, 77 min oct n/l	560, 2,250							

Engine, Nominal/Rated BHP N.R. = Engine Built, Not Flown Or Use in Flight Uncertain	Fuel Spec. – Where Stated (n/l = non-leaded) (TEL = Tetra-ethyl-lead)	Take-Off, S/L BHP, RPM, Max Boost	Normal, Continuous Climb (Rated) Power. BHP, RPM, Max. Boost, Rated Alt.			Maximum Power (Emergency, Combat, 5 Minutes) BHP, RPM, Max. Boost, Altitude			DRY WT LB
			Unsupercharged	Medium Supercharged	Fully Supercharged	Unsupercharged	Medium Supercharged	Fully Supercharged	
Armst Sidd Panther VIA	D. DTD 224, 77 min oct n/l	530, 2,100, +1	560, 2,100, 5,000				625, 2,415, -.375, 6,700		1,068
Armst Sidd Panther VII	D. DTD 224, 77 min oct n/l	555, 2,100, +1.5			565, 2,100, zero, 11,500			638, 2,400, +1.0, 12,000	980
Armst Sidd Panther IXA	G. DTD 230, 87 oct	735, 2,250, +2.5		580/605, 2,100, -125, 3,000			752, 2,655, +??, 4,000		980
Armst Sidd Panther X	G. DTD 230, 87 oct	672, 2,250, +2.5		700, 2,250, + , 3,000			752, 2,600, +1.25, 4,000		1,068
Armst Sidd Panther XI	G. DTD 230, 87 oct	600, 2,100		600, 2,100, + , 5,000			674, 2,450, +??, 6,400		1,068
Armst Sidd Serval I	D. DTD 224, 77 min oct n/l	340, 2,000	334, 1,900			356, 2,200			714
Armst Sidd Serval III	D. DTD 224, 77 min oct n/l	310, 1,820		340, 2,000, 4,000			375, 2,200, 4,500		687
Armst Sidd Serval IIIB	D. DTD 224, 77 min oct n/l	310, 1,820		340, 2,000, 4,000			375, 2,200, +??, 4,500		665
Armst Sidd Serval IV	D. DTD 224, 77 min oct n/l	310, 1,820		340, 2,000, 4,000			368, 2,200, 4,500		645
Armst Sidd Serval V	D. DTD 224, 77 min oct n/l	370, 1, 2,000+		340, 2,000, +1, 6,500			381, 2,300, -0.5, 6,500		730
Armst Sidd Tiger I		570, 1,900							1,044
Armst Sidd Tiger III (N.R.)		610, 2,050		610, 2,050, +??, 2,000			650, 2,350, +??, 4,000		1,185
Armst Sidd Tiger IV		720, 2,150		700, 2,100, +??, 5,000			750, 2,450, +??, 6,000		1,212
Armst Sidd Tiger VI		760, 2,150							1,180
Armst Sidd Tiger VIC	G. DTD 230, 87 oct								
Armst Sidd Tiger VIII	G. DTD 230, 87 oct	918, 2,375, +2.5		840, 2,375, +.5, 6,250	760, 2,200, +.5, 12,750		862, 2,450, +.5, 6,750	782, 2,450, +.5, 14,250	1,294
Armst Sidd Tiger IX	G. DTD 230, 87 oct	830, 2,375, +2.5		775/805, +.25, 6,250			810, 2,450, +.25, 6,500		1,220
Armst Sidd Tiger IXC	G. DTD 230, 87 oct	880, 2,375		805, 2,375, +??, 6,250			805, 2,450, +??, 7,200		1,188
Armst Sidd Tiger X	G. DTD 230, 87 oct								
Armst Sidd Tiger XI	G. DTD 230, 87 oct								
Aspin Flat-four (N.R.)		80, 4,800	80, 4,800			80, 5,000			
Austro-Daimler (90) See also Beardmore	A. Pre-1923, 40-50 octane	82, 1,200	82, 1,200			90, 1,350			316
Austro-Daimler (120) See also Beardmore	A. Pre-1923, 40-50 octane	92, 1,200	92, 1,200			118.4, 1,250			420
Austro-Daimler (160) See also Beardmore	A. Pre-1923, 40-50 octane								
Avro Alpha (90)		90,							
B H P (200)	A. Pre-1923, 40-50 octane	200, 1,350	200, 1,350			235, 1,400			690

Engine, Nominal/Rated BHP. N.R. = Engine Built, Not Flown Or Use in Flight Uncertain	Fuel Spec. – Where Stated (n/l = non-leaded) (TEL = Terra-ethyl-lead)	Take-Off, S/L BHP, RPM, Max Boost	Normal, Continuous Climb (Rated) Power. BHP, RPM, Max. Boost, Rated Alt. Unsupercharged	Medium Supercharged	Fully Supercharged	Maximum Power (Emergency, Combat, 5 Minutes) BHP, RPM, Max. Boost, Altitude Unsupercharged	Medium Supercharged	Fully Supercharged	DRY WT LB
B H P (230) Galloway Adriatic	A. Pre-1923, 40-50 octane	236, 1,400	236, 1,400			250, 1,500			690
B H P (500) Galloway Atlantic	A. Pre-1923, 40-50 octane	500, 1,500	500, 1,500			510, 1,600			1,210
Beardmore (90)	A. Pre-1923, 40-50 octane	90, 1,300	90, 1,300			90, 1,300			
Beardmore (120)	A. Pre-1923, 40-50 octane	133, 1,200	133, 1,200			154, 1,400			545
Beardmore (160)	A. Pre-1923, 40-50 octane	180, 1,350	180, 1,350			186, 1,450			615
Beardmore Simoon I		1,100, 1,250	1,100, 1,250						2,770
Beardmore Tornado III		585, 900	585, 900			720, 1,000			4,197
Beardmore Typhoon I		925, 1,350	925, 1,350						2,233
Beatty (50)	A. Pre-1923, 40-50 octane	40, 1,450	40, 1,450						180
Bentley B.R.1 (A.R.1) (150)	A. Pre-1923, 40-50 octane	158, 1,250	158, 1,250			160, 1,300			408
Bentley B.R.2, (230)	A. Pre-1923, 40-50 octane	230, 1,300	238, 1,300			234, 1,350			475
Bentley B.R.2, (245)	A. Pre-1923, 40-50 octane	245, 1,300	245, 1,300			240, 1,400			498
Blackburn Bombardier 203	DTD 230, 87 oct	203, 2,100	2,000			180, 2,450			325
Blackburn Bombardier 702	DTD 230, 87 oct	180, 2,600	158, 2,300			180, 2,600			350
Blackburn Cirrus Major I	73 OCT n/l	125, 2,100	125, 2,100			135, 2,350			310
Blackburn Cirrus Major II	73 OCT n/l	138, 2,200	145, 2,200			155, 2,450			333
Blackburn Cirrus Major III	DTD 230, 87 oct	138, 2,200	145, 2,200			155, 2,450			333
Blackburn Cirrus Midget		48, 2,300	48, 2,300			55, 2,600			155
Blackburn Cirrus Minor I	73 OCT n/l	82, 2,300	82, 2,300			90, 2,600			200
Blackburn Cirrus Minor II	77 oct DTD224	90, 2,300	90, 2,300			100, 2,600			234
Blackburne Thrush		38, 2,760	30, 2,500						132
Blackburne Tomtit 690 c.c.		26, 3,250	15, 2,000			29, 4,500			79
Bristol Aquila I	C. DTD 134, 73-77 oct, n/l	420, 2,250, FT		420, 2,250, FT, SL			500, 2,600, FT, SL		830
Bristol Centaurus I	J. 100 oct, 100/130 grade	2,000, 2,700, +5.5		1,800, 2,250, +4, 4,500			2,150, 2,650, +5.5, 4,500		
Bristol Centaurus IV	J. 100 oct, 100/130 grade	2,300, 2,700, +8		2,095, 2,400, +6, 5,000	1,850, 2,400, +6, 14,250		2,375, 2,700, +8, 4,000	2,030, 2,700, +8, 13,250	
Bristol Centaurus V	J. 100 oct, 100/130 grade	2,500, 2,700, +8.5		2,150, 2,400, +6, 3,000	1,975, 2,400, +6, 12,750		2,520, 2,700, +8.5, 1,000	2,225, 2,700, +8.5, 11,000	
Bristol Centaurus VI	J. 100 oct, 100/130 grade	2,500, 2,700, +8.5		2,150, 2,400, +6, 3,000	1,975, 2,400, +6, 12,750		2,520, 2,700, +8.5, 1,000	2,225, 2,700, +8.5, 7,000	
Bristol Centaurus VII	J. 100 oct, 100/130 grade	2,400, 2,700, +7.75		2,150, 2,400, +6, 3,000	1,975, 2,400, +6, 12,750		2,440, 2,700, +7.75, 1,750	2,140, 2,700, +7.75, 12,000	

Engine. Nominal/Rated BHP; N.R. = Engine Built, Not Flown; Or Use in Flight Uncertain	Fuel Spec. – Where Stated (n/l = non-leaded) (TEL = Tetra-ethyl-lead)	Take-Off, S/L BHP, RPM, Max Boost	Normal, Continuous Climb (Rated Power). BHP, RPM, Max. Boost, Rated Alt.			Maximum Power (Emergency, Combat, 5 Minutes) BHP, RPM, Max. Boost, Altitude			DRY WT LB
			Unsupercharged	Medium Supercharged	Fully Supercharged	Unsupercharged	Medium Supercharged	Fully Supercharged	
Bristol Centaurus VIII	J. 100 oct, 100/130 grade	2,500, 2,700, +8.5		2,150, 2,400, +6, 3,000	1,975, 2,400, +6, 12,750		2,520, 2,700, +8.5, 1,000	2,225, 2,700, +8.5, 11,000	
Bristol Centaurus IX	J. 100 oct, 100/130 grade	2,500, 2,700, +8.5		2,150, 2,400, +6, 3,000	1,975, 2,400, +6, 12,750		2,520, 2,700, +8.5, 1,000	2,225, 2,700, +8.5, 11,000	
Bristol Centaurus X	J. 100 oct, 100/130 grade	2,500, 2,700, +8.5		2,150, 2,400, +6, 3,000	1,975, 2,400, +6, 12,750		2,520, 2,700, +8.5, 1,000	2,225, 2,700, +8.5, 11,000	
Bristol Centaurus XI	J. 100 oct, 100/130 grade	2,500, 2,700, +8.5		2,150, 2,400, +6, 3,000	1,975, 2,400, +6, 12,750		2,520, 2,700, +8.5, 1,000	2,225, 2,700, +8.5, 11,000 2,695	
Bristol Centaurus XII	J. 100 oct, 100/130 grade	2,300, 2,700, +8.5		2,100, 2,400, +6, 6,000	1,920, 2,400, +6, 18,500		2,400, 2,700, +8.5, 5,500	2,130, 2,700, +8.5, 20,000	
Bristol Centaurus XIV	J. 100 oct, 100/130 grade	2,300, 2,700, +8.5		2,100, 2,400, +6, 6,000	1,920, 2,400, +6, 18,500		2,400, 2,700, +8.5, 5,500	2,130, 2,700, +8.5, 20,000	
Bristol Centaurus XV	J. 100 oct, 100/130 grade	2,300, 2,700, +8.5		2,100, 2,400, +6, 6,000	1,920, 2,400, +6, 18,500		2,400, 2,700, +8.5, 5,500	2,130, 2,700, +8.5, 20,000	
Bristol Centaurus XVI	J. 100 oct, 100/130 grade	2,300, 2,700, +8.5		2,100, 2,400, +6, 6,000	1,920, 2,400, +6, 18,500		2,400, 2,700, +8.5, 5,500	2,130, 2,700, +8.5, 20,000	
Bristol Centaurus XVIII	J. 100 oct, 100/130 grade	2,470, 2,700, +9.5		2,160, 2,400, +6.5, 5,000	1,975, 2,400, +6.5, 15,750		2,550, 2,700, +9.5, 4,000	2,250, 2,700, +9.5, 16,500	
Bristol Centaurus XX Double Installation	J. 100 oct, 100/130 grade	2,360, 2,700, +9.5		2,090, 2,400, +6.5, 5,000	1,900, 2,400, +6.5, 15,750		2,435, 2,700, +9.5, 4,000	2,155, 2,700, +9.5, 16,500 8,390	
Bristol Centaurus 57	J. 100 oct, 100/130 grade	2,470, 2,700, +9.5		2,160, 2,400, +6.5, 5,000	1,975, 2,400, +6.5, 15,750		2,550, 2,700, +9.5, 4,000	2,280, 2,700, +9.5, 16,500	
Bristol Centaurus 58	J. 100 oct, 100/130 grade	2,470, 2,700, +9.5		2,160, 2,400, +6.5, 5,000	1,975, 2,400, +6.5, 15,750		2,550, 2,700, +9.5, 4,000	2,280, 2,700, +9.5, 16,500	
Bristol Centaurus 59	J. 100 oct, 100/130 grade	2,470, 2,700, +9.5		2,160, 2,400, +6.5, 5,000	1,975, 2,400, +6.5, 15,750		2,550, 2,700, +9.5, 4,000	2,280, 2,700, +9.5, 16,500	
Bristol Centaurus 70	J. 100 oct, 100/130 grade	2,470, 2,700, +9.5		2,160, 2,400, +6.5, 5,000	2,550, 2,700, +9.5, 4,000		2,550, 2,700, +9.5, 4,000		
Bristol Centaurus 71	J. 100 oct, 100/130 grade	2,470, 2,700, +9.5		2,160, 2,400, +6.5, 5,000	2,550, 2,700, +9.5, 4,000		2,550, 2,700, +9.5, 4,000		
Bristol Centaurus 100	J. 100 oct, 100/130 grade	2,470, 2,700, +9.5		2,160, 2,400, +6.5, 5,000	1,975, 2,400, +6.5, 15,750		2,550, 2,700, +9.5, 4,000	2,280, 2,700, +9.5, 16,500	
Bristol Centaurus 130	J. 100 oct, 100/130 grade	2,450, 2,700, +10.5		2,090, 2,400, +7.0, 5,500	2,550, 2,700, +10.5, 5,250		2,550, 2,700, +10.5, 5,250		
Bristol Centaurus 165	J. 100 oct, 100/130 grade	2,625, 2,800, +13.5		2,265, 2,500, +9, 5,350	2,110, 2,500, +9, 12,000		2,705, 2,800, +13.5, 4,000		
Bristol Centaurus 173	J. 100 oct, 100/130 grade	2,625, 2,800, +13		2,370, 2,500, +10, 5,000			2,740, 2,800, +13, 5,750		
Bristol Centaurus 175	J. 100 oct, 100/130 grade	2,625, 2,800, +12		2,370, 2,500, +9.5, 5,000			2,740, 2,800, +12, 5,750		
Bristol Centaurus 373	J. 100 oct, 100/130 grade	2,980, 2,800, +14.5		2,570, 2,500, +10.5, 4,500			3,030, 2,800, +14.5, 2,250		
Bristol Centaurus 568	J. 100 oct, 100/130 grade	2,470, 2,700, +9.5		2,160, 2,400, +6.5, 5,000	1,975, 2,400, +6.5, 15,750		2,550, 2,700, +9.5, 4,000	2,280, 2,700, +9.5, 16,500	
Bristol Centaurus 631	J. 100 oct, 100/130 grade	2,450, 2,700, +10.5		2,090, 2,400, +7.0, 5,500			2,550, 2,700, +10.5, 5,250		
Bristol Centaurus 661	J. 100 oct, 100/130 grade	2,625, 2,800, +13.5		2,265, 2,500, +9, 5,500	2,110, 2,500, +9, 12,000		2,705, 2,800, +13.5, 4,000		
Bristol Cherub I	B. BS.121/23, 74 oct, n/l	32, 3,200	31, 2,500, S/L			32, 3,200, S/L			107.5
Bristol Cherub II	B. BS.121/23, 74 oct, n/l	34, 3,200	32, 2,500 S/L			34, 3,200, S/L			
Bristol Cherub III	B. BS.121/23, 74 oct, n/l	36, 3,200	33, 2,900, S/L			36, 3,200, S/L			107.5

Engine, Nominal/Rated BHP N.R. = Engine Built, Not Flown Or Use in Flight Uncertain	Fuel Spec. – Where Stated (nil = non-leaded) (TEL = Tetra-ethyl-lead)	Take-Off, S/L BHP, RPM, Max Boost	Normal, Continuous Climb (Rated) Power. BHP, RPM, Max. Boost, Rated Alt.			Maximum Power (Emergency, Combat, 5 Minutes) BHP, RPM, Max. Boost, Altitude			DRY WT LB
			Unsupercharged	Medium Supercharged	Fully Supercharged	Unsupercharged	Medium Supercharged	Fully Supercharged	
Bristol Draco	C. DTD 134, 73-77 oct, n/l	570, 2,000	530, 2,000, 4,500				650, 2,300, 4,500		1,093
Bristol Hercules I	G. DTD 230, 87 oct	1,325, 2,800, +3.25		1150, 2,400, +1.75, 5,000			1,375, 2,750, +3.25, 4,000		1,845
Bristol Hercules II	G. DTD 230, 87 oct	1,325, 2,800, +3.25		1150, 2,400, +1.75, 5,000			1,375, 2,750, +3.25, 4,000		
Bristol Hercules III	J. 100 oct, 100/130 grade	1,400, 2,800, +4		1,170, 2,400, +2.5, 2,500	1,090, 2,400, +2.5, 14,500		1,425, 2,800, +4, 1,500	1,210, 2,800, +4, 15,000	
Bristol Hercules III	H. 87 oct, higher with 100	1,375, 2,800, +4		1,155, 2,400, +2.5, 4,000	1,070, 2,400, +2.5, 15,000		1,410, 2,800, +4, 2,750	1,250, 2,800, +4, 16,750	
Bristol Hercules IV	G. DTD 230, 87 oct	1,380, 2,800, +3		1,050, 2,400, +.5, 4,500			1,220, 2,800, +.5, 5,500		
Bristol Hercules IVHY	G. DTD 230, 87 oct	1,380, 2,800, +3		1,050, 2,400, +.5, 4,500			1,220, 2,800, +.5, 5,500		
Bristol Hercules V	G. DTD 230, 87 oct	1,380, 2,800, +3		1,050, 2,400, +.5, 4,500			1,220, 2,800, +.5, 5,500		
Bristol Hercules VI	J. 100 oct, 100/130 grade	1,615, 2,900, +8.25		1,400, 2,400, +6, 4,750	1,300, 2,400, +6, 13,500		1,750, 2,800, +8.25, 6,500	1,545, 2,800, +8.25, 15,500	
Bristol Hercules VI	G. DTD 230, 87 oct	1,350, 2,800 +5		1,145, 2,400, +2.5, 9,500	1,045, 2,400, +2.5, 16,500		1,450, 2,800, +5, 8,500	1,265, 2,800, +5, 15,750	
Bristol Hercules VII (N.R.)	J. 100 oct, 100/130 grade	1,700, 2,900, +8.25		1,400, 2,400, +6, 1,500			1,720, 2,900, 8.25, 1,250		
Bristol Hercules VIII	G. DTD 230, 87 oct	1,360, 2,800, +4		1,150, 2,400, +2.7, 7,500	1,070, 2,400, +2, 33,500		1,460, 2,800, +2, 7,000	1,080, 2,800, +4, 36,000	
Bristol Hercules X	G. DTD 230, 87 oct	1,420, 2,800 +4		1,165, 2,400, +2.5, 4,000	1,080, 2,400, +2.5, 15,000		1,460, 2,800, +4, 2,500	1,280, 2,800, +4, 16,000	
Bristol Hercules XI	H. 100 oct, less with 87	1,505, 2,800 +6.75		1,325, 2,500, +3.5, 2,500	1,200, 2,500, +3.5, 14,000		1,575, 2,900, +6.75, 500	1,510, 2,800, +6.75, 11,250	
Bristol Hercules XI	G. DTD 230, 87 oct	1,590, 2,900, +5		1,260, 2,400, +2.5, 4,000	1,135, 2,400, +2.5, 15,500		1,575, 2,800, +5, 1,500	1,590, 2,800, +5, 13,500	
Bristol Hercules XIV	J. 100 oct, 100/130 grade	1,500, 2,800, +3.5		1,185, 2,400, +1.5, 2,000	1,055, 2,400, 33,000		1,500, 2,800, +3.5, S/L		
Bristol Hercules XVMT	J. 100 oct, 100/130 grade	1,650, 2,800,		1,290, 2,400, , 21,000			1,055, 2,800, 33,000		
Bristol Hercules XVI	J. 100 oct, 100/130 grade	1,615, 2,900, +8.25		1,400, 2,400, +6, 4,750	1,300, 2,400, +6, 13,500		1,715, 2,900, +8.25, 6,500	1,545, 2,900, +8.25, 15,500	
Bristol Hercules XVI	G. DTD 230, 87 oct	1,350, 2,800, +5		1,145, 2,400, +2.5, 9,500	1,045, 2,400, +2.5, 16,500		1,450, 2,800, +5, 8,500	1,265, 2,800, +5, 15,750	
Bristol Hercules XVII	J. 100 oct, 100/130 grade	1,725, 2,900, +8.25		1,395, 2,400, +6, 1,500			1,735, 2,900, +8.25, 500		
Bristol Hercules XVII	G. DTD 230, 87 oct	1,690, 2,800, +8.25		1,395, 2,400, +6, 1,500			1,695, 2,800, +8.25, 250		
Bristol Hercules XVIII	J. 100 oct, 100/130 grade	1,700, 2,900, +8.25		1,720, 2,400, +6, 1,250	1,600, 2,400, +6, 10,500		1,820, 2,900, +8.25, 500	1,600, 2,900, +8.25, 10,500	
Bristol Hercules XIX	J. 100 oct, 100/130 grade	1,725, 2,900, +8.25		1,395, 2,400, +6, 1,500			1,735, 2,900, +8.25, 500		
Bristol Hercules XX	J. 100 oct, 100/130 grade	1,700, 2,900, +8.25		1,400, 2,400, +6, 1,500	1,650, 2,400, +6, 9,500		1,920, 2,900, +8.25, 1,250	1,600, 2,900, +8.25, 9,500	
Bristol Hercules 100	J. 100 oct, 100/130 grade	1,675, 2,800, +8.25		1,515, 2,400, +6, 7,750	1,415, 2,400, +6, 16,500		1,800, 2,800, +8.25, 9,000	1,625, 2,800, +8.25, 19,500	
Bristol Hercules 101	J. 100 oct, 100/130 grade	1,640, 2,800, +8.25		1,475, 2,400, +6, 8,000	1,360, 2,400, +6, 16,500		1,765, 2,800, +8.25, 9,250	1,590, 2,800, +8.25, 19,500	
Bristol Hercules 103	J. 100 oct, 100/130 grade	1,640, 2,800, +8.25		1,475, 2,400, +6, 8,000	1,360, 2,400, +6, 16,500		1,765, 2,800, +8.25, 9,250	1,590, 2,800, +8.25, 19,500	

Engine, Nominal/Rated BHP. N.R. = Engine Built, Not Flown. Or Use in Flight Uncertain	Fuel Spec. – Where Stated (n/l = non-leaded) (TEL = Tetra-ethyl-lead)	Take-Off, S/L BHP, RPM, Max Boost	Normal, Continuous Climb (Rated) Power. BHP, RPM, Max. Boost, Rated Alt.			Maximum Power (Emergency, Combat, 5 Minutes) BHP, RPM, Max. Boost, Altitude			DRY WT LB
			Unsupercharged	Medium Supercharged	Fully Supercharged	Unsupercharged	Medium Supercharged	Fully Supercharged	
Bristol Hercules 105	J. 100 oct, 100/130 grade	1,675, 2,800 +7.25		1,495, 2,400, +5, 6,500	1,280, 2,400, +5, 21,750		1,775, 2,800, +7.25, 6,750	1,330, 2,800, +7.25, 27,500	
Bristol Hercules 106	J. 100 oct, 100/130 grade	1,675, 2,800 +10		1,360, 2,400, +6, 8,000	1,280, 2,400, +6, 16,500		1,775, 2,800, +10, 7,250	1,595, 2,800, +10, 17,500	
Bristol Hercules 120	J. 100 oct, 100/130 grade	1,715, 2,800 +8.5		1,440, 2,400, +6, 5,250	1,250, 2,400, +6, 20,250		1,790, 2,800, +8.5, 5,500	1,460, 2,800, +8.5, 22,500	
Bristol Hercules 121	J. 100 oct, 100/130 grade	1,715, 2,800 +8.5		1,440, 2,400, +6, 5,250	1,250, 2,400, +6, 20,250		1,790, 2,800, +8.5, 5,500	1,460, 2,800, +8.5, 22,500	
Bristol Hercules 130	J. 100 oct, 100/130 grade	1,600, 2,800 +7.5		1,485, 2,400, +6.25, 5,250			1,705, 2,800, +7.5, 7,750		
Bristol Hercules 134	J. 100 oct, 100/130 grade	1,690, 2,800 +8.5		1,510, 2,400, +7.25, 3,750			1,780, 2,800, +8.25, 6,500		
Bristol Hercules 216	J. 100 oct, 100/130 grade	1,800, 2,800, +12.5		1,550, 2,400, +8, 10,050			1,925, 2,800, +12.5, 8,950		
Bristol Hercules 230	J. 100 oct, 100/130 grade	1,925, 2,800 +11.5		1,650, 2,400, +9, 3,250			2,000, 2,800, +11.5, 5,000		
Bristol Hercules 234	J. 100 oct, 100/130 grade	1,980, 2,800, +13		1,660, 2,500, +8.5, 4,500			2,020, 2,800, +13, 2,750		
Bristol Hercules 238	J. 100 oct, 100/130 grade	1,980, 2,800, +13		1,660, 2,500, +8.5, 4,500			2,020, 2,800, +13, 2,750		
Bristol Hercules 261	J. 100 oct, 100/130 grade	1,950, 2,800, +12		1,605, 2,400, +8, 2,750	1,535, 2,400, +8, 11,000		1,990, 2,800, +12, 2,750		
Bristol Hercules 264	J. 100 oct, 100/130 grade	1,950, 2,800, +13		1,605, 2,400, +9, 2,750	1,535, 2,400, +9, 11,000		1,990, 2,800, +13, 2,750		
Bristol Hercules 268	J. 100 oct, 100/130 grade	1,950, 2,800, +13		1,670, 2,500, +9, 4,500	1,560, 2,500, +9, 13,250		2,000, 2,800, +13, 3,250		
Bristol Hercules 270	J. 100 oct, 100/130 grade	1,950, 2,800, +11.5		1,650, 2,400, +9, 3,250			2,000, 2,800, +11.5, 5,000		
Bristol Hercules 630	J. 100 oct, 100/130 grade			1,485, 2,400, +6.25, 5,250			1,705, 2,800, +7.5, 7,750		
Bristol Hercules 632	J. 100 oct, 100/130 grade	1,600, 2,800, +8.5		1,510, 2,400, +7.25, 3,750			1,780, 2,800, +8.5, 6,500		
Bristol Hercules 634	J. 100 oct, 100/130 grade	1,600, 2,800, +8.5		1,510, 2,400, +7.25, 3,750			1,780, 2,800, +8, 6,500		
Bristol Hercules 637	J. 100 oct, 100/130 grade	1,690, 2,800, +8		1,530, 2,400, +6.75, 4,000			1,780, 2,800, +8, 6,500		
Bristol Hercules 637-2	J. 100 oct, 100/130 grade	1,690, 2,800, +8		1,530, 2,400, +6.75, 4,000			1,780, 2,800, +8, 6,500		
Bristol Hercules 637-3	J. 100 oct, 100/130 grade	1,690, 2,800, +8		1,530, 2,400, +6.75, 4,000			1,780, 2,800, +8, 6,500		
Bristol Hercules 638	J. 100 oct, 100/130 grade	1,690, 2,800, +8.5		1,530, 2,400, +7.25, 8,750			1,780, 2,800, +8.5, 6,500		
Bristol Hercules 672	J. 100 oct, 100/130 grade	1,690, 2,800, +8		1,530, 2,400, +6.75, 4,000			1,780, 2,800, +8, 6,500		
Bristol Hercules 730	J. 100 oct, 100/130 grade	2,040, 2,800, +13		1,670, 2,500, +8.5, 5,000			2,090, 2,800, +13, 3,000		
Bristol Hercules 733	J. 100 oct, 100/130 grade	2,040, 2,800, +13		1,670, 2,500, +8.5, 5,000			2,090, 2,800, +13, 3,000		
Bristol Hercules 734	J. 100 oct, 100/130 grade	2,040, 2,800, +13		1,660, 2,500, +8.5, 4,500			2,090, 2,800, +13, 3,000		
Bristol Hercules 737	J. 100 oct, 100/130 grade	2,040, 2,800, +13		1,670, 2,500, +8.5, 5,000			2,090, 2,800, +13, 3,000		
Bristol Hercules 738	J. 100 oct, 100/130 grade	2,040, 2,800, +13		1,670, 2,500, +8.5, 5,000			2,090, 2,800, +13, 3,000		
Bristol Hercules 739	J. 100 oct, 100/130 grade	2,040, 2,800, +13		1,670, 2,500, +8.5, 5,000			2,090, 2,800, +13, 3,000		

Engine, Nominal/Rated BHP / N.R. = Engine Built, Not Flown / Or Use in Flight Uncertain	Fuel Spec. – Where Stated (n/l = non-leaded) (TEL = Tetra-ethyl-lead)	Take-Off, S/L BHP, RPM, Max Boost	Normal, Continuous Climb (Rated) Power. BHP, RPM, Max. Boost, Rated Alt. Medium Supercharged	Unsupercharged	Fully Supercharged	Maximum Power (Emergency, Combat, 5 Minutes) BHP, RPM, Max. Boost, Altitude Unsupercharged	Medium Supercharged	Fully Supercharged	DRY WT LB
Bristol Hercules 758	J. 100 oct, 100/130 grade	2,040, 2,800, +13	1,670, 2,400, +8.5, 5,000				2,090, 2,800, +13, 3,000		
Bristol Hercules 759	J. 100 oct, 100/130 grade	2,040, 2,800, +13	1,670, 2,400, +8.5, 5,000				2,090, 2,800, +13, 3,000		
Bristol Hercules 763	J. 100 oct, 100/130 grade	2,080, 2,900, +16.5	1,655, 2,500, +10. 5,750		1,535, 2,500, +10, 16,500		2,140, 2,900, +16.5, 3,750		
Bristol Hercules 773	J. 100 oct, 100/130 grade	1,965, 2,800, +13.75	1,635, 2,500, +9.25, 2,750				1,985, 2,800, +13.75, 1,500		
Bristol Hercules 790	J. 100 oct, 100/130 grade	2,040, 2,800, +13	1,670, 2,500, +8.5, 5,000				2,090, 2,800, +13, 3,000		
Bristol Hydra IM 'Double Octagon'	C. DTD 134, 73-77 oct, n/l	850, 3,000	800, 3,000, +?? ,, 5,000				870, 3,450, 6,000		1,500
Bristol Jupiter II	B. BS.121/23, 74 oct, n/l	385, 2,000, F/T		385, 1,575, S/L		500, 2,000, F/T, S/L		800	
Bristol Jupiter III	B. BS.121/23, 74 oct, n/l	400, 1,625		380, 1,575, S/L		400, 1,625, S/L			729
Bristol Jupiter IV	B. BS.121/23, 74 oct, n/l	430, 1,750		400, 1,575, S/L		430, 1,750, S/L			780
Bristol Jupiter V	B. BS.121/23, 74 oct, n/l	475, 1,825		435, 1,650, S/L		475, 1,825, S/L			
Bristol Jupiter VI	B. BS.121/23, 74 oct, n/l	440, 1,700 GT		477, 1,700, 4,000		515, 1,870			
Bristol Jupiter VIA	B. BS.121/23, 74 oct, n/l	415, 1,700 GT		415, 1,700, 5,000		520, 1,870, 5,000			
Bristol Jupiter VIFH	B. BS.121/23, 74 oct, n/l	420, 1,700 GT		420, 1,700, 4,000		440, 1,870, 4,000			
Bristol Jupiter VIFL (N.R.)	B. BS.121/23, 74 oct, n/l	445, 1,870		445, 1,700, S/L		485, 1,870, S/L			
Bristol Jupiter VIFM	B. BS.121/23, 74 oct, n/l	465, 1,700		465, 1,700, S/L		500, 1,870, S/L			
Bristol Jupiter VIFS (N.R.)	B. BS.121/23, 74 oct, n/l	435, 1,700 GT		435, 1,700, 4,000		465, 1,870, 4,000			
Bristol Jupiter VII	C. DTD 134, 73-77 oct, n/l	375, 1,535, -1.25			440, 1,775, -1.25, 12,000			460, 1,950, -0.75, 15,000	
Bristol Jupiter VIIF	C. DTD 134, 73-77 oct, n/l	450, 1,775, +1			480, 1,775, -.5, 9,000			520, 1,950, +0, 9,000	
Bristol Jupiter VIIF.P.	C. DTD 134, 73-77 oct, n/l	500, 1,950, +1			480, 1,775, -.5, 8,000			530, 1,950, +0, 8,000	
Bristol Jupiter VIII	C. DTD 134, 73-77 oct, n/l	430, 2,000 GT		445, 2,000, 4,000		475, 2,200, 4,000			
Bristol Jupiter VIIIF	C. DTD 134, 73-77 oct, n/l	455, 2,000 -1.75 GT		460, 2,000, 4,000		480, 2,200, 4,000			
Bristol Jupiter VIIIF.P.	C. DTD 134, 73-77 oct, n/l	460, 2,000 -1.75 GT		460, 2,000, 4,000		480, 2,200, 4,000			
Bristol Jupiter IX	C. DTD 134, 73-77 oct, n/l	525, 2,200		465, 2,000, S/L		525, 2,200, S/L			
Bristol Jupiter IXF	C. DTD 134, 73-77 oct, n/l	515, 2,000		515, 2,000, S/L		540, 2,200, S/L			
Bristol Jupiter X	C. DTD 134, 73-77 oct, n/l	470, 2,000, +.5			525, 2,000, +.5, 12,000			545, 2,200, +.5, 16,000	
Bristol Jupiter XF	C. DTD 134, 73-77 oct, n/l	540, 2,000, +.5			525, 2,000, +.5, 11,000			555, 2,200, +.5, 13,000	
Bristol Jupiter XFA	C. DTD 134, 73-77 oct, n/l	483, 2,000, +.5			525, 2,000, +.5, 11,000			550, 2,200, +.5, 11,000	995

Engine, Nominal/Rated BHP N.R. = Engine Built, Not Flown Or Use in Flight Uncertain	Fuel Spec. – Where Stated (n/l = non-leaded) (TEL = Tetra-ethyl-lead)	Take-Off, S/L BHP, RPM, Max Boost	Normal, Continuous Climb (Rated) Power. BHP, RPM, Max. Boost, Rated Alt.			Maximum Power (Emergency, Combat, 5 Minutes) BHP, RPM, Max. Boost, Altitude			DRY WT LB
			Unsupercharged	Medium Supercharged	Fully Supercharged	Unsupercharged	Medium Supercharged	Fully Supercharged	
Bristol Jupiter XFAM	C. DTD 134, 73-77 oct, n/l	580, 2,000, +0		565, 2,000, +0, 4,000			595, 2,200, +0, 4,000		
Bristol Jupiter XFBM	C. DTD 134, 73-77 oct, n/l	580, 2,000, +0		565, 2,000, +0, 4,000			595, 2,200, +0, 4,000		
Bristol Jupiter XFS	C. DTD 134, 73-77 oct, n/l	580, 2,000, +0		565, 2,000, +0, 4,000			595, 2,200, +0, 4,000	575, 2,200, +??, 11,000	
Bristol Jupiter XI	C. DTD 134, 73-77 oct, n/l	460, 2,000							
Bristol Jupiter XIF	C. DTD 134, 73-77 oct, n/l	500, 2,200	460, 2,000, S/L			500, 2,200, S/L			
Bristol Jupiter XIF.P.	C. DTD 134, 73-77 oct, n/l	525, 2,000	490, 2,000, S/L			525, 2,200, S/L			
Bristol Lucifer II	B. BS.121/23, 74 oct, n/l	122, 1,650	118, 1,600, S/L			122, 1,650, S/L			
Bristol Lucifer III	B. BS.121/23, 74 oct, n/l	118, 1,760	115, 1,600, S/L			118, 1,760, S/L			
Bristol Lucifer IV	B. BS.121/23, 74 oct, n/l	128, 1,700	128, 1,700, S/L			140, 1,870, S/L			
Bristol Mercury I	E. 75/25/4 (+4cc/I.G. TEL)	800, 2,500, +8		800, 2,500, +8, S/L			808, 2,500, +8, S/L		680
Bristol Mercury II	F. 80 oct (+5cc/I.G. TEL)	540, 1,850, +4.25			440, 2,000, -.5, 12,500			435, 2,200, -.5, 16,500	
Bristol Mercury IIA	B. BS.121/23, 74 oct, n/l	540, 2,000, +4.25			440, 2,000, -.5, 12,500			455, 2,200, -.5, 16,500	
Bristol Mercury III	B. BS.121/23, 74 oct, n/l	430, 2,250, +.5			490, 2,250, +.5, 13,000			520, 2,475, +.5, 18,000	
Bristol Mercury IV	B. BS.121/23, 74 oct, n/l	430, 2,250, +.5			490, 2,250, +.5, 13,000			520, 2,475, +.5, 10,000	
Bristol Mercury IVA	B. BS.121/23, 74 oct, n/l	530, 2,250, +1			510, 2,250, +0, 13,500			560, 2,600, +1.5, 16,500	
Bristol Mercury IVS.2	C. DTD 134, 73-77 oct, n/l	530, 2,250, +1.5			510, 2,250, +0, 13,000			560, 2,600, +1.5, 16,500	
Bristol Mercury V	C. DTD 134, 73-77 oct, n/l								
Bristol Mercury VI (became Pegasus IU.2)	C. DTD 134, 73-77 oct, n/l								
Bristol Mercury VIA (became Pegasus IU.2)	C. DTD 134, 73-77 oct, n/l	575, 2,400	535, 2,000, S/L			575, 2,000, S/L			
Bristol Mercury VIS	G. DTD 230, 87 oct	620, 2,400, +2.5		605, 2,400, +1, 12,500			645, 2,750, +2.5, 15,500		
1 Bristol Mercury VISP	C. DTD 134, 73-77 oct, n/l	585, 2,400, +1.75		550, 2,400, +0, 13,000			585, 2,750, +1.75, 16,500		
Bristol Mercury VIS.2	G. DTD 230, 87 oct	620, 2,400, +2.5		605, 2,400, +1, 12,500			645, 2,750, +2.5, 15,500		
Bristol Mercury VIIA (became Pegasus IM.2)	C. DTD 134, 73-77 oct, n/l	560, 2,000		555, 2,000, +??, 4,000			575, 2,200, +??, 4,000		
Bristol Mercury VIII	G. DTD 230, 87 oct	725, 2,650, +5		825, 2,650, +5 13,000			840, 2,750, +5, 14,000		
Bristol Mercury VIIIA	D. DTD 224, 77 min oct n/l	535, 2,000	535, 2,000, S/L			575, 2,200, S/L			
Bristol Mercury IX	G. DTD 230, 87 oct	725, 2,650, +5		825, 2,650, +5 13,000			840, 2,750, +5, 14,000		

Engine, Nominal/Rated BHP; N.R. = Engine Built, Not Flown Or Use in Flight Uncertain	Fuel Spec. – Where Stated (n/l = non-leaded) (TEL = Tetra-ethyl-lead)	Take-Off, S/L BHP, RPM, Max Boost	Normal, Continuous Climb (Rated) Power. BHP, RPM, Max. Boost, Rated Alt. — Unsupercharged	Medium Supercharged	Fully Supercharged	Maximum Power (Emergency, Combat, 5 Minutes) BHP, RPM, Max. Boost, Altitude — Unsupercharged	Medium Supercharged	Fully Supercharged	DRY WT LB
Bristol Mercury XI	G. DTD 230, 87 oct	830, 2,650, +3.5		820, 2,400, +3.5, 3,500			890, 2,750, +3.5, 6,000		
Bristol Mercury XII	G. DTD 230, 87 oct	830, 2,650, +3.5		820, 2,400, +3.5, 3,500			890, 2,750, +3.5, 6,000		
Bristol Mercury XV	G. DTD 230, 87 oct	725, 2,650, +5		840, 2,400, +5.5, 5,000	825, 2,650, +3.5, 13,000			840, 2,750, +5, 14,000	
Bristol Mercury XVI	G. DTD 230, 87 oct	1,050, 2,750, F.T.		840, 2,400, +5.5, 5,000			1,075, 2,750, F/T, 2,000		
Bristol Mercury XX	H. 87 oct, higher with 100	820, 2,650 +4.25		810, 2,400, +2.75, 2,500			870, 2,750, +4.25, 4,500		
Bristol Mercury 25	G. DTD 230, 87 oct	730, 2,750, +5			825, 2,650, +5, 13,000			840, 2,750, +5, 14,000	
Bristol Mercury 30	G. DTD 230, 87 oct	830, 2,750, +4.25		810, 2,400, +2.75, 2,500			870, 2,750, +4.25, 4,500		1,065
Bristol Mercury 31	G. DTD 230, 87 oct	820, 2,650, +4.25		710, 2,400, +2.75, 2,500			870, 2,750, +4.25, 4,500		
Bristol Mercury (sh str)	C. DTD 134, 73-77 oct, n/l	420, 2,500, +2			400, 2,500, +.25, 12,000			480, 2,750, +??, 12,000	
Bristol Neptune I	C. DTD 134, 73-77 oct, n/l	295, 1,700	295, 1,700, S/L			320, 1,870 S/L			630
Bristol Orion I		510, 1,870			460, 1,700, 24,000		495, 1,870, 24,000	490, 1,870, 24,000	891
Bristol Pegasus IM.2 was long stroke Mercury VIIA	C. DTD 134, 73-77 oct, n/l	590, 2,000, +1		565, 2,000, +0, 4,500			615, 2,300, +1, 4,500		
Bristol Pegasus IM.3 was long stroke Mercury VIIB	C. DTD 134, 73-77 oct, n/l	590, 2,000, +1		565, 2,000, +0, 4,500	615, 2,300, +1, 4,500				
Bristol Pegasus IS.3 was long stroke Mercury VB	C. DTD 134, 73-77 oct, n/l	545, 2,000, +1.5			530, 2,000, +0, 11,000			580, 2,300, +0, 13,500	
Bristol Pegasus IU.2 was long stroke Mercury VIA	C. DTD 134, 73-77 oct, n/l	550, 1,900	550, 1,900, S/L			630, 2,185, S/L			
Bristol Pegasus III.2P	C. DTD 134, 73-77 oct, n/l	610, 2,000, +1.25		600, 2,000, +.25, 2,000			650, 2,300, +1.25, 2,500		
Bristol Pegasus III.3	C. DTD 134, 73-77 oct, n/l	610, 2,000, +1.25		600, 2,000, +.25, 2,000			650, 2,300, +1.25, 2,500		
Bristol Pegasus IIM	C. DTD 134, 73-77 oct, n/l	620, 2,000, +1.5		580, 2,000, +0, 5,000			635, 2,300, +1.5, 6,500		
Bristol Pegasus IIM.2	C. DTD 134, 73-77 oct, n/l	620, 2,000, +1.5		580, 2,000, +0, 5,000			635, 2,300, +1.5, 6,500		
Bristol Pegasus IIM.3	C. DTD 134, 73-77 oct, n/l	620, 2,000, +1.5		580, 2,000, +0, 5,000			635, 2,300, +1.5, 6,500		
Bristol Pegasus III	G. DTD 230, 87 oct								
Bristol Pegasus IIIM	G. DTD 230, 87 oct								
Bristol Pegasus IIIM.2 became Pegasus VI	G. DTD 230, 87 oct	775, 2,200, +2		690, 2,200, +.5, 3,500			750, 2,525, +.5, 4,750		
Bristol Pegasus III was Pegasus III-M(3) became Pegasus IIIM.3	G. DTD 230, 87 oct	775, 2,200, +2		690, 2,200, +.5, 3,500			750, 2,525, +.5, 4,750		

Engine. Nominal/Rated BHP. N.R. = Engine Built, Not Flown Or Use in Flight Uncertain	Fuel Spec. – Where Stated (n/l = non-leaded) (TEL = Tetra-ethyl-lead)	Take-Off, S/L BHP, RPM, Max Boost	Normal, Continuous Climb (Rated) Power. BHP, RPM, Max. Boost, Rated Alt.			Maximum Power (Emergency, Combat, 5 Minutes) BHP, RPM, Max. Boost. Altitude			DRY WT LB
			Unsupercharged	Medium Supercharged	Fully Supercharged	Unsupercharged	Medium Supercharged	Fully Supercharged	
Bristol Pegasus IV	G. DTD 230, 87 oct	700, 2,250, +2.5			670, 2,250, +.5, 11,500			710, 2,600, +2.5 15,000	940
Bristol Pegasus V (was Pegasus IIIM.4)	G. DTD 230, 87 oct	775, 2,200, +2		690, 2,200, +.5, 3,500			750, 2,525, +.5, 4,750		
Bristol Pegasus VI (was Pegasus IIIM.2)	G. DTD 230, 87 oct	775, 2,200, +2		690, 2,200, +.5, 3,500			750, 2,525, +.5, 4,750		
Bristol Pegasus VIP	G. DTD 230, 87 oct	775, 2,200, +2		690, 2,200, +.5, 3,500			750, 2,525, +.5, 4,750		
Bristol Pegasus IX	G. DTD 230, 87 oct	840, 2,200, F/T		725, 2,200, +.5, 4,500			790, 2,525, +.5, 6,000		
Bristol Pegasus X	G. DTD 230, 87 oct	960, 2,475, +4.5		810/850, 2,250, +2.5, 4,000			875/915, 2,600, +2.5, 6,250		
Bristol Pegasus XC	G. DTD 230, 87 oct	920, 2,475, +3.75		815, 2,200, +1.25, 4,500			830, 2,600, +1.25, 5,250		
Bristol Pegasus XVII (N.R.)	H. 87 oct, higher with 100	965, 2,475 +5.5		815, 2,250, +2.5, 4,750	750, 2,250, +2.5, 14,750		1,000, 2,600, +5.5, 3,000	885, 2,600, +5.5, 15,500	1,135
Bristol Pegasus XVIII	J. 100 oct, 100/130 grade	1,050, 2,600 +6.75		780/815, 2,250, +2.5, 4,750	750, 2,250, +2.5, 14,750		1,065, 2,600, +6.75, 13,000	965, 2,600, +6.75, 13,000	
Bristol Pegasus XVIII	G. DTD 230, 87 oct	965, 2,475, +5.5		780/815, 2,250, +2.5, 4,750	750, 2,250, +2.5, 14,750		1,000, 2,600, +5.5, 3,000	885, 2,600, +5.5, 15,500	
Bristol Pegasus XIX	G. DTD 230, 87 oct	835, 2,475 +4.25		835, 2,250, +3, 8,500				925, 2,600, +4.25, 10,000	
Bristol Pegasus XX	G. DTD 230, 87 oct	835, 2,475 +4.25		835, 2,250, +3, 8,500				925, 2,600, +4.25, 10,000	
Bristol Pegasus 22	G. DTD 230, 87 oct	1,010, 2,600 +6		840, 2,250, +2.5, 4,000			890, 2,600, +6, 6,500		
Bristol Pegasus 22 LR	G. DTD 230, 87 oct	800, 2,600 +2.5		890, 2,250, +2.5, 4,000			890, 2,600, +2.5, 6,500		
Bristol Pegasus 30	G. DTD 230, 87 oct	775, 2,200, +2		690, 2,200, +.5, 3,500			750, 2,525, +.5, 4,750		
Bristol Pegasus 38	J. 100 oct, 100/130 grade	1,010, 2,600, +6.75		805, 2,250, +2.5, 4,750			1,025, 2,600, +6.75, 1,250		1,180
Bristol Pegasus 48	J. 100 oct, 100/130 grade	1,010, 2,600, +6.75		805, 2,250, +2.5, 4,750	720, 2,250, +2.5, 14,750		1,025, 2,600, +6.75, 1,250	925, 2,600, +6.75, 13,000	
Bristol Perseus I.A	C. DTD 134, 73-77 oct, n/l	610, 2,000, F/T		610, 2,000, F/T, S/L			630, 2,300, F/T, 1,000		
Bristol Perseus II-L	G. DTD 230, 87 oct	760, 2,525, F/T		665, 2,000, F/T, S/L			760, 2,525, F/T, S/L		
Bristol Perseus III	G. DTD 230, 87 oct	700, 2,425, +2		720, 2,425, +2, 2,500			740, 2,525, +2, 3,000		
Bristol Perseus VIII	G. DTD 230, 87 oct	815, 2,650, +4		745, 2,400, +2.5, 6,500			890, 2,750, +4, 7,000		
Bristol Perseus X	G. DTD 230, 87 oct	750, 2,650, +3			730, 2,400, +1.5, 14,500			880, 2,750, +3, 15,500	
Bristol Perseus XA	H. 87 oct, higher with 100	880, 2,650, +3		790, 2,400, +1.5, 6,000			950, 2,750, +3, 5,500		
Bristol Perseus XA	J. 100 oct, 100/130 grade	950, 2,650, +5		860, 2,400, +3.5, 2,750					
Bristol Perseus XI (N.R.)	G. DTD 230, 87 oct	830, 2,650 +2.5		745, 2,400, +1.25, 6,500			905, 2,750, +2.5, 6,500		
Bristol Perseus XII	G. DTD 230, 87 oct	830, 2,650 +2.5		745, 2,400, +1.25, 6,500			905, 2,750, +2.5 6,500		
Bristol Perseus XIIC	G. DTD 230, 87 oct	890, 2,700, +3		710, 2,250, +1.25, 4,000			815, 2,600, +1.25, 6,000		

Engine, Nominal/Rated BHP. N.R. = Engine Built, Not Flown Or Use in Flight Uncertain	Fuel Spec. – Where Stated (nil = non-leaded) (TEL = Tetra-ethyl-lead)	Take-Off, S/L BHP, RPM, Max Boost	Normal, Continuous Climb (Rated) Power. BHP, RPM, Max. Boost, Rated Alt.			Maximum Power (Emergency, Combat, 5 Minutes) BHP, RPM, Max. Boost, Altitude			DRY WT LB
			Unsupercharged	Medium Supercharged	Fully Supercharged	Unsupercharged	Medium Supercharged	Fully Supercharged	
Bristol Perseus XIIC1	G. DTD 230, 87 oct	890, 2,700, +3		710, 2,250, +1.25, 4,000			815, 2,600, +1.25, 6,000		
Bristol Perseus XIVC	G. DTD 230, 87 oct	890, 2,700, +3		710, 2,250, +1.25, 4,000			815, 2,600, +1.25, 6,000		
Bristol Perseus XIVC Spl	(N.RG. DTD 230, 87 oct	890, 2,700, +3		710, 2,250, +1.25, 4,000			815, 2,600, +1.25, 6,000		
Bristol Perseus XVI	G. DTD 230, 87 oct	905, 2,750, +3.5		745, 2,400, +1.25, 6,500			955, 2,750, +3.5, 5,000		
Bristol Phoenix I	M. Diesel fuel	380, 2,000	350, 1,900, S/L			380, 2,000, S/L			1,067
Bristol Phoenix IM	M. Diesel fuel	470, 1,900		420, 1,900			485, 2,000		1,090
Bristol Taurus II	G. DTD 230, 87 oct	1,060, 3,100, +4.25		930, 2,700, +2.75 4,000			1,110, 3,100, +4.25, 4,000		1,300
Bristol Taurus III	G. DTD 230, 87 oct	935, 3,300, +4.5			900, 2,800, +2.5, 14,000			1,060, 3,300, +4.5, 14,500	
Bristol Taurus VI	J. 100 oct, 100/130 grade	1,085, 3,110, +4.75		985, 2,800, +3.5, 3,750			1,130, 3,100, +4.75, 3,500		
Bristol Taurus XII	J. 100 oct, 100/130 grade	1,090, 3,100, +4.75		985, 2,800, +3.5, 3,750			1,130, 3,100, +4.75, 3,500		
Bristol Taurus XVI	J. 100 oct, 100/130 grade	1,085, 3,100, +4.75		985, 2,800, +3.5, 3,750			1,130, 3,100, +4.75, 3,500		
Bristol Taurus XX	J. 100 oct, 100/130 grade								
Bristol Titan I (Direct)	B. BS.121/23, 74 oct, n/l	210, 1,800	210, 1,800, S/L			230, 2,000, S/L			500
Bristol Titan IV (Geared)	B. BS.121/23, 74 oct, n/l	220, 1,870	205, 1,700, S/L			220, 2,000, S/L			525
British Salmson 9NG (175)									
British Salmson A.C.7		105, 1,8O0	105, 1,800			112, 2,200			286
British Salmson A.C.9		135, 1,800	135, 1,800			145, 2,000			374
British Salmson A.D.9		50, 2,100	50, 2,100			54, 2,310			160
British Salmson A.D.9R srs III		80, 3,000	80, 3,000			86, 3,300			188
Carden 750 c.c.									
Carden-Ford S.P.1 (40)		37, 3,200		37, 3,200			40, 3,500		
Carden-Ford (31)		31, 3,000	31, 3,000			33, 3,500			130
Caunter B (N.R.)									
Caunter C (N.R.)									
Caunter D (N.R.)									
Cirrus I		60, 1,800	60, 1,800			65, 2,000			268
Cirrus II		75, 1,800	75, 1,800			84, 2,000			280
Cirrus III		85, 1,900	85, 1,900			94, 2,100			285

Engine, Nominal/Rated BHP N.R. = Engine Built, Not Flown Or Use in Flight Uncertain	Fuel Spec. – Where Stated (n/l = non-leaded) (TEL = Tetra-ethyl-lead)	Take-Off, S/L BHP, RPM, Max Boost	Normal, Continuous Climb (Rated) Power. BHP, RPM, Max. Boost, Rated Alt.			Maximum Power (Emergency, Combat, 5 Minutes) BHP, RPM, Max. Boost, Altitude			DRY WT LB
			Unsupercharged	Medium Supercharged	Fully Supercharged	Unsupercharged	Medium Supercharged	Fully Supercharged	
Cirrus IIIA		90, 1,900	90, 1,900			94, 2,100			285
Cirrus Hermes I		105, 1,900	105, 1,900			115, 2,100			300
Cirrus Hermes II		110, 2,000	110, 2,000			118, 2,200			305
Cirrus Hermes IIB		105, 1,900	105, 1,900			115, 2,000			300
Cirrus Hermes IV		120, 2,000	120, 2,000			130, 2,200			300
Cirrus Hermes IVA		120, 2,000	120, 2,000			130, 2,200			300
Clerget 7Z (80)	A. Pre-1923, 40-50 octane	82, 1,200	82, 1,200			95, 1,300			234
Clerget 9B (130)	A. Pre-1923, 40-50 octane	134, 1,250	134, 1,250			135, 1,300			385
Clerget 9Bf (140)	A. Pre-1923, 40-50 octane	140, 1,250	148, 1,250			149, 1,300			394
Clerget 9Z (110)	A. Pre-1923, 40-50 octane	110, 1,180	122, 1,250			123.5, 1,300			367
Clerget 11Eb (200)	A. Pre-1923, 40-50 octane	200, 1,300	197, 1,300			215, 1,350			512
Cosmos Jupiter I	A. Pre-1923, 40-50 octane	450, 1,850, F/T	400, 1,650, S/L			400, 1,850, F/T, S/L		700	
Cosmos Lucifer I	A. Pre-1923, 40-50 octane	100, 1,600, F/T	80, 1,450, S/L			100, 1,600, F/T, S/L		325	
Cosmos Mercury (300)	A. Pre-1923, 40-50 octane	347, 2,000, F/T	315, 1800, S/L			347, 2,000, F/T, S/L		579	
Coventry Victor Neptune		40, 3,000	40, 3,000			40, 3,000			130
Curtiss D12 see Fairey Felix									
Curtiss OX-2 (90)	A. Pre-1923, 40-50 octane 90, 1,300	92, 1,300	92, 1,300			105, 1,400			385
Curtiss OX-5 (90)	A. Pre-1923, 40-50 octane 84, 1,250	84, 1,250	84, 1,250			102, 1,350			375
Curtiss OXX (100)	A. Pre-1923, 40-50 octane 98, 1,300	98, 1,300	98, 1,300			115, 1,400			401
Curtiss VX (160)	A. Pre-1923, 40-50 octane 160, 1,350	160, 1,350	160, 1,350			180, 1,400			695
D.H.Ghost									
D.H.Gipsy I		85, 1,900	85, 2,100			98, 2,300			285
D.H.Gipsy II		95, 2,000	108, 2,120			120, 2,300			298
D.H.Gipsy III		104, 1,900	105, 2,000, S/L			120, 2,300, 2,000			290
D.H.Gipsy IV									
D.H.Gipsy XII Twelve	G. DTD 230, 87 oct	505, 2,600, +3.5	405/420, 2,400, 7,420, 2,400, +0, 7,500				425, 2,450, +0, 7,750		1,058
D.H.Gipsy King I	G. DTD 230, 87 oct	505, 2,600, +3.5	405/420, 2,400, 7,420, 2,400, +0, 7,500				425, 2,450, +0, 7,750		1,058
D.H. Gipsy Major I									

Engine, Nominal/Rated BHP N.R. = Engine Built, Not Flown Or Use in Flight Uncertain	Fuel Spec. – Where Stated (nil = non-leaded) (TEL = Tetra-ethyl-lead)	Take-Off, S/L BHP, RPM, Max Boost	Normal, Continuous Climb (Rated) Power. BHP, RPM, Max. Boost, Rated Alt.			Maximum Power (Emergency, Combat, 5 Minutes) BHP, RPM, Max. Boost, Altitude			DRY WT LB
		Unsupercharged	Medium Supercharged	Fully Supercharged	Unsupercharged	Unsupercharged	Medium Supercharged	Fully Supercharged	
D.H.Gipsy Major srs II									
D.H.Gipsy Major IC	F. 80 oct (+5cc/I.G. TEL)								
D.H.Gipsy Major IF									
D.H.Gipsy Major II (h.c.)		130, 2,100			130, 2,100	142, 2,400			310
D.H.Gipsy Major 7	F. 80 oct (+5cc/I.G. TEL)								
D.H.Gipsy Major 8									
D.H.Gipsy Major 10	F. 80 oct (+5cc/I.G. TEL)	145, 2,100				145, 2,550			310
D.H.Gipsy Major 10/1									
D.H.Gipsy Major 10/2									
D.H.Gipsy Major 30 (N.R.)		160, 2,100			2,100, 2,050	160, 2,500			340
D.H.Gipsy Major 50		197, 2,100					180, 2,400, +??, 7,000		410
D.H.Gipsy Major 200									408
D.H.Gipsy Major 215									408
D.H.Gipsy Minor		80			80, 2,250	90, 2,600			216
D.H.Gipsy Queen I									
D.H.Gipsy Queen II		185, 2,100			185, 2,100	203, 2,350			486
D.H.Gipsy Queen III		185, 2,100			185, 2,100	203, 2,350			
D.H.Gipsy Queen IV/50									
D.H.Gipsy Queen 30		240/250, 2,500			240/250, 2,500				537
D.H.Gipsy Queen 30-2		240/250, 2,500			240/250, 2,500				537
D.H.Gipsy Queen 30-3		240/250, 2,500			240/250, 2,500				537
D.H.Gipsy Queen 30-4		240/250, 2,500			240/250, 2,500				537
D.H.Gipsy Queen 32		240/250, 2,500			240/250, 2,500				537
D.H.Gipsy Queen 34		240/250, 2,500			240/250, 2,500				537
D.H.Gipsy Queen 51		295			185, 2,100		270, 2,400, +??, 7,000		560
D.H.Gipsy Queen 70									
D.H.Gipsy Queen 70-2		365/380, 3,000			342, 2,700		305, 2,700, +??, 6,000		698
D.H.Gipsy Queen 70-3		384/400, 3,000			346, 2,800		305, 2,700, 6,000		698

Engine, Nominal/Rated BHP N.R. = Engine Built, Not Flown Or Use in Flight Uncertain	Fuel Spec. – Where Stated (nil = non-leaded) (TEL = Tetra-ethyl-lead)	Take-Off, S/L BHP, RPM, Max Boost	Normal, Continuous Climb (Rated) Power. BHP, RPM, Max. Boost, Rated Alt.			Maximum Power (Emergency, Combat, 5 Minutes) BHP, RPM, Max. Boost, Altitude			DRY WT LB
			Unsupercharged	Medium Supercharged	Fully Supercharged	Unsupercharged	Medium Supercharged	Fully Supercharged	
D.H.Gipsy Queen 70-4		384/400, 3,000		346, 2,800			305, 2,700, 6,000		660
D.H.Gipsy Queen 71		384/400, 3,000		346, 2,800			305, 2,700, 6,000		686
D.H.Gipsy Six I		180, 2,100	185, 2,100, S/L			200, 2,350, S/L			486
D.H.Gipsy Six I Srs II									
D.H.Gipsy Six II	F. 80 oct (+5cc/I.G. TEL)	191, 2,100	165, 2,100, S/L			205, 2,400, S/L			480
D.H.Gipsy Six R		220, 2,350	220, 2,350			223, 2,400			462
D.H. Iris (40-50)		40/50, 1,500							
Douglas - see Aero Engines									
Douglas 500 c.c.		17, 4,000	10, 2,500			17, 4,000			
Douglas 736 c.c.									
Douglas 750 c.c.									
E.N.V. Type D (35-40)	A. Pre-1923, 40-50 octane								155
E.N.V. Type F (60-80)	A. Pre-1923, 40-50 octane								287
Fairey Felix (D.12)		375, 1,850	375, 1,850			443, 2,200			693
Fairey V-12 Prince I		650, 2,000	650, 2,000, 2,000			670, 2,500, 2,000			
Fairey V-12S Prince II (Super)		680, 2,000			680, 2,000			720, 2,500, 12,000	
Fairey H-16 Prince 3		1,540, 2,800, +3			1,540, 2,000, +2, 9,500			1,600, 3,000, +3, 10,000	2,180
Fairey H-24 Prince 4, Monarch		2,240, 3,000, +??			2,240, 3,000, +??, 9,000			2,240, 3,000, +??,	
Fletcher Empress (50)	A. Pre-1923, 40-50 octane	50, 1,200	50, 1,200						
Galloway - see B.H.P.	A. Pre-1923, 40-50 octane								
General Aircraft V.4	A. Pre-1923, 40-50 octane								
Gnome 7 Omega (50)	A. Pre-1923, 40-50 octane	50, 1,200	50, 1,200						165
Gnome 7 Gamma (70)	A. Pre-1923, 40-50 octane	70, 1,200	70, 1,200						
Gnome 7 Lambda (80)	A. Pre-1923, 40-50 octane	65, 1,150	65, 1,150			67.5, 1,250			212
Gnome 9 Delta (100)	A. Pre-1923, 40-50 octane	100, 1,200	100, 1,200						297
Gnome 14 Gamma-Gamma (140)	A. Pre-1923, 40-50 octane	140, 1,200	140, 1,200						
Gnome 14 Lambda-Lambda (160)	A. Pre-1923, 40-50 octane	160, 1,200	160, 1,200						
Gnome 14 Omega-Omega (100)	A. Pre-1923, 40-50 octane	120, 1,200	120, 1,200						

Engine, Nominal/Rated BHP N.R. = Engine Built, Not Flown Or Use in Flight Uncertain	Fuel Spec. – Where Stated (nil = non-leaded) (TEL = Tetra-ethyl-lead)	Take-Off, S/L BHP, RPM, Max Boost	Normal, Continuous Climb (Rated) Power. BHP, RPM, Max. Boost, Rated Alt.			Maximum Power (Emergency, Combat, 5 Minutes) BHP, RPM, Max. Boost, Altitude			DRY WT LB
			Unsupercharged	Medium Supercharged	Fully Supercharged	Unsupercharged	Medium Supercharged	Fully Supercharged	
Gnome Monosoupape 7 A (80)	A. Pre-1923, 40-50 octane	65, 1,150	65, 1,150			80, 1,250			212
Gnome Monosoupape 9B-2 (100)	A. Pre-1923, 40-50 octane	113, 1,250	113, 1,250			115, 1,300			303
Gnome Monosoupape 9N (150)	A. Pre-1923, 40-50 octane	154, 1,350	154, 1,350			156, 1,350			320
Green (80/100)		82, 1,100	82, 1,100			82, 1,100			
Green C4 (30-35)	A. Pre-1923, 40-50 octane	30-35, 1,390	30-35, 1,390			52.5, 1,460			184
Green D.4 (50-60)	A. Pre-1923, 40-50 octane	50-60, 1,050	50-60, 1,050			70, 1,200			310
Green E.6 (100-120)	A. Pre-1923, 40-50 octane	102, 1,200	102, 1,200			120, 1,300			440
Green (260)	A. Pre-1923, 40-50 octane	250, 1,200	250, 1,200			270, 1,300			900
Hart (35) (N.R.)	A. Pre-1923, 40-50 octane								
Hart (150)	A. Pre-1923, 40-50 octane								
Hispano-Suiza 8 (140)	A. Pre-1923, 40-50 octane								
Hispano-Suiza 8Aa (150)	A. Pre-1923, 40-50 octane	150, 1,600	165, 1,600			185, 1,800			440
Hispano-Suiza 8Ab (180)	A. Pre-1923, 40-50 octane	180, 2,000	200, 2,000			232, 2,100			460
Hispano-Suiza 8B (200)	A. Pre-1923, 40-50 octane	220, 2,000	220, 2,000			232, 2,100			515
Hispano-Suiza 8Ba (200)	A. Pre-1923, 40-50 octane	208, 2,000	208, 2,000			215, 2,100			515
Hispano-Suiza 8Bb (200)	A. Pre-1923, 40-50 octane	200, 2,200	208, 2,000						515
Hispano-Suiza 8Bc (220)	A. Pre-1923, 40-50 octane	220	460						
Hispano-Suiza 8Bd (220)	A. Pre-1923, 40-50 octane	220	515						
Hispano-Suiza 8Be (220)	A. Pre-1923, 40-50 octane	220	515						
Hispano-Suiza 8Cb (220)	A. Pre-1923, 40-50 octane	515							
Hispano-Suiza 8F (300)	A. Pre-1923, 40-50 octane								
Hispano-Suiza 8Fb (300) (N.R.)	A. Pre-1923, 40-50 octane	308, 1,850	308, 1,850			318, 1,950			595
Isaacson (60)	A. Pre-1923, 40-50 octane	60, 1,200	60, 1,200						245
Jameson FF-1 (110)		106, 3,050	106, 3,050			106, 3,050			290
J.A.P. (9)		9							150
J.A.P. (20)		20, 1,300							
J.A.P. (40)		40, 1,500							
J.A.P. J-99 (Aeronca)		36, 2,400	36, 2,400			40, 2,500			

Engine, Nominal/Rated BHP N.R. = Engine Built, Not Flown Or Use in Flight Uncertain	Fuel Spec. – Where Stated (n/l = non-leaded) (TEL = Tetra-ethyl-lead)	Take-Off, S/L BHP, RPM, Max Boost	Normal, Continuous Climb (Rated) Power. BHP, RPM, Max. Boost, Rated Alt.			Maximum Power (Emergency, Combat, 5 Minutes) BHP, RPM, Max. Boost, Altitude			DRY WT LB
			Unsupercharged	Medium Supercharged	Fully Supercharged	Unsupercharged	Medium Supercharged	Fully Supercharged	
Le Rhone 7 (50)	A. Pre-1923, 40-50 octane	50, 1,200	50, 1,200			50, 1,200			183
Le Rhone 9C (80)	A. Pre-1923, 40-50 octane	92, 1,250	92, 1,250			92, 1,300			268
Le Rhone 9Ja (110)	A. Pre-1923, 40-50 octane	110, 1,200	131, 1,300			135, 1,350			323
Le Rhone 9Jb (130)	A. Pre-1923, 40-50 octane	130, 1,280	130, 1,280			148, 1,280			343
Le Rhone 9Jby (130)	A. Pre-1923, 40-50 octane	130, 1,280	130, 1,280			148, 1,280			343
Le Rhone 9R (170)	A. Pre-1923, 40-50 octane	168, 1,360	168, 1,360			180, 1,360			
Liberty 12A (H.C.) (400)	A. Pre-1923, 40-50 octane	405, 1,650	421, 1,750			449, 1,940			844
Liberty 12N (350)	A. Pre-1923, 40-50 octane	396, 1,650	400, 1,650			418, 1,750			825
Luton Anzani-see Anzani (Br)									
N E C (50)	A. Pre-1923, 40-50 octane								
Napier Cub	A. Pre-1923, 40-50 octane	996, 1,800	1,000, 1,800 S/L			1,074, 2,000, S/L			2,450
Napier Culverin	M. Diesel fuel	720, 1,700	720, 1,700, S/L			820, 2,050, S/L			1,785
Napier Lion I	B. BS.121/23, 74 oct, n/l	450, 1,950	450, 2,000, 5,000			468, 2,100, 5,000			840
Napier Lion II (High Comp)	B. BS.121/23, 74 oct, n/l	450, 1,950	450, 2,000, 5,000			480, 2,200, 5,000			960
Napier Lion II (Low Comp)	B. BS.121/23, 74 oct, n/l	425, 1,950	425, 2,000, 5,000			460, 2,200, 5,000			960
Napier Lion IIB	B. BS.121/23, 74 oct, n/l	470, 2,000	470, 2,000, 5,000			502, 2,200, 5,000			966
Napier Lion III	B. BS.121/23, 74 oct, n/l	460, 2,000				490, 2,200			
Napier Lion IV	B. BS.121/23, 74 oct, n/l	460, 2,000				490, 2,200			
Napier Lion V	B. BS.121/23, 74 oct, n/l	425/440, 2,050	450, 2,050, 5,000			470, 2,200, 5,000			970
Napier Lion VA	B. BS.121/23, 74 oct, n/l	480, 2,250	500, 2,250, 5,000			540, 2,475, 5,000			970
Napier Lion VB		580							
Napier Lion V*		460, 2,000				490, 2,200, 5,000			
Napier Lion VI		480, 2,250, S/L	500, 2,250, S/L			530, 2,475, 5,000			920
Napier Lion VII	25/75 + 10.75 cc TEL/I.G.	680, 2,600	700, 2,700			700, 2,700			750
Napier Lion VIIA	25/75 + 10.75 cc TEL/I.G.	875, 3,300	875, 3,300			875, 3,300			850
Napier Lion VIIB	25/75 + 10.75 cc TEL/I.G.	875, 3,300	875, 3,300			875, 3,300			930
Napier Lion VIID	25/75 + 10.75 cc TEL/I.G.	1,320, 3,600	1,320, 3,600,	1,170					
Napier Lion VIII		535, 2,350	535, 2,350			560, 2,585, S/L			930

Engine, Nominal/Rated BHP. N.R. = Engine Built, Not Flown Or Use in Flight Uncertain	Fuel Spec. – Where Stated (n/l = non-leaded) (TEL = Tetra-ethyl-lead)	Take-Off, S/L BHP, RPM, Max Boost	Normal, Continuous Climb (Rated) Power. BHP, RPM, Max. Boost, Rated Alt.			Maximum Power (Emergency, Combat, 5 Minutes) BHP, RPM, Max. Boost, Altitude			DRY WT LB
			Unsupercharged	Medium Supercharged	Fully Supercharged	Unsupercharged	Medium Supercharged	Fully Supercharged	
Napier Lion IX		460, 2,000				490, 2,200			
Napier Lion X		460, 2,000				490, 2,200			
Napier Lion XA		460, 2,000				490, 2,200			
Napier Lion XI	C. DTD 134, 73-77 oct, n/l	540, 2,350	5540, 2,350, 5,000			580, 2,585, 5,000			980
Napier Lion XIA	D. DTD 224, 77 min oct n/l	530, 2,350	530, 2,350, 5,000			570, 2,585, 5,000			995
Napier Lion XIA Special		505, 2,350	525, 2,350, 5,000			560, 2,585, 10,500			1,095
Napier Lion XIB		570							
Napier Lion XV (N.R.)		555, 2,350	555, 2,350			605, 2,600			1,013
Napier Nomad N.Nm.7	M. Diesel fuel	3,467, 2,100, +89			2,443, 1,950, +76				3,580
Napier-Halford Sabre I	J. 100 oct, 100/130 grade	2,060, 3,700, +7							2,375
Napier-Halford Sabre I (Special)		2,560, 4,000, +9.2					2,560, 4,000, +9.2		
Napier-Halford Sabre II	J. 100 oct, 100/130 grade	2,300, 3,700, +7		3,500, +6	3,500, +6		3,700, +7	3,700, +7	
Napier-Halford Sabre IIA	J. 100 oct, 100/130 grade	1,995, 3,750, +7		2,065, 3,700, +7, 4,750	1,735, 3,700, +7, 17,000		2,235, 3,700, +9, 2,500	1,880, 3,700, +9, 15,250	
Napier-Halford Sabre IIB	J. 100 oct, 100/130 grade	2,010, 3,850, +11		2,065, 3,700, 4,750	1,735, 3,700, 17,000		2,400, 3,850, S/L, +11	2,045, 3,850, 13,750, +11	
Napier-Halford Sabre IIC	J. 100 oct, 100/130 grade	2,065, 3,850, +17.25		2,235, 3,700, 8,500	1,960, 3,700, 18,250		3,055, 3,850, +17.25, 2,250	2,760, 3,850, +17.25, 12,450	2,540
Napier-Halford Sabre III	J. 100 oct, 100/130 grade	2,250, 4,000		1,890, 3,500, 5,000	1,630, 3,500, 16,500		2,310, 4,000, 2,500	1,920, 4,000, 16,000	
Napier-Halford Sabre IV	J. 100 oct, 100/130 grade	2,240, 4,000, +9		2,240, 4,000, +9, 8,000					
Napier-Halford Sabre V	J. 100 oct, 100/130 grade	2,300, 3,850, +12		2,165, 3,650, 6,500	1,930, 3,650, 15,750		2,600, 3,850, 2,500	2,300, 3,850, 12,750	2,500
Napier-Halford Sabre VA	J. 100 oct, 100/130 grade	2,300, 3,850, +15		2,165, 3,650, 6,500	1,930, 3,650, 15,750		2,600, 3,850, 2,500, +15	2,300, 3,850, 12,750, +15	2,490
Napier-Halford Sabre VI	J. 100 oct, 100/130 grade	2,310, 3,750							
Napier-Halford Sabre VII	J. 100 oct, 100/130 grade	3,000, 3,850, +17.25		2,235, 3,700, +17.25	1,960, 3,700, 18,250		3,055, 3,850, +17.25, 2,250	2,760, 3,850, +17.25, 12,450	2,540
Napier-Halford Sabre VII (wet)	J. 100 oct, 100/130 grade	3,500, 3,850, +20		2,235, 3,700, 8,500	1,960, 3,700, 18,250		3,055, 3,850, +20, 2,250	2,760, 3,850, +20, 12,450	2,540
Napier-Halford Sabre VIII		3,000,							
Napier-Halford Sabre E.118									
Napier-Halford Dagger I	G. DTD 230, 87 oct	715, 3,500, +3							
Napier-Halford Dagger II	G. DTD 230, 87 oct	700, 3,500, +3.5			695, 3,500, +1.5, 10,000			725, 4,000, +3, 12,500	1,302
Napier-Halford Dagger IIIM	G. DTD 230, 87 oct			725, 3,500, +2.25, 3,500			825, 4,000, +2.25, 4,000		1,358
Napier-Halford Dagger VII	G. DTD 230, 87 oct	955, 4,200, +6		925, 4,000, +6, 9,000			1,000, 4,200, +6,		1,390

Engine, Nominal/Rated BHP N.R. = Engine Built, Not Flown Or Use in Flight Uncertain	Fuel Spec. – Where Stated (nil = non-leaded) (TEL = Tetra-ethyl-lead)	Take-Off, S/L BHP, RPM, Max Boost	Normal, Continuous Climb (Rated) Power. BHP, RPM, Max. Boost, Rated Alt.			Maximum Power (Emergency, Combat, 5 Minutes) BHP, RPM, Max. Boost, Altitude			DRY WT LB
			Unsupercharged	Medium Supercharged	Fully Supercharged	Unsupercharged	Medium Supercharged	Fully Supercharged	
Napier-Halford Javelin I		150, 2,000	150, 2,000			170, 2,300			410
Napier-Halford Javelin III		160, 2,100	160, 2,100			172, 2,325			420
Napier-Halford Javelin IIIA		160, 2,100	160, 2,100			172, 2,325			420
Napier-Halford Rapier I		301, 3,500		301, 3,500					640
Napier-Halford Rapier II		295, 3,500			305, 3,500, 10,000			355, 3,900, 10,000	710
Napier-Halford Rapier IV		325, 3,50/CO		340, 3,500, +??, S/L			385, 3,900, +??, S/L		726
Napier-Halford Rapier V	G. DTD 230, 87 oct	335, 3,500, +3.0			315, 3,500, +1.5, 13,000			330/340, 4,000, +3, 13,000	720
Napier-Halford Rapier VI	G. DTD 230, 87 oct	365, 3,500, +3.5		370, 3,650, +2.5, 4,750			395, 4,000, +3.5, 6,000		707
Packard V-1650 - see R-R									
Pobjoy Cataract I		75, 2,900, S/L	75, 2,900, S/L			80, 3,200 S/L			135
Pobjoy Cataract II		84, 3,200, S/L	84, 3,200, S/L			90, 3,500, S/L			148
Pobjoy Cataract III		90, 3,000, S/L	90, 3,000, S/L			90, 3,500, S/L			130
Pobjoy Niagara I		84, 3,200	84, 3,200, S/L			90, 3,500, S/L			157
Pobjoy Niagara II		84, 3,200	84, 3,200, S/L			90, 3,500, S/L			157
Pobjoy Niagara III		85, 3,300	88, 3,300, S/L			93, 3,625, S/L			148
Pobjoy Niagara IV		98, 3,300	98, 3,300, S/L			98, 3,625, S/L			130
Pobjoy Niagara V		125, 4,000	125, 4,000, S/L			142, 4,600, S/L			175
Pobjoy P-1		60, 3,000	60, 3,000			67.5, 3,300, S/L			119
Pobjoy R		75, 3,000	75, 3,000			85, 3,300, S/L			143
R.E.P. (60)	A. Pre-1923, 40-50 octane	60, 1,100	60, 1,100						330
Rednup Fury II	A. Pre-1923, 40-50 octane	85, 2,200	85, 2,200						200
Renault (60)	A. Pre-1923, 40-50 octane	60, 1,800	60, 1,800						373
Renault WB, WC (70)	A. Pre-1923, 40-50 octane	70, 1,750	75, 1,800						396
Renault WS (80)	A. Pre-1923, 40-50 octane	80, 1,800	80, 1,800			104, 1,900			463
Renault (160)	A. Pre-1923, 40-50 octane	160							
Renault (190) 8Gd (N.R.)	A. Pre-1923, 40-50 octane	190							
Renault 12Fe (220)	A. Pre-1923, 40-50 octane	220, 1,400	260, 1,400			290, 1,600			805
Rollason Ardem 4CO2-1		34,							

Engine, Nominal/Rated BHP N.R. = Engine Built, Not Flown Or Use in Flight Uncertain	Fuel Spec. – Where Stated (n/l = non-leaded) (TEL = Tetra-ethyl-lead)	Take-Off, S/L BHP, RPM, Max Boost	Normal, Continuous Climb (Rated) Power. BHP, RPM, Max. Boost, Rated Alt.			Maximum Power (Emergency, Combat, 5 Minutes) BHP, RPM, Max. Boost, Altitude			DRY WT LB
			Unsupercharged	Medium Supercharged	Fully Supercharged	Unsupercharged	Medium Supercharged	Fully Supercharged	
R-R Buzzard IMS (N.R.)	C. DTD 134, 73-77 oct, n/l	825, 2,000	825, 2,000, 2,000				955, 2,300, 2,000		1,540
R-R Buzzard IIMS	C. DTD 134, 73-77 oct, n/l	825, 2,000	825, 2,000				825, 2,000, 2,000	955, 2,300, 2,000	1,540
R-R Buzzard IIIMS	C. DTD 134, 73-77 oct, n/l	825, 2,000	825, 2,000				840, 2,000, 2,000	937, 2,300, 2,000	1,540
R-R Condor I (600)		610, 1,750	610, 1,750			656, 2,000			1,350
R-R Condor IA		650, 1,900	650, 1,900			675, 2,000			1,606
R-R Condor II		650, 1,900	650, 1,900			2,100			1,606
R-R Condor IIA									1,606
R-R Condor III (N.R.) ??		745, 1,900	665, 1,900, 3,000			797, 2,100			1,400
R-R Condor III		650/670, 1900	650, 1,900			707, 2,100			1,336
R-R Condor IIIA		665, 1,900 GT	665, 1,900, 3,000			797, 2,100 S/L			1,380
R-R Condor IIIB		665, 1,900 GT	665, 1,900, 3,000			797, 2,100 S/L			1,395
R-R Condor IV		750, 2,000	700, 2,000			785, 2,200 S/L			1,300
R-R Condor IVA (N.R.)		750, 2,000							1,250
R-R Condor V (N.R.)									1,250
R-R Condor VII (N.R.)									1,250
R-R Condor C.I.	M. Diesel fuel	480, 1,900	480, 1,900			480, 1,900			
R-R Eagle I (225)	A. Pre-1923, 40-50 octane	254, 1,800	254, 1,800			256, 1,900			900
R-R Eagle II (250)	A. Pre-1923, 40-50 octane	267, 1,800	267, 1,800			267, 1,900			907
R-R Eagle III (250)	A. Pre-1923, 40-50 octane	285, 1,800	285, 1,800			286, 1,980			907
R-R Eagle IV (250)	A. Pre-1923, 40-50 octane	285, 1,800	285, 1,800			286, 1,900			905
R-R Eagle V (275)	A. Pre-1923, 40-50 octane	307, 1,800	307, 1,800			315, 1,900			910
R-R Eagle VI (275)	A. Pre-1923, 40-50 octane	322, 1,800	322, 1,800			330, 1,900			960
R-R Eagle VII (275)	A. Pre-1923, 40-50 octane	322, 1,800	322, 1,800			330, 1,900			960
R-R Eagle VIII (300)	A. Pre-1923, 40-50 octane	360, 1,800	360, 1,800			368, 1,900			960
R-R Eagle IX (360)	A. Pre-1923, 40-50 octane	360, 1,800	360, 1,800			368, 1,900			965
R-R Eagle X (360) (N.R.)	A. Pre-1923, 40-50 octane	360, 1,800	360, 1,800			368, 1,900			965
R-R Eagle XV (360) (N.R.)	A. Pre-1923, 40-50 octane	360, 1,800	360, 1,800			368, 1,900			965
R-R Eagle XVI (N.R.)	A. Pre-1923, 40-50 octane								

Engine, Nominal/Rated BHP; N.R. = Engine Built, Not Flown; Or Use in Flight Uncertain	Fuel Spec. – Where Stated (nil = non-leaded) (TEL = Tetra-ethyl-lead)	Take-Off, S/L BHP, RPM, Max Boost (Unsupercharged)	Normal, Continuous Climb (Rated) Power. BHP, RPM, Max. Boost, Rated Alt. — Unsupercharged	Medium Supercharged	Fully Supercharged	Maximum Power (Emergency, Combat, 5 Minutes) BHP, RPM, Max. Boost, Altitude — Unsupercharged	Medium Supercharged	Fully Supercharged	DRY WT LB
R-R 46H Eagle I (N.R.)	J. 100 oct, 100/130 grade								3,900
R-R 46H Eagle II (N.R.)	J. 100 oct, 100/130 grade								3,900
R-R 46H Eagle Srs 22	L. 100 oct, 100/150 grade	3,500, 3,500, +21		3,150, 3,500, +21, 2,750	3,150, 3,500, +21, 14,250		2,600, 3,300, 9,500	2,410, 3,300, 19,500	3,900
R-R Exe		1,150, 4,200, +4.5		1,050, 3,600, +3.5, 4,000	925, 3,600, +3.5, 13,250		1,100, 3,800, +3.5, 5,000	950, 3,800, +3.5, 15,000	1,530
R-R Falcon I (230)	A. Pre-1923, 40-50 octane	230, 2,000	234, 2,100			234, 2,100			710
R-R Falcon II (253)	A. Pre-1923, 40-50 octane	253, 2,000	253, 2,000			263, 2,250			710
R-R Falcon III (285)	A. Pre-1923, 40-50 octane	285, 2,200	285, 2,200			288, 2,300			715
R-R Goshawk I	D. DTD 224, 77 min oct n/l	600, 2,600, +							975
R-R Goshawk II	D. DTD 224, 77 min oct n/l	615, 2,600, +3			600, 2,600, +1.5, 12,000			720, 3,000, +1.5, 12,500	
R-R Goshawk III	G. DTD 230, 87 oct	600, 2,500						+1.5 14,000	
R-R Goshawk VIII	G. DTD 230, 87 oct								
R-R Griffon I (N.R.)	J. 100 oct, 100/130 grade								
R-R Griffon II	J. 100 oct, 100/130 grade	1,720, 2,750, +12		1,735, 2,750, +9, 1,000	1,495, 2,750, +9, 14,500		1,735, 2,600, +12, 1,000	1,495, 2,600, +12, 14,500	1,790
R-R Griffon IIB	J. 100 oct, 100/130 grade	1,720, 2,750, +12		1,735, 2,750, +9, 1,000	1,495, 2,750, +9, 14,500		1,735, 2,600, +12, 1,000	1,495, 2,600, +12, 14,500	1,790
R-R Griffon III	J. 100 oct, 100/130 grade	1,720, 2,750, +12		1,735, 2,750, +9, 1,000	1,495, 2,750, +9, 14,500		1,735, 2,600, +12, 1,000	1,495, 2,600, +12, 14,500	1,790
R-R Griffon IV	J. 100 oct, 100/130 grade	1,720, 2,750, +12		1,735, 2,750, +9, 1,000	1,495, 2,750, +9, 14,500		1,735, 2,600, +12, 1,000	1,495, 2,600, +12, 14,500	1,790
R-R Griffon VI	J. 100 oct, 100/130 grade	1,950, 2,750, +15		1,475, 2,600, +9, 6,500	1,340, 2,600, +9, 14,800		1,850, 2,750, +15, 2,000	1,630, 2,750, +15, 10,500	1,800
R-R Griffon VIII (N.R.)	J. 100 oct, 100/130 grade	1,820, 2,750, +15		1,475, 2,600, +9, 6,500	1,340, 2,600, +9, 14,800		1,850, 2,750, +12, 2,000	1,630, 2,750, +15, 10,500	2,020
R-R Griffon XII	J. 100 oct, 100/130 grade	1,815, 2,750, +15		1,520, 2,600, +12, 3,250	1,330, 2,600, +9, 15,750		1,800, 2,750, +15, 1,000	1,645, 2,750, +15, 11,500	1,800
R-R Griffon 26	J. 100 oct, 100/130 grade	1,815, 2,750, +15		1,520, 2,600, +12, 3,250	1,330, 2,600, +9, 15,750		1,800, 2,750, +15, 1,000	1,645, 2,750, +15, 11,500	1,800
R-R Griffon 29	J. 100 oct, 100/130 grade	1,815, 2,750, +15		2,600, +9lb	2,600, +		1,665, 2,750, +	2,750, +	2,020
R-R Griffon 35 (N.R.)	J. 100 oct, 100/130 grade			2,600, +	2,600, +			2,750, +	
R-R Griffon 36 (N.R.)	J. 100 oct, 100/130 grade	2,200, 2,750, +18		1,680, 2,600, +12, 6,500	1,580, 2,600, +12, 13,500		2,050, 2,750, +18, 2,000	1,870, 2,750, +18, 11,000	1,980
R-R Griffon 37	J. 100 oct, 100/130 grade	2,200, 2,750, +18		1,680, 2,600, +12, 6,500	1,580, 2,600, +12, 13,500		2,050, 2,750, +18, 2,000	1,870, 2,750, +18, 11,000	1,980
R-R Griffon 56		2,000, 2,750, +							
R-R Griffon 57	L. 100 oct, 100/150 grade	2,500, 2,750 +25(S)		1,590, 2,600, +18, S/L	1,540, 2,600, +18, 12,500		2,030, 2,750, +18, 1,750	1,830, 2,750, +18, 10,000	2,050
R-R Griffon 57A	L. 100 oct, 100/150 grade	2,500, 2,750 +25(S)		1,590, 2,600, +18, S/L	1,540, 2,600, +18, 12,500		2,030, 2,750, +18, 1,750	1,830, 2,750, +18, 10,000	2,050
R-R Griffon 59	L. 100 oct, 100/150 grade								

Engine, Nominal/Rated BHP. N.R. = Engine Built, Not Flown Or Use in Flight Uncertain	Fuel Spec. – Where Stated (n/l = non-leaded) (TEL = Tetra-ethyl-lead)	Take-Off, S/L BHP, RPM, Max Boost	Normal, Continuous Climb (Rated) Power. BHP, RPM, Max. Boost, Rated Alt.			Maximum Power (Emergency, Combat, 5 Minutes) BHP, RPM, Max. Boost, Altitude			DRY WT LB
			Unsupercharged	Medium Supercharged	Fully Supercharged	Unsupercharged	Medium Supercharged	Fully Supercharged	
R-R Griffon 61	J. 100 oct, 100/130 grade	1,900, 2,750 +18		1,480, 2,600, +9, 13,500	1,345, 2,600, +9, 26,100		2,005, 2,750, +18, 6,000	1,810, 2,750, +18, 20,500	1,980
R-R Griffon 61	L. 100 oct, 100/150 grade	1,900, 2,750 +18						2,300, 2,750, +25, 650	1,980
R-R Griffon 62	J. 100 oct, 100/130 grade	1,900, 2,750 +18		1,480, 2,600, +9, 13,500	1,345, 2,600, +9, 26,100		2,005, 2,750, +18, 6,000	1,810, 2,750, +18, 20,500	1,980
R-R Griffon 62	L. 100 oct, 100/150 grade	1,900, 2,750 +18						2,300, 2,750, +25, 650	1,980
R-R Griffon 64	J. 100 oct, 100/130 grade	1,900, 2,750 +18		1,480, 2,600, +9, 13,500	1,345, 2,600, +9, 26,100	2,005, 2,750, +18, 6,000	1,810, 2,750, +18, 20,500		1,980
R-R Griffon 64	K. 115/145 grade	1,900, 2,750 +18						2,300, 2,750, +25, 650	1,980
R-R Griffon 65	J. 100 oct, 100/130 grade	1,900, 2,750 +18		1,480, 2,600, +9, 13,500	1,345, 2,600, +9, 26,100	2,005, 2,750, +18, 6,000	1,810, 2,750, +18, 20,500		1,980
R-R Griffon 65	K. 115/145 grade	1,900, 2,750 +18						2,300, 2,750, +25, 650	1,980
R-R Griffon 66	J. 100 oct, 100/130 grade	1,900, 2,750 +18		1,480, 2,600, +9, 13,500	1,345, 2,600, +9, 26,100	2,005, 2,750, +18, 6,000	1,810, 2,750, +18, 20,500		1,980
R-R Griffon 66	K. 115/145 grade	1,900, 2,750 +18						2,300, 2,750, +25, 650	1,980
R-R Griffon 67	J. 100 oct, 100/130 grade	1,900, 2,750 +18		1,480, 2,600, +9, 13,500	1,345, 2,600, +9, 26,100	2,005, 2,750, +18, 6,000	1,810, 2,750, +18, 20,500		1,980
R-R Griffon 67	L. 100 oct, 100/150 grade	1,900, 2,750 +18						2,300, 2,750, +25, 650	1,980
R-R Griffon 68 (N.R.)	J. 100 oct, 100/130 grade	2,750 +18		2,600, +	2,600, +		2,750, +18,	, , 2,750, +	1,980
R-R Griffon 69	J. 100 oct, 100/130 grade	1,900, 2,750 +18		1,480, 2,600, +9, 13,500	1,345, 2,600, +9, 26,100	2,005, 2,750, +18, 6,000	1,810, 2,750, +18, 20,500		1,980
R-R Griffon 69	K. 115/145 grade	1,900, 2,750 +18						2,300, 2,750, +25, 650	1,980
R-R Griffon 70 (N.R.)	J. 100 oct, 100/130 grade	2,750 +18		2,600, +	2,600, +		2,750, +25,	, , 2,750, +	1,980
R-R Griffon 71	J. 100 oct, 100/130 grade	1,765, 2,750 +18		1,510, 2,600, +9, 7,600	1,410, 2,600, +9, 20,500	2,050, 2,750, +18, 700	1,900, 2,750, +18, 15,000		1,980
R-R Griffon 71	L. 100 oct, 100/150 grade	1,765, 2,750 +18						2,190, 2,750, +25, 9,900	1,980
R-R Griffon 72	J. 100 oct, 100/130 grade	1,765, 2,750 +18		1,510, 2,600, +9, 7,600	1,410, 2,600, +9, 20,500	2,050, 2,750, +18, 700	1,900, 2,750, +18, 15,000		1,980
R-R Griffon 72	K. 115/145 grade	1,765, 2,750 +18						2,190, 2,750, +25, 9,900	1,980
R-R Griffon 73	J. 100 oct, 100/130 grade	1,765, 2,750 +18		2,600, +	2,600, +	1,665, 2,750, +18, 11,000	2,245, 2,750, +18 2,020		1,980
R-R Griffon 73	L. 100 oct, 100/150 grade	1,765, 2,750 +18							
R-R Griffon 74	J. 100 oct, 100/130 grade	1,765, 2,750 +18		1,510, 2,600, +9, 7,600	1,410, 2,600, +9, 20,500	2,050, 2,750, +18, 700	1,900, 2,750, +18, 15,000		1,980
R-R Griffon 74	K. 115/145 grade	1,765, 2,750 +18						2,190, 2,750, +25, 9,900	1,980
R-R Griffon 83	J. 100 oct, 100/130 grade	1,900, 2,750 +18		1,480, 2,600, +9, 13,500	1,345, 2,600, +9, 26,100	2,005, 2,750, +18, 6,000	1,810, 2,750, +18, 20,500		1,980
R-R Griffon 83	K. 115/145 grade	1,900, 2,750 +18						2,300, 2,750, +25, 650	1,980
R-R Griffon 85	J. 100 oct, 100/130 grade	1,900, 2,750 +18		1,480, 2,600, +9, 13,500	1,345, 2,600, +9, 26,100	2,005, 2,750, +18, 6,000	1,810, 2,750, +18, 20,500		1,980
R-R Griffon 85	K. 115/145 grade	1,900, 2,750 +18						2,300, 2,750, +25, 650	1,980

Engine, Nominal/Rated BHP. N.R. = Engine Built, Not Flown. Or Use in Flight Uncertain	Fuel Spec. – Where Stated (n/l = non-leaded) (TEL = Tetra-ethyl-lead)	Take-Off, S/L BHP, RPM, Max Boost	Normal, Continuous Climb (Rated) Power. BHP, RPM, Max. Boost, Rated Alt.			Maximum Power (Emergency, Combat, 5 Minutes) BHP, RPM, Max. Boost, Altitude			DRY WT LB
			Unsupercharged	Medium Supercharged	Fully Supercharged	Unsupercharged	Medium Supercharged	Fully Supercharged	
R-R Griffon 86	J. 100 oct, 100/130 grade	1,900, 2,750 +18		1,480, 2,600, +9, 13,500	1,345, 2,600, +9, 26,100		2,005, 2,750, +18, 6,000	1,810, 2,750, +18, 20,500	1,980
R-R Griffon 86	L. 100 oct, 100/150 grade	1,900, 2,750 +18						2,300, 2,750, +25, 650	1,980
R-R Griffon 87	J. 100 oct, 100/130 grade	1,900, 2,750 +18		1,480, 2,600, +9, 13,500	1,345, 2,600, +9, 26,100		2,005, 2,750, +18, 6,000	1,810, 2,750, +18, 20,500	1,980
R-R Griffon 87	K. 115/145 grade	1,900, 2,750 +18						2,300, 2,750, +25, 650	1,980
R-R Griffon 88	J. 100 oct, 100/130 grade	1,900, 2,750 +18		1,480, 2,600, +9, 13,500	1,345, 2,600, +9, 26,100		2,005, 2,750, +18, 6,000	1,810, 2,750, +18, 20,500	1,980
R-R Griffon 88	K. 115/145 grade	1,900, 2,750 +18						2,300, 2,750, +25, 650	1,980
R-R Griffon 89	J. 100 oct, 100/130 grade	1,900, 2,750 +18		1,480, 2,600, +9, 13,500	1,345, 2,600, +9, 26,100		2,005, 2,750, +18, 6,000	1,810, 2,750, +18, 20,500	1,980
R-R Griffon 89	K. 115/145 grade	1,900, 2,750 +18						2,300, 2,750, +25, 650	1,980
R-R Griffon 90	J. 100 oct, 100/130 grade	1,900, 2,750 +18		1,480, 2,600, +9, 13,500	1,345, 2,600, +9, 26,100		2,005, 2,750, +18, 6,000	1,810, 2,750, +18, 20,500	1,980
R-R Griffon 90	L. 100 oct, 100/150 grade	1,900, 2,750 +18						2,300, 2,750, +25, 650	1,980
R-R Griffon 91 (N.R.)	J. 100 oct, 100/130 grade	1,765, 2,750 +18		1,510, 2,600, +9, 7,600	1,410, 2,600, +9, 20,500		2,050, 2,750, +18, 700	1,900, 2,750, +18, 15,000	1,980
R-R Griffon 91 (N.R.)	K. 115/145 grade	1,765, 2,750 +18						2,190, 2,750, +25, 9,900	1,980
R-R Griffon 92 (N.R.)	J. 100 oct, 100/130 grade	1,765, 2,750 +18		1,510, 2,600, +9, 7,600	1,410, 2,600, +9, 20,500		2,050, 2,750, +18, 700	1,900, 2,750, +18, 15,000	1,980
R-R Griffon 92 (N.R.)	K. 115/145 grade	1,765, 2,750 +18						2,190, 2,750, +25, 9,900	1,980
R-R Griffon 94 (N.R.)	J. 100 oct, 100/130 grade	2,750 +							
R-R Griffon 101	K. 115/145 grade	1,900, 2,750 +25		See Text	See Text		See Text	See Text	2,100
R-R Griffon 102	K. 115/145 grade	1,900, 2,750 +25		See Text Griffon 101.	See Text Griffon 101.	See Text, Griffon	See Text, Griffon 101.	See Text Griffon 101.	2,100
R-R Griffon 105	K. 115/145 grade	1,900, 2,750 +25		See Text Griffon 101.	See Text Griffon 101.	See Text, Griffon	See Text, Griffon 101.	See Text Griffon 101.	2,100
R-R Griffon 121	K. 115/145 grade	1,900, 2,750 +25		See Text Griffon 101.	See Text Griffon 101.	See Text, Griffon	See Text, Griffon 101.	See Text Griffon 101.	2,100
R-R Griffon 122	K. 115/145 grade	1,900, 2,750 +25		See Text Griffon 101.	See Text Griffon 101.	See Text, Griffon	See Text, Griffon 101.	See Text Griffon 101.	2,100
R-R Griffon 130 (N.R.)	K. 115/145 grade	1,900, 2,750 +25		See Text Griffon 101.	See Text Griffon 101.	See Text, Griffon	See Text, Griffon 101.	See Text Griffon 101.	2,100
R-R Hawk I (75)	A. Pre-1923, 40-50 octane	75, 1,350	91, 1,500			95, 1,600			406
R-R Hawk II (100) (N.R.)	A. Pre-1923, 40-50 octane	100, 1,500							
R-R F.X (Kestrel prot)	C. DTD 134, 73-77 oct, n/l		760						
R-R Kestrel IA	C. DTD 134, 73-77 oct, n/l	490, 2,500	490, 2,250, 2,000			560, 2,700, 3,000			865
R-R Kestrel IIA	C. DTD 134, 73-77 oct, n/l	490, 2,250	490, 2,250, 2,000			560, 2,700, 3,000			865
R-R Kestrel IIIA	C. DTD 134, 73-77 oct, n/l	490, 2,250	490, 2,250, 2,000			560, 2,700, 3,000			865
R-R Kestrel IB	D. DTD 224, 77 min oct n/l	546, 2,250	480, 2,250, 3,000			600, 2,700, 3,000			865

Engine, Nominal/Rated BHP N.R. = Engine Built, Not Flown Or Use in Flight Uncertain	Fuel Spec. – Where Stated (n/l = non-leaded) (TEL = Tetra-ethyl-lead)	Take-Off, S/L BHP, RPM, Max Boost	Normal, Continuous Climb (Rated) Power. BHP, RPM, Max. Boost, Rated Alt.			Maximum Power (Emergency, Combat, 5 Minutes) BHP, RPM, Max. Boost, Altitude			DRY WT LB
			Unsupercharged	Medium Supercharged	Fully Supercharged	Unsupercharged	Medium Supercharged	Fully Supercharged	
R-R Kestrel IB3 (N.R.)	D. DTD 224, 77 min oct n/l	546, 2,250	480, 2,250, 3,000						865
R-R Kestrel IB4 (N.R.)	D. DTD 224, 77 min oct n/l	546, 2,250	480, 2,250, 3,000						865
R-R Kestrel IB5 (N.R.)	D. DTD 224, 77 min oct n/l	546, 2,250	480, 2,250, 3,000						865
R-R Kestrel IIB	D. DTD 224, 77 min oct n/l	546, 2,250	480, 2,250, 3,000			530, 2,700, 3,000			865
R-R Kestrel IIIB	D. DTD 224, 77 min oct n/l	546, 2,250	480, 2,250, 3,000			530, 2,700, 3,000			865
R-R Kestrel IMS (N.R.)	D. DTD 224, 77 min oct n/l	525, 2,250 +1.375		500, 2,250, +1.375, 3,000			620, 2,700, +1.5, 3,000		900
R-R Kestrel IIMS	D. DTD 224, 77 min oct n/l	525, 2,250 +1.375		500, 2,250, +1.375, 3,000			620, 2,700, +1.5, 3,000		900
R-R Kestrel IIMS Pusher	D. DTD 224, 77 min oct n/l	525, 2,250 +1.375		500, 2,250, +1.375, 3,000			620, 2,700, +1.5, 3,000		900
R-R Kestrel IIMS.2	D. DTD 224, 77 min oct n/l	525, 2,250 +1.375		500, 2,250, +1.375, 3,000			620, 2,700, +1.5, 3,000		900
R-R Kestrel IIMS.5	D. DTD 224, 77 min oct n/l	525, 2,250 +1.375		500, 2,250, +1.375, 3,000			620, 2,700, +1.5, 3,000		900
R-R Kestrel IIMS.6	D. DTD 224, 77 min oct n/l	525, 2,250 +1.375		500, 2,250, +1.375, 3,000			620, 2,700, +1.5, 3,000		900
R-R Kestrel IIIMS	D. DTD 224, 77 min oct n/l	525, 2,250 +1.375		500, 2,250, +1.375, 3,000			620, 2,700, +1.5, 3,000		900
R-R Kestrel IIIMS Pusher	D. DTD 224, 77 min oct n/l	525, 2,250 +1.375		500, 2,250, +1.375, 3,000			620, 2,700, +1.5, 3,000		900
R-R Kestrel IIIMS.2 (N.R.)	D. DTD 224, 77 min oct n/l	525, 2,250 +1.375		500, 2,250, +1.375, 3,000			620, 2,700, +1.5, 3,000		900
R-R Kestrel IIIMS.4 (N.R.)	D. DTD 224, 77 min oct n/l	525, 2,250 +1.375		500, 2,250, +1.375, 3,000			620, 2,700, +1.5, 3,000		900
R-R Kestrel IIIMS.6	D. DTD 224, 77 min oct n/l	525, 2,250 +1.375		500, 2,250, +1.375, 3,000			620, 2,700, +1.5, 3,000		900
R-R Kestrel IS	D. DTD 224, 77 min oct n/l	480, 2,250 +1.75			480, 2,250, -.5, 11,500			550, 2,700, +1.75, 13,000	900
R-R Kestrel IIS	D. DTD 224, 77 min oct n/l	480, 2,250 +1.75			480, 2,250, -.5, 11,500			550, 2,700, +1.75, 13,000	900
R-R Kestrel IIS Pusher	D. DTD 224, 77 min oct n/l	480, 2,250 +1.75			480, 2,250, -.5, 11,500			550, 2,700, +1.75, 13,000	900
R-R Kestrel IIIS	D. DTD 224, 77 min oct n/l	480, 2,250 +1.75			480, 2,250, -.5, 11,500			550, 2,700, +1.75, 13,000	900
R-R Kestrel V	G. DTD 230, 87 oct	745, 2,500 +6			600, 2,500, +1.5, 11,000			640, 2,900, +1.5, 14,000	975
R-R Kestrel VDR	D. DTD 224, 77 min oct n/l	692, 2,500 +2.25			673, 2,350, +0, 12,000			508, 2,350, -.35, 12,000	975
R-R Kestrel VI	G. DTD 230, 87 oct	745, 2,500 +6			600, 2,500, +1.5, 11,000			640, 2,900, +1.5, 14,000	975
R-R Kestrel VII (N.R.)	G. DTD 230, 87 oct	700, 2,375, +4.5 FT		675, 2,500, +2.625, 3,000			730, 2,900, +2.625, 5,250		975
R-R Kestrel VIII Pusher	G. DTD 230, 87 oct	700, 2,375, +4.5 FT		675, 2,500, +2.625, 3,000			730, 2,900, +2.625, 5,250		975
R-R Kestrel IX Tractor	G. DTD 230, 87 oct	700, 2,375, +4.5 FT		675, 2,500, +2.625, 3,000			730, 2,900, +2.625, 5,250		975
R-R Kestrel X	G. DTD 230, 87 oct	500/525, 2,500,	560/585, 2,500			610/635, 2,900			918
R-R Kestrel XDR	D. DTD 224, 77 min oct n/l	520/545, 2,500,	560/585, 2,500			610/635, 2,900			918

Engine, Nominal/Rated BHP N.R. = Engine Built, Not Flown Or Use in Flight Uncertain	Fuel Spec. – Where Stated (nil = non-leaded) (TEL = Tetra-ethyl-lead)	Take-Off S/L BHP, RPM, Max Boost	Normal, Continuous Climb (Rated) Power. BHP, RPM, Max. Boost, Rated Alt. Unsupercharged	Medium Supercharged	Fully Supercharged	Maximum Power (Emergency, Combat, 5 Minutes) BHP, RPM, Max. Boost, Altitude Unsupercharged	Medium Supercharged	Fully Supercharged	DRY WT LB
R-R Kestrel XI (N.R.)	G. DTD 230, 87 oct	520/545, 2,500,	560/585, 2,500			610/635, 2,900			918
R-R Kestrel XII (N.R.)	G. DTD 230, 87 oct	520/545, 2,500,	560/585, 2,500			610/635, 2,900			918
R-R Kestrel XIV (N.R.)	G. DTD 230, 87 oct	670, 2,225 +6			690, 2,600, +3.25, 11,000			745, 3,000, +3.25, 14,500	975
R-R Kestrel XV (N.R.)	G. DTD 230, 87 oct	670, 2,225 +6			690, 2,600, +3.25, 11,000			745, 3,000, +3.25, 14,500	975
R-R Kestrel XVI	G. DTD 230, 87 oct	670, 2,225 +6			690, 2,600, +3.25, 11,000			745, 3,000, +3.25, 14,500	975
R-R Kestrel XVIDR	G. DTD 230, 87 oct	670, 2,225 +6			690, 2,600, +3.25, 11,000			745, 3,000, +3.25, 14,500	975
R-R Kestrel XVI(Spl) (N.R.)	G. DTD 230, 87 oct	670, 2,225 +6			690, 2,600, +3.25, 11,000			745, 3,000, +3.25, 14,500	975
R-R Kestrel XVI(VP)	G. DTD 230, 87 oct	670, 2,225 +6			690, 2,600, +3.25, 11,000			745, 3,000, +3.25, 14,500	975
R-R Kestrel XXX	G. DTD 230, 87 oct	720, 2,750 +5			550, 2,400, +.5, 11,750			585, 2,750, +.5 12,000	990
R-R Merlin Prot P V 12	G. DTD 230, 87 oct	3,000 +							1,177
R-R Merlin B	G. DTD 230, 87 oct	3,000 +							
R-R Merlin C	G. DTD 230, 87 oct	890, 2,850 +6			950, 2,600, +6 11,000			1,100, 3,000, +6, 12,500	
R-R Merlin E	G. DTD 230, 87 oct	890, 2,850 +6.25							
R-R Merlin F	G. DTD 230, 87 oct	890, 2,850 +6			990, 2,600, +6.25			1,030, 3,000, +6.25, 16,250	1,375
R-R Merlin G	G. DTD 230, 87 oct	890, 2,850, +6.25			990, 2,600, +6.25, 12,250			1,030, 3,000, +6.25, 16,250	1,375
R-R Merlin I	G. DTD 230, 87 oct	890, 2,850 +6			990, 2,600, +6.25			1,030, 3,000, +6.25, 16,250	1,375
R-R Merlin II	G. DTD 230, 87 oct	890, 2,850, +6.25			990, 2,600, +6.25, 12,250			1,030, 3,000, +6.25, 16,250	1,375
R-R Merlin II Special	G. DTD 230, 87 oct	2,160, 3,200 +27				2,160, 3,200 +27, S/L	1,370		
R-R Merlin III	G. DTD 230, 87 oct	890, 2,850, +6.25			990, 2,600, +6.25, 12,250			1,030, 3,000, +6.25, 16,250	1,375
R-R Merlin IV		890, 3,000, +9-12						1,030, 3,000, +6.25, 16,250	1,375
R-R Merlin V		890, 3,000, +9-12						1,310, 3,000, +12, 9,000	1,375
R-R Merlin VIII		1,275, 3,000, +5.75	1,025, 2,850, +4, 6,500				1,060, 3,000, +4, 7,500		1,420
R-R Merlin X	H. 87 oct, higher with 100	1,065, 3,000, +5.75	1,035, 2,600, +5.75, 2,250				1,130, 3,000, +5.75, 5,250	1,010, 3,000, +5.75, 17,750	1,450
R-R Merlin XII	H. 100 oct, less with 87	1,175, 3,000, +12.5			2,850, +9, 13,000			1,280, 3,000, +9, 10,500	1,420
R-R Merlin XII	G. DTD 230, 87 oct	3,000 +7			2,850, +7, 13,000			3,000, +7, 10,000	1,420
R-R Merlin XX	J. 100 oct, 100/130 grade	1,280, 3,000, +12		1,125, 2,850, +9, 9,500	1,130, 2,850, +9, 16,750		1,460, 3,000, +14, 6,500	1,430, 3,000, +16, 11,000	1,450
R-R Merlin 21	J. 100 oct, 100/130 grade	1,280, 3,000, +12		1,125, 2,850, +9, 9,500	1,130, 2,850, +9, 16,750		1,460, 3,000, +14, 6,250	1,430, 3,000, +16, 11,000	1,450
R-R Merlin 22	J. 100 oct, 100/130 grade	1,390, 3,000, +14		1,125, 2,850, +9, 9,500	1,130, 2,850, +9, 16,750		1,460, 3,000, +14, 6,250	1,430, 3,000, +16, 11,000	1,450

Engine, Nominal/Rated BHP N.R. = Engine Built, Not Flown Or Use in Flight Uncertain	Fuel Spec. – Where Stated (n/l = non-leaded) (TEL = Tetra-ethyl-lead)	Take-Off. S/L BHP, RPM, Max Boost	Normal, Continuous Climb (Rated) Power. BHP, RPM, Max. Boost, Rated Alt.			Maximum Power (Emergency, Combat, 5 Minutes) BHP, RPM, Max. Boost, Altitude			DRY WT LB
			Unsupercharged	Medium Supercharged	Fully Supercharged	Unsupercharged	Medium Supercharged	Fully Supercharged	
R-R Merlin 22A (N.R.)	J. 100 oct, 100/130 grade	1,390, 3,000, +14		1,125, 2,850, +9, 9,500	1,130, 2,850, +9, 16,750		1,460, 3,000, +14, 6,250	1,430, 3,000, +16, 11,000	1,460
R-R Merlin 23	J. 100 oct, 100/130 grade	1,390, 3,000, +14		1,125, 2,850, +9, 9,500	1,130, 2,850, +9, 16,750		1,460, 3,000, +14, 6,250	1,430, 3,000, +16, 11,000	1,450
R-R Merlin 23A (N.R.)	J. 100 oct, 100/130 grade	1,390, 3,000, +14		1,125, 2,850, +9, 9,500	1,130, 2,850, +9, 16,750		1,460, 3,000, +14, 6,250	1,430, 3,000, +16, 11,000	1,460
R-R Merlin 24	J. 100 oct, 100/130 grade	1,610, 3,000, +18		1,125, 2,850, +9, 9,500	1,130, 2,850, +9, 16,750		1,630, 3,000, +18, 2,500	1,510, 3,000, +18, 9,250	1,455
R-R Merlin T.24/2	J. 100 oct, 100/130 grade	1,610, 3,000, +18		1,125, 2,850, +9, 9,500	1,130, 2,850, +9, 16,750		1,630, 3,000, +18, 2,500	1,510, 3,000, +18, 9,250	1,460
R-R Merlin T.24/4	J. 100 oct, 100/130 grade	1,610, 3,000, +18		1,125, 2,850, +9, 9,500	1,130, 2,850, +9, 16,750		1,630, 3,000, +18, 2,500	1,510, 3,000, +18, 9,250	1,465
R-R Merlin 25	J. 100 oct, 100/130 grade	1,610, 3,000, +18		1,125, 2,850, +9, 9,500	1,130, 2,850, +9, 16,750		1,630, 3,000, +18, 2,500	1,510, 3,000, +18, 9,250	1,455
R-R Merlin 27	J. 100 oct, 100/130 grade	1,610, 3,000, +18		1,125, 2,850, +9, 9,500	1,130, 2,850, +9, 16,750		1,630, 3,000, +18, 2,500	1,510, 3,000, +18, 9,250	1,455
R-R Merlin 28 (V-1650-1)	J. 100 oct, 100/130 grade	1,390, 3,000, +14		1,125, 2,850, +9, 9,500	1,130, 2,850, +9, 16,750		1,460, 3,000, +14, 6,250	1,430, 3,000, +16, 11,000	1,460
R-R Merlin 29	J. 100 oct, 100/130 grade	1,390, 3,000, +14		1,125, 2,850, +9, 9,500	1,130, 2,850, +9, 16,750		1,460, 3,000, +14, 6,250	1,430, 3,000, +16, 11,000	1,460
R-R Merlin 30	J. 100 oct, 100/130 grade	1,300, 3,000, +12.5							1,420
R-R Merlin 31	J. 100 oct, 100/130 grade	1,390, 3,000, +14		1,125, 2,850, +9, 9,500	1,130, 2,850, +9, 16,750		1,460, 3,000, +14, 6,250	1,430, 3,000, +16, 11,000	1,460
R-R Merlin 32	J. 100 oct, 100/130 grade	1,620, 3,000, +18		1,335, 2,850, +12, 5,100	1,130, 2,850, +9, 16,750		1,620, 3,000, +18, 1,500	1,430, 3,000, +18, 1,500	1,430
R-R Merlin 33	J. 100 oct, 100/130 grade	1,390, 3,000, +14		1,125, 2,850, +9, 9,500	1,130, 2,850, +9, 16,750		1,460, 3,000, +14, 6,250	1,430, 3,000, +16, 11,000	1,450
R-R Merlin T.34 (N.R.)	J. 100 oct, 100/130 grade	1,610, 3,000, +18		1,125, 2,850, +9, 9,500	1,130, 2,850, +9, 16,750		1,630, 3,000, +18, 2,500	1,510, 3,000, +18, 9,250	1,460
R-R Merlin 35	J. 100 oct, 100/130 grade	1,250, 3,000, +12		970, 2,650, +7, 9,500			1,225, 3,000, +9, 11,500		
R-R Merlin 38	J. 100 oct, 100/130 grade	1,390, 3,000, +14		1,125, 2,850, +9, 9,500	1,130, 2,850, +9, 16,750		1,460, 3,000, +14, 6,250	1,430, 3,000, +16, 11,000	1,450
R-R Merlin 45	J. 100 oct, 100/130 grade	1,230, 3,000, +12			1,200, 2,850, +9, 16,000			1,230, 3,000 +12, 18,000	1,385
R-R Merlin 45M	J. 100 oct, 100/130 grade	1,230, 3,000, +12			1,155, 2,850, +9, 10,000			1,585, 3,000, +18, 3,000	1,385
R-R Merlin 46	J. 100 oct, 100/130 grade	1,120, 3,000, +12			1,160, 2,850, +9, 18,000			1,190, 3,000, +9, 23,000	1,385
R-R Merlin 47	J. 100 oct, 100/130 grade	1,120, 3,000, +12			1,160, 2,850, +9, 18,000			1,190, 3,000, +9, 23,000	1,385
R-R Merlin 50	J. 100 oct, 100/130 grade	1,230, 3,000, +12			1,200, 2,850, +9, 16,000			1,230, 3,000 +12, 18,000	1,385
R-R Merlin 50A	J. 100 oct, 100/130 grade	1,120, 3,000, +12			1,160, 2,850, +9, 18,000			1,190, 3,000, +9, 23,000	1,385
R-R Merlin 50M	J. 100 oct, 100/130 grade	1,230, 3,000, +12			1,155, 2,850, +9, 10,000			1,585, 3,000, +18, 3,000	1,385
R-R Merlin 55	J. 100 oct, 100/130 grade	1,230, 3,000, +12			1,200, 2,850, +9, 16,000			1,230, 3,000 +12, 18,000	1,385
R-R Merlin 55A	J. 100 oct, 100/130 grade	1,230, 3,000, +12			1,200, 2,850, +9, 16,000			1,230, 3,000 +12, 18,000	1,385
R-R Merlin 55M	J. 100 oct, 100/130 grade	1,230, 3,000, +12			1,155, 2,850, +9, 10,000			1,585, 3,000, +18, 3,000	1,385
R-R Merlin 55MA	J. 100 oct, 100/130 grade	1,230, 3,000, +12			1,155, 2,850, +9, 10,000			1,585, 3,000, +18, 3,000	1,385

Engine, Nominal/Rated BHP (N.R. = Engine Built, Not Flown Or Use in Flight Uncertain)	Fuel Spec. – Where Stated (n\l = non-leaded) (TEL = Tetra-ethyl-lead)	Take-Off, S/L BHP, RPM, Max Boost	Normal, Continuous Climb (Rated) Power. BHP, RPM, Max. Boost, Rated Alt.			Maximum Power (Emergency, Combat, 5 Minutes) BHP, RPM, Max. Boost, Altitude			DRY WT LB
			Unsupercharged	Medium Supercharged	Fully Supercharged	Unsupercharged	Medium Supercharged	Fully Supercharged	
R-R Merlin 56 (N.R.)	J. 100 oct, 100/130 grade	1,120, 3,000, +12			1,160, 2,850, +9, 18,000			1,190, 3,000, +9, 23,000	1,385
R-R Merlin 60	J. 100 oct, 100/130 grade	1,390, 3,000, +12					1,280, 3,000, +9, 8,750	1,125, 3,000, +9, 29,000	1,550
R-R Merlin 61	J. 100 oct, 100/130 grade	1,280, 3,000, +12		1,330, 2,850, +12, 12,000	1,130, 2,850, +12, 17,000		1,530, 3,000, +15, 13,000	1,340, 3,000, +15, 23,500	1,640
R-R Merlin 61	L. 100 oct, 100/150 grade	1,280, 3,000, +12						1,810, 3,000, +21, 6,250	1,640
R-R Merlin 61 V-1650-3	J. 100 oct, 100/130 grade	1,280, 3,000, +12		1,330, 2,850, +12, 12,000	1,130, 2,850, +12, 17,000		1,530, 3,000, +15, 13,000	1,340, 3,000, +15, 23,500	1,640
R-R Merlin 62	J. 100 oct, 100/130 grade	1,280, 3,000, +12		2,850, +12	2,850, +12,		1,560, 3,000, +15, 12,000	1,370, 3,000, +15, 24,000	1,640
R-R Merlin 63	J. 100 oct, 100/130 grade	1,280, 3,000, +12		1,335, 2,850, +12, 12,500	1,175, 2,850, +12, 23,500		1,680, 3,000, +18, 8,500	1,400, 3,000, +18, 15,000	1,645
R-R Merlin 63	L. 100 oct, 100/150 grade	1,280, 3,000, +12						1,810, 3,000, +21, 6,250	1,645
R-R Merlin 63A	J. 100 oct, 100/130 grade	1,280, 3,000, +12		1,335, 2,850, +12, 12,500	1,175, 2,850, +12, 23,500		1,680, 3,000, +18, 8,500	1,400, 3,000, +18, 15,000	1,645
R-R Merlin 63A	L. 100 oct, 100/150 grade	1,280, 3,000, +12						1,810, 3,000, +21, 6,250	1,645
R-R Merlin 64	J. 100 oct, 100/130 grade	1,280, 3,000, +12		1,335, 2,850, +12, 12,500	1,175, 2,850, +12, 23,500		1,680, 3,000, +18, 8,500	1,400, 3,000, +18, 15,000	1,665
R-R Merlin 64	L. 100 oct, 100/150 grade	1,280, 3,000, +12						1,810, 3,000, +21, 6,250	1,665
R-R Merlin 65	J. 100 oct, 100/130 grade	1,330, 3,000, +12		1,410, 2,850, +12, 8,500	1,310, 2,850, +12, 18,000		1,750, 3,000, +18, 5,250	1,625, 3,000, +18, 12,500	1,645
R-R Merlin 65	L. 100 oct, 100/150 grade	1,330, 3,000, +12						1,860, 3,000, +25, 11,000	1,645
R-R Merlin 66 V-1650-7	J. 100 oct, 100/130 grade	1,330, 3,000, +12		1,410, 2,850, +12, 8,500	1,310, 2,850, +12, 18,000		1,750, 3,000, +18, 5,250	1,625, 3,000, +18, 12,500	1,645
R-R Merlin 66 V-1650-7	L. 100 oct, 100/150 grade	1,330, 3,000, +12					2,000, 3,000, +25, 5,250	1,860, 3,000, +25, 11,000	1,645
R-R Merlin 67 (N.R.)	J. 100 oct, 100/130 grade	1,330, 3,000, +12		1,410, 2,850, +12, 8,500	1,310, 2,850, +12, 18,000		1,750, 3,000, +18, 5,250	1,625, 3,000, +18, 12,500	1,645
R-R Merlin 67	L. 100 oct, 100/150 grade	1,330, 3,000, +12						1,860, 3,000, +25, 11,000	1,645
R-R Merlin 68 V-1650-7	J. 100 oct, 100/130 grade	1,315, 3,000, +18							1,690
R-R Merlin 68A	J. 100 oct, 100/130 grade	1,315, 3,000, +12		2,850, +12			1,705, 3,000, +18, 5,750	1,580, 3,000, +18, 18,500	1,690
R-R Merlin 69	J. 100 oct, 100/130 grade	1,315, 3,000, +12							1,645
R-R Merlin 70	J. 100 oct, 100/130 grade	1,225, 3,000, +12		1,210, 2,850, +12, 13,500	1,210, 2,850, +12, 24,500		1,700, 3,000, +18, 10,500	1,475, 3,000, +18, 22,500	1,640
R-R Merlin 70	L. 100 oct, 100/150 grade	1,225, 3,000, +12						1,940, 3,000, +25, 5,500	1,640
R-R Merlin 71	J. 100 oct, 100/130 grade	1,225, 3,000, +12		1,210, 2,850, +12, 13,500	1,210, 2,850, +12, 24,500		1,700, 3,000, +18, 10,500	1,475, 3,000, +18, 22,500	1,640
R-R Merlin 71	L. 100 oct, 100/150 grade	1,225, 3,000, +12						1,940, 3,000, +25, 5,500	1,640
R-R Merlin 72	J. 100 oct, 100/130 grade	1,210, 3,000, +12		1,335, 2,850, +12, 12,500	1,175, 2,850, +12, 23,500		1,680, 3,000, +18, 8,500	1,400, 3,000, +18, 15,000	1,645
R-R Merlin 72	L. 100 oct, 100/150 grade	1,280, 3,000, +12						1,810, 3,000, +21, 6,250	1,645
R-R Merlin 73	J. 100 oct, 100/130 grade	1,280, 3,000, +12		1,335, 2,850, +12, 12,500	1,175, 2,850, +12, 23,500		1,680, 3,000, +18, 8,500	1,400, 3,000, +18, 15,000	1,645

Engine, Nominal/Rated BHP N.R. = Engine Built, Not Flown Or Use in Flight Uncertain	Fuel Spec. – Where Stated (n/l = non-leaded) (TEL = Tetra-ethyl-lead)	Take-Off, S/L BHP, RPM, Max Boost	Normal, Continuous Climb (Rated) Power. BHP, RPM, Max. Boost, Rated Alt.			Maximum Power (Emergency, Combat, 5 Minutes) BHP, RPM, Max. Boost, Altitude			DRY WT LB
			Unsupercharged	Medium Supercharged	Fully Supercharged	Unsupercharged	Medium Supercharged	Fully Supercharged	
R-R Merlin 73	L. 100 oct, 100/150 grade	1,280, 3,000, +12						1,810, 3,000, +21, 6,250	1,645
R-R Merlin 76	J. 100 oct, 100/130 grade	1,225, 3,000, +12		1,210, 2,850, +12, 13,500	1,210, 2,850, +12, 24,500		1,700, 3,000, +18, 10,500	1,475, 3,000, +18, 22,500	1,640
R-R Merlin 76	L. 100 oct, 100/150 grade	1,225, 3,000, +12						1,940, 3,000, +25, 5,500	1,640
R-R Merlin 77	J. 100 oct, 100/130 grade	1,225, 3,000, +12		1,210, 2,850, +12, 13,500	1,210, 2,850, +12, 24,500		1,700, 3,000, +18, 10,500	1,475, 3,000, +18, 22,500	1,640
R-R Merlin 77	L. 100 oct, 100/150 grade	1,225, 3,000, +12						1,940, 3,000, +25, 5,500	1,640
R-R Merlin 85	J. 100 oct, 100/130 grade	1,330, 3,000, +12		1,410, 2,850, +12, 8,500	1,310, 2,850, +12, 18,000		1,750, 3,000, +18, 5,250	1,625, 3,000, +18, 12,500	1,645
R-R Merlin 85	L. 100 oct, 100/150 grade	1,330, 3,000, +12						1,860, 3,000, +25, 11,000	1,645
R-R Merlin 85B (N.R.)	J. 100 oct, 100/130 grade	1,330, 3,000, +12		1,410, 2,850, +12, 8,500	1,310, 2,850, +12, 18,000		1,750, 3,000, +18, 5,250	1,625, 3,000, +18, 12,500	1,645
R-R Merlin 85B (N.R.)	L. 100 oct, 100/150 grade	1,330, 3,000, +12						1,860, 3,000, +25, 11,000	1,645
R-R Merlin 86	J. 100 oct, 100/130 grade	1,330, 3,000, +12							1,740
R-R Merlin 102	J. 100 oct, 100/130 grade	1,635, 3,000, +18		2,850, +			1,810, 3,000, +20, 5,750	1,660, 3,000, +20, 17,500	1,750
R-R Merlin 102A	J. 100 oct, 100/130 grade	1,635, 3,000, +18		2,850, +			1,810, 3,000, +20, 5,750	1,660, 3,000, +20, 17,500	1,660
R-R Merlin 104 (N.R.)	J. 100 oct, 100/130 grade	1,635, 3,000, +18		2,850, +			2,030, 3,000, +25, 1,250	1,890, 3,000, +25, 13,750	1,660
R-R Merlin 110 (N.R.)	J. 100 oct, 100/130 grade	1,530, 3,000, +18		1,380, 2,850, +12, 15,500	1,200, 2,850, +12, 30,000		1,685, 3,000, +18, 13,000	1,440, 3,000, +18, 27,000	1,660
R-R Merlin 112 (N.R.)	J. 100 oct, 100/130 grade	1,530, 3,000, +18		1,380, 2,850, +12, 15,500	1,200, 2,850, +12, 30,000		1,685, 3,000, +18, 13,000	1,440, 3,000, +18, 27,000	1,660
R-R Merlin 113	J. 100 oct, 100/130 grade	1,530, 3,000, +18		1,380, 2,850, +12, 15,500	1,200, 2,850, +12, 30,000		1,685, 3,000, +18, 13,000	1,440, 3,000, +18, 27,000	1,660
R-R Merlin 113A	J. 100 oct, 100/130 grade	1,530, 3,000, +18		1,380, 2,850, +12, 15,500	1,200, 2,850, +12, 30,000		1,685, 3,000, +18, 13,000	1,440, 3,000, +18, 27,000	1,660
R-R Merlin 114	J. 100 oct, 100/130 grade	1,530, 3,000, +18		1,380, 2,850, +12, 15,500	1,200, 2,850, +12, 30,000		1,685, 3,000, +18, 13,000	1,440, 3,000, +18, 27,000	1,660
R-R Merlin 114A	J. 100 oct, 100/130 grade	1,530, 3,000, +18		1,380, 2,850, +12, 15,500	1,200, 2,850, +12, 30,000		1,685, 3,000, +18, 13,000	1,440, 3,000, +18, 27,000	1,660
R-R Merlin 130	J. 100 oct, 100/130 grade	1,670, 3,000, +18		1,430, 2,850, +12, 11,000	1,280, 2,850, +12, 14,000		1,850, 3,000, +20, 6,250	1,625, 3,000, +20, 11,000	1,665
R-R Merlin 130	L. 100 oct, 100/150 grade	1,670, 3,000, +18						2,090, 3,000, +25, 2,000	1,665
R-R Merlin 131	J. 100 oct, 100/130 grade	1,670, 3,000, +18		1,430, 2,850, +12, 11,000	1,280, 2,850, +12, 14,000		1,850, 3,000, +20, 6,250	1,625, 3,000, +20, 11,000	1,665
R-R Merlin 131	L. 100 oct, 100/150 grade	1,670, 3,000, +18						2,090, 3,000, +25, 2,000	1,665
R-R Merlin 132 (N.R.)	J. 100 oct, 100/130 grade	1,670, 3,000, +18		1,430, 2,850, +12, 11,000	1,280, 2,850, +12, 14,000		1,850, 3,000, +20, 6,250	1,625, 3,000, +20, 11,000	1,665
R-R Merlin 132 (N.R.)	L. 100 oct, 100/150 grade	1,670, 3,000, +18						2,090, 3,000, +25, 2,000	1,665
R-R Merlin 133 (N.R.)	J. 100 oct, 100/130 grade	1,670, 3,000, +18		1,430, 2,850, +12, 11,000	1,280, 2,850, +12, 14,000		1,850, 3,000, +20, 6,250	1,625, 3,000, +20, 11,000	1,665
R-R Merlin 133 (N.R.)	L. 100 oct, 100/150 grade	1,670, 3,000, +18						2,090, 3,000, +25, 2,000	1,665
R-R Merlin 134	J. 100 oct, 100/130 grade	1,670, 3,000, +18		1,430, 2,850, +12, 11,000	1,280, 2,850, +12, 14,000		1,850, 3,000, +20, 6,250	1,625, 3,000, +20, 11,000	1,665

Engine, Nominal/Rated BHP. N.R. = Engine Built, Not Flown Or Use in Flight Uncertain	Fuel Spec. – Where Stated (n/l = non-leaded) (TEL = Tetra-ethyl-lead)	Take-Off, S/L BHP, RPM, Max Boost	Normal, Continuous Climb (Rated) Power. BHP, RPM, Max. Boost, Rated Alt.			Maximum Power (Emergency, Combat, 5 Minutes) BHP, RPM, Max. Boost, Altitude			DRY WT LB
			Unsupercharged	Medium Supercharged	Fully Supercharged	Unsupercharged	Medium Supercharged	Fully Supercharged	
R-R Merlin 134	L. 100 oct, 100/150 grade	1,670, 3,000, +18						2,090, 3,000, +25, 2,000	1,665
R-R Merlin 135	J. 100 oct, 100/130 grade	1,670, 3,000, +18		1,430, 2,850, +12, 11,000	1,280, 2,850, +12, 14,000	1,850, 3,000, +20, 6,250	1,625, 3,000, +20, 11,000	1,665	1,665
R-R Merlin 135	L. 100 oct, 100/150 grade	1,670, 3,000, +18						2,090, 3,000, +25, 2,000	1,665
R-R Merlin 140	J. 100 oct, 100/130 grade	1,725, 3,000, +18		2,850, +			1,780, 3,000, +20, 4,500	1,650, 3,000, +20, 16,750	1,660
R-R Merlin 150 (N.R.)	J. 100 oct, 100/130 grade	1,725, 3,000, +20		1,175, 2,650, +9, 10,000	1,175, 2,850, +9, 20,275		1,770, 3,000, +20, 4,500	1,640, 3,000, +20, 15,750	1,750
R-R Merlin 224	J. 100 oct, 100/130 grade	1,610, 3,000, +18		1,125, 2,850, +9, 9,500	1,130, 2,850, +9, 16,750		1,630, 3,000, +18, 2,500	1,510, 3,000, +18, 9,250	1,455
R-R Merlin 225	J. 100 oct, 100/130 grade	1,610, 3,000, +18		1,125, 2,850, +9, 9,500	1,130, 2,850, +9, 16,750		1,630, 3,000, +18, 2,500	1,510, 3,000, +18, 9,250	1,455
R-R Merlin 228 (N.R.)	J. 100 oct, 100/130 grade	1,390, 3,000, +14		1,125, 2,850, +9, 9,500	1,130, 2,850, +9, 16,750		1,460, 3,000, +14, 6,250	1,430, 3,000, +16, 11,000	1,460
R-R Merlin 266 V-1650-7	J. 100 oct, 100/130 grade	1,315, 3,000, +18		2,850, +12	2,850, +12		1,750, 3,000, +18, 5,100	1,580, 3,000, +18, 16,000	1,646
R-R Merlin 266	L. 100 oct, 100/150 grade								
R-R Merlin 300 V-1650-7 (N.R)	J. 100 oct, 100/130 grade	1,660, 3,000, +18		2,850, +			1,850, 3,000, +20, 6,250	1,690, 3,000, +20, 18,400	1,660
R-R Merlin 301 (N.R.)	J. 100 oct, 100/130 grade	1,660, 3,000, +18							1,660
R-R Merlin 500	J. 100 oct, 100/130 grade	1,660, 3,000, +18		1,125, 2,850, +9, 9,500	1,130, 2,850, +9, 16,750		1,630, 3,000, +18, 2,500	1,510, 3,000, +18, 9,250	1,455
R-R Merlin 500/29	J. 100 oct, 100/130 grade	1,660, 3,000, +18		1,125, 2,850, +9, 9,500	1,130, 2,850, +9, 16,750		1,630, 3,000, +18, 2,500	1,510, 3,000, +18, 9,250	1,455
R-R Merlin 500/45	J. 100 oct, 100/130 grade	1,660, 3,000, +18		1,125, 2,850, +9, 9,500	1,130, 2,850, +9, 16,750		1,630, 3,000, +18, 2,500	1,510, 3,000, +18, 9,250	1,455
R-R Merlin 501	J. 100 oct, 100/130 grade	1,660, 3,000, +18		1,125, 2,850, +9, 9,500	1,130, 2,850, +9, 16,750		1,630, 3,000, +18, 2,500	1,510, 3,000, +18, 9,250	1,455
R-R Merlin 502	J. 100 oct, 100/130 grade	1,660, 3,000, +18		1,125, 2,850, +9, 9,500	1,130, 2,850, +9, 16,750		1,630, 3,000, +18, 2,500	1,510, 3,000, +18, 9,250	1,455
R-R Merlin 600	J. 100 oct, 100/130 grade	1,725, 3,000, +20		1,175, 2,650, +9, 10,000	1,175, 2,850, +9, 20,275		1,770, 3,000, +20, 4,500	1,640, 3,000, +20, 15,750	1,750
R-R Merlin 600A	J. 100 oct, 100/130 grade	1,725, 3,000, +20		1,175, 2,650, +9, 10,000	1,175, 2,850, +9, 20,275		1,770, 3,000, +20, 4,500	1,640, 3,000, +20, 15,750	1,750
R-R Merlin 620	J. 100 oct, 100/130 grade	1,725, 3,000, +20		1,175, 2,650, +9, 10,000	1,175, 2,850, +9, 20,275		1,770, 3,000, +20, 4,500	1,640, 3,000, +20, 15,750	1,750
R-R Merlin 621	J. 100 oct, 100/130 grade	1,725, 3,000, +20		1,175, 2,650, +9, 10,000	1,175, 2,850, +9, 20,275		1,770, 3,000, +20, 4,500	1,640, 3,000, +20, 15,750	1,750
R-R Merlin 622	J. 100 oct, 100/130 grade	1,725, 3,000, +18		2,850, +			1,770, 3,000, +20, 4,000	1,655, 3,000, +20, 16,500	1,700
R-R Merlin 623	J. 100 oct, 100/130 grade	1,610, 3,000, +18		2,850, +			1,635, 3,000, +18, 2,250	1,510, 3,000, +18, 9,250	1,740
R-R Merlin 624	J. 100 oct, 100/130 grade	1,610, 3,000, +18		2,850, +			1,635, 3,000, +18, 2,250	1,510, 3,000, +18, 9,250	1,745
R-R Merlin 626-1	J. 100 oct, 100/130 grade	1,760, 3,000, +20.5		2,850, +	2,850		3,000, +20.5	3,000, +20.5	1,740
R-R Merlin 626-12	J. 100 oct, 100/130 grade	1,760, 3,000, +20.5		2,850, +	2,850		3,000, +20.5	3,000, +20.5	1,740
R-R Merlin 722	J. 100 oct, 100/130 grade	3,000		2,850, +		3,000, +		3,000, +	1,740
R-R Merlin 724-1 (N.R.)	J. 100 oct, 100/130 grade	3,000		2,850, +		3,000, +		3,000, +	1,740

Engine, Nominal/Rated BHP. N.R. = Engine Built, Not Flown Or Use in Flight Uncertain	Fuel Spec. – Where Stated (n/l = non-leaded) (TEL = Tetra-ethyl-lead)	Take-Off, S/L BHP, RPM, Max Boost	Normal, Continuous Climb (Rated) Power. BHP, RPM, Max. Boost, Rated Alt.			Maximum Power (Emergency, Combat, 5 Minutes) BHP, RPM, Max. Boost, Altitude			DRY WT LB
			Unsupercharged	Medium Supercharged	Fully Supercharged	Unsupercharged	Medium Supercharged	Fully Supercharged	
R-R Merlin 724-1C	J. 100 oct, 100/130 grade	3,000		2,850, +			3,000, +	3,000, + 1,740	
R-R Merlin 724-10	J. 100 oct, 100/130 grade	3,000		2,850, +			3,000, +	3,000, + 1,740	
R-R Peregrine I	H. 100 oct, less with 87	880, 3,000, +9		2,850, +9	2,850, +9		3,000, +9		1,140
R-R Peregrine I	G. DTD 230, 87 oct	3,000, +6.75		2,850, +6.75			3,000, +6.75		1,140
R-R 'R' Type, 1929	N. Banks Racing 'Cocktail'	1,900, 3,000, +13.5					1,900, 3,000, +13.5		1,530
R-R 'R' Type, 1931, Schneider	N. Banks Racing 'Cocktail'	2,350, 3,200, +17.5					2,350, 3,200, +17.5		1,640
R-R 'R' Type, 1931, Record	N. Banks Racing 'Cocktail'	2,530, 3,200, +17.6					2,530, 3,200, +17.6		1,640
R-R Vulture I	J. 100 oct, 100/130 grade	1,800, 3,200, +6		1,780, 2,850, +6, 4,000	1,650, 2,850, +6, 13,500		1,845, 3,000, +6, 5,000	1,710, 3,000, +6, 15,000	
R-R Vulture II	J. 100 oct, 100/130 grade	1,800, 3,200, +6		1,780, 2,850, +6, 4,000	1,650, 2,850, +6, 13,500		1,845, 3,000, +6, 5,000	1,710, 3,000, +6, 15,000	
R-R Vulture V	J. 100 oct, 100/130 grade	1,690							
R-R/Pack V-1650-1 Merlin 28	J. 100 oct, 100/130 grade	1,390, 3,000, +14		2,850, +9	2,850, +9,		1,460, 3,000, +14, 6,250	1,435, 3,000, +16, 11,000	1,470
R-R/Pack V-1650-3 Merlin 63	J. 100 oct, 100/130 grade	1,280, 3,000, +12		2,850, +12	2,850, +12,		1,530, 3,000, +16, 15,750	1,300, 3,000, +16, 26,500	1,690
R-R/Pack V-1650-5 Merlin	J. 100 oct, 100/130 grade								
R-R/Pack V-1650-7 Merlin 266	J. 100 oct, 100/130 grade	1,315, 3,000, +12		2,850, +12	2,850, +12,		1,705, 3,000, +18, 5,750	1,580, 3,000, +18, 13,500	1,645
R-R/Pack V-1650-9 Merlin 100	J. 100 oct, 100/130 grade	1,380, 3,000, +14		2,850, +			1,920, 3,000, +20, 9,500	1,620, 3,000, +20, 21,750	1,690
R-R/Pack V-1650-9A Merlin 100	J. 100 oct, 100/130 grade								
R-R/Pack V-1650-11 Merlin	J. 100 oct, 100/130 grade	1,380, 3,000, +14		2,850, +			1,920, 3,000, +20, 9,500	1,620, 3,000, +20, 21,750	1,690
R-R/Pack V-1650-21 Merlin	J. 100 oct, 100/130 grade	2,850, +							
R-R/Pack V-1650-23 Merlin	J. 100 oct, 100/130 grade	2,850, +							
R-R/Pack V-1650-25 Merlin	J. 100 oct, 100/130 grade	2,850, +							
R.A.F. 1 (90) (N.R.)	A. Pre-1923, 40-50 octane	90, 1,750							440
R.A.F. 1a (90)	A. Pre-1923, 40-50 octane	108, 1,800	108, 1,800			112, 1,900			450
R.A.F. 1b (110)	A. Pre-1923, 40-50 octane	110, 1,800	110, 1,800			118, 1,950			450
R.A.F. 1c (N.R.)	A. Pre-1923, 40-50 octane								
R.A.F. 1d (N.R.)	A. Pre-1923, 40-50 octane					150, 2,000			418
R.A.F. 1e (N.R.)	A. Pre-1923, 40-50 octane								
R.A.F. 2 (120)	A. Pre-1923, 40-50 octane	120,							
R.A.F. 3 (200) (N.R.)	A. Pre-1923, 40-50 octane	200				230, 1,700			780

Engine, Nominal/Rated BHP N.R. = Engine Built, Not Flown Or Use in Flight Uncertain	Fuel Spec. – Where Stated (n/l = non-leaded) (TEL = Tetra-ethyl-lead)	Take-Off, S/L BHP, RPM, Max Boost	Normal, Continuous Climb (Rated) Power. BHP, RPM, Max. Boost, Rated Alt.			Maximum Power (Emergency, Combat, 5 Minutes) BHP, RPM, Max. Boost, Altitude			DRY WT LB
			Unsupercharged	Medium Supercharged	Fully Supercharged	Unsupercharged	Medium Supercharged	Fully Supercharged	
R.A.F. 3a (200)	A. Pre-1923, 40-50 octane	260, 1,750	260, 1,750			278, 1,900			780
R.A.F. 4 (150) (N.R.)	A. Pre-1923, 40-50 octane	150, 1,800	150, 1,800						680
R.A.F. 4a (150)	A. Pre-1923, 40-50 octane	163, 1,800	163, 1,800			173, 2,000			680
R.A.F. 4d (180)	A. Pre-1923, 40-50 octane	180, 1,800	180, 1,800			200, 2,000			660
R.A.F.4e (240) (N.R.)	A. Pre-1923, 40-50 octane	240							
R.A.F. 5 (140)	A. Pre-1923, 40-50 octane	150, 1,800	150, 1,800			158, 1,950			670
R.A.F. 5b (170) (N.R.)	A. Pre-1923, 40-50 octane	170							
R.A.F.7 (300) (N.R.)	A. Pre-1923, 40-50 octane	300							
R.A.F. 8 (300)Siddeley-Deasy	A. Pre-1923, 40-50 octane	300							
Salmson (C-Unne) B.9 (140)	A. Pre-1923, 40-50 octane	140, 1,250	140, 1,250						
Salmson (C-Unne) M.9 (140)	A. Pre-1923, 40-50 octane	140, 1,250	140, 1,250			1,300			555
Salmson (C-Unne) 9ZM (250)	A. Pre-1923, 40-50 octane	258, 1,500	258, 1,500			278, 1,650			
Salmson (C-Unne) R.9 (160)	A. Pre-1923, 40-50 octane	155, 1,300	155, 1,300			160, 1,350			704
Salmson (C-Unne) (200)	A. Pre-1923, 40-50 octane	200							
Scott Flying Squirrel		16, 3,200	16, 3,200			28, 4,000			85
Siddeley-Deasy Puma (236)	B. BS.121/23, 74 oct, n/l	250, 1,400	250, 1,400			265, 1,500			645
Siddeley-Deasy Puma HC (290)	B. BS.121/23, 74 oct, n/l	290, d/r 240, 1,400	276, 1,700			260 appr, 1,500			636
Siddeley-Deasy Pacific (500)	B. BS.121/23, 74 oct, n/l	500, 1,400	500, 1,400			520 appr, 1,500			636
Siddeley-Deasy Tiger (600)	A. Pre-1923, 40-50 octane	600, 1,600	600, 1,600			660, 1,700			1,400
Smith (150)	A. Pre-1923, 40-50 octane	150							
Sunbeam Afridi (200)	A. Pre-1923, 40-50 octane	200							745
Sunbeam Amazon (160)	A. Pre-1923, 40-50 octane	160, 2,000	165, 2,000			170, 2,100			640
Sunbeam Arab I (200)	A. Pre-1923, 40-50 octane	212, 2,000	212, 2,000			220, 2,100			550
Sunbeam Arab II (200)	A. Pre-1923, 40-50 octane	200, 2,000	517						
Sunbeam Cossack (320)	A. Pre-1923, 40-50 octane	350, 2,000	350, 2,000			364, 2,100			1,145
Sunbeam Crusader (150)	A. Pre-1923, 40-50 octane	150, 2,500							480
Sunbeam Dyak (100)	A. Pre-1923, 40-50 octane	100, 1,200							399
Sunbeam Gurkha (240) (N.R.)	A. Pre-1923, 40-50 octane	240							

Engine, Nominal/Rated BHP N.R. = Engine Built, Not Flown Or Use in Flight Uncertain	Fuel Spec. – Where Stated (n/l = non-leaded) (TEL = Tetra-ethyl-lead)	Take-Off, S/L BHP, RPM, Max Boost	Normal, Continuous Climb (Rated) Power. BHP, RPM, Max. Boost, Rated Alt.			Maximum Power (Emergency, Combat, 5 Minutes) BHP, RPM, Max. Boost, Altitude			DRY WT LB
			Unsupercharged	Medium Supercharged	Fully Supercharged	Unsupercharged	Medium Supercharged	Fully Supercharged	
Sunbeam Manitou (300) (N.R.) A. Pre-1923, 40-50 octane		315, 2,000	315, 2,000			333, 2,100			790
Sunbeam Maori I (250)	A. Pre-1923, 40-50 octane	270, 2,100	270, 2,100			284, 2,200			890
Sunbeam Maori II (250)	A. Pre-1923, 40-50 octane	270, 2,100	270, 2,100			284, 2,200			890
Sunbeam Maori III (250)	A. Pre-1923, 40-50 octane	270, 2,100	270, 2,100			284, 2,200			905
Sunbeam Matabele (400)	A. Pre-1923, 40-50 octane	420, 2,000							1,000
Sunbeam Mohawk (225)	A. Pre-1923, 40-50 octane	225, 2,000							905
Sunbeam Nubian (155)	A. Pre-1923, 40-50 octane	168, 2,100	168, 2,100			170, 2,200			575
Sunbeam Viking (450) (N.R.)	A. Pre-1923, 40-50 octane	450							1,430
Sunbeam Zulu (160)	A. Pre-1923, 40-50 octane	160							
Sunbeam (110)	A. Pre-1923, 40-50 octane	110							
Viale (35)	A. Pre-1923, 40-50 octane	35							
Viale (45)	A. Pre-1923, 40-50 octane	45							
Viale (70)	A. Pre-1923, 40-50 octane	70							
Villiers-Hay Maya I		120, 2,300	120, 2,300			135, 2,700			280
Weir - see Aero Engines									
Wicko F (Mod. Ford V-8)									
Wolseley Aquarius I		155, 2,250	155, 2,250			170, 2,475			375
Wolseley A.R.9 Aries I		185, 2,200	200, 2,475			203, 2,420			452
Wolseley A.R.9 Aries II		205, 2,250	205, 2,475			205, 2,475			460
Wolseley A.R.9 Aries III		205, 2,250		205, 2,475			225, 2,475		510
Wolseley Scorpio I		230, 2,250, zero		230, 2,250, zero			250, 2,475, +1.5		538
Wolseley Scorpio II		230, 2,250, zero		230, 2,250, zero			250, 2,475, +1.5		538
Wolseley W.4A Python I (150)	A. Pre-1923, 40-50 octane	150, 1,500	156, 1,500			165, 1,600			455
Wolseley W.4A Python II (180)	A. Pre-1923, 40-50 octane	180, 1,500	180, 1,500			190, 1,600			460
Wolseley W.4A* Viper (200)	A. Pre-1923, 40-50 octane	200, 2,000	220, 2,000			225, 2,100			500
Wolseley W.4B Adder I (200)	A. Pre-1923, 40-50 octane	208, 2,000	208, 2,000			215, 2,100			570
Wolseley W.4B* Adder II (200)	A. Pre-1923, 40-50 octane	208, 2,000	208, 2,000			215, 2,100			570
Wolseley W.4B* Adder III (200)	A. Pre-1923, 40-50 octane	208, 2,000	208, 2,000			215, 2,100			570

Engine. Nominal/Rated BHP N.R. = Engine Built, Not Flown Or Use in Flight Uncertain	Fuel Spec. – Where Stated (n/l = non-leaded) (TEL = Tetra-ethyl-lead)	Take-Off, S/L BHP, RPM, Max Boost	Normal, Continuous Climb (Rated) Power. BHP, RPM, Max. Boost, Rated Alt.			Maximum Power (Emergency, Combat, 5 Minutes) BHP, RPM, Max. Boost, Altitude			DRY WT LB
			Unsupercharged	Medium Supercharged	Fully Supercharged	Unsupercharged	Medium Supercharged	Fully Supercharged	
Wolseley (60)	A. Pre-1923, 40-50 octane	55, 1,150	55, 1,150			60, 1,800			385
Wolseley (80)	A. Pre-1923, 40-50 octane	80, 1,150	80, 1,150			85, 1,800			420
Wolseley (160)	A. Pre-1923, 40-50 octane	126, 1,150	126, 1,150			131.5, 1,200			

Appendix 1

Aviation Fuel

Aviation fuel is a material designed to produce the maximum mechanical energy for the minimum of weight. Its major constituents include Heptane, Iso-Octane and may include Aromatics or Olefins. Sam Heron, whose contribution to engine development was immense, has claimed that aviation fuels made practically no progress until the engineer began to have an elementary understanding of their chemistry. Before then, the fuel chemist who thought he understood chemistry also thought he understood engines, a view which Heron considered to be correct in the case of 0.1 per cent of the chemists involved. Aviation fuels are associated with synthesized branched chain paraffin hydrocarbons but were not in fact developed specifically for aviation purposes.

Although in the description of the rotary engine, the mixture within all crankcases (except the Monosoupape) was described as 'explosive' (which indeed it was), it is important not to consider the power stroke in a piston engine's cylinder as the result of an explosion, even though the crack of its exhaust may sound like it. In reality of course, it is the result of very carefully controlled burning. Explosions can occur within an engine, as detonations, the 'pinking' or 'knocking' of a motor vehicle engine when it is overloaded on an uphill struggle. This is highly damaging, if not destructive and is to be avoided if possible. Detonation in a high-powered aero-engine is even more damaging and destructive and were it to occur in certain critical circumstances such as take-off, it may not be possible to avoid very serious consequences. Fortunately, with the use of correct modern fuels, this is improbable, wherein lies much of the answer to the problem.

Fuel, a hydro-carbon, has a very complex chemistry and, as a result, is a subject not to be regarded lightly nor gone into here in any great depth. All fuel burns at a rate which is governed by circumstances and the correct combination of fuel with oxygen in an engine's cylinder may be looked at in the following way. When a bomb such as a grenade detonates, a small charge of explosive combines instantly with oxygen, violently releasing its energy, disintegrating its case and causing considerable destruction, accompanied by flame, over a very small but concentrated area.

By comparison, a piece of artillery has a similar but opposite function. As much as possible of the energy released upon firing the charge needs to be used up within the barrel, accelerating its shell for as long as it is contained within, the shell emerging from the muzzle at the desired velocity. The length of the barrel is designed so as to match the charge with the weight of the projectile and the cordite charge is calculated to give the muzzle velocity to achieve the range required for a given weight of projectile. The ammunition therefore has to burn relatively slowly and at a reliably known rate, so that the resultant range can accurately be calculated. Hence the high muzzle velocity and long range of the shell from the long barrel. This diversion into the magic of artillery may be unexpected but has a point, although the comparison must end there, because there are obviously other considerations for the gunner as well as significant similarities.

The fuel/air mixture in an internal combustion engine is designed to achieve a somewhat similar effect, the controlled burning of suitable fuel driving the power stroke for exactly the length of time required and at exactly the expansion rate required before the cylinder has to be evacuated again. There are many other complications of course, such as evacuating all the burnt remains of combustion out of the cylinder, making way for the next charge and scavenging the cylinder. As it all happens very rapidly indeed,

occasionally at well over 3,500 rpm, (although most engines will only operate safely at far lower figures than this), the engine is obviously a very skilfully designed machine. Complications occur when both exhaust and inlet valves are open at the same time and Appendix 2, on valve overlap, contributed by an expert on the subject is included for those who wish to delve further into its complexities.

The very important knocking, peculiar to petrol, was investigated in 1906 by H.R. Ricardo, then about to graduate from Cambridge and working with Professor Hopkinson. The Professor attributed the knock to an explosion wave inside the combustion chamber. He believed this to be the cause, rather than pre-ignition resulting from local overheating. The latter cause was a widely held belief until 1912 but, since this was not encountered in a gas engine, he suggested that the knock was probably a characteristic of the primitive petrol fuel then in use, little better than paraffin. Fuel chemistry was yet to be fully understood, as were the characteristics of its burning and the proper use of the energy thus released.

Ricardo, having subsequently studied an engine whose compression ratio was well below 4:1, observed a sudden and abrupt pressure rise following ignition and concluded that the knock in the petrol engine was caused by spontaneous combustion or detonation of part of the working fluid. He deduced that this was due to compression by and radiation from the rapidly advancing flame front. The degree to which this took place depended upon the ability of the remainder of the unburnt charge to shed its heat to the cylinder wall. This was desirable before the damaging 'knocking', or super-compression occurred, caused by the burning and expanding gas behind the flame raising its temperature to a level which would induce spontaneous detonation, even before the flame could reach it.

The slow-burning of the fuel charge was similar to the cordite in a gun barrel, whereas detonation was more like the behaviour of fulminate of mercury. Pre-ignition had to be avoided. If, at the same time, detonation or knock could be prevented, a much higher compression could be used, with attendant gains in power and efficiency.

Ricardo found, after testing petrol samples from various oilfields in 1917, that petrol from Borneo had noticeably better anti-knock properties, both in terms of compression and supercharging, than oil found elsewhere at that time. The tests showed that fuel from this source had a much greater specific gravity and higher proportion of aromatics than others. As a result, much of it was being burned to waste because its specific gravity was considered too high to meet existing specifications. From such a very undesirable situation, Ricardo proposed blending this highly aromatic fuel with petrol from other sources and with anti-detonants. So began the lengthy process of refinement, progressively making possible a reduction in the tendency of fuel to detonate, (in other words, increasing the anti-knock value) and, at the same time, improving the product as a whole.

Coincidentally, the alternative use of the then new benzole (or benzol), an aromatic hydrocarbon derived from coal, produced 20% more power but no trace of knocking, even at 5:1 compression. Paraffin clearly had the worst knocking characteristics, aromatics having the best. By 1913, Ricardo was satisfied that it was detonation which was most important in limiting compression ratios and therefore the efficiency and power output of the spark-ignition engine. The finding and manufacture of suitable fuels, based on this most important conclusion was to have a fundamental influence upon future engine design. Charles Kettering, of Delco (a General Motors subsidiary) had investigated the same phenomenon in the United States in 1911 and the search there for the cause and cure began in earnest in 1917.

In Britain, Ricardo and consultant physicists H.T. (later, Sir Henry) Tizard and D.R. Pye conducted investigations into detonation and overheating, continuing studies made at Farnborough in 1915 by Professor A.H. Gibson. In the United States, the discovery of the knocking properties of branched chain paraffin was an academic exercise, much of it a result of private enterprise. The shortage of petrol during the war had caused paraffin to be used in the United States for house-lighting generating sets but had resulted in complaints about engine knocking and consequent damage. The first explanation that detonation was a phenomenon of fuel chemistry came from Ricardo.

Working for General Motors, C.F. Kettering and Thomas Midgeley's discovery and development, in 1926, of tetra-ethyl-lead (TEL) as an anti-detonant was a result of commercial competition in the United States but had little to do with aviation. The increasing use of lead was largely the result of the U.S. Government's pressure on industry to improve their engine designs so that they could use leaded fuels. When the importance of branched chain paraffins and the addition of lead was established the same year, the development of suitable manufacturing methods was begun and this too was a commercial initiative. Octane, after having been synthesized in America by Dr Graham Edgar, changed from a laboratory curiosity to being a valuable component of fuel. However, the market for military fuel in peacetime was small and the greatest impetus for fuel improvement came from the motor car industry. In the tense years and months leading up to the Second World War, the pressure on industry by inter-governmental competition for improvements in engine performance provided the necessary financial support for the expensive production processes. It is a long and complex story.

The Octane number scale, in relation to the detonation characteristics of pure hydrocarbons, was worked out in 1927 by Graham Edgar who realized that Heptane would detonate under almost any conditions, whereas Iso-Octane had the highest resistance to knocking of any of the hydrocarbons which he had tested. Edgar therefore proposed a scale, in which normal Heptane would be at the bottom, as zero, and Iso-Octane at the top, as 100.

On the Octane rating scale therefore and using the basis for calculating the Octane number as Heptane = 0 and Iso-Octane = 100, *the Octane number is the percentage, by volume, of Iso-Octane in a mixture of Iso-Octane and normal Heptane* and it describes the fuel in 'anti-knock' characteristics (these having been tested under specified conditions, the higher the proportion of Heptane present, the lower the resistance to knock). So, for example, a mixture of 96 parts Iso-Octane + 4 parts Heptane = 96-Octane. By this definition, 100-Octane therefore consists of almost pure Iso-Octane but with the addition of tetra-ethyl-lead (TEL). By increasing the TEL proportion, higher anti-knock values than 100 are obtainable and it is more usual to quote all grades above 100 in Performance Numbers (PN). Fuel is quoted in grades appropriate to mixture strength and this gives a clue to the possible output of an engine when cruising in weak mixture or at full throttle in rich mixture and it needs to be taken into consideration in conjunction with engine compression ratios and supercharging, the possible variations in fuel being both numerous and complex.

By the start of the Second World War, Royal Air Force squadrons were flying mostly on leaded 87 Octane fuel. It contained 20% of aromatics, a natural content of the Borneo fuel supplied by Shell and for which British engines were suitable. Such fuel was suitable for boost pressures up to the +6 lb/sq inch then produced by the Kestrels and early Merlins, without risking detonation. In a lecture given in 1937, F.R.Banks had drawn attention to the advisability of making provision for the use of 100 Octane fuel for the highly-supercharged engines clearly on the horizon. However, it was known in Britain that the U.S. Government was ordering large quantities of 100 Octane and, in the same year, the Director of Technical Development accepted that alterations to certain British engines

could be made, so as to be able to run on this type of fuel and that the ability to use it was becoming essential. This would take time, war was looming and it was also imperative that the fuel should be made in Britain.

For testing purposes at Derby, Bristol and Farnborough, a small amount of 100 Octane was imported from the United States in 1938. It was known that American fuel was restricted to not more than about 2 per cent of aromatic content, because of its detrimental effect on rubber tubing. Clearly, as imported, American 100 Octane was unsuitable for British engines which were designed to run on 20 per cent aromatics and would not give the rich mixture response needed with straight American fuel. Thanks to the foresight and initiative of Dr Bill Sweeney, who blended a 100 Octane mixture which would provide the rich response required for British supercharged engines, a tanker loaded with 100 Octane fuel arrived in Britain from the States a bare three months before the declaration of war on 3 September 1939. As a result of satisfactory trials, in March 1940, it was decided to switch Fighter Command to 100 Octane fuel, followed by Bomber Command about a year later.

The war was obviously a tremendous spur to the continual improvements of fuel, particularly to accommodate the immense boost pressures which technology could produce and, as a result, effectively doubled the power delivered by engines in the top power bracket. For such engines, it was essential for the knock value to be high, to prevent detonation. As engine technology advanced and power went up, airframe technology advanced with it, making possible ever greater speeds and climb. The demands for ever better fuel increased in step. The whole process was a rolling exercise in damage limitation, while extracting the utmost energy from the fuel.

Fuel's Major Constituents

Heptane has a straight chain molecule with a low knock rating, a high Cetane number and a low Octane number. With this feature, the fuel can safely withstand a very much higher compression (and is the basis for diesel fuel) but its response can be improved with the addition of an anti-detonant such as tetra-ethyl-lead (TEL).

TEL, in its pure form, is a highly toxic and dangerous substance and, from its inception in the United States, its manufacture has been carefully controlled. Traces of it (in high concentrations of motor car exhausts) contribute significantly to air pollution. It originally tended to foul sparking plugs and burn exhaust valves and seats but brominated compounds, added to the TEL before mixing with the fuel, reduced these disadvantages and made TEL safer. This resulted in ethylene dichloride being added to motor car fuel as a lead scavenger and the more expensive and more volatile and effective ethylene dibromide to aviation fuel.

Iso-Octane, with a low Cetane number, having a branched chain paraffin molecule, is more compact with a higher resistance to knock, or higher knock rating, giving it a high Octane number and a lower need, in normal circumstances, for the addition of TEL.

Olefins have the more compact and dense molecules. They also have an even higher knock rating but are subject to oxidisation and polymerisation, which may produce gums and lacquers in the fuel tanks and system. It is also expensive to refine out this effect.

Aromatics, of which Benzene, or commercial benzole is the most important, are ring-chain compounds, having a compact molecules. Aromatics are very stable and have a high knock value but react with elastomers in the fuel, causing carbon deposits and are therefore prone to pre-ignition.

Fuel Specifications Key

See also Performance Tables.

Fuel; British Standard, Octane number rating or grade, DTD Specifications, Performance Numbers (PN) and Tetra-ethyl-lead (TEL) additive.

A   Early motor spirit-type fuel, up to 1922-3. Approximately 40-50 Octane.

B   74 Octane approximately, to British Specification 121/1923. 80/20 fuel = 80 per cent British Standard Aviation Spirit +20 per cent benzole — non-leaded.

C DTD 134. 73 Octane (minimum) — 77 Octane, non-leaded. 60/40 fuel = 60 per cent British Standard Aviation spirit + 40% benzole (Note: Anglo-Persian spirit, as used particularly in Iraq, 1928–1930).

D DTD 224, 77 Octane (minimum), non-leaded.

E 75/25/4 fuel = 75 per cent British Standard Aviation Spirit + 25 per cent benzole + 4 cc TEL/Imperial gallon.

F 80 Octane (e.g. Pratt's Ethyl spirit) +5.5 cc TEL/Imperial gallon.

G DTD 230, 87 Octane, + 5.5 cc TEL/Imperial gallon. Correct designation, Grade 87 (5.5). From 25 October 1944 this Fuel Spec. became DED 2473.

H 100 Octane fuel performance figures are quoted in some instances but engines were operated at reduced bhp and boost when using DTD 230, 87 Octane. Similarly, when DTD 230, 87 Octane fuel figures are quoted in some instances, engines could be operated at increased bhp and boost with 100 Octane.

J 100/130 grade, 100 Octane. (Lower figure for weak mixture, upper figure rich) + 5.5 cc TEL/Imperial gallon, DED 2475.

K 115/145 grade, 115PN/145PN. (Lower figure for weak mixture, upper figure rich) + 5.5 cc TEL/Imperial gallon.

L 100/150 grade, 100 Octane. (Lower figure for weak mixture, upper figure rich) + 7.2 cc TEL/Imperial Gallon. This was a special fuel, containing mono-methyl-aniline, developed at the end of the Second World War, permitting very high boost and giving a lot more power, without detonation, for chasing flying bombs. The S.U.-type carburettor was cleared potentially for + 21 lb boost on 150 grade fuel which became available in 1944. It enabled the use of + 25 lb boost on certain types of engine and would have been cleared for +30 lb, had the war not finished.

M Diesel fuel (high heptane content).

N Racing (sprint) 'Cocktails' devised by F.R. Banks. The ultimate fuel in 1931 was 60 per cent methanol, 30 per cent benzole, 10 per cent acetone, plus TEL.

ENGINE PERFORMANCE RELATED TO HEIGHT

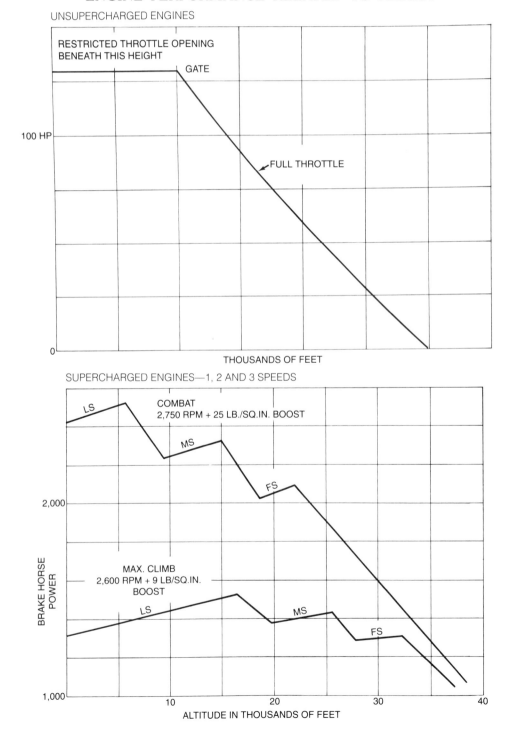

Appendix 2
A Note on Valve Timing

The author is greatly indebted to Alec Harvey-Bailey for the following comments on the important subject of valve overlap.

There are two basic approaches to achieve high horse powers from piston engines, setting aside the issue of supercharging. One can either have a relatively small cubic capacity unit running at high rpm or a large cubic capacity engine running at low rpm. In the development of piston engines, racing cars have moved down the scale in cubic capacity, using high rpm, while aero-engines for high-performance aircraft have taken the route of large cubic capacity with designs featuring lightweight construction.

In racing car engines since before the First World War there was a move to twin overhead camshaft units with bucket tappets, aimed at running at high speed. To obtain high specific powers entailed a free breathing induction system and, as engine speeds rose, the use of 'long' valve openings and considerable valve overlap. That involves, having both inlet and exhaust valves open simultaneously towards the end of the exhaust stroke and the start of the inlet stroke, to promote good gas flow and effective scavenging of the combustion chamber. In racing engines, this can mean as much as 90 degrees of valve overlap and some 300 degrees of inlet valve opening. Such an engine will produce high power outputs at the top end of the performance range but will give poor torque and ragged running at low rpm.

It is not unusual for current racing engines, depending upon the category or class, to run anywhere between 10,000 and 14,000 rpm. At the upper limit, some form of variable valve timing may be necessary to give reasonable operation at low rpm.

The aero-engine, running at much lower rpm, while employing high valve lifts will use shorter opening periods for valves and only a small degree of overlap. Poppet valve in-line or vee engines generally employ single overhead cam layouts, using rockers to actuate the valves, because this gives a cleaner engine from the point of view of installation. The object of the large aero-engine is to obtain good breathing and, therefore, torque not only at maximum power but at cruising and climb ratings as well. The engine has to swing a large propeller and even with a reduction gear ratio reducing propeller rpm to below half engine speed, there will be propeller tip speed limitations.

In considering valve durations, in the opening and closing phases of a valve, importance is placed on the form of the cam ramps, which allow relatively gentle acceleration and deceleration, reducing opening and closing loads. A timing diagram can therefore give the impression of a much longer useful duration in terms of gas flow than is the case. On high-revving racing engines, it is normal practice to check valve timing with a given amount of lift on the valve so that it is at a point of high acceleration and avoids the difficulty of the slower-opening ramp.

Supercharging increased the mass-flow through the engine, which enables long valve durations to be exploited, but if waste of charge flow is to be avoided valve overlap should be lower than on a normally aspirated engine. Development testing can show the right compromise in overlap to provide good scavenging of the combustion chamber, with the minimum waste of charge flow.

On poppet valve radial engines, similar considerations of charge flow apply, but the method of valve actuation is different. The camshaft is replaced by a cam sleeve at the core of the engine, working the valve via push-rods and rockers in the cylinder heads. The sleeve valve aero-engine, whether in radial or in-line cylinder form, obtains its timing via a sleeve drive mechanism in place of a cam. As the opening and closing of the valve is in a complex sliding action, it avoids the loadings associated with the action of the cam on a poppet valve, which is an advantage. It does, however, introduce problems of sleeve wear, which can lead to serious engine failure, and the development of reliable sleeve operation was a long and difficult task. In Commercial aviation, however, very long engine lives have been achieved at modest level of cruise power but on a world widebasis, poppet valve engines were much more widely used until gas turbines took over.

Measurements, Calculations and Conversion Factors

For calculating Swept Volume — (bore/stroke), either in inches and cubic inches, or centimetres and cubic centimetres, use one of the following methods:-

Pi x d/2 x d/2 x stroke x n (no of cylinders), or
22/7 x d x d/4 x stroke x n

where d (diameter) = cylinder bore, n = number of cylinders.

For converting, multiply by:
   Inches to Centimetres 2.54

Centimetres to Inches	0.3937
Feet to Metres	0.3048
Metres to Feet	3.2808
Square Inches to Square Centimetres	6.452
Square Centimetres to Square inches	0.155
Cubic Inches to Cubic Centimetres	16.387
Cubic Inches to Litres	0.0164
Litres to Cubic Inches	61.024
Cubic Centimetres to Cubic Inches	0.0610
Pound to Kilogramme	0.454
Kilogramme to Pound	2.205

PART 6
BIBLIOGRAPHY

AUTHOR	TITLE	PUBLISHER	DATE
	Aero, The	Iliffe & Sons Ltd, London	1909-10
Andrews, C.F.,	Vickers Aircraft since 1908	Putnam & Co Ltd, London	1969
Andrews, C.F. & Morgan, E.B.,	Supermarine Aircraft since 1914	Putnam & Co Ltd, London	1981
Angle, Glenn D.,	Aerosphere	Aircraft Publishers, New York	1939
Banks, Air Commodore F.R.(Rod),	I Kept No Diary	Putnam & Co Ltd, London	1978
Barnes, C.H.,	Bristol Aircraft since 1910	Putnam & Co Ltd, London	1964
Barnes, C.H.,	Handley Page Aircraft since 1907	Putnam & Co Ltd, London	1976
Barnes, C.H.,	Shorts Aircraft since 1900	Putnam & Co Ltd, London	1967
Beamont, Wing Commander Roland P.	Testing Years	Ian Allan Ltd, Shepperton	1980
Birch, David,	Rolls-Royce and the Mustang	Rolls-Royce Heritage Trust, Derby	1987
Boughton, Terence,	British Light Aeroplane, Story of the	John Murray (Publishers), London	1963
Brooks, Peter W.,	Cierva Autogiros	Smithsonian Institution Press, Washington	1988
Brooks, Peter W.,	Zeppelin: Rigid Airships 1893-1940	Putnam & Co Ltd, London	1992
Brown, Don.L.,	Miles Aircraft since 1925	Putnam & Co Ltd, London	1970
Bruce, J.M.,	Aeroplanes of the Royal Flying Corps (Military Wing)	Putnam & Co Ltd, London	1982
Bruce, J.M.,	Warplanes of the First World War, Fighters, 5 vols	Macdonald, London	1965-1972
Burls, G.A.,	Aero Engines	Benn Brothers Ltd, London	1917
Burton, Mike,	Piston Engines and Supercharging	Airlife Ltd, Shrewsbury	1991
Cook, Ray,	Armstrong Siddeley -The Parkside Story 1896-1939	Rolls-Royce Heritage Trust, Derby	1988
Crosby Warren, J.A.,	Flight Testing of Production Aircraft	Putnam & Co Ltd, London	1943
Gibbs-Smith C.H.,	Aeroplane, The — An Historical Survey	H.M.S.O., London	1960
Gunston, W.T.,	By Jupiter!	R.Ae.S., London	1978
Gunston, W.T.,	Rolls-Royce Aero Engines	Patrick Stephens Ltd, Sparkford	1989
Gunston, W.T.,	World Encyclopaedia of Aero Engines	Patrick Stephens Ltd, Sparkford	1986
Harvey-Bailey, Alec,	Merlin in Perspective	Rolls-Royce Heritage Trust, Derby	1983
Harvey-Bailey, Alec & Evans, Michael H.	Rolls-Royce – The Pursuit of Excellence	Rolls-Royce Heritage Trust, Derby	1984
Hooker, Sir Stanley,	Not Much of an Engineer	Airlife Ltd, Shrewsbury	1984
Jackson, A.J.,	Avro Aircraft since 1908	Putnam & Co Ltd, London	1965
Jackson, A.J.,	Blackburn Aircraft since 1909	Putnam & Co Ltd, London	1968
Jackson, A.J.,	British Civil Aircraft since 1919 (3 vols)	Putnam & Co Ltd, London	1973
Jackson, A.J.,	De Havilland Aircraft since 1915	Putnam & Co Ltd, London	1962
James, Derek N.,	Gloster Aircraft since 1917	Putnam & Co Ltd, London	1971
James, Derek N.,	Westland Aircraft since 1915	Putnam & Co Ltd, London	1991
Jefford, Wing Commander C.G.,	R.A.F. Squadrons	Airlife Ltd, Shrewsbury	1988
Judge, A.W.,	Aircraft Engines	Chapman & Hall Ltd, London	1942, 1947
King, H.F.,	Sopwith Aircraft 1912-1920	Putnam & Co Ltd, London	1981
Knott, E.W. (Ed),	Aeroplane Maintenance & Operation	George Newnes Ltd, London	1939, circa
London, Peter,	Saunders & Saro Aircraft since 1917	Putnam & Co Ltd, London	1988
Mason, Francis K.,	Hawker Aircraft since 1920	Putnam & Co Ltd, London	1961

AUTHOR	TITLE	PUBLISHER	DATE
Mason, Francis K.,	Hawker Typhoon and Tempest	Aston Publications, Bourne End, Bucks	1988
Morgan, E.B. & Shacklady, E,	Spitfire, The History	Key Publishing, Stamford	1987
Morse, William,	Rotary Engines of World War One	Nelson & Saunders Aviation Collection	1987
Ransom, Stephen & Fairclough, Robert,	English Electric Aircraft & their Predecessors	Putnam & Co Ltd, London	1987
Ricardo, Sir Harry,	Pattern of my Life	Ricardo Consulting Engineers Ltd	1990
Riding, Richard,	Ultralights, The Early British Classics	Patrick Stevens Ltd	1987
Rubbra, A.A.,	Rolls-Royce Piston Aero Engines	Rolls-Royce Heritage Trust, Derby	1990
Russell, Sir Archibald,	Span of Wings, A	Airlife Ltd, Shrewsbury	1992
Schlaifer, R; Heron, S.D.,	Development of Aircraft Engines & Aviation Fuels	Harvard University, Harvard	1950
Stinton, Darrol,	The Anatomy of the Aeroplane	G.T. Foulis, Sparkford	1966
Stokes, Peter,	From Gipsy to Gem – With Diversions 1926-1986	Rolls-Royce Heritage Trust, Derby	1987
Tagg, A.E.,	Power for the Pioneers	Crossprint, Isle of Wight	1990
Tapper, Oliver,	Armstrong Whitworth Aircraft since 1913	Putnam & Co Ltd, London	1973
Taylor, H.A.,	Airspeed Aircraft since 1931	Putnam & Co Ltd, London	1970
Taylor, H.A.,	Fairey Aircraft since 1915	Putnam & Co Ltd, London	1974
Taylor, H.A.,	Test Pilot at War	Ian Allan Ltd, Shepperton	1970
Thetford, Owen G.,	British Naval Aircraft since 1912	Putnam & Co Ltd, London	1962, 1991
Wallace, John,	Design of Aeroplane Engines	Benn Brothers Ltd, London	1920
Wilkinson, Paul H.,	Aircraft Engines of the World 1951	Sir Isaac Pitman Ltd, London	1951
Wilkinson, Paul H.,	Aircraft Engines of the World 1960-61	Paul H.Wilkinson, New York	1960-61
Wilkinson, Paul H.,	Aircraft Engines of the World 1964-65	Paul H.Wilkinson, New York	1964-65
Wilson, Charles & Reader, William,	Men & Machines, D.Napier & Son 1908-1958	Weidenfeld and Nicholson	1958
Wixey, Kenneth E.,	Parnall Aircraft since 1914	Putnam & Co Ltd, London	1990

PART 7

General Index

Note. The General Index refers to page numbers. Pages in italics refer to illustrations. In addition to illustrations of people and places, a selection of the illustrations which refer to certain technical aspects of engines is also included in the General Index. Many items, such as Cooling, Carburation, Supercharging, Propeller Reduction Gears etc, which are common to most, if not all engines and would lead to a very large number of similar entries if all cases were specified. These Index entries are simply intended to lead into the subject. Each engine is then dealt with individually. Similarly, Power-curves mentioned in the Reports from the A. & A.E.E. and M.A.E.E. are only recorded under the relevant engine entries. See also acknowledgements.